General Business
For Economic Understanding
Tenth Edition

S. Joseph DeBrum *Professor of Business*
San Francisco State College

Peter G. Haines *Professor of Business and Distributive Education*
Michigan State University

Dean R. Malsbary *Professor of Business Education*
University of Connecticut

Ernest H. Crabbe *Editor Emeritus*
South-Western Publishing Company

Published By

G13 **SOUTH-WESTERN PUBLISHING CO.**

Cincinnati Chicago Dallas New Rochelle, N.Y. Burlingame, Calif. Brighton, England

Standard Book Number: 0-538-07130-3

Library of Congress Catalog Card Number: 70-142754

K 8 7 6 5 4 3

Printed in the United States of America

PREFACE

More than ever before, all people need to understand the business and economic environment in which they live and work. As consumers we depend upon business to satisfy our needs and wants. As producers we derive our income from business or from sources that depend on business. As citizens we engage in activities and make decisions that affect our economic welfare. Yet many persons, both adults and students, are economically naive.

This Tenth Edition of *General Business for Economic Understanding* is dedicated to helping students develop an understanding and appreciation of our American business system and the economic setting in which it functions. This knowledge is vital to a balanced education.

One of the major purposes—if not *the* major purpose—of a course in general business is to improve economic citizenship through study of our business and economic environment. The authors interpret economic citizenship in this context to mean the development of individuals who are: (1) knowledgeable about the American business system as part of our total economic environment; (2) skillful in selecting and using the goods and services that are available from business, industry, and government; and (3) competent in managing their personal and business affairs. In this text, a four-phase sequence is used to strengthen the student's understanding and behavior as an economic citizen.

DEVELOPING ECONOMIC CITIZENSHIP

Phase 1: The Economic Setting of Business. Unit 1, "Our Economic World," and Unit 2, "The Nature of American Business," comprise the first phase of the sequence. Through this phase, the student will realize that most of our economic needs and wants are met through businesses that operate within the framework of our American economic system.

Phase 2: The Services of Business. Units 3 through 9 comprise the second phase of the sequence. Here the student will identify and assess many of the services provided by banks, stores, credit agencies, insurance companies, investment firms, savings institutions, transportation companies, and other enterprises. In this phase, the student will acquire skills and insights that will enable him to be a more efficient user of business services.

Phase 3: The Relationships of Business to Government, Labor, and International Trade. Unit 10 provides the thrust for the third phase. Through the readings, discussions, and activities related to this phase, the student will realize that businesses, governments, workers, and individual nations must depend on each other in varying degrees for economic growth and well-being.

Phase 4: The Individual in Our Economy. Unit 11, "Living and Working in Our Economy," brings the course to an appropriate close. Here the focus is on the most important group associated with the study of general business: the students. Emphasis is placed on how each student can plan for a successful future in our economic world.

STUDENT ACTIVITIES

At the end of each part of *General Business for Economic Understanding* are activities carefully planned for teaching and for learning. These activities involve students in writing, investigating, interviewing, problem-solving, demonstrating, explaining, reporting, and other behavioral responses. These varied and challenging experiences allow teachers to provide for a wide range of student abilities and interests. The end-of-part activities are divided into the following sections:

1. *Developing Your Business Vocabulary.* This section fulfills an important objective—that of increasing the student's word power by expecting him to identify definitions of commonly used business and economic terms.
2. *Checking Your Understanding.* This section aims to measure the student's comprehension through oral or written responses to questions directly related to the content of each part.
3. *Applying What You Have Learned.* Through the activities in this section, the student applies what he has learned in problem situations relevant to him and his everyday life.

4. *Solving Business Problems.* By solving the business-economic problems in this section, the student strengthens and refines his abilities in basic mathematics.

5. *Enriching Your Business Understanding.* The activities in this section are intended mainly, but not exclusively, as optional experiences for students. Their solution requires students to exercise careful thought, to investigate sources of information beyond the textbook, and in some cases to conduct studies using basic and practical research methods. Students may be expected to report on their findings and to make decisions or recommendations. This section is designed particularly for the more able or resourceful students.

BACKGROUND AND GUIDANCE FOR FUTURE STUDY

The content of the textbook is of immediate value to all students in their personal, family, and community living. In addition, it provides a foundation for the study of advanced business and economics courses, whether such study is undertaken in the later high school years or in college. Since various fields of business are explored, students should also obtain an understanding of their own aptitudes, abilities, and interests concerning many kinds of occupations. Thus, vocational guidance is given throughout the text as students learn about functions and services of business and about qualities needed for successful job performance.

PREPARING THE TENTH EDITION

By canvassing a random sample of general business teachers throughout the United States, the authors obtained much helpful information about general business teaching methods and course content. As part of the survey, teachers were asked to react to some 60 general business topics and to indicate whether they believed that in a general business textbook these topics should be "discussed fully," "discussed briefly," or "omitted." Teachers were also asked to respond to an open-end question by detailing other topics they would like a general business textbook to contain. Responses were received from more than 3,600 general business teachers representing all our 50 states.

In planning this Tenth Edition, the authors gave serious consideration to the opinions and recommendations of this national representation of general business teachers. Many of the improvements in this revision reflect the judgments of a majority of the teachers who participated in the survey.

This edition is an extensive revision of the widely used previous edition. Much of the significant and tested content of the preceding edition has been retained; but this content has been thoroughly updated, with greater attention to forceful and idiomatic language. Some of the topics treated in previous editions have been reduced in coverage or eliminated to make way for new material that is more relevant for today's students.

The following parts in the Tenth Edition are new: Part 1, "Business Meets Economic Needs and Wants"; Part 2, "Features of Our Economic System"; Part 3, "How Our Economy Is Changing"; Part 6, "Men and Machines in Business"; Part 19, "Understanding Types of Sales Credit"; Part 32, "Investment Clubs and Mutual Funds"; Part 37, "The Rising and Falling Values of Money"; Part 48, "The American Tax System"; and Part 50, "World Trade and Our Economy." Many of the other parts have been rewritten and relevant new material added to them.

An added dimension has been given to this text by a completely new and modern format and by an almost entirely new selection of graphs, charts, photographs, and other illustrative materials. Color is attractively and functionally used throughout the text.

ACKNOWLEDG-MENTS

Specialists from all levels of the teaching profession have read manuscripts, offered suggestions, and otherwise contributed to the improvement of this book. Authorities from business and government helped significantly in updating content and illustrations relating to insurance, banking, social security, labor, credit, investments, and other topics.

Many pages would be required to give deserving and proper recognition to each individual who has contributed in some way to the production of this textbook. Although it is not feasible to mention individual acknowledgments in this preface, the authors are deeply grateful for the encouragement and constructive suggestions they have received from each of the many contributors.

S. Joseph DeBrum
Peter G. Haines
Dean R. Malsbary
Ernest H. Crabbe

CONTENTS

Unit 1

Our Economic World

PART 1
Business Meets Economic Needs And Wants

It's a Saturday afternoon, and you're window-shopping downtown. How many different things that you'd like to own do you see in the store windows? A just-released record album, maybe, or a sweater. Perhaps a camera, a pair of boots, a radio, a wall poster.

We never stop needing and wanting things. *Needs* are those things we must have to survive. Food, clothing, and shelter are usually thought of as our three basic needs. *Wants* are those things which we could live without, but which make living much more fun. All the stores that you pass during your Saturday window-shopping exist to satisfy your needs and wants.

We satisfy most of our needs and wants by buying goods and services. A *business* is an organization that supplies us with goods or services that we want. Most of the goods and services that we use are supplied by businesses. Others are supplied by such institutions as hospitals, government agencies, and schools.

Goods or *products* are the tangible things we use in our everyday lives. Some goods, like food, are used up at one time. Other goods, like cars, may be used over and over again for a long time. *Services* are those things that others do for us. We are using services when we mail letters, fly in a plane, call a plumber, or get clothes dry-cleaned.

WE USE GOODS AND SERVICES

As a user of goods and services, you are a *consumer*. So is every person you know. But organizations can also be consumers. Your school buys and uses desks, chalkboards, lab supplies, and many other items. Your local, state, and federal governments buy many kinds of goods, from courtroom furniture to street lights. Businesses, which supply goods and services to us, are also consumers. The owner of a service station, for example, buys and uses many goods supplied by other businesses. He needs a cash register, display cases, gasoline pumps, and many other items.

WE MUST DEPEND ON EACH OTHER

The pioneer family in our country was quite self-sufficient. There were few chances to trade with other people, since the nearest family often lived many miles away. Each home was a factory. Meats were smoked, pickled, or dried to preserve them. Each family ground its own grain and made its own bread. Pioneer families made their own furniture and cloth. They raised sheep, sheared them, spun the wool into yarn, and wove the yarn into cloth. They were very independent, but the goods and services they had were limited mostly to what they could produce in or near their homes.

Today we are not so much independent as we are interdependent. A person can still produce by himself some of the goods and services he needs or wants. But the number that one

Illus. 1-1. Because they buy and use goods and services, these girls are consumers. So are businesses, government, and other organizations.

General Electric

UNIT 1 / OUR ECONOMIC WORLD

person alone can produce is very small. Clothing is a basic need, and many women today sew their own clothes. But do you know anyone who spins the thread and weaves her own cloth?

The efforts of many people are required to supply us with the things we need and want. Inventors think up new ways of doing and making things. Businessmen organize firms to sell us the goods and services we want. Investors lend money to start businesses and keep them operating because they believe in inventors' ideas and in businessmen's abilities to make a profit. Government passes laws to help businesses operate by rules that are fair to everyone. Many persons are needed to work on farms, in stores, and in factories to produce the goods and services we want.

You can see, then, that modern business requires the cooperation of many people to satisfy the needs and wants of all of us.

THE THREE KINDS OF ECONOMIC RESOURCES

Goods and services don't just come out of thin air. We cannot create goods from nothing or provide services without some effort. The means with which we produce the things we need and want are called *economic resources*. There are three kinds of economic resources: natural resources, capital resources, and human resources.

Natural resources are materials supplied directly by nature. Trees, minerals, water, and wildlife are some important natural resources. Natural resources must be taken from the earth and refined before they can be used in producing goods and services.

Capital resources include tools, machinery, and other equipment used to convert natural resources into goods and services. Factory buildings, power plants, tractors, and typewriters are examples of capital resources.

Human resources are the people who work to produce goods and services. Labor is another name for human resources. Human resources include the men and women who run our farms, mines, and factories, who transport products to places where they are needed, who perform business and government services for other people, and who manage businesses. Natural and capital resources would have little value without human resources to use them in producing goods and services.

OUR ECONOMIC RESOURCES

NATURAL RESOURCES

CAPITAL RESOURCES

HUMAN RESOURCES

UNLIMITED WANTS AND LIMITED RESOURCES

Wants are peculiar; there is no limit to them. Satisfying one want usually gives rise to new ones. Buy a camera, and you want film, flash cubes, maybe a tripod, perhaps a developing outfit. There is a limit, though, to economic resources.

We do not have an endless supply of coal, oil, timber, and other such raw materials. We are also realizing that, because of pollution, we do not have an endless supply of clean air, water, and land. In addition, we will probably never have enough dentists, teachers, secretaries, and other such persons with the skills to satisfy our unlimited wants. And since our natural and human resources are limited, our man-made capital resources are also limited.

Because our economic resources are limited, we need to be "economical" in using them. We must use these resources as wisely as we can if our unlimited wants are to be satisfied as fully as possible. All countries have a shortage of economic resources. Some have fewer economic resources than others. A major problem facing every nation is how best to use its limited economic resources so that it satisfies as many as possible of its people's needs and wants.

Every nation has developed some plan for making decisions on how best to use its economic resources. Each nation's plan is known as its *economic system* or *economy*. In the next part, you will learn about some features of our country's economic system and some features of other countries' economic systems.

WE MUST BALANCE OUR RESOURCES WITH OUR WANTS

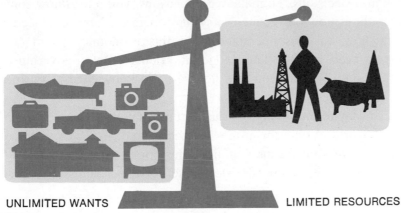

Illus. 1-3. Our wants are unlimited, but not our resources. How do we solve the problem? We "economize" in the use of our resources.

UNLIMITED WANTS   LIMITED RESOURCES

WE MUST ALL MAKE ECONOMIC DECISIONS

A nation makes economic decisions, and so do you. As a consumer, you decide how best to use your own personal economic resources to satisfy your needs and wants. Suppose someone gives you $3. If you spend it for snacks after school, you won't have enough left to go to the movie Friday night. So you must make an economic decision. You have to decide which want—the snacks with your friends or the movie—is more important to you.

As consumers, we decide what products businesses will make and what services they will offer. We do this by buying—or by not buying—certain goods and services. When you buy something, you are casting an economic vote. You are saying to a business: "I like your product or service, and I'm willing to pay for it."

If enough people buy a product or service, the businessman supplying it will produce more of it. If people don't buy, the businessman will either have to improve his product or service or stop supplying it. You can find many examples of how this economic voting affects our whole economic system. For example, laundromats, drive-in restaurants, and shopping centers were all built in large numbers when consumers showed—by spending their dollars—how much they wanted them. Banks changed their hours, and discount stores grew up like mushrooms because of consumers' economic votes.

Each person in our country is important when it comes to making economic decisions. Neither wealth, race, religion, nor age can keep a person from making significant economic decisions.

WHAT YOU CAN GAIN FROM THIS COURSE

You owe it to yourself and to your society to make wise economic decisions. To make wise decisions, you must know something about how our economic system operates. You also need to know how business operates within this economic system. Just as you need a basic knowledge of science, math, government, history, and English, you also need a basic knowledge of business and economics.

In day-to-day living, you are a part of our business and economic world. You use business services, and you face problems in managing your business affairs. This course can help you learn how to make economic decisions and solve problems like these:

1. How can banks and other financial institutions help me in planning a savings program and in using checking account services?
2. Where can I get reliable information about goods I want to buy?
3. When is it wise to pay cash for goods and when should I buy on credit?
4. How can I plan an insurance program for myself? What kinds and what amounts of insurance should I carry?
5. How should I plan a savings program? What effect will a possible change in the price level have on this program?
6. What records of my business transactions should I keep?
7. How can I use communication and transportation services most effectively?

Illus. 1-4. Every time you buy something, you are casting an economic vote. This course can help you learn how to "vote" wisely.

H. Armstrong Roberts

8. Why are taxes paid? What is done with the tax money that is paid to local, state, and federal governments?

9. What kinds of jobs are open to high school graduates? How can I best prepare for these jobs?

These are only a few of the many business and economic problems for which you will need answers from time to time. No doubt you have already experienced some of these problems. An important purpose of *General Business* is to introduce you to our business and economic system and help you understand your everyday business problems. In this way, you can become a better manager of your own business activities.

Developing Your Business Vocabulary

The following italicized terms should become part of your business vocabulary. For each numbered statement, find the italicized term that has the same meaning.

business	*human resources*
capital resources	*natural resources*
consumer	*needs*
economic resources	*services*
economic system or *economy*	*wants*
goods or *products*	

1. Those things that humans must have to survive.
2. Those things that are not necessary to survival but that make life much more enjoyable.
3. An organization that supplies persons with the goods or services they want.
4. The tangible things we use in our everyday lives.
5. Those things that other people do for us.
6. One who uses goods and services.
7. All the means with which we produce the things we need and want.
8. Materials supplied directly by nature and that may be used in producing goods and services.
9. Tools, machinery, and other equipment used to convert natural resources into goods and services.
10. The people who work to produce goods and services.
11. The plan that a nation develops for making decisions on how best to use its economic resources.

Checking Your Understanding

1. Explain the difference between needing things and wanting things.
2. Do most of us today depend upon business for most of the things we need and want? Explain.
3. Are business firms and government agencies also consumers? Explain.
4. "Pioneer families were much more self-sufficient and independent than families are today." Do you agree with this statement? Give reasons for your answer.
5. Give at least two examples each of natural resources, capital resources, and human resources.
6. Why is it necessary for most of us to make economic decisions in buying goods and services?
7. Explain how our economic votes can mean success or failure to a businessman.
8. Every person should have a basic understanding of how our business and economic system operates. Why is this true?

Applying What You Have Learned

1. Prepare a list of at least four different goods and services that are supplied by businesses for two of the following: your school basketball team, your family car, a family pet, or a club or church to which you belong.
2. "Satisfying one want often gives rise to other wants." Give an example from your personal experience or your family's experience in support of this statement.
3. Ask your parents or some older friends to help you prepare a list of 10 goods and services that are available today but that were not in existence 20 or 30 years ago.
4. Mention at least four businesses in your community that sell goods; four that sell services; and four that sell both goods and services.
5. "A service that is rendered by someone can be a personal service to an individual and a business service to a business firm." Is this statement correct? Give reasons for your answer.
6. Modern families are using more services than they ever have in the past. Make a list of services that a family may have obtained within the last few weeks.
7. Suppose that you and a few friends were stranded on a small Pacific island. How would the problem of satisfying your needs and wants on this island differ from that problem in your community? Be as specific as you can in explaining this situation.
8. Would your economic needs change if you moved from Florida to northern Minnesota? Why or why not?

Solving Business Problems

1. The actual land of the United States is one of our most important economic resources. The area of land in our country is listed below in millions of acres:

Total land in U.S. 2,266
Owned by the federal government   766
Owned by the states 103
Owned by counties and cities 19

   (a) In figures, what is the total amount of government-owned land?
   (b) The remainder, privately owned, amounts to a total of how many acres?
   (c) What percent of all our land is privately owned? (Round answer to nearest whole number.)
   (d) What percent of all our land is publicly owned?

2. Three segments of our economy account for most of the spending for goods and services. These three segments are individuals, businesses, and government. The table below shows what each of these segments spent in 1969 and what each segment is expected to spend in 1980. Study the table, then answer the questions.

	1969	1980
Spending by people	$578 billion	$896 billion
Spending by businesses	140 billion	233 billion
Spending by government	212 billion	287 billion

   (a) In dollars, how much more will total spending be in 1980 than it was in 1969?
   (b) What is the increase in total spending expressed as a percentage?
   (c) In dollars, how much more will each segment spend in 1980 than it spent in 1969?
   (d) What is the increase in spending by each segment, expressed as a percentage?

3. In a recent year, the population and land area in square miles for the whole United States and for six different states were:

	Population	Area in Square Miles
United States	203,000,000	3,541,000
Alaska	282,000	566,400
California	19,400,000	156,500
New York	18,300,000	47,900
New Jersey	7,100,000	7,500
Texas	11,200,000	263,000
North Dakota	615,000	69,300

(a) What is the density (number of people per square mile) of population in the United States as a whole?

(b) What is the density of population in each of the six states?

Enriching Your Business Understanding

1. Natural resources, capital resources, and human resources are generally called the three basic economic resources. What do you think would happen if any of these three resources were not available to us?

2. Water is one of our most important natural resources. With increases in population and industry, there will be an increased demand for water. How can our water supply be protected and even increased?

3. Select a product that you often eat or use. Show how each of our three basic economic resources was necessary for the production of that product.

4. Collect four or five advertisements that are designed to create new wants. Mount the ads on heavy paper or arrange them on the bulletin board. Tell the class how these ads attempt to get the public to want what is advertised.

5. Goods are frequently classified as consumer goods when they are used in their final stage to satisfy human wants. If goods are used to produce other goods or services, they are often classified as capital or producer goods. Explain how each of the following may be classified as a product for consumer use as well as for capital use: typewriter, automobile, camera, basketball, pair of scissors. Draw a form similar to that shown below. In the first column, list each product. In the second and third columns, give briefly an example of how the product is used.

Item	Used as a Consumer Good	Used as a Capital Good

PART 2
Features Of Our Economic System

When you turn on the TV to watch a favorite show, do you ever wonder how many other people in the world can enjoy the same pleasure? Or when you pick up the phone and dial a friend's number, do you stop to think that not all teenagers in the world can do the same thing? Do you suppose that every family in the world or even in our country has its own car?

For many people in our country, TV sets, phones, cars, automatic washers, refrigerators, and many other things are very much a part of their daily lives. These things are so much a part of their lives that they forget—or just do not realize that other people may not have them.

Why does our economic system work so well in comparison with those of other countries? Why do we have more of life's comforts than do people in many other places? Why do we have such a good educational system? How are we able to produce more and more goods and services and yet shorten the work week and lengthen vacations? How are we able to provide health services for our citizens? There are no simple answers to these questions. In this part, you will learn about some of the things that make our economic system work as well as it does. But first we will discuss three basic questions that every economic system, including ours, must answer.

THREE ECONOMIC QUESTIONS MUST BE ANSWERED

What goods and services should be produced? How should goods and services be produced? For whom should goods and services be produced? These three basic questions face every society. *Economics* is the study of the activities that people perform in answering these questions and in using their economic resources to produce goods and services.

Think about the first economic question: What goods and services should be produced? In Part 1, you learned that economic resources are limited. A society's people must decide which goods and services are most important to them. The limited economic resources are then used to produce these goods and services. A nation might decide to use most of its economic resources to produce guns, planes, missiles, and other military supplies. But if it does this, there likely won't be enough resources left to provide better medical care or housing or many cars, TV sets, and other such things for its people. The nation must decide which kinds of goods and services are most important to it.

Now, think about the second question: How should goods and services be produced? Economic resources can be combined in different ways to produce the same goods and services. For example, a country could hire many workers to do hand labor in building a road. Or it could hire a few workers to run machines such as bulldozers and power shovels. In the first case, the country is using many units of human resources and few of capital resources. In the second case, it is using many units of capital resources and few of human resources. In either case, the road will get built. But the second combination is more efficient, and the road should be finished much sooner.

Now, the third economic question: For whom should goods and services be produced? This really means: How should goods and services be divided among the people? Some persons believe that the goods and services a society produces should be shared equally by all the people. Most persons, though, believe that people who contribute more to producing the goods and services should be able to get a larger share of them. In our economic system, the share of goods and services that a person is able to obtain is determined largely by the amount of money he has to spend. The amount of money that a person receives in wages or salary is affected by many factors, including his own abilities.

THREE BASIC ECONOMIC QUESTIONS

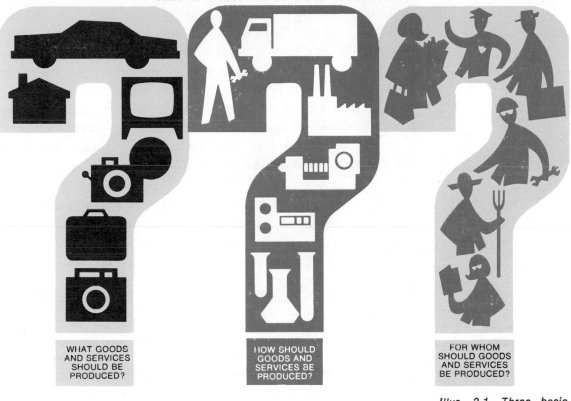

WHAT GOODS AND SERVICES SHOULD BE PRODUCED?

HOW SHOULD GOODS AND SERVICES BE PRODUCED?

FOR WHOM SHOULD GOODS AND SERVICES BE PRODUCED?

Illus. 2-1. Three basic economic questions that must be answered by every society.

OUR ECONOMIC SYSTEM IS CALLED CAPITALISM

When people talk about economic systems, they usually compare socialism, communism, and capitalism. The main difference between these three systems is in who owns the capital resources or, simply, capital. In our economic system, capital resources are mostly owned and managed by individuals rather than by government. Our economic system is called *capitalism*. Later in this part, you will learn something about socialism and communism.

Three important features of capitalism are private property, private enterprise, and freedom of choice. Businessmen are free to offer goods and services at a price, time, and place of their choice. You are free to buy or not to buy. Through this free market system, most of our "what," "how," and "for whom" questions are answered.

THE BASIC RIGHT OF PRIVATE PROPERTY

The right of *private property* is the right to own, use, or sell things of value. In our country, you can own any item and do what you want to with it, so long as you don't break a law. You also have the right to own, use, and sell what you invent or create.

You own the clothes you're wearing and probably many other items. Later, you may want to own such things as a car, house, or boat. Businessmen also have the right to own property. This property includes land, buildings, tools, and the goods they produce. Just as you do, they have the right to sell what they own and to keep the money that comes from sales.

THE BASIC RIGHT OF PRIVATE ENTERPRISE

In our country, a person is free to decide what business to enter and what goods or services to produce. He has the right to start any business so long as he obeys the law in doing so. The right to decide what business to enter and what goods and services to produce is the right of *private enterprise*. This right is very important to the success of our economic system. Because of it, our economic system is sometimes called the private enterprise or free enterprise system.

Under the right of private enterprise, people are entitled to make a profit from their businesses. *Profit* is the difference between what it costs a person to run his business and what his sales bring in. Businessmen are entitled to profits because when they start a business, they run the risk of losing the money they've invested. Also, extra work and extra headaches go with owning and running a business.

The desire to work for profit is often called the *profit motive*. It helps make our economic system strong. Because of it, people invest money in businesses and businessmen develop new products to satisfy consumers' needs and wants. But the profit motive is not the only motive for putting time, money, and effort into businesses. Some people take great pride in bringing out new products or improving existing ones. Many people get pleasure from knowing that the goods or services they produce make people's lives happier. Other people thrive on the excitement of starting and running new businesses.

The right of private enterprise and the profit motive produce competition among businesses. Look at the ads crammed into a

H. Armstrong Roberts

Illus. 2-2. Our entire business world is built on the important rights of private property and private enterprise.

Sunday newspaper. And think of how many commercials you see in just one evening of watching TV. Businesses are always trying to lure customers away from other businesses. Each business tries to build loyalty to the goods or services it sells. This rivalry among businesses is called *competition*. One business may compete with another in several ways. It may lower the prices of its products. It may improve the quality of its products. Or it may offer more services. As a consumer, you benefit from competition.

We have been discussing two very important rights in our economic system: the right to own property and the right to enter the business of our choice. We also have other rights that give us economic freedom of choice. Here are some of them:

OTHER RIGHTS GIVE US FREEDOM OF CHOICE

1. We have the right to buy where and what we please, except for those things that the government declares to be harmful to us. If you don't like the goods and services of one business, you can go to another.
2. We have the right to choose what we will do for a living. We're free to do any kind of work that is not against the law.
3. We have the right as workers to organize. Through organization, we can strive to improve our working conditions.

4. We have the right to travel when and where we please in our country and in many other countries.
5. We have the right to express our opinions in newspapers, over radio and television, and in talking with others.

Our country has been blessed with plentiful natural resources. We also have great capital resources and the ability to use them effectively. In addition, we have the many creative talents of our people. But these are not the only reasons for our economic success. Perhaps most important of all are the personal rights or freedoms that you have just learned about. These give every American the chance to use his abilities to the utmost.

FEATURES OF OTHER ECONOMIC SYSTEMS

It is very hard to define capitalism, socialism, and communism and explain how they work. This is true partly because none of them exists anywhere in a pure form. Under pure capitalism, for example, all enterprises would be privately owned and managed. Under pure communism, all enterprises would be owned and run by the government. Features of economic systems vary from country to country, even though several countries may call their economic systems by the same name.

Under *socialism* today, the government may own and operate such basic enterprises as steel mills, railroads and airlines, power plants, radio and TV stations, and banks. However, the extent of government ownership and control is decided by the people. If they want more government control, they can vote for it. If they want less, they can vote against it. Some enterprises are also privately owned, but there is less chance for private business ownership than in our country. In some socialistic countries, such as England and Sweden, the people have many of the economic freedoms we have.

Under *communism,* the government has tight control over the economic resources. Farms, mines, factories, stores, newspapers, railroads, telephone services—all are owned and run by the government. Government decides what goods and services are to be produced, and it decides how they are to be produced. It is true that people are free to buy whatever goods and services are offered for sale. But the prices and supply of such products as clothing, TV sets, watches, and cars are set by the government.

Illus. 2-3. In our economic system, consumers are free to buy what they want, and businesses are free to produce almost anything they want. Under communism and, to some extent, under socialism, economic resources are controlled by the government.

Most people living under communism do not have the freedom to decide how far they will go in school or what job they will have. Job opportunities and wages to be paid are mostly fixed by government. Government may even tell a person how large an apartment or house he may live in.

In our country, there is some government regulation of business. There are also some government-operated enterprises such as post offices and schools. Our economic system is not pure capitalism, so it is often called modified capitalism. In Unit 10, you will learn about how government and business work together in our economic system.

Most Americans feel that they are very lucky to be living under our economic system. The precious rights of private property, private enterprise, and those other rights giving economic freedom of choice are yours. The only restrictions are laws made to prevent unfair competition, to ensure fair dealing, and to give each person equal business opportunities.

Developing Your Business Vocabulary

The following italicized terms should become part of your business vocabulary. For each numbered statement, find the italicized term that has the same meaning.

<table>
<tr><td>capitalism</td><td>private property</td></tr>
<tr><td>communism</td><td>profit</td></tr>
<tr><td>competition</td><td>profit motive</td></tr>
<tr><td>economics</td><td>socialism</td></tr>
<tr><td>private enterprise</td><td></td></tr>
</table>

1. The study of how people decide what, how, and for whom goods and services should be produced.
2. An economic system in which individuals own most of the capital resources and carry on business activities with a minimum of government control.
3. The right to own, use, or sell things of value.
4. The right of individuals to start or invest in any legal business with the hope of earning fair profits.
5. The amount left over from sales after the costs of running a business have been paid.
6. The desire to benefit financially from investing time and money in a business, realizing that there is risk of loss.
7. The rivalry among businesses to sell their goods and services to buyers.
8. An economic system in which the government owns and operates a number of basic industries and provides for some degree of private property and private enterprise.
9. An economic system in which government owns most of the property and has tight control over the production and distribution of goods and services.

Checking Your Understanding

1. What are three basic economic questions that every economic system must answer?
2. If a nation spends all its economic resources to produce consumer goods, it may not be able to provide adequate police and fire protection, sidewalks and roads, and health and sanitation services. Do you agree? Give reasons for your answer.
3. What are three important features of capitalism?

4. Our economic system is often called a private enterprise or free enterprise system. Why?
5. "People go into business for only one reason: to make a big profit." Tell why you agree or disagree with this statement.
6. State three ways in which consumers may benefit from competition among businesses.
7. What are some important rights, in addition to those of private property and private enterprise, that give us economic freedom of choice?
8. An important difference between capitalism, socialism, and communism is in who owns the capital resources. Explain who owns the capital resources in each of these economic systems.
9. Why is it really more accurate to refer to our economic system as modified capitalism rather than as capitalism?

Applying What You Have Learned

1. How is the problem of what goods and services to produce chiefly determined under socialism, communism, and capitalism?
2. Some persons say that our economic system is able to provide many more of life's comforts for its people largely because it has been blessed with plentiful natural resources. Do you agree or disagree that the presence of many natural resources is the main reason why our economy has been so successful? Explain your answer.
3. Select two of the rights mentioned on pages 17 and 18. If these rights were taken away from you and other Americans, what changes would take place in the way you live?
4. We have the freedom to own and use property as we wish, so long as we don't interfere with the rights of others. Can you think of some restrictions that are placed upon the use of property we own? Who imposes these restrictions? Why are these restrictions imposed?
5. If several businesses in your community fail during the year, how might the welfare of individual consumers, workers, other businesses, and government be affected?
6. Americans enjoy many freedoms, among them the right to choose almost any kind of work we want to do for a living. Why, then, doesn't any person have the freedom to open a law office, be a pharmacist, practice medicine, or be an airline pilot when he believes he is ready to do so?
7. Can you think of ways in which competition among businesses might work to the disadvantage of consumers?

Solving Business Problems

1. Dan Klassen was offered $95 for his used motorcycle. He decided that he could get a much better price if he made some repairs on the motorcycle. He did all the work himself and bought these parts and materials:

Item	Price
New rear tire and tube	$16.50
Brake lever	1.90
Spark plugs	1.15
Set of points	2.38
Seat cover	5.42
Can of lacquer paint .	3.75
Pair of handle grips ..	1.40

After making the improvements, Dan sold the motorcycle for $140.

(a) Dan had to pay a sales tax of 4% on the total cost of the parts and materials he bought. What were his total costs, including parts and materials and sales tax?

(b) How much more money did he receive by waiting to sell the repaired motorcycle?

(c) Assume that Dan spent 16 hours working on the motorcycle. How much did he make per hour?

2. In Russia, consumer goods are not as plentiful as they are in this country. Most items, especially home furnishings and appliances, are very expensive when compared with costs in the United States. Assume that to earn enough money to buy a 23-inch color TV set, the average Russian worker would have to put in 1,320 working hours. Assume that the average American worker would have to put in 120 hours to earn enough to buy a comparable TV set.

(a) The Russian worker has to work how many times as long as the American worker to earn enough money to buy the TV set?

(b) How many 8-hour days of work are required for each of the two workers?

(c) If the American worker receives $3.10 an hour, what would be the cost of the TV to him?

(d) If the American worker had to put in as many hours as the Russian worker, how much would he be paying for the set?

3. United States automobile manufacturers have competition from automobile manufacturers in foreign countries who export cars for sale in this country. The table on page 23 shows the production of automobiles in the United States and the number of cars imported into this country from 1965 through 1969.

Year	U.S. Production	Imports
1965	9,340,000	560,000
1966	8,600,000	910,000
1967	7,410,000	1,020,000
1968	8,850,000	1,620,000
1969	8,220,000	1,850,000

(a) How many more cars were produced and imported in 1969 than in 1965?

(b) Imports were what percentage of U.S. production in each of the five years given in the table?

(c) Of all new cars (those made here plus imported ones) that were available for sale in this country in 1969, what percentage was produced in foreign countries?

Enriching Your Business Understanding

1. What does the term *laissez faire* mean? How does it relate to capitalism? Do you feel that we in the United States could improve our economic system by adopting *laissez faire* principles? Explain.

2. Interview a man in your community who owns and manages his own business. Find out why he has invested his money and time in operating a business of his own. Ask him also if it would not be easier and less worrisome to work for someone else at a salary that would bring him about as much income as he now receives. If he agrees, ask him why he doesn't seek such a position.

3. People sometimes get into arguments about whether or not our government should control prices of the things we buy. For each of the following items, tell whether you consider government control of prices to be important and give reasons for your answers:

milk	water
haircuts	shoes
bus fares	electricity
magazines	postage stamps
gasoline	services of physicians
long-distance phone calls	high school football games

4. Select a nation, preferably one in Asia, Africa, South America, or Europe, and do research on this nation or interview someone who has lived or traveled in that nation. Find out how the country compares with the United States in as many different respects as you can. The items listed on page 24 are some that you may wish to cover, but you will no doubt think of others.

Characteristics of the economic system
Amount of goods and services that are available
Ability of people to buy the things they need and want
Economic and political freedom
Educational opportunities
Job opportunities
Government ownership and controls

Organize and outline your notes neatly in detail. Then be prepared to present a 10- to 20-minute oral report to the class on the most important and interesting facts obtained in your research.

5. There is much more government regulation in our country now than there was 50 or 100 years ago. Why do you suppose there has been an extension of government activities in our economic life?

PART 3

How Our Economy Is Changing

Every economy must look toward and build for the future. Behind us are two of the most challenging decades in our country's history: the 50's and 60's. Ahead of us are even more challenging years. How far have we come in this century? Where do we go from here? And just how do you—now as a teenager and in the future as a voting citizen—fit into the whole scene? This part will try to answer these questions.

As nations go, ours is relatively young, but our economic growth has been remarkable. Today more than 80 million Americans work in thousands of different jobs and produce thousands of different goods and services. Jelly beans, snowmobiles, garbage collection, nail polish, haircuts, fire engines, carry-out chicken dinners, rock concerts—you could name many more. The total of all the goods and services that Americans produce is the output or production of our nation. We have only about 7% of the world's land and about 6% of the world's population, but our output accounts for about 33% of all goods and services produced in the world.

One way to find out how well our economy is doing is to compare outputs from year to year. The federal government

WE CAN MEASURE THE GROWTH OF OUR ECONOMY

supplies estimates of our national output. The most widely used estimate is the *gross national product* or GNP. The GNP is the total value of all goods and services produced in our country during a year.

GNP includes what we consumers spend for food, clothing, and housing. It includes what businessmen spend for buildings, equipment, and supplies. It also includes what government agencies spend to pay employees and buy supplies. If the GNP increases from year to year, this is a good sign that our economy is growing.

ITEMS IN GROSS NATIONAL PRODUCT

Illus. 3-1. These are the elements that make up our Gross National Product.

Let's go one step further. An even better way to measure economic growth is to find out what the *per capita* (or per person) *output* is. For example, suppose that there is no change in GNP this year over last. But suppose that the population increases. You can see that the same output would have to be divided among more people. So each person would produce and have, on the average, less than before.

The per capita output can easily be found by dividing the GNP by the total population. An increase in per capita output usually means that our economy is growing. A decrease may mean that our economy is having troubles. Adjusting for price changes, today's per capita output is about four times what it was at the turn of the century.

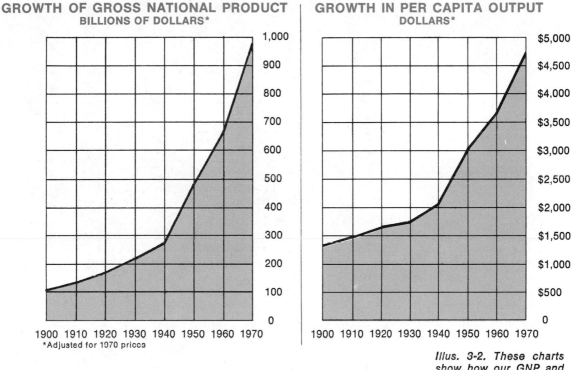

GROWTH OF GROSS NATIONAL PRODUCT
BILLIONS OF DOLLARS*

1,000
900
800
700
600
500
400
300
200
100
0

1900 1910 1920 1930 1940 1950 1960 1970
*Adjusted for 1970 prices

GROWTH IN PER CAPITA OUTPUT
DOLLARS*

$5,000
$4,500
$4,000
$3,500
$3,000
$2,500
$2,000
$1,500
$1,000
$500
0

1900 1910 1920 1930 1940 1950 1960 1970

Illus. 3-2. These charts show how our GNP and our per capita output have increased since 1900.

Another important measure of how our economy is growing is the *output per man-hour* or *productivity*. This is the amount of goods that one worker, on the average, can produce in one hour. In the 1960's, output per man-hour increased almost 35%. A major reason why our productivity has increased so much is that we now use many modern machines and efficient methods of producing goods and services. You will learn about some of these modern machines and production methods in Part 6.

Our economic history shows that as workers produce more items per hour, they earn more per hour. As workers produce more at less cost, the employer can pass some of the savings on to them in the form of higher wages. And as the costs of production decrease, many products are reduced in price. Try to imagine how much you would pay today for a car built entirely by hand with only the simplest tools.

INDEXES OF OUTPUT PER MAN-HOUR

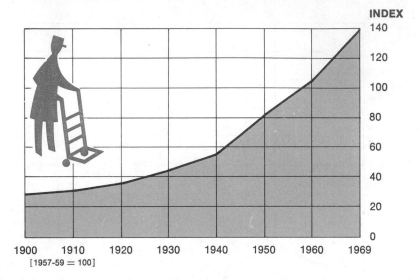

Illus. 3-3. Through the use of modern machinery and production methods, we have greatly increased our productivity.

Our ability to produce more and more has also made it possible to reduce the number of hours in a work week. In the early 1890's, an average worker put in more than 55 hours a week. Today the average work week is a little less than 40 hours. But even though we work fewer hours and have more leisure time, we produce more and earn more than our labor force ever has before.

STYLES OF LIVING CHANGE AS THE ECONOMY GROWS

Because of modern production methods, we are able to provide more goods and services for consumers and higher earnings for workers. We can thus enjoy a higher style of living. *Style of living* refers to the goods or services that an individual, family, or even a nation regularly obtains. A person's style of living depends mainly on two things: the amount of income he has, and how wisely he makes economic decisions. A person's style of living is influenced by his values, customs, likes, and dislikes.

How is style of living measured? Persons may measure another person's style of living by the kind of house he lives in, whether his family owns one car or two, what kind of clothes he wears, where he works, whether he takes a vacation to Canada this summer, and many other things. Our style of living as a nation not only includes an abundance of goods and services but also such important things as opportunities for education and leisure time. It includes highways and sidewalks that everyone can use. It includes police and fire protection, parks, social security payments, and all the other services that government provides.

Most people in our country have enough income to buy the goods and services that make up at least a minimum style of living. But some of our people are not able to do this. Some have not had the education or training necessary to obtain employment. Others live in rural areas where few jobs are available. This situation must be corrected. In a nation as rich as ours, everyone should be able to obtain at least a minimum style of living.

Soon you'll have responsibilities as a wage earner, perhaps as head of a family, and certainly as a voting member of a community. With the growth of our economy go some trends that will affect you very much in these new roles.

A LOOK AT OUR GROWING ECONOMY

Our population has increased by more than 35% since 1950, and about 180,000 more people are added to our nation every month. People are living longer today, too. A child born in 1920 could expect to live only to about age 55. Thanks to better diets and better medical care, a child born today can expect to live to about age 70. The great increases in our population mean that we must use our economic resources more wisely than ever before. There must be enough land to live on, food to eat, and clothes to wear for all these new Americans.

Our population is often said to be a young one. Right now, about 46 out of every 100 Americans are under 25. Within the next 10 years, the group of people between 20 and 35 will grow twice as fast as the rest of the population. So you and everyone else who is a teenager today will have a lot to say about where our economy goes from here. Even today, you're an important part of our economy. Teenagers today have more money to spend than they have ever had before. And you have quite an influence on the spending habits of your families. Many businesses depend upon teenage spending for most of their income. The record industry, for example, would not be nearly as large as it is today if it were not for teenage buying.

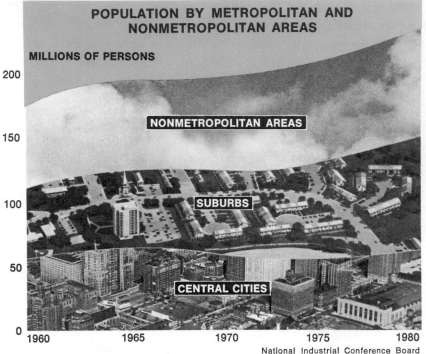

POPULATION BY METROPOLITAN AND NONMETROPOLITAN AREAS

MILLIONS OF PERSONS

200

150

NONMETROPOLITAN AREAS

100

SUBURBS

50

CENTRAL CITIES

0

1960   1965   1970   1975   1980

National Industrial Conference Board

Illus. 3-4. Where our population will be by 1980.

If our population is a young one, it is also a mobile one. We're a nation of travelers. Thousands of motels, travel agencies, drive-in restaurants, and many other kinds of service businesses have sprung up in the last decade. Manufacturers of trailers and campers are doing a booming business. Jet planes make coast-to-coast flights almost as easily as a trip across town.

We Americans still have some pioneer spirit left. Many of us think nothing of pulling up stakes and moving to another part of the country if we have a chance for a better life. About one-fourth of our population moves in any one year. If you live in either the West or the Southwest, you're living in one of the fastest-growing parts of our country. And if you live in a city or suburb, you have plenty of company. Most of our population is concentrated there rather than in rural areas.

Today our people have more money to spend than they have ever had. They also have more free time in which to spend it. The average family income is over $9,000. By 1980, it should be about $12,000. We earn this income working fewer hours than we've ever worked before. And we also have many gadgets that cut down on the routine chores we do. In the kitchen alone, blenders blend, carving knives carve, toasters toast, ice crushers crush. Your mother can buy almost any kind of packaged food from instant mashed potatoes to frozen breakfasts to applesauce raisin cake mix. With the extra leisure time we have, we can play tennis, go to the movies, learn to waterski, or do just about anything else we want to do.

Another important feature of our growing economy is the education explosion. It's been going on for the last 25 or 30 years, but it will be even more "explosive" in the next decade. Thirty years ago, only about 12% of all high school graduates went on to college. In many parts of the country now, almost 70% of the high school graduates receive some type of education or training beyond high school. This percentage is expected to go even higher. The extra education pays off. Our labor force is becoming more skilled and more resourceful. Less emphasis is being placed on musclepower, and more emphasis is being placed on brainpower. Estimates are that 50% more technical and professional workers will be needed within the next 10 years.

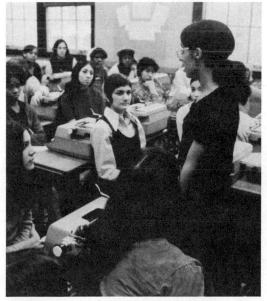

Chemical Bank

Illus. 3-5. In the next few years, more and more high school graduates will be receiving some type of education or training beyond high school. The extra education pays off.

YOU CAN HELP BUILD OUR ECONOMIC FUTURE

What lies ahead for our economy? No one knows for sure. Robots doing most of the routine work in factories? Housekeeping done entirely by machines? Mining and farming under the ocean? Space colonies on the moon? Two-way pocket telephones and three-dimensional TV? Germproof, tornadoproof, earthquakeproof, soundproof, fireproof, burglarproof houses? These are some of the things scientists have predicted for the year 2000.

We've come a long way under our private enterprise system. We know it works well. We also know it can be made to work even better. In our country, there are still some people who do not have good food, decent housing, and proper health care. All of us are being harmed by what is happening to our environment. Air and water are being polluted by gases, smoke, and waste coming from industry and from the products we buy and use. This is one problem that we must solve. Government now is responding to the people's demand for action, and businesses are cooperating so that we can keep our environment healthy for future Americans.

Another problem is that of providing proper housing for all our people, especially in large cities. Already much slum housing is being remodeled or torn down and rebuilt. Efforts are being made to solve traffic problems in large cities, and new shopping and cultural centers are being built.

As Americans, we realize that we have some shortcomings. And as a nation, we are working to eliminate economic hardship for our people. Much needs to be done to control disease and reduce human suffering. There are great responsibilities to conserve our natural resources. Ideas are needed on how to continue to improve our government and on how to live in peace with our fellow men. Much remains to be done in education, aviation, and space exploration.

To provide for a better life for everyone, each of us has the responsibility of gaining a basic understanding of how our economic system works, of having an awareness of our problems, and of wanting to help solve our problems. The economic frontier calls for: better housing, safer highways, a clean environment, improved working conditions, more efficient production to raise everyone's style of living. How our country conquers this economic frontier depends in part on you.

Developing Your Business Vocabulary

The following italicized terms should become part of your business vocabulary. For each numbered statement, find the italicized term that has the same meaning.

gross national product or *GNP*   *per capita output*
output per man-hour or *productivity*   *style of living*

1. The total value of all goods and services produced in a country during a year.
2. The figure that results from dividing the GNP of a country by the population of that country.
3. The amount of goods that one worker, on the average, can produce in one hour.
4. The quality and quantity of goods or services, plus economic and social advantages, that are available to individuals, families, and even nations.

Checking Your Understanding

1. "One way of finding out how well our economy is doing is to compare outputs from year to year." What does this statement mean? Do you agree with it?
2. Is GNP determined entirely by what individual consumers spend for goods and services?
3. If the GNP remains the same from one year to another but the population increases by about 10%, has there been economic growth? Explain.
4. How has our increased productivity changed our style of living?
5. Besides the many goods and services that we are able to buy, what other things contribute to our style of living?
6. Give several characteristics of our growing, changing economy.
7. Why do people live longer today than they did 50 or more years ago? Can you give any reasons for this besides those mentioned in your textbook?
8. Why can teenagers be considered an influential group in our economy?
9. Is there room for improvement in our economic system? Can you think of several economic problems that need solving?

Applying What You Have Learned

1. The GNP of Country A is $200 million. The GNP of Country B is $400 million. Does this mean that the per capita output of Country B is about twice that of Country A? Explain.
2. What does the term "style of living" mean to you? Does every person in a particular community have about the same style of living? Explain.
3. Recently our GNP was over $900 billion. Five years before, it was nearly $700 billion. And in less than five years from now, our GNP is expected to go beyond the trillion dollar mark. What difference does it make to you and to other people in your community whether the GNP is increasing or decreasing?
4. Various products, services, and conditions contribute to one's style of living. List at least ten different things that you consider important to attain and maintain a good style of living for yourself.
5. Why is it possible for the style of living of one person to be much higher than that of another person when both of them have about the same income, live in the same neighborhood, and live in homes of equal value?
6. Some people say that young Americans today have more opportunities for pioneer work than did people in almost any other time in our history. Do you agree? Why?
7. Do you think the world of the future—say, around the year 2000—will be considerably different from the world we live in now? Explain.

Solving Business Problems

1. In a recent year, the gross national product of the United States was composed mainly of these three parts:

   Amount spent by consumers for goods and services, $577.5 billion
   Amount spent by businesses for equipment, buildings, and other capital resources, $139.8 billion
   Amount spent by government to pay for services and products, $212.2 billion

   (a) What was the total GNP?
   (b) What percent of the total GNP was accounted for by the value of consumer purchases?
   (c) What percent of the total GNP was accounted for by the value of business purchases?
   (d) What percent of the total GNP was accounted for by the value of government purchases?

2. At the end of a recent year, U.S. population was estimated to be about 203 million. Using the GNP figure from Problem **1a,** determine the per capita output of the United States for that year.

3. It has been estimated that our population will increase 20% from 1970 to 1980. At 1970 prices, how much would our GNP have to grow if we did nothing more than keep up with our 1970 per capita output?

4. The table below gives data on the gross national product and population for six countries in a recent year. The countries are ranked from the highest to lowest in terms of GNP. On a separate sheet of paper, copy this chart. (Or use the form in your *Activities and Projects.*) Add two columns with the headings "Per Capita Output" and "Per Capita Rank." For each country, enter its per capita output and then determine the rank order according to per capita output.

Country	GNP (In millions of dollars)	GNP Rank	Population (In millions)
Italy	$66,958	1	52
Canada	57,329	2	20
Australia	26,692	3	12
Mexico	24,112	4	46
Peru	3,507	5	12
Ghana	2,052	6	8

Enriching Your Business Understanding

1. Comparing gross national products from year to year is one way of finding out whether or not we are making economic progress. What are some other available facts that might indicate how well our economy is doing?

2. Look through some recent economics textbooks and find out what "opportunity cost" means. Then, by giving illustrations, indicate how this concept can affect our style of living.

3. Make a case history of a product that has been on the market for many years. Compare today's product with the same kind of product sold many years ago. Consider such things as changes in appearance and form, new features and uses, differences in price, methods of production, and so on.

4. Discuss with your grandparents or with some friends about your grandparents' age how they lived when they were your age. Try to find out what their style of living was. What advantages do you

have today that they did not have? What advantages did they have that you do not have? Organize your findings into a written report.

5. In determining our gross national product, only *final* goods and services are included. This avoids having some items counted more than once. For example, a mining company sells iron ore to a company that makes steel. The steel company sells the steel to an automobile manufacturer who produces finished cars. The iron ore is not counted at each step. Its value is included only once: in the price paid for the final product, the car.

Below is a list of things produced in our economy. Tell whether you think each item should be counted as part of our GNP. If you do not think it should be counted, tell why.

(a) Electric toaster for newlyweds.
(b) Telephone in a private home.
(c) Telephone in a government office.
(d) Tires sold to a company that makes motorcycles.
(e) Haircuts.
(f) Paper sold to the publisher of this book.
(g) Automobile for a family's use.
(h) Automobile for a highway patrolman's use.
(i) Sidewalks paid for by a city.
(j) Soap sold to a laundry.
(k) Peaches sold to a cannery.

Unit 2

The Nature of American Business

PART 4
Business In Our Economy

Look around your classroom. Almost everything you see was supplied by business. Your desk, your pencil, your books, your clothes, the chalkboard—the list could go on and on. Yesterday you might have ridden to school on the bus, bought lunch, gone shopping for new school clothes. Can you think of a single day when you didn't come in contact with business?

From our point of view as consumers, the purpose of business is simple: to supply us with the goods and services that we need and want but cannot supply ourselves. It is impossible to separate our business world from our economic system. Our economic system is the framework in which business operates, and there couldn't be one without the other.

There are millions of different businesses in this country, but in one way they are all alike. They all add some kind of utility to a good or a service. Utility is a characteristic of a good or service that helps to make it useful to consumers. In other words, utilities of various types make it possible for goods and services to satisfy our needs and wants. There are four kinds of utility: form, place, time, and possession utility. From your point of view, a good must usually have all four utilities before it can satisfy a need or want.

BUSINESSES ADD UTILITY TO GOODS AND SERVICES

Suppose that your mother sends you to the store to buy corn flakes. An ear of corn on a stalk in the middle of Iowa has no value to you. The corn must be picked and processed into a form you can use. When the corn is ground and made into flakes, it has acquired *form utility*.

So now there are corn flakes, but they still aren't in your kitchen. They have form utility, but they have no other utility for you if they are packed in cartons in Battle Creek, Michigan. The next utility that must be added is *place utility*. The corn flakes must be shipped to your local grocery store so that you can buy them.

The corn flakes must also be in your local store when you want them, that is, they must have *time utility*. After the grocer receives the corn flakes, he stores them in his warehouse and eventually places them on the display shelves so that they will be available at the time you want them.

Finally, the corn flakes must have *possession utility* for you. Suppose that they are in the grocery store and the grocery store is open, but you left your money at home. The corn flakes have three of the four kinds of utility, but that still doesn't do you any good because you don't have the money to buy them.

You can see, then, that most of the goods you buy must have the four kinds of utility—form, place, time, and possession. Form utility can be added only to goods, but the other three kinds of utility can be added to services as well.

Illus. 4-1. Most of the goods that we buy as consumers must have the four kinds of utility.

Extractors, manufacturers, marketing businesses, and service businesses are the basic kinds of businesses. They all add one or more kinds of utility to goods or services.

Businesses that grow products or take raw materials from nature are called *extractors*. Farmers and fishermen are two important extractors. So are those who dig copper out of Montana, pump oil out of Texas, and run lumber camps in Washington. Sometimes the extractor's products are ready to be sold just as they come from the earth or the sea, like the crabs sold on San Francisco's Fisherman's Wharf. But most food products and raw materials need some processing or change in form before the consumer can use them.

The manufacturer takes the extractor's products or raw materials and changes them into a form that consumers can use. Some manufacturers are only a part of the total process of adding form utility to the extractor's products. For example, a textile mill takes the cotton grown on an Alabama farm, spins it into yarn, and makes the yarn into cloth. Another plant in New England takes the cloth and dyes or prints it. A garment factory in New York buys the cloth and makes it into shirts. Together, extractors and manufacturers add form utility to goods. They are usually referred to as producers.

Mobil Oil Corporation

Illus. 4-2. Extractors, like the company that operates this offshore oil-drilling rig, take raw materials from nature.

Marketing businesses add place and time utility to goods. Most producers are too busy growing or making their products to have time to supply consumers directly. And most consumers are too busy at their own jobs or too far away from the producer to go directly to him. Bridging the gap between the producer and the consumer can be a very complex process. The services of many businesses are often needed before goods actually reach consumers. All the activities that are involved in moving goods from producers to consumers are called *marketing* or *distribution*. All persons or businesses which supply this service of moving goods from producers to consumers are called *middlemen* or *distributors*. Because marketing is so important in making sure that you can obtain the goods to satisfy your needs and wants, it will be discussed in more detail in Part 7.

Illus. 4-3. The middleman that is probably most familiar to most consumers is the retailer. A large shopping center like this one may contain many different retail stores.

Ewing Galloway

Service businesses are perhaps the fastest-growing segment of our business world. As people come to have more leisure time and more money to spend, they want more and more businesses to do things for them. Some service businesses serve individual consumers. Some serve other businesses. And some serve both individual consumers and other businesses. Today you can find a service business to: move you from Maine to Oklahoma; cut your hair; wash your car; figure your income tax; board your dog; give you guitar lessons; clean your clothes; rent you a pair of skis; pull a tooth; take you on a tour; and almost any other thing you can think of.

There are many different types and sizes of businesses. A business may be as small as a newspaper stand on a neighborhood corner, or as large and complex as an oil company which has wells, refineries, and pumping stations in many different countries. Although individual businesses may be very different in the way they operate, most of them perform basically the same kinds of activities. Some of these important activities are: (1) buying goods and services; (2) selling goods and services; (3) storing goods; (4) handling money and keeping records; (5) extending credit to customers; (6) providing services to customers; (7) packaging and dividing goods; and (8) training employees.

(1) Businesses buy goods and services both for resale and for their own use. The owner of a men's clothing store, for instance, must buy slacks, jackets, suits, coats, and other items for his stock. The store owner also needs sales tickets, a cash register, display cases, and other supplies. He needs services offered by other businesses, such as advertising space in a newspaper or a window cleaner to wash his display windows.

(2) Businesses must sell goods and services if they expect to stay in operation. Some businesses—grocery stores, hardware stores, jewelry stores, and others—sell goods. Other businesses— telephone companies, airlines, and so on—sell services. Doctors, dentists, lawyers, and architects all offer professional services.

(3) Goods must be stored until they are sold or until the customer wants them delivered. For example, toys are produced the year round, but most of them are stored until retail merchants order for Christmas. Manufacturers need storage yards and ware-houses to store raw materials, supplies, and finished parts. Some businesses handle products that need special storage. A meat market, for example, must have refrigerators and freezers.

(4) All businesses must handle money and keep records. Every businessman needs to know how much his sales have been, how much of what he sold was returned by unhappy customers, and how much he owes to others. He needs to know how much he is spending for building repairs, rent, salaries, and other expenses. He needs records of the property he uses in his business, such as display cases, adding machines, and delivery trucks. His records show whether his business is making or losing money and give him information he needs for government reports.

Control Data Corporation

Illus. 4-4. Large businesses keep records involving huge quantities of data. To speed up their recordkeeping, they use complex electronic equipment such as this.

(5) Most businesses today extend credit to their customers. Few middlemen would be able to operate if manufacturers and other middlemen did not extend credit to them. And retail merchants find that most customers today expect credit at stores where they shop.

(6) Almost all businesses give certain services with the goods they sell to customers. Often a customer will buy from the business that offers the most service. A firm that makes air conditioners for factories, for example, may offer help in installing the air conditioners. A department store may provide parking space, lounges, a coffee shop, telephones, delivery service, and other things to make shopping easier and more pleasant.

(7) Many businesses package and divide goods to meet customer needs. For example, manufacturers design packages to protect goods and make them more attractive. Retailers package goods to protect them while they are being delivered or to make them attractive as gifts. Businesses that market goods may buy them in large quantities and divide them into small quantities for customers. A middleman might buy tomatoes by the bushel and package them into trays of three tomatoes each, which is a more convenient size for the customer. The trays are then sold to supermarkets which in turn sell them to consumers.

(8) Businessmen usually find that they must train people they hire to work for them. Every business operates a little differently from every other business, and a new employee must learn the procedures in the business he is working for. Businessmen know that trained employees can earn more both for themselves and for the business. In some firms, new employees are trained by more experienced ones. Larger firms may have training departments or may even operate special schools. Some firms pay expenses of sending an employee to evening classes.

Not all businesses are successful. Some fail because of the risks taken. Some of these risks cannot be controlled by the owner or manager of a business. For example, a farmer may lose his crops because of drought. A strike of transportation workers may seriously harm other industries. Poor economic conditions may harm business in general.

PROFITS ARE REWARDS FOR BUSINESS RISKS

All businessmen take risks. When a man decides to start a business, he plans to use his time and energy in running it. He also decides to put into that business the money he has saved and the savings of others who have confidence in him. He will need to answer important questions such as these:

1. What kind of business will it be?
2. How much money will I need?
3. How much money may I safely borrow?
4. Where shall I locate my business?
5. What goods and services shall I offer my customers?
6. What prices shall I charge?
7. How much merchandise shall I carry in stock?
8. Shall I sell for cash or credit?
9. Shall I take on a partner or set up some other organization plan?
10. How much shall I spend on advertising?

Businessmen are entitled to profits because of the risks they take in investing their money and because of the extra work and responsibility that go with ownership and management. But most businesses do not make the huge profits that some people suppose. Competition with other businesses helps keep prices and profits down to a reasonable figure. Then, too, some people misunderstand gross profit and net profit. *Gross profit* or *margin* is the difference between the selling price and the cost price of an article. *Net profit* is what is left after all expenses have been paid. Suppose Ken Irwin, owner of a camera shop, sells a camera for $20. He bought the camera from a wholesaler for $12, so he has a gross profit of $8. But out of this $8 he must pay for rent, supplies, advertising, taxes, and many other expenses. His records show that all expenses related to the sale of the camera amount to $7. He has therefore made a net profit of $1 on the camera—or a net profit of 5% ($1 ÷ $20) on the selling price.

Illus. 4-5. Most businesses do not make the huge profits sometimes supposed. This chart shows profits, after taxes, of large corporations in various industries In a recent year.

INDUSTRY	PROFITS AS % OF SALES
All industries	4.6%
Selected industries	
Aircraft and parts	3.5%
Apparel	3.6%
Food and beverages	2.7%
Office machinery, including computers	6.3%
Motor vehicles and parts	3.9%
Shipbuilding, railroad equipment, mobile homes	4.2%
Pharmaceuticals (drugs, medicines)	9.2%
Paper and wood products	5.1%
Soaps, cosmetics	7.5%

SOURCE: Fortune Directory of 500 Largest U.S. Industrial Corporations, May, 1970

HOW BUSINESSES HELP A COMMUNITY

Almost everyone is pleased when a new business opens in a community. Why? Because a new business benefits the community in several ways. Perhaps the most important benefit is that a new business creates jobs. This means that the people who work directly for it have incomes to support themselves and their families. As they spend their incomes for goods and services, there is a multiplier effect.

Let's see how this multiplier effect works. The money that workers spend is in turn spent by those who receive it. This creates more jobs and income in the community. For example, part of each worker's income is spent for food. The food store manager pays out part of this money for his stock. He also pays part of it to his employees, who in turn spend their money somewhere else for goods and services. If new people come to the community to work, more houses will probably be needed. This means that local builders will hire more men and buy more materials. As each dollar is spent, each businessman is likely to buy more goods and hire more people to meet his customers' demands. So when a new job is created in a community, each dollar paid to workers is said to multiply itself.

Another benefit from a new or expanded business is that it pays taxes to the community. This means that the community has more money to build new schools, repair its streets, provide better police and fire protection, and improve other services such as parks.

As you learned earlier, business firms are themselves consumers. When a new business comes to a community, it buys such things as electricity, office furniture and supplies, equipment, and tools. Some of these will be bought from firms in other towns, but much will be bought locally. This gives income to local businesses and, in turn, paychecks to their employees.

Businesses also tend to attract other businesses. When one business settles in a community, other businesses often come to supply it. This is especially true when a large firm comes to a community. For example, small factories may spring up to supply a large factory with such things as small parts, office supplies, cleaning services, and advertising services. Each of these smaller firms hires people and buys goods and services. So more jobs and more income are created in the community.

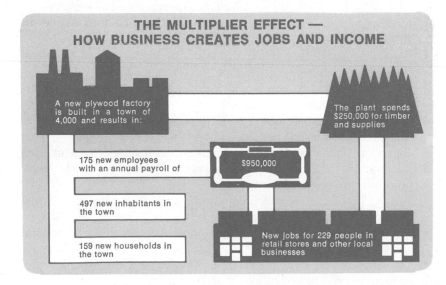

THE MULTIPLIER EFFECT —
HOW BUSINESS CREATES JOBS AND INCOME

A new plywood factory is built in a town of 4,000 and results in:

The plant spends $250,000 for timber and supplies

175 new employees with an annual payroll of

$950,000

497 new inhabitants in the town

159 new households in the town

New jobs for 229 people in retail stores and other local businesses

Illus. 4-6. A new business can benefit almost everyone in a community. Here is how the multiplier effect works.

BEGIN THINKING ABOUT YOUR FUTURE CAREER

As you read and study other parts of this book, you will learn more about various types of businesses and will get a better idea of the kind of employees they need. In Unit 11 you will learn about the job market and about the opportunities open to you if you decide on a career in business.

As you progress in this course, try to choose a few occupations that seem attractive to you. Then learn what you can about them and about the kinds of work done in them. It is in your best interest to find the job that is suited to your abilities and your personality.

Developing Your Business Vocabulary

The following italicized terms should become part of your business vocabulary. For each numbered statement, find the italicized term that has the same meaning.

extractors	*net profit*
form utility	*place utility*
gross profit or *margin*	*possession utility*
marketing or *distribution*	*time utility*
middlemen or *distributors*	

1. Usefulness that is added to materials by changing their shape or structure.
2. Usefulness added to goods and services by being shipped to where they are wanted.
3. Usefulness added to goods and services by being made available when they are wanted.
4. Usefulness that comes from owning or having the right to use a particular good or service.
5. Businesses that grow products or take raw materials from nature.
6. The various activities that are involved in moving goods from producers to consumers.
7. Persons or businesses which supply the various services in moving goods from producers to consumers.
8. The difference between the selling price and the cost price of an article.
9. The amount left over after the cost price and all expenses are deducted from the selling price of an article.

Checking Your Understanding

1. "There are many different kinds of businesses in this country, and all of them are alike in that they add some kind of value or usefulness to goods and services." In general, do you agree with this statement? Why?
2. Name several products that we use that do not need to have form utility added to their original state.
3. Name four kinds of extractors and mention at least two products that may be provided by each.
4. How does a manufacturer differ from an extractor?
5. What two kinds of utilities are made possible mainly by businesses engaged in marketing activities?
6. Explain why farmers who grow peaches, for example, are so directly dependent upon manufacturers or processors and middlemen for their success.
7. Why are service businesses among the fastest growing of our various types of businesses?
8. List at least seven kinds of activities that are commonly carried on by both large and small businesses.
9. Some people believe that businesses make from 50% to 100% profit on everything they sell. Is this a fair assumption? Give specific reasons for your answer.
10. Explain how the multiplier effect of new businesses can result in more jobs and income in a community.

Applying What You Have Learned

1. Daniel Mattos is a young dairy farmer. Explain under what conditions he might be considered as: (a) solely an extractor; (b) an extractor and a distributor; (c) an extractor and a manufacturer (or processor); and (d) an extractor, manufacturer, and distributor.
2. Illustrate how Daniel Mattos might add form, place, time, and possession utility to his products.
3. Explain the storage problems of each of the following types of businesses:

   (a) Jewelry store   (e) Service station
   (b) Supermarket   (f) Photographer
   (c) Flower shop   (g) Coffee shop
   (d) Used-car dealer   (h) Pet shop

4. How does a merchant decide what he should buy to offer for sale in his store?
5. If a business has a large gross profit, is it assured of having a net profit? Defend your answer.

6. Businessmen try to locate stores where they can be of greatest service to customers. For each location listed below, name two types of businesses that usually may be found there and give one good reason why each business is located there.

(a) Airport
(b) Hospital zone
(c) College campus
(d) Highway intersection
(e) Residential area

7. Select a business that you know something about, such as a store, garage, or bank. Prepare a list of different kinds of jobs held by people working in that business.

8. Think now about the kind of work you would like to do. Divide a sheet of paper into two columns. In the left-hand column, list the occupations in which you are interested. In the other column, write opposite each occupation a brief explanation of why you think you would be successful in that kind of work.

Solving Business Problems

1. The cost price and the percent of gross profit (based on cost price) for a number of items are given below:

	Cost Price	Percent of Gross Profit (based on cost)
Radio	$ 40	30%
Record album	4	25
Motorcycle	325	20
Watch	27	33⅓
Television set	190	23

(a) What is the amount of gross profit on each item?
(b) What is the selling price of each item?

2. The selling price and the percent of gross profit (based on selling price) for a number of items are given below:

	Selling Price	Percent of Gross Profit (based on selling price)
Typewriter	$120	20%
Camera	36	30
Baseball glove	14	26
Perfume	6	40
Shoes	12	37½

(a) What is the amount of gross profit on each item?
(b) What is the cost price of each item?

3. The Angelo Catelani Company is considering building a cannery in Santa Rosa. The company's accountants estimate the monthly income and expenses for the new plant to be:

Income from sales $96,000
Expenses:
    Salaries $48,000
    Raw materials purchased $30,000
    Rent on equipment .... $ 3,000
    Miscellaneous expenses ...... $ 2,000
    Taxes .... $ 4,000

(a) What is the total amount of the cannery's estimated monthly expenses, including taxes?

(b) What will be the cannery's net profit if the estimates are accurate? (Calculate net profit by subtracting the total estimated expenses and taxes from estimated income.)

(c) If taxes were reduced 20%, how much would they be each month?

(d) What percentage of income does the firm pay in salaries?

(e) Salaries account for what percentage of the total expenses, not including taxes?

4. During the first month of its second year of operation, the Angelo Catelani cannery had total sales of $114,500. The net profit for the month was $7,328. This profit was what percentage of sales?

5. Joe Raintree, a sophomore at Big Valley High School, decides to go into the lawn mowing business to earn money. He buys the following equipment for this personal business venture:

1 power lawn mower $87.50
1 rake 3.19
1 hoe 2.99
1 pair of trimming shears 3.25
1 hand edger 6.45
1 light wheelbarrow 10.20
2 pairs of work gloves, each at ... 1.71

(a) How much does Joe have invested in equipment?

(b) If he mows lawns for an average price of $3 each, how many does he have to mow to pay for his equipment, assuming that he has no other expenses?

(c) Assume that Joe mows 10 lawns a week and saves 70% of his income for 12 weeks. How much will he have saved at the end of that time?

(d) On the average, it takes Joe 18 hours each week to mow the 10 lawns. How much more (or less) would he earn per week if he worked on the basis of $2 per hour?

Enriching Your Business Understanding

1. Most of the things you have at home or use in school were supplied by various kinds of businesses. Can you list some items that you use at home or school that were not obtained from businesses?

2. Select an item of clothing that you wear. Trace its development from the original materials from which it was made. Tell how the original materials, while being transformed into the finished product, acquired four types of utility.

3. List up to ten firms in your community that can be classified mainly as service businesses. Set this up in table form: one column for the names of the businesses, and one column summarizing briefly the types of services offered by the businesses.

4. Each year thousands of businesses fail in this country. Prepare an outline listing some of the reasons for such failures. (Search through business management books, check the *Readers' Guide* for articles, or interview an official of your bank or chamber of commerce. In your report, cite your sources of information.)

5. Be prepared to give an oral report about an interview with the owner of a local business firm. Plan carefully in advance for your interview. Ask the businessman questions such as these:

   (a) Why did you choose to go into this particular kind of business?
   (b) What risks do you take in operating your own business?
   (c) What methods do you use to compete with similar businesses for customers?
   (d) What training and experience should a person have before attempting to start his own business?

6. Listed below are a number of factors that a firm might consider before locating in a community:

   Low taxes
   Good schools
   Plentiful supply of skilled labor
   Highway, rail, and air transportation facilities
   Parks and other recreational facilities
   Other firms of the same type nearby
   Water and power available at low rates

   (a) Which of the factors do you think are most important? Why?
   (b) Are some factors more important to some kinds of businesses than to others? Give examples.

PART 5
How American Businesses Are Organized

Cantor's Garage, Dan's Barber Shop, Boyd and Hart Hardware, Bechtel Manufacturing Company, Fashion Fair Department Store. What do these names have in common? They are all names of businesses.

Study the names of various businesses in your community, and you may find clues about the type of ownership each has. The names of some smaller ones, such as Cantor's Garage and Dan's Barber Shop, suggest that each is owned by one person. Boyd and Hart Hardware may be a firm owned by two or more persons. The Bechtel Manufacturing Company and the Fashion Fair Department Store are probably owned by many people who have invested money in them.

Besides differing in type of ownership, businesses also differ greatly in size. A local automobile dealer might employ only four people to help him: a salesman, two mechanics, and an office worker. But the company that makes his cars may employ over 100,000 people and may be owned by even more investors.

THREE TYPES OF BUSINESS OWNERSHIP

The three major types of business ownership are the sole proprietorship, the partnership, and the corporation. Later in the part, you will learn about another type of business ownership, the cooperative.

A *sole proprietorship* is a business owned by one person. Most sole proprietorships are small firms such as grocery stores, restaurants, gas stations, barber shops, and drugstores.

A *partnership* is owned and managed by a small group, often not more than two or three people who become "partners." By written agreement, these partners share the profits or losses and the responsibilities of their business.

A *corporation* is a business owned by a number of people and operated under a state-issued charter or license. It acts as a single individual in behalf of its owners. By buying shares of stock, people become owners of corporations. They are then known as *stockholders* or *shareholders*. A corporation may have very few owners, but most corporations have many owners. The American Telephone and Telegraph Company, for example, has more than 3 million owners. Even if you own just one share of stock in this giant company, you are still one of its owners. Most mining, manufacturing, and transporting of goods is done by corporations. And many of our consumer goods are supplied by supermarkets, department stores, and other businesses organized as corporations.

The size and the nature of a business are key factors in choosing the best type of ownership and organization for it. To help you understand each type of ownership, the next few pages tell a story of how a young man started a business and worked to make it grow.

MAJOR TYPES OF BUSINESS OWNERSHIP

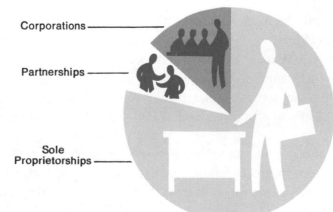

Corporations

Partnerships

Sole
Proprietorships

Illus. 5-1. The three major types of business ownership are the sole proprietorship, the partnership, and the corporation. Note that the majority of businesses in our country are operated as sole proprietorships.

During his first years in high school, Roger Selsback held a number of different part-time jobs after school and on Saturdays. He thought about retailing as a career and took business courses in school. In his senior year, he became a part-time sales trainee in the sporting goods department of a large department store. After graduation, he accepted a full-time job with the store.

In the next few years, Roger worked hard and was successful as a salesman. He prepared for advancement by taking several evening school courses. Soon he was promoted to assistant manager of the sporting goods department. By this time he was married, earning a good salary, and saving some of it. But he wanted to own his own business. He liked the idea of earning profits for himself while being his own boss. So he resigned his job in the department store and started to plan his own business.

Because of his experience and his interest in selling sporting goods, Roger wanted to open a sporting goods store. He chose the name All-Seasons Sports Shop. He rented a small store in a shopping center and bought showcases and other equipment. With the help of a bank loan, he bought his stock of merchandise.

Illus. 5-2. Roger Selsback is the sole owner or proprietor of this store. Many of the businesses in your community may be of this type.

Roger had learned a lot about selling sporting goods in the department store, but he found that a one-man business required long hours and much decision making. He ordered merchandise, built window displays, and did most of the selling and the stock work. His wife helped him keep his business and tax records. A student was employed part-time. Roger owned the business by himself, so it was a sole proprietorship. All the profits—or losses—were his.

SELSBACK AND HUMBER FORM A PARTNERSHIP

The All-Seasons Sports Shop was a success. Roger paid his bills on time and paid himself a fair salary. Each month he made payments on his bank loan until it was paid off. Profits were put aside in a savings account.

Soon Roger felt that it was time to expand the business, but he needed more money than he had saved. He also needed the help of someone who knew more about advertising and book-keeping than he did. A friend, Bert Humber, was a salesman in another store and had studied advertising and other business subjects in junior college. Roger invited Bert to become a part owner of the All-Seasons Sports Shop.

With their combined skills, experience, money, and other property, they could afford to offer a larger variety of sporting goods. They could also afford to add a new line of merchandise—sportswear—to draw trade from a larger area. With a lawyer's help, Selsback and Humber drew up a written agreement called the *articles of partnership*. Among other things, this agreement provided that:

1. The name of the firm will be the All-Seasons Sports Center.
2. Selsback will invest $18,000 in cash and property. Humber will invest $9,000 in cash.
3. Each partner will draw a salary of $800 a month.
4. Profits and losses after salaries are paid will be shared in proportion to each partner's investment: two-thirds to Selsback and one-third to Humber.
5. Selsback will have main responsibility for sales, selection and purchase of merchandise, and customer and community relations. Humber will handle financial records, payroll, store maintenance, advertising and sales promotion, and other details of operating the business.
6. In the event of the death or the necessary withdrawal of one partner, the remaining partner will have the right to purchase the departing partner's share of the business.

Before Selsback and Humber signed the articles of partnership, their lawyer pointed out some of the legal responsibilities of partners. For example, each partner could be held personally responsible for all the debts of the business. This would even include debts incurred by the other partner without the first partner's consent. Each partner was also bound by the agreements made for the business by the other partner. To avoid problems, Selsback and Humber agreed to talk over all important business matters, such as hiring people or buying new equipment.

Illus. 5-3. Selsback and Humber remodel and enlarge the old All-Seasons Sports Shop by taking over the store next door. They add a sportswear department and a camping and vacation supplies section.

At the end of the first year, the Selsback and Humber partnership showed a net profit of $4,200 after the partners' salaries had been paid. Since they had agreed to share profits in proportion to their investment in the business, Selsback received two-thirds or $2,800, and Humber received one-third or $1,400.

SELSBACK AND HUMBER FORM A CORPORATION

The All-Seasons Sports Center continued to grow under the Selsback and Humber partnership, and the partners considered the possibility of expanding the business even more. A new shopping center was being built on the other side of town. Should they open a branch store there? Should they also enlarge the present store? Should they add new sales and storage space and also lines of outdoor furniture and boats? Selsback and Humber found themselves asking these questions. To do these things, they needed more money, so they thought about adding more partners. However, they decided against this. They reasoned that they did not need partners to help them manage the business since they could hire qualified assistant managers. Also, there would be personal risks in being responsible for the actions of other partners.

Their lawyer advised them that if they formed a corporation, each member would not be personally responsible for the business' debts. In case of a business failure, each member could lose only the amount he had invested. With their lawyer's help, Selsback and Humber dissolved the partnership and drew up a plan for a corporation—the All-Seasons Sports Center, Incorporated. The corporation was to represent a total investment of $90,000. Their financial records showed that the partnership was worth $60,000, so they needed to raise another $30,000.

Selsback and Humber decided to divide the $90,000 into 9,000 shares, each with a value of $10. Based on the partnership agreement and the corporation plans, they divided the 9,000 shares this way: (1) Selsback received 4,000 shares worth $40,000; (2) Humber received 2,000 shares worth $20,000; and (3) they offered for sale 3,000 shares valued at $30,000.

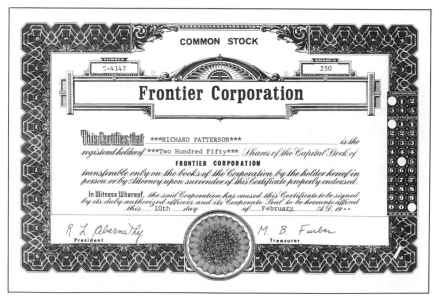

Illus. 5-4. A stock certificate, like this one, is evidence of ownership in a corporation.

The information about the division of shares of stock and other information about the corporation was put in an application submitted to the state government. The application asked permission to operate as a corporation. After approving the application, the state issued a *charter* authorizing the formation of the All-Seasons Sports Center, Incorporated.

Illus. 5-5. If any stockholder of the All-Seasons Sports Center, Inc., wants to withdraw his investment, he can sell his shares of stock to anyone else without affecting the organization and life of the business.

Selsback and Humber were no longer owners of the partnership. They had sold their partnership to the new corporation. In return they had received 6,000 shares of stock, or a part ownership amounting to $60,000. These 6,000 shares were divided in proportion to the investment in the former partnership. Selsback received two-thirds or 4,000 shares, and Humber received one-third or 2,000 shares. The 3,000 shares offered for sale were sold to 30 people who had confidence in the new corporation. The corporation, then, had 32 different stockholders.

Selsback and Humber called a meeting of the stockholders to elect officers, to make plans for opening a branch store, and to transact other business. Each stockholder had one vote for each share of stock that he owned. Since Selsback and Humber together owned 6,000 of the 9,000 shares, they had enough votes to control the business' operation.

At the stockholders' meeting, these persons were elected as directors of the corporation: Greg Snyder, Constantine Raboli, Kenneth Grover, JoAnn McCline, Bert Humber, Paulette Mc-Kenna, and Roger Selsback. These seven persons made up the *board of directors*. The board's responsibility was to manage the corporation properly. The board's first act was to elect the executive officers of the corporation. The directors elected Roger Selsback as president, Kenneth Grover as vice-president, JoAnn McCline as secretary, and Bert Humber as treasurer.

At the end of a year, after all taxes were paid, the corporation had a net profit of $10,300. The board of directors voted to keep $4,000 of this in the business for expansion and to divide the other $6,300 among the stockholders. Since the corporation had issued 9,000 shares, each of the 32 stockholders received 70 cents for each share of stock that he owned ($6,300 ÷ 9,000). The part of the profits that each stockholder received was called a *dividend*. Selsback received $2,800 ($.70 × 4,000 shares), and Humber received $1,400 ($.70 × 2,000 shares).

CORPORATIONS MAY BE NONPROFIT ORGANIZATIONS

When driving into towns, you have probably seen signs like "Bluefield—Incorporated." An incorporated town is called a *municipal corporation*. It is organized not to make a profit but rather to provide services for its citizens. It has its own officials, its own schools, and its own police and fire departments. It repairs its own streets; and it provides its own water supply, its own street lighting system, and other services for its citizens. It levies taxes and passes rules and regulations to operate effectively.

Certain other groups are organized as nonprofit corporations. Among these are churches, private colleges and universities, the American Red Cross, Boy Scouts of America, Future Business Leaders of America, and Distributive Education Clubs of America.

SOME BUSINESSES ARE ORGANIZED AS COOPERATIVES

Sometimes people join together to operate a business known as a *cooperative*. There are two main types of cooperatives. One type is a consumers' cooperative, an organization of consumers who buy goods and services more cheaply together than each person could individually. For example, farmers and members of labor unions may form cooperatives to buy such products as groceries and gasoline and such services as insurance and electricity. Farmers also form cooperatives from which they buy products needed to run their farms, such as feed and fertilizer.

A second type of cooperative is a producers' cooperative. It is usually a farmers' organization that markets such products as fruits, vegetables, and grains. Some cooperatives not only sell a farmer's products for him but also store and transport them. Sometimes the cooperative operates processing plants such as canneries. A producers' cooperative lets small farmers band together for greater bargaining power in selling their products.

A cooperative is much like a corporation. It must obtain a charter from the state. It may sell one or more shares of stock to each of its members. A board of directors may be chosen by the members to manage the cooperative. But a cooperative differs from a corporation in that each member of a cooperative has an equal voice in controlling the cooperative's affairs. Each member has only one vote, no matter how many shares he owns. In a corporation, a person has one vote for each share he owns.

Most consumers' cooperatives sell to nonmembers as well as members. Prices in cooperative stores that sell to nonmembers are set at about the same level found in other local stores. If a cooperative is successful, it makes a net earning. Most of this net earning may be refunded directly to members at the end of the business year.

THE SIZE OF COOPERATIVE BUSINESSES IN THE U.S.

KIND OF CO-OP	PURPOSE	NUMBER OF CO-OPS	MEMBERS	ANNUAL BUSINESS
Credit unions	Thrift and credit	22,796	18,007,000	$10,138,433,000* 9,115,840,000*
Co-op-oriented insurance companies	Financial security	10	11,750,000	580,000,000
Farm purchasing	Production and Home supplies	3,050	3,200,000	3,150,000,000**
Farm marketing	Higher returns for producers	5,100	3,700,000	12,750,000,000**
Electric co-ops	Rural electricity	993	5,600,000	1,021,914,409
Farm Credit System Land bank associations	Land, production, and co-op credit	707	390,000	1,337,000,000
Production credit associations		466	545,000	4,813,000,000
Banks for cooperatives		13	2,972 (cooperatives)	1,664,000,000
Major consumer goods centers	Food and home supplies	116	240,000	160,000,000
Housing co-ops	Homes	640	165,000	235,000,000

*Net annual increase   **Does not include intercooperative business
SOURCE: The Cooperative League of the USA.

Illus. 5-6. This chart gives some statistics on various kinds of cooperatives for a recent year.

Illus. 5-7. Most consumers' cooperatives, like this one, sell to nonmembers as well as to members.

Assume that your parents are members of the Hillsdale Consumers' Cooperative. The total sales of this business amount to $500,000 for the year. After all expenses are paid, there is $10,000 left. In other kinds of businesses, the $10,000 would be a net profit. Of this amount, taxes would be paid; and the balance would be available for dividing among stockholders or other owners. But in a cooperative the "profits" are considered as savings to be paid back to member-customers in proportion to their purchases. Members may also vote to retain part or all of the profits within the cooperative for expansion purposes.

The board of directors of the Hillsdale Consumers' Cooperative may decide to refund the $10,000 to its members. Since $10,000 is 2% of the total sales of $500,000, each member will receive 2 cents for every dollar he spent at the cooperative. If your parents bought $1,000 worth of merchandise at the cooperative during the year, they will receive a return of 2% or $20. This return is called a *patronage refund*. Only members are entitled to patronage refunds.

Developing Your Business Vocabulary

The following italicized terms should become part of your business vocabulary. For each numbered statement, find the italicized term that has the same meaning.

articles of partnership   *municipal corporation*
board of directors   *partnership*
charter   *patronage refund*
cooperative   *sole proprietorship*
corporation   *stockholder* or *shareholder*
dividend

1. A business owned by one person.
2. An association of two or more persons operating a business as co-owners and sharing profits or losses according to a written agreement.
3. A business made up of a number of owners but authorized by law to act as a single person.
4. A person who owns stock in a corporation.
5. A written agreement made by partners in forming their business.
6. A document, generally issued by a state government, granting permission to start a corporation.
7. A group of people elected by stockholders to manage a corporation.
8. The part of the profits of a corporation that each stockholder receives.
9. An incorporated town or city.
10. A business that is owned by the members it serves and is managed in their interest.
11. Earnings that are returned to a member of a cooperative in proportion to the amount of his purchases.

Checking Your Understanding

1. What do you consider to be some of the most important advantages and disadvantages of a one-owner business?
2. What are some of the important provisions that should be included in a written partnership agreement?
3. How does the management of a partnership differ from the management of a sole proprietorship?

4. What are some of the major advantages and disadvantages of having a business organized as a partnership?

5. When Selsback and Humber needed additional funds to expand their business, why did they change from a partnership to a corporation?

6. What loss may be suffered by a stockholder of a corporation that fails? By the owner of a sole proprietorship that fails? By the members of a partnership that fails?

7. Summarize the advantages and the disadvantages of having a business organized as a corporation.

8. Are all corporations organized for the purpose of making a profit? Explain.

9. Give some of the differences as well as some of the similarities between a cooperative and a business corporation.

10. How are the earnings of cooperatives shared by the members?

11. If anyone is permitted to buy from a particular cooperative, why do some people choose to become members of that organization?

Applying What You Have Learned

1. John Favero states that it would be possible for a drugstore to be a sole proprietorship, a partnership, a corporation, or a cooperative. Do you agree with John? Why?

2. In the United States there are many more sole proprietorships than corporations, but the corporations do a much larger volume of business. Give an explanation for this situation.

3. Assume that you would like to form a partnership with one other person and go into the business of operating a service station. In selecting your partner, what personal qualities and strengths would you like him to have?

4. Could the policies and the management of a corporation with more than 10,000 stockholders be controlled by just one stockholder? Give reasons for your answer.

5. There are many businesses organized as corporations whose stock is owned by thousands of stockholders. Do you believe that if these businesses were organized as partnerships they could have as many partners? Explain.

6. Mark Reid and his partner, Kenneth Bailey, fail in business. The debts are about $8,000 greater than the value of the business. Mr. Reid has personal property worth more than $10,000, but his partner has nothing. How much of the debts of the business will Mr. Reid probably have to pay?

7. Why is it important for dentists, physicians, lawyers, writers, singers, artists, actors, and other professional workers to develop

an understanding of business principles and practices? Try to include some specific examples in your answer.

8. Suppose that an opportunity for part-time and summer work as a retail clerk is available to you in either a small one-owner grocery store, in one of several large supermarkets operated by a corporation, or in a big market operated by a local consumers' cooperative. By which one of these businesses would you prefer to be employed? Why?

Solving Business Problems

1. Refer to the discussion of the Selsback and Humber partnership on pages 58 and 59.

   (a) If at the end of the second year of operation, this partnership had made a net profit of $5,481 after payment of the partners' salaries, how much would be each partner's share of the profit?

   (b) If the business had instead incurred a loss of $1,920, what would have been each partner's share of the loss?

2. Partners divide profits according to different plans. Investments in one partnership were: O'Brien, $10,000; Rossi, $8,000; and Weinstein, $6,000. In one year the partnership had net earnings of $6,000. How much did each partner receive:

   (a) If the earnings were divided in proportion to investment?

   (b) If each partner received 6% on his investment, with the remainder divided equally?

   (c) If O'Brien received 1/3, Rossi received 2/5, and Weinstein received 4/15?

3. Refer to the discussion of the All-Seasons Sports Center, Inc., on pages 59-62. Assume that at the end of a year this corporation had a net profit of $12,600. The board of directors voted to retain $7,740 of this amount to expand the business. The rest was to be divided among the stockholders as a dividend.

   (a) What sum would be available for dividends?

   (b) What would be the dividend for each of the 9,000 shares of stock of the corporation?

   (c) How much would Roger Selsback receive?

   (d) How much would Bert Humber receive?

4. Frank Moore, Lucille Arata, and Hugh Garrison formed a corporation with a beginning investment of $300,000.

   (a) How many shares of stock with a value of $25 would have to be sold to provide this amount?

   (b) How many shares could Mr. Moore buy for $160,000?

   (c) How much would Mrs. Arata have to pay for 500 shares?

Enriching Your Business Understanding

1. In most partnerships the partners are general partners, but sometimes there are limited partners and silent partners. Explain the difference between each of these types. (Refer to business law and business principles textbooks in your library.)

2. Select a business block in your town and list the names of the various business firms (street-level only) in that block. List these on a chart with such headings as: Name of Business, Services Provided by the Business, and Form of Organization (sole proprietorship, partnership, corporation, cooperative, or nonprofit corporation). If the firm is a branch of a large organization, indicate where the home office is located if you can conveniently obtain such information.

3. A small group of people can very easily form a corporation and can buy all of the stock themselves. On the other hand, if a large corporation wishes to sell stock to many people, it must comply with regulations of the federal government and must provide information in printed form for prospective stockholders. Why do you believe the selling of stock of large corporations is so carefully regulated?

4. Franchising is becoming a popular way of going into business. Franchise businesses are being established in all sorts of fields, but they are particularly common in the motel, restaurant, and prepared-food fields.

    (a) Explain what franchises are.

    (b) List the names of four or five franchise businesses in your area and describe the services rendered by two of the firms on your list.

    (c) What are the advantages and disadvantages of this way of going into business?

5. What is Junior Achievement, Inc.? Look into the nearest Junior Achievement program in your area. If possible, visit some of the Junior Achievement "companies" that are in operation. Be prepared to report orally to the class on the results of your investigation.

PART 6
Men and Machines In Business

Suppose that every item sold in the All-Seasons Sports Center had to be made by hand. Think of the time it would take to make just one golf ball! Then think how much that golf ball would probably cost if you had to pay for the many hours of a worker's time.

In Part 1 you learned that the efforts of many people are needed to supply us with the goods and services we demand. People organize businesses to provide us with goods and services. But these goods and services could not be produced in the quantities we demand or at prices we could afford if it were not for modern machines and efficient production methods.

In the past, each family provided for most of its own needs and wants. Most of the goods a family produced met basic needs; there were few luxuries. But as our economy developed, the demand for more and better products also grew. Faster, cheaper methods of making goods were needed to keep up with the demand for goods. As an example, imagine the time it took to make just one coat when a person had to raise the sheep, shear it, card the wool, spin it into yarn, weave the yarn into cloth, and make the cloth into a coat.

THE MACHINE AGE STARTED WITH THE INDUSTRIAL REVOLUTION

Around the middle of the 18th Century, imaginative men started inventing machines to do much of the work of producing goods. Gradually many more goods were produced by machine than by hand. This period was known as the Industrial Revolution, and its symbol was the steam engine because the steam engine was a source of power for machines.

Once machines were operating and producing large quantities of goods, the demand for raw materials increased. Sometimes this demand resulted in the invention of other machines. Take cotton, for example. There were machines to spin thread and weave cloth. Farmers in our country were able to grow large amounts of cotton. But seeds still had to be removed from the cotton by hand, and this slowed down the whole process of making cotton cloth. So the cotton gin was invented to remove the seeds.

Men invented—and are still inventing—machines to keep up with the demands for goods and services. In many ways, the Industrial Revolution is still going on. Businesses are always looking for newer, faster, and better ways of producing goods. The machines and skills needed to make a car did not exist a hundred years ago. And think of the number of goods and services being sold today that did not exist even ten years ago.

Today's worker can produce six times more goods than a worker could produce at the beginning of this century. This great increase in productivity is due mainly to advancements in business management, science, and technology. *Technology* is the application of scientific and technical knowledge and methods to the production of goods and services. In our industries today, technology places emphasis on the efficient use of modern tools and machinery, especially automated equipment.

MASS PRODUCTION IS A RESULT OF THE INDUSTRIAL REVOLUTION

Before man invented machines and harnessed the power to run them, he had to produce goods and services by using his own power and animal power. Thousands of people worked for many years to build the pyramids in Egypt. These same pyramids could be built today in much less time by a few hundred men using cranes, bulldozers, and other power-driven machines.

Power-driven machinery makes it possible for industry to engage in *mass production*. This is the production, by machine, of great numbers of the same kind of article. With mass production, many more items can be produced at a lower cost than if they were made by hand. In the 1800's, for example, tin cans were made by hand at the rate of about six an hour. The cans were so expensive that they were saved and used over and over again. Today mass production enables one worker operating one machine to produce more than 20,000 tin cans an hour.

In mass production, no one person does all the work needed to make any one product. Instead, many workers are involved in making a single product such as a stereo, watch, or car. Each worker is highly skilled in operating a machine that makes one part or is skilled in fitting parts together. This specialization of work is called *division of labor*.

H. Armstrong Roberts

Illus. 6-1. The techniques of mass production and division of labor are essential in making many of the products we use every day.

Businesses also specialize in their production. One business may make only motors for automatic washers. Another may make only automobile mufflers. Larger businesses may divide production among several plants that they own. For example, one plant may make only automobile transmissions. Another may make only automobile bodies. Parts produced in one plant are then shipped to another plant and assembled into an automobile.

Usually no two handmade products are alike. If an artist paints two pictures of the same scene, those two pictures will be different in some way. The sky, for instance, may be a slightly different shade of blue in one picture. But with mass production, products are standardized. This means that whether a machine turns out five or five thousand items in a day, each of those items will be just like all the others.

Because products are standardized, their parts are standardized. Suppose that you buy a Model Z watch. That watch is like every Model Z watch the manufacturer sells. And each part in each Model Z watch is exactly the same. So if one part of the watch breaks, you don't have to throw the watch away and buy a new one. A jeweler can order a duplicate part and replace the broken one. You can see how important *interchangeable parts* are every time you need to replace tubes in a radio or spark plugs in a car.

MACHINES DO PHYSICAL AND MENTAL WORK FOR US

Many increases in productivity are the result of automation. *Automation* is the use of electronic or mechanical equipment to produce goods and services with a minimum of human effort. Factories use a great deal of automatic machinery. In automobile plants, for example, huge presses automatically form the tops of cars in one operation. In making ballpoint pens, machines automatically perform 36 different operations in assembling the ball and tip.

Automatic machines can do more than just reduce the amount of physical work needed to produce goods. They can also reduce the amount of mental work needed. Many businesses today use automatic machines to process information (or data) and to prepare reports. Processing data by using automatic machines that require little human attention is called *automated data processing*.

The invention of automated data processing machines, like the invention of the steam engine, was the result of an inventor meeting a need. It took seven and a half years to complete the 1880 census. Our Constitution requires that a national census be taken every ten years. So the Census Bureau was afraid that the 1890 census might not be completed before the 1900 census began unless a better way could be found to compile the data.

The Bureau called on Dr. Herman Hollerith, a noted statistician of the time. He developed a card on which data could be recorded in the form of punched holes. By 1890 when the census was to begin, he had invented a series of machines that could sort the punched cards and summarize the data they contained. Using Dr. Hollerith's invention, the 1890 census took only two and a half years to complete. The population, though, had actually increased by 13 million people between 1880 and 1890.

The punched card is now widely used for recording data for processing by automatic machines. The card has 80 columns, and certain areas of the card are designed for recording certain kinds of data. You have probably noticed that bills for gas and electricity or bills for credit purchases are often in punched-card form. Each hole punched in the card represents a certain kind of information.

INPUT
Information on the source documents to be processed is punched into cards or tape in code form. Common office machines with card-punch or tape-punch attachments or a card-punch machine may be used. Ordinarily, a machine called a verifier is used to check the accuracy of the punched cards before they are processed.

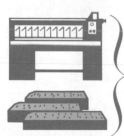

PROCESSING AND STORAGE
The cards are sorted and grouped according to the information desired. This is an automatic process handled by a machine known as a sorter. The cards are then ready for further processing.

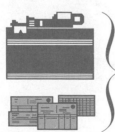

OUTPUT
The grouped cards are run through a machine known as a tabulator. The tabulator selects the data desired from the punched cards and prints the information on output media such as sales reports, statements, and checks.

Illus. 6-2. A summary of the procedures involved in processing data by automatic machines.

THE COMPUTER IS A SERVANT OF BUSINESSES

Automated data processing is not always fast enough for businesses that must process a great deal of data in a hurry. So the electronic computer was developed to meet the need for a faster method of processing data. It is a machine that receives information; stores it; "remembers" it; adds, subtracts, multiplies, and divides with it. Based on the data fed into the computer, problems are solved and reports are prepared. The processing of data by electronic computers is called *electronic data processing* or simply *EDP*.

The first workable computer went into operation in 1946. However, it was not used in business until 1953. Since then, computers have changed very much. Today's computer can transmit and process data much faster than any earlier computer. Its features have astonished many people and have caused them to refer to the computer as an "electronic brain." But a computer is basically an arrangement of wires, switches, and magnets; and it can do only what a person has planned for it to do. It cannot think. A computer can store data, recall them instantly, and combine them with other data to produce a report or give the answer to a difficult problem. But it can do this only if a person has first given it a plan—called a *program*—to follow. If an incorrect plan for processing the data or if incorrect information is given to a computer, the computer will give out incorrect answers.

Illus. 6-3. A computer can do many things for us, but it cannot think.

(Reprinted by permission from *Sales Management, The Marketing Magazine* © by Sales Management, Inc., 1968)

Businesses use computers in many ways. A computer can prepare payrolls and can even write paychecks. It can keep a daily record of the goods a business has sold or has on hand. Airline and hotel reservations can be made or confirmed in a few seconds, thanks to the computer. Computers can help insurance companies keep track of when premiums are due for millions of insured persons. Computers help the government figure taxes and social security payments. They can help banks keep records and can prepare monthly checking account statements for a bank's customers. Some computers can even read words printed in a foreign language and translate them into English. And they can help a physician diagnose the illnesses of his patients.

Almost any kind of data that occurs over and over again can be easily handled by a computer. Scientists are continually finding new applications for the computer. There are no doubt many as yet undiscovered ways in which the computer can help us in factories, offices, hospitals, schools, and almost every other place in which we obtain goods and services.

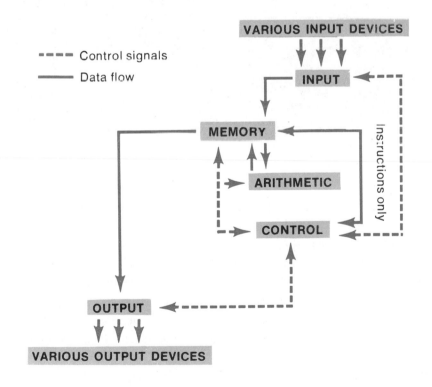

Illus. 6-4. Here are the components of a computer. The solid lines and arrows show the path the data take.

MACHINES ARE AFFECTING JOBS AND WORKERS

The many complex machines that we use to produce today's goods and services would have little value if there were no skilled people to operate them. Human resources are necessary in every phase of production. It is true, though, that advancements in technology have changed the nature of many jobs. Technological change creates new jobs, causes others to be no longer needed, and alters the nature of many others. Many new jobs are quite technical in nature and require knowledge of mathematics and science. Others, including many in the office and marketing fields, require that workers have more education because the jobs are complex.

Illus. 6-5. Modern machines would be useless without skilled, well-trained people like these to operate them.

Control Data Corporation

As more and more automated machines take over the routine tasks in the factory and in the office, there will be greater demand for more highly skilled and educated workers. There will be less demand for the less skilled and less educated workers. This means that a person must be prepared for the job he wants, either by completing high school or college or by getting vocational training. And because technology is always causing changes in jobs, the worker must expect to continue his education for most of his working life. To keep up with changes, he can enroll in company training programs, attend adult education classes, and study on his own at home.

Developing Your Business Vocabulary

The following italicized terms should become part of your business vocabulary. For each numbered statement, find the italicized term that has the same meaning.

automated data processing   *interchangeable parts*
automation   *mass production*
division of labor   *program*
electronic data processing or *EDP*   *technology*

1. The application of scientific and technical knowledge and methods to the production of goods and services.
2. The use of machines to produce goods in large quantities.
3. Specialization by workers in performing certain portions of a total job.
4. Parts that are made precisely the same so that they can be used to replace similar parts that are worn out or broken.
5. The process of using electronic or mechanical equipment to perform a series of operations with a minimum of human effort.
6. Processing data by using automatic machines that require little human attention.
7. The use of computers to process data and produce reports or solve problems based on that data.
8. A set of detailed instructions that directs the operation of a computer.

Checking Your Understanding

1. "In many ways, the Industrial Revolution is still going on." Do you agree with this statement? Give reasons for your answer.
2. Explain why mass production is highly dependent upon power-driven machinery.
3. Why does mass production enable us to produce goods at a much lower cost than was possible in earlier times?
4. Many different businesses are often engaged in the production of a consumer good. Give examples to show how businesses specialize in production.
5. Give several examples of division of labor in the production of a consumer good.
6. Why is the computer sometimes referred to as an "electronic brain"?
7. List at least five ways in which computers are used by business and government.

8. Describe some of the general effects that technological change has on jobs and on the requirements for workers who fill these jobs.

9. Perhaps more than ever before, workers today and in the future will need to keep up with the technical and scientific changes taking place in jobs. Suggest several ways in which a person can continue his education and training during his working years.

Applying What You Have Learned

1. Mass production as we know it today would not be possible without the use of interchangeable parts. Explain.

2. Give specific examples to show why the concept of interchangeable parts is of great benefit to: (a) a housewife; (b) a farmer; (c) an automobile manufacturer; (d) an automobile owner; and (e) a proprietor of a hardware store.

3. Because of modern mass production methods, Americans can buy an almost countless number of products at a reasonable cost. Most of these products are satisfactorily made in great quantities by machinery. Why, then, do some people prefer to buy hand-tailored suits, custom-made furniture, and other individually made items?

4. Automation is not just the same thing as using a source of power to make a machine operate, such as an electric typewriter or a motor scooter. How, then, does automation differ from the ordinary use of much of our labor-saving machinery in factories, offices, and homes?

5. An important characteristic of automation is that electronic or mechanical equipment is used to operate or control other equipment. The thermostat that turns on the furnace in a home is an example. Give several other examples of automation that may exist in your home or the homes of people you know.

6. More and more, automation makes it possible for us to receive quicker and more efficient services from business and government. Describe some of these services.

Solving Business Problems

1. The Russell Beach Corporation manufactures aluminum kitchen utensils. With its present equipment, it can turn out 4,000 units a week at an average unit cost of 85¢. By installing newer machines, including automated equipment, the company estimates that it will be able to produce 7,000 units a week at a unit cost of 78¢. Assume that these utensils have been, and would continue to be, sold at $1.50 per unit.

(a) What is the total cost of a week's production when units are produced for 85¢ each?

(b) What is the total cost of a week's production when units are produced for 78¢ each?

(c) What is the gross weekly income (based on sales price) when the production cost is 85¢ a unit and the entire week's production is sold?

(d) What would be the gross weekly income when the production cost is 78¢ a unit and the entire week's production is sold?

(e) What would be the gross yearly increase in income made possible by the installation of the new machinery?

2. The president of the Russell Beach Corporation realized that installing new equipment would be very expensive. Before making a decision on whether or not to buy the new machinery, he asked his accounting department to make a cost study. The following information was presented:

Cost of new equipment	$125,750
Necessary remodeling and installation costs	32,150
Trade-in value of old equipment	12,500
Estimated life of new equipment	8 years

If the cost of buying and installing the equipment is to be spread over its estimated life, what will be the estimated annual cost of putting in the new equipment?

3. Production of goods is high in our country because industry provides workers with efficient tools, machinery, and other facilities. The table below shows, for a recent year, the total amount invested in plants and equipment by several businesses and the number of workers in each business.

Kind of Business	Total Investment	Number of Workers
Cannery	$ 8,439,000	485
Printing business	348,800	32
Chemical company	4,267,200	127
Clothing manufacturer ..	3,111,700	841
Automobile manufacturer	171,032,400	7,404

(a) How much did each business have invested in plant and equipment for each employee?

(b) Why are modern industries always on the lookout for better equipment? Who benefits from this action?

Enriching Your Business Understanding

1. Find out where the term "manufacturing" comes from. Contrast the original definition of this word with today's definition.

2. As our population has increased, the proportion of workers engaged in agriculture has decreased sharply. In 1840 when our population was 17,000,000, about 80% of the workers were employed in farming. Now, with a population of about 206,000,000, less than 6% of American workers are in agriculture. What reasons can you offer to explain why, in relation to our total population, fewer farm workers are needed today to produce the food we consume?

3. Each of the following persons is a noteworthy inventor:

Marconi	Whitney	Matzeliger
McCormick	Morse	Galileo
Daimler	Sholes	Howe
Goodyear	Rillieux	Roentgen

   (a) What important invention is commonly attributed to each?

   (b) Explain how each invention has aided business in producing needed consumer goods or services.

4. Interview two persons who have been employed for some time. Ask each how his job has changed over the years. Find out what caused these changes. Also find out what changes there may have been in qualifications for the job, such as skills, training, or experience.

5. Collect "Help Wanted" advertisements from the classified section of newspapers (and possibly from other sources such as magazines and leaflets) pertaining to job opportunities in the data processing field. Analyze these advertisements and make a summary of the types of jobs for which workers are needed.

6. Prepare a written report—or a detailed outline for an oral report to your class—on the contributions that computers and other modern automated equipment are making in special fields. Select one of the topics below or, with the help of your teacher, choose another field in which computers are important.

   How can computers help in the management of a business firm?
   The computer and income tax reports.
   The computer and medical and hospital care.
   How the computer helps in crime detection and crime prevention.
   Could our astronauts have reached the moon without computer help?
   How are computers used in the operation of schools?

Unit 3

Business and the Consumer

PART 7

How Goods Reach the Consumer

It takes more than efficient machinery and production methods to satisfy all your needs and wants for goods and services. It also takes a marketing system to give you the kind of goods you want, when you want them, where you want them, and at prices you are willing to pay.

Suppose that you live in a small Colorado town and a blizzard completely isolates your town. What happens? No trucks or trains can reach the stores, so very quickly all fresh bread, milk, and pastries will be gone from the store shelves. Within a few days, most fresh and preserved meats will be gone. Before long, most canned goods will also be gone.

This situation isn't likely to happen today because someone would probably come to your town's rescue very shortly. But it does show how we depend upon businesses to keep us supplied with the goods we need every day. You have already learned that we are a very interdependent people. Most of us produce few goods and services for ourselves. Many of the goods we want come to us from far away. Thus, an important link between the producer and you as a consumer is the middleman. Without middlemen, our style of living would be quite different from what it is now.

MARKETING HELPS BOTH PRODUCERS AND CONSUMERS

Middlemen buy goods at one price and sell them to other middlemen or to consumers at a higher price. If you pay $1 for a ballpoint pen, less than 50 cents goes to the business that made the pen. The rest goes to the businesses that moved the pen from the producer to you. Why can't we buy everything directly from producers? Why must we pay middlemen to handle our goods?

Think how hard it would be for you to buy a few ounces of pepper from its producer. You would probably have to travel all the way to the East Indies for it. And think how much those few ounces of pepper would cost you under those conditions. If each of us tried to buy everything we use directly from producers, we would have little time to do anything else. And if producers had to sell all their products directly to consumers, they would have little time to make more products.

When a manufacturer creates form utility by taking steel and other materials and making them into a refrigerator, he adds value to the original materials. Our marketing system also adds value to products. Cereal stored in a manufacturer's warehouse has some value. But its value increases when middlemen move it to a grocery store where you can buy it. Toys manufactured in May take on greater value when a middleman stores them and delivers them to department stores in time for the Christmas rush. So marketing adds value to products by bringing them where the consumer is, at the time he wants them, in the assortment he wants, and at prices he is willing to pay.

Our advanced technology and our skilled labor force enable producers to make thousands of different products at a reasonable cost. But if these products cannot be sold to consumers, they are of no use to producers. And if these products are not available when and where consumers want to buy them, they are of no use to consumers. Marketing, then, keeps our economy moving.

GOODS TRAVEL THROUGH CHANNELS OF DISTRIBUTION

When Columbus discovered America, he was really looking for a shorter trade route to India. In fact, many of the explorers you've learned about were looking for better trade routes for goods. Finding the best route for goods to travel from the producer to the consumer is a problem now just as it was in Columbus' day. Every item you see on a store shelf has its own trade route. If you knew the complete history of any one item—a box of tea, for

General Electric

Illus. 7-1. Without marketing, these many labor-saving products would be of little value to the consumers.

example—you would probably find that its trade route was quite complex.

Trade routes of many of the goods we use reach halfway around the world. Much of the coffee that we use comes from South America; tin and rubber come from the Far East. No nation is entirely self-sufficient. Each country must buy some products from other countries, and each country sells products to other countries in exchange. Nations, like the people of our country, are interdependent.

When we talk about the trade route of a product, we generally use the term *channel of distribution*. A product's channel of distribution is the path it takes on its way from the producer to the consumer. A channel of distribution may have no middlemen, one middleman, or more than one middleman. Sometimes more than one type of channel is used for the same type of product.

Although most of the goods we buy are handled by middlemen, we do buy some goods directly from producers. For example, a channel of distribution with no middlemen may be used when the freshness of a product is very important to the consumer. You or your family may have bought fruits or vegetables from a farmer's roadside stand in the country. Or you may have shopped at a central produce market in town where farmers set up stalls of their products.

SOME GOODS ARE BOUGHT DIRECTLY FROM PRODUCERS

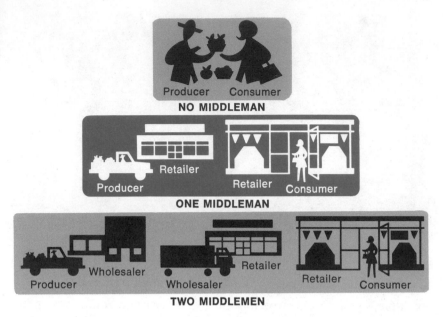

Producer — Consumer
NO MIDDLEMAN

Producer — Retailer — Retailer — Consumer
ONE MIDDLEMAN

Producer — Wholesaler — Wholesaler — Retailer — Retailer — Consumer
TWO MIDDLEMEN

SOME GOODS ARE HANDLED BY ONE MIDDLEMAN

Sometimes producers send their own salesmen to call on consumers. A dairy may have route salesmen to sell milk, cream, and other dairy products from door to door. Manufacturers of such products as brushes, spices, books, magazines, and cosmetics may also employ door-to-door salesmen. A few producers, such as sewing machine manufacturers, even operate their own retail stores.

Some producers also sell directly to the consumer by mail. They may send out booklets describing their products and including order blanks. Shoes and some types of clothing, for example, are sometimes sold by mail by their producers.

Most clothing, furniture, appliances, and cars travel through channels of distribution with one middleman—a retailer. A *retailer* is a middleman who sells directly to ultimate consumers (final users) of a product. To most of us, the most familiar part of our marketing system is the retail store.

In the small towns of a hundred years ago, the general store was about the only retail store around. It carried all kinds of merchandise, from crackers to horse collars, and was a combination of meeting place, social hall, and post office. There are few general stores left today, but there are many other kinds of retail stores.

Every retailer knows that different people have different buying habits. Some like to shop downtown because the stores are usually larger and may have better selections of goods. Others prefer suburban stores because their locations are convenient and because they offer plenty of free parking space. Some people like the convenience of self-service; others like to be waited on. No one kind of retail store appeals to everyone, so businessmen have established many different kinds of retail stores. Visit a shopping center today, and you are likely to find examples of single-line stores, department stores, variety stores, supermarkets, and discount stores.

Single-line stores carry only one kind of merchandise or a couple of related kinds. A shoe store is an example of a single-line store. When a single-line store sells only men's or women's clothing, it is usually called a specialty shop.

Department stores are like a number of single-line stores grouped under one roof and under one management. Because a department store offers many different kinds of merchandise, it allows people to do most of their shopping in one place.

Variety stores are much like department stores except that they are smaller than most department stores, sell lower-priced goods, and sell few bulky items such as furniture. The Woolworth or Grant store where you may buy school supplies is a variety store.

Supermarkets sell mainly food items and are usually entirely self-service. As they sell huge quantities of goods, do not deliver, and usually do not offer credit, they can generally afford to sell goods at lower prices than can small grocery stores.

Discount stores have grown up in large numbers in recent years. They stock many different kinds of merchandise and operate on a self-service basis. They generally sell goods at lower prices than do other stores, such as department stores, which sell the same goods.

Mail-order houses represent yet another form of retail enterprise. They sell goods through catalogs and ship the ordered goods directly to the customer. Some mail-order houses sell general merchandise; others sell only a few kinds of merchandise, such as hobby supplies.

The Vendo Company

SOME GOODS ARE HANDLED BY MORE THAN ONE MIDDLEMAN

All of us buy from retailers and are familiar with their services. But many of us don't know about the important services that wholesalers provide. A *wholesaler* is a middleman who buys goods in large quantities from a producer and sells them in smaller quantities to retailers. Products such as fruits and vegetables, candy, hardware, paint, magazines, and toys are often handled by both a wholesaler and a retailer before they reach the consumer.

A wholesaler may buy canned fruit, cereal, or coffee by the carload and sell to retailers a few cases or cartons at a time. In doing this, the wholesale business becomes a vast warehouse that gathers products from many manufacturers. A retailer can often order from one wholesaler hundreds of different items that are produced in many different places.

Wholesalers also perform other important functions. They store goods until the retailer needs them. They may buy toys or Christmas tree ornaments from the manufacturer in the summer and sell them to the retailer for December delivery. Wholesalers usually extend credit to retailers, sometimes by allowing them to pay for the goods after they have been sold. Wholesalers may also help retailers advertise their goods and may even train the retailer's sales force.

Marketing is one of the fastest growing areas of employment in this country. People are constantly demanding more and more goods and services, and marketing is essential in providing these goods and services. More than 25 million people today work in retailing, wholesaling, and service businesses. There are almost 2 million retail firms in this country, and these firms employ more than 10 million people. In retailing, a person might start as a salesperson, stockkeeper, or cashier. These jobs often lead to promotions. A salesperson who can get along with customers and fellow workers, who knows his merchandise, and who has basic selling skills can earn a good income. Successful salespeople may be promoted to buyers, department heads, assistant store managers, or even managers.

Other kinds of marketing businesses also offer fine job opportunities. For example, a person might become a professional salesman in an area such as insurance or real estate. Or he might become a highly paid manufacturer's sales representative. Career opportunities can also be found in advertising, traffic management, sales management, hotel management, and many other fields.

Eli Lilly and Company

Illus. 7-4. A respected position in the field of selling is that of a manufacturer's sales representative.

Developing Your Business Vocabulary

The following italicized terms should become part of your business vocabulary. For each numbered statement, find the italicized term that has the same meaning.

channel of distribution   *single-line store*
department store   *supermarket*
discount store   *variety store*
mail-order house   *wholesaler*
retailer

1. The path that a product takes on its way from the producer to the consumer.
2. A middleman who sells directly to ultimate consumers.
3. A retail store that carries only one kind of merchandise or a few related kinds.
4. A large retail store that is organized into departments and that sells many different kinds of merchandise.
5. A retail store that is similar to a department store but that sells lower-priced goods and fewer bulky items.
6. A retail store that sells mainly food items and is characterized by self-service.
7. A self-service retail store that sells general merchandise at lower prices than those of other stores selling the same merchandise.
8. A retail firm that sells merchandise through catalogs and ships goods directly to customers.
9. A middleman who buys goods in large quantities from producers and sells them in smaller quantities to retailers.

Checking Your Understanding

1. Why is marketing so important in satisfying our needs and wants for goods and services?
2. How does marketing benefit producers as well as consumers?
3. Name three channels of distribution and three items distributed through each channel.
4. Mention two ways in which consumers today obtain goods directly from producers.
5. Are most of the goods we use received directly or indirectly from producers? Which appears to be the better plan today?

6. Name as many different kinds of retail businesses as you can. Why do we have so many different kinds?
7. What activities do wholesalers perform in helping to market goods?
8. About how many persons are engaged in selling in this country?
9. Give some examples of job opportunities in marketing other than sales jobs.

Applying What You Have Learned

1. Prepare a list of 12 items that you as a consumer could not possibly obtain from the original producer or that you could obtain only with great difficulty. Give reasons for each selection.
2. As well as you can, trace the channel of distribution for three of the following items: a can of tomatoes, a dozen eggs, an automobile tire, a watch, a bunch of bananas, a quart of milk, a gallon of gasoline, a man's suit, or a box of candy.
3. From your own knowledge gained through experience, reading the newspaper, listening to the radio, or watching TV, tell who helps distribute goods in case of a disaster. Describe how goods are distributed in such a situation.
4. Assume that you are planning to buy each of the following items: a pair of shoes, a camera, an automobile tire, popular records, and a radio. Would you prefer to buy each item from a single-line store, a department store, a variety store, a discount store, or a mail-order house? Give reasons for your answers.
5. In almost every community, you will find one or more of the following businesses: retailer, wholesaler, manufacturer, public utility (such as gas, electricity, and telephone companies), transportation, communication, and personal service. Draw a form similar to the one shown below. In the first column, write the names of four of the different types of businesses just mentioned. In the second column, write the exact names of at least two businesses in your community that represent each of the four different types. In the third column, write the main item of merchandise or the service that each business sells.

Type of Business	Name of Business	Goods or Services Sold

6. Name at least six items that probably will never be sold through vending machines. Give reasons for your selections.

7. Since many competing retail stores carry the same or similar product brands, they frequently must offer special services to attract customers.

(a) For what kinds of customers and stores would it be important to offer many special services?

(b) Some retailers offer very few services. How are they able to compete effectively?

8. What social and economic changes are taking place in our country to cause more and more people to want to buy services rather than perform them for themselves? What changes will this likely cause in our marketing system?

Solving Business Problems

1. A factory sells small electrical appliances to a wholesaler at $12 per unit. The appliances are sold to retailers at the wholesaler's cost plus 20%. To pay his expenses and still make a reasonable net profit, the retailer has to sell the appliances to consumers at cost plus 50%.

(a) What does the retailer pay for each appliance?

(b) What is the amount of the retailer's gross profit?

(c) What does the consumer pay for the appliance?

(d) Assume that the retailer's total expenses for selling each appliance amounted to $6.12. How much net profit would there be?

(e) What would this net profit be as a percentage of sales?

2. The owner of the Maple Road Supermarket sometimes allows producers of nonfood items to place their goods in his store for sale. The store does not buy the goods but agrees to try to sell them in return for a commission on each sale. During one month, the supermarket made sales for three different companies as follows:

Company	Amount of Sales	Rate of Commission
Lawn Furniture Co.	$426.00	8%
Ace Novelty Co.	153.00	15%
Hill and Dale Iron Works	395.00	12½%

(a) How much did the Maple Road Supermarket earn on the sale of merchandise for each company?

(b) What was the total amount earned by the supermarket?

(c) What was the net amount paid to each company?

(d) What was the total amount paid to all three companies?

3. The owner of a music store can buy 100 radios for $50 each. If he buys 200 radios, he can get them for $47.50 each. He believes that he can sell 100 radios at $75 each; but to sell 200 radios, he will need to offer them at $62.50 each.

   (a) How much profit will he make if he decides to buy and sell 100 radios?
   (b) How much will he make if he decides to buy and sell 200 radios at $62.50 each?
   (c) Which is the better proposition? How much better?

4. Near the end of the summer, Jablonski's Garden Store marked down a number of items for quick sale. The regular selling price, marked-down price, and cost of each item to the store are shown below. Each item was sold at the marked-down price.

Item	Regular Price	Marked-Down Price	Cost
21-inch power mower	$ 79.50	$ 63.60	$ 50.88
Riding lawn mower	308.00	246.40	220.00
Electric hedge trimmer	42.00	37.80	36.00
Deluxe barbeque grill	54.75	32.85	34.58
Lawn furniture set	139.99	93.33	79.99

   (a) By what amount was each item marked down?
   (b) How much profit or loss was realized on each item?
   (c) What was the total profit realized on the five items?

Enriching Your Business Understanding

1. Mr. Graham and Mr. Chambers are having an argument over the place of middlemen in our marketing system. Mr. Graham believes that if we had fewer middlemen, prices would be lower. Mr. Chambers contends that no businessman, middleman or otherwise, can stay in business unless he renders an important service that consumers are willing to pay for. Discuss in class or prepare a written report telling whether you agree with Mr. Graham or with Mr. Chambers. Give reasons for your stand on the issue.

2. Business firms spend millions of dollars each year developing new products and marketing them. In a recent year, almost 10,000 new consumer products were introduced. Only a small percentage of them sold profitably. (a) Why do so many new products appear each year when the majority of them do not sell profitably? (b) Name several new products that you have seen in the marketplace, tell whether you think they will sell profitably, and give reasons for your choices.

3. In earlier years in this country, producers of fruit, vegetables, and meats brought their products to a central marketplace in larger towns and cities and there sold them directly to consumers. Today most of these marketplaces have disappeared. Generally our foods go through the hands of several processors and middlemen before we buy them. (a) What are some advantages and disadvantages of a central market system? (b) Why has this system largely disappeared in this country?

4. Through research, find out what kinds of marketing jobs are available in your community. Find out what kind of education or training beyond high school is necessary to do well on these jobs and also find out about the salaries that are offered. Be ready to report your findings in class.

5. Mr. Aglamesis feels that it is foolish to buy radios, TV sets, refrigerators, and other expensive items at retail prices. He says that he has a friend who can get anything you want at wholesale prices. (a) What additional information would you want before agreeing to make a purchase through Mr. Aglamesis? (b) If you did make the purchase, in what ways might you lose money?

6. Although most of the goods we buy at retail come from stores, many of us enjoy buying at auctions. Selling through auctions is a form of retail selling. Mrs. Holyoke attended an auction of used furniture. She saw a chair in which she was very interested. Two other bidders wanted the same chair, but Mrs. Holyoke was determined that she would have it and kept bidding until the other bidders dropped out. The chair cost her $42.75. (a) How could you find out if Mrs. Holyoke paid a fair price for the chair? (b) What are some advantages and disadvantages of buying goods at auctions?

PART 8
How Incomes Are Spent

Today the producers and the marketers in this country offer you goods and services that your grandparents never dreamed of. Try to imagine the years when your grandparents were your age. At that time, most homes were heated by coal-burning furnaces. Every day a block of ice was delivered for the icebox in the kitchen. In many homes, the smells of apples, peaches, and tomatoes being canned was part of every summer. There were no such things as power steering, power brakes, or air-conditioning in cars. But times have changed, and so have our styles of living.

So far you have learned something of how our economic system works, the nature of business in this country, and how American businesses are organized. You have also learned how mass production and our complex marketing system make available the kinds of goods you want, when you want them, where you want them, at prices you can afford. As a people, we have a better style of living than we have ever had before. Most of us have more money to spend than we have ever had. Yet one thing hasn't changed: our wants are still unlimited. Satisfy one, and another comes to take its place.

Few of us have incomes that enable us to buy everything we want. No doubt we would all like to be richer so that we could buy more goods and services. But most of us probably never will have enough income to buy every single thing we want, because we never stop wanting things. There is a way, though, to get the most for every dollar that you have to spend: buy wisely. In the rest of this unit, you will be given some guidelines for buying goods and services wisely. They can help you get the most goods and services for the money you have to spend.

WE CAN'T SPEND ALL WE EARN

Usually a person doesn't have a chance to spend all that he earns. Certain amounts are taken out of most paychecks before employees ever see them. For example, laws require employers to deduct income taxes and social security taxes from employees' salaries. Sometimes an employer is required to withhold union dues from an employee's pay. And the employee himself may ask that money be withheld from his pay and put into health or life insurance or into a savings plan. The net amount that an employee receives after all deductions are made from what he earns is called *take-home pay.*

YOU SPEND PART OF YOUR INCOME TO MEET NEEDS

Everyone spends at least part of his income to meet basic needs, and some people must spend all their income to meet basic needs. As you learned in Part 1, the basic needs are usually considered to be food, shelter, and clothing. Most people also consider education, medical care, and transportation as basic needs.

No two people's needs are exactly the same. A family's needs may depend partly on the number and the ages of the people in it. A family's needs may also depend partly on where it lives. A family living in Miami, Florida, for instance, will have very different transportation and clothing needs from a farm family living near Fargo, North Dakota. Also, no two families—though they may be alike in many ways—will see their needs in exactly the same way. One family may feel that it "needs" a large house with a big yard. Another family of the same size may feel that an apartment will do nicely.

THE REMAINING INCOME CAN BE SPENT FOR WANTS

After basic needs have been met, a family or an individual must decide how to use the remaining income most wisely. Suppose that Earl Turner feels he must have a yearly income, after taxes, of at least $7,200 to meet the basic needs of himself and his family. If the Turners can increase their income to $9,000 after taxes, they will have one-fifth of their income left after meeting their basic needs.

The Turners may decide to use this extra income to meet their basic needs more adequately. They may buy or rent a larger house. They may buy a newer, more dependable car. They may buy more life insurance. And they may want to save or invest some of this income.

Much of the extra income, though, will probably be spent to satisfy some of the family's wants. How people spend their money to satisfy their wants gives some indication of the values they consider important. Some persons will use extra income to buy a color TV set. Others will go out to eat more often or will entertain lavishly. Still others will use the money to buy books. In this country, a person is free to spend his income on whatever he pleases.

Illustration 8-1 shows how an average family living in an urban area in this country spends its income. Urban areas include cities and their suburbs and towns over 2,500 in population. About seven out of ten Americans live in urban areas. The spending patterns of people who live in rural areas may not be exactly the same, but they are probably quite similar.

HOW AN AVERAGE URBAN FAMILY SPENDS ITS INCOME

HOW AN AVERAGE URBAN FAMILY SPENDS ITS
INCOME (AFTER TAXES)

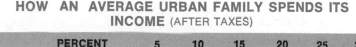

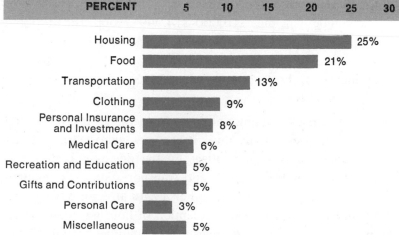

SOURCE: *Survey of Consumer Expenditures, Supplement 2, BLS Report, U.S. Department of Labor, Bureau of Labor Statistics.*

Illus. 8-1. The average urban family spends almost half of its income for food and shelter.

You can see from the chart that the average urban family spends the most for housing—about 25 cents out of every dollar. This expense includes such items as utilities, fuel, repairs, and home furnishings. The next largest expense is food—about 21 cents out of every dollar. So you can see that food and shelter together use up almost half of the average urban family's income. The next largest expense is transportation. About 13 cents out of every dollar goes toward owning and maintaining a car or paying for public transportation.

Now almost two-thirds of the income has been used up. Of the remaining income, about 9 cents out of every dollar is spent for clothing and about 8 cents is spent for personal insurance and investments. About 6 cents goes for medical care; and the other 18 cents is spent for recreation and education, gifts and contributions, personal care, and miscellaneous items.

SPENDING PATTERNS OF FIVE DIFFERENT INCOME GROUPS

How Americans in different income groups spend their income is shown in Illustration 8-2. This table shows the distribution of spending for five groups with annual incomes ranging from $3,000-$4,999 to $15,000 and over. The amounts are given after income taxes and social security taxes have been deducted. In each case, the average amount spent is given in dollars and as a percentage of the total.

As you examine this table, you will note that for all types of spending the amounts spent increase as the income increases. For example, families in the $10,000-$14,999 group spend about twice as much for food as do those in the $3,000-$4,999 group. But note that even though the dollar amount of each type of spending increases, the percentage of total income spent may either increase or decrease.

As income rises, the amount spent for personal insurance and investments increases rapidly until it becomes almost 30% of the total. This increase is largely offset by the decrease in the percentages spent for housing, food, and transportation. The changes in the percentages spent for all other items are not very large. We may conclude that, with the exception of housing, food, transportation, and insurance and investments, families in all of the income groups tend to use their income in much the same way.

AS INCOMES RISE, SPENDING PATTERNS CHANGE
URBAN FAMILIES BY INCOME GROUPS (AFTER TAXES)

INCOME (AFTER TAXES)	$3,000 $4,999	$5,000 $7,499	$7,500 $9,999	$10,000 $14,999	$15,000 AND OVER
Housing					
% of Income	29.1	26.2	23.6	22.0	19.0
Amount	$1,294	$1,710	$2,094	$2,628	$4,368
Food					
% of Income	25.3	22.2	20.5	18.3	12.2
Amount	$1,126	$1,449	$1,825	$2,186	$2,809
Transportation					
% of Income	13.8	13.6	13.6	13.4	9.1
Amount	$617	$888	$1,210	$1,596	$2,097
Clothing					
% of Income	9.0	9.1	9.6	9.7	7.9
Amount	$402	$597	$849	$1,160	$1,823
Personal Insurance and Investments					
% of Income	0	6.4	10.3	13.0	28.2
Amount	0	$416	$915	$1,547	$6,481
Medical Care					
% of Income	6.7	5.9	5.5	5.0	4.1
Amount	$298	$385	$483	$599	$930
Recreation and Education					
% of Income	4.7	5.1	5.5	6.5	5.3
Amount	$211	$339	$491	$778	$1,226
Gifts and Contributions					
% of Income	3.5	4.1	4.4	5.1	7.7
Amount	$153	$269	$390	$615	$1,762
Personal Care					
% of Income	2.9	2.6	2.4	2.2	1.5
Amount	$131	$171	$217	$264	$351
Miscellaneous					
% of Income	5.0	4.8	4.6	4.8	5.0
Amount	$223	$312	$411	$568	$1,160

SOURCE: Survey of Consumer Expenditures, Supplement 2, BLS Report 237-38, U. S. Department of Labor, Bureau of Labor Statistics

Illus. 8-2. As incomes rise, spending patterns change. Even though the dollar amount spent in a category may increase a great deal as income increases, the percentage spent may decrease.

Very often we don't think our incomes are large enough to meet all our needs and wants. But people today are earning more than people ever have before. Illustration 8-3 on page 102 helps to point out that income levels are increasing. It shows the percentage of all families in various income groups for the years 1958 and 1968. Note the increase in the three higher groups during this time period and the decrease in the three lower groups.

The figures in Illustration 8-3 are given in terms of *money income.* This is the amount of money a family or an individual earns in a definite period of time, such as a year. If you receive $7,000 a year, you have a money income of $7,000. As incomes have been increasing, prices of goods and services have also been increasing. Today you cannot buy the same amount of goods and services with $5 that you could buy ten years ago. *Real income* refers to the amount of goods and services you can buy with the amount of money you receive during a certain period of time.

INCOME LEVELS ARE INCREASING

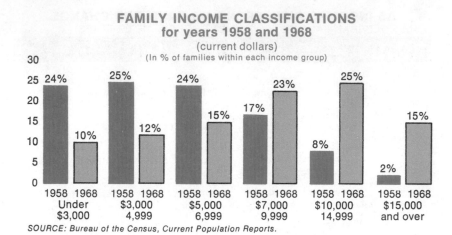

FAMILY INCOME CLASSIFICATIONS
for years 1958 and 1968
(current dollars)
(In % of families within each income group)

Illus. 8-3. This chart shows family income classifications for 1958 and 1968. Incomes are measured in current dollars.

SOURCE: Bureau of the Census, Current Population Reports.

Suppose that your salary stays at $7,000 for a period of two years. Also, suppose that prices of goods and services double during that time. Your real income would actually decrease by half because it would buy fewer goods and services at the end of the time period than it would buy at the beginning. This is true even though your money income has stayed the same.

Now look at Illustration 8-4. It is about the same as Illustration 8-3, except that it is given in terms of real income. You can see that there is less difference in the sizes of the highest and lowest income groups. Still, between the years 1958 and 1968 there was a marked decrease in the number of families in the lower income groups and a marked increase in the number of families in the higher income groups.

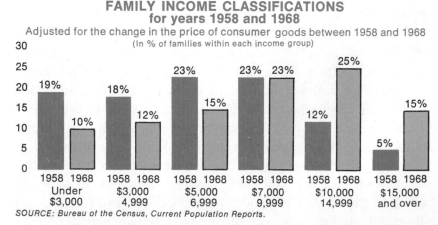

FAMILY INCOME CLASSIFICATIONS
for years 1958 and 1968
Adjusted for the change in the price of consumer goods between 1958 and 1968
(In % of families within each income group)

Illus. 8-4. In this chart, incomes have been adjusted for the changes in the price of consumer goods between 1958 and 1968.

SOURCE: Bureau of the Census, Current Population Reports.

The increase in real income levels is due mainly to our increased productivity. New production methods continue to make more goods and services available. Our country's producers are ably supported by our marketing system. Because of competition, producers and middlemen strive to increase their sales by improving products and decreasing costs. Together, mass production and competition within our marketing system tend to reduce costs so that a person can actually buy more with his income.

A reason for the increase in our productivity is the rising level of education among our people. More and more people are graduating from high school, and more and more are continuing their education after high school. A high level of education helps people to get good jobs and to keep them. It also enables them to become more effective workers and managers. Also, it gives them new tastes that increase their desires for higher styles of living.

A larger income can mean that a person will be able to achieve a higher style of living. However, this is likely to happen only if he learns how to plan carefully and buy wisely. Even if a person's income suddenly doubled, there would probably still be many goods and services he would want but wouldn't have enough money to buy. To get the most from our incomes, each of us must learn how to make the best choices of goods and services.

Developing Your Business Vocabulary

The following italicized terms should become part of your business vocabulary. For each numbered statement, find the italicized term that has the same meaning.

money income   *real income*   *take-home pay*

1. The net amount of money that an employee receives after all deductions are made from what he earns.
2. The amount of money that a family or an individual earns during a certain period of time.
3. The amount of goods and services that a family or an individual can buy with the amount of money earned during a certain period of time.

Checking Your Understanding

1. What is meant by "deductions from wages or salaries"? Give examples.
2. What are some necessary expenditures in addition to those for food, shelter, and clothing?
3. How would the location and the climate in which a family lives affect the amount they would have to spend to meet their basic needs?
4. What arc the three largest areas of spending for the average American family? What are the three smallest areas of spending?
5. As family incomes increase, for what type of spending is there the greatest increase in dollars? For what type of spending is there the greatest increase in percent of the total income?
6. As family incomes increase, for what types of spending is there a decrease in the percent of the total income?
7. Which income group shown in Illustration 8-3 decreased the most in size from 1958 to 1968? How much was the decrease?
8. Which income group shown in Illustration 8-3 increased the most in size from 1958 to 1968? How much was the increase?
9. Why does Illustration 8-4 show a smaller difference between the sizes of the income groups for 1958 and 1968 than does Illustration 8-3?
10. How does a higher level of education help increase a person's chances for a larger income?

Applying What You Have Learned

1. Suppose that the Harvey Maupin family and the Lawrence Pope family both have incomes of $6,600. The Maupins live in a city that has a sales tax; the Popes do not. The Maupins have two children; the Popes have none. (a) Will both families have the same take-home pay? (b) What might account for differences in the way the two families spend their incomes?
2. Alan and Janet Aronoff have been married for four years and have a two-year-old child. They feel that they must have more income than Alan earns if they are to be able to buy a home. Janet thinks that she could earn about $375 a month (take-home pay) as a secretary. What expenses might the Aronoffs have if Janet works that would probably not exist if she were not to work?

3. In a recent year, the percentages of family income accounted for by a working wife were:

Total Income	Percent Earned by Wife
$ 2,000-$ 2,999	12.2%
$ 3,000-$ 4,999	15.6%
$ 5,000-$ 6,999	17.0%
$ 7,000-$ 9,999	26.1%
$10,000-$15,000	28.7%
$15,000 and over	20.8%

How might you account for the steadily rising percentage figures and then the sudden drop in the "over $15,000" income group?

4. The table below shows how much some popular consumer goods and services changed in price in a ten-year period. Study the table, then answer the questions.

Item	Approximate % of Change in Price
Automobiles, new	+ 2%
Automobiles, used	+32%
Gasoline, regular and premium	+18%
Auto insurance rates	+57%
Radios, portable and table	−24%
Tape recorders, portable	− 8%
Phonograph records, stereo	− 3%
Bowling balls	− 2%
Indoor movie admissions	+96%
Drive-in movie admissions	+56%
Dentists' fees	+43%
Physicians' fees	+53%
Men's suits	+48%
Women's blouses, cotton	+23%
Baby-sitter service	+32%

Source: U.S. Department of Labor, Bureau of Labor Statistics

(a) Which goods and services showed the greatest price increases?
(b) What reasons can you give for stereo records and tape recorders decreasing in price when most items increased in price?
(c) Which items, if any, do you believe might have increased in quality so as to partially account for the price increases?

5. Most people feel that education pays off in terms of increased income. Study the chart on page 106. Then answer the questions.

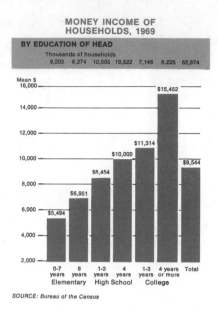

**MONEY INCOME OF
HOUSEHOLDS, 1969**

BY EDUCATION OF HEAD
Thousands of households
9,203 8,274 10,505 19,522 7,146 8.225 62,874

SOURCE: Bureau of the Census

Do you agree that education pays off in terms of increased income?
Explain your answer.

Solving Business Problems

1. Frank Homan earns $3.70 an hour and is paid every two weeks.
   During one two-week pay period, he worked 80 hours plus 10
   hours overtime at time-and-a-half. Deductions from his paycheck
   were:

Deduction	Amount
Income tax	$35.77
Social security taxes	5.2% of total earnings
Union dues	2.50
Hospital insurance	5.20
Stock purchase plan	10.00
Group life insurance	3.90

   (a) What was Mr. Homan's total income for the pay period?
   (b) What was the amount of the required deductions? What percentage was this of Mr. Homan's total earnings?
   (c) What percentage of total deductions did the voluntary deductions (hospital insurance, stock purchase plan, and group life
   insurance) represent?
   (d) What is the amount of Mr. Homan's take-home pay? What
   percentage is this of his total earnings?

2. The members of the Lavely family have the following jobs and regular monthly incomes:

Member	Income
Mr. Lavely, factory worker	$620
and part-time house painter	95
Mrs. Lavely, office worker	325
Jim Lavely, newspaper route	62
Linda Lavely, part-time waitress	70

(a) What is the total monthly family income?

(b) What percentage of the family income does Mr. Lavely provide?

(c) What is the total yearly income earned by both parents?

3. Ron and Libby McCarthy find that at the end of the year, their total income, after taxes, was spent as follows:

Expenditure	Amount
Housing	$1,801.80
Food	1,365.65
Transportation	929.50
Clothing	443.30
Personal insurance and investments	743.60
Medical care	457.60
Recreation and education	521.95
Gifts and contributions	321.75
Personal care	278.85
Miscellaneous	286.00

(a) What was the total amount of income, after taxes, earned by the family?

(b) What percentage of the total income does each expenditure represent?

4. In one county, the number of households in each income group was:

Group	Income	Number of Households
A	$ 0 -$2,499	490
B	$ 2,500-$3,999	1,285
C	$ 4,000-$6,999	3,713
D	$ 7,000-$9,999	3,070
E	$10,000 and over	2,142

(a) What percentage of the households was in each income group?

(b) Assume that the average family in this county needed an income of $4,000 to meet basic needs. What percent of the families did not have enough income to meet these needs?

Enriching Your Business Understanding

1. Rick Emery and Nancy Moran are discussing in class what should be considered as "income." Rick says that income should include only money earned, including salary, interest, and dividends. Nancy says that "things in kind" that are worth money, such as meals a waitress eats on the job or uniforms furnished by an employer, should also be considered as income.

   (a) Who is correct as far as reporting income for tax purposes is concerned?
   (b) Are things furnished by an employer in any way a kind of income? If so, why?
   (c) Make a list of "things in kind" that might be received by an employee in addition to his salary.

2. Find out the meaning of the word "median" in a table of figures. Then use the *Statistical Abstract of the United States* in answering these questions:

   (a) What is the median income of families in your state?
   (b) Is the median in your state more or less than the median for the United States as a whole?
   (c) How much has the median income in your state increased in recent years? Is that percent of increase more or less than that for the United States as a whole?
   (d) Now look up the definition of "mean" as used in statistics. In what way is "mean" different from "median"?

3. Suppose that consumers spend 95% of their income this year and save only 5% of it. Also suppose that next year they spend only 90% of their income and save 10% of it. What effects might this change in spending patterns have on our economy?

4. Discretionary income is the amount left to spend after all taxes have been paid and basic needs have been provided for. Discretionary income is most often used to satisfy a person's or a family's wants.

   (a) Why would a businessman be interested in the amount of additional discretionary income that goes with increased income levels?
   (b) If consumers gained more discretionary income, what businesses selling what kinds of goods and services would most likely gain greater sales volume?

PART 9

Face Up To Buying Problems

What kind of buyer are you? Are you an impulse buyer, buying items that suddenly strike your fancy without really thinking much about what you are doing? Many of us do this. Did you ever go downtown or to a shopping center with a few dollars you had earned and come home without much left? Perhaps you bought something and later wondered why you bought it, or wished that you had bought something else.

The smart consumer plans how to get the most benefit from his income. Few of us are ever able to have all the things we would like to have. But by planning how to use our incomes and by buying wisely, we can have many of the things we want.

How many times have you heard someone say, "Well, it's nice, but I'd never pay that much for it," or "I'd rather spend my money for something else"? Statements like these show that different people have different values. The *value* of any good or service is how much a person is willing to pay for it. The *price*, of course, is the amount that he actually has to pay.

Whenever you think about buying something, you weigh values. You weigh the value of what you have to spend against the value of what you are thinking of buying. A prospector lost without water in a desert might be willing to give up a fortune

YOU WEIGH VALUES WHEN YOU BUY

in uranium for a canteen of water. The water has more immediate value to him than the uranium does. But if you had a dozen pencils, you would probably not want to buy another one, because another pencil would have little value for you.

Suppose that you had saved your money and were thinking of taking a vacation trip to Hawaii. What would be the cost of this vacation to you? The answer to this question, in terms of weighing values, would depend largely on what you deprived yourself of in order to pay for the trip. For example, you might also like to buy a motorcycle or a new wardrobe or perhaps add to your savings account for college. They could be bought with the money you had saved for the Hawaiian trip. In this case, the cost of the Hawaiian trip to you would be a motorcycle, a new wardrobe, or perhaps even a portion of your college education. Would such a cost be too high? Only you are able to answer this in terms of your personal values.

What do you mean when you say that an article costs too much? You mean that for you the article does not have enough value to make you willing to pay its price. You may mean that you must give up too much of your money for it. You may mean that the item is of poor quality. You may mean that you don't really need it. You may mean that you can buy it somewhere else for less money. Or you may mean that you do not want to do without other things that you could buy with the same money.

Illus. 9-1. You weigh values in deciding how to spend your income. The Rand Youth Poll reports these spending patterns of teenagers in the 16- to 19-year-old group.

BOYS SPEND WEEKLY:

Movies, dating	$ 4.45
Gas and Auto	3.25
Clothing	3.10
Candy, Ice Cream, Snacks	1.65
Personal Grooming	.95
Magazines, Paperbacks, Records	1.40
Hobbies	.85
	$15.65
Savings	2.70
	$18.35

GIRLS SPEND WEEKLY:

Movies, Entertainment	$ 2.15
Gas and Auto	1.60
Clothing	4.20
Candy, Ice Cream, Snacks	.80
Personal Grooming	4.60
Magazines, Paperbacks, Records	2.00
Jewelry, Notions	1.50
	$16.85
Savings	2.65
	$19.50

SOURCE: CHANGING TIMES, The Kiplinger Magazine

The next time you think about buying something, ask yourself this: "Am I weighing my own values or someone else's when I buy this article?" Many people try to obtain status by buying material goods—a new house, a sports car, or a mink coat, for example. They try to impress people by what they own. This is called *conspicuous consumption*.

Almost everyone engages in conspicuous consumption at some time. It becomes a problem only if people don't know when to stop trying to "keep up with the Joneses." They can become so concerned with buying goods to impress other people that they do without things they really need, such as proper food. For example, there are probably many people today who drive expensive new cars but who don't have enough money left to buy life insurance to protect their families in case the breadwinner dies.

Conspicuous consumption often shows up in the desire to own the latest fashions. Many of us want other people to notice and to be impressed by the fact that we are wearing the latest fashions in clothes or driving the latest model car. Many people are willing to discard perfectly good products just because they are "out of fashion." Keeping up with fashion change costs money. Of course, a person may feel that keeping up with fashion change is worth the money. The consumer must decide what he values and what he is willing to pay for.

As consumers in today's marketplace, we face two principal buying problems. One of these problems is that we lack adequate knowledge about most of the products the market offers. A second problem is that we are, in a way, lazy shoppers. We are too busy doing other things to take the time—or even care about taking the time—to gather product information and to shop carefully.

You have learned how our technology and our marketing system make available thousands of different consumer goods and services. Walk into a large department store, and you will see a huge array of goods for sale. Brightly colored packages, animated signs, and eye-catching displays all say, "Buy this product." Every year, hundreds of new products are introduced. Modern merchants offer a wide choice of many items and many varieties of just one item. Today's supermarket, for example, may carry more than 6,000 different items.

Shopping today is complicated. Take shampoo, for example. You might think, "How complicated can it be to buy one bottle of shampoo?" Not too complicated, unless you want to make sure that you're getting the best value for your money and for your needs. Walk into a drugstore and look at the number of different brands of shampoo on the shelves. You may see as many as 10 or 15 different brands. You have probably seen some of the brands advertised on TV or in magazines. They are likely to be somewhat more expensive than the other private brands you may not recognize. The different shampoos come in plastic bottles, plastic tubes, and glass bottles of all shapes and sizes. One brand of shampoo may come in four or five different sizes, each sold at a different price. There's shampoo for oily hair, dry hair, fine hair, tinted hair, bleached hair. How do you know which is the best value?

When people used to produce many of the goods they used, such as clothing, they knew a lot about the goods and about how to judge the quality of goods. Most of us don't have time for that any more. We would rather be doing something else instead of spending the time and effort to learn about what to look for in different products and to shop for the best buys. We are lazy shoppers. And, of course, that is our choice. But we should understand that our lack of product knowledge and our unwillingness to take the time or effort to shop cost us money.

SOURCES THAT CAN HELP WITH BUYING PROBLEMS

Where can you gather the product information that you need to buy wisely? There are a number of sources open to you. Sometimes it is wise to get an expert's advice on what to look for in a product. This is especially true when you have never before bought a particular item. Consult specialists who know quality. For example, a painter or a contractor can advise you on paints. Repairmen and mechanics can tell you what to look for in appliances, cars, and hardware. Doctors can advise you on medicines; dentists can advise you on toothpastes. You will still need to make your own buying decisions, but a specialist can help you gather product information.

Advertising is another source of product information. Today advertising is so much a part of our lives that we almost take it for granted. Newspapers, billboards, magazines, radio, television, circulars—they bombard us with advertising. Some people say that

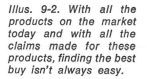

"Is this supposed to be any good?"

Copyright 1968 by the Kiplinger Washington Editors, Inc.

Illus. 9-2. With all the products on the market today and with all the claims made for these products, finding the best buy isn't always easy.

advertising creates problems because it can persuade us to buy things we don't really want or need. But for the person who knows how to use it, advertising can be valuable.

Ads vary widely in the amount of useful information they provide. Most praise the attractive features of a certain product. Some do this in general terms and others do it in great detail. By studying detailed descriptions, you can learn about what features to look for when you are comparing different brands. From advertising you can learn about (1) new products on the market, (2) how products may be used, (3) important features of products, (4) values useful in comparing competing items, (5) prices, and (6) special sales. Studying ads can save you a good deal of shopping time and energy.

A reliable merchant and his salespeople can often give you helpful product information. Tell the merchant or his salesperson what your needs are and what you want a certain article to do. Ask him which article he thinks is best if there is a choice of several price lines. For certain products, booklets describing product features and uses are available. Manufacturers of some products, such as furniture and carpeting, can supply you with printed material on what to look for in buying their type of product. Agencies of the federal government also prepare literature of interest to consumers.

Illus. 9-3. Reputable merchants and knowledgeable salespeople can be good sources of product information.

Today there are a number of private organizations which can help people become more completely informed shoppers. Two such organizations are Consumers' Research, Inc., and Consumers Union of the United States, Inc. They test consumer goods and report on their quality. Consumers' Research publishes its findings in a magazine called *Consumer Bulletin*. Consumers Union publishes its findings in a magazine called *Consumer Reports*.

Some magazines also test and rate products. For example, magazines devoted to stereo equipment may analyze new models of speakers and report on their quality. Magazines devoted to cars often report test results and rate new models. Such ratings are generally reliable, but they should be used only as guides for buying. Magazines and newspapers have also begun to carry articles of help to consumers. Newspapers often run weekly columns on "best food buys" written by home economists. Other articles may deal with such things as how to shop for credit, what to look for in a used car, and how to make sound investments.

Another source of information is the Home Economics Cooperative Extension Service. This is a cooperative service of the federal government and the land-grant college or university in each state. Each county in the United States has the services of a county agent and a cooperative extension office. The county agent is a trained home economist who gives information at meetings, answers questions by telephone and mail, and perhaps writes newspaper columns or appears on radio and TV broadcasts. The Cooperative Extension office at the land-grant college or university also publishes many free bulletins for consumers.

The sources you have just read about will give you a good starting point for gathering the product information you need to buy wisely. But there are many other sources that you will find for yourself as you become a more experienced shopper. Even with all the aids that are available, few of us can take the time and make the effort to be certain that every single thing we buy is the best possible purchase we could make. We can, though, develop the habit of using good judgment when we buy.

Whenever you buy anything, you must make a number of important decisions. Among these decisions are:

1. Would I rather buy this type of item than another item which I could buy for the same money?
2. Which dealer should I go to?
3. What quality of merchandise do I want to buy?
4. What price am I willing to pay?
5. Should I pay cash or use some kind of credit plan?
6. Do I really need this item now, or can I wait awhile?
7. If I make this purchase, what other important item may I have to do without?

Each purchase should be judged according to whether it will give you more pleasure than something else you might have bought instead. Purchases must be guided by the relationship between the need or want for one article and the possible needs or wants for others.

Developing Your Business Vocabulary

The following italicized terms should become part of your business vocabulary. For each numbered statement, find the italicized term that has the same meaning.

conspicuous consumption
price
value

1. The worth of a good or service to a consumer, measured in terms of how much he is willing to pay for it.
2. The amount a consumer must pay to obtain a good or service.
3. The practice of buying goods and services to impress others.

Checking Your Understanding

1. Do various goods and services have the same value for all people? Give examples of the values that different people might place on the same product, such as a coat.
2. What may you mean when you say that an article costs too much?
3. What problems does conspicuous consumption create for consumers? Does this also apply to you?
4. Describe at least two major buying problems that the American consumer has and tell which one you think is the most difficult.
5. Give several examples of how specialists can help you in making some purchases.
6. What are six important kinds of information about goods and services that you may be able to obtain from advertisements?
7. Explain how a reliable merchant or salesperson can help you in making your purchases.
8. How do private consumer testing services aid the consumer?
9. In what ways do magazines and newspapers help consumers become better informed shoppers?
10. List six important buying decisions that a person makes every time he plans to buy a product or service.

Applying What You Have Learned

1. Suppose that you were given the money to buy a portable stereo. From what sources could you get information about quality features to look for in stereo sets?
2. From a magazine or newspaper, select three advertisements of new products. For each advertisement, write a brief statement on important information given about each product. What important items of information about the product are missing?
3. Some people feel that all conspicuous consumption is bad. Can you defend the idea that some people get psychological value from such purchases, even though they may pay a high price for them?
4. All of us need to make many buying decisions each day. In each of the following cases, select the purchase you would make and give reasons for your choice.

   (a) A new foreign car, or a good domestic used car, each costing about $2,000.
   (b) A theater ticket in the orchestra section for $3.50, or a balcony ticket for $2.50.
   (c) A football ticket on the 50-yard line for $2.75, or a ticket in the end zone for $1.50.
   (d) Nationally known gasoline for 37 cents a gallon, or cut-rate gasoline sold by an independent dealer for 33 cents a gallon.

5. Describe in your mind the kinds of people who live in your neighborhood or near your home. Consider their incomes and the values they appear to place on goods and services. (a) What do you think are their major problems as consumers? (b) If you had the power, what would you do to help them become better consumers?

6. Some people tend to buy newer styles of products; others prefer to buy last year's styles or to buy at the end of the season. For example, some persons will buy new models of cars as soon as they come on the market; others buy leftover new cars after the newer models come on the market. Present as many arguments as you can for and against each practice. Which practice do you favor? Why?

Solving Business Problems

1. Suppose that by careful planning a family can save 2¢ out of every 50¢ formerly spent for family necessities. In the past, the family usually spent about $5,750 a year for necessities.

   (a) How much can be saved in one year under this careful spending plan?
   (b) What percent is this of the amount formerly spent?
   (c) How much can be saved in five years?

2. Mr. Overbaugh decides to buy two new snow tires for his car. The blackwall snow tires sell for $29.95 each, while the whitewall snow tires sell for $33.95 each.

   (a) How much can he save by buying the blackwall tires?
   (b) If he drives the tires 10,000 miles, what is the cost per mile for each tire?

3. Assume that your high school drama club is planning to sell season tickets for a series of plays. The treasurer of your club has set up the following schedule of prices and the probable number of tickets that will be sold at each price.

Price of Season Ticket	Probable Number of Tickets That Will Be Sold
$1.50	120
2.25	100
3.00	50
4.50	25

   (a) If the treasurer's estimates are correct, which price will bring the greatest income?
   (b) How much money will be taken in at this price?
   (c) How much more money will be taken in at this price than at the next most profitable price?

4. The Foster Furniture Company offered for sale certain items of furniture. If these items were purchased separately, they could be bought at the following prices:

Item	Price
6-piece living room suite	$325
4-piece bedroom suite	245
Dinette group	110
Refrigerator	177
Gas range	90

These items could be bought as a group for $662.90; or the first three items could be bought for $544.00.

(a) What is the total cost of all items if they are bought separately?
(b) How much is saved by buying the entire group? What percent?
(c) How much is saved by buying the first three items as a group? What percent?

Enriching Your Business Understanding

1. Find out all you can about the activities of Consumers' Research, Inc., Consumers Union of the United States, Inc., or your Home Economics County Extension Service. Present a summary report of your findings.
2. Outside of class, look through several newspapers and magazines for articles or columns that give consumer information on such things as buying certain products, budgeting, credit, or law for consumers. Make a list showing the publication's name and the type of information given. If possible, bring the publication to class or cut out samples of consumer information. Show these samples to the class and report on them.
3. Mr. and Mrs. Lansing are planning to buy a living room rug. They find one priced at $175 that they feel will be satisfactory. They are also shown another rug priced at $350. The second rug is little, if any, more attractive than the first, but the Lansings are assured that it will wear more than twice as long. What should the Lansings consider before they decide which rug to buy?
4. Through research in your library, find out what is meant by the "consumer movement." Find out what it is, how it got started, and how it affects individual consumers. Present your findings in report form.
5. The 1960's have been called by some people "the decade of the consumer." Why do you think this is true?

PART 10
Become A Sharp Shopper

You probably know some people who have invested a great deal of time and energy in becoming very skilled at something. Some are good hunters or golfers, some know a lot about music, some are good at sewing, others know a lot about the stock market. But very few people today take the time or spend the energy to learn how to become skilled shoppers.

What should you buy? How can you use your money wisely and shop so that you receive good value and get your money's worth? The competition in our economic system helps you. Most merchants try to give good values and honest service to attract your patronage and to hold your buying loyalty. But you can help buy wisely and avoid costly mistakes by following some general rules of buying.

TAKE YOUR TIME ABOUT BUYING

Time is precious for most of us, but sharp shoppers are willing to take their time. Sometimes consumers get impatient. They want to buy right now, and often this costs them money. Being willing to wait means postponing a purchase until you have saved enough money to pay cash, until you can afford to make a larger down payment, or until you know a special sales event is coming.

Waiting to buy also means slowing down and giving yourself a chance to look for the best values. If you learn to pace yourself sensibly, you will probably find that your money goes farther toward buying the things you need and want. The sharp shopper plans carefully and refuses to be hurried into buying anything. In this way, he avoids buying merchandise that he really does not need at all or that does not serve his purposes.

LOOK FOR THE GENUINE SALES

You have probably seen "Sale" signs a thousand times. They are used so much as gimmicks to try to sell more goods that many shoppers no longer know when a real sale is going on. Many so-called "sales" are not really sales at all, and you should check them carefully. Sometimes they consist of regular goods at regular prices being heavily promoted with the word "sale." When an item is really "on sale," it is offered at a price lower than its normal selling price. Department stores may regularly have January linen sales, February furniture sales, or August coat and fur sales. Grocery stores may have sales of canned goods in July or August.

Retailers run two main types of sales: promotional sales and clearance sales. In the *promotional sale*, the merchant tries to promote the sale of his regular merchandise by making a temporary price reduction. He may do this to build acceptance of a new product by offering it at a low introductory price. He hopes that customers will buy the product at the reduced price, like it, and buy it regularly in the future. The retailer also uses promotional sales to draw trade. He hopes that the customer who buys the sale merchandise will buy other products at the regular price.

Clearance sales are used to "clear" merchandise that a retailer no longer wants. This may be shopworn stock, leftovers such as odd sizes and models, or a line of merchandise that he is no longer going to carry. Clearance sales usually offer some real bargains, but it is important to be sure that you can really use a sale item before you buy it. Also, you should be sure that the merchant did not buy low-quality merchandise especially for the sale.

To be able to take advantage of real sales, sharp shoppers keep some extra money available rather than letting themselves be strapped for cash. Having cash available lets you take advantage of a special sale and buy items you had planned on buying later. Often you can make some real savings.

You can keep from making costly buying mistakes partly by avoiding *impulse buying*. This happens when you see an item and decide suddenly, "That's nice; I'll buy it." When you see some item attractively displayed, it is natural to want it. Buying an occasional candy bar or ice cream cone on impulse is part of life. The cost is small and the value is usually worth the price. But buying other items like clothing, records, or cosmetics just on a whim can be costly. You may not really need the item, for one thing. Or it might not be the best value for the price, as you would have discovered if you had shopped around.

Making a shopping list or plan and sticking to it can help stop impulse buying. Research firms often study customers to find out why they buy. Such firms found out that in supermarkets people without shopping lists buy many more items and also buy more luxury items than do people with shopping lists. Most consumers are open to suggestion. An attractive display of products, for example, can tempt you to buy something that you had not planned to buy. But you can save money if you buy from a shopping list. Using a shopping list also saves the time and trouble of making trips back to the store for something you needed but forgot to buy.

When your mother goes to the grocery store, she can tell a lot about the quality of the vegetables offered for sale. She knows if the lettuce is wilted, the tomatoes are too ripe, the carrots are withered, or the grapefruit is too green. Shoppers can do the same thing with many items that they buy. If your father buys a used car, for example, he can have an expert mechanic check it over and give it a test drive.

Always try to examine what you buy. Even if you are not an expert, you can often tell whether one item is better than another or whether it is exactly what you want. Also learn to use the sources of product information that you learned about in Part 9. They will help you learn what to look for in examining goods. As you continue to study and examine goods, you will learn to recognize differences in quality. For example, you will learn to recognize good quality in clothing by looking for such things as wide seams and matching of patterns.

TRY TO AVOID IMPULSE BUYING

TRY TO EXAMINE WHAT YOU BUY

Illus. 10-1. Always try to examine what you buy. Sometimes you may actually be able to try out the product, such as a typewriter.

Litton Industries

As you examine the quality of merchandise, you should remember an important rule of buying: "Don't buy quality you don't need." This means that the intended use of the product determines how high a quality you need. For example, you wouldn't need to buy expensive finished walnut if you were building a doghouse. Rough lumber would do just as well. But if you were building a bookshelf for your room, you might want the walnut rather than the rough lumber.

BUY FROM A MERCHANT WHOM YOU CAN TRUST

You should make every effort to judge quality for yourself. But sometimes you may have no way of proving for yourself exactly what you are getting. One of the best guarantees you can have that the things you buy are of good quality is to buy from merchants of established reputation. Repeat business is a merchant's bread and butter, and the wise merchant knows that the best customer is a satisfied customer. He knows the uses and the quality of the goods he is offering for sale. He is also concerned about matching the proper goods to his customers' needs. If you buy from merchants of established reputation, you can usually rely on them and their salespeople to help you make your merchandise selections.

It is important that you let a merchant know what you expect from an article. Many buyers are unhappy with what they buy because they had hoped that an item would be better than they had any right to expect. For example, a very low-priced tire simply will not last long at high-speed driving. If you buy lower quality items than a merchant recommends, you may not get the results you want.

Many goods are advertised nationally and are sold in almost every community. Among these goods are shoes, tools, canned foods, toothpaste, cosmetics, furniture, and appliances. Manufacturers of such goods often place special *brand names* on the items they make. "Coke," for example, is the brand name of a world-famous soft drink.

LEARN TO KNOW BRAND NAMES

Learning to recognize brand names can help you in several ways. First, you can usually expect uniform quality even when brand name goods are bought in different stores. This is especially helpful in buying goods that are difficult to inspect for quality, such as canned goods. Second, brand names make it possible for you to do comparison shopping at several stores to find the best price and service. Third, brand name items often have better guarantees behind them. It is true, of course, that some unbranded items are comparable in quality to brand name items and are less expensive. They can be good buys if you know how to examine goods for quality.

Look for labels on goods and read them carefully. *Labels* describe the content, quality, and quantity of food and drugs in packages, cans, and other containers. Retailers and manufacturers have worked with consumer groups over the years to develop more informative labels. Manufacturers particularly have found that labels, tags, and pamphlets in packages help the consumer know better how to use and care for his purchases, thus making him a more satisfied customer.

STUDY LABELS ON MERCHANDISE

Labels often tell what grade of merchandise you are buying. One company grades its merchandise as "good, better, and best." This is simple, yet it gives the shopper some idea about the quality of what he is buying. But grading is not always as simple as this. Sometimes it is extremely difficult to tell which is the top grade. Foods are sometimes marked Grade A, B, C, choice, prime, and so on. But Grade A may not always be the top grade; there may

ANOTHER FUN FABRIC FROM PEERLESS MILLS!

CONTENTS: 100% Perlan Acrylic fiber

ADVANTAGES: The fiber in this garment offers smooth comfort and is ideal either for outerwear or next to the skin. Little shrinkage or stretchage. Delightfully warm, yet lightweight. Easy to care for; excellent washability; little or no ironing needed. Moth and mildew-proof, nonallergenic.

WASHING INSTRUCTIONS: Remove oily stains before washing. Wash by machine at low temperature. Dry by machine at low temperature or hang up to dry. If ironing is desired, use cool iron only.

Peerless Mills   Raleigh, North Carolina

Illus. 10-2. Product labels can often be good sources of information.

be a Grade AAA. Automobile tires bear such names as Champion, Deluxe, Safety, Thorobred, Premium, and Life-Saver. Actually, such terms do not mean much unless you can associate a reputation for quality with each of the names used.

Labels may also bear seals of approval from organizations or magazines that test products. The familiar U. L. label or tag on electrical products shows that the product has been tested and meets safety standards of the Underwriters Laboratories of the National Board of Fire Underwriters. The *Good Housekeeping* or *Parents Magazine* seal of approval on a product label means that the product has been tested and meets the magazine's standards of performance.

Even if the goods you are buying are labeled, you should examine them if you can. You may have confidence in your merchant; but you must remember that his stock of goods was assembled to please many people, and the wants of everyone are not the same.

COMPARE PRICES AND SERVICES

Except for utilities, such as water, electricity, and telephone service, or for very specialized goods, there are few things that are not produced or sold by more than one business. Competition and a desire to gain a larger share of the market see to that. Therefore, you have a choice of where to buy, and you can compare prices and services in different stores.

Whenever and whatever you buy, you will want to get your money's worth. Quality merchandise generally costs more, but sometimes merchandise of poor quality is priced too high. Buying low quality merchandise can sometimes turn out to be expensive. For example, if you paint a house with a poor grade of paint, it may last only a year or two. A good grade of paint, though, may outlast two or three paintings with a poor grade.

In comparing prices, the sharp shopper should be wary of some merchants who mark so-called artificial list prices on their merchandise. These are prices that are more than the merchandise usually sells for. They are accompanied by a marked-down "sale" price, and the artificial list price is intended to make the customer think he is getting a bargain. This practice is unethical but not illegal.

Sharp shoppers are also wary of ads that use such phrases as "normally sells for" or "sold elsewhere for." Sometimes these are honest ads of marked-down items. But sometimes the prices mentioned in them are really artificial list prices. The sharp shopper follows the rule of comparing prices so that he knows when he is being offered a true reduction in price.

The sharp shopper also compares services from store to store. Reputable merchants try to give good service, but the types of service differ. Some merchants sell for cash only; others extend credit. Some merchants deliver goods; others do not. Some have very large stocks from which a selection may be made; others have smaller stocks.

Good service may make up for a difference in selling price. For example, it might be possible to buy a TV set from one dealer for $30 less than it could be bought somewhere else. But if the lower selling price does not include delivery, installation, and a guarantee, the cost of these services might amount to more than $30.

Service is important, but one should not pay for more service than he actually needs, just as he should not pay for more quality than he actually needs. The good buyer knows what he wants, seeks out what he wants, and buys what he wants at the best prices.

Developing Your Business Vocabulary

The following italicized terms should become part of your business vocabulary. For each numbered statement, find the italicized term that has the same meaning.

brand name   *label*
clearance sale   *promotional sale*
impulse buying

1. Selling items below regular cost to increase the sales of regular merchandise or to draw trade.
2. Using a price reduction to sell items that a merchant no longer wishes to carry in stock.
3. The purchase of goods that a consumer had not planned to buy but was prompted to buy because he saw the goods attractively displayed.
4. A trade name placed on merchandise by manufacturers or middle-men.
5. A statement attached to merchandise describing its nature or contents.

Checking Your Understanding

1. What are two possible advantages of being willing to postpone a purchase rather than buying at the first opportunity?
2. What is meant by a "genuine sale"?
3. Give several examples of items that are often bought on impulse. How can sharp shoppers guard against unwise impulse buying?
4. Name at least five items of merchandise for which quality is very difficult to determine, even by close examination. Name five items for which quality can be seen by an experienced shopper.
5. Many items are now packaged so that the goods inside are difficult to examine. How does the package often influence the buyer?
6. Explain what is meant by the statement, "Don't buy quality you don't need."
7. "In dealing with reliable merchants, you usually get what you pay for." Discuss this statement.
8. Explain how brand names can be helpful to a shopper.
9. What important items of information can be obtained by studying the labels and tags attached to merchandise?
10. How does the consumer benefit when the goods he buys are graded?

11. Give several examples of special services that merchants may offer to shoppers. Why do merchants offer such services, since they add to the costs of doing business?

12. Why is it wise to shop around and compare prices and services before making important purchases?

Applying What You Have Learned

1. Mrs. Stiles and Mrs. Greenberg were discussing different buying practices. Mrs. Stiles said that she always bought from the same merchant, regardless of the prices charged. Mrs. Greenberg said that she always bought at the lowest price she could find, regardless of who the merchant was. (a) Discuss possible reasons for each point of view. (b) Which plan do you prefer? Why?

2. A discount store advertises for sale certain well-known products at less than the regular prices.

   (a) Does this mean that the prices of all products in the store are less than the regular prices in other stores?
   (b) Do you recommend buying at discount stores or cut-rate stores? Why?
   (c) If you do purchase at discount stores or cut-rate stores, what are some precautions that you might take?

3. Mr. Sniders prefers to buy a suit at the beginning of the season so that he will have a larger variety to choose from. Mr. Laone prefers to buy a suit during the end-of-season sales so that he will be able to buy at a low price. Which of the two men do you think is following the better policy? Justify your answer.

4. In trying to make a sale to a customer, a salesperson used the following statements: "It's the buy of a lifetime"; "It's worth twice what I'm asking for it"; "Buy it, try it, and if you don't like it, return it"; "I'm offering this at a special price to you only." (a) Which of these statements do you consider to be the most reliable? (b) The least reliable? Why?

5. Some people think that they can be sharp shoppers and save money by buying in large quantities.

   (a) Mention three common items that are less expensive per unit when they are bought in large amounts.
   (b) What precautions would you need to take in storing these three items?
   (c) How could buying in large quantities actually be more costly than buying smaller amounts more frequently?

6. Paul's Diner sells a full-course roast beef dinner for $1.75. Directly across the street, the Normandy Hotel sells a similar dinner for $3.25. Both have a fair share of business.

   (a) Why doesn't Paul's Diner get all the business?
   (b) What services might customers get in the Normandy Hotel that they couldn't get in Paul's Diner?
   (c) Are those who buy the more expensive dinner poor money managers? Explain.

7. Would you expect to find a great difference between the original selling price and the end-of-season sale price for: (a) men's shoes or women's shoes? (b) women's raincoats or women's hats? (c) boys' swim trunks or boys' overshoes?

Solving Business Problems

1. At the end of the holiday season, the Westwood Appliance Store placed the following items on sale:

Item	Regular Price	Sale Price
Electric toaster	$17.50	$12.60
Tea service	79.95	47.97
Engraved mirror	24.95	19.96

   (a) Calculate the amount that each item was reduced.
   (b) Calculate the percent by which each item was reduced.

2. The Apex TV Shop advertised a black and white TV set for $220, including an antenna and delivery and installation service. The Economy TV Shop advertised the same TV set less a 10% discount, but charged $5 for delivery, $15 for the antenna, and $12 for installation.

   (a) Which is the better deal if the TV set is to be delivered and installed? How much better?
   (b) What percent of the total cost of the less expensive set is saved by making the better purchase?

3. Dave and Ellen Kerr are a young couple living in a small apartment with little storage space. They try to save money on their purchases, but buying in too large quantities results in spoilage. They can buy potatoes in different quantities at the prices listed below. The estimated spoilage for the different quantities is shown at the right.

Quantity	Price	Estimated Spoilage
5 pounds	$0.49	None
10 pounds	.89	½ pound
25 pounds	1.70	2 pounds

(a) Calculate the cost per pound for the purchase of each different quantity, before spoilage. Have your answers correct to the nearest one-tenth of a cent.

(b) Calculate the cost per pound of each different quantity, after spoilage.

4. The advertisement below appeared in a newspaper during the month of March:

CLEARANCE SALE
SAVE, yes SAVE ½ and more!
Buy NOW! Buy for Next Year!
A small deposit will hold your
  selection!
Don't miss these fine values!

	Regular Price	Sale Price
Fur-Trimmed Coats	$157	$43.75
Finer Winter Coats	$99.95	$36.25
Zip-Coats	$62.50 to $74.95	$23.75
Raincoats	$24.95	$ 8.95

(a) How much were the fur-trimmed coats reduced?

(b) How much were the finer winter coats reduced?

(c) How much were the raincoats reduced?

Enriching Your Business Understanding

1. Bring to class labels from several different products. Be prepared to describe the information each label provides and tell whether or not you think the label gives enough information.

2. Retail stores often run sales at the same times year after year. For example, department stores have January white sales every year. Such regular sales allow shoppers to plan their purchases ahead of time and take advantage of real sales events. Name as many such regularly scheduled retail sales events in your community as you can.

3. Describe the merits of each of the following buying practices:

(a) Mrs. Grabowski always makes her purchases at the same stores where, as she says, "I have learned to know them and they have learned to know me."

(b) Mr. and Mrs. Landon live in a small town but drive to a nearby city to do most of their shopping because city stores offer wider selections.

(c) Mrs. Barbera does much of her shopping by phone after studying advertisements and catalogs of retail merchants.

(d) Mrs. Cannady says she believes in being loyal to local stores. If they don't have what she wants, "they'll order it for me."

(e) Mrs. Michaelson usually buys off-brand merchandise because "less money is spent for advertising and prices are cheaper."

4. For each article listed below, tell whether you would choose to buy a higher priced item or whether you would choose a lower priced item. Give reasons for each choice.

(a) Outdoor paint for a two-story frame house.

(b) Tires for the car your father drives a few miles into town to work each day.

(c) A tie to go with a sport coat that you wear often.

(d) A billfold to give to your father, who is a salesman.

(e) A ballpoint pen for school use.

5. This part gives eight rules for becoming a sharp shopper. Copy each of the rules in one column on a separate sheet of paper. In a second column, opposite each rule, tell whether you "usually follow" that rule or whether you "usually do not follow" that rule. Ask others in your class to compare their ratings with yours. As a class project, consider having each person ask a parent or neighbor to rate themselves, then tally all the ratings and see which rules most people follow and which ones they do not follow.

PART 11
Your Rights
As a Buyer

If you watched television last night, you probably saw at least four or five commercials in an hour. In today's newspaper, you will find many ads for many kinds of products. The vast number of goods and services offered for sale often makes your selection difficult. Businesses compete for our shopping dollars, and some firms may "oversell" as they promote their goods. Many of us shop in stores where we do not know the owner, and we may accept as fact the many claims made for a product.

Most sellers follow honest, ethical sales practices. But some products do not always live up to the manufacturer's claims, and a few businesses are not always honest with their customers. You should be aware of your rights as a buyer and know what you are entitled to expect when you make a purchase.

When you ask to buy five gallons of gasoline, you are entitled to five full gallons of gasoline. If a label states that the net content of a container is ten ounces, two quarts, or some other quantity, you are entitled to receive that amount. Local, state, and federal governments have passed laws regarding full measure. For example, most state governments inspect for accuracy such things as gasoline pumps, scales, and sizes of milk and soft drink bottles.

YOU ARE ENTITLED TO FULL MEASURE

YOU SHOULD GET CLEAR TITLE TO GOODS YOU BUY

The word *title*, as used here, means the same as ownership. "Title" may also refer to the form that is evidence of ownership. For example, the form that a car buyer receives to show his ownership is called the title to the car. When a person buys a house, he receives a form showing his ownership, but this title is called a *deed*. Most of the things you buy do not have written titles, but you have the right to receive a good title from the seller. If you do not receive a good title, you have a claim against the seller for the amount you paid plus any damages you have suffered.

YOU MAY BUY GOODS ON TRIAL

Sometimes you may not be sure that a certain item will serve your purpose. So the dealer may sell it to you *on trial* or *on approval*. This means that it is not your property until you have given your approval. Of course, you must give your approval within a reasonable time. Otherwise, it is assumed that you want the merchandise and it then becomes yours.

You may also buy an item with the "right to return" it in a few days if it is not satisfactory. In such a transaction, you get title to the article when you buy it. If the article is unsatisfactory, you may return it. But if you do not return it within the time agreed upon, you lose your right to do so. While you possess merchandise on a trial basis, you are obligated to treat it well and not damage it.

ALL GOODS MUST BE MERCHANTABLE

A merchant must offer for sale only *merchantable goods*. These are goods that are not defective, spoiled, damaged, or otherwise unfit for use by the consumer. Food products, particularly, must be merchantable goods.

A dealer does have the right to sell defective, soiled, faded, or damaged items if the items are so marked. Such merchandise is advertised and sold "as is." This means that you, the buyer, are accepting the item as you see it and that you recognize such defects as dents and scratches. By labeling the item "as is," the merchant tells you that he does not guarantee it to be in any better condition than you see it. Such items can be good values if you can use them in the condition they are in.

Product descriptions that appear in ads and on labels can give you valuable information. But you should learn to tell the difference between helpful descriptions and meaningless statements or catchy slogans. Examples of meaningless statements are: "Best on the market." "Worth twice as much." "Best buy in town." "Good as new." "Contains a secret ingredient." "$10 value for $7.50."

GOODS MUST BE AS DESCRIBED BY THE SELLER

Sometimes we buy carelessly. We may not weigh the facts given in advertising or by a salesperson, and we blame the seller for our poor purchases. There are times, though, when false information is given to a customer in an effort to make a sale. This misrepresentation is known as *fraud*.

To be defrauded, you must actually be deceived. Suppose that you are looking at a used car. If the salesman tells you that it is a late '70 model but you know that it is a '69 model, there is no fraud. You were not deceived even though the salesman was not telling the truth. When a salesman puffs up his product—says "it's the best" or "it's a great value"—he is not guilty of fraud. If, however, the salesman tells you that the car has just had a complete engine overhaul when, in fact, the engine is almost worn out, there is fraud.

A *guarantee* is a promise by the manufacturer or dealer, usually in writing, that a product is of a certain quality or that defective parts will be replaced. A guarantee is also called a *warranty*. Statements like these are guarantees: "This garment is guaranteed not to shrink more than 1%." "Contains 50% new wool." "Defective tubes will be replaced within 30 days without charge."

GUARANTEED ITEMS MAY BE REPLACED

You should insist on seeing a copy of the warranty when you buy an item that is guaranteed. And you can require the store to put in writing any other guarantees that have been offered. Warranties are sometimes spelled out in ads for the product. You should keep a copy of the ad as evidence of the warranty. Read the warranty carefully to find out just what is guaranteed and what period of time is covered. The guarantee may apply to the entire item or only to some parts of it. No guarantee will cover damages caused by misuse. You should also find out who will service the product during the warranty period.

WARRANTY

This appliance is guaranteed for one year against electrical and mechanical defects in material and workmanship. Repairs or parts required as a result of such defects will be made free of charge during this period. The guarantee does not cover damage caused by misuse, negligent handling, or use on current or voltage other than that stamped on the appliance. This guarantee is in lieu of any other warranty, either expressed or implied. If service is required, send the appliance prepaid to the nearest Astron Appliance Company service station. Please write a letter explaining your difficulty.

Astron Appliance Company is under no obligation to extend this warranty to any appliance for which an Astron warranty registration card has not been completed and mailed to the Company within fifteen days after date of delivery.

ASTRON COMPANY   ST. LOUIS, MISSOURI

Illus. 11-1. You should ask to see a copy of the warranty for any item that is guaranteed.

Many products are sold with a warranty card attached. To validate the warranty, you must fill out the warranty card and return it to the manufacturer or dealer. There is usually a time limit for returning the warranty card.

UNORDERED MERCHANDISE MAY BE KEPT

You have probably received through the mail an invitation to join a record or book club. If you join, a monthly selection is usually sent to you unless you tell the club that you do not want that selection. This kind of agreement between you and the club is legal and is a convenience to you.

There are firms, however, which ship unordered merchandise to individuals in the hope that persons will buy the merchandise. These unethical firms sometimes send unordered goods "on approval" to a person and include an "approval invoice" that states the price of the items. This "approval invoice" also includes a request for payment. If payment is not made, the firm sends a series of notices demanding payment.

You are under no obligation to pay for unordered merchandise unless you intend to use it or decide to buy it. Neither are you obligated to return the merchandise nor keep it intact.

PRIVATE GROUPS HELP PROTECT BUYERS' RIGHTS

Today there are a number of private organizations which help to protect your rights as a buyer. Sometimes businessmen form *trade associations*. These are organizations of firms engaged in one line of business. Many trade associations establish standards of quality for the products that their members manufacture. These standards of quality help assure the consumer that he is getting a good buy for his money when he buys that type of product. For example, the American Institute of Laundering sets up standards of washability for fabrics. If a fabric's tag bears the seal of this association, this means that the fabric has met the association's standards. Some trade associations also publish codes of ethics that members are urged to follow.

Local businessmen often work together to help protect themselves and their customers from unethical or dishonest business practices. In many cities, local businesses finance a nonprofit organization called a Better Business Bureau. The Bureau warns consumers of dishonest schemes being practiced in the community and promotes fair advertising and selling practices. The Bureau also investigates complaints about unethical or dishonest business practices. In communities which have no Better Business Bureau, the local chamber of commerce may perform much the same function of protecting consumers.

Business - Consumer Relations Code

We reaffirm the responsibility of American business to:

1. Protect the health and safety of consumers in the design and manufacture of products and the provision of consumer services. This includes action against harmful side effects on the quality of life and the environment arising from technological progress.

2. Utilize advancing technology to produce goods that meet high standards of quality at the lowest reasonable price.

3. Seek out the informed views of consumers and other groups to help assure customer satisfaction from the earliest stages of product planning.

4. Simplify, clarify, and honor product warranties and guarantees.

5. Maximize the quality of product servicing and repairs and encourage their fair pricing.

6. Eliminate frauds and deceptions from the marketplace, setting as our goal not strict legality but honesty in all transactions.

7. Ensure that sales personnel are familiar with product capabilities and limitations and that they fully respond to consumer needs for such information.

8. Provide consumers with objective information about products, services, and the workings of the marketplace by utilizing appropriate channels of communication, including programs of consumer education.

9. Facilitate sound value comparisons across the widest possible range and choice of products.

10. Provide effective channels for receiving and acting on consumer complaints and suggestions, utilizing the resources of associations, chambers of commerce, better business bureaus, recognized consumer groups, individual companies, and other appropriate bodies.

Chamber of Commerce of the United States

Illus. 11-2. This code of business-consumer relations has been adopted by the Chamber of Commerce of the United States.

GOVERNMENT PROTECTS BUYERS' RIGHTS

State, federal, and local governments are very concerned that the products available to the consumer are safe for him to buy and use and that his rights as a buyer are protected. The federal government has set up various agencies to protect the consumer. The National Bureau of Standards, for example, tests goods, sets up standards, and controls weights and measures. The Department of Agriculture sets up standards for grading farm products sold in interstate commerce. It also controls the processing of meats, inspects them, and stamps meat and meat products with grades according to their quality. State and local governments are also active in inspecting food processing plants.

Two more important agencies that help protect the consumer are the Food and Drug Administration and the Federal Trade Commission. The Food and Drug Administration, among other things, makes sure that food, drug, and cosmetic products are not harmful to consumers and that labels of these products do not mislead the consumer. The Federal Trade Commission protects consumers and businessmen against unfair business practices and unfair competition. It regulates the labeling of products other than food, drugs, and cosmetics, and is alert to deceptive, fraudulent, or misleading advertising.

The Post Office Department also helps protect consumers by investigating and stopping fraudulent use of the mails. Postal inspectors guard against such schemes as lotteries, sale of worthless stock, and fraudulent sale of land.

States and cities often require that merchants obtain licenses to sell products such as drugs or to operate such businesses as restaurants and barber shops. Businesses that handle food must meet sanitation requirements. New plumbing and electrical installations must be approved by the proper officials.

Most states and a few cities have developed consumer-protection programs. Deceptive sales practices are a prime target of these programs. The concern of agencies responsible for these programs is that the consumer be given a fair shake for the dollars he spends. In some states, court action has been brought against businesses which have violated the consumer's rights.

As a buyer, you are often responsible for what you buy if the merchant has been honest with you. When dissatisfaction occurs because of faulty merchandise or misleading advertising which may have influenced you to buy the merchandise, you should first talk with the merchant who sold the item. If you fail to obtain the kind of adjustment you would like, you may:

1. Contact the Better Business Bureau and report what happened.
2. Contact the State Bureau of Consumer Affairs or the State Attorney General's office.
3. Contact your social welfare agency if you or your family is receiving government financial aid.
4. Contact a lawyer or the Legal Aid Society if the problem is quite serious.
5. In larger cities, file a claim for damages in the Small Claims Court. Claims may be filed in any court, but this court is operated for the filing of small claims only.

Developing Your Business Vocabulary

The following italicized terms should become part of your business vocabulary. For each numbered statement, find the italicized term that has the same meaning.

deed	*on trial* or *on approval*
fraud	*title*
guarantee or *warranty*	*trade association*
merchantable goods	

1. Ownership of goods or services, or the form that is evidence of ownership.
2. A form showing ownership of a house.
3. A sale in which goods do not become the buyer's property until he has given his approval of them.
4. Goods that are fit to be used by the buyer.
5. The act of deceiving or misrepresenting.
6. A promise that a product is of a certain quality or that defective parts will be replaced.
7. An organization of firms engaged in one line of business.

Checking Your Understanding

1. Describe four important rights that you have as a buyer.
2. How do local, state, and federal governments help assure that you will receive full measure when you buy?
3. If you do not receive a good title for an item you buy, what action may you take?
4. If a sale is made on trial or on approval, when does the buyer get title to the goods? If a sale is made with the "right to return," when does the buyer get title to the goods?
5. Under what conditions can a merchant sell defective, soiled, faded, or damaged articles? Is it ever wise to buy such articles?
6. What are some things to remember when buying an item that is guaranteed?
7. Have you or members of your family ever received unordered merchandise through the mail? What is your legal obligation in regard to unordered merchandise that you receive?
8. What services does a trade association provide for consumers?
9. Give examples of ways in which the following government agencies help the consumer: (a) the Bureau of Standards, (b) the Department of Agriculture, (c) the Food and Drug Administration, (d) the Federal Trade Commission, and (e) the Post Office Department.
10. If your buying rights are violated, what action may you take?

Applying What You Have Learned

1. Examine a number of ads published in a newspaper or magazine. Study the statements made in these ads and classify them into three groups: (a) helpful statements; (b) meaningless statements; and (c) statements that are guarantees.
2. "A buyer cannot receive good title to stolen property, even if he knew nothing about the theft." Explain this statement.
3. If there were a Better Business Bureau in your community, what services would you expect it to provide for you? For businessmen?
4. Why do merchants often accept merchandise returned by dissatisfied customers, even though the law might not require them to do so?
5. Suppose that you were buying an appliance or some other expensive item. The salesman demonstrates the product and makes certain claims about it, saying that it performs better and will last longer than other brands sold elsewhere. Later, after you have used the item, you believe that the salesman's claims were not true. (a) Do his statements give you a claim against the seller on the basis of fraud? (b) How could you go about getting your money back?

6. Why do state and city governments require that some individuals and businesses have licenses in order to sell certain goods and services? Mention several different goods or services for whose sales licenses are required.

7. "Almost 98% of the purchases which consumers make are a matter of faith between buyer and seller, and most problems can be settled by simple discussion between the two parties." This statement has been made about the American free-market system. Explain why you believe the statement to be true or not true.

Solving Business Problems

1. Saul Hames bought a used motorcycle from a friend for $335. He paid $50 down and agreed to pay $30 per month on the balance.

   (a) How much did he owe after making the down payment?
   (b) How many payments will he make?
   (c) What will be the amount of the final payment?

2. The Mark Edwards Construction Company submits a bid to build a small office building of 4,000 square feet at $44 a square foot. The bid is accepted and states that the company will complete the building in 90 days or will pay a 1% penalty for each day that it is late.

   (a) How much is the Edwards bid?
   (b) If the company is 10 days late in completing the building, how much will it be penalized?
   (c) If the company fails to complete the building and is penalized for 20% of the contract, what will be the amount of the penalty?

3. Phil Mayo is a high school student who has a career goal of becoming a retail store manager. He enrolls in the Distributive Education Cooperative Program in which he studies marketing subjects in his morning classes and receives on-the-job training in a retail store in the afternoon. He signs a training agreement with the school and his employer to meet the occupational experience requirement of the cooperative program. He will work in the store 15 hours each week for 40 weeks and will receive $1.50 per hour.

   (a) If Phil is not absent from work during the 40 weeks, what will his income be?
   (b) A 1% city payroll tax is deducted from his salary each week. What is the amount of this tax for the week?
   (c) If Phil works 10 hours overtime during each of the four weeks of Christmas selling and during one week at Easter, how much

will he earn in overtime pay if overtime pay is 1½ times the regular rate?

(d) What will be Phil's total income in this program? Calculate the amount of his income after the city payroll tax deduction.

4. The Direct Nursery Sales Company guarantees that its products will satisfy the customer or that the purchase price plus postage will be refunded. Last year's sales and returns were:

Total sales	$120,000
Products returned for refund	5,400
Cost of postage on returned goods	60

(a) What percent of sales is made up of products returned for refund?

(b) What is the cost of postage for returned products as a percentage of sales?

(c) What is the total amount of sales after refunds?

Enriching Your Business Understanding

1. "An advertisement is not an offer to sell the goods advertised." Explain this statement. (You will find discussions of this subject in business law textbooks in the section dealing with contracts and under the title "Offer" or "Offer and Acceptance.")

2. Assume that a person came to your home offering a bargain on painting the house, installing a new furnace, or making some other home improvement. As the buyer, you think that the deal is too good to be true. How could you check on the salesman's claims about his deal?

3. Many times, misunderstanding occurs between a buyer and a seller because each does not understand what the other said or meant. What should both parties do when there is an apparent disagreement?

4. Joe Polski read an advertisement for a product that was being reduced 10% from its usual selling price. Thinking he would save money, Joe rushed down and bought the item. The next day, he saw an ad in which the store stated that it was clearing out its stock of the product at 50% of the original price. Joe went to the store and demanded an adjustment of the price he had paid. (a) Does Joe have any legal claim to a price adjustment? (b) If you were the store manager, would you make an adjustment?

5. What do you think are the buyer's responsibilities in handling merchandise, paying bills, returning goods, making complaints about products or services, and otherwise dealing with merchants?

Unit 4

Banks and Banking Services

PART 12
Why Banks Are Needed

When you hear the word "bank," you probably think first of a place to keep money safely. And a bank is this. If we place money in a bank, we are confident that we can get it back whenever we need it. But a bank is more than a place to keep money safely. A bank is a business, just as are the stores and factories in your community. It hopes to make a profit for its owners by performing certain services for customers.

The services of a bank may be very simple, such as changing a quarter for five nickels or helping someone start a savings program with only a few dollars. Or the services may be very complex, such as making up a business firm's payroll involving thousands of dollars, or arranging a multi-million dollar loan to build a new factory. Simple or complex, all of a bank's services are important in helping people carry out their daily business transactions.

Suppose that Gary Marshall, a high school student, has a summer job that pays him $60 a week. He plans to save most of his wages, partly to pay next year's school expenses and partly to build a fund for future college expenses. Gary knows that if he carries the money with him or keeps it at home, he may be tempted to spend it or it may be lost or stolen.

BANKS ACCEPT DEPOSITS

To protect his money, Gary may put most of his weekly pay in the bank. When he puts money in the bank, he makes a *deposit* and becomes a *depositor*. The record that the bank keeps of a customer's deposits is known as an *account*. When Gary puts his money in the bank, he is said to have an account in the bank.

BANKS OFFER CHECKING ACCOUNT SERVICES

After Gary Marshall has deposited his money in the bank, he may want to use part of it to pay bills. He may go to the bank and withdraw the necessary cash. Or he can use his money to pay bills by writing orders directing the bank to pay out his money. This makes it unnecessary for him to go to the bank to withdraw in person the amount that he needs. A depositor's written order directing a bank to pay out money for him is called a *check*. Anyone who has a bank account against which he can write checks is said to have a *checking account*. A depositor cannot call the bank on the phone and order it to pay out money for him; the order must be written as a check. This gives the bank a record to show that it was ordered to pay out the depositor's money.

Illus. 12-1. After a person has deposited money in a checking account, he can write checks directing the bank to pay out money for him.

Transamerica Corporation

As Gary earns more than he needs to pay his immediate bills, he may decide to put part of his earnings in a *savings account*. There are two important differences between savings accounts and checking accounts. First, checks may be written on checking accounts but not on savings accounts. Second, the bank pays *interest* on deposits in savings accounts but not on deposits in checking accounts.

If the bank pays 4% interest on savings accounts, Gary will receive 4 cents for each dollar deposited in his account for one year. A few cents may not sound like much; but if Gary's summer savings amount to $600 and he does not withdraw any money, his interest for one year will be $24—enough to buy some new fall school clothes.

Besides offering a place where money can be kept safely, banks offer a place where other valuables can be kept safely. Banks usually have vaults that contain many *safe-deposit boxes*. Since these boxes are well guarded, they are the safest place for persons to keep such valuables as jewelry, bonds, wills, birth records, and insurance policies. Not even the bank has the right to open a customer's safe-deposit box. The box can be opened only by the customer himself or by someone who has been given the right to open it for him.

Bank of America

Illus. 12-2. Banks have large vaults, protected by massive doors, in which customers' safe-deposit boxes are kept.

BANKS MAKE LOANS TO CUSTOMERS

Many business firms, individuals, and government units need to borrow money at some time. For example, a business may be able to buy merchandise at a good price provided it makes payment right away. But it may not have enough money to do this. In such a case, the business may borrow from a bank. The loan can be repaid some 30 or 60 days later, after much or all of the merchandise has been sold. Or a family may not have enough money to buy something it needs or wants, such as a car. It can postpone buying the car until it has saved the money it needs. Or it may borrow from the bank, buy the car, and repay the loan as the car is being used.

Banks are glad to lend money to those who need to borrow, if it seems reasonably likely that the loans will be repaid when due. In fact, a bank needs to make such loans. It receives most of its income from the interest that it charges borrowers.

A bank can help customers with money problems other than borrowing money wisely. Officers of a bank can advise customers on whether it is wise to buy a certain house, how to send money safely through the mail, how to build a good credit rating, how to invest their money, and many other matters.

BANKS OFFER HELP WITH INVESTMENTS

Anyone may buy federal government bonds through a bank. If a depositor wants to buy bonds regularly—such as once a month—his bank will do this for him and charge the cost of the bonds to his account. A bank will also cash government bonds for its customers and pay them whatever interest has been earned. There is no charge for these services.

Banks will also buy for their customers bonds issued by businesses and by state and local governments, including school districts. Banks will give advice and help their depositors make other kinds of investments, and they will help depositors sell any investments they want to sell.

MANY BANKS HAVE TRUST DEPARTMENTS

Many banks manage investments for their customers. When they do this, the money or other property that is turned over to them for investment is said to be held in trust. Banks that perform only this kind of service are called *trust companies*. Many banks have trust departments that perform the same services as trust companies.

Trust departments are used by people of all ages, but they are especially useful for the very young or the very old. If a very young person inherits money, he may not have the skill and experience to manage it wisely. The inheritance may then be turned over to a bank's trust department. The bank will make sure that the money is invested wisely. It will also assist in seeing that the income earned is properly used. An older person who no longer wants to be bothered with making investments himself may also place his money in trust with a bank. The bank will take care of all investments and regularly make payment to the customer.

Illus. 12-3. In many banks, counselors can give persons help with their investments.

Gamble-Skogmo

BANKS ARE ORGANIZED FOR SPECIAL PURPOSES

Some banks offer all the services discussed in this part. Other banks are organized for special purposes. *Savings banks,* for example, are organized to handle savings accounts for individuals and to make loans to home buyers. Trust companies, as you have learned, serve individuals by managing their money and property for them. *Investment banks* help large corporations obtain money for new buildings, machinery, and other long-term needs.

Most banks are organized as *commercial banks*. Commercial banks handle checking accounts, make loans to individuals and businesses, and provide other banking services such as those you have been reading about. Often a commercial bank will perform services similar to those of banks organized for special purposes.

These services may be handled in different departments of a commercial bank, such as a savings department, a trust department, a real estate department, a personal loan department, or an investment department. The commercial bank today is a "department store" of banking because it offers so many different banking services.

BANKS EXPECT TO EARN PROFITS

Banks expect to earn profits for their owners just as any other business does. Some banking services, such as selling government bonds, are free; but a bank earns part of its income by charging for its services. For example, customers usually pay a charge for using checking account services. A bank receives most of its income from interest charged for lending money to customers.

A bank does not promise to return to a customer exactly the same bills or coins he deposited, but simply an equal amount. It is unlikely that all of a bank's customers would want to withdraw all their money at the same time. So a bank is able to invest part of the money deposited with it. The loans and investments that it makes help many people and organizations: government, businesses, and individuals. A bank's earnings are used to pay its expenses (such as employees' salaries), to pay interest on savings accounts, and to provide profits for the bank's owners.

OUR GOVERNMENT REGULATES BANKS

A bank's operations are regulated more strictly than are the operations of most other businesses. *State banks* operate under the banking laws of the state in which they are located. *National banks* operate under the banking laws passed by the federal government as well as those of the state in which they are located. Banks are regularly inspected by bank examiners and are required to publish in local newspapers periodic statements of their financial condition. Government regulation of banks is necessary to assure the safety of depositors' money.

The federal government established the *Federal Reserve System* to help banks serve the public most efficiently. Under this system, the United States is divided into 12 areas called Federal Reserve Districts. A Federal Reserve bank is located in each district. All national banks are required to join the Federal Reserve System, and state banks may become members. Banks that join the System are known as member banks.

THE FEDERAL RESERVE SYSTEM

LEGEND

—— Boundaries of Federal Reserve Districts   —— Boundaries of Federal Reserve Branch Territories

★ Board of Governors of the Federal Reserve System   ■ Federal Reserve Bank Cities   ● Federal Reserve Branch Cities

Illus. 12-4. The Federal Reserve System.

A Federal Reserve bank is a banker's bank. Its relationship to member banks is similar to that of any bank to its own customers. It receives deposits from member banks and makes loans to them. A Federal Reserve bank does not handle individual checking or savings accounts or make loans directly to individuals and businesses.

BANKS HELP COMMUNITIES GROW

From what you have learned so far about banks, you can see that banks are important to all of us. Almost a million people work in America's 36,000 banking establishments. Banking services help build homes, start new businesses, plant crops, finance educations, and buy goods. Banking services help a community pave its streets, build hospitals and public buildings, and buy new equipment. These services are made possible because of the savings of many people.

Bank deposits do not remain idle in bank vaults; they are put to work. When you make a deposit in your bank, you are making your money work for you and for your community.

Developing Your Business Vocabulary

The following italicized terms should become part of your business vocabulary. For each numbered statement, find the italicized term that has the same meaning.

account	*investment bank*
check	*national bank*
checking account	*safe-deposit box*
commercial bank	*savings account*
deposit	*savings bank*
depositor	*state bank*
Federal Reserve System	*trust company*
interest	

1. Money that is placed in a bank account by a customer.
2. One who places money in a bank account.
3. The record that a bank keeps of a customer's deposits.
4. An order written by a depositor directing a bank to pay out money for him.
5. A bank account against which a depositor may write checks.
6. A bank account on which interest is paid.
7. An amount paid for the use of money.
8. A compartment in a bank vault for the storing of valuables.
9. A bank that manages the money and property of others.
10. A bank that accepts only savings deposits.
11. A bank that handles the transactions of businesses that need to obtain large amounts of money.
12. A bank that handles checking accounts, makes loans to individuals and businesses, and provides other banking services.
13. A bank that operates under the banking laws of the state in which it is located.
14. A bank that operates under banking laws of the federal government.
15. A nationwide banking plan set up by our federal government to assist banks in serving the public more efficiently.

Checking Your Understanding

1. Why might a high school student find it desirable to have a checking account?
2. What are the important differences between a checking account and a savings account?
3. Give a reason why a business may borrow from a bank.

4. Give a reason why an individual may borrow from a bank.

5. How can banks help individuals with their money problems?

6. Give an example of a situation in which it might be advisable for the trust department of a bank to handle a person's money.

7. A brief description of different kinds of banks follows. Identify each type of bank.

   (a) A bank that specializes in accepting accounts on which interest is paid.

   (b) A bank that manages money and property for customers.

   (c) A bank that aids businesses in obtaining large amounts of money.

   (d) A bank that offers miscellaneous services through different departments.

   (e) A bank organized under the banking laws of a particular state.

   (f) A bank operating under banking laws passed by the federal government.

8. How do banks earn most of their income?

9. What is one important difference between a Federal Reserve bank and your local bank?

10. Mention several ways in which banks help communities grow.

Applying What You Have Learned

1. Every year thousands of dollars are lost by individuals who keep large amounts of money on their persons or in their homes.

   (a) Why might these people keep large amounts of cash?

   (b) List the hazards of keeping money in the house.

   (c) What are some arguments you could use to encourage such persons to place their money in banks?

2. The Mayer and Sons Company keeps only a small amount of money in its safe. Most of its cash receipts are deposited in a bank each day. Suggest reasons why this method is followed.

3. Almost everyone uses the services of banks at one time or another, but different individuals and groups often use different kinds of services. For each of the following, mention the types of banking services they are most likely to use and tell why you think so: (a) your class in school, (b) a retired person, (c) a service station operator, (d) a car buyer, and (e) a church.

4. A Federal Reserve bank is sometimes referred to as a "bankers' bank." Explain.

5. Try to imagine a community without a bank. Explain how people in the community might solve each of the money problems mentioned on page 154.

(a) What might they do with the money they saved?

(b) How might an employer pay his employees?

(c) How might a home buyer obtain funds to purchase a house?

(d) How might a farmer pay for some farm machinery that he wanted to buy?

(e) How might citizens pay their taxes?

Solving Business Problems

1. Dick Melvin had a bank balance of $640 at the beginning of a month. During the month he made deposits of $170 and $210; he wrote checks for $46.50, $112.00; $49.83, $16.75, and $125.10. What was his balance at the end of the month?

2. The General Business students of Anderson High School set up a savings plan for the members of the class. The teacher served as banker. The deposit and withdrawal records of three students over a period of one month were:

Tom Riegert:

10/1	Deposited	$4.00
10/11	Withdrew	1.50
10/18	Deposited	2.25
10/25	Deposited	1.25
10/31	Deposited	.75

Carmen Rizzo:

10/4	Deposited	$6.50
10/11	Deposited	3.00
10/16	Withdrew	1.30
10/22	Withdrew	.60
10/25	Withdrew	1.00
10/30	Deposited	4.50

Anne Bryce:

10/1	Deposited	$2.25
10/8	Deposited	2.15
10/15	Deposited	2.00
10/22	Deposited	2.75
10/25	Withdrew	1.30
10/29	Deposited	2.25

(a) What amount did each student have on deposit at the end of the month?

(b) What was the total amount on deposit in the three accounts?

(c) Which student has the best saving habits? Explain.

3. Carl Hansen's average bank balance during the past year was $500. The bank was successful in lending 70% of this amount at

the average rate of 6%. The expenses of the bank were 80% of the total income. The net profit (total income less expenses) was 20% of the total income.

(a) What amount was the bank able to lend from Mr. Hansen's account?

(b) How much was earned from lending this amount?

(c) How much of this interest earned was net profit? (Assume that the net profit was the same percent of the interest earned as the net profit of the bank as a whole.

4. Jack Mooney operated a small grocery store. He was careful to keep on hand only as much money as was needed to make change. He deposited his daily receipts in the bank at the close of every business day. He kept a careful record of his daily deposits for four weeks and was interested in knowing how his deposits varied from day to day and from week to week. To obtain this information, he used the plan illustrated below:

Days	1st Week	2nd Week	3rd Week	4th Week
Monday	$167.06	$176.14	$143.50	$159.63
Tuesday	179.78	191.29	163.57	171.58
Wednesday	89.68	96.14	79.70	81.57
Thursday	163.69	159.78	144.83	164.52
Friday	203.45	222.97	191.46	197.54
Saturday	280.94	296.93	264.27	287.34

(a) Find the total of Mr. Mooney's deposits for each of the four weeks.

(b) Find the total deposited on each day of the week for the four-week period.

5. Mike Crowley works as a cashier in Westendorf's Grocery Store. At the end of one business day, Mr. Westendorf asked Mike to help him prepare the cash receipts for deposit in the bank. Mike was told to count and wrap the coins in rolls as follows: 50 pennies; 40 nickles; 50 dimes; and 40 quarters. When Mike had finished, he found that he had:

7 rolls of pennies, with 12 left over
9 rolls of nickels, with 3 left over
6 rolls of dimes, with 23 left over
4 rolls of quarters, with 17 left over

(a) What was the total value of all coins?

(b) If Mr. Westendorf deposited in the bank only the wrapped coins, what was the amount deposited?

(c) What was the total value of the unwrapped coins?

Enriching Your Business Understanding

1. Some money and banking terms have interesting origins. Using an unabridged dictionary or an encyclopedia, look up the original meaning of the following terms. If possible, explain the relationship between the original meaning and the current meaning of the term:

   (a) cent   (c) capital   (e) money   (g) currency
   (b) bank   (d) dime   (f) dollar   (h) pecuniary

2. At one time almost anyone who wanted to do so could start a bank about as easily as he could set up a grocery store or other type of business. Today the establishment and operation of banks are regulated by the state or federal governments. (a) Give possible reasons for this government regulation. (b) Is this a restriction upon the rights of an individual living in a free country? Explain.

3. All officials who carry major responsibilities in a bank are bonded.

   (a) What does being "bonded" mean?
   (b) In what way is bonding important to the bank? To customers of the bank?
   (c) Can you think of other kinds of businesses in which the bonding of certain kinds of employees is desirable? Explain.

4. Prepare a list of the names and addresses of your local banks. Also, secure the following information about each bank:

   (a) Is it a state bank or a national bank?
   (b) Does it belong to the Federal Reserve System?
   (c) Is it a commercial bank, or has it been organized for a special purpose?
   (d) Does it provide safe-deposit facilities for its customers?

5. Banks hire employees to do different kinds of work. By reading or by talking to parents or others who have information about banks, find out the titles of jobs held by workers in banks and try to get detailed information about one of these jobs. What qualities do you think are especially needed by workers in banks?

6. Be prepared to report to the class about one or more functions of Federal Reserve banks. A high school economics textbook should be a good source of such information.

PART 13

Opening a Checking Account

You have probably read newspaper stories about sizable sums of money being lost, stolen, or destroyed in a fire. Such stories show that whenever money is handled, there is always some risk of loss. You cannot entirely avoid this risk, for you must always use some money. But you can limit the risk by keeping only a small amount of money on hand. As you learned in Part 12, you can deposit money in a savings account and go to the bank to withdraw sums when they are needed. Or you can deposit money in a checking account and then pay most of your bills with checks.

Using a checking account is both safe and convenient. With a checking account, you do not need to keep a lot of money on hand and risk losing it. You can pay your bills by mail and can avoid the trouble of going to each business that sent you a bill to make payment. You can safely send a check through the mail because it can be cashed only by the person or the business to which it is made payable. If it is lost, it may be replaced without cost. Also, after a check is paid by a bank, it is returned to the person who wrote it. The paid check is evidence that payment was actually made.

CHECKING ACCOUNTS ARE SAFE AND CONVENIENT

At one time there was a real risk in depositing money in banks. There was always the chance that banks might fail and that depositors would lose part or all of the money they had on deposit. In 1933, however, the federal government removed this danger by establishing the *Federal Deposit Insurance Corporation (FDIC)*. This is a government corporation, but the money for its operation is provided by banks rather than by the government.

The FDIC guarantees each account in an insured bank up to $20,000. Suppose that a depositor had $22,000 in an insured bank that failed. He would receive only $20,000 from the FDIC. He might or might not receive an additional part of the $2,000 owed him, depending on whether the value of the bank's property was enough to repay him and other depositors. On the other hand, a depositor who had $10,000 in the same bank would receive all of his deposit back from the FDIC.

All banks that are member banks of the Federal Reserve System are required to join the FDIC. State banks that are not members of the Federal Reserve System may become members of the FDIC by meeting certain requirements. Most banks are members of the FDIC. Each insured bank posts signs stating that it is a "Member of the Federal Deposit Insurance Corporation." Depositors can place money in these banks with the assurance that it will be safe, up to the maximum amount of insurance coverage.

DEPOSITORS SIGN SIGNATURE CARDS

A bank will withdraw from a customer's account only the amount of those checks that are signed by him. Therefore, the bank must keep each depositor's signature on record to compare with the signature on the depositor's checks. For this reason, a person opening a checking account is asked to fill out a *signature card*.

A bank account used by two or more persons is called a *joint account*. When such an account is used, each person who is to write checks on the account must sign the signature card. A joint account is often used by a husband and wife. Illustrations 13-1 and 13-2 show the signature cards for an individual account and for a joint account. The signature card for a business would be similar to these, but it would show the name of the business and the signatures of all persons authorized to sign checks for the business.

ACCOUNT NUMBER 63-180-23   Date *Nov. 7, 19—*
(Herein Called The Account)

INDIVIDUAL CHECKING

Mr.
Mrs. *Samuel Alcott*
Miss

THIS ACCOUNT IS SUBJECT TO THE AGREEMENT SET FORTH BELOW

AGREEMENT

The Fifth Third Bank is hereby authorized to recognize the signature executed above for the withdrawal of funds or the transaction of any other business of depositor.

This account shall be subject to such rules and regulations as may be established from time to time by The Fifth Third Bank and to all applicable banking laws, Clearing House regulations, recognized banking practices and customs and such service charges as may be established from time to time by the Bank and shall be further subject to the terms appearing below.

Should this account be closed at any time by the withdrawal of the balance of the account and later reopened, such reopened account shall be subject to all the terms and conditions hereof.

In case of overdraft or overpayment on this account, whether by error, mistake, inadvertence or otherwise, Depositor shall be liable to The Fifth Third Bank for the overdraft or overpayment.

Illus. 13-1. Signature card for an individual account.

JOINT AND SURVIVORSHIP CHECKING
ACCOUNT AGREEMENT

Account Number 590-72003   Date *Dec. 10, 19—*
(herein called The Account)

(1) Signature   Mr.
               Mrs. *Ben T. Shuler*
               Miss

(2) Signature   Mr.
               Mrs. *Linda P. Shuler*
               Mrs.

We, the above signed (herein called Joint Depositors), and The Fifth Third Bank, located in Cincinnati, Ohio (herein called Bank) agree to the following terms.

All amounts now on deposit or hereafter deposited by either or both of the Joint Depositors in The Account and all accumulations thereon shall be owned by the Joint Depositors jointly with the right of survivorship and shall be subject to withdrawal by or on the checks of either or the survivor of the Joint Depositors upon the signature of either of them, in spite of the incapacity of either of them.

Each Joint Depositor appoints the other Joint Depositor as his attorney with power to deposit in The Account moneys of the other and for that purpose to endorse any check, draft, note or other instrument which is payable to the other or both Joint Depositors and with power to make withdrawals from The Account by or on the check of the other, as stated above.

In case of overdraft or overpayment on The Account, whether by error, mistake, inadvertence or otherwise, Joint Depositors shall be jointly and severally liable for repayment to Bank the amount thereof plus interest thereon which Bank may impose at 6% per annum from the time thereof until time of repayment.

The Joint Depositors shall be jointly and severally liable for payment of any service charge which Bank may from time to time impose (without notice), including charges with respect to The Account for failure to maintain a compensating balance, for return or payment of a check postdated or for return or payment of a check drawn against insufficient or uncollected funds. Depositors shall be subject to rules in the Pay-by-Check checkbook, if applicable.

Bank shall be discharged from any liability by payments to or on the check of either or the survivor of the Joint Depositors.

Payments to or on the check of the survivor shall be subject to any applicable estate or inheritance tax law.

Joint Depositors may not modify or terminate this agreement, especially the rights and authority of Bank, except by written notice to Bank, which shall not affect transactions made before receipt of such notice.

If The Account is closed by the withdrawal of the balance and later reopened, such reopened account shall be subject to this agreement.

This agreement shall be subject to the rules and regulations of Bank as may be established from time to time all applicable banking laws, all clearing house regulations, and all recognized banking practices and customs.

Illus. 13-2. Signature card for a joint account.

When a person deposits money in his checking account, he lists the items deposited on a *deposit ticket* or *deposit slip*. The depositor should fill out this form and give it to the bank clerk or teller with the items—coins, paper money, or checks—that are being deposited.

Each deposit ticket should show the depositor's name and account number, the date, the items deposited, and the total amount of the deposit. Some banks print the depositor's name and account number on the deposit tickets furnished him. Other banks provide deposit tickets with blank spaces for this information. On the deposit ticket, the items deposited may be classified under the headings "cash and checks" or under the headings "currency, coins, and checks." Each check is listed separately to assist the bank clerk in verifying the amount.

Illustration 13-3 shows a deposit ticket made out by Ray Armstrong, a depositor in the Citizens National Bank. His deposit consisted of $46.25 in cash and four checks. Each check is identified by the number of the bank on which it was drawn. Sometimes checks are identified by the name of the person from whom the check was received or by the name of the bank on which it was drawn. The depositor should use the method his bank prefers.

The American Bankers Association has a system by which each commercial bank in this country can be identified by a number as well as a name. Study Illustration 13-4. The first part of the number above the line indicates the city or state in which the bank is located. The second part is the number assigned to the individual

DEPOSITS ARE LISTED ON A DEPOSIT TICKET

BANKS ARE KNOWN BY NUMBERS

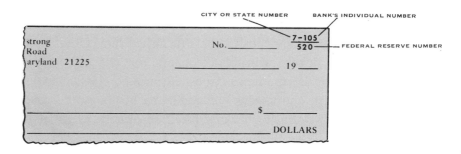

CHECKING ACCOUNT DEPOSIT TICKET		DOLLARS	CENTS
	CURRENCY	45	00
	COIN	1	25
NAME RAY ARMSTRONG	CHECKS 1 74-67	19	85
	2 24-60	140	00
DATE April 10 19--	3 4-57	15	78
	4 1-731	36	61
	TOTAL FROM OTHER SIDE		
This deposit is accepted subject to verification and to the rules and regulations of this Bank.	TOTAL	258	49

IF MORE THAN 4 CHECKS, LIST ON REVERSE SIDE. ENTER TOTAL HERE.

FOR BANK'S USE ONLY

LIST CHECKS SINGLY • ENDORSE EACH ITEM

CITIZENS NATIONAL BANK
Baltimore, Maryland

ACCOUNT NUMBER 326-01622

Illus. 13-3. Note how this deposit ticket is filled out.

bank. The number below the line is a Federal Reserve number that banks use in sorting checks. It is not used in listing checks on a deposit slip.

In the illustration, the numbers 7-105 represent the *ABA number,* the number assigned to the bank by the American Banking Association. The checks listed on the deposit slip in Illustration 13-3 were drawn on banks identified as Nos. 74-67, 24-60, 4-57, and 1-731.

CITY OR STATE NUMBER   BANK'S INDIVIDUAL NUMBER

strong
Road
aryland 21225

No. _____

7-105
520 —— FEDERAL RESERVE NUMBER

19 ____

$ _____

DOLLARS

Illus. 13-4. Each commercial bank in this country can be identified by its ABA number.

BANKS ISSUE RECEIPTS FOR DEPOSITS

When a person makes a deposit in his checking account, the teller gives him a receipt. This receipt may be printed by a machine at the same time that it registers the deposit in the bank's records. Or an acknowledgement of the deposit may be written or stamped on a duplicate copy of the deposit slip. Some banks give each customer a book, known as a *bankbook* or *passbook,* in which the teller enters each deposit. The entries in this book serve as receipts.

When a person cannot conveniently visit his bank to make a deposit, the deposit may be sent through the mail. Such a deposit should not include money, because money might be lost. It should include only checks and similar forms, to be discussed later, that can be replaced if they are lost. If the bank is closed for the day, a deposit may be placed in an envelope and dropped into a depository—built something like a mailbox—found near the entrance of many banks. In either case, the bank acknowledges the deposit by mailing a receipt to the depositor.

Banks supply their depositors with blank checks bound in *checkbooks*. Checkbooks are often supplied to depositors without charge, but banks may make a charge when a depositor's name and address are printed on each of his checks.

DEPOSITORS ARE SUPPLIED WITH CHECKBOOKS

A checkbook contains both blank checks and forms on which a depositor can keep a record of deposits he makes and checks he writes. In some checkbooks, this record is kept on the *stub* for each check. The stub is bound in the checkbook and is separated from the check by a perforated line (see Illustration 13-6). Another type of checkbook provides a register form for recording deposits and checks (see page 168). Some checkbooks also contain deposit tickets.

When checks are printed, the bank number and the account number can be printed in magnetic ink. These magnetic ink numbers enable banks to sort checks quickly with machines that "read" the numbers, thus avoiding much sorting by hand. Note the magnetic ink numbers in the lower left corner of Illustration 13-6.

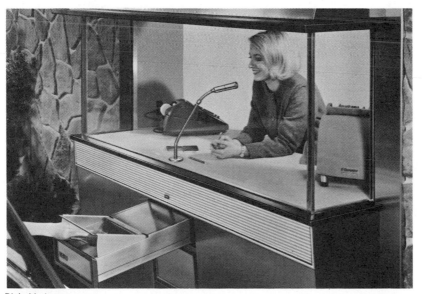

Diebold, Inc.

Illus. 13-5. Many banks offer the convenience of drive-in windows like this one. Customers can make deposits without leaving their cars.

```
No._____ $_____        Ray M. Armstrong                    No._____  7-105
Date_____ 19____        121 Oxford Road                                  520
To_____        Baltimore, Maryland  21225           _____ 19____

For_____
_____          PAY TO THE
                             ORDER OF_____ $_____
         |DOLLARS|CENTS|
Bal. Bro't For'd|    |       _____ DOLLARS
Amt. Deposited  |    |
        TOTAL   |    |        CITIZENS NATIONAL BANK
Amt. this Check |    |           Baltimore, Maryland      _____
Bal. Car'd For'd|    |
                            ⑆0520⑈0105⑆  326⑈0⑆6⑆22⑆
```

Illus. 13-6. A bank check and stub.

DEPOSITS ARE ENTERED ON THE CHECK STUB OR CHECK REGISTER

As soon as a customer makes a deposit in his checking account, he should enter the amount of the deposit on the check register or check stub. Illustration 13-7 shows the deposit information entered on a check stub. On April 10, Ray Armstrong deposited $258.49. (See the deposit ticket on page 160.) This amount is now entered on the line opposite "Amt. Deposited." Since Mr. Armstrong is opening a new account, there is no balance to be entered on the "Bal. Bro't For'd" line. The deposit is the amount against which checks can be written. The amount $258.49 is thus entered on the "Total" line.

```
No._____ $_____
Date_____ 19____
To_____

For_____
_____
                |DOLLARS|CENTS|
Bal. Bro't For'd|       |     |
Amt. Deposited  |  258  |  49 |
        TOTAL   |  258  |  49 |
Amt. this Check |       |     |
Bal. Car'd For'd|       |     |
```

Illus. 13-7. A check stub with a deposit recorded.

Ray Armstrong is now ready to write checks on the account that he has opened with Citizens National Bank. In the next part, you will learn how this is done.

Developing Your Business Vocabulary

The following italicized terms should become part of your business vocabulary. For each numbered statement, find the italicized term that has the same meaning.

ABA number   *deposit ticket* or *deposit slip*
bankbook or *passbook*   *Federal Deposit Insurance Corporation*
checkbook   *joint account*
check stubs   *signature card*

1. An organization that guarantees bank deposits up to $20,000 for each account.
2. A card, kept by a bank, that shows the signatures of persons authorized to draw checks against the account.
3. A bank account that is used by two or more persons.
4. A form that accompanies a deposit and shows the items deposited.
5. The number assigned to a bank by the American Bankers Association.
6. A depositor's book in which a bank enters his deposits.
7. A bound book containing blank checks and check stubs or a check register.
8. Forms in a checkbook on which a depositor keeps a record of his deposits and checks.

Checking Your Understanding

1. Give three reasons for having a checking account in a bank.
2. Why is the Federal Deposit Insurance Corporation important for depositors in commercial banks?
3. Why does a bank require a depositor to sign a signature card?
4. Would you suggest that a depositor sign his name in three or four different ways on the signature card? Why?
5. What is a joint account? Who should sign the signature card for a joint account?
6. Name five different kinds of information that appear on a deposit ticket.
7. Why is each check listed separately on the deposit ticket?
8. Explain the meaning of the following numbers that appear on a bank check: $\frac{71\text{-}227}{712}$. Which of these numbers may be written on the deposit ticket when a check is deposited?

9. What different forms of receipts do banks give to customers when they make deposits?
10. Why do banks supply depositors with checkbooks?
11. Checkbooks are usually divided into two parts. What are the two parts? Why are these two parts necessary?
12. Explain the procedure followed by a depositor in entering his deposit on the check stub.

Applying What You Have Learned

1. Some organizations require that, in addition to the name of the organization, the signatures of two officials appear on the check. Why might more than one signature be required?
2. A depositor signed her name on a signature card in this way: "Katherine M. Stuart." Later she signed a check in this way: "Katie Stuart." Should the bank pay this check? Discuss.
3. Large businesses and other organizations often open checking accounts in several different banks. Can you suggest at least two good reasons for doing this?
4. Why is it desirable to show an account number on a deposit ticket?
5. If there are several banks in your community, will the first number in the numerator of the ABA number be the same for all banks? Will the second number be the same for all banks? Explain.
6. By the end of a school day, the treasurer of the South Page High School had received the following amounts of money: Girls' Athletic Association, $39.40; Library Club, $7.20; Senior Class, $52.65; Business Club, $16.80; and Art Club, $4.35.

   (a) What was the total amount received by the treasurer?
   (b) Is it better to deposit this money in one account in the bank or in five different accounts? Why?
   (c) If the money is put in one account, how can each organization know from time to time how much it has in the bank?
   (d) Is it better for the treasurer to deposit this money in the bank at once, or should he make deposits once a week after a larger amount of money has accumulated? Why?

Solving Business Problems

1. John Mazlon deposited the items listed below and on page 165 in his account, 176-54381, in the Clermont County Bank:

   Cash: $78.23
   Checks:
   Denver State Bank, 23-107, $11.31
   Second National Bank, 56-35, $8.34

Provident Bank and Trust Company, 80-71, $40.94
Public National Bank, 37-54, $2.23
Central Trust Company, 45-23, $17.88

Prepare a deposit ticket for Mr. Mazlon's deposit, using the current date.

2. Marcia Lee deposited the items listed below in her account, 250-136-6, in the Mercantile National Bank:

Cash: $52.38
Checks:
    Mercantile National Bank, 13-94, $10.05
    City Bank of Commerce, 35-71, $16.37
    Citizens State Bank, 79-228, $6.25
    Western Park Bank, 71-225, $14.30
    Union National Bank, 56-61, $81.95

Prepare a deposit ticket for Miss Lee's deposit, using the current date.

3. The treasurer of the Seneca Township High School kept a record of money received from each school organization. At the end of the month, he deducted from each organization's account the total amount of checks written for that organization. His record of receipts and checks written for one month is given below.

(a) Find the total amount available in each account during the month, including the balance on hand on the first of the month.
(b) What was the amount of the balance in each account at the end of the month?
(c) What was the total of the balances at the beginning of the month?
(d) What was the total of the balances of all the accounts at the end of the month?

Record of Receipts and of Checks Written

Date	Explana-tion	Girls' AA	Boys' AA	Senior Class	Junior Class	Soph. Class	Bus. Club	Art Club	Music Club	Dram. Club
Nov. 1	Balance	15.63	215.68	145.25	65.50	23.68	7.32	3.44	17.12	15.75
Nov. 6	Received	90.25	. . . . .	. . . . .	24.18	. . . .	. . . .	2.28	. . . .	. . . .
Nov. 8	Received	. . . .	119.88	5.88	. . . .	. . . .	2.50	. . . .	2.12	1.06
Nov. 12	Received	17.88	. . . . .	. . . . .	2.38	2.68	2.50	.94	3.25	. . . .
Nov. 15	Received	. . . .	108.31	37.00	. . . .	. . . .	1.88	. . . .	. . . .	. . . .
Nov. 20	Received	40.81	91.75	. . . . .	31.48	20.38	.68	. . . .	. . . .	3.45
Nov. 26	Received	. . . .	. . . . .	11.80	. . . .	. . . .	. . . .	9.90	12.90	. . . .
Nov. 29	Received	5.15	65.90	. . . . .	. . . .	2.85	2.50	. . . .	. . . .	53.95
Nov. 30	Checks Written	54.20	197.45	54.45	22.28	15.60	5.47	2.40	3.44	71.18

Enriching Your Business Understanding

1. In the earlier days of this country, it was not uncommon for depositors to make a "run on the bank." (a) Explain what is meant by a "run on the bank." (b) Why is a "run on the bank" not likely to happen today?

2. Your class in school, your school clubs, your athletic teams, and other groups from time to time receive funds that are deposited in the bank. For one such group, prepare a report explaining who makes the bank deposits, when the money is deposited, how checks are signed, and the reasons for the method or methods used in signing checks.

3. Obtain a deposit ticket from a bank. (a) Fill it out for a deposit of $76.25 in cash; and two checks, one on the Merchants National Bank, Seattle, 19-108, for $13.50, and one on the People's National Bank, Trenton, 55-76, for $31.89. (b) On the back of the deposit ticket, write a brief report telling whether the bank prefers checks to be identified by the names of banks, by cities, or by ABA numbers.

4. The denominator of an ABA number is a Federal Reserve number used by banks in sorting checks. Read about check routing symbols in a textbook on money and banking or consult a banker to find the meaning of each digit in the denominator. Then prepare a report explaining the exact meaning of each digit in the denominator of the ABA number on: (a) the check in Illustration 13-6 and (b) a check of one of your local banks.

PART 14
Making Payments By Personal Check

In Part 13 you learned how Ray Armstrong opened a checking account with the Citizens National Bank of Baltimore, Maryland. He received a checkbook from the bank and entered the amount of his deposit, $258.49, on the first check stub. Now Mr. Armstrong is ready to write checks.

The check stub should always be filled out before the check is written. Otherwise, the writer of the check may forget to fill out the stub and later on may not remember the amount of the check or to whom it was written. In that case, he may not know the amount against which he may write other checks.

Study Illustration 14-1. This shows that Mr. Armstrong has written a check for $15.95 payable to Grammer's Shoe Store. The left portion of the illustration shows the stub properly filled out for this first check. Note carefully the information recorded on the upper and the lower parts of the stub. The balance at the bottom of the stub is carried forward to the stub of the next check. This amount is entered on that stub opposite the heading "Bal. Bro't For'd." It is shown properly entered on the stub for Check No. 2 in Illustration 14-3.

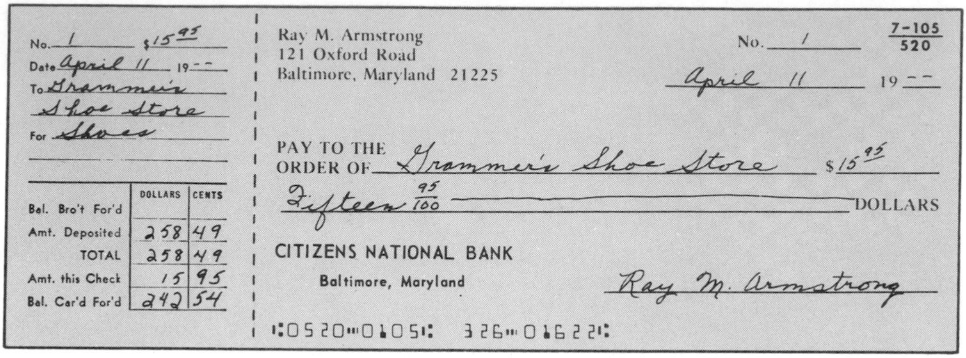

No. 1 $15.95
Date April 11 19--
To Grammer's Shoe Store
For Shoes

	DOLLARS	CENTS
Bal. Bro't For'd		
Amt. Deposited	258	49
TOTAL	258	49
Amt. this Check	15	95
Bal. Car'd For'd	242	54

Ray M. Armstrong
121 Oxford Road
Baltimore, Maryland 21225

No. 1 7-105/520

April 11 19--

PAY TO THE ORDER OF Grammer's Shoe Store $15.95

Fifteen 95/100 DOLLARS

CITIZENS NATIONAL BANK
Baltimore, Maryland

Ray M. Armstrong

⑆0520⑈0105⑆ 326⑈01622⑆

Illus. 14-1. A properly filled out check and check stub.

As you learned in Part 13, a *check register* may be used instead of check stubs. Illustration 14-2 shows a check register as it would appear if Ray Armstrong had used it instead of a check stub. Note that the information recorded is much the same, but the arrangement is different.

CHECK NO.	DATE 19--	CHECK ISSUED TO	AMOUNT OF CHECK		✓	DATE OF DEP.	AMOUNT OF DEPOSIT		BALANCE	
						4/10	258	49	258	49
1	4/11	Grammer's Shoe Store	15	95					242	54
2	4/13	Cash	40	00					202	54
						4/16	20	50	223	04
3	4/22	Griffin Co.		88					222	16

Illus. 14-2. A check register may be provided in a checkbook instead of check stubs.

HOW TO WRITE A CHECK

Since a check is an order directing a bank to pay out money, the check must be filled out completely and accurately. A check must contain: (1) the check number, (2) the date, (3) the name of the payee, (4) the amount, and (5) the depositor's signature.

(1) Checks and check stubs are numbered consecutively. These numbers help a depositor compare with his check stub records those checks that have been paid and returned. Numbers

are usually printed on all checks. If they are not printed, they should be written in by the depositor.

(2) The date is entered in the proper space on the check just as it was entered on the stub.

(3) The person or business to whose order payment is to be made is the *payee*. In Illustration 14-1, the payee is Grammer's Shoe Store. This name is written on the line following "Pay to the order of." A check may also be made payable to "Cash" or to "Bearer." Anyone can cash a check made out in this manner. If such a check is lost, it can be cashed by whoever finds it. For this reason, a check should not be made payable to "Cash" or "Bearer" unless it is to be cashed right after it is written.

(4) The amount of a check is written twice. It is first written in figures after the printed dollar sign following the payee's name. The amount should be written close to the dollar sign so that a dishonest person cannot *raise the check* by inserting another figure between the amount and the dollar sign. Cents figures are usually written somewhat smaller so that the amount in dollars and the amount in cents can easily be distinguished. The cents figures should be written close to the dollar figures so that no additional numbers can be inserted.

The amount is then written a second time on the line below the payee's name. The amount in dollars is written in words; the amount in cents is written as a fraction of a dollar, or as so many

Illus. 14-3. A check made payable to "Cash." Note how the stub is filled out when a balance is brought forward and no additional deposit is recorded.

hundredths of a dollar. The writing should begin at the far left end of the line so that the amount cannot be changed by adding a word at the beginning of the line. A line should be drawn from the fraction to the printed word "Dollars" to fill all unused space.

If the amount written in figures does not agree with the amount written in words, the bank may pay the amount written in words. But if there is a serious difference between the two amounts, the bank may call the customer and ask for his instructions concerning payment.

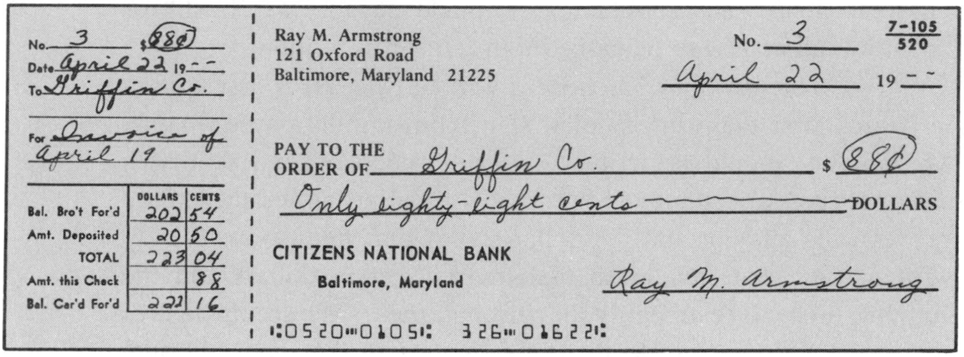

No. 3 $ 88¢
Date April 22 19--
To Griffin Co.
For Invoice of April 19

	DOLLARS	CENTS
Bal. Bro't For'd	202	54
Amt. Deposited	20	50
TOTAL	223	04
Amt. this Check		88
Bal. Car'd For'd	222	16

Ray M. Armstrong
121 Oxford Road
Baltimore, Maryland 21225

No. 3 — 7-105/520

April 22 19--

PAY TO THE ORDER OF Griffin Co. $ 88¢

Only eighty-eight cents DOLLARS

CITIZENS NATIONAL BANK
Baltimore, Maryland

Ray M. Armstrong

⑆0520⑈0105⑆ 326⑈01622⑆

Illus. 14-4. A check is seldom written for an amount less than one dollar. But if such a check is written, this form should be used.

(5) The person who signs a check is called the *drawer.* In the checks you have just studied, Ray Armstrong is the drawer. A drawer should sign his checks with the same signature that he wrote on his signature card. A married woman should use her given name in signing checks. For example, she should sign as Jean S. Harmon, not as Mrs. William Harmon.

On checks issued by a business or other organization, the firm's name may appear as either a printed or a handwritten signature followed by the word "By." The person who signs the check writes his name after the word "By." This indicates that the check should be charged to the firm and not to the person who signs his name. Examples of such signatures are given in Illustrations 14-5 and 14-6.

Illus. 14-5. Signature for a business.

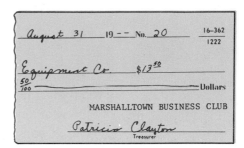

Illus. 14-6. Signature for a school organization.

The bank may subtract from the depositor's balance only the amounts of checks that the depositor has actually signed. If it cashes a check signed by someone who had no right to use the depositor's signature, the bank may be held responsible. A check on which the depositor's signature was written by someone without the depositor's authority is known as a *forged check*. The writing of such a check is a crime called forgery.

Anyone who writes checks has a great deal of responsibility. But if you observe the following eight precautions, there is little likelihood of your losing money because of poorly written checks.

(1) Write checks only on forms supplied to you by your bank. Theoretically, you could write a check on just about anything—even a shingle. But millions of checks are written every day. Sorting these checks and exchanging them among banks is a tremendous task. This task can be completed at a reasonable cost only by the use of machines that sort the checks according to the numbers printed in magnetic ink in the lower left corner. If a check does not have these numbers, the sorting will be interrupted, the check may be delayed, and a charge for handling the check may be made.

(2) Destroy all checks on which you make errors. Do not erase or try to retrace your writing as you fill out checks. No one who handles the check after it leaves your hands can be sure whether the changes were made by you or by someone who had no right to make them.

(3) Always sign checks with the same signature which is recorded on your signature card. Otherwise, the bank may refuse to honor your checks.

BE CAREFUL WHEN YOU WRITE CHECKS

(4) Don't sign checks with the amount left blank. You may be held responsible for amounts filled in by others.

(5) Don't overdraw your checking account balance. A bank is not expected to cash checks for more than the amount you have in your account. Writing checks for more money than you have in your account is against the law except under certain credit-check plans. When two persons are using the same account, each must know the amount against which he can write checks. Otherwise, the account might be overdrawn. To avoid overdrawing the account, the two persons may use the same checkbook. If each prefers to use a separate checkbook, the beginning balance and the amount of each deposit may be divided between the checkbooks.

(6) Record every check. Some people carry blank checks in their wallets so that they can use them when they do not have their checkbooks with them. When such a check is used, the drawer should make a note of it and as soon as possible record it on a check stub or check register. Otherwise, he may completely forget about the check and write other checks for more than he has on deposit.

(7) Don't post-date checks. A *post-dated check* is, for example, one written on October 1 but dated October 15. A person might post-date a check because he did not have enough money on deposit on October 1 to cover the check but planned to deposit money by October 15. This is not a desirable business practice because a person who post-dates a check with the intention of making a deposit later may not be able to make it. As a result, his account may be overdrawn.

(8) Write all checks in ink. A bank is supposed to charge a depositor's account only for the amounts he has written on his checks. But a depositor who writes a check in pencil may still incur a loss. Someone may be able to raise the check without making a detectable erasure. In that case, the drawer may be charged for the larger amount because he cannot prove that the check was not written for this amount. Businesses often use *check protectors* to guard against possible changes in the amount of a check. Such a machine stamps the amount on the proper line of the check so that the amount cannot be changed.

Todd Company Division,
Burroughs Corporation

Illus. 14-7. This check-writer prints the amount of the check, the date, and the signature. It guards against possible changes in the amount of a check by dishonest persons.

STOPPING
PAYMENT
ON A CHECK

The checks that a depositor writes are not charged against his account until they have been returned to his bank and paid. If, before a check is paid, he directs the bank not to pay it, the bank will refuse to honor it when it is presented for payment. This is called stopping payment on a check. Suppose that a person loses a check that you have given him. He probably will ask you for another check. But before you give him a new check, you should stop payment on the first one. Most banks make a charge for this service.

When a bank is asked to stop payment on a check, it should be given complete information about the check. In an emergency, a bank will temporarily stop payment on a check in answer to a telephone call. It requires, however, that a written notice to stop payment be given as soon as possible. This written notice includes the date, the number, and the amount of the check, as well as the name of the payee. This written notice is called a *stop-payment order*.

CITIZENS NATIONAL BANK

June 5, ____ 19 --

Received: Office_____ Date_____ 19____ Time_____

☒ Please STOP PAYMENT on the following described check, issued by the undersigned

Amt. $45.67	Date 6/1/--	Ck. No. 30	Payee Joseph Fields

It is understood that you agree to indemnify us for said amount and losses, expenses and costs incurred by us arising from our compliance with the above order.

☐ Please cancel the above stop payment.

Date_____ 19____

Signature_____

Account Name and Address

Account Number____326-01622____

Ray M. Armstrong
121 Oxford Road
Baltimore, Maryland   21225

Signature _Ray M. Armstrong_

AUTHORIZATION

Illus. 14-8. A form for stopping payment on a check.

Stopping payment on a check is a privilege that should be used only for good and legal reasons. Once you have issued a check, it may be passed from one person to another. You can be held responsible for damages that your stopping payment on a check may cause to rightful holders of the check.

Developing Your Business Vocabulary

The following italicized terms should become part of your business vocabulary. For each numbered statement, find the italicized term that has the same meaning.

check protector	*payee*
check register	*post-dated check*
drawer	*raised check*
forged check	*stop-payment order*

1. A form used instead of check stubs for a record of checks written.
2. The person to whom a check is made payable.
3. A check whose amount was increased by a dishonest person.
4. The person who signs a check.
5. A check signed by someone without the authority to do so.
6. A check dated later than the date of issue.
7. A machine that imprints the amount of the check on the check form.
8. A written order instructing a bank not to make payment on a certain check.

Checking Your Understanding

1. Why should the check stub always be filled out before a check is written?
2. What is the difference between check stubs and a check register? Which do you consider preferable? Why?
3. What five important items should the drawer write on a check?
4. Explain why checks and check stubs are numbered.
5. When is it proper to make a check payable to "Cash" or to "Bearer"? Why?
6. Why is the amount of a check usually written twice, once in figures and once in words?
7. Why should the amount in figures be written close to the dollar sign on a check? Illustrate with an example.
8. Suppose that the amount is written on a check in figures as $98.00 and in words as ninety-four dollars. Which amount will the bank pay?
9. The word "By" sometimes precedes a part of the signature on a check. Explain when the word "By" is used.
10. Why should checks be written only on forms supplied to the drawer by the bank?
11. If you make an error in writing the amount of a check, should you correct it? Why?
12. Describe a situation in which you might stop payment on a check. How would this be done?

Applying What You Have Learned

1. Mrs. Holly does not record any information on her check stubs. She says that she does not wish to be bothered with keeping unnecessary records. What reasons could you give Mrs. Holly to show her that it is poor practice to write checks without filling out the corresponding check stubs?
2. Compare the information written on a check with the information written on a check stub. What items of information are included: (a) on both? (b) only on the check? (c) only on the check stub?
3. Larry Walters fills out a check stub before he writes the corresponding check. Grant Michaels writes a check and then fills out the stub. Which practice do you think is the better one? Why?
4. Dick Parker never carries his checkbook with him but always keeps a few blank checks in his wallet to use in case he runs short of cash. (a) How may this practice cause him trouble in keeping an accurate record of the checks he has written? (b) Can you suggest a plan whereby he might follow this practice but still be reasonably sure of having an accurate record?

5. Ellen Browning placed an order with a mail-order firm. Since she did not know what the total amount of the purchase would be, she filled out a check with the amount left blank. She asked the mail-order firm to complete the check for her. Was this procedure desirable? Explain.

6. At a time when Ken Grigsby's bank balance was $225, he wrote a check for $320. Later he was notified by the payee of the check that the bank had refused to pay the check. Mr. Grigsby then complained to the bank that he had not been treated fairly. He had kept a checking account with the bank for several years and felt that the bank should know that he paid his debts. He thought that the bank should have paid the check and allowed him to make up the difference later. Do you agree?

7. Can you think of any circumstances under which post-dating a check might be desirable? Is such a situation likely to occur often?

8. Mr. and Mrs. Hoffman decide that it would be more convenient for them to have a joint checking account. They open such an account in their bank with a deposit of $300. At the end of three weeks, Mr. Hoffman is notified that the account is overdrawn. He finds that he has written checks totaling $150 and that Mrs. Hoffman has written checks totaling $200. How can similar trouble be prevented in the future?

9. Mrs. Haymes gave a check for $10.60 to a person who claimed to be a door-to-door kitchenware salesman. Mrs. Haymes was in a hurry and wrote the check with a pencil. When the check was returned by the bank, she found that the amount had been changed to $110.60. Is there anything Mrs. Haymes could do to recover the loss?

Solving Business Problems

1. Assume that you are treasurer of the Westchester High School Student Council. Fill out check stubs and write checks for the following transactions of the Student Council. If forms are not available, rule forms similar to that shown in Illustration 14-1 on page 168. The beginning balance is $167.43. Use the current date. Number the stubs and checks beginning with 28.

   (a) Pay $4.25 to the Ohio Book Store for the book *Parliamentary Procedure*.
   (b) Pay 98 cents to Sandy Geiger for a record book.
   (c) Pay $12.50 to Latimer's Sporting Goods for a basketball trophy.
   (d) Pay $11.92 to Don Schloemer for his traveling expenses to the state convention of Student Councils.

2. On September 1, Jim Lansbury had a balance of $478.25 in his checking account. During the month he wrote the checks and made the deposits listed below. Record the beginning balance, the checks, and the deposits in a check register similar to the one in Illustration 14-2 on page 168.

Sept.

3	Check #133 to Danville Public Utilities	$ 8.95
4	Check #134 to Moyer Realty Company	89.00
6	Deposit	175.24
9	Check #135 to J. F. Brunsman, M.D.	18.90
13	Check #136 to Vonderbrink's Clothing Store	64.22
16	Check #137 to Boman Brothers Hardware	42.20
18	Deposit	95.25
20	Check #138 to Bushelman Fuel Company	42.60
24	Check #139 to Vogel's Supermarket	23.94
28	Check #140 to United Appeal	35.00
30	Check #141 to Klein's Drugs	13.11

3. Assume that you are treasurer of the Dramatics Club of your school. Fill out the stubs and write the checks for the following transactions. The beginning balance is $132.56. Use the current date. Number the stubs and checks beginning with 26.

(a) Pay $18.75 to Cherokee Costume Shop for rental of costumes.
(b) Pay $9.25 to Fischer-Hardy Company for a gift for the sponsor of the Dramatics Club.
(c) Pay $17.50 to the Bayside Printing Company for the printing of playbills.
(d) Pay $2.65 to the Columbia Stationery Store for a new book for recording minutes.

Enriching Your Business Understanding

1. Listed below and on page 178 are errors that were made in filling out checks. Explain which errors would probably not affect the validity of the checks and which would probably void the checks.

(a) The check number was omitted.
(b) The check stub was not filled out.
(c) The drawer forgot to sign the check.
(d) The check was dated January 3, 1981 instead of January 3, 1971.
(e) The drawer forgot to fill in the name of the payee.
(f) The payee's name was misspelled.
(g) The amount of the check was $54.50. It should have been $45.50.

(h) The drawer omitted the amount of the check since he did not have the information, and in a letter instructed the payee to fill in the correct amount.

2. Harvey Graham owed Leonard Saunders a debt of $58. He wrote a check to Mr. Saunders and mailed it to him. Later Mr. Graham decided that he did not want to pay the debt at once. He therefore asked the bank to stop payment on the check. Do you think it was advisable for Mr. Graham to make this request?

3. A check is a "negotiable instrument." Refer to a business law textbook and look up the meaning of the word "negotiable." In terms of what you read, explain why a check is negotiable.

4. Refer to a business law textbook and answer the following questions:

   (a) Must checks be written only on forms provided by a bank?
   (b) What makes a check a valid instrument?
   (c) Could you write a valid check on a piece of your notebook paper?

5. Obtain a blank check form printed on a special kind of paper to make changes difficult. Then perform the following activities:

   (a) Write a few figures on the check with ink and then erase them.
   (b) If a liquid ink eradicator is available, use it and observe what effect it has on the paper.
   (c) Prepare a report showing that the use of this special paper provides protection for the drawer of the check and for the bank.

PART 15
Using a Checking Account

A bank provides many checking account services for each depositor. It records his deposits; it supplies him with a checkbook; it cashes his checks; it keeps a record of his account; and it sends him a copy of this record at regular intervals. A bank also keeps enough cash on hand so that it will always be able to pay for the checks drawn by the depositor. These services are performed by a number of employees using expensive equipment. Maintaining a depositor's account, therefore, is a costly process for the bank.

If a depositor keeps a large balance in his account, the bank can lend part of the money to someone else. The bank can thus earn enough interest to handle the checking account without any direct charge to the depositor. But if the account balance is not large, the bank makes a charge for checking account services.

The charge that a bank makes for checking account services is known as a *service charge*. A service charge may be made up of: (1) a fixed monthly charge for maintaining the account, called a *maintenance charge*, and (2) a charge for each check written and often for each check deposited. The service charge may also include the bank's charge for stopping payment on a check. The amount of this charge is often $1.

SERVICE CHARGES ON REGULAR ACCOUNTS

Some banks make no service charge for regular checking accounts as long as the account balance does not fall below a certain amount during a month. This minimum balance is not the same in all banks. In some, it may be $500 or more; in others, it may be as little as $100. Often banks figure the charges for services rendered and then, to offset part or all of these charges, give credit based on the average balance of the account. This credit may be called *service credit*.

Suppose that the Wilcox State Bank computes service charges on regular checking accounts as follows: monthly maintenance charge, $1.00; amount charged for each check written, 8 cents; amount charged for each check deposited, 6 cents. A credit of 15 cents is given for each $100 in the average balance for the month. This credit, given for even $100's only, is applied to the total charge for the month.

Now suppose that a depositor in the Wilcox State Bank writes 20 checks, deposits 2 checks, and has an average bank balance of $450. His service charge is found in this way:

Maintenance charge	$1.00
20 checks written at 8 cents each	1.60
2 checks deposited at 6 cents each	.12
Total charges	$2.72
$450 average balance at 15 cents each even $100 ..	.60
Net service charge	$2.12

Different banks have different rates and different methods of charging for checking account services. A depositor may obtain a rate schedule from his own bank.

SERVICE CHARGES ON SPECIAL ACCOUNTS

Some depositors write only a few checks each month and maintain only small bank balances. For such depositors, banks commonly offer special checking accounts. These accounts may be given distinctive names, such as Pay-by-Check Account, Handi-Check Account, Thrift-Check Account, or Tenplan Checking Account.

Not all banks make the same charge for special checking accounts, but here is a typical example. Suppose that the Wilcox State Bank makes a monthly charge of 75 cents for maintaining a special checking account and charges 10 cents for each check written. No charge is made for receiving deposits. If a depositor writes 10 checks a month, his total service charge for the month is:

Maintenance charge . . . . $ .75
10 checks at 10 cents each 1.00
Total service charge $1.75

Some banks have no maintenance charge for a special checking account, but they are likely to make a larger charge for each check written. For example, one bank that has no maintenance charge for a special checking account charges 15 cents for each check written.

BANKS ISSUE STATEMENTS TO DEPOSITORS

At regular intervals, usually monthly, a bank gives each depositor a statement of his account known as a *bank statement*. Statements for special accounts are sometimes issued at three-month intervals. The bank statement a depositor receives shows:

1. The balance at the beginning of the month.
2. The deposits made during the month.
3. The checks paid by the bank during the month.
4. The service charge or other charges for the month, if there were any.
5. The balance at the end of the month.

Study Illustration 15-1 to see how bank statements may be prepared.

With the bank statement, the bank gives the depositor the checks that it has paid for him. It also gives him a form showing the service charge for the period. Before the bank returns the depositor's checks, it cancels each check, usually with a machine that punches holes in or stamps the check. The paid checks are called *canceled checks*.

RECONCILING THE BANK BALANCE

As you have learned, the depositor's record of his checking account is kept on check stubs or a check register form. His bank statement gives him a copy of the bank's record of his account. A mistake may have been made in either record, so he should compare the two. But even if no error has been made, the balance on the check stubs and the balance on the bank statement are usually different. Bringing the two balances into agreement is

CITIZENS NATIONAL BANK

Baltimore, Maryland

ACCOUNT NUMBER

326-01622

Ray M. Armstrong
121 Oxford Road
Baltimore, Maryland 21225

CHECKS	CHECKS	DEPOSITS	NO. OF CHECKS	DATE	BALANCE
				April 10	258.49
40.00	15.95		2	April 14	202.54
		20.50		April 16	223.04
.88			1	April 23	222.16
		160.00		April 23	382.16
16.30	6.22		2	April 24	359.64
25.78	18.95		3	April 26	249.58
65.33					
33.46	24.33		4	April 27	173.14
5.80	12.85				
		160.00		April 29	333.14
4.25			1	April 30	328.89
1.25SC				April 30	327.64

CC—Certified Check   EC—Error Corrected   OD—Overdrawn
CM—Credit Memo   LS—List of Checks   RT—Returned Item
DM—Debit Memo   NC—Check Not Counted SC—Service Charge

Illus. 15-1. A bank statement.

known as reconciling the bank balance. The statement showing how the two balances were brought into agreement is known as the *bank reconciliation.*

There are several reasons why the balances shown by the check stubs and the bank statement may differ:

(1) Some of the checks that were written and subtracted from the balance on the check stubs may not have been presented to the bank for payment before the bank statement was made. These checks have, therefore, not been deducted from the bank statement balance. Such checks are known as *outstanding checks.*

(2) A service charge may be shown on the bank statement but may not have been recorded on the check stubs.

(3) A deposit may have been mailed to the bank but may not have been received and recorded when the bank statement was made.

Let us see how a bank reconciliation is made. On May 4, Ray Armstrong received the bank statement shown in Illustration 15-1. He found that his bank statement showed a balance of $327.64 and that his check-stub balance on April 30 was $280.39. He then sorted, according to their numbers, all the canceled checks that were returned with his statement. He found that checks Nos. 8, 10, and 11 were outstanding. Next he made a bank reconciliation by which he proved his checkbook balance.

In the bank reconciliation, shown in Illustration 15-2, Mr. Armstrong proved the accuracy of the bank statement and his record (1) by subtracting the total of the outstanding checks from the bank statement balance and (2) by subtracting the service charge from his checkbook balance. In some cases, other additions or subtractions might have to be made in the reconciliation. For example, a charge made for stopping payment on a check should be subtracted from the checkbook balance. Also, a deposit made so late in the month that it did not appear on the bank statement should be added to the balance on the bank statement. If two checkbooks are being used by persons having a joint account, the bank statement should be reconciled with the total of the two checkbooks.

```
                          BANK RECONCILIATION

Bank balance, April 30 . . . . . $327.64   Checkbook balance, April 30,
                                              before subtracting the
                                              service charge . . . . . . . $280.39
Less checks outstanding:

   #8 . . . . . . . . . . $10.00
   #10. . . . . . . . . .  21.00
   #11. . . . . . . . . .  17.50

Total checks outstanding . . . .  48.50   Less service charge. . . . . . .    1.25

Available bank funds . . . . . . $279.14   Correct checkbook balance. . . . $279.14
```

Illus. 15-2. Study this bank reconciliation carefully.

Suppose that the available funds as shown by the bank statement and the corrected checkbook balance are not the same. Either the depositor or the bank has made a mistake. In this case, the depositor should compare his canceled checks with those listed on the bank statement and with those recorded on his check stubs.

He should then carefully go over the calculations on his check stubs. If he does not find an error, he should take the matter up with the bank.

After the bank statement has been reconciled, any errors that have been made on the check stubs should be corrected. The service charge should then be subtracted from the balance on the check stub so that the stub will show the correct balance before the depositor writes more checks.

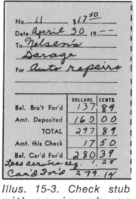

Illus. 15-3. Check stub with service charge deducted.

The bank reconciliation should be filed so that it will be on hand when the next bank statement is received. When the next reconciliation is to be made, the depositor will need the record of the checks that were outstanding at the beginning of the preceding month so that he can determine quickly whether those checks have been returned.

CANCELED CHECKS SHOULD BE SAVED   A depositor should keep his canceled checks as evidence that payments have been made. The canceled check, not the check stub, is valuable as evidence. The check stub is the depositor's own record of the check, but it does not prove that the payee actually received the check. The canceled check, on the other hand, is evidence that the payee received payment. This is true because the payee must sign his name on the back of a check before he cashes it. Such a signature is called an endorsement.

When you pay by check, you have evidence as to whom you paid, how much you paid, and when you paid. Your check stub should also show why payment was made.

In an average day, some 50 million checks are written by individuals and businesses in this country. If someone stacked together the checks written in a single year, they would cover a whole football field to the depth of 15 to 20 feet. Handling this vast number of checks has been estimated to cost between $3 billion and $4 billion a year. As the volume of checks increases, the cost of handling them also increases. Banks are spending large sums of money to develop time-saving and labor-saving methods of handling checks. They hope to improve their service to customers and yet reduce the number of checks required.

It is fairly easy to eliminate the need for checks when a depositor is making regular payments to his own bank. For example, assume that a depositor borrows $2,000 from his bank to pay for a car and agrees to repay the debt in monthly payments of $75. Each month he may write a check for $75 payable to his bank. Or he may authorize the bank to make a monthly charge of $75 to his account. If the latter plan is followed, the loan may be completely paid without the borrower's having written a single check.

In a similar way, a depositor may authorize his bank to pay some of his regular bills for him. For example, the bank may pay his monthly insurance premiums or his bills at various retail stores. It can do this by charging the depositor's account and crediting the account of the insurance company or the store. A business may likewise eliminate the need for payroll checks. It may authorize a bank to charge its account for the total amount of each payroll and to credit each employee for the amount that he has earned.

Transactions such as these are handled most easily when the person making payment and the person being paid have accounts in the same bank. In that case, the bank need only transfer an amount from one account to another in its own books. But the transactions can also be handled when the two persons have accounts in different banks. By using modern electronic equipment, banks are able to transfer among themselves charges and credits to customers' accounts. These transfers can be made quickly and at a reasonable cost.

Banks are having some success in reducing the number of checks needed. Their possible continued success has caused some people to refer to the future as a "checkless society" when checks would not be used. It is probable, however, that great numbers of checks will continue to be used. The new methods of handling checks will accomplish much if they slow down or stop the increase in the number of checks used, although this number will continue to be very large.

Developing Your Business Vocabulary

The following italicized terms should become part of your business vocabulary. For each numbered statement, find the italicized term that has the same meaning.

bank reconciliation   *outstanding check*
bank statement   *service charge*
canceled check   *service credit*
maintenance charge

1. A charge made by a bank for checking account services.
2. A fixed monthly charge made by a bank for maintaining an account.
3. A decrease in the service charge, allowed for a bank account with a large balance.
4. A report given by a bank to a depositor showing the condition of his account.
5. A check that has been paid by a bank.
6. A statement showing how the checkbook balance and the bank statement balance were brought into agreement.
7. A check given to the payee but not yet returned to the bank for payment.

Checking Your Understanding

1. Why does a bank make a service charge for some checking accounts but not for others?
2. What two separate charges may make up a service charge?
3. What are the principal differences between a regular checking account and a special checking account?
4. How frequently are bank statements prepared?
5. What are five important items of information that appear on a bank statement?
6. Why do banks cancel checks returned to them for payment?

7. Ordinarily the balance shown on a depositor's bank statement and the balance on his check stubs are not the same. Explain why this is true.
8. If, after making a bank reconciliation, the available bank funds and the corrected checkbook balance are not the same, what should the depositor do?
9. When should service charges be entered on the check stub?
10. What should be done with canceled checks that are returned to depositors?
11. How may the need for checks be eliminated when a depositor is making regular payments to his own bank?
12. How may the need for checks be eliminated when a depositor authorizes a bank to pay some of his regular bills for him?

Applying What You Have Learned

1. Sheila Vilas usually writes about 6 checks a month and deposits 2 checks a month. Her average bank balance is about $150. (a) Which would be the less expensive plan for Miss Vilas: to have a regular checking account and pay the charges given on page 180, or to have a special checking account with no service charge but pay $2 for a book of 20 checks? (b) How much cheaper is the better plan?
2. The bank at which Norman Morrow maintains his account makes no service charge on a checking account that always has a balance of $300 or more. If the balance falls below $300 at any time during a month, a charge of 10 cents a check is made for each check written in that month. Mr. Morrow's checking account balance often falls below $300. He has a savings account that pays interest at the rate of 4%. Will it be advisable for Mr. Morrow to withdraw money from his savings account to maintain a $300 checking account balance if: (a) He writes an average of 30 checks a month? (b) He writes an average of only 5 checks a month?
3. Edward Graves has received his bank statement for the month of May. The bank statement shows a balance of $401.19, but his checkbook shows a balance of only $364.52.

    (a) Give three possible reasons why these two figures do not agree.
    (b) What are two calculations that Mr. Graves must make to prove the accuracy of these figures?
    (c) If these two figures still do not agree, what additional steps are necessary?

4. Mrs. Devaney says that she saves all of her canceled checks. Mrs. Lambert says that she destroys her canceled checks after she

reconciles her bank balance since they are of no further use to her. Which is the better plan? Why?

5. Listed below are a number of errors made by Andrew Paine in using his checkbook. For each item, tell if the error will increase or decrease the true amount to be carried forward on the stub or if the error will have no effect on the true amount to be carried forward. Explain your answers.

(a) Forgot to write down the number of the check.
(b) Forgot to enter a deposit on the stub.
(c) Wrote a check for $45.50, but entered $54.50 on the stub.
(d) Forgot to write the date of the check on the check stub.
(e) Deposited $167.80, but wrote $176.80 on the stub.
(f) Wrote a check for $35 on a check that he carried in his wallet and forgot to enter the amount on a stub.
(g) Subtracted a check for $19.85 from a total of $271.58 and got $262.73.
(h) Received a notice of a service charge made by his bank, but did not enter the amount of the charge on a check stub.

Solving Business Problems

1. The Northeast State Bank uses the following plan to calculate service charges on checking accounts: monthly maintenance charge, 75 cents; amount charged for each check written, 7 cents; amount charged for each check deposited, 7 cents. A service credit is given at the rate of 14 cents for each $100 of average balance, with no allowance for a fraction of $100.

During the month of July, Ben Marshall completed the following transactions:

July	1	Deposited 3 checks
	5	Wrote 2 checks
	8	Deposited 2 checks
	11	Wrote 4 checks
	14	Deposited 1 check
	18	Wrote 3 checks
	24	Wrote 2 checks
	29	Deposited 2 checks
	30	Wrote 1 check

All checks written by Mr. Marshall were paid by the bank, with the exception of the check written on July 30. Assume that Mr. Marshall's average balance during the month was $350. Calculate the service charge for the month.

2. During the months of March, April, and May, Charles Adamson completed the following transactions with his bank:

March: He wrote 6 checks, deposited 2 checks, and had an average balance of $150.

April: He wrote 7 checks, deposited 2 checks, and had an average balance of $200.

May: He wrote 15 checks, deposited 4 checks, and had an average balance of $600.

All the checks were paid by the bank in the month in which they were written.

(a) Using the rates given in Problem 1, what was the service charge for each month and the total for the three months?

(b) How much cheaper or more expensive would it have been for Mr. Adamson to have used during these three months a special checking account in which he paid $1.50 for a book of 10 blank checks and paid no other service charges?

3. Bruce Tucker is planning to open a checking account in the Wilcox State Bank. The service charges for a regular checking account and a special checking account in this bank are given on pages 180 and 181. Which type of checking account will be more economical for him if he expects to:

(a) Have an average balance of $50, deposit 2 checks, and write 5 checks?

(b) Have an average balance of $100, deposit 1 check, and write 11 checks?

(c) Have an average balance of $600, deposit 4 checks, and write 20 checks?

4. In October Leo Kishman received a bank statement that showed a balance of $378.65. The service charge amounted to 85 cents. Mr. Kishman found that the following checks were outstanding: No. 31, $7.16; No. 34, $15.10; and No. 35, $9.95. His checkbook balance at the end of October was $347.29. Reconcile the bank balance.

Enriching Your Business Understanding

1. Below and on page 190 are a number of arguments for not having a checking account that people have used on occasion. For each argument given, present at least one good reason in favor of having a checking account.

(a) "It's too much bother."

(b) "The amount of money we are able to deposit is too small."

(c) "Checking accounts are expensive."

(d) "I can never keep an accurate record—my checkbook balances never agree with the bank statement balances."

(e) "Someone may forge my signature; then I'll have nothing."

2. Give reasons for your answers to the following questions:

(a) Do checks ever circulate as money?

(b) Why are checks unsatisfactory as money?

(c) Are some checks better than others?

3. On page 184 the statement is made that canceled checks are "evidence that payments have been made." Look up the meaning of the terms "evidence" and "proof." (a) What is the difference in meaning? (b) Can you think of a case in which a canceled check would not be proof that a particular debt was paid?

4. Find out and explain the meaning of each of the terms listed below. Use each term in a sentence.

(a) overdraft   (d) voucher check

(b) specie   (e) insufficient funds

(c) dishonored check   (f) voided check

5. From one of your local banks, obtain the following information:

(a) Does the bank make no service charge, regardless of the number of checks written, if the customer's account balance does not fall below a fixed amount? If so, what is this amount?

(b) If a service charge is calculated on a regular account, what are the charges made? What credit is given for the average account balance?

(c) If the bank offers a special account, by what name is the account known? How do the charges compare with those for a regular checking account?

PART 16
Special Means Of Making Payments

When you want to pay a bill or make some other kind of payment to another person or business, you will probably write a personal check. More than nine-tenths of the "money" that flows in and out of banks every day is in the form of checks. There are times, however, when a personal check cannot be used conveniently. For example, you may want to pay a bill but do not have a checking account and so cannot write a check. Or perhaps the person to whom payment is being sent does not know you and is unwilling to accept your personal check.

When using personal checks is not entirely satisfactory, you may use a special means of making payment. Special means of making payments include: (1) certified checks, (2) bank drafts, (3) cashier's checks, (4) bank money orders, (5) postal money orders, (6) telegraphic money orders, (7) express money orders, and (8) travelers checks.

Suppose that Margaret Sandman wants to make a payment in the form of a check. This payment is to go to someone who does not know her and who may hesitate to accept her personal check. In this case, Miss Sandman may have the bank certify her check as shown in Illustration 16-1. A *certified check* is a personal check on which the bank has written its guarantee that the check will be paid.

CHECKS MAY BE CERTIFIED

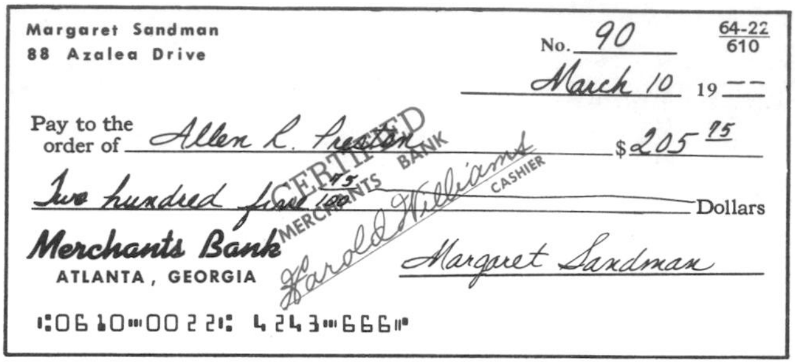
Margaret Sandman
88 Azalea Drive

No. 90 — 64-22/610

March 10 19--

Pay to the order of Allen L. Preston $205 95/100

Two hundred five 95/100 Dollars

CERTIFIED MERCHANTS BANK CASHIER Harold Williams

Merchants Bank
ATLANTA, GEORGIA

Margaret Sandman

⑆0610⑉0022⑆ 4243⑈666⑈

Illus. 16-1. A certified check.

When the bank writes its guarantee across the face of a check to certify it, the amount of the check is immediately subtracted from the depositor's account. This makes it impossible for the depositor to draw out the money or to use it for other checks.

BANK DRAFTS MAY BE PURCHASED

Banks usually deposit part of their funds in other banks. An official of a bank may draw checks on these deposits in the same way that an individual may draw on funds that he has deposited in his bank. A check that a bank official draws on the bank's deposits in another bank is known as a *bank draft*. Banks will sell bank drafts to anyone. A person who buys such a draft pays the bank the exact amount of the draft plus a small charge for issuing the draft.

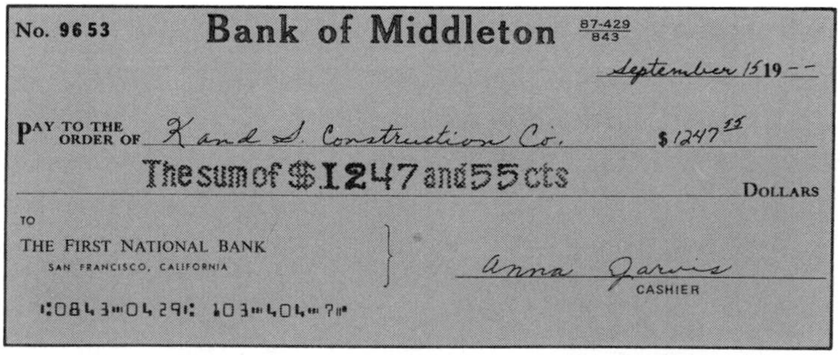
No. 9653 — Bank of Middleton — 87-429/843

September 15 19--

PAY TO THE ORDER OF K and S. Construction Co. $1247 55/100

The sum of $1247 and 55 cts DOLLARS

TO
THE FIRST NATIONAL BANK
SAN FRANCISCO, CALIFORNIA

Anna Jarvis
CASHIER

⑆0843⑉0429⑆ 103⑈404⑈7⑈

Illus. 16-2. A bank draft.

CASHIER'S CHECKS MAY BE PURCHASED

A check that a bank draws on its own funds is usually called a *cashier's check*. It has this name because such checks were originally drawn by an officer of the bank known as a cashier. Now such a check is often drawn by another officer. Some banks refer to checks drawn on their own funds as officer's checks, treasurer's checks, or manager's checks, depending on who is authorized to draw them. In our discussion the term "cashier's check" will refer to all checks drawn by a bank on its own funds.

Banks commonly use cashier's checks in paying their own expenses. They also sell such checks to customers just as they sell bank drafts. If the customer has no preference as to whether he obtains a bank draft or a cashier's check, the bank will recommend one or the other. The choice depends on where the payment is to be sent.

As with bank drafts, the person who is buying the cashier's check pays the bank the amount of the check plus a service fee. Both bank drafts and cashier's checks are commonly used to make rather large payments. These banker's checks are more acceptable than the personal checks of an individual whom the payee may not know.

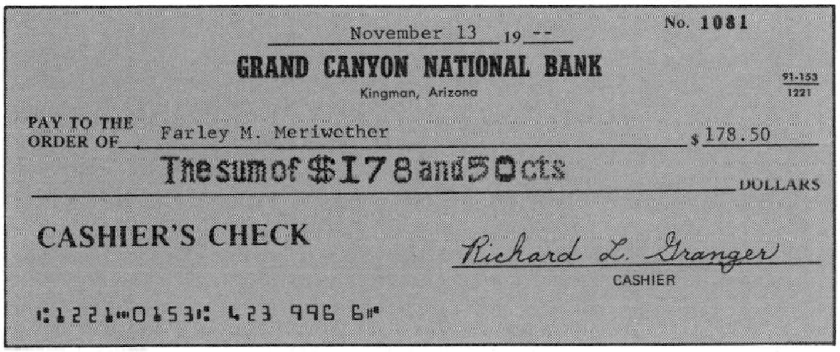
No. 1081
November 13 19 --
GRAND CANYON NATIONAL BANK
Kingman, Arizona
91-153
1221
PAY TO THE ORDER OF Farley M. Meriwether $ 178.50
The sum of $178 and 50 cts DOLLARS
CASHIER'S CHECK
Richard L. Granger
CASHIER

Illus. 16-3. A cashier's check.

YOU MAY BUY A BANK MONEY ORDER

Banks often sell money orders to persons who do not have checking accounts but want to send money payments through the mail. For payments under $100, money orders are more often used than are bank drafts or cashier's checks because they cost less. The purchaser of a *bank money order* pays the bank clerk the amount of the money order plus a small fee.

A bank money order is shown in Illustration 16-4. In this example, Tony Guardino is sending $22.50 to the Grolier Corporation. He pays the bank $22.50 plus a 25-cent charge for the service. The bank then stamps the amount of the money order on the form and gives it to Mr. Guardino. He fills in the date, the name of the payee, and his own name and address.

When this money order has been paid, it will not be returned to Mr. Guardino as a canceled check would be. It will, however, be returned to the bank that issued it. The money order can then

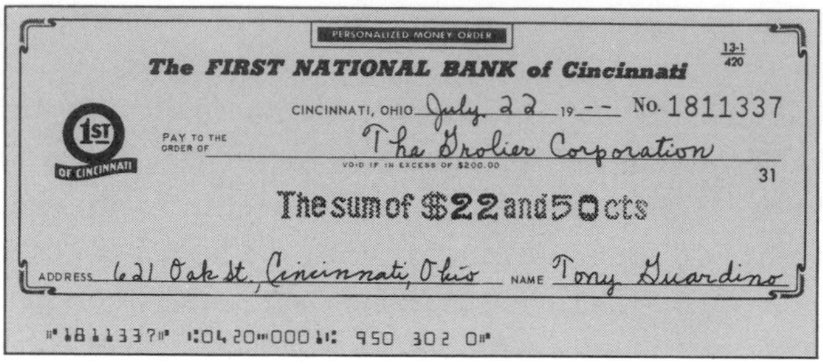

PERSONALIZED MONEY ORDER

The FIRST NATIONAL BANK of Cincinnati 13-1/420

CINCINNATI, OHIO July 22 19-- No. 1811337

PAY TO THE ORDER OF The Grolier Corporation

VOID IF IN EXCESS OF $200.00

31

The sum of $22 and 50 cts

ADDRESS 621 Oak St, Cincinnati, Ohio NAME Tony Guardino

Illus. 16-4. Money order issued by a bank.

be referred to if it is desirable to prove that payment was made. Since bank practices in issuing money orders vary, you should check with your bank to find out what its practice is before you buy a money order.

A POST OFFICE SELLS MONEY ORDERS

A post office is obviously not a bank, but it, like a bank, sells money orders. A *postal money order* is a form issued by a post office directing that money be paid to a business or a person, or to his order. When you buy a postal money order, the postal clerk fills out the money order with the exception of the payee's name and the sender's name and address. The sender then enters this information.

A postal money order can be sent safely through the mail because it can be cashed only when it is signed by the payee. If a money order is lost or stolen or if the payee denies having received it, the receipt portion of the money order may be used in making a claim with the post office. The payee of a postal money order may cash it at a post office or a bank, or he may transfer it

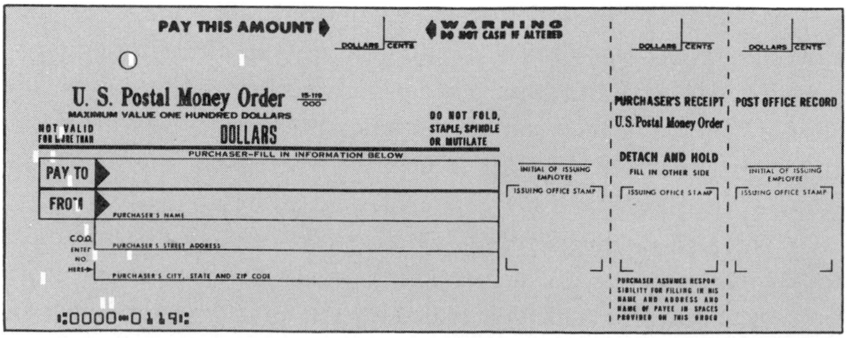

PAY THIS AMOUNT DOLLARS CENTS

WARNING DO NOT CASH IF ALTERED

U. S. Postal Money Order

MAXIMUM VALUE ONE HUNDRED DOLLARS

DOLLARS

DO NOT FOLD, STAPLE, SPINDLE OR MUTILATE

PURCHASER–FILL IN INFORMATION BELOW

PAY TO

FROM PURCHASER'S NAME

PURCHASER'S STREET ADDRESS

PURCHASER'S CITY, STATE AND ZIP CODE

INITIAL OF ISSUING EMPLOYEE

ISSUING OFFICE STAMP

PURCHASER'S RECEIPT U.S. Postal Money Order

DETACH AND HOLD FILL IN OTHER SIDE

PURCHASER ASSUMES RESPONSIBILITY FOR FILLING IN HIS NAME AND ADDRESS AND NAME OF PAYEE IN SPACES PROVIDED ON THIS ORDER

POST OFFICE RECORD

Illus. 16-5. A postal money order.

by endorsement to another person. Information about the endorsement of postal money orders is printed on the back of each order.

The maximum amount for which a postal money order may be issued is $100. If a person wants to send a larger amount, he may buy two or more orders. Fees for postal money orders vary with the amounts that are sent.

EXPRESS MONEY ORDERS

Money orders issued by the American Express Company are known as *express money orders*. They are similar to bank money orders and postal money orders. Express money orders may be bought at more than 32,000 places, including offices of the American Express Company, many Western Union Telegraph and REA Express offices, and many retail stores.

The maximum amount for which an American Express money order can be drawn is $200, but a person may buy as many orders as he wants. Charges are about the same as for postal money orders. The buyer of an express money order is given a receipt, and he should keep it as long as he may need proof that he bought the money order.

Bank drafts, postal money orders, and express money orders may all be used in sending payments to foreign countries. Information about the methods of sending payments to foreign countries may be obtained from the bank or the office where the money order is purchased.

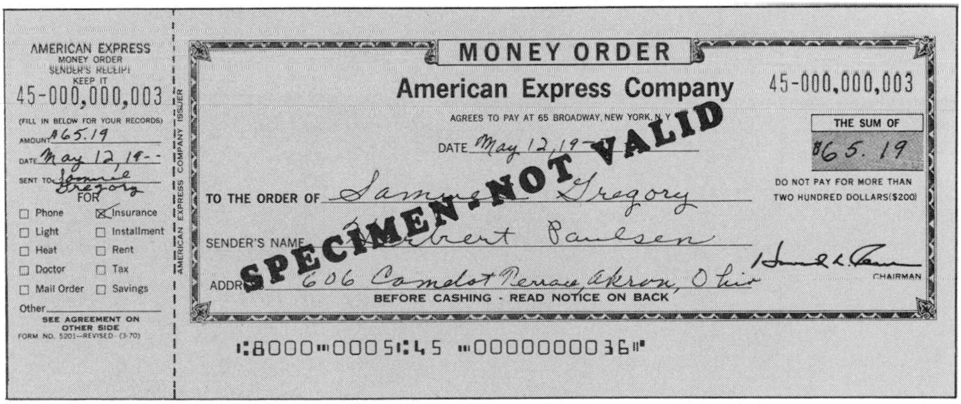
AMERICAN EXPRESS
MONEY ORDER
SENDER'S RECEIPT
KEEP IT
45-000,000,003
(FILL IN BELOW FOR YOUR RECORDS)
AMOUNT $65.19
DATE May 12, 19--
SENT TO Sammie Gregory
FOR
☐ Phone ☒ Insurance
☐ Light ☐ Installment
☐ Heat ☐ Rent
☐ Doctor ☐ Tax
☐ Mail Order ☐ Savings
Other
SEE AGREEMENT ON OTHER SIDE
FORM NO. 5201—REVISED (3-70)

AMERICAN EXPRESS COMPANY ISSUER

MONEY ORDER
American Express Company
45-000,000,003
AGREES TO PAY AT 65 BROADWAY, NEW YORK, N.Y.
THE SUM OF
DATE May 12, 19--
$65.19
TO THE ORDER OF Sammie Gregory
DO NOT PAY FOR MORE THAN TWO HUNDRED DOLLARS ($200)
SENDER'S NAME Herbert Paulsen
ADDRESS 606 Camelot Terrace Akron, Ohio
CHAIRMAN
BEFORE CASHING - READ NOTICE ON BACK
SPECIMEN-NOT VALID
⑆8000⑈0005⑆45 ⑈0000000036⑈

Illus. 16-6. Express money order. The receipt at the left should be detached by the sender and retained as his record of the transaction.

YOU MAY BUY A TELEGRAPHIC MONEY ORDER

A *telegraphic money order* is a message directing a telegraph office to pay a sum of money to a certain person. Suppose that Rod Bennett, while applying for work in another city, finds that he needs more money to pay his traveling expenses. He may go to the nearest telegraph office and send a telegram to his father asking that money be sent to him. His father pays the money to the telegraph company, and a return telegram is sent ordering the first telegraph office to pay Rod a certain amount. The telegraph company will make immediate payment to Rod. If the return message is sent promptly, Rod should have the money soon after the first telegram is sent.

The telegraph company charges a fee for handling payment of the money. This fee depends on the amount to be paid. Another charge is made for any messages sent with the money order. Obtaining money in this way is somewhat expensive when one considers the cost of the telegrams both ways and the cost of the money order. However, this service is very helpful in an emergency.

Illus. 16-7. A telegraphic money order. Note the information it contains.

UNIT 4 / BANKS AND BANKING SERVICES

It is risky for a traveler to carry a large sum of money, since it can be easily lost or stolen while he is moving about and staying in strange places. It is also inconvenient for him to try to pay his traveling expenses with personal checks, since he will be dealing largely with strangers who will not know whether his checks are good. Even money orders and bank drafts may not be entirely satisfactory, as the traveler may not be able to get the identification that is necessary in cashing such forms.

Special forms for making payment have been designed for the traveler's use. These forms are known as *travelers checks*. They can be bought at banks, offices of express companies, travel bureaus, and many Western Union offices. A reasonable charge, in addition to the face value, is made for travelers checks. They can be bought in convenient denominations such as $10, $20, $50, and $100.

TRAVELERS CHECKS ARE SAFE AND CONVENIENT

Illus. 16-8. A book of travelers checks.

The travelers check provides two spaces for the traveler's signature. When he buys the checks, the traveler signs each in the presence of the agent. When a check is cashed, it is signed again in the presence of the person cashing it. The similarity of the two signatures provides adequate identification.

Travelers checks are commonly accepted by banks, transportation companies, hotels, restaurants, stores, and other organizations throughout the world. Almost anyone is willing to accept a travelers check since there is little chance of its not being signed by the right person.

When you buy travelers checks you should immediately record the serial number of each check on a form that is generally furnished by the issuing agency. Then, on the form you should also note the place and date of each check cashed. This record should be kept separately from your checks so that you can refer to it if your checks are lost or stolen. If the checks are lost or stolen, you should notify at once the nearest bank or office where such checks are sold. The company that issued the checks will replace them.

Developing Your Business Vocabulary

The following italicized terms should become part of your business vocabulary. For each numbered statement, find the italicized term that has the same meaning.

bank draft *express money order*
bank money order *postal money order*
cashier's check *telegraphic money order*
certified check *travelers checks*

1. A personal check that is guaranteed by a bank.
2. A check that a bank draws on its deposits in another bank.
3. A check that a bank official draws on funds in his own bank.
4. A form often purchased from banks for use in making small payments.
5. A form issued by a post office for use in making payments.
6. A form purchased from an express company for use in making payments.
7. A message directing a certain telegraph office to pay a specific amount of money to a particular person.
8. Forms sold by banks, express companies, and various other establishments to take care of the financial needs of travelers.

Checking Your Understanding

1. Describe two situations in which you could not conveniently make payments by personal check.
2. If you were offered a certified check signed by someone unknown to you, would you accept it? Explain.
3. Explain how banks certify checks.
4. Assume that you do not have a checking account and that you wish to send a payment to a mail-order house. Can you buy a certified check from a bank for this purpose?

5. What is the difference between a personal check, a bank draft, and a cashier's check?
6. Banks usually charge a small fee for issuing money orders to their customers. Why do banks charge for this service?
7. If you do not have a checking account but would like to send a payment through the mail, are you more likely to buy a bank draft or a bank money order? Why?
8. What is the largest amount of money that may be sent by a single postal money order? How might a customer send larger amounts?
9. If you received a postal money order as a gift, where might you go to get the money?
10. Explain how an express money order is different from a bank money order and a postal money order.
11. May money orders be used to send money to other countries? Where could you obtain information about proper forms to use and the rates charged?
12. Explain how money payments may be sent by telegraph.
13. What are the special advantages of travelers checks?

Applying What You Have Learned

1. Dennis Ogilvy paid his dues for October in the Downtown Youth Club. He sent through the mail two $1 bills with a letter addressed to the treasurer. The letter was never delivered, and Dennis was required to make payment a second time. How could the loss have been prevented?
2. Suppose that you wish to send $3 by mail to the Novelty Hobby Shop. You have no checking account. Would you prefer to make payment with a postal money order, an express money order, or a bank money order? Explain.
3. Tell in your own words how you would purchase and send a postal money order for $7.28.
4. Ted Dugan is in Philadelphia. He has lost his billfold and is without money. Suggest how he may get money in the shortest time from his father in Atlanta.
5. Listed below and on page 200 are some of the money payments that the Farrell family of Des Moines, Iowa, was required to make during a 6-month period. In each case, tell what method of making payment you would recommend.

   (a) Paid telephone bill at local office.
   (b) Made monthly payment on house at local bank.
   (c) Paid state income tax.

(d) Paid federal income tax.

(e) Bought automobile license.

(f) Paid $125 for goods they ordered from a Chicago mail-order house. Wanted the goods shipped at once, but had never bought goods from the firm previously.

(g) Mr. Farrell had an automobile accident 300 miles from home. Was sent $250 by fastest method.

(h) Bought postage stamps, $4.50.

(i) Paid for automobile repairs at local garage, $14.75.

(j) Mr. Farrell sent $100 to his daughter, who is attending college in another city.

(k) The family moved to Zanesville, Ohio, and transferred its bank account, $1,385, to a Zanesville bank.

Solving Business Problems

1. Mr. and Mrs. Dromboski have a joint checking account. On December 30, Mr. Dromboski's check stub shows a balance of $238.53, and Mrs. Dromboski's check stub shows a balance of $117.81. They receive a statement from their bank showing a balance of $301.11.

In checking back over their business transactions with the bank, Mr. Dromboski discovered the following items that he neglected to enter on his check stubs: he wrote a check transferring $40 to his savings account; he had asked the bank to buy two $25 Series E government bonds at a cost of $37.50.

Mrs. Dromboski discovered the following items that were not entered on her check stubs: a deposit of $42.25; a service charge of 25¢ for a cashier's check.

(a) What is the correct amount of Mr. Dromboski's check-stub balance?

(b) What is the correct amount of Mrs. Dromboski's check-stub balance?

(c) What is the total of the two balances?

(d) Is this total the same as the balance on the bank statement? More? Less? How much more or less?

(e) What additional steps should be taken to reconcile the total of the check-stub balances and the balance shown on the bank statement?

2. Mr. and Mrs. Ray Kendall have a joint checking account. At the beginning of March, their joint balance was $563.82. During the month of March, they wrote checks and made deposits as follows:

Mr. Kendall:

March   1   Deposit, $197.40
          3   Check #136, $61.50
          9   Check #137, $10.00
        11   Check #138, $49.75
        15   Check #139, $17.50
        16   Deposit, $199.70
        27   Check #140, $46.23
        30   Deposit, $15.70

Mrs. Kendall:

March   2   Check #161, $4.50
          6   Check #162, $21.50
          9   Check #163, $8.78
        16   Check #164, $4.30
        21   Check #165, $75.20
        28   Check #166, $9.40

At the end of March, Mr. and Mrs. Kendall received a bank statement that showed a bank balance of $675.96. The service charge amounted to $1.40. Check No. 166 was outstanding. Reconcile the bank balance.

3. The following transactions were completed by Richard Blaine during May of the current year:

May   1   The balance was $494.20.
       1   Gave Check #143 for $51.33 to the Avon Furniture Store for furniture.
       1   Gave Check #144 for $31.40 to Dr. R. F. Alf for dental work.
       4   Deposited cash, $85.40; a check on the Farmers State Bank, Wichita, Kansas, 40-8, $42.97.
       5   Gave Check #145 for $15 to J. A. Glenheimer, Treasurer, for club dues.
       8   Gave Check #146 for $29.31 to Chan's Specialty Food Shop for groceries.
     11   Gave Check #147 for $7.50 to Meadowbrook Farms for dairy products.
     12   Deposited cash, $99.30; a check on the First City Bank, Chicago, 2-53, $26.80.
     19   Gave Check #148 for $30 to the United Appeal.
     22   Gave Check #149 for $49.78 to Hawkins Hardware Store for electrical fixtures.
     26   Gave Check #150 for $12.48 to K and K Garage for repairs on his car.

The bank statement that Mr. Blaine received at the end of the month showed a balance of $563.52. A service charge of 83¢ for the month was included on the statement. Checks #148 and #150 were outstanding.

(a) Write the check stubs, the checks, and the deposit tickets for the transactions.
(b) Reconcile the check-stub balance with the bank-statement balance.

Enriching Your Business Understanding

1. On the telegraphic money order illustrated on page 196, there is a space labeled "Test Question." From a local telegraph office, find out for what this space is used. Under what circumstances would you consider its use desirable?
2. At a time when the fee for issuing travelers checks was usually 1% of the face value of the checks, one bank advertised that, for a limited time, it would issue $5,000 of travelers checks for only $5. What did the bank have to gain from the sale of the checks for $5 instead of the usual $50?
3. Prepare as complete a list as possible of places in your community where money orders can be purchased. What is the cost of each kind of money order for $10? For $25?
4. Suppose that you are using each of these special means of making payment to send a rather large sum of money through the mail: (a) certified check, (b) bank draft, (c) cashier's check, (d) bank money order, (e) postal money order, and (f) express money order. Also, suppose that the person to whom the payment is being sent never receives it. In each case, what can you do?

PART 17
Receiving Payment By Check

When you receive a check that reads "Pay to the Order of (Your Name)," you are the payee of that check. The check is payable only upon your order. You can do one of three things with the check: (1) cash it at a bank, (2) deposit it in your account, or (3) transfer it to another person or business either for cash or as payment of a bill.

Before doing any of these things, you should write your name on the back of the check, near the left end. Such a signature is called an *endorsement*. Your endorsement is written evidence that you received payment from the bank or that you transferred your right of receiving payment to someone else.

HOW TO WRITE AN ENDORSEMENT

In endorsing a check, the payee should sign his name in ink exactly as it is written on the face of the check. If Donald F. Scheaffer received a check made payable to D. F. Scheaffer, he should endorse it "D. F. Scheaffer." He should not sign his name "Don Scheaffer" or even "Donald F. Scheaffer."

If his name is not given correctly on a check, the payee should first endorse the check exactly as the name is given and should then write his name correctly as a second endorsement. If Mr. Scheaffer's check had been made payable to "D. R. Scheaffer," Mr. Scheaffer should endorse it as shown in Illustration 17-1.

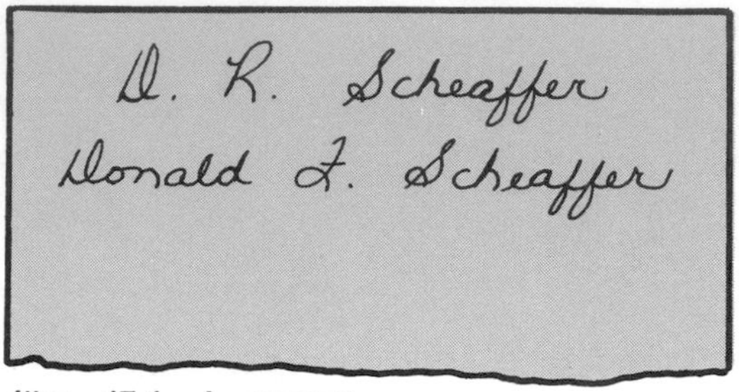

Illus. 17-1. A correctly written endorsement.

Illus. 17-2. A blank endorsement.

YOU MAY USE A BLANK ENDORSEMENT

Different endorsements serve different purposes. An endorsement that consists of only the endorser's name is called a *blank endorsement*. The endorsements "Nancy Brooks" in Illustration 17-2 and "Donald F. Scheaffer" in Illustration 17-1 are blank endorsements. A blank endorsement makes a check payable to anyone who has possession of it. A blank endorsement may be used whenever a check is to be transferred, but sometimes other endorsements are preferable.

YOU MAY USE AN ENDORSEMENT IN FULL

Suppose that you have received a check made payable to you. You want to make it payable to Alan Friedman of another city. If you use a blank endorsement and send it to him, he can cash the check when he receives it. But if it should be lost before it reaches him, anyone who finds it can cash it.

To make sure that no one except Mr. Friedman will be able to cash the check, you may use an *endorsement in full*. With this endorsement, you place before your signature the words "Pay to the order of Alan Friedman." Mr. Friedman's signature is required before the check can be cashed.

YOU MAY USE A RESTRICTIVE ENDORSEMENT

A *restrictive endorsement* limits the use of a check to the purpose given in the endorsement. For example, you may have several checks that you want to mail to the bank. If you use a blank endorsement, they may be lost and cashed by someone else. But if you place the words "For deposit only" above your signature, you have restricted the use of each check so that it can only be deposited to your account. If a check with such an endorsement is lost, it cannot be cashed by the finder.

Many businesses use rubber stamps for restrictive endorsements that require checks to be deposited to their accounts. A check so endorsed cannot be cashed but can only be deposited to the endorser's account. A business thus has no risk of loss if an unauthorized person uses the stamp to endorse a check.

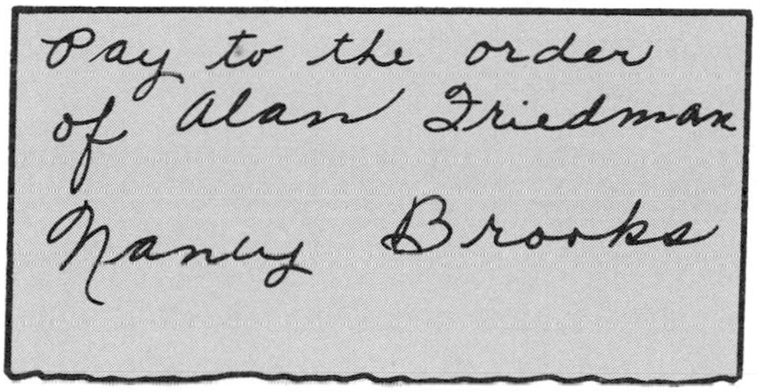

Illus. 17-3. Endorsement in full.

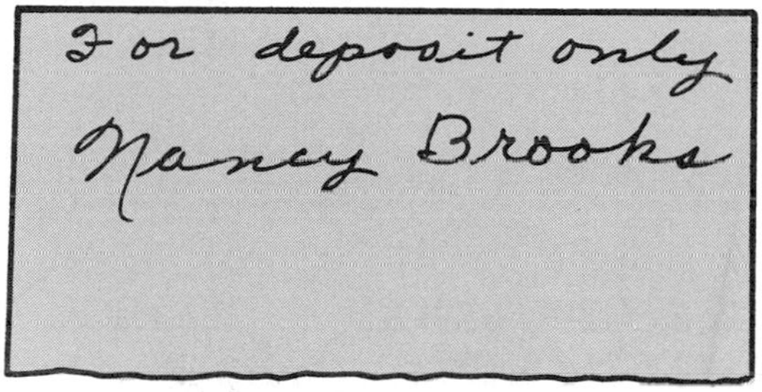

Illus. 17-4. Restrictive endorsement.

WHAT YOU PROMISE AS AN ENDORSER

When you endorse a check, your responsibilities are almost as great as if you had written the check yourself. As an endorser, you are actually making this promise: "If this check is not paid, I will pay it." After endorsing a check, the payee usually cashes it or deposits it in a bank. But the payee may transfer the check to another person, who in turn may transfer it to someone else, and so on. Each person who transfers a check should be required to endorse it, for his endorsement is another promise that the check will be paid.

An endorsement serves as a promise only to persons who receive the check after the endorsement is written. It does not apply to persons who held the check before the endorsement. For example, suppose that Bill Whitfield signs a check and gives it to Sam Corbett and that Corbett endorses it and gives it to you. Suppose also that you endorse the check and give it to Harry Paulsen. If the bank later refuses to pay the check for any reason, Paulsen may collect the amount from the drawer (Whitfield) or from either of the two endorsers (Corbett or you). If he collects from you, you have a claim against the drawer (Whitfield) and against the first endorser (Corbett). But if Paulsen collects from either of them, neither has a claim against you.

CLEARING CHECKS THROUGH THE SAME BANK

A check may be passed from person to person by endorsement. But sooner or later it is returned to the drawer's bank to be paid and charged to his account. Suppose that both Reuben Carter and Louis Wingate have checking accounts in the West Fork National Bank. Suppose that Mr. Carter writes a check for $25 and gives it to Mr. Wingate and that Mr. Wingate then deposits the check in his account. How does the transfer of funds take place? This is done by a simple bookkeeping record in which the bank subtracts $25 from Mr. Carter's account and adds it to Mr. Wingate's account. The bank then cancels the check and returns it to Mr. Carter with his bank statement.

CLEARING CHECKS BETWEEN BANKS IN A SMALL TOWN

Illustration 17-5 shows how a local check may be paid when there are two banks in a small town. In this case, George Endicott has an account with the West Fork National Bank. He writes a check and makes it payable to Cushing's Garage. He sends the check to Cushing's Garage, which endorses and deposits the check in its account with the Citizens Trust Company. When the Citizens Trust Company receives the check, it adds $58 to the account of Cushing's Garage, endorses the check, and sends it to the West Fork National Bank for payment. After the West Fork National Bank receives the check, it pays the Citizens Trust Company $58 and subtracts that amount from George Endicott's account. The check is then canceled by the West Fork National Bank and returned to Mr. Endicott as his record of payment.

Actually, where there are two or more banks in a small town, each bank may cash daily hundreds of checks drawn on the other banks. It would not be very practical for a bank to send a clerk to some other bank to get its money every time it cashed a check drawn on that bank. Instead, banks in the same town agree on a certain time of day to clear the checks.

Each bank makes up packages of its paid checks which were drawn on the other banks—one package for each bank. A messenger may travel from bank to bank exchanging packages of checks and paying to or receiving from each bank the difference in the dollar amounts of the packages exchanged. Or, representatives of the different banks may meet in one place to exchange checks.

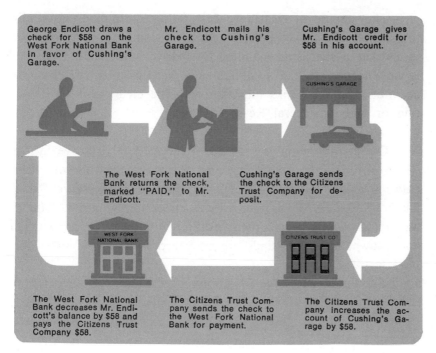

George Endicott draws a check for $58 on the West Fork National Bank in favor of Cushing's Garage.

Mr. Endicott mails his check to Cushing's Garage.

Cushing's Garage gives Mr. Endicott credit for $58 in his account.

The West Fork National Bank returns the check, marked "PAID," to Mr. Endicott.

Cushing's Garage sends the check to the Citizens Trust Company for deposit.

The West Fork National Bank decreases Mr. Endicott's balance by $58 and pays the Citizens Trust Company $58.

The Citizens Trust Company sends the check to the West Fork National Bank for payment.

The Citizens Trust Company increases the account of Cushing's Garage by $58.

Illus. 17-5. The path traveled by a check. If the Citizens Trust Company and the West Fork National Bank were in a city having a clearinghouse, the check would be sent from one bank to the other through the clearinghouse. If they were in different cities, the check would be sent from one bank to the other through a Federal Reserve bank.

Suppose that when the bank representatives meet, it is found that (1) the Citizens Trust Company has checks totaling $4,000 drawn on the West Fork National Bank and that (2) the West Fork National Bank has checks totaling $4,250 drawn on the Citizens Trust Company. The Citizens Trust Company thus owes the West Fork National Bank $250. It may pay this amount in cash, but usually a method is worked out that makes the handling of cash unnecessary. For example, both banks may maintain accounts with the same bank in a neighboring city. In this case, the city bank may be notified to transfer $250 from the account of the Citizens Trust Company to the account of the West Fork National Bank.

CLEARING CHECKS BETWEEN BANKS IN LARGE CITIES

In large cities where there are many banks, it would not be practical for each bank to present checks for payment to all the banks on which they were drawn. Usually city banks are members of an association which operates a *clearinghouse* for member banks. Member banks send all local bank checks to the clearinghouse daily.

The method of clearing checks in a clearinghouse is similar to the method followed between banks in a small town, except that thousands of checks are handled for many banks. Here, also, cash is not needed to make settlements. Entries may be made in accounts that the banks maintain with the clearinghouse association or with a Federal Reserve Bank.

CLEARING CHECKS BETWEEN BANKS IN DIFFERENT CITIES

One of the valuable services of the Federal Reserve System, which you learned about in Part 12, is the clearing of checks between banks in different cities. The Federal Reserve System has set up methods so that (1) a check drawn on a bank in another city may be returned promptly to the bank on which it was drawn, and (2) funds are transferred between banks when necessary.

The Federal Reserve System handles millions of checks every day. Because of its services, checks can be used to make payments in any part of the country as easily as they can be used locally.

BE CAREFUL IN ACCEPTING AND CASHING CHECKS

It is important that you understand your responsibility as a signer and as an endorser of checks. According to law, a check is payable on demand; that is, at the time the holder of the check presents it for payment at the bank on which it is drawn. But a bank may refuse to accept a check if it is presented for payment long after the date on which it was written. So you should present a check for payment within a reasonable time after you receive it.

A check is valuable only when it is drawn on a bank in which the drawer has money on deposit. For this reason you should accept checks only when they are drawn or endorsed by people whom you know and trust. A check received from a stranger may turn out to be worthless, and it may be impossible for you to find him and collect from him.

Just as you should not cash checks for strangers, you should not expect strangers to cash checks for you. If you must ask a stranger to cash a check, you may have to prove your identity. You may do this by showing your driver's license or some other form of identification. Checks are used so commonly instead of money that you will usually have no trouble cashing them where you are known, but no one is legally required to accept your checks.

Developing Your Business Vocabulary

The following italicized terms should become part of your business vocabulary. For each numbered statement, find the italicized term that has the same meaning.

blank endorsement *endorsement in full*
clearinghouse *restrictive endorsement*
endorsement

1. Writing on the back of a check that transfers ownership of the check.
2. An endorsement consisting of a name only.
3. An endorsement including the name of the person to whom the check is transferred.
4. An endorsement that limits the use of a check to a specific purpose.
5. A place where banks exchange checks drawn on each other.

Checking Your Understanding

1. In what three possible ways may you use a check that is made payable to you?
2. Why is it necessary for the payee of a check to endorse it before transferring it to another person or company?
3. Where should the endorsement be written on a check?
4. Give an example of a blank endorsement, an endorsement in full, and a restrictive endorsement. Explain the purpose of each.
5. As an endorser of a check, what promise do you make to other holders of the check?
6. Is your endorsement on a check a promise to persons who held the check before you, to those who will hold it after you, or to both? Explain.
7. Explain briefly how checks are cleared: (a) in the same bank; (b) between different banks in a small town; (c) between different banks in a large city; and (d) between banks in different cities.
8. How soon after a check has been received by the payee should he present it for payment? Can you think of any exceptions to this?
9. What are several precautions you should observe in accepting checks? Explain each.
10. Why might you have some difficulty cashing a check in a town where you are not known? What are possible ways that you might establish your identity?
11. Does a stranger have the right to refuse to cash your check even if you properly identify yourself? Explain.

Applying What You Have Learned

1. Several different kinds of endorsements were explained in this part. For each of the situations listed below, name and describe the type of endorsement that should be used. Give your reason in each case.

    (a) Lloyd Wright is in the bank and wants to cash a check of which he is the payee.
    (b) Douglas Bishop wants to pay a bill by sending through the mail a check he received from Mr. Sloan.
    (c) Carol Dorrmann wants to make a deposit in her bank by mail.
    (d) T. R. Baker uses a check received from Mark Christian to buy some groceries.
    (e) Patricia Parks gives two checks to a friend, Marilyn King, who is to deposit them in Patricia's account.
    (f) M. S. Leeds receives a check on which his name has been misspelled as M. S. Leads.

2. A check was endorsed in succession by J. J. Getz, M. L. Ainsley, and P. B. Todd. Mr. Todd deposited the check in his bank. Later it was found that the check was worthless and that the original drawer could not be located. Who lost the value of the check?

3. Ron McMillan wishes to give you a check in exchange for money. Since you do not know him, you hesitate to accept his check. Joel Foreman, who knows both you and Mr. McMillan, offers to endorse the check. Will this make you more willing to accept Mr. McMillan's check? Explain.

4. Some businesses use a rubber stamp in endorsing checks that they receive. Under what circumstances do you consider an endorsement made with a rubber stamp satisfactory? Give reasons for your answer.

5. Mr. Campbell, a merchant, frequently cashes checks for customers. He says that he is not much interested in who has signed these checks, but he is very much interested in who endorses them at the time they are cashed. Why is Mr. Campbell so much more interested in knowing the endorser of a check than he is in knowing the drawer?

6. Burt Engles maintains a checking account at the Fulton Trust Company. He drew a check on his account for $15.35 and gave it to the Edison Electric Company. The Edison Electric Company deposited the check in the Fifth National Bank, which in turn sent the check to the Fulton Trust Company for payment. Assuming that all parties concerned were located in the same city, draw a chart similar to that on page 207 showing the movement of the check from the time it was issued by Mr. Engles until it was returned to him.

Solving Business Problems

1. David Ackers drew a check payable to Gene Fleming and gave it to Mr. Fleming. Mr. Fleming endorsed the check with a blank endorsement and gave it to Margaret Bridges. Miss Bridges in turn endorsed the check so that it would be payable to the order of Henry Olden. Mr. Olden mailed the check to the bank so that it could be deposited to his account. Before mailing the check, Mr. Olden wrote a restrictive endorsement. Show how the various endorsements appeared on this check.

2. Write the following endorsements as they should be written on the backs of checks:

   (a) Laura Merrill endorsed a check in the simplest possible manner and transferred it to the Specialty Food Shop. The Specialty Food Shop endorsed this check for deposit.

   (b) Margo White, treasurer of a women's club, endorsed a check so that it was payable to the order of Lyle Hibbler.

   (c) Cliff Brennan endorsed a check with the simplest form of endorsement. He sent it to Rod Franklin, who endorsed it so that it was payable to the Miami Equipment Company.

   (d) Barbara Larkin endorsed a check so that it was payable to the order of Emily Schmidt. Miss Schmidt endorsed the check with a blank endorsement and gave it to Maxine Owens. Miss Owens endorsed the check so that it could be sent safely through the mail for deposit.

3. When the four banks in the town of Butler prepared to clear checks one day, they found that they had paid checks on one another as shown in the table below:

Checks Held By	Drawn On			
	First National	Farmers' Trust	Merchants' Mutual	Butler Bank
First National	. . . . . .	$938.57	$644.63	$1,158.64
Farmers' Trust	$443.74	. . . . . .	$711.44	$ 208.45
Merchants' Mutual	$304.35	$522.82	. . . . . .	$ 639.28
Butler Bank	$988.95	$326.31	$783.30	. . . . . .

Assuming that each bank makes an individual settlement with every other bank, calculate the amount that each bank will either pay to or receive from every other bank.

Enriching Your Business Understanding

1. Gilbert Coors, who is well known to you, offers you a check signed by Dale Maxwell that has been made payable to "Cash." Would you accept the check from Mr. Coors without his endorsement? Explain.

2. It has been said that the more endorsements that appear on a check, the more valuable it becomes. Do you agree with this statement? Explain circumstances under which this might or might not be true.

3. Assume that you are a cashier in a supermarket and that one of your responsibilities is approving customers' checks. Which of the following checks would you cash and which would you not cash? What additional information might you want in some cases?

    (a) A stranger presents a check made out to him and signed by one of the store's best customers.

    (b) An occasional customer presents a check signed by an unknown person and drawn on an out-of-town bank.

    (c) A 12-year-old boy brings in his father's paycheck to pay the grocery bill. The check was endorsed by his father.

    (d) A customer, unknown to you, presents a check written with a pencil.

    (e) A regular customer presents a $35 check dated six months ago.

    (f) A stranger offers a $75 check, drawn on a local bank, to pay for a $5.80 grocery bill. He requests change for the difference.

4. Debbie Jansen received a check made payable to her order. Debbie lost the check. It was found by another person, who wrote Debbie's name as an endorsement and cashed the check at the bank on which it was drawn. Can Debbie require the bank to pay her the amount of the check?

5. In this part you learned about three kinds of endorsements. Other kinds of endorsements can also be used on some occasions. Refer to a business law textbook and obtain information about other kinds of endorsements. Briefly describe each of these endorsements and explain when it might be used.

Unit 5

Using Credit Wisely

PART 18

Credit Helps Buyers Meet Needs and Wants

Bill Stulke came to work without his lunch money on Tuesday. But he didn't have to go without lunch because the cafeteria supervisor agreed that he could pay for the lunch on Wednesday. That day, Bill's sister, Mary Kay, borrowed 75 cents from her friend Sue to buy a lipstick she wanted. That week, Bill's dad bought a new refrigerator and agreed to pay for it in monthly installments of $18.75. The appliance dealer who sold the refrigerator needed to order more to replenish his stock and agreed to pay the manufacturer for the refrigerators 10 days after receiving them. And Mrs. Stulke went to a school board meeting where the board agreed to sell bonds to raise money to build a new junior high school.

Similar situations take place many times every day in this country. They show how individuals, businesses, and government use credit to obtain goods and services. *Credit* means promising to pay at a future time for something of value that is received now.

Anyone who buys on credit or receives a loan is known as a *debtor*. The one who sells on credit or makes the loan is called the *creditor*. Our credit system operates on a basis of trust between debtor and creditor. The creditor trusts that the debtor will honor

ALL CREDIT IS BASED ON TRUST

his promise to repay the loan or pay later for the goods and services he has obtained and used. The cafeteria supervisor trusted Bill Stulke enough to let him buy his lunch on credit. Sue trusted Mary Kay to repay the 75 cents. The retailer trusted Mr. Stulke to pay for the refrigerator while the Stulke family was using it. If there were no trust in buyer-seller relationships, our credit system would not work.

Usually the trust between debtor and creditor is expressed in a formal written agreement. The debtor signs some type of statement promising to repay the loan or pay for the purchase. When Mr. Stulke agreed in writing to pay for the refrigerator, he was entering a formal agreement. At other times, the trust between debtor and creditor is an informal agreement. For example, Sue believed Mary Kay when she said, "I'll pay you back the 75 cents on Friday." Whether the agreement is formal or informal, credit represents a promise to pay.

MOST OF US USE CREDIT AT SOME TIME

Almost everyone uses credit at some time or other. Every year individuals, businesses, government units, and other organizations buy billions of dollars worth of goods and services on credit. It has been said that credit in our economy is like fuel in an engine: it makes our economy go.

The American consumer uses credit often and for many reasons. Consumers use credit most often to buy products which are fairly expensive and will last for quite a while, such as a house, a car, furniture, or appliances. They also use credit for convenience in making small everyday purchases. They may use credit to pay for services, such as medical care or travel. And they use credit when they borrow to pay taxes or pay off another debt. Credit helps consumers enjoy the style of living they want at the time they want it. With credit, consumers can obtain and use those things that they could not have until much later if they could buy only for cash.

Businesses also rely on credit. Business firms may borrow over a number of years to buy land, construct buildings, and buy costly equipment. They also use short-term credit, usually from 30 to 90 days, to meet temporary needs for cash. For example, merchants buy goods on credit, and manufacturers buy raw materials and supplies on credit. Many firms also borrow to meet

's Cafe

WE HONOR ALL CREDIT CARDS

WE ALSO ACCEPT CASH

Illus. 18-1. Credit is used in many different businesses, by many different people, at many different times.

payrolls for their employees. Businesses are willing to borrow on a short-term basis to get cash while they wait for goods to be sold and for customers to pay.

Local, state, and federal government units use credit often in providing for the public welfare. Your school was probably built on credit; bonds may have been sold so that it could be paid for while it is being used. The same is true of many of our highways, hospitals, public buildings, parks, and airports. Government units also borrow cash from banks to pay current expenses while they wait to collect taxes.

Although credit is very important to business and to government, most of our discussion in this unit will focus on consumer credit.

ADVANTAGES OF USING CREDIT

Few businesses could operate today without the use of credit. Sellers grant credit because they believe that by doing so they can increase sales and profits more than enough to offset the added expense of granting credit. But when the customer buys on credit, he is not thinking of aiding business; he is thinking of his own personal benefits. Four important advantages that customers can gain from using credit are: (1) buying on credit is convenient; (2) credit customers may get better service than cash customers; (3) credit customers may receive advance notice of sales and so obtain good merchandise buys; and (4) buying on credit enables a person to establish a credit rating.

(1) Perhaps the most important reason why customers use credit is that it is convenient. A customer of a department store, for example, can make a number of purchases during a month and pay for them with only one check at the end of the month. Also, the credit customer needs to carry little cash with him and thus avoids the risk of losing money.

Credit allows a person to have immediate possession of an item that he wants. A family can buy a new dishwasher on credit and begin using it instead of having to wait until enough money is saved to pay cash. In some cases, a person may not want to withdraw money from a savings account to make a necessary purchase because interest on the savings will be lost. So it may be better to charge purchases for a short time.

Sometimes credit is more of a necessity than a convenience. No matter how carefully a person manages his money, there will be times when he has little or no money on hand to pay for necessities. An automobile tire may blow out and have to be replaced right away. With credit, the customer who is short of ready cash can charge a new tire for a few weeks or a month and keep on driving the car.

(2) Some persons feel that credit customers get better service than cash customers do. For example, goods that have been bought on credit and that turn out to be unsatisfactory may often be more easily exchanged or returned than if they were bought for cash. This situation is probably not true in all stores, but many customers feel that it is true in some stores.

(3) Some stores, especially department and furniture stores, send notices of a special sale to their credit customers several days before the sale is advertised to the public. Credit customers thus have first choice of the merchandise and may obtain good values. Stores can send out advance notices to credit customers because they have the names and addresses of these customers but usually have no record of cash customers.

(4) A person who buys on credit and pays his bills when they are due gains a reputation for being dependable. He thus establishes a good *credit rating*. This credit rating is valuable when a person must borrow money to meet emergencies or to make a major purchase such as a house. It is also valuable in obtaining credit when he moves to another community. If a person buys

H. Armstrong Roberts

Illus. 18-2. Credit allows persons to buy products and begin using them immediately without waiting until they have saved enough money to pay cash.

only for cash, he will never establish a credit rating. Merchants will not know whether he would pay promptly if he were to use credit.

Buying on credit is easy and convenient, but it can also be troublesome. Here are three problems of using credit: (1) credit customers may overbuy; (2) credit customers may buy at the wrong time or place; and (3) credit prices may be higher than cash prices.

(1) Overbuying is one of the most common hazards in using credit. There are several ways in which a credit customer may overbuy. One way is to buy a more expensive item than he can afford. A man may buy a suit for $125 if he can say, "Charge it," while he might not be willing to pay more than $85 for a suit if he had to pay cash.

The credit customer may also be tempted to buy items that he doesn't really need. Everyone has had the experience of looking in store windows or reading advertisements and seeing many things he would like to have. Suppose that a lady is window-shopping and sees a pair of shoes that she especially likes. If she has a charge account with the store, she may buy the shoes on impulse, even though she had given no thought before to buying a pair

SOME PROBLEMS IN USING CREDIT

of shoes. She may not need the shoes and later may decide that they aren't as attractive as she first thought. If a person has to part with money at the time he buys, he is less likely to buy things he really does not need.

(2) Customers may become lazy shoppers because credit is so easy to use. They may buy at the wrong time or the wrong place. The smart shopper knows that at certain times of the year, prices of goods go down. This may be during a special sale, such as an August furniture sale, or an end-of-season sale. He also knows that items are priced higher when they are first put on the market than they are later after they become popular and more of them are made. The year-round presence of credit sometimes tempts a customer not to wait for a better price on an item he wants. It may also tempt him to buy only in stores which offer credit, even though those merchants may charge higher prices or give less reliable service.

(3) Stores that sell only for cash can sometimes sell at lower prices than stores which offer credit. Granting credit is expensive. It requires a lot of bookkeeping to keep a record of each charge sale and each payment on account. And if a customer does not pay promptly, there is the extra expense of collecting what is owed.

Every merchant who sells on credit will have some *uncollectible accounts*. No matter how carefully merchants choose their credit customers, a few customers do not pay what they owe. Losses

Illus. 18-3. Overbuying is one of the most common problems in using credit.

"It's simple . . . if we skip two payments on the washer and one on the car, we'll have the down payment on a color TV."

Copyright 1969 by the Kiplinger Washington Editors, Inc.

on accounts that cannot be collected must be considered as one of the costs of doing business. No merchant can stay in business very long if he "carries too much on his books." The overextension of credit is a common cause of business failures.

All the costs of granting credit must either be added to the selling price of the merchandise or must be subtracted from the profits. It is possible, however, that offering credit may increase a merchant's sales enough so that he does not have to raise the prices of merchandise to cover the costs of granting credit.

GUIDELINES FOR USING CREDIT

People are very different in their needs and wants for goods and services, in their savings habits, and in their incomes. It is impossible to tell anyone exactly how to use credit. There are, though, some pointers which have been set down by persons experienced in granting credit:

(1) Use credit for those goods which have a price much higher than you can afford with one or two paychecks. Avoid using credit for small items which you buy frequently. It is easy to use credit for small everyday purchases and to spend your cash for luxuries.

(2) Use credit mainly for goods which have a useful life longer than the time you need to pay for them. It is discouraging to pay over many months for things which you use up quickly, such as a vacation.

(3) Know what your income will be. If it varies from month to month, set a spending limit on yourself equal to the smallest paycheck you receive. Avoid buying on credit in the hope that you can make more money later in the year to pay for it.

(4) Make as large a down payment as you can without robbing yourself of cash to buy necessities. Larger down payments can reduce the total amount of money you pay in interest for receiving credit.

(5) Estimate your future income and expenses to be sure that you will have enough money in the future to pay a debt that you incur now. It is dangerous to use credit without knowing that you will have the money to pay debts when they are due.

(6) Do not be tempted to buy one item on credit just because you have finished paying for another one. For example, avoid buying a new car just because you have paid off your current model.

(7) Avoid the temptation to use credit at times when you feel like splurging. For example, buying expensive Christmas presents on credit may be a real problem in January when the bills come due.

If a person gets into credit difficulties, he should talk to his creditors. He should admit his problem so that they can help. Most merchants want customers' future business and also want to be paid—even slowly—rather than have to take back the goods purchased.

Also, the credit customer should not be rushed into a credit transaction. He should not be embarrassed to ask that every detail of a credit transaction be explained to him.

Developing Your Business Vocabulary

The following italicized terms should become part of your business vocabulary. For each numbered statement, find the italicized term that has the same meaning.

credit   *debtor*
creditor   *uncollectible account*
credit rating

1. Promising to pay at a future time for something of value received now.
2. One who buys or borrows and promises to pay later.
3. One who sells or lends on another's promise to pay in the future.
4. An individual's reputation for paying his debts on time.
5. Amounts owed by credit customers who do not pay their bills.

Checking Your Understanding

1. Why is it said that credit is basically a matter of trust?
2. Give several examples of ways in which consumers use credit.
3. Give several examples of ways in which businesses use credit.
4. Give several examples of ways in which local, state, and federal government units use credit.
5. Why do merchants sell on credit?
6. How can credit be a real help to a family? How can it be a hindrance? Explain carefully.

7. "Credit is not something that a merchant gives to a customer but rather something that a customer earns." Explain.
8. "If a person buys for cash only, he may have difficulty in establishing a credit rating." Explain.
9. "No merchant can stay in business very long if he carries too much on his books." Explain.
10. Name at least six guidelines for the wise use of credit.
11. What should a person do if he encounters difficulties in using credit?

Applying What You Have Learned

1. Below are a number of statements expressing different attitudes toward the use of credit. Examine these statements and tell whether or not you agree. Explain why in each case.

   (a) "The use of credit increases sales, helps business, and makes jobs; therefore, I should buy as many things on credit as possible."
   (b) "Credit is best when it is not abused."
   (c) "If things were sold for cash only, in the long run business would be just as good as it is when things are sold on credit."
   (d) "A person should buy on credit regularly to keep a good credit rating which he may need in an emergency."
   (e) "Buying on credit aids in character development because it develops in a person a sense of responsibility."
   (f) "Credit is a worrisome thing and should be avoided except in cases of emergency."
   (g) "Credit should be used only for buying high-priced items such as houses and cars and not for buying low-priced items such as food and clothing."

2. Listed below are ten items that most consumers use frequently. (a) Which of these items are commonly sold on credit? Tell why in each case. (b) Which are almost always sold for cash? Tell why in each case.

Houses	Ice cream sodas
Theater tickets	Television sets
Newspapers	Refrigerators
Automobiles	Groceries
Postage stamps	Pencils

3. Mr. Nelson buys all he can possibly buy on credit. If he has no money to pay his bills when they come due, he borrows the money. Mr. Porter never buys anything on credit; he buys only after he

has saved enough cash to pay for what he wants. (a) Do you favor Mr. Nelson's plan or Mr. Porter's plan? (b) What suggestions about the wise use of credit might you make to both men?

4. Mr. Stoner and Mr. Bissell got into an argument over the use of credit. Mr. Stoner argued that if everyone saved money as he should, no one would ever need to buy on credit. Mr. Bissell contended that this was not a very practical idea; that customers, business, and the country are better off because of credit purchases. What do you think about this? Support your point of view with examples.

5. Mr. Harolds believes that he has been given poor service by the Southern Department Store. He therefore decides to let the store wait just as long as possible before he pays his bill. (a) Why is this poor money management on the part of Mr. Harolds? (b) How may his attitude affect his credit rating in other stores?

6. Some kinds of businesses regularly sell on credit. Others rarely or never sell on credit. (a) Mention several businesses in your community which fit into each of these two groups. (b) Explain why two of the businesses never sell on credit.

Solving Business Problems

1. Mrs. Tregoe planned to spend $190 to buy new clothing for her children at the start of the school year. She bought the clothing at several department stores, where she charged these amounts: $40.62; $25.34; $35.78; $20.33; $50.71; and $44.77.

   (a) What was the total of the amounts that Mrs. Tregoe charged?
   (b) How much more was this amount than the amount she had planned to spend?
   (c) By what percent did Mrs. Tregoe exceed the amount she had planned to spend?

2. Stan Butcher bought a hardware store and used credit to do the following things:

Buy new store fixtures	$1,500
Buy a delivery truck	$2,200
Order goods to replenish inventory	$3,800
Remodel the store	$6,400

   (a) What is the total amount Mr. Butcher owes?
   (b) If his monthly payment for fixtures is $125, how many months will it take to pay what he owes?
   (c) If he pays for the delivery truck in 11 months, what will be the amount of his monthly payment?

(d) If he makes four equal payments per year for four years to pay for the remodeling, what will be the amount of each payment?

(e) If Mr. Butcher makes annual payments of $3,550, what percentage will this be of sales of $100,000?

3. The Charles Company has annual sales of $500,000. Its losses from uncollectible accounts are .15% of its sales.

(a) How much are its annual losses from uncollectible accounts?

(b) Assume that the net profits of the business are 6% of the sales. How many dollars of sales are required to provide profits equal to the loss from uncollectible accounts?

4. Wholesalers sometimes offer cash discounts to retailers to encourage them to pay their bills promptly. These terms appeared on an invoice received by Kane's Hardware: 5/10, 2/20, n/30. The term 5/10 means that a 5% discount will be allowed if the invoice is paid within 10 days. The term 2/20 means that a 2% discount will be allowed if the invoice is paid within 20 days. The term n/30 means that it is expected that the bill will be paid no later than 30 days after the date of the invoice.

(a) The amount of the invoice was $526.70. If Kane's Hardware paid the bill within 5 days, what was the amount of the check written?

(b) What was the amount of the check if the invoice was paid on the 15th day? On the 25th day?

Enriching Your Business Understanding

1. It has been said that when a person uses credit, he "mortgages his future." **(a)** What does this statement mean? **(b)** In what ways do you think it is true or untrue?

2. The table below shows how much consumer credit was outstanding in 1969. Study it, then answer the questions on page 228.

Consumer Credit Outstanding, End of 1969
(in billions of dollars)

Installment		$ 98.2
Automobile paper	$36.6	
Other consumer goods paper	27.6	
Repair and modernization loans	4.1	
Personal loans	29.9	
Noninstallment		$ 24.3
Single-payment loans	$ 9.1	
Charge accounts	8.2	
Service credit	7.0	
Total		$122.5

(a) What does the term *outstanding* mean?

(b) Which type of credit was apparently most used? Which was least used?

(c) If almost all people in this country were able to increase their incomes by at least 25% and prices stayed the same, which type of credit, if any, do you think would be used more? Used less? Why?

3. A family with a relatively low income and little property might have a better credit rating than a family with a large income and considerable property. Likewise, a small business might have a better credit rating than a much larger business owning millions of dollars worth of property. Explain the circumstances under which each of these conditions might exist.

4. Dick Hoffner owns and operates a record shop in a rented building located along a main street. Business is good, but Mr. Hoffner is considering adding a line of radios, tape recorders, and stereos to his stock. He sells for cash only. How might granting credit help or hurt his business?

5. Suppose that you and your parents decide to open a snack shop near your school to sell light lunches, soft drinks, and various kinds of snacks. Most of the customers will be junior and senior high school students. Since many students will forget to bring money or will want to treat friends when they haven't enough money, they will often ask you to charge their purchases. Make up a set of rules for extending credit to your teenage customers.

PART 19
Understanding Types of Sales Credit

Charge it! American consumers say that for millions of dollars of purchases a year. Today so many different businesses offer credit that a person can buy almost any item he wants on credit. For example, several thousand different credit cards are available from retail stores, oil companies, airlines, banks, and independent credit-card firms. Most people carry more than one credit card, and one businessman even gained national publicity for holding 87 different credit cards, carried in special pockets sewn into his suits.

To a newcomer on the consumer credit scene, the great variety of plans and terms offered can be bewildering. Everywhere businesses are urging you to "buy now and pay later." But there are really only a few basic types of consumer credit. Learn what they are and how they work, and you will be in a better position to use the type of credit plan which is best for you.

BASIC TYPES OF CONSUMER CREDIT

Consumer credit can be classified in two basic ways: as loan credit versus sales credit, or as installment credit versus non-installment credit.

Loan credit is credit used to borrow money. Borrowing money will be discussed in Part 20; in this part we will be concerned mainly with sales credit. *Sales credit* is credit used to acquire goods and services and pay for them at a later time. When sales credit is used specifically to acquire services such as those of a doctor or plumber, it may be called *service credit.*

Installment credit is the plan by which one can pay back a debt in a number of payments. For example, a home loan which is paid back in monthly payments is installment credit. Paying for a car or stereo in a series of payments is installment credit. If you agree to pay back a loan or pay for a purchase in only one payment, this is *noninstallment credit.*

Sales credit can be either installment or noninstallment. Perhaps the most familiar type of sales credit is that used to buy goods on a noninstallment basis. This usually takes the form of a charge account. With a charge account, a customer buys on credit during a month or other specified period of time and is expected to pay for his purchases in full at the end of the time period. If he does not pay in full, he may be assessed a finance charge. A *finance charge* covers the merchant's cost of handling a particular account.

There are many varieties of noninstallment sales credit plans. Some of the most common plans are: (1) open charge accounts, (2) budget accounts, (3) revolving charge accounts, (4) travel and entertainment plans, (5) bank credit card plans, and (6) teenage accounts.

OPEN ACCOUNTS

With an *open charge account,* the seller agrees to let the buyer purchase what he wants during the "open" period and expects payment in full at the end of the period. The open period is usually a month, but it could also be from one payday to the next or until the end of the harvest season or some other similar period. Sometimes the seller sets a limit on the total amount that may be charged during a given period. Open accounts are used mostly for everyday needs such as food, clothing, and gasoline.

Some merchants still write out a sales ticket for each purchase and keep these sales tickets in the customer's file. But most merchants use *credit cards* to identify customers who have valid accounts. Credit cards, like those in Illustration 19-1, are identification cards. They show that the customer is one who pays his

Illus. 19-1. Credit cards identify customers who have credit accounts. Some persons carry many different credit cards.

debts and is entitled to charge his purchase. Sometimes the salesperson will call the credit office when a credit card is presented. This is to make sure that the customer is not charging goods in excess of the credit limit which he and the merchant may have agreed upon.

BUDGET ACCOUNT PLANS

Some merchants offer *budget plans* which are similar to open charge accounts but spread payments over several months. One type of budget plan is the *90-day* or *3-pay plan.* Under this plan, the customer charges an item and pays for it in equal payments over a period of three months. There is usually no finance charge if payments are made on time. A few merchants also offer 60-day plans of a similar nature.

In another type of budget plan, an estimate is made of how much the customer will buy during a certain period of time, such as a year, and payments are spread over a given number of months. For example, a homeowner may arrange with a fuel oil company to pay a given amount each month over a year's time for all the fuel delivered during that period.

Many customers like budget plans because they spread the cost of large purchases over several months and also avoid high finance charges. Such a plan helps the customer average his monthly expenses. Many merchants like budget plans because they encourage large purchases which the customer might postpone if he had to pay interest on an installment purchase.

REVOLVING CHARGE ACCOUNTS

The *revolving charge account* has become very popular in recent years. It is like an open account in some ways but also has some added features. Any purchase can be charged, usually with a limit on the total amount that can be owed to the merchant at one time. A payment is due once a month, but the entire amount owed need not be paid at one time. An interest charge is added to the customer's bill if it is not paid in full at the end of the month. This charge is a percentage of the unpaid balance, which is the amount owed on the date the customer is billed. Interest charges are often as much as $1\frac{1}{2}\%$ per month.

Revolving accounts are convenient, but they can tempt the customer to overbuy. When a customer continually charges low-priced, frequently purchased items, the revolving account can become expensive. Also, many customers never pay the amount in full. They remain always in debt to the seller.

BANK CARD PLANS

Central bank credit card plans have also become very popular in recent years. With such a plan, a bank or group of banks sets up the plan and issues credit cards to individuals whose credit ratings meet the banks' standards. Such a credit card, in effect, guarantees that the credit rating of the cardholder is good. Then the banks make agreements with various merchants so that they will accept the customer's credit card.

Briefly, here is how a bank card plan works. A customer makes a purchase using his credit card, and a credit sales ticket or sales draft is prepared. The merchant collects all sales drafts he issues during a day or other time period and forwards them to the bank. At this point, two things happen.

First, the bank charges each customer's account with his purchases and bills the customer once a month for all purchases made during the month. The customer usually does not pay a finance charge if he pays his bill in full. However, if he pays only part of his bill, he pays interest on the unpaid balance.

Second, the bank totals all the sales drafts from each merchant and pays him the amount of his sales less the amount of a fee. This fee is usually about 4%. Thus, if a merchant submits sales drafts totaling $1,000, he gets back $1,000 less 4% ($40) or $960. This discount or fee covers the bank's expenses of processing the sales drafts, billing and collecting from customers, and losing on uncollectible accounts. The bank is doing the work which the firm otherwise would have its own credit department do.

The bank card plans have found much favor with merchants, especially small ones, because they provide prospective customers who are judged to be good credit risks. Also, they relieve merchants of much of the trouble and expense of granting credit. Customers like such a plan because the bank card is valid at so many businesses and because they receive only one bill rather than many.

BANKAMERICARD DIRECT INQUIRIES TO 7584634

TO PAY YOUR ACCOUNT IN INSTALLMENTS / IN FULL

MINIMUM PAYMENT DUE			NEW BALANCE
PAST DUE	CURRENT DUE	MINIMUM PAYMENT	
.00	10.00	10.00	147.30

STATEMENT DATE 04-03-71 * DATE PAYMENT DUE 04-28-71

445-123-456-789 AMOUNT PAID ________
ACCOUNT NUMBER

PLEASE NOTE ANY CHANGE OF ADDRESS

Mr. John E. Doe
456 Main Street
Anytown, U.S.A. 40001

® SERVICE MARKS OWNED AND LICENSED BY BANKAMERICA SERVICE CORPORATION © BANKAMERICARD SERVICE CORPORATION (2-62) (6-69)

PLEASE RETURN THIS PORTION AND CHECK, PAYABLE TO ABOVE NAMED BANK

BANK REFERENCE	DATE	DESCRIPTION	PURCHASES AND ADVANCES	PAYMENTS AND CREDITS
16201	3-12	Friendly Inn	25.60	
03426	3-16	Payment		40.45
12701	3-17	Fly Away Airlines	65.20	
17206	3-27	Golden Gourmet Restaurant	20.50	
46501	3-28	ABC Dept. Store	36.00	

CREDIT LIMIT		PREVIOUS BALANCE	PAYMENTS	CREDITS	FINANCE CHARGE	PURCHASES AND ADVANCES		NEW BALANCE
TOTAL	UNUSED					NO.	AMOUNT	
500	353	40.45	40.45	.00	.00	4	147.30	147.30

ACCOUNT NUMBER	TIME BALANCE	STATEMENT DATE	* DATE PAYMENT DUE	ANNUAL PERCENTAGE RATE	MINIMUM PAYMENT
445-123-456-789	.00	04-03-71	04-28-71	.00	10.00

Applicable rates used to compute your **Finance Charge**

PURCHASES		CASH ADVANCES
$0 - $600.	OVER $600.	
1.50(18.00)	1.00(12.00)	1.25(15.00)

PERIODIC RATE **(ANNUAL PERCENTAGE RATE)**
*Payment in full of New Balance must be made by Date Payment Due to avoid additional **Finance Charges.**

NOTICE: See Reverse Side For Important Information

The Fifth Third Bank, Cincinnati, Ohio

Illus. 19-2. This is the statement received monthly by persons taking part in one bank card plan. Note the kinds of information it contains. The two largest and best-known bank card plans are Master Charge and BankAmericard.

TRAVEL AND ENTERTAINMENT CARD PLANS

Travel and entertainment card plans are central charge plans, like bank card plans. But in a T&E plan, an independent firm performs the functions that a bank performs in a bank card plan. The T&E plans are used to buy such services as lodging in hotels and motels, meals, and tickets to types of entertainment. Examples of nationally known T&E cards are Diners' Club, Carte Blanche, and American Express. A person who holds a T&E card pays an annual fee for the privilege of using the card. His purchases are billed like those of the bank card plans.

Travelers especially like the T&E cards because they do not have to carry much cash with them; the cards are good at many different businesses in all parts of the country. Firms who take part in T&E plans often find that their sales increase. They are able to attract more customers, and customers will often buy more with a T&E card than they might buy if they had to pay cash.

TEENAGE ACCOUNTS

As the teenage population has grown, teenagers have come to have more and more buying power in the marketplace. Some merchants today are granting credit to teenagers. Teenage accounts usually have a limit on the amount which can be charged during a given month. Generally the parent must agree to stand behind the debt, and sometimes the parent must also have an account with the firm granting the credit. But the teenager has his own credit card and can buy an item without his parents' permission.

Teenage accounts give the teenager freedom in buying. But he needs to learn to use this privilege wisely. This is especially true since it is often his first venture onto the credit scene.

INSTALLMENT SALES CREDIT

The kinds of sales credit you have been reading about up to this point represent short-term credit. Installment sales credit is usually long-term. This may be more than six months and often is up to 36 months. With installment credit, the buyer repays his debt in a series of payments, usually of equal size. Installment credit requires that the buyer sign a sales contract. This states the conditions of the sale, the payment period, and the interest or finance charges.

An installment credit sale differs from a charge account sale in the following ways:

1. The buyer must sign a written agreement covering the terms of the purchase.
2. The buyer receives the goods at the time he buys but usually does not obtain title to them until all payments have been made.
3. A *down payment*—a payment of part of the purchase price— is usually made at the time of the purchase.

4. The amount that remains unpaid is in a sense a loan from the merchant who sold the goods.
5. Regular payments must be made at stated times, usually weekly or monthly. For example, if a total of $60 is to be repaid in 12 monthly installments, $5 is paid at the end of each of 12 months.
6. The merchant has the right to take back the goods if payments are not made according to the agreement.
7. In some installment contracts, all payments come due at once if only one payment is missed.

Developing Your Business Vocabulary

The following italicized terms should become part of your business vocabulary. For each numbered statement, find the italicized term that has the same meaning.

budget plan	*90-day or 3-pay plan*
credit card	*noninstallment credit*
down payment	*open charge account*
finance charge	*revolving charge account*
installment credit	*sales credit*
loan credit	*service credit*

1. Credit that is used to borrow money.
2. Credit that is used to acquire goods and services and pay for them at a later time.
3. Sales credit that is used to acquire services.
4. A type of credit in which a debt is repaid in a series of payments.
5. A type of credit in which a debt is repaid in one payment.
6. The charge that covers a merchant's cost of handling a particular credit account.
7. A credit plan in which a customer may charge a purchase at any time but must pay the amount owed in full at the end of a specified period.
8. A card which identifies a person and gives him the privilege of obtaining goods and services on credit.
9. A credit plan which is similar to an open charge account but spreads payment over a few months.
10. A type of budget plan in which a customer makes a purchase and pays for it in equal payments over a period of three months.
11. A credit plan in which purchases can be charged at any time and at least part of the debt must be paid each month.
12. Part of the purchase price of an item, paid at the time of buying.

Checking Your Understanding

1. What are two basic ways of classifying consumer credit?
2. How does an open account plan differ from a budget plan? What items are most often purchased on an open account plan?
3. Explain how a credit card is used.
4. Describe two types of budget plans. Why do merchants and customers like budget plans?
5. How does a revolving charge account differ from an open account?
6. What are the dangers for the customer in a revolving charge account plan?
7. Describe briefly how a bank credit card plan works. What are the two largest bank card plans?
8. Give several examples of T&E cards and describe briefly how a T&E card plan works.
9. Why is it important that teenagers learn how to buy wisely before using teenage charge accounts?
10. What are the main differences between a charge account sale and an installment credit sale?

Applying What You Have Learned

1. Different people have different attitudes toward the use of sales credit. Expressions of different attitudes are found in the statements below. Which of these attitudes most nearly matches yours? Tell why. Then explain why you do not agree with the others.

   (a) "If I can't pay cash, I know I can't afford it; and I won't buy it."
   (b) "I buy on credit only those things for which I can pay within one month."
   (c) "I pay cash for all small items and use credit mostly to buy durable and expensive items."
   (d) "I buy everything I possibly can on credit in order to live a fuller life."

2. Clip from your local newspaper at least four advertisements, each describing a different kind of sales credit plan. Be prepared to explain briefly how each of the plans operates.
3. Why are the bank credit cards, such as Master Charge and Bank-Americard, sometimes called "universal credit cards"?
4. Scotty Wood operates a small neighborhood clothing store and thinks he knows his customers well. They are mostly hourly-paid factory workers who buy for themselves and their families. He says that it does not make any difference what kind of credit he gives since all his customers want is to buy now and pay later when they

get their weekly checks or Christmas bonuses. (a) Is Scotty right in thinking that customers do not care about what type of credit they are granted? Explain. (b) Assume that you are a credit consultant. Tell Scotty which of the credit plans discussed in this part would appeal most to Scotty's customers.

5. Prepare three lists of reasons concerning the value of teenage credit plans: (a) reasons why the teenager might think they are valuable; (b) reasons why parents might be concerned about the plans; and (c) reasons why merchants might like or dislike such plans.

Solving Business Problems

1. From his first full-time job, Art Blair had saved enough money to buy a watch. He saw an advertisement of a watch selling for $16.45 and a band selling for $5.50. After examining the watch and band, he thought them quite satisfactory. The salesman told him that his credit was good and encouraged him to buy a better watch for $32.99 and a band for $6.52. Art bought both of them.

   (a) How much more did Art spend than he had originally intended?
   (b) What percent more?

2. Julie and Rick Piper decided to buy their mother some glassware for her birthday. The pieces they decided upon cost $28.75. They were able to make a down payment of $6, and the merchant agreed to hold the glassware for them if they would pay $1.50 a week until it was paid for.

   (a) After they made the down payment, what additional amount was owed?
   (b) How many weeks were required to pay for the glassware?
   (c) What was the amount of the last payment?

3. In one day an appliance dealer sold the following five items to five different customers:

Item	Installment Price	Down Payment
Television set	$205.00	$45
Washing machine	276.00	60
Radio	46.00	2
Record player	42.80	None
Electric mixer	27.20	None

   (a) What was the balance owed by each customer?
   (b) How much was each payment if each item was to be paid for in 8 equal payments?

4. John and Helen Franklin have an open account at Holmes' Department Store. Payments are due by the 20th of each month, and a 1½% finance charge is made on the balance of any past-due account. In a recent month, the Franklins made the following purchases: 2 men's sport shirts, $5.95 each; one pair of children's shoes, $10.95; and costume jewelry, $1.15.

How much will the Franklins save if they pay the total amount owed at the time it is due?

Enriching Your Business Understanding

1. Businesses often give special names to their credit plans in order to attract customers. One department store, for example, may call its revolving charge account plan a Basic Charge Account plan. Another store may give another name to its revolving charge account plan. Find two businesses in your community which offer both open accounts and revolving charge accounts. (a) What names do each of these businesses give to their open accounts and revolving accounts? (b) How do the plans of the two businesses differ?
2. Norm Stekatee manages a restaurant, and the owner has asked for his advice about whether they should join a central bank credit plan to attract more customers.

    (a) What might be the advantages of the plan for the restaurant?
    (b) If the restaurant joins the plan, what services will the plan probably provide?
    (c) If the restaurant must pay in fees 1.5% of its billings of $125,000, how much will it cost to belong to the plan?
3. Some firms mail credit cards to people who did not request them.

    (a) If you keep unsolicited credit cards but do not intend to use them, are you liable for purchases made with them?
    (b) If you keep them, are you liable for purchases if they are lost or stolen and used by someone else?
    (c) If you do not want the cards, how can you protect yourself from liability?
4. Before revolving charge account plans became widely offered, layaway plans were often used by customers.

    (a) What is the layaway plan?
    (b) Is the layaway plan still used by stores in your community?
    (c) What are the advantages of such a plan for the customer?
    (d) How does easy credit affect the customer's willingness to put an item in storage and wait to use it until it is paid for?

PART 20

Borrowing In Order To Buy

On the late, late show you may have seen a movie melodrama in which the villain waited at the door of a poor widow's house, ready to seize her property if she failed to repay a loan. As the seconds ticked away, the hero, carrying the money, was fighting all kinds of obstacles to get there in time.

Borrowing money may not often have the hazards of the melodrama. Borrowing, though, does require repayment and that often is difficult for the borrower. But regardless of the hardships that may be caused by the necessary paying of bills, people do borrow for many purposes. Individuals borrow money to pay for houses, cars, furniture, hospital bills, college educations, and many other things. A retail merchant may borrow to buy a larger stock of merchandise, add a new department to his store, or buy new furniture or equipment. A manufacturer may borrow to buy auto-mated equipment to increase production.

But why not buy on credit instead of borrowing? Perhaps the person from whom a customer wants to buy sells only for cash. Or if he does give credit, he might not give it to that customer because he does not know him or is unsure of the customer's ability to repay him. Also, the cost of borrowing may sometimes be less than the cost of sales credit.

WHERE LOANS MAY BE OBTAINED

Money can be borrowed from a number of different sources. Banks, insurance companies, credit unions, savings and loan associations, and consumer finance companies are some of these sources. These organizations and others make a business of lending money. Lending agencies earn a profit by requiring borrowers to pay interest or other charges for this service.

Commercial banks usually do a large business in consumer and business loans. Investment banks also help businesses with their borrowing needs. As you have learned, banks make loans to earn money to pay interest to their depositors and make a profit for themselves. For consumers, banks are a good source of loans for the purchase of cars and other durable goods. Bank lending requirements are usually very strict, but bank loans can be one of the least expensive means of borrowing.

The funds of a *savings and loan association* or *building and loan association* are loaned to those who want to build or buy homes. These loans are usually paid back in regular monthly installments. It is generally possible to borrow from a savings and loan association an amount equal to three-fourths of the value of a house and lot.

A *credit union* is organized by a group of people who have a common interest, such as employees of one firm or members of a labor union. A credit union accepts deposits from its members and makes loans to them. It cannot do business with anyone who is not a member. A loan to a member may be made for any purpose that is considered to be of benefit to the borrower. Credit unions are good sources of loans because they know their customers well and are willing to help them out. Their interest charges may be somewhat lower than those of banks.

A person may also borrow from *consumer finance companies*. These companies make a business of lending small amounts of money, usually up to $1,000, without requiring the borrower to put up security. Other lending agencies often will not make small loans to persons with weak credit ratings, but consumer finance companies take the risk of making loans to such persons. For taking this risk, though, they usually charge higher interest rates than do banks or credit unions.

When a person borrows money, he is usually required to give his written promise to repay it at a certain time. This written promise is called a *promissory note* or, more briefly, a *note*. Usually a special printed form is used for notes. However, a note may be in the form of a letter or may be written on any piece of paper as long as it contains the necessary information.

Special names are given to the different parts of a note. You should study Illustration 20-1 carefully to learn these terms and their meanings.

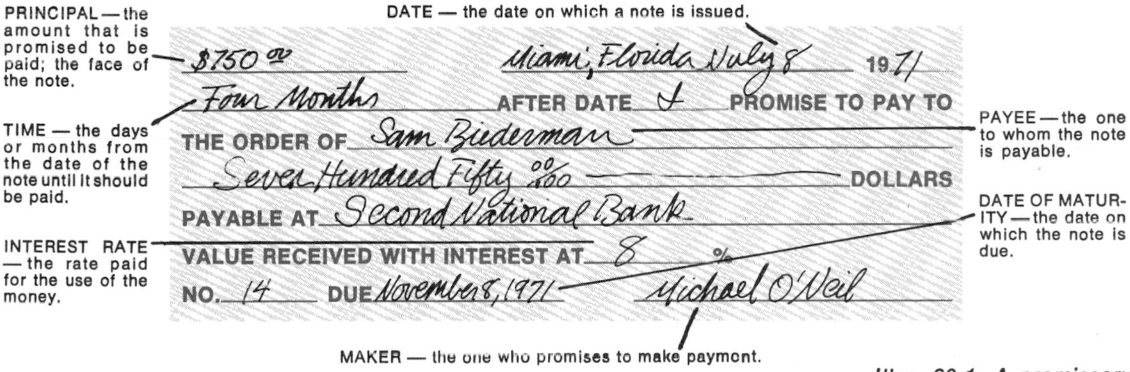

PRINCIPAL—the amount that is promised to be paid; the face of the note.

DATE — the date on which a note is issued.

$750 00   Miami, Florida July 8   19 71

Four Months   AFTER DATE ✓   PROMISE TO PAY TO

TIME — the days or months from the date of the note until it should be paid.

THE ORDER OF Sam Biederman

Seven Hundred Fifty 00/100 ———— DOLLARS

PAYABLE AT Second National Bank

INTEREST RATE — the rate paid for the use of the money.

VALUE RECEIVED WITH INTEREST AT 8 %

NO. 14   DUE November 8, 1971   Michael O'Neil

PAYEE—the one to whom the note is payable.

DATE OF MATURITY—the date on which the note is due.

MAKER — the one who promises to make payment.

Illus. 20-1. A promissory note.

A lender must have some assurance that each loan will be repaid. A person with an excellent credit rating may be able to borrow money just by signing a note. Loans made on this basis are sometimes called *signature loans*. In many cases, however, the borrower will be asked to offer some kind of *security*.

Sometimes security is in the form of property. If the borrower owns a car, a home, or other property of value, he may be able to offer it as security for a loan. In this case, he gives the lender a *mortgage*. This is a legal paper signed by the borrower and giving the lender a claim against the borrower's property in case the principal, the interest, or both are not paid. A borrower who has no property to offer as security may sign an agreement that gives the lender the right to collect part of the borrower's wages if the loan is not paid when it is due.

What if a borrower does not have a good enough credit rating or enough property to borrow money on a note for which he alone is responsible? In this case, he may get a friend or relative who

BORROWERS MAY NEED TO OFFER SECURITY

has property or a good credit rating to endorse the note. The *endorser* is responsible for payment of the note if the original borrower does not pay on the due date.

BORROWERS MUST PAY INTEREST ON MONEY BORROWED

If a person has money in a savings account, he will be paid interest on it. But if he borrows money, he must pay interest. The amount of interest paid depends on the amount borrowed, the time for which it is borrowed, and the rate of interest charged.

Most people today do not do the arithmetic needed to calculate the interest on their loans. Instead they rely on the printed interest tables used by the lending agency. The good money manager, though, should be able to determine interest rates that are at least approximately correct. This enables him to compare the cost of one loan with the cost of another and to check the interest charged to see whether it is correct.

There are two kinds of loans. One kind is the *single-payment loan* in which the borrower agrees to pay the amount of the loan, plus interest, at the end of a definite time, such as 60 or 90 days or on demand. The other kind is the *installment loan* in which the borrower repays the loan, with interest, in monthly installments extending over a period of several months or even several years. In the rest of this part, you will learn how interest is calculated on these two types of loans. Additional information on calculating interest is given in Appendix B.

CALCULATING THE INTEREST ON SINGLE-PAYMENT LOANS

In calculating interest, there are three basic things to remember: (1) the rate of interest must be expressed in the form of a fraction; (2) interest is charged for each dollar, or part of a dollar, borrowed; and (3) the interest rate is based upon one year of time.

(1) Interest is expressed as a part of a dollar. This part of a dollar, or percent, is called the rate of interest. For example, an interest rate of 6% means that 6 cents must be paid for every dollar borrowed. Before using a percent rate in a problem, you must change it to either a common or a decimal fraction. For example, a rate of interest of 6% would be changed to a common fraction of 6/100 or a decimal fraction of .06.

(2) When a rate of interest is expressed as, say, 6% per annum or per year, the borrower must pay 6 cents for each dollar

he borrows for a year. At this rate, if he borrows $1, he pays 6 cents. If he borrows $2, he pays 12 cents. If he borrows $10, he pays 60 cents, and so on. The amount of the interest charge is found by multiplying the principal by the rate of interest. Suppose that a person borrowed $100 for a year at 6% per annum. The amount of interest would be figured in this way:

$$\$100 \times .06 = \$6.00$$

(3) If a person borrows $100 at 6% for 1 year, he must pay back the $100 plus $6 interest, as you have just seen. If he borrows the same amount of money at the same rate of interest for 2 years, he pays twice as much interest, or $12. If the money is borrowed for 3 years, he pays $18, and so on. The amount of interest on $100 borrowed at 6% for 2 years would be figured in this way:

$$\$100 \times .06 \times 2 = \$12.00$$

How is interest found if money is borrowed for less than 1 year? The amount of interest is calculated on the fractional part of the year. The fraction may be expressed either in months or in days. A month is considered to be one-twelfth of a year, regardless of the number of days in the particular month. Suppose that a person had borrowed $100 at 6% for 1 month. Here is how the interest would be figured:

$$\$100 \times .06 \times 1/12 = \$.50$$

When a loan is made for a certain number of days, such as 30, 60, or 90 days, the interest is determined by days. To make the calculation easy, it is customary to use 360 days as being a year. Suppose that a person had borrowed $100 at 6% for 60 days. Here is how the interest would be figured:

$$\$100 \times .06 \times 60/360 = \$1.00$$

INTEREST MAY BE CHARGED IN ADVANCE

Sometimes interest is subtracted from the amount borrowed at the same time the loan is made. Interest paid in advance in this manner is called *discount*. The borrower does not actually receive the amount on the face of the note he signs. He receives the face of the note less the discount. The amount that he receives is called the *proceeds*. The note itself is called a discounted note.

```
$ 1,000.00                        Atlanta, Georgia _____ July 9 _____ 19_--_
-----------Sixty days--------------- AFTER DATE ----I----- PROMISE TO PAY TO
THE ORDER OF Second National Bank of Atlanta, Georgia _____
             PAYABLE AT  SECOND NATIONAL BANK
One thousand 00/100------------------------------------------ DOLLARS
AND INTEREST AT---6---% after September 7, 19--
No. 46  DUE Sept.7, 19--        Carl Blackwood
```

Illus. 20-2. A discounted note.

Suppose that on July 9 Carl Blackwood signs a note for $1,000 to be repaid in 60 days. Suppose also that the bank deducts interest at the rate of 6% from the face of the note. The discount will be $10 ($1,000 × .06 × 60/360 = $10). So the proceeds— the amount that Mr. Blackwood will receive on July 9—will be $990. Instead of deducting a discount, the lender may add the amount of the interest to the amount borrowed and have the borrower sign a note for the total.

When interest is charged in advance, the note does not call for the payment of additional interest when the note is due. But if the note is not paid on the date of maturity, interest is charged from that date. How is the date of maturity found? When the time of the note is stated in months, the date of maturity is the same day of the month as the day of the note. If a note is dated January 15 and is to run 1 month, it will be due February 15. If it were to run 2 months, it would be due March 15, and so on.

When the time of the note is given in days, the exact number of days must be counted to find the date of maturity. This can be done (1) by finding the number of days remaining in the month when the note was written and then (2) by adding days in the following months until the total equals the required number of days. Suppose that you wanted to find the date of maturity of a 90-day note dated March 3. Here is how it would be done:

March 28 (31 − 3 = 28)
April 30
May   31
June   1 (due date)
    90 days

Ordinary interest, as you have just learned, is calculated on the basis of 1 year of time. Consumer finance companies and credit unions may charge a monthly interest rate on unpaid balances. You can see that interest at 1% a month is the same as 12% for 1 year. If you borrowed $100 at 2% for 1 year at ordinary interest, you would pay back $102 ($100 principal + $2 interest) at the end of 1 year. But if you borrowed $100 at a monthly rate of 2%, at the end of 1 month you would also pay back $102. Your interest charge, however, would be at the rate of 24% a year (2% × 12 months) since you had the use of the money for only 1 month.

On installment loans, interest may be charged only on the amount that is unpaid at the end of each month. Suppose that Bill Hand borrowed $100 and agreed to repay the loan at $20 a month plus 2½% each month on the unpaid balance. Illustration 20-3 shows the schedule of payments that was set up. The interest rate on the loan was 30% a year (2½% per month × 12 months).

MONTHS	THE LOAN AND UNPAID BALANCE	INTEREST PAID ON BALANCE	MONTHLY PAYMENTS ON PRINCIPAL	TOTAL MONTHLY PAYMENTS
First	$100	$2.50	$ 20	$ 22.50
Second	80	2.00	20	22.00
Third	60	1.50	20	21.50
Fourth	40	1.00	20	21.00
Fifth	20	.50	20	20.50
Totals	——	$7.50	$100	$107.50

Illus. 20-3. The schedule of payments set up for Bill Hand's $100 loan.

When money is borrowed from a commercial bank, the amount of the interest is usually added to the amount received by the borrower, and he signs a note for the total amount. The note may then be repaid in equal monthly installments. Suppose that Sylvia Merkle borrowed $100, signed a note for $108, and agreed to repay the loan in 12 monthly installments of $9. What annual rate of interest did she pay for the use of the $100 that she actually received?

Illus. 20-4. Installment loans are made by consumer finance companies, banks, credit unions, and similar organizations.

The Sperry & Hutchinson Company

If Sylvia had borrowed $100 for one year and paid $8 interest, the interest rate would have been 8% ($8 ÷ $100 = .08, or 8%). But Sylvia repaid the loan in monthly installments, so she had the use of $100 for only one month and a smaller amount each succeeding month. For the entire year she had the use of only about one-half the original amount. As a result, the actual interest rate was about twice the rate calculated on the full amount, or about 16%.

How is the interest rate found when installments are paid over a period other than one year? Suppose that Steve Allworth borrowed $120, signed a note for $126, and agreed to repay the loan in 8 monthly installments of $15.75. If Steve had borrowed $120 for 8 months for $6 interest, the interest rate would have been found as follows:

$$\$6 \div \$120 \times 12/8 = .075, \text{ or } 7.5\%$$

But since Steve repaid the loan in installments, he had the use of only about half the original amount throughout the period. The rate would therefore be about twice the rate on a loan of $120 for the entire eight months, or about 15%.

When a loan is paid off in equal monthly payments over a period of one year, the annual rate of interest paid is about twice the stated rate of interest. Some lending agencies may add other service charges to the interest charge. When this is done, the annual rate paid for the use of money is higher than twice the stated interest rate.

Developing Your Business Vocabulary

The following italicized terms should become part of your business vocabulary. For each numbered statement, find the italicized term that has the same meaning.

consumer finance company   principal
credit union   proceeds
date of maturity   promissory note
discount   savings and loan association
endorser   security
installment loan   signature loan
maker   single-payment loan
mortgage

1. An organization that provides savings account services for its depositors and makes loans to individuals for use in buying homes.
2. A cooperative association which accepts deposits and makes small loans to its members.
3. A company which specializes in making small loans without requiring the borrower to put up security.
4. A written promise to repay borrowed money at a definite time.
5. The amount of money borrowed.
6. The date on which a note comes due and must be paid.
7. The person who signs a note and promises to make payment.
8. A small loan obtained for a short time just by signing a note.
9. Something of value pledged to insure payment of a loan.
10. A legal paper giving a lender a claim against a borrower's property in case the borrower does not repay a loan.
11. The person who endorses a note and is responsible for payment if the original borrower does not pay.
12. A loan repaid with interest at the end of a definite time.
13. A loan repaid with interest in a series of payments.
14. Interest deducted in advance from the total amount borrowed.
15. The net amount of money a borrower receives after the discount is subtracted from the principal.

Checking Your Understanding

1. Mention at least three different lending agencies from which individuals may borrow money. Who would be most likely to borrow from each of these agencies?
2. How do lending agencies make profits by lending money?

3. Why do lending agencies require borrowers to sign promissory notes or other forms of written promises?
4. Why do lenders of money usually require some form of security from borrowers? What types of security might be offered?
5. What three basic things must one remember in calculating interest?
6. Explain what is meant by "rate of interest."
7. Explain two methods used to calculate interest for less than one year.
8. What is the difference between "interest" and "discount"?
9. How is the date of maturity of a note found (a) when the time of the note is stated in months and (b) when the time of the note is stated in days?
10. What is the approximate annual rate that is actually paid if the stated interest rate on an installment loan to be paid in one year is 8%? 7½%? 9%? 6½%? Under what circumstances might the rates actually paid be even higher?

Applying What You Have Learned

1. Mr. and Mrs. Patterson are planning to buy a home freezer. They are undecided about whether to borrow the money to buy it now or whether to save the necessary money to buy it next year for cash. What are some things they should consider before deciding?
2. Glenn Malloy owned real estate and other property worth $50,000. He wanted to borrow $1,000 from his bank. The bank was willing to lend him the money and requested him to sign a note. He resented this request because he felt that his oral promise to pay should be enough. Explain why his note was requested.
3. Do you feel that offering future wages as security for a loan is a wise policy? Why? Under what conditions might this be necessary?
4. Vince Patrice wants to borrow $300. If Paul Manious endorses a note signed by Mr. Patrice, Mr. Patrice will be able to borrow this amount from his bank. Assume that Mr. Manious has $300 that he could lend to Mr. Patrice. If you were Mr. Manious, would you prefer to endorse Mr. Patrice's note or to lend him the money? Why?
5. Find the date of maturity for each of the following notes:

Date of Note	Time To Run
March 15	4 months
May 26	3 months
July 31	5 months
April 30	30 days
October 5	45 days
November 2	120 days

6. Mr. Stauber can borrow $100 at 12% for 1 year and repay the principal and the interest at the end of the year; or he can borrow $100 and repay it in 12 monthly payments of $9.50.

   (a) Under what circumstances might he prefer the first plan?
   (b) Under what circumstances might he prefer the second plan?
   (c) How much will each of these loans cost?
   (d) What rate of interest will he pay under the second plan?

7. Mr. Eugene Emerson bought a new car for $3,400. He offered his used car as a trade-in and received $1,400 for it. The $2,000 balance was financed by an installment loan company which charged him 18% interest. Why would Mr. Emerson be willing to pay 18% on borrowed money when the local lending agencies charged rates as follows: installment loan department of a bank, 10%; regular bank loan, 6%; credit union, 12%?

8. Bill Sanker is thinking seriously about attending a technical institute for two years after he finishes high school in order to become a radio and TV repairman. Since he does not have the money now, he is considering two plans to obtain the money to go to school. He could borrow the needed money, or he could work for a few years until he had saved enough money to pay for his training.

   (a) What are some advantages and disadvantages of borrowing the money?
   (b) What may happen if he takes a job in order to earn the needed money?
   (c) Which plan would you recommend?

Solving Business Problems

1. Write four notes, using the information given below and on page 250. In each case, use the current year as part of the date.

   (a) Maker, B.R. Doellman, of Keokuk, Iowa. Payee, Keokuk State Bank. Date, July 3. Time, 2 months. Principal, $275. Interest rate, 7%. Payable at the Keokuk State Bank. No. 5.
   (b) Clement P. Mehring, of Middletown, Ohio, borrowed $750 from Robert Schearer. He gave Mr. Schearer a 60-day note for this amount. The note (No. 13) was dated March 15, bore interest at 12%, and was payable at the First National Bank.
   (c) Maker, Nora Yeager, of Concord, New Hampshire. Payee, Lawrence and Lawrence, Inc. Date, October 3. Time, one year. Principal, $424.85. Interest rate, 8%. No. 8. Where the note was payable was not shown.

(d) On May 16 Don Bassarab discounted his $600 note at 7% at the Citizens National Bank, Dallas, Texas. The time of the note (No. 16) was 30 days. The note was payable at the bank. If the note was not paid at maturity, interest after that date was to be at the rate of 9%.

2. Calculate the interest charge on each of the following notes:

	Face of Note	Interest Rate	Time to Run
(a)	$225	8%	1 year
(b)	$650	6%	3 years
(c)	$240	8%	3 months
(d)	$520	7%	5 months
(e)	$460	9%	60 days
(f)	$720	6½%	90 days

3. The schedule of payments made by Bill Hand on a $100 loan, with interest of 2½% a month on the unpaid balance, is shown on page 245. Assume that Mr. Hand was required to pay 3% a month on the unpaid balance.

(a) Calculate the monthly interest charge and the total payment made each month.
(b) What total amount would Mr. Hand have paid at this rate?
(c) What annual rate of interest would he have paid?

4. A consumer finance company advertised loans at the rates shown below.

Cash You Get	Monthly Payments for		
	18 Months	12 Months	6 Months
$ 100	....	$ 9.75	$ 17.95
200	$13.44	19.01	35.80
300	20.11	28.46	53.65
500	32.71	46.65	88.54
750	47.86	68.76	131.56
1,000	62.85	90.72	174.40

(a) What rate of interest was charged by this company on a loan of $100 payable in 6 monthly payments?
(b) What rate of interest was charged on a loan of $200 payable in 12 monthly payments?
(c) What rate of interest was charged on a loan of $1,000 payable in 18 monthly payments?

5. Before borrowing $200, Lloyd Brock visited a small loan company and the small loan department of a commercial bank. At the small

loan company he found that he could borrow the $200 if he agreed to sign a note and pay back the balance in 6 equal monthly installments of $36.25. At the commercial bank, he could secure the money by signing a note for $208 and repaying the balance in 6 equal monthly payments.

(a) What would be the cost of the loan at the small loan company?
(b) What annual rate of interest would be paid if Mr. Brock borrowed at the small loan company?
(c) What would be the cost of the loan at the commercial bank?
(d) What annual rate of interest would be paid if Mr. Brock borrowed at the commercial bank?

Enriching Your Business Understanding

1. People borrow money for many different reasons. Some borrow money to consolidate their debts.

   (a) What is meant by "consolidating debts"?
   (b) Is there any advantage in consolidating debts and making a single monthly payment on a single loan?
   (c) How might consolidating debts reduce the amount of each payment? Does this mean that the borrower would be saving money?

2. In one community, the cost of loans from different lending agencies was: credit union, 1% per month; small loan department of a bank, 9%; consumer finance company, 2½% per month; and regular bank loan, 6%.

   (a) Which of these is the most expensive loan? The least expensive?
   (b) How can a company remain in business if it charges a much higher interest rate than another? Explain.
   (c) How does the amount of interest a person can secure on savings or investments compare with the interest paid on money that is borrowed?

3. At some time or other, people will come to you and ask to borrow money. Perhaps they have already done so. These borrowers may be good friends.

   (a) How can you be reasonably sure that the money you lend to others will be paid back to you?
   (b) Would your attitude toward lending the money be any different if the borrower is a close friend or merely an acquaintance? Explain.

4. In many cities there are businesses known as pawnshops. They lend money on goods left with them as security. They also sell goods which they have bought from their customers. Some people believe that most pawnshop loans are not really loans and that these firms charge extremely high rates of interest. Make a report on how a pawnshop operates.

5. Mr. Gregory borrowed $500 from his bank, signing a note promising to pay the face amount plus 6% interest at the end of 90 days. At the end of 90 days, Mr. Gregory explained to the loan clerk that he could pay only $300. The loan clerk accepted the $300, plus interest, and asked Mr. Gregory to sign another 90-day note for $200. The $500 note was stamped "Paid" and returned to Mr. Gregory.

   (a) Explain the meaning of the word "Paid" as stamped on the $500 note.
   (b) Since Mr. Gregory was unable to fulfill his contract, why was the bank willing to accept $300 in part payment?
   (c) Is this good business from the point of view of the bank? From Mr. Gregory's point of view?
   (d) Under what circumstances might the bank not be willing to accept another note as part payment? If the bank did not accept the note, how might it collect the remaining $200?

6. The federal government supports a plan by which college students can borrow money to finance their educations. Some state governments also have such a plan, and some banks offer educational loans. Write a report on sources of loans to finance education beyond high school. Give information about costs of such loans, repayment rules, and eligibility for the loans.

PART 21
Buying on Installments

Only "$9 down—up to 20 months to pay!" "$12 down, balance on easy payment plan!" "No money down—name your own monthly terms!" Pick up almost any newspaper, and you are likely to see advertising statements such as these. They encourage you to buy now and to pay for purchases over a period of weeks, months, or even years. Buying in this way is known as buying on the installment plan, or *installment buying*.

Consumers usually buy on the installment plan those items that are expensive and quite durable: cars, furniture, TV sets, and appliances, for example. But jewelry, clothing, and almost all types of merchandise except food are sometimes bought on the installment plan. In department stores that offer installment buying privileges, almost one-fourth of the merchandise sold is sold on the installment plan.

Installment credit, as you learned in Part 19, is the paying back of a debt in a number of payments. Borrowing money and repaying the loan in installments is one form of installment credit. When a person borrows money in the manner explained in Part 20, he actually receives the cash from the lending agency. He takes the cash to the seller to buy what he wants, or he uses it to pay his bills.

THE TWO TYPES OF INSTALLMENT CREDIT

Installment buying is also a type of installment credit. The difference is that the seller provides the credit; the customer does not pay the seller for his purchase by getting a loan somewhere else. With installment buying, the customer goes to a merchant and buys the article he wants. He signs a contract which requires him to make periodic payments to the seller.

YOUR COSTS FOR BUYING ON INSTALLMENTS

Installment purchases cost more than cash purchases because the seller is a lender who has his money tied up for some time. He has the expense of collecting money in small amounts and of recording payments. Sometimes he loses money because debts cannot be collected. He is entitled to collect interest on the money that he has, in effect, loaned to his customers.

You should know how much extra you are paying for the privilege of buying on installments. This advertisement appeared in a newspaper: "Deluxe power mower, $104.95. No down payment. Pay only $9 a month." Some important information was missing: (1) the number of months over which payments will be made, and (2) the total amount to be paid.

Different stores use different plans for quoting prices. Some quote only the cash price; some quote only the credit price; others may quote both the cash price and the credit price. Before you decide to buy on the installment plan, you should find out for yourself how much it will cost you. Stated prices, even if they include all charges, are not always the best guide for making a buying decision. For example, one dealer may advertise a rate of 8% and include other things such as insurance or free servicing for a year. Another dealer may advertise a rate of 6% but include no such services.

Whatever the particular installment plan may be, you should know whether you are paying 5% or 50% for the use of the seller's money. If the extra cost is too high, the purchase should be made elsewhere or on some other credit plan.

FINDING THE COST OF BUYING ON INSTALLMENTS

When you buy on the installment plan, you are really borrowing money. You will continue to use borrowed money until the last installment has been paid. The rate of interest that you are paying can be found in much the same way that the amount of interest on installment loans was found in Part 20.

Suppose that Ted Hammond wanted to buy a TV set from the Uptown Appliance Shop. The cash price was $184. He did not have this much money, but he learned that he could buy the TV set on the installment plan for $204 if he made a down payment of $24 and paid $18 a month for 10 months. The cost of buying on the installment plan would thus be $20 ($204 — $184). This cost seemed reasonable for the privilege of paying for the TV set over a period of 10 months, but Mr. Hammond wanted to know what rate of interest he was paying. If he had borrowed $160 for 10 months for $20 interest (the cost of buying on the installment plan), the interest rate would have been found as follows:

$$\$20 \div \$160 \times 12/10 = .15, \text{ or } 15\%$$

But since he made a payment each month, he had the use of only about half the original amount throughout the period. The rate would therefore be about twice the rate on a loan of $160 for the entire ten months, or 30%.

The cost of $20 for buying on installments might have seemed reasonable at first, but Mr. Hammond was paying interest at the rate of 30% a year. This rate is much more than a person could ordinarily earn on any money he could invest, so it might have been wise for Mr. Hammond to defer the purchase until he had saved enough money to pay cash for the TV set.

A person buying on installments is required to sign an agreement known as an *installment contract*. Usually the contract is *conditional*. This means that the buyer can take possession of the article and use it. But legally it still belongs to the seller, and he can *repossess* it (take it back) if payments are not made promptly. The buyer usually is responsible for keeping the article in good repair and insuring it against damage or theft.

STUDY THE CONTRACT BEFORE SIGNING

In a typical installment purchase, Michael E. Hodges bought a used car for $1,995. He traded in his old car, for which he received an allowance of $900, and made a down payment of $200. He also signed an installment contract calling for regular monthly payments of $41.50 for 24 months. The charge for financing the purchase of the car was $93.50. The interest rate, found by the method explained on page 246, was about 10% per year.

Most automobile dealers do not themselves grant credit to finance all the cars they sell. They arrange to have credit granted by a bank or a sales finance company of the customer's choice. The customer then makes his monthly payments to the bank or finance company, not to the dealer.

If Mr. Hodges could not make his payments according to his contract, the car might be repossessed by the finance company. Actually, only between 3% and 5% of all cars sold on the installment plan are repossessed. If an honest buyer has difficulty making his payments, most banks and reputable finance companies are willing to arrange for him to make smaller payments.

CREDIT LAWS VARY AMONG THE STATES

In the past, the legal regulation of consumer credit was left up to each state legislature. As a result, there has been a hodge-podge of laws. Maximum interest rates vary among states. In some cases, consumers have little protection against unethical businessmen. The poor and the uneducated have been led into unwise credit transactions, and they have had few means of getting fair adjustments.

In recent years, state and federal laws have been passed mainly to protect the consumer but also to protect the businessman who grants credit. In 1968 Congress passed the Truth-in-Lending Act. It affects all businesses which give credit. The law does not set maximum interest rates that can be charged or regulate the terms of installment credit contracts. This is left up to the states.

The Truth-in-Lending Act is mainly a disclosure law. This means that it is intended to improve a customer's knowledge of credit terms by requiring sellers to tell him about credit costs. This increases his ability to compare credit terms available from various sources. The two most important disclosures that the law requires businesses to make are:

1. The annual rate of interest and the annual amount of dollars of interest. It is not enough now to say something like, "Only 1½% per month."
2. The total number of dollars which must be paid as the finance charge on an installment sale.

The disclosures must appear on the installment contract that the customer signs, and he must be told this information before he signs.

FULL DISCLOSURE OF TERMS OF A CREDIT UNION LOAN
FEDERAL TRUTH-IN-LENDING LAW

MSU EMPLOYEES	CREDIT UNION	LOCATION	EAST LANSING	MICH.
			CITY	

BORROWER'S NAME	ACCOUNT NUMBER	DATE
John Doe	0000-0	4-20-71
		MONTH, DAY, AND YEAR

	← PERMITTED CHARGES →	DEDUCTIONS				
	DESCRIPTION	DESCRIPTION	DESCRIPTION			
AMOUNT OF LOAN	FF			AMOUNT FINANCED	FINANCE CHARGES TOTAL INTEREST WHEN LOAN IS PAID AS PLANNED	TOTAL PAYMENTS LOAN PLUS INTEREST
$ 1001.25	AMOUNT $ 1.25	AMOUNT $	AMOUNT $	$ 1001.25	$ 127.95	$ 1129.20

INTEREST IS CALCULATED AT AN ANNUAL PERCENTAGE RATE OF 12.8 %

| X | THIS LOAN IS SECURED BY A SECURITY AGREEMENT COVERING COLLATERAL CHECKED BELOW | SECURITY AGREEMENT WILL SECURE FUTURE OR OTHER INDEBTEDNESS, AND COVER AFTER ACQUIRED PROPERTY | ☐ THIS LOAN IS NOT SECURED BY A SECURITY AGREEMENT | P A Y M E N T | S C H E D U L E | FIRST PAYMENT IS DUE ON | 5-15-71 |

		FREQUENCY OF PAYMENTS	NUMBER OF PAYMENTS	AMOUNT OF PAYMENTS
X	CAR: MAKE Ford YEAR 1968	☒ MONTHLY	24	$ 47.05
	Household furnishings as disclosed and described by borrower on Schedule "B". Copy returned to borrower.	☐		$

| X | SAVINGS WHICH BORROWER NOW HAS OR HEREAFTER MAY HAVE IN HIS ACCOUNTS· EXCEPT, HOWEVER, SUMS IN EXCESS OF ► $ | 5.00 | MAY BE WITHDRAWN PROVIDING LOAN PAYMENTS ARE CURRENT |

THE FOLLOWING LATE CHARGES MAY BE APPLIED IF LOAN IS NOT PAID AS SCHEDULED

VOLUNTARY DEPOSIT		
I REQUEST THAT ► $	FROM THIS LOAN BE PLACED IN MY SAVINGS .	BORROWER'S INITIALS
REQUIRED DEPOSIT		
I understand that ► $	deducted from this loan and placed in my savings will be wholly applied toward payment of this loan when the balance has been reduced to the amount of said deposit, unless, at that time, I instruct the Credit Union to the contrary.	BORROWER'S INITIALS

No charge for Loan Protection Insurance (Credit Life) which is provided for eligible borrowers.

(I HAVE RECEIVED A COPY OF THIS STATEMENT)
X John Doe (SIGNATURE OF BORROWER)

Michigan State University Employees Credit Union

Illus. 21-1. This form is given to a person obtaining an automobile loan. It tells him the total amount of interest he is paying, the number of payments, and the annual interest rate.

A Uniform Consumer Credit Code has also been prepared, and states can use it as a model to enact new credit laws. The Code may result in more uniform credit laws among the states, provide better protection for consumers, and protect honest businessmen from harmful competition with unethical ones.

BE CAREFUL IN BUYING ON INSTALLMENTS

Buying on installments enables the consumer to obtain goods right away with little or no cash for a down payment. He can thus use the item while he is paying for it. In some cases this is very desirable. For example, suppose that Russell Barton has the chance to get a job as a machinist in a nearby city. The job is permanent and will pay him $16 a week more than he can earn near home. But he needs a car to get back and forth. He locates a good used car that he can buy for $900. By offering rides to other workers traveling to the same plant, he finds that their contributions pay for his gasoline and car insurance. In a little more than a year, the car will be paid for. In the meantime, his family has a car for pleasure driving.

The cautious buyer will purchase on the installment plan only durable goods which may be used for several years, such as furniture or a car. The length of time over which payments are made should be no longer than the life of the item purchased. It is very discouraging to continue making payments on an item that is of no further use.

Although installment purchases can be made with little or no down payment, the good money manager will try to make a down payment of one-half or one-third the purchase price. This gives him a feeling of immediate part ownership, and future payments will be less of a burden. The installment buyer should be especially cautious about overbuying. The careless buyer can easily find himself obligated in too many "easy payment plans."

The good money manager knows that he must fulfill his contracts. Thus, he is careful not to sign agreements that he does not fully understand. If he is not certain about what parts of a contract mean, he should have them explained to him by a lawyer or someone else who is familiar with such agreements.

Developing Your Business Vocabulary

The following italicized terms should become part of your business vocabulary. For each numbered statement, find the italicized term that has the same meaning.

conditional sales contract　　　*installment contract*
installment buying　　　*repossess*

1. Buying merchandise and promising to make weekly or monthly payments on it.
2. The written agreement signed by a customer buying on the installment plan.
3. A contract under which the ownership of the goods remains with the seller until the buyer completes all payments.
4. To take back what was sold on the installment plan if payments are not made as agreed.

Checking Your Understanding

1. What kinds of items are most often bought on the installment plan? Why are they bought on the installment plan?
2. Explain the difference between an installment loan and an installment purchase.
3. Why are the costs of buying on the installment plan more than those of paying cash?

4. Why should the buyer find out for himself the interest rate charged on purchases that he expects to make on the installment plan?
5. If you make a purchase on the installment plan, when do you receive the article purchased? When do you get ownership of the article? Explain the difference between possession and ownership.
6. What are the two main requirements of the Truth-in-Lending Act?
7. What is the Uniform Consumer Credit Code?
8. Give reasons why nondurable goods should not be purchased on the installment plan.
9. If a buyer does not understand parts of an installment contract, what should he do?

Applying What You Have Learned

1. Connie Ammerman can buy a rebuilt typewriter either by paying $80 in cash or by making a down payment of $25 and paying $5 a month for 12 months. What amount of money would she pay for buying on the installment plan?
2. Which of the following items might be wisely purchased on the installment plan? Which would you advise not buying on the installment plan? Why? (a) Vacation trip; (b) electric train; (c) car; (d) rug; (e) refrigerator; (f) man's suit; (g) pet dog; (h) TV set.
3. How may buying on the installment plan improve a buyer's credit rating? How may it harm his credit rating?
4. Tim Wells wants to buy a drum so that he can join the high school band. The cash price of the drum is $30. He has saved $10 of the money he earned from his paper route. In one store, he can pay $10 down and $2 a month for 12 months. In another store, he does not have to make a down payment but must pay $3 a month for 12 months. Which plan do you think Tim should choose?
5. Andy Rowan bought a television set from the Sparky Electric Company, paying $26.50 down and agreeing to pay the balance in 10 monthly installments of $20 each. He made two monthly payments and then neglected to make additional payments. Several days later, two men from the Easy Finance Company came to his house to take the TV set. Mr. Rowan claimed that they had no right to take the set since he had bought it from the Sparky Electric Company. Do you think it is probable that the Easy Finance Company had this right?
6. Study each of the statements below. Which statement gives you the most complete information? Explain.

   (a) $15 down, balance on easy payment plan.
   (b) No money down, pay $12 a month for 15 months.
   (c) $12 down, pay only $11 a month until paid for.

Solving Business Problems

1. Sandy Wilson bought a rug for $350. She made a down payment of $50 and agreed to make 12 monthly payments of $25 each. The rug could have been purchased for cash for $330.

   (a) How much did Miss Wilson pay for the privilege of buying on the installment plan?

   (b) What was the rate of interest paid for installment buying?

2. Tom Brumfield can buy a TV set for $260 in cash. He has, however, only $60 in cash to apply on the purchase. He is considering two plans. Under the first plan, he would make a down payment of $60 and make 15 monthly payments of $15 each. Under the second plan, he would pay cash after borrowing $200 from a small loan company and would repay the loan in 20 monthly payments of $12.20.

   (a) How much more than the cash price would he pay for the installment buying privilege under the first plan?

   (b) What annual rate of interest would he pay under the first plan?

   (c) How much more than the cash price would he pay for the installment loan under the second plan?

   (d) What annual rate of interest would he pay under the second plan?

3. A department store offers an easy-payment plan for installment purchases. Part of the payment schedule is shown below. Down payments are required for items costing more than $50.

Cash Price	Add for Easy Payments	Monthly Payments
No down payment required		
$ 30.01-$ 35.00	$ 3.50	
35.01- 40.00	4.00	
40.01- 45.00	4.50	$5.00
45.01- 50.00	5.00	
$5 down payment required		
$ 50.01-$ 55.00	$ 6.50	
55.01- 60.00	7.00	
60.01- 65.00	7.50	6.00
65.01- 70.00	8.00	
$10 down payment required		
$120.01-$130.00	$19.00	
130.01- 140.00	21.00	
140.01- 150.00	23.00	8.00
150.01- 160.00	26.00	

In one day, customers bought six articles on the installment plan. The cash price of each of the articles is shown below. In each case, the minimum down payment was made.

Article	Cash Price
Electric fan	$ 31.50
Metal kitchen cabinets	63.50
Bicycle	69.00
Record player	127.00
Bunk beds	133.00
Fiber furniture suite	160.00

For each article find:

(a) The amount to be added for the privilege of buying on the installment plan.

(b) The total price to be paid on the installment plan.

(c) The amount of the down payment.

(d) The balance owed, to be paid in installments.

(e) The number of months over which installments will have to be paid.

(f) The rate of interest to be paid for the privilege of buying on the installment plan. (Remember that in finding the interest rate, the amount that is considered to be borrowed from the merchant is the difference between the cash price and the down payment. For example, the amount borrowed in purchasing the third item is the cash price, $69, minus the down payment, $5, or $64.)

4. Jim Steffen wants very much to buy a new car. He is offered a deal in which his trade-in is worth $950 on a car priced at $3,250, including taxes and license. Interest on his new loan is $460.

(a) If Jim completes the deal, how much will he owe?

(b) If Jim drives his new car 30,000 miles and gets $1,200 when he trades again, how much will he have paid for each mile driven?

(c) If Jim pays off his loan in 24 months, how much will he pay per month?

Enriching Your Business Understanding

1. It is sometimes argued that buying merchandise on the installment plan encourages people to be thrifty. It is also sometimes argued that it raises their style of living. Do you agree or disagree with these points of view? Explain your answer.

2. It has been said that we are living in an "installment age." Almost everything we buy can be purchased on the installment plan: furniture, cars, houses, TV sets, vacation trips, insurance, education, and so on. If we go too deeply into debt, we can borrow money to pay the debts, and we can pay off the loan on the installment plan.

   (a) Explain how this easy payment plan may be helpful to an individual. How may it be harmful?
   (b) How may the easy payment plan be helpful to businesses? Under what circumstances may offering easy payment plans be harmful to business?

3. Every person should understand any installment contract he signs. If a person signs a contract, he cannot later avoid meeting its terms by saying that he did not understand the terms. Below are five statements from an installment contract. Study each of the statements and be prepared to explain its meaning in your own words.

   (a) "Title to said property shall not pass to purchaser until said amount is fully paid in cash."
   (b) "In case of any default in the performance of the terms hereof, the seller shall have the right to declare the full unpaid amount immediately due and payable."
   (c) "Purchaser shall not transfer any interest in this contract or said property."
   (d) "If seller deems the property in danger of misuse or confiscation, seller or any officer of the law may take immediate possession of said property."
   (e) "No warranties, expressed or implied, representations, promises, or statements have been made by the seller unless endorsed hereon in writing."

4. Every person needs to be cautious about the contracts he signs, as well as to be sure that he understands all of the contract terms. Now that you have learned something about installment credit, prepare a checklist of items to be looked for by anyone who plans to sign an installment contract.

PART 22
Writing Your Credit Record

Some people are very uneasy about applying for credit. Some feel insecure or embarrassed. Some are afraid of the questions that may be asked and dislike revealing personal information to a credit interviewer. Some feel that they are asking a favor when they ask for credit. But they should remember that credit is a necessary part of our business and economic system. A lending agency or a merchant is careful in extending credit because he wants to insure payment and prevent bad risks as much as possible. At the same time, he wants to complete the sales transaction, whether on a cash or a credit basis. Most merchants believe that their customers expect them to offer credit. They are convinced that they will be more successful if they offer credit than if they do not.

When a customer applies for credit, he should expect to give the seller information about property he owns, his income, the debts that he owes others, and his reputation for paying his debts. He should not object if the seller questions him about these facts because the seller has a right to expect repayment. The customer should give all the information needed to prove his willingness and ability to repay.

A seller probably will not ask a credit applicant whether he pays his bills promptly, but he will ask for the names of other

YOU MUST GIVE PERSONAL DATA WHEN YOU APPLY FOR CREDIT

firms from whom the applicant has bought on credit. These businesses can then be contacted to find out whether the applicant pays his bills on time.

Most credit applicants are required to fill out a special form. The seller uses the information given on this form in deciding whether the applicant should be given credit privileges. A typical application is shown in Illustration 22-1.

TO WHOM WILL SELLERS EXTEND CREDIT?

Before a seller grants credit to a prospective customer, he wants some assurance that the customer can and will pay his bills promptly. In deciding whether or not to extend credit, he may consider the three C's: character, capacity, and capital.

Character has to do with the customer's honesty and probable willingness to pay. What is his reputation for paying his bills? What is his standing in the community? If the answers to such questions are favorable, the merchant will be inclined to grant credit. How a person will pay his bills in the future can be judged to some extent by how he has paid them in the past.

Capacity has to do with the customer's ability to earn. Is his income large enough so that he can probably continue to pay his bills promptly? If his income is too small or is unsteady, it may not be wise to grant him additional credit even though he has had a good credit rating in the past. On the other hand, his income

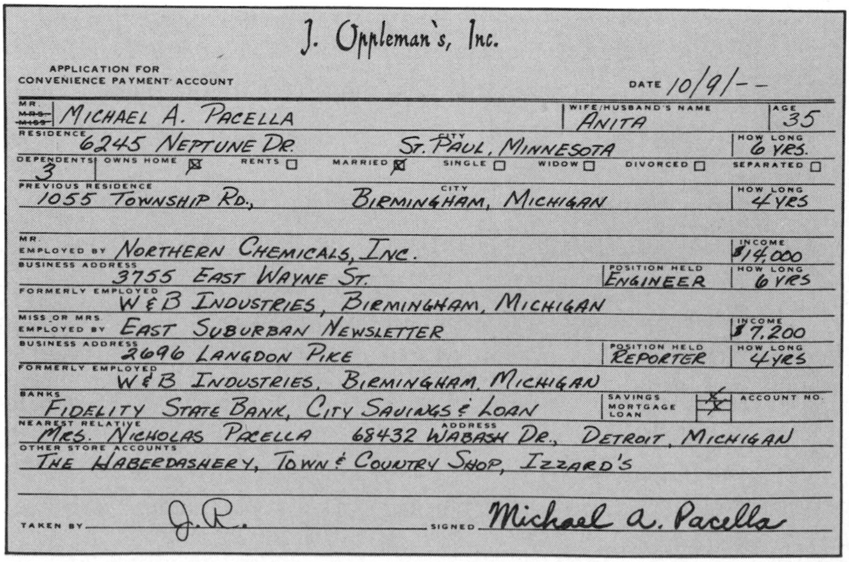
J. Oppleman's, Inc.

APPLICATION FOR CONVENIENCE PAYMENT ACCOUNT

DATE 10/9/--

MR. MICHAEL A. PACELLA — WIFE/HUSBAND'S NAME ANITA — AGE 35

RESIDENCE 6245 NEPTUNE DR. — CITY ST. PAUL, MINNESOTA — HOW LONG 6 YRS.

DEPENDENTS 3 — OWNS HOME ☒ — RENTS ☐ — MARRIED ☒ — SINGLE ☐ — WIDOW ☐ — DIVORCED ☐ — SEPARATED ☐

PREVIOUS RESIDENCE 1055 TOWNSHIP RD., — CITY BIRMINGHAM, MICHIGAN — HOW LONG 4 YRS

MR. EMPLOYED BY NORTHERN CHEMICALS, INC. — INCOME $14,000

BUSINESS ADDRESS 3755 EAST WAYNE ST. — POSITION HELD ENGINEER — HOW LONG 6 YRS

FORMERLY EMPLOYED W & B INDUSTRIES, BIRMINGHAM, MICHIGAN

MISS OR MRS. EMPLOYED BY EAST SUBURBAN NEWSLETTER — INCOME $7,200

BUSINESS ADDRESS 2696 LANGDON PIKE — POSITION HELD REPORTER — HOW LONG 4 YRS

FORMERLY EMPLOYED W & B INDUSTRIES, BIRMINGHAM, MICHIGAN

BANKS FIDELITY STATE BANK, CITY SAVINGS & LOAN — SAVINGS ☒ MORTGAGE LOAN ☒ — ACCOUNT NO.

NEAREST RELATIVE MRS. NICHOLAS PACELLA — ADDRESS 68432 WABASH DR., DETROIT, MICHIGAN

OTHER STORE ACCOUNTS THE HABERDASHERY, TOWN & COUNTRY SHOP, IZZARD'S

TAKEN BY J.R. — SIGNED Michael A. Pacella

Illus. 22-1. Application for a charge account. Note the types of information that the merchant wishes before he decides to grant credit.

may be very high but he may have many debts. In this case, his ability to pay off new debts may be limited.

Capital has to do with the property the customer owns. How much is he worth? He may have nothing except his current income. Or he may have his car paid for and a large amount paid on his home. He may have a checking account, some savings, and perhaps some investments. The money and property that a person owns are his "capital." Having capital is further assurance that a person will continue to be able to pay his bills.

A reputable seller checks an applicant's credit record before he extends credit. This is especially true if he does not know the applicant or if the applicant has just moved into the community. The seller usually contacts the references given on the application form and asks what type of person the applicant is. The seller also checks to see if the applicant is employed as he says he is and to see how much he earns. The references and other data given on a credit application are very important.

Besides checking the applicant's references, the seller often checks with the local *retail credit bureau*. This organization keeps records on persons in the area who have done business on credit with local firms. A local credit bureau is usually linked with similar organizations in other communities in the same state and in other states. It can call and get an applicant's credit record from the community where he used to live. If it is asked, the credit bureau gives the seller a report on the credit applicant. The report grades the applicant as a credit risk and describes what he owes now and how his payment record has been in the past. A person's credit record is confidential. It can be given out only to legitimate businesses from which the person is seeking credit or to businesses that are considering hiring him for a job.

SELLERS CHECK THE APPLICANT'S CREDIT RECORD

When a retail merchant sells goods on credit, he makes a record of the sale on a sales ticket. He usually makes two or more copies of each sales ticket. One copy is given to the customer. The other copy or copies are kept by the merchant for billing purposes or sent to a central collection agency if he belongs to a central charge plan. When one business sells to another business—as when a wholesaler sells to a retailer—a form similar to

BUSINESS FORMS USED IN CREDIT TRANSACTIONS

THE HOBBY SHOP				
Canton, Ohio				

Sold To	MR. HARRY CALLOWAY		Date	12/14/--
Street	225 GREENFIELD DRIVE		Emp.	KATHY
City	CANTON, OHIO		How Sold	CASH-SEND

QUANTITY	DESCRIPTION	PRICE	
2	FUN FILM KITS, X495M, @ $3.98	7	96
1	PAINT-BY-NUMBER KIT, 3986J	6	98
1	ARTIST'S EASEL, RA695	15	50
	TOTAL	30	44
	TAX	1	37
	TOTAL AMOUNT OF SALE	31	81

Illus. 22-2. A sales ticket.

Invoice

MARK PUBLICATIONS, INC.

3451 BROOKHURST ROAD, ANAHEIM, CALIFORNIA 92836

Sold To	Marshall's Book Store	Date	January 15, 19--
	6801 Main Street	Our Order No.	77654
	Sausalito, California 94965	Your Order No.	13355
Terms	2/10, n/30	Shipped By	Eagle Truck Lines

25 copies	P6789	4.75	118.75
10 copies	B23972	9.50	95.00
50 copies	L52321	5.20	260.00
30 copies	R6645	2.75	82.50
			556.25

Illus. 22-3. An invoice.

Cincinnati Bell

LOCAL TELEPHONE SERVICE	6 90
LONG DISTANCE CALLS	60
TAXES	75
ADDITIONAL LOCAL CALLS	
OTHER CHARGES AND CREDITS	
DIRECTORY ADVERTISING	
BALANCE FROM LAST BILL	

PLEASE RETURN THE ENCLOSED CARD AND THIS AMOUNT ➡ 8 25

BILL IS PAYABLE UPON RECEIPT — THANK YOU
CHECKS SHOULD BE MADE PAYABLE TO "CINCINNATI BELL"
TO CALL THE COMPANY
RESIDENCE CUSTOMERS: 396-9900
BUSINESS CUSTOMERS: 421-5900
WILLIAMSTOWN OFFICE: 824-3313
HARRISON OFFICE: 634-3121

	TELEPHONE NO.
Thomas R. Bosley ———	562-6453
275 Ritchie Avenue ———	DATE OF BILL
Cincinnati, Ohio 45241	Nov 23 70

DATE	CODE	LONG DISTANCE CALLS	AMOUNT
903	1	Olean NY 716 372-5379	60
		US Tax .06 Total Excl Tax	60

LONG DISTANCE CODE
1. DIALED DIRECT
2. CREDIT CARD
3. BILL TO 3RD NUMBER
* CAN BE DIALED DIRECT

Illus. 22-4. A telephone bill.

No. **95**

Credit Memorandum

Date January 29, 19--

MARK PUBLICATIONS, INC.
3451 BROOKHURST ROAD
ANAHEIM, CALIFORNIA 92836

To   Marshall's Book Store
      6801 Main Street
      Sausalito, California 94965

YOUR ACCOUNT HAS BEEN CREDITED FOR:

50 copies Stock No. L52321 returned on our invoice of January 15   260.00

Illus. 22-5. A credit memorandum.

a sales ticket is prepared. This form is known as an *invoice.* An invoice usually contains more complete information about the sale.

The term *bill* is often used to mean the same as "invoice" or "sales ticket." But in business "bill" is used more commonly to refer to a charge for services rather than for goods. Thus, we speak of an invoice or sales ticket for merchandise and a bill for the services of a telephone company or a dentist.

Buyers sometimes return goods to the seller for credit. The term "credit" as used here refers to reductions made in the buyer's sales ticket or invoice. Goods may be returned because they were sent by mistake or because they are unsatisfactory. When a return is made, the merchant may give the customer a detailed record of the return on a form known as a *credit memorandum.* Also, if a customer has been overcharged on an invoice or a sales ticket, or if the goods have not been received in good condition, the seller may give the buyer a credit memorandum for the difference between the actual value and the amount charged.

A credit memorandum should be placed with the invoice or sales ticket for the transaction if payment has not yet been made. If payment has been made, the credit memorandum should be kept where future invoices or sales tickets will be filed. This should be done so that the amount of the credit memorandum can be subtracted from a future payment. The credit memorandum might also be presented to the seller for a cash return.

At regular intervals, usually monthly, a business sends to each credit customer a record of the transactions that he completed with the business during the billing period. This record is known as a *statement of account* or, more briefly, a *statement.* This form shows:

UNDERSTANDING MONTHLY CREDIT STATEMENTS

1. The balance that was due when the last statement was mailed.
2. The amounts charged to the customer during the month for merchandise sold to him.
3. The amounts credited to the customer during the month for payments or for merchandise returned.
4. The current balance, which is the balance from the previous statement, plus the amounts charged to the customer, less the amounts credited to the customer.

Illustration 19-2 on page 233 is an example of a statement of account.

Statements may be prepared by special bookkeeping machines or by a computer. Some statements list separately each item that was purchased. Some list only the totals purchased, paid, and owed. Merchants usually send a copy of each credit sales ticket to the customer to give him information about each purchase.

A statement serves two purposes: (1) it shows the customer how much he owes, and (2) it gives him a complete record of his transactions with the business. The customer can prove the accuracy of the statement by comparing it with his copies of invoices and sales tickets and with his record of payments and credit memorandums. If an error is discovered, it should be called to the seller's attention at once.

MAKING PAYMENTS AND KEEPING RECORDS

As soon as a customer receives a sales ticket, invoice, bill, or statement, he should examine it to make sure that it is correct. A business may by mistake charge a person for goods he did not actually buy. Or it may fail to give him credit for a payment or for goods that were returned. The date when payment is due should also be carefully noted. When payment is made, the date, the method of payment, and the check number, if a check is used, should be written on the face of the form. All such sales tickets and bills should be kept. They will be valuable in the future if any question arises as to whether or not they have been paid.

It is not enough for a person to know that he has paid an invoice or a bill. He should be able to show that payment was made. Otherwise, he may be required to make payment a second time. In studying about checks, you learned that a canceled check is valuable as evidence that payment has been made because it bears the endorsement of the payee. When a person does not pay by check, he needs some other method of showing that he has made payment.

A written form which acknowledges that payment was made is called a *receipt*. Receipts are sometimes bound in books, along with stubs like check stubs. The receipt form provides spaces for entering the number of the receipt, the date, the name of the person making payment, the amount of the payment in words, the reason for the payment, the amount in figures, and the signature of the person receiving payment. The stub is filled out to show the same information.

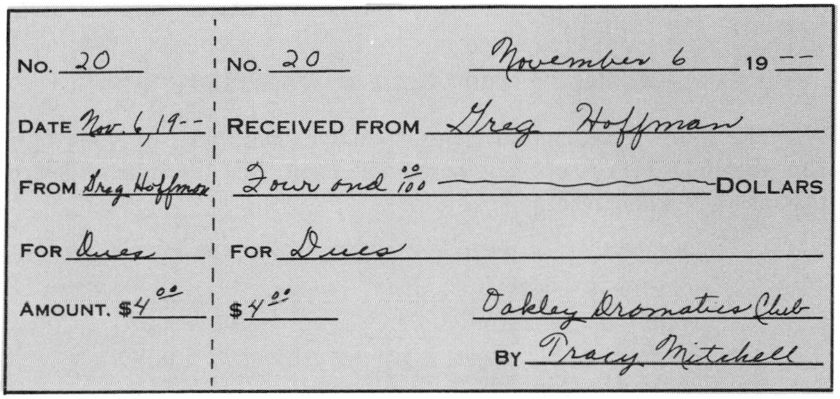
No. 20
Date Nov. 6, 19--
From Greg Hoffman
For Dues
Amount. $4.00
No. 20
November 6 19--
Received from Greg Hoffman
Four and 00/100 Dollars
For Dues
$4.00
Oakley Dramatics Club
By Tracy Mitchell

Illus. 22-6. Study this illustration to see how a receipt form and its stub are filled out.

The information recorded on a receipt stub may later be needed by the one issuing the receipt to determine whether a customer has paid and when. Each stub and receipt is numbered so that the customer's receipt can easily be compared with the stub if there is a dispute about the amount paid. Some books of receipt forms do not have stubs; in this case, a carbon copy is made when the receipt is written.

Sometimes the acknowledgement of payment is written or stamped on the invoice or statement, and the form is returned to the person making payment. And of course, there are situations when you do not need evidence that payment was made, such as when the complete transaction was made for cash and no one made a record of it. For example, if you buy your lunch in the school cafeteria, you do not need anything to show that payment was made. Cash was paid on the spot, and the cashier did not record either your name or what you bought.

Receipts, canceled checks, receipted bills, and all other forms showing that payments have been made should be kept. If a receipt is lost, the one making payment may have to pay again, since he may not be able to give evidence that the debt was paid. In all cases, a receipt should be kept until the one making payment is sure that he will never have to prove that payment was made. If a monthly statement is received and is found to be correct, there is usually no point in keeping sales tickets or receipts for the preceding months. The current statement shows the amount owed at the beginning of the month and is evidence that only that amount is to be paid.

Developing Your Business Vocabulary

The following italicized terms should become part of your business vocabulary. For each numbered statement, find the italicized term that has the same meaning.

bill	*invoice*
capacity	*receipt*
capital	*retail credit bureau*
character	*statement of account*
credit memorandum	

1. The factor in credit that has to do with a customer's honesty and probable willingness to pay.
2. The factor in credit that has to do with a customer's ability to earn.
3. The factor in credit that has to do with the property a customer owns.
4. An organization which keeps records on persons in a community who have done business on credit with local firms.
5. A form used by wholesalers and manufacturers for listing items sold to retailers.
6. A form generally used to show charges for services.
7. A form used to show the value of merchandise returned or an allowance for unsatisfactory merchandise.
8. A form sent to customers showing a complete record of business transactions for a period, such as a month.
9. A written acknowledgement that money has been received.

Checking Your Understanding

1. Is it right that some people should feel insecure or embarrassed in asking for credit? Explain.
2. What information is a credit applicant likely to be asked to supply?
3. Name the three C's of credit. Why is each one important in the decision to grant or not to grant credit?
4. If you apply for credit, whom is the seller likely to contact to determine your standing as a credit risk?
5. Examine the credit application form on page 264. Give possible reasons why each item of information was included on the form.
6. Why is more than one copy made of sales tickets? Of what value is a sales ticket to a customer and to a business?
7. What should a customer do with credit memorandums that he receives?

8. What important information is usually shown on the statement of account sent to customers?

9. How can a customer prove the accuracy of statements he receives? What should he do if he finds an error on a statement received from a merchant?

10. What information should be written on a sales ticket, bill, or other forms when they are paid? Why?

11. What evidence can a person give to prove that he has paid his debt?

Applying What You Have Learned

1. Some writers speak of the four C's of credit. They include the three mentioned in this part plus a fourth, collateral. Find the meaning of the word "collateral" as it is used in connection with credit and explain how it is used.

2. Mr. Ballinger operates a retail grocery store. One day Mr. Stark, a total stranger, approaches him and asks if he may buy a week's supply of groceries on credit. Mr. Stark explains that he has just moved into town that day, that the moving expenses took all of his cash, but that he has a good job and will be able to pay Mr. Ballinger in a week or ten days. (a) What should Mr. Ballinger do? (b) If he decides to extend credit to Mr. Stark, what precautions do you think he should take?

3. Mr. Saxon wants to open an account in the Grandin Road Department Store. He objects, however, to giving the credit manager information about such things as where he has other charge accounts, whether he owns real estate, where he works, and in which bank he maintains an account. (a) Does the credit manager have a right to ask for this information? (b) Should Mr. Saxon object?

4. Examine the sales ticket on page 266 and answer these questions:

    (a) Who is the seller?
    (b) Who is the buyer?
    (c) What is the date of the sale?
    (d) How is the salesperson identified?
    (e) Is this a cash sale or a credit sale?
    (f) What is the total amount of the sale?

5. Examine the invoice on page 266 and answer these questions:

    (a) What is the name and address of the seller?
    (b) What is the name and address of the buyer?
    (c) How is the merchandise to be shipped?
    (d) What are the terms of the sale?
    (e) What is the total amount of the sale?

6. Mary Korski, a secretary, examined her statement of account and found that two items she had returned had not been credited and that two items charged to her account had not been purchased by her. She was furious at what she thought were the store's mistakes. (a) Was it possible that the store was correct and that Mary was not? (b) What actions should Mary take to correct what she believes are errors?

7. Mrs. Leyman never saves the sales tickets listing merchandise that she buys for cash. Mrs. Dunbar saves her sales tickets for at least a week. Who is following the better business practice?

8. Below is a list of some everyday business transactions. Assuming that you are paying cash (no check) in each case, for which payments would you wish to have receipts and for which payments are receipts unimportant? Tell why in each case.

   (a) Bought 10 gallons of gasoline.
   (b) Bought a bus ticket.
   (c) Bought a newspaper.
   (d) Paid for shoe repairs.
   (e) Paid the garage bill.
   (f) Paid club dues.
   (g) Bought a sandwich at a drive-in.
   (h) Bought a ticket to a football game.
   (i) Paid the telephone bill.

9. Bring to class two or three different kinds of receipt forms received by your parents. Compare them with the forms illustrated in this part and explain how they are alike and how they are different. What is the purpose of each item appearing on the receipt forms?

Solving Business Problems

1. For the following charge sales, prepare sales tickets similar to the one illustrated on page 266. Use your initials in the space headed "Sold By" and use the current date.

   (a) Store: Sansone's, 795 Galbraith Road
       Customer: Mrs. Laura Dwyer, 1299 Cypress Drive
       Department: G (Grocery Department)
       Items Sold: 1 can frozen orange juice, 59¢; 3 quarts milk @ 28¢ a quart; 1 loaf bread, 31¢; 5 pounds potatoes, 79¢; 1 jar pickles, 48¢.
   (b) Store: M and R Variety Store, 335 West Third Street
       Customer: Mrs. Carl Dominica, 6504 Cottonwood Lane
       Department: H (Housewares)

Items Sold: 1 glass coffee maker, $5.25; 3 boxes thumbtacks @ 10¢ a box; 1 can opener, $4.95; 1 pastry board, $1.39; 1 set refrigerator dishes, $4.69; 1 dish rack, $1.79.

2. The Dyna-Con Products Company, 810 Lexington Drive, Detroit, Michigan 48236, sold the items listed below to Eagle Electric Service, 4467 Colerain Avenue, Flint, Michigan 48507. The items were purchased on terms of 2/15, n/30. Shipment was by Lancer Motor Freight.

  60 Single Pole Mercury Toggle Switches @ $.42 each
400 feet No. 10, 2-wire, Outdoor Cable @ $.22½ per foot
  16 12-inch Steel Reflectors @ $.85 each
120 Duplex Outlets @ $.44 each
   8 Water Heater Control Switches, 100 amp., @ $6.60 each
800 Solderless Connectors @ $.92½ per 100

Prepare invoice No. 763, using the form on page 266 as a guide. Use the current date.

3. As treasurer of the Anderson Athletic Club, you receive payments from members for dues, locker fees, and supplies (such as tennis balls, handballs, and baseball gloves) which are sold on credit by the club. The details of four receipts are given below. Prepare receipts and stubs similar to the one shown on page 269. Use the current date.

(a) No. 209, R. R. Cipollone, $7.50 dues for the year.
(b) No. 210, A. D. Hessler, $7.50 for dues and $3 for the locker fee for the year.
(c) No. 211, M. B. Abbinante, $4.75 for supplies.
(d) No. 212, J. J. Pearson, $7.50 for dues for the year and $5.25 for the balance owed for the purchase of supplies.

Enriching Your Business Understanding

1. "Whenever anything is bought on credit, the agreement to pay for the purchase should be placed in writing; whenever anything is bought for cash, no record of the purchase is necessary." Do you agree with the above statements? Why or why not?
2. For many years it was customary for department stores to send bills or statements to their credit customers at the end of each month. Today many stores use a "cycle billing" system. (a) What is cycle billing? (b) What are advantages and disadvantages of cycle billing to the store and to the customer?

3. One credit bureau charges a fee to provide a local business with a credit report on a potential customer. Why would a firm be willing to pay such a fee rather than do its own investigating?

4. In many communities there are firms known as credit collection agencies or as credit counselors. Make a report on collection agencies, including information on the services they perform for creditors, the fees they charge, and how they help customers who are in credit trouble.

5. Some people believe that collection agencies often try to pressure people into paying. If you were trying to collect a debt, what would you say to a person to encourage him to pay?

6. Because credit is so widely used, there is a great deal of paperwork involved in billing customers and crediting payments. Often, it seems, mistakes are made which annoy customers. Make a survey of adults you know and determine what problems they have had with errors in being billed or in not receiving credit for payments. Report on their answers and on what effect you believe these customers' attitudes would have on their feelings toward a particular merchant.

Unit 6

Economic Risks and Insurance

PART 23
Insuring Against Economic Risk

Scan the front page of today's newspaper, and you may see headlines like these: "Two Persons Injured in Downtown Auto Crash," "Fire Destroys Home of Local Family," "$700 Stolen in Service Station Robbery." The people involved in these incidents have all suffered some kind of financial loss. Every person has possessions that he values, and every person runs the risk of losing them. If he owns a home, it may be destroyed by fire or by a tornado. If he owns a car, it may be stolen or wrecked. If he injures others or damages their property, he may be required to pay a large amount of money to them.

To many people, the ability to earn a living is even more important than the property they own. But earning power may be limited or even lost because of an accident, sickness, or old age. A person may lose his job just because business conditions are poor. Or family income may disappear or be greatly reduced because of the death of the breadwinner.

All these risks of loss of property or earning power are called *economic risks*.

WE CAN SHARE ECONOMIC RISKS

No matter how careful we are, economic risks cannot be completely removed. We can, however, avoid a large financial loss at one time by sharing the risks with others. Suppose that you and 29 other people belong to a club for motorbike owners. Also, suppose that you wreck your motorbike, which is worth $150. If you are bearing your own risk, you lose the entire $150 investment. The other club members lose nothing. But if all the club members had agreed to share all losses, each of the 30 members would chip in $5 to make up your total loss of $150.

You can see that under the first plan, you lose a sizable sum of money. Under the second plan, each of the 30 members loses a little. By sharing an economic risk, you and your fellow members helped each other. When you wrecked your motorbike, you were promptly paid for the loss. The other members know that they will receive the same prompt payment if they have a similar loss.

INSURANCE LETS PEOPLE SHARE ECONOMIC RISKS

It would not be practical for all sharing of economic losses to be handled as it was by the motorbike club. There are too many kinds of risks and too many people to be protected. Such protection must be planned carefully, and the plans must be carried out by specialists. *Insurance* is the protection provided by the sharing of economic risks. The companies that make this protection service available are called *insurance companies*.

An insurance company agrees to assume a certain economic risk for a person and to pay him if and when a loss occurs. The person for whom the risk is assumed is known as the *insured* or the *policyholder*. To show that risk has been assumed, the company provides the insured with a policy. A *policy* is a contract which is evidence of the agreement between the company and the policyholder. The policy sets forth certain conditions which the insurance company and the policyholder have agreed to. For example, the policyholder may agree not to keep gasoline or other flammable substances in his house, not to allow a teenager to drive his car, or not to engage in certain other practices.

In return for assuming a risk, the insurance company requires the policyholder to pay a certain amount of money at certain intervals. He may make payments once a month, once every four months, once every six months, once a year, or sometimes even less frequently. The amount that the policyholder must pay is called a *premium*. The premiums from all the policyholders that the company insures make up the funds from which the company pays losses.

MIDWESTERN INSURANCE COMPANY

DECLARATIONS
INSURED'S NAME AND MAILING ADDRESS

Knipp, Lawrence G. and Roberta L.
168 Forrest Avenue
Muscatine, Iowa 52761

No. 35-67 73 23

INCEPTION DATE 5/13/71	POLICY PERIOD 12 mo.	EXPIRATION OF POLICY PERIOD 5/13/72

[X] THIS POLICY WILL BE RENEWED AUTOMATICALLY, SUBJECT TO PROVISIONS OF THE FORMS THEN CURRENT, FOR EACH SUCCEEDING POLICY PERIOD THEREAFTER AND IS SUBJECT TO TERMINATION BY THIS COMPANY ONLY AFTER TEN (10) DAYS' WRITTEN NOTICE TO INSURED AND MORTGAGEE. THE PREMIUM FOR SUCCEEDING POLICY PERIODS WILL BE COMPUTED AT THIS COMPANY'S RATES THEN CURRENT.

DESCRIPTION OF DWELLING
THE DWELLING IS OF FRAME CONSTRUCTION WITH APPROVED ROOF, OCCUPIED BY NOT MORE THAN TWO FAMILIES. EXCEPTIONS IF ANY ARE:

LOCATION OF PREMISES (IF DIFFERENT THAN SHOWN ABOVE)	CONSTRUCTION	TYPE OF ROOF	NUMBER OF FAMILIES
	Brick		

HOMEOWNERS POLICY [X]	STANDARD FIRE POLICY
INSURANCE IS PROVIDED ONLY WITH RESPECT TO THOSE OF THE FOLLOWING COVERAGES WHICH ARE INDICATED BY A SPECIFIC LIMIT OF LIABILITY APPLICABLE THERETO.	INSURANCE IS PROVIDED AGAINST THOSE PERILS AND FOR ONLY THOSE COVERAGES INDICATED BELOW BY A PREMIUM CHARGE AND AGAINST OTHER PERILS AND FOR OTHER COVERAGES ONLY WHEN ENDORSED HEREON OR ADDED HERETO.

PREMIUM		PROPERTY AND COVERAGES	POLICY LIMITS OF LIABILITY	POLICY LIMITS OF LIABILITY	PROPERTY	PERILS AND COVERAGES	RATE	PREMIUM
BASIC POLICY PREMIUM $ 53.00		A. DWELLING	$ 21,500	$	DWELLING	FIRE AND LIGHTNING		$
ADDITIONAL PREMIUM $	SECTION I	B. UNSCHEDULED PERSONAL PROPERTY	$ 8,600	$	CONTENTS			$
CREDIT FOR EXISTING INS $		C. ADDITIONAL LIVING EXPENSE	$ 4,300	$				$
PREPAID PREMIUM (Automatic Renewal or 3 Year Term Policies) $ 53.00				$				$
					OTHER PERILS AND COVERAGES			
TOTAL POLICY PREMIUM (If Paid In Installments)	SECTION II	E. COMPREHENSIVE PERSONAL LIABILITY (EACH OCCURRENCE)	$ 25,000	$ X X X X	EXTENDED COVERAGE			$
$		F. MEDICAL PAYMENTS (EACH PERSON)	$ 500	$				$
INSTALLMENT PREMIUM $		G. PHYSICAL DAMAGE TO PROPERTY OF OTHERS (EACH OCCURRENCE)	$ 250	$				$

Illus. 23-1. Part of an insurance policy.

A person can buy insurance against almost every legal economic risk if he is willing to pay the premiums for it. Individuals organizing a county fair, for example, may buy insurance against rain. Singers can insure their voices, and a professional pianist can insure his hands. Such special kinds of insurance, though, are obviously not bought by the general public. The kinds of insurance that will be most important to most people are: automobile insurance, property and liability insurance, life insurance, health insurance, and insurance for income security.

Everyone should know exactly what protection is provided by the kinds of insurance policies he has. Some people have failed to notify their insurance companies about losses for which they should have been paid just because they did not know their policies covered those losses. Other people have assumed that losses they suffered were covered by their insurance, only to find out by reading their policies that the losses were not covered.

HOW THE COST OF INSURANCE IS DETERMINED

An insurance company must collect enough money through premiums to pay the losses of its policyholders and to pay its operating expenses. The premium for each individual policy is determined partly by the experiences of insurance companies in paying losses of the kind covered in that policy. The premium must be set high enough so that the insurance company will be able to pay all the losses that it expects to occur and still have a reserve amount to cover any unusually heavy losses that are not expected but that may occur. The funds that an insurance company keeps to pay losses that may occur in the future are invested. To some extent, the earnings from these investments make it possible to provide insurance at a lower cost.

If the losses paid by insurance companies decrease, premiums may also decrease. Some insurance experts state that life insurance premiums could be cut by as much as 30% if cures for cancer and heart disease were developed. However, if the losses paid by insurance companies increase, premiums will probably also increase. For example, the rising cost of automobile insurance is due in large part to the increasing number of accidents and the financial losses resulting from them.

Everyone benefits if the losses covered by insurance are decreased. Assume that fewer losses are caused by fire and that fire insurance premiums are reduced. If your family owns a house and has fire insurance on it, you gain directly because you pay lower premiums. If you rent a home, lower premiums paid by the landlord may result in a lower rent. If a businessman pays lower premiums, his expenses will be less and his prices on goods may be less. Anything that you can do to decrease losses covered by insurance helps not only you but the entire community.

WHERE ONE MAY BUY INSURANCE

Individuals can buy some kinds of insurance through their employers, but most people buy insurance through an *insurance agent*. He is a person who works for an insurance company or for an independent agency which sells many kinds of policies from a number of different companies. You can learn a lot about insurance by reading about it, but it is hard for anyone to know about all the types of coverage that are available. The best thing to do is to select a reliable insurance agent who can explain the various policies to you.

Some points to consider in choosing an insurance agent are:

1. What kind of reputation does his company have for settling claims?
2. What kind of reputation does he have for helping policyholders when they suffer a loss?
3. Does he obtain enough essential background information about you to recommend the right policy?
4. When recommending a particular policy, does he explain why he feels it is most suitable for you?
5. Does he show that he is concerned about your welfare?

There really is no one best insurance policy. Insurance companies offer different types of policies to meet the needs of different people or to meet the needs of one person at different times. Anyone who buys insurance is interested mainly in making sure that his economic risks are properly covered and that his claim will be paid promptly in case of loss.

Insurance is important to all of us because it gives us some measure of personal security. Without insurance, most of us could take care of small losses such as those resulting from minor accidents. But without insurance, a large loss from a big fire or a serious illness could be a real financial hardship. Protection against major hazards gives everyone a feeling of security.

WHY INSURANCE IS IMPORTANT TO ALL OF US

Insurance is also important because of its contributions to the business world and to our economy. Insurance makes it possible for many persons and businesses to undertake activities they otherwise could not consider. Suppose that a person wants to buy a $25,000 home but can make only a $5,000 down payment. He needs to borrow $20,000. It is extremely doubtful that anyone would lend him this amount at a reasonable interest rate unless the house was insured. Money to buy a new car couldn't be borrowed at a reasonable rate unless the car was insured against such risks as theft and collision.

You have learned that part of the money collected in premiums is invested. Many insurance companies, mainly life insurance companies, make loans to build homes, office buildings, factories, roads, schools, and many other government and private business projects which help our economy grow. Insurance companies also perform educational services by conducting campaigns on safety, health, and accident prevention.

Developing Your Business Vocabulary

The following italicized terms should become part of your business vocabulary. For each numbered statement, find the italicized term that has the same meaning.

economic risk   *insured* or *policyholder*
insurance   *policy*
insurance agent   *premium*
insurance company

1. The chance of losing the financial value of something.
2. The protection provided by the sharing of economic risks.
3. A firm that makes insurance available to others.
4. One who carries insurance.
5. A contract between one who buys insurance and one who makes it available.
6. The amount paid for insurance.
7. A person who sells insurance.

Checking Your Understanding

1. Name several economic risks that are of concern to the average person or his family.
2. Can an individual avoid economic risks by being especially careful in handling his own affairs?
3. How do insurance companies help people share economic risks? Illustrate by giving an example.
4. Name four kinds of insurance that are very important to most people.
5. What two important financial obligations must be covered by the premiums an insurance company collects?
6. What determines the cost of insurance? How may costs be reduced?
7. Assume that a person carries fire insurance on a house for many years but never has a loss. What has he received for his premiums?
8. In selecting an insurance agent, what qualifications would you consider important?
9. "If it were not for insurance, many people would not be able to buy a home or a new car." Do you agree with this statement? Explain.

Applying What You Have Learned

1. The members of a local businessmen's club have been told that only about 60% of the money that a fire insurance company receives in premiums is used to pay losses. The company uses the balance to pay operating expenses and other costs. The club members believe that they can reduce their insurance expenses by insuring each other. They feel that this arrangement will keep them from having to pay for the insurance company's operating costs. So they agree to share equally in losses that any member may suffer as a result of a fire. Do you think that this is a good plan?

2. Explain how the careful safety practices of a family or a community can reduce insurance costs. Give several examples.

3. The Eastern Hardware Company operates 1,800 small hardware stores. It also has 10 large warehouses from which the stores obtain their supplies. The company carries no insurance on the merchandise or equipment in its retail stores, but the warehouses are fully covered by insurance. Why does the company consider it unnecessary to insure the 1,800 stores but necessary to insure the 10 warehouses?

4. Gordon Wilson owns a hardware store that is about the same size as one of the Eastern Hardware Company's branch stores. He does not carry fire insurance on merchandise because the Eastern Hardware Company does not carry fire insurance on its retail stores. Is his decision a wise one? Why or why not?

5. Most families who own their own homes carry insurance against loss from fire or windstorm but do not carry insurance against loss from flood. Why is this so?

6. Tony and Peggy Armstrong are annoyed with the insurance agent who has just talked with them. They feel that the agent asked too many personal questions, particularly about their financial situation. Do you think that the Armstrongs are right in feeling as they do?

Solving Business Problems

1. In a recent year, the economic losses from motor vehicle accidents in the United States amounted to about $17 billion. In the same year, about 27 million drivers were involved in accidents. What was the average cost for each driver involved in accidents?

2. In a recent year, the total losses from fire in the United States amounted to about $1,952 million. At that time, the population was about 203 million.

   (a) What was each person's share of the total fire loss?
   (b) What would be the share of this total loss for a family of four?

3. Ed O'Leary is planning to obtain a fire insurance policy on his home. He learns that a one-year policy will cost $42 and that a three-year policy will cost $105.

   (a) What is the yearly cost of the two policies?

   (b) How much would he save each year by buying a three-year policy instead of three separate one-year policies?

4. The Dewand Skeen family pays the following insurance premiums for the year: first life insurance policy, $180; second life insurance policy, $190; insurance on house and household goods, $80; automobile insurance, $140.

   (a) What is the total cost of the insurance premiums paid?

   (b) If the Skeen family keeps a monthly budget, how much should the monthly allowance for insurance be?

Enriching Your Business Understanding

1. Vernon Schlattman feels that all insurance rates are too high, so he has set up what he calls a "self-insurance program." Every month he deposits $100 in the bank for the special purpose of covering any financial losses he might have. He carries no insurance against such losses. **(a)** Is there any merit in Mr. Schlattman's self-insurance plan? **(b)** What are the major weaknesses in the plan?

2. Compare the common economic risks of today with those that your grandparents faced. **(a)** What new risks exist now that did not exist then? **(b)** What risks did they face which have decreased or which no longer exist?

3. Be prepared to give a 10-minute oral report on the early history of insurance. In preparing the report, you may refer to encyclopedias and books on insurance in your school and public libraries. A local insurance agency may also be able to help you find information on this topic.

4. Write a brief report on the regulation of insurance prices and practices in your state. Give some reasons why your state feels it is necessary to regulate insurance companies. Do you feel that such regulation is desirable?

5. As you study this unit, think of job possibilities in the field of insurance. Insurance companies employ many stenographers, typists, bookkeepers, and other office workers. They also provide many career opportunities in such positions as actuary, adjuster, agent, appraiser, and broker. **(a)** Do any of these positions appeal to you? Why? **(b)** How would you prepare yourself for this kind of position?

PART 24
Automobile Insurance

This year, more than 55,000 Americans will die in automobile accidents. More than 150 will be killed today, if this is an average day. Besides the large number who will be killed, one out of every 40 persons will be injured in an automobile accident this year. Driving a car, even if you're only going two blocks to the neighborhood drugstore, is risky. Because of the high risk of being involved in an accident, every driver should carry insurance to protect himself and others. Some states have even passed laws requiring persons to carry automobile insurance before they can legally drive a car. All 50 states have passed *financial responsibility laws*. These laws provide that if a driver causes an accident and cannot pay for damages either through insurance or through his own savings or property, his driver's license will be suspended or revoked.

A person can buy insurance to protect his car from almost everything that could happen to it except wearing out. Even more important, though, he can buy insurance to protect himself against financial loss if he injures someone else or damages someone else's property in an automobile accident. Sometimes an accident is unavoidable, and no one can be directly blamed for it. In most cases, however, someone is at fault. The person who is found to be at fault is responsible for damages resulting from the accident.

PROTECTION PROVIDED BY AUTOMOBILE INSURANCE

Even a driver who thinks he is completely innocent may be sued. If he is insured, his insurance company will give him protection in the form of legal defense. If the court decides that he is legally liable for injuries and damages to property, his insurance company will pay the costs up to the limits stated in his insurance policy.

The kinds of driving protection that are available through automobile insurance are explained in the following paragraphs. These coverages are available in several combinations and for varying amounts. Although some of the basic coverages can be bought separately, many car owners prefer a package policy which includes most or all of the coverages.

BODILY INJURY LIABILITY INSURANCE

Bodily injury liability insurance protects the policyholder from claims resulting from injuries or deaths caused by the car he drives. This kind of insurance covers persons in other cars, guests riding with the driver, and pedestrians. It does not cover the policyholder or, in most cases, his immediate family. Amounts of bodily injury coverage are generally expressed as 10/20, 25/50, 100/300, and so on. The first number refers to the limit, in thousands of dollars, that the insurance company will pay for injuries of any one person in any one accident. The second number is the maximum, in thousands of dollars, that will be paid for all the injuries resulting from any one accident. In most states, 10/20 is the minimum amount that can be purchased; several states have higher minimums ranging up to 20/40.

Car owners should consider carrying larger amounts of bodily injury liability insurance than the minimums that state financial responsibility laws require. It is not unusual for juries to award an injured person $25,000 or more. If this happened to you and you had only 10/20 coverage, your insurance company would pay the $10,000 limit and you would have to pay the rest. Since large claims do not occur as often as small claims, the cost for extra coverage is reasonable.

MEDICAL PAYMENTS INSURANCE

Bodily injury liability insurance provides protection mainly when the policyholder's car is involved in the injury of other persons. Injuries suffered by the policyholder himself are not covered. However, car owners who carry bodily injury insurance may obtain medical expense protection for themselves and their families by buying *medical payments insurance*. This coverage applies to the car owner and his immediate family if they are injured when riding in his car, when riding in someone else's car, or if struck by a car while walking. Guests riding in the insured person's car are also protected.

With medical payments insurance, the insurance company agrees to pay the costs of reasonable and necessary medical, surgical, dental, ambulance, hospital, nursing, and funeral services. Payment, up to the limit stated in the policy, is made regardless of who is at fault in the accident. Medical payments coverage is available in the minimum amount of $500 for each person. For rather small additional costs, the coverage may be increased up to a limit of, generally, $5,000.

Sometimes injuries are caused by hit-and-run drivers or by drivers who have no insurance and no money to pay claims. Therefore, insurance companies make available a coverage called *uninsured motorists protection*. This coverage is available only to those persons who carry bodily injury liability insurance. It protects the insured person and members of his family at all times. It also protects the insured's guests, providing that they are in his car when they are injured.

UNINSURED MOTORISTS PROTECTION

The amount of coverage provided by uninsured motorists protection is limited to the liability that state financial responsibility laws require. In most states, this is at least 10/20. Unlike medical payments insurance, uninsured motorists protection covers the insured person only if the uninsured motorist is legally responsible for the accident. However, uninsured motorists protection gives broader coverage than does medical payments insurance. For example, a person who has uninsured motorists protection may be compensated for a loss of earnings while he is recovering from an accident. He may also be compensated for permanent damage to an eye or some other part of his body as a result of the accident. Death benefits may be paid to beneficiaries of the insured person.

In most states, uninsured motorists protection does not pay for damage to the insured's car. Such coverage is available through collision insurance, which is discussed later in this part.

PROPERTY DAMAGE LIABILITY INSURANCE

Property damage liability insurance protects a person when his car damages someone else's property. The damaged property is usually another car, but it may also be such property as telephone poles, water hydrants, and buildings. The coverage of property damage liability insurance does not include damage to the insured person's car.

Car owners often buy property damage insurance to provide $5,000 worth of protection in any one accident. Additional coverage, though, may be bought for little extra cost. State financial responsibility laws define minimum coverage for property damage liability. Thus, one should find out what this minimum coverage is to make sure that he complies with state laws.

COMPREHENSIVE PHYSICAL DAMAGE INSURANCE

A sensible car owner wants to be sure that he is protected if he injures someone else or damages someone else's property. He also wants protection against damage to his own car. Such protection is available through *comprehensive physical damage insurance*. This coverage protects a car owner against almost all losses except those caused by a collision or by turning over. Such financial losses as those resulting from theft, fire, tornadoes, windstorms, glass breakage, and falling objects are covered by comprehensive physical damage insurance.

If a car is totally destroyed or is stolen, the amount paid to the insured is not necessarily equal to the cost of the car. Rather, it is equal to the car's estimated value at the time of the loss. Suppose that a new car costing $3,000 is stolen soon after the policyholder buys it. The insurance company will probably pay the policyholder almost as much as the car cost, perhaps $2,800. But if the car is stolen ten months after it was bought, the insurance company may pay the policyholder only $2,400. As the car has grown older, its value has decreased.

COLLISION INSURANCE

Collision insurance pays for damages to a policyholder's car caused by a collision with any object or by turning over. It does not cover injuries to people or damage to others' property. Most collision insurance is written with a $50 or $100 *deductible clause*. This means that the insured person agrees to pay the first $50 or $100 of damage to his car in any one collision, and the insurance company agrees to pay the rest. Full collision insurance is available, but it is considerably more expensive and is not often sold. A person can usually pay for minor repairs and so does not greatly need insurance against small losses. Buying collision insurance on a deductible basis enables a person to carry the insurance at a reasonable cost, yet to be protected against major losses.

As with comprehensive physical damage insurance, collision insurance does not provide for payment of damages greater than the car's value. It is usually foolish for persons to pay premiums for collision insurance if their cars are not worth much. Some insurance companies will not even sell collision insurance for cars of little value.

Both collision insurance and comprehensive physical damage insurance will be required if you buy a car on credit. This protects the firm which gave you the credit. That firm really owns the car until you have completely paid back the money lent you. If someone else, such as the car dealer, obtains the insurance for you, it is important to find out whether insurance for bodily injury and personal damage liability is included. If it is not, you should not drive until this important protection has been obtained.

A SUMMARY CHART OF AUTOMOBILE INSURANCE COVERAGE

Illus. 24-1. A summary of automobile insurance coverages.

COVERAGES	PRINCIPAL APPLICATIONS	
Bodily Injury Coverages	Policyholder	Other Persons
Bodily Injury Liability	NO	YES
Medical Payments	YES	YES
Protection Against Uninsured Motorists	YES	YES
Property Damage Coverages	Policyholder's Automobile	Property of Others
Property Damage Liability	NO	YES
Comprehensive Physical Damage	YES	NO
Collision	YES	NO

SOURCE: Insurance Information Institute

The cost of automobile insurance is not the same for every person. Some of the factors that an insurance company considers in determining the cost of a particular type of coverage are:

WHAT DOES AUTOMOBILE INSURANCE COST?

1. The community in which the insured person lives.
2. The value of the car.

3. Whether the car is used for business or pleasure.
4. The average number of miles driven in a year.
5. The age of the driver.
6. The driver's safety record.

The more accidents that insured drivers have, the more claims insurance companies must pay. The more dollars paid in claims, the higher the overall cost of automobile insurance.

Illustration 24-2 gives rates for four different types of coverage on one type of car in five different cities. All conditions of driving are the same except the cities in which the car owners live. You can see that the rate for bodily injury liability insurance is about 60% more in San Francisco than it is in New York. One may assume, then, that the amounts insurance companies pay out in claims are also greater in San Francisco than in New York.

Illus. 24-2. These rates are for a new car costing about $3,000, with bodily injury insurance of $10,000 for one person injured in one accident or $20,000 for two or more persons injured in one accident, and with property damage insurance of $5,000. These rates may be changed at any time.

TYPE OF INSURANCE	RATES IN SELECTED CITIES				
	CLEVELAND	NEW ORLEANS	NEW YORK	PHOENIX	SAN FRANCISCO
Bodily Injury Liability	$59	$79	$52	$68	$84
Property Damage Liability	37	37	33	31	54
Comprehensive Physical Damage	25	25	26	35	31
Collision ($100 deductible)	47	61	59	45	104

The value of an insured person's car naturally has an important effect on the cost of insurance. Premiums for collision insurance and comprehensive physical damage insurance must be higher for a car worth $3,500 than for a car worth only $1,000. The insurance company runs the risk of paying out much more to the insured if the $3,500 car is destroyed or stolen.

The purpose for which a car is used and the miles that it is driven in a year are also important in determining insurance rates. Cars used for business purposes are generally driven more miles in a year than are cars driven for pleasure and so are more likely to be involved in an accident. Insurance companies often give car owners a reduced rate if the car being insured is driven less than 20 miles a day to work or is used only for short pleasure trips.

The cost of insurance is usually higher when one of the drivers in the insured's family is under 30 than it is if all family drivers are over 30. Generally speaking, the younger the drivers in the family, the higher the insurance rates. The extra amount charged for young drivers may be decreased if they have completed approved driver education courses. Also, a discount is sometimes available to students who maintain a good scholastic record.

Most insurance companies give discounts to drivers who have not been involved in accidents where they were at fault and who have not been convicted of serious traffic violations. If an individual has a clean driving record for at least one to three years, he may receive a discount of 10% to 20% on the price of a certain policy. A poor driving record has the opposite effect.

Every person who buys automobile insurance must explain his insurance needs and wants to his agent so that he obtains the proper kind of coverage. Not all policies that are supposed to offer the same type of protection have exactly the same provisions. For example, a policy may or may not protect the owner if his car is driven by a minor who is not a member of the family. Usually the car owner is protected by his insurance if his car is being driven with his permission by any licensed driver. Also, a person whose car is insured is generally protected if he drives another car on which there is no insurance. Such protection may or may not apply to other members of his family.

It is important that a policyholder understand his policy so that he can be certain about the extent of his protection. Too many people do not realize the limits of their protection until it is too late.

Insurance on motorcycles, motorbikes, and motorscooters is similar to automobile insurance, but there are several important differences that limit protection. Here are some common restrictions:

MOTORCYCLE INSURANCE

1. Insurance does not apply when the cycle is engaged in speed or riding contests.
2. Persons who operate a borrowed cycle are not covered by the owner's insurance.
3. Passengers are not insured, even if they are riding with the owner.
4. Medical payments for injuries to the operator are not covered.

Weight and horsepower are important factors in determining the cost of motorcycle insurance. The bigger the cycle, the higher the cost. Otherwise, the cost of cycle insurance is determined by the same factors—such as age and driving record—that apply to automobile insurance. Because of the variation in motorcycle insurance among different companies, details of each policy should be discussed with the insurance agent.

Developing Your Business Vocabulary

The following italicized terms should become part of your business vocabulary. For each numbered statement, find the italicized term that has the same meaning.

*bodily injury
  liability insurance*
collision insurance
*comprehensive physical
  damage insurance*

deductible clause
financial responsibility laws
medical payments insurance
property damage liability insurance
uninsured motorists protection

1. Laws providing that if a driver causes an accident and cannot pay for damages either through insurance or through his own savings or property, his driver's license will be suspended or revoked.
2. Insurance protecting the insured person against claims resulting from accidental injuries or deaths he is responsible for.
3. Insurance providing medical expense protection for those persons injured while in the insured person's car.
4. Insurance protecting the policyholder against losses if he is injured by a hit-and-run driver or by a driver who carries no insurance.
5. Insurance providing protection against claims of damage to other people's possessions.
6. Insurance covering losses of or damages to the insured automobile, except those caused by collision or by turning over.
7. Insurance covering damage to one's car caused by collision or by turning over.
8. A part of an insurance policy which states that the policy pays only a certain percent of any loss or that the policy does not cover losses below a certain amount.

Checking Your Understanding

1. How do state governments help protect drivers from losses arising from automobile accidents?
2. If an insurance company charges a car owner $67 for the minimum amount of bodily injury liability insurance, why is the company able to double the amount of protection for an extra $6?
3. Tell whether benefits will be paid in the following situations if the driver is protected by medical payments insurance:

    (a) A passenger in his car is injured.
    (b) He himself is injured in an accident for which he is legally at fault.
    (c) A neighbor driving his own car is injured in a collision with the insured driver's car.
    (d) The insured person is crossing the street and is injured by a passing car.

4. What determines the limits of the amount of coverage provided by uninsured motorists protection?
5. Tell whether a person who has comprehensive physical damage insurance can collect from the insurance company if:

    (a) The car is stolen.
    (b) The tires are stolen while the car is parked on the street.
    (c) The car is destroyed by fire.
    (d) The windshield is broken.
    (e) A fender is damaged when the driver is backing out of his garage.
    (f) The car skids and runs into a tree.

6. In the case of a collision between two cars, is a person who holds a collision insurance policy protected from losses arising from damages to his car? Is he protected from losses arising from damages to the other person's car?
7. One insurance company charged $146 to cover all losses over $25 to the insured's car resulting from collision. If losses up to $200 are not covered, the premium is only $50. Why is there so great a difference in cost between these deductible amounts?
8. What factors determine the insurance rates charged by an insurance company?
9. Why is the cost of automobile insurance higher when one of the drivers of the car is 18 years old than it would be if all drivers were over 30?
10. Tell whether the driver of the car is usually protected by automobile insurance in the situations described on page 296:

(a) A licensed driver who has no insurance of his own drives an insured car with the owner's permission.

(b) A licensed driver who has no insurance of his own drives an insured car without the owner's permission.

(c) A licensed driver who has insurance on his own car drives another car on which there is no insurance.

11. In what ways is motorcycle insurance different from automobile insurance?

Applying What You Have Learned

1. "Property damage liability insurance is less necessary than bodily injury liability insurance." Do you agree or disagree with this statement? Explain your answer.

2. Maury Rosenberg owns an old car which he figures is worth only about $100. He carries no collision insurance on it because the premium he would have to pay would be more than the car is worth. What insurance coverage do you think he should have? If you omit certain types of coverage, give reasons for not including them.

3. Nettie Garber's car was involved in a collision in which both cars were seriously damaged. Mrs. Garber was not sure who was at fault. However, when she found out how badly the other person was worried about the accident, she said: "I'll take the blame and ask my insurance company to settle with you." Should Mrs. Garber have done this? Why or why not?

4. Ned Gorkin is the principal owner in a prosperous business, the Gorkin Wholesale Company. R. L. Kirkpatrick is a salesman who has just begun working for that company. Both Mr. Gorkin and Mr. Kirkpatrick buy new cars for use partly in business and partly for pleasure. For which of the two men do you consider collision insurance to be more important? Why?

5. What can be done to reduce the costs of automobile insurance or at least to prevent rates from continuing to increase?

6. Outline arguments for and against this proposition: Every owner of a car should be made by law to carry bodily injury liability and property damage liability insurance.

Solving Business Problems

1. Bill Hunter was involved in an accident in which two persons in the other car were injured. Bill was at fault, so his insurance company was required to pay the damages. A court awarded one

person $14,500 for his injuries. The second person was awarded $8,000. Bill had 10/20 bodily injury liability coverage.

(a) How much will his insurance company pay in damages?
(b) How much will Bill have to pay?

2. Juan Martinez bought a new car for $3,400 and immediately obtained insurance on it, including comprehensive physical damage insurance. The insurance company estimates that the car will decrease in value $800 the first year, $550 the second year, and $425 for each of the following two years. How much will Mr. Martinez collect from the insurance company if the car is destroyed by fire:

(a) At the end of the first year?
(b) At the end of the second year?
(c) At the end of the third year?
(d) At the end of the fourth year?

3. The table on page 292 shows the cost (for one type of car) for bodily injury liability, property damage liability, comprehensive physical damage, and collision insurance in five different cities.

(a) What is the total cost of the four types of insurance in each of the five cities?
(b) What is the amount of the difference between the highest and lowest totals?
(c) What is the average cost in the five cities for each type of coverage?

4. During a five-year period, James Nameth carried collision insurance with a $50 deductible clause and an annual premium of $82. During that time, he had two accidents which were covered by his collision insurance. In one accident, the loss was $50. In the other accident, the loss was $360.

(a) Was the amount the insurance company paid for damages as a result of these two accidents more or less than Mr. Nameth had paid in premiums during the five-year period?
(b) What would have been the difference between the premiums paid and the amounts received if he had had a $100 deductible policy costing $68 a year?
(c) What would have been the difference between the premiums paid and the amounts received if he had had a $150 deductible policy costing $59 a year?
(d) What would have been the difference between the premiums paid and the amounts received if he had had a $250 deductible policy costing $46 a year?

Enriching Your Business Understanding

1. Interview a friend or relative who has benefited from having automobile insurance. Prepare a brief written report describing the situation.
2. Find the cost in your community of property damage liability, comprehensive physical damage, and collision ($100 deductible) insurance for a new car costing about $3,000. Also find the cost of 10/20 bodily injury liability insurance. How do these rates compare with those for the five cities given on page 292?
3. Check with an insurance agent to find out what should be done about insurance coverage if:

    (a) An insured person sells his car and buys a new one.
    (b) An insured person sells his car four months before his policy expires and does not plan on getting another car.
    (c) Conditions of driving change, such as use of the car, number of drivers of the car, or a move to another location.

4. Summarize the provisions of the financial responsibility law in your state.
5. Tell what the driver of a car should do if he is involved in the following accidents:

    (a) His car has a minor scratch on a fender and the other car does not appear to be damaged at all.
    (b) The other car has a small scratch on a fender but his car does not seem to be damaged.
    (c) Both cars are seriously damaged, but neither driver seems to be hurt.
    (d) The driver of the other car is injured slightly.
    (e) A passenger in the other car is seriously injured.

PART 25

Insurance For the Home

Count off 13 seconds. While you're counting, at least one fire will break out somewhere in America. Fire is the biggest single threat to the property, other than cars, that people own. But property owners also face other hazards, such as losses from theft, floods, and windstorms. A property owner also runs the risk of being sued by persons who are injured on his property and of being found liable for damages. Because the risks of loss in such situations are high, property owners should—and most do—carry property insurance.

A property owner must first determine what should be insured and how much it should be insured for. Property attached to the land, such as a house or a garage, is known as *real property*. Property not attached to the land, such as furniture or clothing, is known as *personal property*. Real and personal property may be protected by separate policies or by a combination policy.

Property owners can buy separate insurance policies covering specified kinds of risks, or they can combine several kinds of insurance into a package policy to meet their insurance needs. Today most persons are buying a combination that is popularly known as a *homeowners policy*. The number of perils covered by a homeowners policy depends on whether the insured chooses the basic form, the broad form, or the comprehensive form.

THERE ARE SEVERAL KINDS OF PROPERTY INSURANCE

The broad form of a homeowners policy is the most widely purchased. It insures property against 18 different perils, which are given in Illustration 25-1. The basic form is limited to the first 11 perils shown in the illustration. The comprehensive form covers all perils shown in the illustration and many more. For this reason, it is sometimes referred to as an all-risks policy. Actually, such a policy insures against all perils except those named at the right of the illustration. Liability insurance, which will be discussed later in this part, is included in a homeowners policy. Also, a homeowners policy pays for a family's added living expenses if it is forced to live elsewhere because of fire or any other peril stated in the policy.

PERILS AGAINST WHICH PROPERTIES ARE INSURED HOMEOWNERS POLICY

FORMS

COMPREHENSIVE

BROAD

BASIC

PERILS

1. fire or lightning
2. loss of property removed from premises endangered by fire or other perils
3. windstorm or hail
4. explosion
5. riot or civil commotion
6. aircraft
7. vehicles
8. smoke
9. vandalism and malicious mischief
10. theft
11. breakage of glass constituting a part of the building

12. falling objects
13. weight of ice, snow, sleet
14. collapse of building(s) or any part thereof
15. sudden and accidental tearing asunder, cracking, burning, or bulging of a steam or hot water heating system or of appliances for heating water
16. accidental discharge, leakage or overflow of water or steam from within a plumbing, heating or air-conditioning system or domestic appliance
17. freezing of plumbing, heating and air-conditioning systems and domestic appliances
18. sudden and accidental injury from artificially generated currents to electrical appliances, devices, fixtures and wiring (TV and radio tubes not included)

All perils EXCEPT: earthquake, landslide, flood, surface water, waves, tidal water or tidal wave, the backing up of sewers, seepage, war, and nuclear radiation.

Illus. 25-1. Perils against which properties are insured by a homeowners policy.

SOURCE: Insurance Information Institute

With a homeowners policy, the insured person is protected as he would be if he bought several different policies. Yet the cost of a homeowners policy is usually 20% to 30% less than if the same amount of coverage were obtained by buying separate policies. Also, there is the convenience of having only one policy and one premium to be concerned about. Persons who do not own their own homes can obtain a similar package policy to protect their personal property.

If he prefers, a property owner can buy separate policies which insure against certain kinds of perils. For example, it is possible to buy a *standard fire policy* which insures against losses caused by fire or lightning. Such a policy also generally covers losses caused by smoke and water, by damage resulting from firemen's efforts to put out a fire, and by damage to articles moved from a burning building. For an additional premium, one can have *extended coverage* included in his standard fire policy. This expands the coverage to include damage from wind, hail, smoke, riot, vehicles, and falling aircraft. Other individual policies are available to meet the special protection needs of property owners.

Each person who would lose money if a certain piece of property were damaged or destroyed is said to have an *insurable interest* in that property. If a person has no insurable interest in a property, he is not paid for any damage to that property, even though he has paid for an insurance policy on it. It is not enough that an insurable interest existed when the policy was bought. The insurable interest must exist at the time of the loss.

THERE MUST BE AN INSURABLE INTEREST IN THE PROPERTY

Suppose that Vincent Mueller's house is insured for $18,000 under a policy that expires on September 30. If Mr. Mueller sells his house on June 1, his insurable interest expires at that time. If the house is destroyed by fire on July 15, he cannot collect on any insurance, even though his policy is still in effect. If the insurable interest expires before the policy does or if the policy is canceled, the insured may be able to obtain a partial refund of the premium he has paid.

An insurance company agrees to pay the insured for any losses covered by his policy. However, the company does not agree to pay the insured more than the amount of his loss, no matter what the amount of his insurance. Suppose that Elbert Garcia owns a house valued at $25,000 but insured for $40,000. If his house burns to the ground, Mr. Garcia will receive a payment of not more than $25,000. Now suppose that Mr. Garcia had insured his house for $25,000 with one insurance company and $25,000 with another. If the house is destroyed, the two companies share the loss equally. Each company would pay Mr. Garcia only $12,500. Thus, he would receive a total of $25,000 even though he was carrying $50,000 worth of insurance.

COVERAGE IS TO BE BASED ON THE PROPERTY'S CURRENT VALUE

If a homeowner wants adequate protection, the amount of insurance on his real property should be based on the property's current value. Suppose that Robert Ketcham built his house in 1960 for $20,000 and that he has it insured for this amount. It would probably cost $30,000 to build a similar house today, so his house has a replacement value of $30,000. Yet if Mr. Ketcham's house is completely destroyed by fire, the insurance company is obligated to pay him only $20,000.

Construction costs and property values in general have increased tremendously in recent years. As a result, many homes are underinsured. That is, if they were put up for sale, they would bring more money than they are insured for. It is wise for a homeowner to review the value of his house and the amount of his insurance every few years. This will enable him to determine the current cost of replacing his house and to adjust his policy so that he has enough protection.

Special care should be taken to estimate the value of personal property. This kind of property includes many different items, some of which may be overlooked if a careless estimate of value is made. The value of personal property that is collected bit by bit over the years is often surprisingly high.

FINDING THE COST OF PROPERTY INSURANCE

The cost of property insurance is usually low in comparison with the amount of protection received. Cost depends on the estimated danger of loss. It is affected by such things as:

1. The construction of the building; that is, whether it is made of brick, wood, or concrete and whether the roof has wood or composition shingles.
2. The nature of the surroundings; that is, whether there is danger of fire from neighboring buildings.
3. The efficiency of the local fire department.
4. The length of time for which the policy is being written.

In rural areas, the cost may also be affected by how far the property is located from a source of water.

Property insurance policies are generally written for either a one-year or a three-year period. Yearly premiums for three-year policies are less than the premiums for one-year policies. Because of the savings that can be made, property insurance policies are most often sold for a period of three years.

When an insured building is damaged or destroyed by fire, the insurance company can easily estimate the amount of loss and determine how much should be paid to the insured. But when personal property such as furniture and clothing is destroyed, the insurance company's job is much harder. The company cannot easily judge what the property cost originally or what it was worth at the time of the loss.

Before an insurance company makes payment under a policy, the insured must furnish the company with *proof of loss*. If the insured is to prove the amount of the loss, he obviously must know the value of each article damaged or destroyed. This means that he must know (1) the original cost of each article, and (2) how long he had owned the article. The time of ownership is quite important. As property becomes older, it gradually wears out and decreases in value. This decrease in value is known as *depreciation*. To estimate how much his property was worth at the time it was damaged or destroyed, the insured subtracts from the value of similar new property the estimated decrease in value due to time or use.

It is important for the policyholder to keep a list of the personal property that is insured. Such a list, known as an *inventory*, should be kept up-to-date and should give the cost of each item and the time it was bought. An inventory provides evidence of loss and enables the insured to prepare a complete record of loss. Without an inventory, the insured may not recall some of the items that were destroyed.

Insurance companies can provide policyholders with inventory forms and with information on how to submit claims for losses.

In Part 24, you learned that bodily injury liability insurance and property damage liability insurance are essential for all drivers. Persons can also be held legally responsible for injuries to other persons and damages to property resulting from causes other than driving a car. Consider, for example, the following situations: (1) a guest falls down the stairs in your house and hurts his back; (2) your dog bites the mailman, and (3) you accidentally hit a baseball through your neighbor's picture window.

In each of these three cases, the property owner could be sued, and he could be required to pay a good deal of money to

HOW IS PAYMENT FOR LOSSES OBTAINED?

THE PROTECTION OF PERSONAL LIABILITY INSURANCE

Household Inventory					
Living Room	Date of Purchase	Cost	Bedroom	Date of Purchase	Cost
Sofa	1967	$359.95	Bed	1967	$150.95
Chair	1967	235.00	Mattress & box springs	1967	200.00
Coffee table	1967	89.98	Double dresser	1967	280.00
Boston rocker	1968	54.95	Night stand	1967	45.00
End table	1968	50.00	Table lamp	1967	36.95
Hanging lamp	1970	89.95	Chest	1970	110.75
Screen	1970	159.95	Chair	1970	65.50

Illus. 25-2. A completed inventory should be kept in a safe-deposit box or some other place outside the home. Then, if the house is destroyed, the inventory will be available for preparing a claim for losses.

the injured party. Protection against such risks can be obtained through *personal liability insurance.* This insurance protects the property owner and members of his family from claims arising from injuries to other people or damages to other people's property. Personal liability insurance is automatically included in homeowners policies, but it may also be bought separately.

Personal liability insurance offers the insured and his family three kinds of coverage: comprehensive personal liability coverage, medical payments coverage, and coverage for physical damage to property. If a guest falls down the stairs in the insured's house and hurts his back, the comprehensive personal liability provision of the insured's policy will cover payment of damages to the guest. However, the insurance company will not make payment until it is convinced that the insured is legally liable. The limit of coverage is usually $25,000 for each occurrence.

If the insured's dog bites the mailman, the medical payments provision of the insured's policy will pay the claims of the injured party. Medical payments coverage applies no matter who is at fault in an accident. The limit of coverage for each person is usually $5,000. The insured and his family are not included in this coverage.

If the insured's son hits a baseball through the neighbor's picture window, claims will be paid through the provision in the insured's policy that covers physical damage to others' property. This provision applies whether or not the accident happens on the insured's property and regardless of who is at fault. The limit that will be paid is usually $250 for each occurrence.

Developing Your Business Vocabulary

The following italicized terms should become part of your business vocabulary. For each numbered statement, find the italicized term that has the same meaning.

depreciation *personal liability insurance*
extended coverage *personal property*
homeowners policy *proof of loss*
insurable interest *real property*
inventory *standard fire policy*

1. Property attached to the land.
2. Property not attached to the land.
3. A package policy covering a wide range of risks for the owners of homes.
4. A basic type of property insurance that protects against loss resulting from fire or lightning damage to a home.
5. Additional protection of property against losses from such causes as windstorms, explosions, riots, and vehicles.
6. A financial interest in insured property.
7. The evidence which the insurer requires of the insured in order to establish the loss and determine the extent of liability.
8. The decrease in the value of property caused by time and use.
9. A list of goods showing the cost of each item and the time it was bought.
10. Insurance against loss because of one's responsibility for injury to other persons or for damage to property.

Checking Your Understanding

1. Give examples of losses against which property may be insured.
2. Give at least three examples of real property and five examples of personal property.
3. How does the comprehensive form of a homeowners policy differ from the standard form and the broad form?
4. Does an insurable interest in property always extend for the same length of time as the insurance policy covering the property? Give an example.
5. If a loss occurs after the insurable interest in a property has ended, is the insurance company legally bound to fulfill the agreements in the policy?

6. Why is it wise for a property owner to review his home's value every few years?
7. Why are fire insurance rates higher in some cities than in others?
8. Why may the fire insurance rate on one building be higher than the rate on another similar building in the same city?
9. How could you prove the value of the furnishings that were in a house when it was destroyed by fire?
10. Why does depreciation have to be considered when the value of property damaged by fire is determined?
11. Explain why personal liability insurance is very important for homeowners. Mention at least four events, other than car accidents, that could make one liable for injuries to others or for damages to their property.

Applying What You Have Learned

1. Frank Polewski and his family live in a rented apartment which they have furnished themselves. Since the owner of the apartment building carries property and liability insurance, Mr. Polewski insists that it is not necessary for him also to carry property and liability insurance. Do you agree with his point of view? Give reasons for your answer.
2. Ronald Latin wants to make sure that he is more than fully protected against the loss of his new $20,000 home. Therefore, he decides to buy two $15,000 standard fire policies, each from a different company. Is this a sensible decision?
3. Jack Yamamoto bought a house and lot for $25,000. Before moving into his new home, he wanted to take out an insurance policy covering both the house and his personal property. Thus, he needed an estimate of the value of both his real and personal property. (a) How do you think he should proceed in estimating the value of his house? (b) How do you think he should proceed in estimating the value of his personal property?
4. On January 2, Jim Galloway took out a fire insurance policy on his house. The policy provided $20,000 of coverage and was to run for one year. On December 1, Mr. Galloway sold his house. On December 29, four days before his policy expired, the house burned. Could Mr. Galloway collect on the insurance?
5. J. C. Henderson has an office in a large office building and carries insurance on his office furniture. The furniture was bought two years earlier for $1,750. A fire destroys the building in which Mr. Henderson's office is located, and his furniture is also destroyed. Although he has a list of the articles of furniture and can prove how much he paid for each, he receives only $1,500 from the insurance company. Why does he not receive the full cost price?

Solving Business Problems

1. The home furnishings listed below were so badly damaged in a fire that they were valueless:

Article	Total Cost
dining room table	$150
6 dining room chairs	$ 30
couch	$360
3 floor lamps	$ 35
9′ x 12′ rug	$225
4 throw rugs	$ 14
occasional chair	$105

Because the furnishings were no longer new, the insurance company did not pay their total cost but rather only $700.

(a) What was the original cost of all the furnishings that were damaged?

(b) How much was the depreciation considered to be?

(c) What percent of the original cost did the insurance company pay?

2. On a warehouse that he owns, Larry Wong carries fire insurance policies with two different companies. Company A insured the warehouse for $15,000. Company B insured it for $20,000. Suppose that a fire causes a loss of $14,000. The two insurance companies share this loss in proportion to the amounts of the policies. What amount will Mr. Wong receive from each company?

3. Harold O'Rourke has his house and its contents protected by insurance through a $16,500 fire and extended coverage policy. His premium for one year is $48.

(a) If the premium for a three-year policy is 2.7 times that for a one-year policy, what premium would Mr. O'Rourke pay for a three-year policy?

(b) How much money would he save by buying a three-year policy instead of three one-year policies?

(c) Stated in another way, this saving would be the same as a discount of what percent?

(d) Assume that Mr. O'Rourke takes out a three-year policy. At the end of one year, he sells his home and cancels his insurance. In applying for a refund on the three-year premium, Mr. O'Rourke is told that the insurance company will keep 37% of the amount he has already paid and that the rest will be returned to him. What refund can Mr. O'Rourke expect to receive?

(e) In canceling the three-year policy at the end of one year, what is the actual cost of insurance protection for the year?

(f) How does this cost compare with the premium on a one-year policy?

(g) If Mr. O'Rourke had known that he would probably need insurance for only one year, would it have been wiser for him to buy a one-year policy instead of a three-year policy?

Enriching Your Business Understanding

1. Once every five or six years, usually in the spring, several fields on Christopher Bixby's farm are flooded by a nearby river. In flood years, Mr. Bixby is not able to farm these fields as profitably as he normally would. On rare occasions, farm crops in Mr. Bixby's area have been so severely damaged by hail that they were almost an entire loss. However, Mr. Bixby's crops have never suffered hail damage. Should Mr. Bixby be more interested in obtaining insurance against loss from floods or insurance against loss from hail?

2. If insurance premiums on a certain property are the same no matter who pays them, why does it make any difference whether a person insuring that property has an insurable interest in it?

3. In determining the amount of loss on insured property, both the original cost of the article and the depreciation of the article must be considered. For the following items, tell what percent of the original cost you think the annual depreciation rate would be: **(a)** a car; **(b)** a stereo; **(c)** an automatic washer; **(d)** a watch; and **(e)** living room furniture.

4. Property insurance policies usually set certain limits on the amount of protection allowed for such personal property as stamp and coin collections, jewelry, furs, and rare paintings. Why are such limitations established? If a person wants to be covered for the full value of such property, what can he do?

5. Here are six rather unusual terms used in the insurance field: **(a)** attractive nuisance; **(b)** extra living expense; **(c)** floater policies; **(d)** friendly fire; **(e)** hostile fire; and **(f)** rider. Define as many of these terms as you can and try to show, by example, how each applies to an insurance situation. Write these definitions in paragraph form and be prepared also to report orally to the class.

PART 26
Life
Insurance

Phil Campanella is considering his economic risks and those of his family. He estimates that their house is worth $16,000 and that their furniture and other household goods are worth about $3,000. The Campanellas could lose as much as $19,000 if their home and belongings were destroyed, so their homeowners policy protects them for that amount.

When Mr. Campanella began his study of economic risks, he thought that their home was their most valuable possession. But as he continues to study their financial situation, he realizes this is not true. His salary is $9,400 a year. His earnings for only two years will about equal the value of the house and its contents. If he should die, the loss of his earning power would cause great hardship to his family. Thus, Mr. Campanella feels that from his family's point of view, insurance on his life is even more important than insurance against loss of property. He plans to keep his home-owners policy in force, but he decides that he should also buy life insurance to give financial protection for his dependents.

The person named in the policy to receive the insurance benefits is called the *beneficiary*. For example, a man with a wife and two small children may name his wife as the beneficiary of his life insurance policy. Persons other than the beneficiary, though,

LIFE INSURANCE REQUIRES AN INSURABLE INTEREST

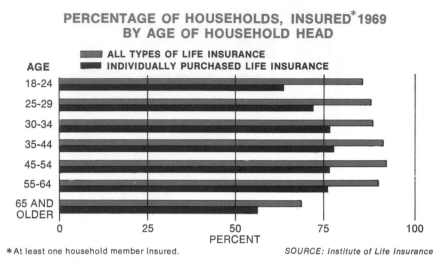

PERCENTAGE OF HOUSEHOLDS, INSURED*1969
BY AGE OF HOUSEHOLD HEAD

ALL TYPES OF LIFE INSURANCE
INDIVIDUALLY PURCHASED LIFE INSURANCE

Illus. 26-1. A national survey conducted by the Institute of Life Insurance produced these results.

*At least one household member insured.

SOURCE: Institute of Life Insurance

benefit indirectly from life insurance. Children are protected indirectly, since insurance provides money that will help the wife to support them if their father dies.

A person may insure not only his own life but also the life of any other person in whom he has an insurable interest. To have an insurable interest in the life of another person, one must derive some kind of financial benefit from that person's continued life. You have, for example, an insurable interest in the lives of your parents. You do not have an insurable interest in a stranger's life. The insurable interest must exist at the time the policy is taken out, but it need not exist at the time of loss.

No two people need exactly the same kind of protection from life insurance. Their ages differ, their incomes and financial obligations differ, the number of their dependents differ. To provide all the different types of protection that are needed, insurance companies offer a variety of policies.

PEOPLE MAY BUY TERM INSURANCE

Term insurance provides protection only for a definite period (term) of time. Policies may run for a period of one year, five years, ten years, or twenty years. If the insured dies during the period for which the insurance was taken, the amount of the policy is paid to the beneficiary. If the insured does not die during the period for which the policy was taken, the insurance company is not required to pay anything. Protection ends when the term of years expires.

By paying a slightly higher premium, a person can buy term insurance with renewable or convertible provisions in the contract. If the policy is *renewable*, the policyholder can continue it for one or more terms without taking a physical examination to determine whether he is still a satisfactory risk physically. If the policy is *convertible*, the insured can have it changed into some kind of permanent insurance without taking a physical examination.

Term insurance policies may be either level term or decreasing term. With *level term insurance*, the amount of protection remains the same during the term. With *decreasing term insurance*, premiums remain the same during the term but the amount of protection gradually decreases. Premiums for a decreasing term policy are lower than for a level term policy of the same amount.

An example of decreasing term insurance is *mortgage insurance*. It protects homeowners from losing their homes in case the insured person dies before the mortgage is paid off. Suppose that the Don Reese family bought a $25,000 house on which they paid down $5,000 and took a 20-year mortgage for the remaining $20,000. Mr. Reese wants to be sure that the mortgage will be paid off if he should die, so he takes out a $20,000 mortgage insurance policy. This assures Mrs. Reese that she will receive the necessary amount of money to pay off the mortgage if Mr. Reese should die before the debt has been paid. The amount of coverage decreases as the Reeses repay what they have borrowed, so the coverage corresponds to the balance of the debt.

Whole life insurance is permanent insurance that extends over the lifetime of the insured. One type of whole life insurance is called *straight life insurance* or *ordinary life insurance*. Premiums for straight life insurance remain the same as long as the policyholder lives. Some whole life insurance policies are intended to be paid up in a certain number of years and are called *limited-payment policies*. They may also be designated by the number of years the insured agrees to pay on them, such as 20-payment life policies. They are like straight life policies except that premiums are paid for a limited number of years—20 or 30, for example—or until a person reaches a certain age—say, 60 or 65. Limited-payment policies free the insured from paying premiums during retirement when his income may be small.

PEOPLE MAY BUY WHOLE LIFE AND ENDOWMENT INSURANCE

Endowment life insurance is really a savings plan which also gives insurance protection. An endowment policy may provide a fund of money for the insured at the end of a certain period, such as 10 or 20 years, or at a certain age, such as 60 or 65. If the insured dies before the end of the endowment period, the face value of the policy is paid to the beneficiary.

Assume that Gary Estes wants to make sure that money will be available to send each of his children to college. When each child is born, he takes out a $5,000 endowment policy on his own life. Each policy is to mature in 17 years and will be payable to Mr. Estes if he is living at the end of the 17-year period. If he dies before that time, it will become an educational fund for the child. In either case, the face value of the policy—$5,000—will be available for the child's education.

A recent important development in personal life insurance is the *guaranteed insurability option*. This enables the policyholder to buy additional insurance even though he has become uninsurable. This option is generally offered with the purchase of a straight life or endowment policy by persons under age 40. Additional insurance may be purchased every three or four years—usually in the same amount as the original policy, but often no more than $10,000 each time.

COMBINING POLICIES TO MEET SPECIAL NEEDS

Every person has different economic risks and should be able to protect himself against exactly those risks of concern to him. The basic life insurance policies you have just learned about can be combined or modified to meet individual needs.

A combination plan that is particularly popular with young married couples is the *family income policy*. It is really a whole life insurance policy that has attached to it a decreasing term rider. A *rider* is a special provision attached to a standard policy. In the family income policy, the rider usually covers a definite number of years. It agrees to pay a specified monthly income to the family from the time the insured dies until the end of the period specified by the rider. The monthly income is paid from the term insurance part of the policy. The whole life insurance part of the policy can be taken in a lump sum or can be paid in an additional series of monthly payments.

Group life insurance gives protection to each individual in a certain group, with the group acting as a single unit in buying the insurance. Most group life insurance contracts are issued through employers. Some policies, though, are available through unions, professional associations, and other similar organizations. Group life insurance has become very important in recent years and now makes up about one-third of all life insurance in force in the United States.

PEOPLE MAY BUY GROUP LIFE INSURANCE

Group life insurance is almost always issued on a term basis, but whole life policies may be offered. If a person leaves the group in which he is insured, he usually does not have to drop his insurance. He can convert his group insurance to some kind of individual policy if he does so within a given period of time, such as 30 days. No physical examination is required, but his premium is based upon his age at the time he converts his policy.

The cost of group life insurance is less than the cost of a similar amount of protection bought individually. This lower cost is possible because insurance for many people can be handled economically in one policy. The employer and the employee usually share the cost of group insurance, but one or the other may pay the entire cost under some plans. The amount of protection available to an individual under a group insurance plan is generally limited. Many persons, therefore, supplement their group insurance with policies of their own.

To buy at least a minimum amount of insurance, some people find it necessary to make premium payments in smaller amounts and at more frequent intervals than is required with ordinary insurance. Life insurance that is offered under this arrangement is called *industrial insurance*. It gets its name from the fact that it was originally offered for workers in industrial occupations who received weekly wages.

PEOPLE MAY BUY INDUSTRIAL INSURANCE

Industrial insurance is usually issued in amounts of less than $1,000. Physical examinations are generally not required. Agents usually call at the insured's home weekly or monthly to collect the premiums. Because of the extra work in collecting premiums and in keeping records, the cost of industrial insurance is higher than the cost of an equal amount of ordinary life insurance.

COMPARING COSTS OF DIFFERENT POLICIES

Different types of insurance policies have different premiums; and persons of different ages will be required to pay different premiums, even on the same type of policy.

Premiums for straight life insurance are higher than those for term insurance, but the annual premium stays the same throughout the insured's life. Illustration 26-2 gives a comparison of the premiums for straight life insurance and for a five-year renewable term policy. You can see that the premiums on the term policy at ages from 15 to 40 are less than the premiums on the straight life policy taken at age 15. After 40, though, the premiums on the term policy increase very rapidly. By the time a person is 60, the premium for a term policy is almost four times the premium on the straight life policy. After 65, term insurance is so expensive that most companies do not offer it.

The premiums on limited-payment life insurance are higher than those for straight life insurance, but they are payable for only a limited number of years. Although the premiums on a 20-payment life policy are payable for only 20 years, the policy remains in force for the lifetime of the insured.

The premiums on endowment policies are higher than the premiums for limited payment life, straight life, or term insurance policies. Endowment policies are payable on the death of the insured and are also payable to the insured at the end of the policy period. Thus, the insurance company must collect enough in premiums to: (1) give the insured protection in case he dies before the end of the policy period, and (2) pay to the insured the amount of the policy if he is living at the end of the period.

Many insurance companies offer what are known as *participating insurance policies*. The premiums for these policies are

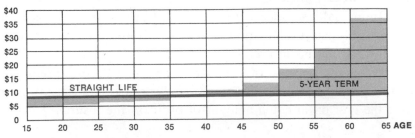

PREMIUMS FOR STRAIGHT LIFE AND 5-YEAR TERM INSURANCE BEGINNING AT AGE 15

Illus. 26-2. A comparison of premiums for $1,000 policies of straight life insurance taken at age 15 and term insurance.

UNIT 6 / ECONOMIC RISKS AND INSURANCE

higher than the company expects to need under normal conditions. At the end of the year, the difference between the premiums paid and the amount actually needed to provide protection is returned to the policyholders as *dividends*. Dividends on participating policies are not real earnings but rather are a refund of part of the premiums. Dividends may be taken in cash by the insured, deducted from future premiums, or left on deposit with the company. Dividends left with the company can be used to increase the amount of the insurance or to pay up the policy before it normally would be paid up according to the terms of the policy. The option of what shall be done with dividends is left to the policyholder.

Policies that are not entitled to dividends are known as *nonparticipating policies*. The premiums on such policies are lower than the premiums on participating policies. When the dividends on participating policies are considered, the cost of the two types of policies is about the same.

As long as they are kept in force, whole life policies and endowment policies accumulate a cash surrender value or, simply, *cash value*. If the insured gives up or surrenders his policy, he is paid the amount of the cash value. The longer the policy is kept, the higher its cash value will be. If a person needs money but does not wish to cancel his policy, he can borrow from the insurance company an amount not exceeding the cash value. If the policyholder should die before the loan could be repaid, the amount yet unpaid would be deducted from the amount that the beneficiary would otherwise have received.

MOST POLICIES BUILD UP CASH VALUES

The cash value may be either more or less than the total premiums paid to the company, depending on the age of the insured, the type of policy, and the length of time the policy has been in force. Suppose that a person who is 15 years old obtained four different policies—term, straight life, 20-payment life, and 20-year endowment—and that each had a face value of $1,000. Illustration 26-3 shows the annual premiums for each of these policies, the total premiums paid during a 20-year period, the cash value at the end of 20 years, and the difference between total premiums and cash value.

Note that at the end of 20 years, the cash value of the endowment policy is $172.80 more than the total of the premiums. This

	5-YR. RENEWABLE TERM	STRAIGHT LIFE	20-PAYMENT LIFE	20-YEAR ENDOWMENT
Annual Premiums	$ 6.52	$ 9.29	$ 17.08	$ 41.36
Premiums Paid in 20 Years	130.40	185.80	341.60	827.20
Cash Value at End of 20 Years	NONE	184.00	359.00	1,000.00
Cost for 20 Years	130.40	1.80	—17.40	—172.80

is because the insurance company invests the premiums it receives so that they will earn interest. The premiums on a 20-year endowment policy are larger than those on other policies, so they earn more interest when they are invested. Also, when a person is only 15, the risk of his dying in the next 20 years is not very great and so the premiums he pays are relatively low. But if he should take out a policy when he is much older, perhaps 50, the premiums he would pay in 20 years would be greater than the cash value at the end of 20 years.

Term insurance accumulates no cash value. Both straight life and 20-payment life accumulate cash values, but in each case the values are somewhat less than the total of the premiums paid over the 20-year period.

Developing Your Business Vocabulary

The following italicized terms should become part of your business vocabulary. For each numbered statement, find the italicized term that has the same meaning.

beneficiary
cash value
convertible policy
decreasing term insurance
dividend
endowment life insurance
family income policy
group life insurance
guaranteed insurability option
industrial insurance
level term insurance

limited-payment policy
mortgage insurance
nonparticipating policy
participating policy
renewable policy
rider
straight life insurance or
ordinary life insurance
term insurance
whole life insurance

1. The person named in an insurance policy to receive the insurance benefits.
2. A life insurance policy that only protects against risk for a specified period of time.
3. A term life insurance policy that the policyholder can continue for one or more terms without taking a physical examination.
4. A term life insurance policy that may be changed into another type of insurance.
5. Term life insurance on which the amount of protection remains the same during the term.
6. Term life insurance on which the premiums remain the same during the term but the amount of protection gradually decreases.
7. A life insurance policy that assures the payment of debts on real property if the insured dies.
8. Permanent life insurance that includes premium payments either for a lifetime or for a limited number of years.
9. Permanent life insurance on which the insured pays unchanged premiums throughout his life.
10. Permanent life insurance on which premiums are paid only for a stated number of years.
11. A life insurance policy payable to the beneficiary if the insured should die or payable to the insured himself if he lives beyond the number of years in which premiums are paid.
12. A provision that enables the holder of a straight life or endowment policy to buy additional insurance even though he has become uninsurable.
13. A policy that combines a standard whole life insurance policy with a decreasing term rider.
14. A special provision attached to a standard insurance policy.
15. Life insurance issued to members of a group as a unit.
16. Insurance sold in small amounts and for which premiums are often collected weekly or monthly.
17. An insurance policy that entitles the policyholder to a refund of part of the premium at the end of the policy year.
18. Part of the premium returned to the holder of a life insurance policy.
19. A policy that does not pay dividends to the policyholder.
20. The amount that an insurance company will pay to the insured if a policy is given up.

Checking Your Understanding

1. Is loss of income or loss of property more serious to the average family in which there are small children?
2. What is the essential difference between the insurable interest in life insurance and in property insurance?

3. How do term life insurance and straight life insurance differ?
4. Why should a term policy that is renewable or convertible cost more than one that is not?
5. In what respect is a limited payment life policy similar to a straight life policy? In what respect is it different?
6. How does an endowment policy differ from a limited-payment life policy? Why is the endowment policy more expensive?
7. If a person leaves a group in which he is insured, what choice does he have about his insurance policy?
8. What is the difference between a participating policy and a non-participating policy? How do the two differ in cost to the insured?
9. Illustration 26-2 shows that the annual cost of a term insurance policy taken out by a person 60 years old is almost four times as much as the annual cost for a policy taken out by a person 15 years old. What accounts for this difference?
10. Ray Mulligan has a participating insurance policy, and each year the insurance company pays dividends on the policy. What choices does Mr. Mulligan have about the dividends paid to him?
11. Suppose that Jane Harris carries for a period of ten years three $1,000 policies: a term policy, a whole life policy, and a 20-payment life policy. At the end of that time, which of these policies will have the greatest cash surrender value? the least?

Applying What You Have Learned

1. Can Greg Templeman take out an insurance policy on the life of his father? Can he take out an insurance policy on the life of his uncle, who is paying his college expenses?
2. Michael Kardos is 22 years old. He is earning a good salary and is saving part of it every week. After considering buying life insurance, he decides against it. No one is dependent on him for support, so he sees no need for insurance. Do you think he is making a wise decision? Why?
3. Harris Nussbaum purchased a convertible term policy. After carrying it for ten years, he converted it to a straight life policy. For what reasons might he have changed the form of his policy?
4. Tell what kind of insurance policy you would recommend be purchased in each of the following cases:

   (a) Dan Rawlings, age 26, wishes to buy a policy on which the premiums will be as low as possible for the next 10 years.
   (b) Tony Ribera, working full time as a mechanic, wishes maximum protection for his invalid and widowed mother.
   (c) Gene Tarr, age 35, wishes to buy a policy that will not require payment of any premiums after he retires.

5. Endowment insurance is sometimes called an insured savings plan. Can you explain why it is given this title?

6. For which of the four policies listed in Illustration 26-3 is the cash value at the end of 20 years (a) greater than the total amount of premiums paid or (b) less than the total amount paid? Why should the difference between the total premiums paid and the cash value not be the same for all kinds of policies?

7. If a person buys an insurance policy for himself, he is ordinarily required to take a physical examination. But when a person buys a policy as a member of a large group, no physical examination is ordinarily required. Why does this difference exist?

Solving Business Problems

1. Martin Schmidt borrowed $1,500 to finish his college education. He agreed to pay $300 on the principal each year, plus interest of 7% a year on the unpaid balance. To be sure that his debt would be paid if he should die, he took out a $1,500, five-year term insurance policy with an annual premium of $7.00.

(a) How much did Martin pay in premiums and interest each year?

(b) What was the total cost of premiums and interest for the five years?

2. When Phillip Bell took out a life insurance policy, he was told that he could pay the premiums monthly, quarterly, semiannually, or annually. Monthly premiums were $14.56; quarterly premiums were $42.86; semiannual premiums were $84.48; and annual premiums were $164.85.

(a) How much would Mr. Bell save by paying the premiums annually instead of semiannually?

(b) By paying the premiums annually instead of quarterly?

(c) By paying the premiums annually instead of monthly?

3. Mr. and Mrs. Jim Komack have a 20-year, $20,000 mortgage on their home. They will repay their mortgage debt in monthly installments. In the first year, $500 will be paid on the principal; in the second year, $600 will be paid on the principal. To assure that the debt will be repaid if he should die, Mr. Komack takes out a mortgage insurance policy to cover the debt.

(a) How much insurance protection do the Komacks have at the time the policy is taken out?

(b) At the end of the first year?

(c) At the end of the second year?

4. Allen Orler, who is 30 years old, is considering taking out several different kinds of life insurance policies. He obtained the following information from one insurance company:

Type of Policy	Premium	Cash Surrender Value at End of 20 Years	Cash Surrender Value at End of 35 Years
Straight life	$16.94	$303	$ 560
20-payment life	$29.40	$549	$ 716
Endowment at 65	$24.10	$451	$1,000

(a) Prepare a table similar to the one in Illustration 26-3 and show for each of the three types of policies the annual premium, the premiums paid in 20 years, the cash surrender value at the end of 20 years, and the cost for 20 years.

(b) Prepare another table and show for each policy the annual premium, the premiums paid in 35 years, the cash surrender value at the end of 35 years, and the cost for 35 years.

Enriching Your Business Understanding

1. A life insurance policy is said to be for a definite amount, such as $1,000, $5,000, or $10,000. This amount may be paid to the beneficiary in the event the insured dies. Does the entire amount have to be taken by the beneficiary at one time?

2. Find out from two or three of your relatives or friends what types of group life insurance are offered through their employers or through organizations to which they belong. Make a list of these various kinds of insurance and describe briefly the benefits provided by each kind.

3. Suppose that a person is temporarily unable to pay the premium on a life insurance policy that has a cash value. He may, if he wishes, borrow from the insurance company enough to pay the premium. But suppose that a person is unable or unwilling to pay any premiums in the future. What may he do then?

4. In some instances, life insurance premiums are higher for someone who works at a dangerous job.

(a) Find out from a local life insurance agent what are considered to be hazardous occupations.

(b) How much more will the premium on a term insurance policy be for a person working in such an occupation than for the same person working in a standard occupation?

(c) Suppose that a person who is a standard risk later transfers to a hazardous occupation. Will he be obligated to report this change to the insurance company?

PART 27
Health
Insurance

What would happen to a family if the wage earner became disabled and his income stopped? There probably would not be enough money available to take care of the medical bills, much less cover the family's regular living expenses. A wealthy family could meet such costs; but for most people the result of an unexpected, prolonged illness could be financial disaster.

Although health care is one of our most important needs, it is an expense that is difficult to budget for. Suppose that a family sets aside $500 a year to cover health care costs, including services of hospitals, doctors, and dentists, medicines, and other medical needs. This $500 may be more than enough to take care of ordinary costs if all members of the family stay in reasonably good health. But it might not meet the expenses of a serious injury or a long illness for just one member of the family. Such an injury or illness might cost hundreds or even thousands of dollars.

The best way to protect against unexpected medical expenses is through health insurance. Such insurance can help a person financially if he is faced with high costs for health care and with loss of income because of illness or injury.

THE IMPORTANCE OF HEALTH INSURANCE

FIVE BASIC KINDS OF HEALTH INSURANCE

Since the needs and wants for health insurance differ considerably among individuals and families, insurance companies offer different types of policies. These policies can be classified into five basic kinds of health insurance: (1) hospital expense insurance, (2) surgical expense insurance, (3) regular medical expense insurance, (4) major medical expense insurance, and (5) comprehensive major medical insurance. Variations and combinations of these basic policies may be designed to meet people's special needs.

(1) *Hospital expense insurance* pays part or all of the charges for room, board, and other hospital expenses. A specific amount is allowed for each day spent in a hospital up to a maximum number of days. Payments are also made for such items as use of the operating room, anesthesia, and drugs. More people carry hospital expense insurance than any other kind of health insurance.

(2) *Surgical expense insurance* is frequently bought in combination with hospital expense insurance. Surgical expense insurance pays part or all of a surgeon's fee for an operation. The typical surgical policy gives a list of operations that it covers and states the amount allowed for each operation. Some policies allow larger amounts for operations than others do. This, of course, requires that a higher premium be paid.

(3) *Regular medical expense insurance* pays part or all of a physician's ordinary bills, such as his calls at the patient's home or at a hospital or a patient's visits to his office. The policy specifies the amount payable for each call and the maximum number of calls covered. This type of insurance is often bought along with hospital and surgical insurance. The protection offered by these three policies is often referred to as *basic health coverage*.

(4) *Major medical expense insurance* provides protection against the very large costs of a serious or long illness or injury. In a sense, it takes over where other medical coverage leaves off. Major medical expense insurance covers part of physicians' fees, hospital bills, nursing care, drugs, and practically every other expense rising out of treatment in a hospital or at home. Benefits may run as high as $15,000 or more, amounts that most people could not afford to pay out of their earnings and savings.

Most major medical policies contain a deductible clause similar to the deductible clause in automobile collision insurance.

In this clause, the insured agrees to pay the first part—perhaps $200 or $500—of the expense resulting from sickness or injury. Major medical policies also usually contain a *coinsurance clause*. This means that the insured person will be expected to pay a certain percentage—generally 20 or 25%—of the costs over and above the deductible amount.

The deductible clause helps discourage the filing of minor claims. The coinsurance clause encourages the insured to keep his medical expenses as reasonable as possible. Thus, both clauses help to make lower premiums possible because they help to keep down insurance payments.

All major medical policies are not the same. The terms of the coinsurance clause may be different, and the deductible amount may vary. Also, policies may differ considerably as to the maximum amounts allowed for surgical and hospital expenses. A person who wants major medical expense protection should study various policies and compare carefully the costs and the protection offered.

(5) *Comprehensive major medical insurance* is another health insurance plan that is becoming increasingly popular. It is a single policy that combines basic health coverage with major medical protection. Such insurance pays for most or all of one's medical expenses above a low deductible amount. Each policy states the maximum amount that the insurance company will pay.

NUMBER OF PEOPLE WITH HEALTH INSURANCE PROTECTION

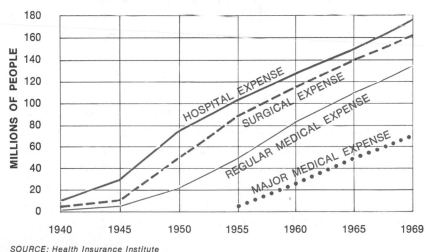

SOURCE: Health Insurance Institute

Illus. 27-1. The number of people having health insurance protection has increased greatly in recent years.

WHERE AND HOW TO BUY HEALTH INSURANCE

Health insurance may be bought by an individual on his own, or it may be bought by an individual who is part of a group. Individual policies are more expensive than group policies. They may require a physical examination, and they usually require the insured to give his medical history when he applies for the insurance. In some cases, persons with a long history of illnesses or injuries will not be insured on an individual basis.

Most Americans are protected under *group health insurance.* Like group life insurance, such policies are made available by employers to their employees, by unions to their members, and by other organizations to their members. The company, union, or other organization receives a master policy or contract. Those persons insured under the plan get certificates to indicate their participation in the plan. Companies that sponsor group policies often pay part or all of the premium costs for their employees. The cost of group health insurance is lower than the cost of a comparable individual policy. This is possible because insurance companies can administer group plans more economically, thus lowering costs for each individual in the group.

Health insurance may be purchased from insurance companies or from nonprofit organizations sponsored by hospitals, doctors, and medical societies. A little more than half of all health insurance is purchased from insurance companies. Most of the rest is purchased through nonprofit organizations. The best-known nonprofit organizations are Blue Cross and Blue Shield. Both are operated as state or regional organizations but are coordinated throughout the country. Rates charged and services offered may vary from one location to the next, since each organization stays relatively independent.

Blue Cross plans provide hospital care benefits for their subscribers up to a specified number of days. The hospital care includes room and board, regular nursing care, use of needed facilities such as operating rooms and X-ray equipment, medications, and other services as set forth in the contract. Blue Cross plans usually pay hospitals directly for care provided to their subscribers. If specialized or additional care is needed beyond that authorized by the local Blue Cross organization, the patient must pay the hospital directly for the extra charges.

Blue Shield plans are concerned mainly with medical and surgical treatment rather than hospital care. They are sponsored by groups of physicians. Most Blue Shield plans list the maximum amounts that will be paid for different types of surgery. These plans also cover charges for physicians' care in the hospital, and some plans pay for a physician's services in his office or in the insured's home. In many areas, Blue Cross and Blue Shield combine their resources to provide major medical expense protection similar to that sold by regular insurance companies.

Our local, state, and federal governments undertake and encourage activities that improve the health of our entire population. For example, public health is safeguarded through public sanitation services such as sewage disposal, garbage collection, and street cleaning. Various public health agencies provide valuable services by inspecting food, testing water supplies, licensing doctors and druggists, and enforcing health and safety laws. Some hospitals receive part of their funds from taxes, and a few of them operate almost entirely with public funds.

HEALTH INSURANCE PROVIDED BY THE STATES

An especially important health insurance program provided by our state governments is *workmen's compensation.* Accidents may occur on almost any job, but some jobs are more hazardous than others. Employees may suffer injuries or may get some disease as a result of their working conditions. Thus, all states have passed legislation known as workmen's compensation laws. These laws provide medical benefits to employees who are injured on the job or become ill as a direct result of their working conditions. These laws protect the welfare of employees and of employees' families. Under these laws, most employers are required to provide and pay for insurance for their employees.

The benefits provided through workmen's compensation vary according to state laws. In some states, all necessary expenses for medical treatment are paid. In others, there is a stated limit of payment. Usually there is a waiting period of a few days before a worker is eligible for loss-of-income benefits. If he is unable to return to his job after this waiting period, he is paid a certain proportion of his wages. This proportion often amounts to about two-thirds of the worker's wages, but no one is paid 100%

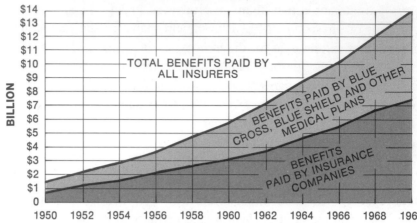

HEALTH INSURANCE BENEFIT PAYMENTS

TOTAL BENEFITS PAID BY ALL INSURERS

BENEFITS PAID BY BLUE CROSS, BLUE SHIELD AND OTHER MEDICAL PLANS

BENEFITS PAID BY INSURANCE COMPANIES

BILLION: $14 $13 $12 $11 $10 $9 $8 $7 $6 $5 $4 $3 $2 $1 0

1950 1952 1954 1956 1958 1960 1962 1964 1966 1968 1969

SOURCE: Health Insurance Institute

Illus. 27-2. This chart shows the upward trend in health insurance benefit payments.

of his earnings. Payments are also made to dependents if the worker is killed in an accident while on the job. Benefits for injury to or death of a worker are usually paid without regard to whether the employee or the employer was at fault.

A person who is covered by workmen's compensation should not feel that he does not need other health insurance for himself and his family. There are limits to the benefits available under workmen's compensation. Every employee should find out whether his employer is required to provide for workmen's compensation and, if so, to what extent he is protected.

A second important health insurance program provided by state governments is *Medicaid*. For years, state and local governments have been paying the cost of medical services to families with little income. In 1965, the federal government agreed to share the cost of providing health benefits to families receiving welfare payments and to other medically needy families. A medically needy family has been defined as one whose income provides for life's basic necessities but who could not afford adequate medical care or pay large medical bills.

Medicaid specifies that at least five basic services must be provided to medically needy persons: (1) in-patient and out-patient hospital care, (2) physician's care, (3) X-rays, (4) lab tests, and (5) nursing-home benefits. States may provide additional services if they wish.

UNIT 6 / ECONOMIC RISKS AND INSURANCE

In 1965, Congress amended the nation's social security laws to provide a broad national program of health insurance. This program is known as *Medicare*. It has two basic parts: hospital insurance and medical insurance.

Nearly every American 65 or over is covered by a basic hospital insurance plan under social security laws. The major provisions of this plan are:

1. Up to 90 days of hospital care for a single illness, with the patient paying the first $52 of the bill and paying $13 a day for each day from the 61st to the 90th day.
2. Up to 100 days of extended care—following a stay of three or more days in a hospital—in an approved nursing home. The plan pays for 20 days of skilled nursing care and all but $6.50 daily for an additional 80 days.
3. Home health care—after the patient has been treated for three or more days in a hospital or nursing home—of up to 100 visits by part-time nurses, physical therapists, and other health workers (not including doctors).

The medical insurance portion of Medicare is often called supplementary or voluntary insurance. It pays for physicians' bills and certain other services not covered by hospital insurance. Almost everyone over 65 may qualify for hospital insurance without having to pay premiums. Medical insurance, though, is available only to persons over 65 who are willing to pay a small monthly premium for it.

The services covered under medical insurance include:

1. Physicians' services such as surgery, consultations, and home, office, and hospital calls.
2. Visits by nurses and other health workers to the patient's home under conditions not covered by the basic hospital plan.
3. Other services not covered in the basic plan, such as special tests, ambulance service, and use of medical equipment (wheelchairs, braces, and oxygen tents, for example).

The premiums for medical insurance are currently $5.30 a month, and the federal government contributes an equal amount to help cover the program's full cost. If medical costs rise substantially in the future or if greater protection is demanded, premiums will no doubt have to be increased. Persons who take part in the medical insurance program pay the first $50 of their total yearly bills for services covered by the program. The program pays 80% of the reasonable charge of remaining bills, and the insured pays the other 20%. This arrangement is similar to the deductible and coinsurance provisions in other health policies.

Developing Your Business Vocabulary

The following italicized terms should become part of your business vocabulary. For each numbered statement, find the italicized term that has the same meaning.

basic health coverage
coinsurance clause
*comprehensive major
    medical insurance*
group health insurance
hospital expense insurance
*major medical
    expense insurance*

Medicaid
Medicare
*regular medical
    expense insurance*
surgical expense insurance
workmen's compensation

1. Insurance that pays part or all of the charges for room, board, and other hospital expenses that the insured person incurs.
2. Insurance that provides benefits to cover the cost of operations.
3. Insurance that provides for payment of a physician's ordinary bills.
4. A combination of hospital, surgical, and regular medical expense insurance.
5. Insurance designed to help offset very heavy medical expenses resulting from serious or long ailments.
6. A provision in which a person agrees with his insurance company to pay a percentage of his medical expenses.
7. A combination insurance policy that includes basic health coverage and major medical protection.
8. Health insurance available to members of a group as a unit.
9. Payments made to employees for injury and loss of income caused by accidents on the job.
10. Medical expense assistance provided by state governments.
11. Health insurance provided under social security laws.

Checking Your Understanding

1. Why is it so difficult to budget ahead of time for health care expenses?
2. Name five basic kinds of health insurance. Which kind is most frequently purchased?
3. If a person has regular medical expense insurance, why should he consider buying surgical expense insurance?
4. To be adequately protected, should a person buy the basic health coverage policies if he carries comprehensive major medical insurance? Explain.
5. How do the deductible clause and the coinsurance clause in major medical expense policies help to make lower premiums possible?
6. Why is the cost of group health insurance lower than the cost of a comparable individual policy?
7. Where may health insurance be purchased?
8. How do Blue Cross and Blue Shield differ in the health-care services they offer?
9. Who must make payments into the fund created by workmen's compensation laws?
10. Under provisions of Medicaid, what five basic services are provided to medically needy families?
11. What two types of health insurance are provided under Medicare? Describe each briefly.

Applying What You Have Learned

1. Marcia Klein is studying to be an elementary school teacher and has a part-time job to help pay her college expenses. She carries no health insurance because she feels she cannot afford it and also feels that she does not really need it. (a) Do you think Marcia should protect herself with some type of health insurance? (b) What possibilities might she have to obtain a policy at a reasonable premium?
2. Eric Grueter found that he could buy major medical expense insurance with a maximum coverage of $5,000 for about the same cost as regular medical expense insurance with a maximum coverage of about $1,000. Why is the cost of the two types of insurance about the same when the maximum coverage is so different?
3. Several of Wayne Harding's friends have suffered large financial losses because they were not covered by health insurance when they were struck by serious illness. Mr. Harding does not want to risk such a loss himself, so he plans to buy hospital, surgical, and

regular medical expense insurance as well as a comprehensive major medical policy. (a) Do you believe Mr. Harding is making wise choices? (b) If not, what insurance do you recommend to meet his desire for full health protection?

4. Lynn Knox has an individual hospital expense insurance policy that costs $46 a year. Her friend Leslie Gibson, who lives in another part of the country, also has an individual hospital expense policy; but she pays $92 a year for it. Is Lynn's policy a better buy because its premium is so much less than Leslie's? Explain your answer.

5. The workmen's compensation laws of the various states provide for payments to employees or their families in the event of injuries or death resulting from accidents that happen on the job. If state governments require protection against accidents occurring on the job, why should they not require protection against accidents of all kinds?

Solving Business Problems

1. In a recent year, American consumers spent $492.2 billion for goods and services. Of this amount, $33.96 billion was spent for medical care, including insurance.

   (a) Medical care constituted what percent of the total amount spent by consumers?
   (b) If the total amount spent for medical care had been distributed equally among the population, which was then about 200 million, what would have been the average share of this expense for a family of four?

2. Carl Byerly has a major medical expense policy with these conditions: expenses paid by hospital and surgical expense insurance are deducted before benefits from this policy are determined; an additional $100 of the expense is to be paid by Mr. Byerly; 20% of all expenses over the deductible amount are to be paid by Mr. Byerly. Assume that Mr. Byerly has medical expenses of $1,950. His hospital expense insurance and surgical expense insurance will pay $650 of this amount.

   (a) How much will the insurance company pay to Mr. Byerly under his major medical expense policy?
   (b) If the deductible clause in this policy had been $200, how much would have been paid by the insurance company?
   (c) If the deductible clause had been $500, how much would have been paid by the insurance company?

3. Study the table below to get a mental picture of the kinds of information given. Then refer to the table for specific answers to the questions that follow.

WORK DAYS LOST DUE TO ACUTE CONDITIONS IN THE UNITED STATES IN A RECENT YEAR

ACUTE CONDITIONS	NUMBER OF WORK DAYS LOST (000,000 OMITTED)			WORK DAYS LOST PER EMPLOYED PERSON		
	All ages 17 and older	Age 17-44	Age 45 and older	All ages 17 and older	Age 17-44	Age 45 and older
All acute conditions	256.0	159.3	96.8	3.4	3.5	3.2
Infective and parasitic diseases	19.6	15.1	4.6	0.3	0.3	0.2
Respiratory conditions	110.8	63.8	47.0	1.5	1.4	1.6
Digestive system conditions	15.9	9.5	6.4	0.2	0.2	0.2
Injuries	79.0	51.8	27.2	1.0	1.1	0.9
All other acute conditions	30.7	19.1	11.6	0.4	0.4	0.4

SOURCE: Health Insurance Institute

(a) What type of ailment was responsible for the greatest number of lost work days?

(b) What was the total number of work days lost because of infective and parasitic diseases?

(c) Among workers 45 years or older, how many work days were lost due to digestive system conditions?

(d) Considering all workers and all illnesses and injuries, how many work days were lost per employed person?

(e) Do workers who are 45 and older lose more work days than workers who are under 45?

(f) Which group appears to lose more work days per capita because of injuries—younger workers (ages 17-44) or older workers (45 and older)?

(g) Injuries accounted for what percent of the total acute conditions?

Enriching Your Business Understanding

1. Suppose that a favorite relative learns that you are not protected by any form of health insurance. He offers to buy one policy as a gift for you. You can choose hospital expense, surgical expense, regular medical expense, or major medical expense insurance.

(a) Which of these four policies would you select? Give reasons for your choice.

(b) You soon decide that you want additional health insurance protection, so you plan to buy one additional policy. What type of policy would you buy as your second choice? Again, give reasons for your choice.

2. Ask your parents, a relative, or a friend to let you summarize the provisions of a health insurance policy they might have. Do not bring the policy to class. In examining the policy, look for answers to these questions:

(a) What type of health insurance is it?
(b) What risks are covered and what are excluded?
(c) What are the maximum benefits, and what are the limits in the amounts paid and in the time covered?
(d) When does the policy expire, and can it be renewed?
(e) What instructions are given in regard to making claims?
(f) Are there other special provisions or limitations in the policy?

3. Many private and public agencies and organizations contribute in important ways to improving our health practices and conditions. Here are some of these agencies and organizations: American Cancer Society, American Heart Association, Blood Bank, Christmas Seals Committee, Community Chest or United Appeal, March of Dimes, Red Cross, Safety Council, U. S. Department of Public Health, U. S. Food and Drug Administration, and Veteran's Administration. You may know of other agencies and organizations that could be added to this list. For example, you might add a community or county hospital supported by public funds or your local public health department.

Select one agency or organization which is working to improve public health standards. Then prepare a report describing the services it provides that relate directly to the prevention, care, or elimination of disease, sickness, accidents, and other health matters.

4. From the topics that follow, select the one that interests you most. Obtain all the information you can about the topic and report your findings in written outline form. Also, be prepared to tell the class about the points you consider most important.

(a) Health insurance for your school's athletes.
(b) Provisions of your state's workmen's compensation laws.
(c) A description of workmen's compensation benefits received by someone you know.
(d) How employers benefit from sponsoring health plans for their employees.

5. Contact your local public health department to determine the nature of the Medicaid program in your community. Find out requirements for participation in the program, how much of the funds for the program comes from the federal government, and how much comes from state sources.

PART 28
Insurance For Income Security

Jim Brolin, a student at McCauley High School, remarked to a friend: "I don't see why I should learn anything about insurance for income security. That won't affect me for a long time—not until I'm in my 60's, if I live that long." The truth is, the need for income security affects all of us from the time we are born until we die. As children, we are affected if our parents lose the ability to earn an income. As young adults, we are concerned about how we would exist if we were injured or disabled. At middle age, we are concerned about how our children would be supported and educated if one parent died or became disabled. Elderly people often worry about expenses because they can't work and are living on incomes considerably lower than those they earned before retirement. So at all stages of your life, you are directly concerned with making sure that there will be enough money to live on in case you are unable to work or want to retire.

LOSS OF INCOME INSURANCE

Loss of income insurance, sometimes called *disability income insurance*, helps to replace income that stops when a person cannot work because of illness or injury. Since one must be sick or injured to collect this kind of insurance, some people think of it as a form of health insurance. However, its main purpose is to provide for income security.

It is possible to obtain loss of income insurance that pays benefits from the first day a person is out of work. However, most policies specify a waiting period of a week, a month, or even longer before payments start. Today many workers receive sick-leave pay from their employers or have income from other sources to cover short absences from work. Thus, a limited waiting period generally does not cause financial hardship.

There are many different loss of income insurance policies. The provisions for the amount of each payment, the duration of the waiting period, and the length of time that payments are desired should be chosen on the basis of the needs of each family. The more benefits provided for, the higher premiums will be.

STATES OFFER UNEMPLOYMENT INSURANCE

When an employee loses his job, his family's income may be cut off entirely or at least greatly reduced. The wage earner may lose his job through no fault of his own. People are out of work at different times due to such causes as business failures, changes in methods and in equipment used in industry, and the temporary or seasonal nature of certain jobs.

To decrease the risk of financial loss because of unemployment, every state has an *unemployment insurance* program which it operates in cooperation with the federal government. Through this plan, an unemployed person is helped to find other employment. But if no suitable job is readily available, he may receive payments to replace part of his lost wages. The duration of such payments varies, but most states will pay for as long as 26 weeks of unemployment after a one-week waiting period.

Unemployment insurance is sometimes confused with workmen's compensation, which you read about in Part 27. Workmen's compensation covers medical expenses of employees injured or disabled on the job, and it also covers part of the loss of income while they are unable to work. Unemployment insurance is completely different. It is designed to provide income to a healthy worker who is temporarily out of a job through no fault of his own. Both plans are financed by employers, except in a very few states where employees may also be required to contribute to unemployment insurance.

Privately organized programs also contribute to our income security. Many employers offer plans that provide monthly payments, or *pensions*, to retired workers. Similar plans are often established by professional and trade associations or by unions.

To qualify for a pension under most private plans, a person must work for the same company or belong to the same organization for a minimum number of years. This may be a drawback to individuals who want or need to change jobs from time to time. Pensions are commonly paid not only to retired workers of industries but also to retired workers of institutions such as schools, hospitals, and government units. It is possible for some workers to retire on pensions which, together with social security benefits, yield an income of up to half or more of their earnings during employment.

MANY EMPLOYERS OFFER PRIVATE PENSION PLANS

If an individual chooses to do so, he can enter into a contract with an insurance company to provide him with a regular future income. The individual arranges to pay the insurance company a certain amount of money either in a lump sum or in a series of payments. In return, the company agrees to pay the person a regular income beginning at a certain age and continuing for life or for a specified number of years. The amount of money that the insurance company will pay at definite intervals to a person who has previously deposited money with the company is called an *annuity*.

ANNUITIES ASSURE FUTURE INCOME

"Yes, there is a catch to our retirement plan. First you have to get hired."

Copyright 1968 by the Kiplinger Washington Editors, Inc.

Illus. 28-1. Many business firms provide pension plans for their employees.

Annuity contracts are sold by life insurance companies and are often thought to be a form of life insurance. However, they are really quite different. A person buys life insurance mainly to protect his dependents; he buys an annuity to protect himself against not having an adequate income in retirement years. It has been said that "life insurance insures against dying too soon and an annuity insures against living too long."

MOST PERSONS ARE COVERED BY SOCIAL SECURITY

Much of the protection for income security is provided through social security laws. The Medicare program which you learned about in Part 27 is one important part of the social security laws. The other important part is *retirement, survivors, and disability insurance*. This insurance provides pensions to retired workers and their families, death benefits to survivors of workers, and benefits to disabled workers and their families.

To pay for social security benefits, a tax on earnings is collected. The employee and the employer share equally in this tax. Each employee's tax is deducted from his wages each payday. The employer contributes an equal amount and then sends the total to the government. If a person is self-employed—as many farmers, retail merchants, and professional workers are—he pays the entire tax. But this amount is somewhat less than the total amount paid by both the employer and the employee on the same income. The self-employed person pays his tax when he files his income tax return.

SOCIAL SECURITY CONTRIBUTION RATE SCHEDULE
(IN PERCENT OF COVERED EARNINGS)

Illus. 28-2. Beginning with January, 1968, the social security tax was levied on the first $7,800 of a person's yearly earnings. Note that tax rates increase gradually in later years. Both the amount subject to the tax and the rates may be changed by law at any time.

EMPLOYEES AND EMPLOYERS, EACH				SELF-EMPLOYED PEOPLE			
Years	For Retirement, Survivors, and Disability Insurance	For Hospital Insurance	TOTAL	Years	For Retirement, Survivors, and Disability Insurance	For Hospital Insurance	TOTAL
1969-70	4.2	.6	4.8	1969-70	6.3	.6	6.9
1971-72	4.6	.6	5.2	1971-72	6.9	.6	7.5
1973-75	5.0	.65	5.65	1973-75	7.0	.65	7.65
1976-79	5.0	.7	5.7	1976-79	7.0	.7	7.7
1980-86	5.0	.8	5.8	1980-86	7.0	.8	7.8
1987 AND AFTER	5.0	.9	5.9	1987 AND AFTER	7.0	.9	7.9

UNIT 6 / ECONOMIC RISKS AND INSURANCE

Under social security laws, three types of monthly payments are available: retirement benefits, survivor's benefits, and disability benefits. These payments are not automatically paid when people are entitled to them. To draw any of these benefits, one must apply at a social security office.

Men and women who are covered by social security can receive the full amount of the monthly payments to which they are entitled when they reach age 65. But if they choose, they can retire as early as 62 by accepting lower payments. These payments are scaled down to take into account the longer period of time they will be collecting benefits. If benefits start at age 62, the amount of each monthly payment will be 80% of what it would be at age 65. There are several exceptions to these general retirement regulations. Widows may draw full benefits at age 62 and may draw lower benefits at age 60. Men and women may be entitled to full benefits if they become disabled at any age before 65.

When an insured worker qualifies for social security benefits, monthly payments may be obtained as follows:

1. For himself as long as he lives.
2. For his wife if she does not qualify for higher benefits as an insured worker on her own account. The wife may begin to receive benefits at age 62, but her monthly benefits will be larger if they do not begin until she is 65.
3. For unmarried children under 18 (or up to age 22 if they are full-time students) and for children of any age if they were disabled before age 18.
4. For a wife, regardless of age, who is caring for a child who is under 18 or disabled.
5. For a dependent husband 62 or older.

If an insured worker dies, monthly payments are also available as follows:

1. For a widow who is 60 years old, but with larger benefits if payments begin at age 62.
2. For unmarried children under the same conditions as described in No. 3 above.
3. For a widow of any age caring for a child who is under 18 or disabled.
4. For a dependent widower 62 years old or over.

5. For dependent parents who have reached retirement age (62 years for both men and women).

6. For a widow as early as 50 who is disabled; and for a widower as early as 50 who is disabled and who was supported by his spouse.

If an insured worker dies, a lump-sum payment (up to a maximum of $255) will be made to help take care of burial expenses, even though monthly benefits are also payable. Workers and their families should keep in touch with local social security representatives about other benefits and regulations not mentioned in this part.

Examples of monthly benefits under social security are given in Illustration 28-3. These examples indicate merely the types of benefits that may be obtained. The exact amounts may be changed by law at any time, and they will differ according to the average monthly earnings of the worker.

Illus. 28-3. Some changes may be made in the future in the benefits paid; but even if they are, these figures will be helpful in indicating the approximate amounts that different beneficiaries may receive.

EXAMPLES OF MONTHLY CASH SOCIAL SECURITY PAYMENTS

AVERAGE MONTHLY WAGES	$200.00	$300.00	$400.00	$550.00	$650.00*
Retired workers benefits, age 65	116.40	146.20	176.70	218.40	250.70
Total benefits, both retired worker and his wife, age 65	175.50	219.30	265.10	327.60	376.10
Total benefits, widow of worker (under 62) and one child under 18	175.40	219.40	265.20	327.60	376.20
Benefit for a surviving child (unmarried and under 18, disabled, or under age 22 if full-time student)	87.70	109.70	132.60	163.80	188.10
Benefit for a widow (age 62), widower, or dependent parent	96.50	120.70	145.80	180.20	206.90
Highest family benefit (this might apply to a widow and two or more children under 18)	175.40	240.00	322.40	395.60	434.40

*The monthly average of $650 is equal to $7,800 a year, the maximum on which social security taxes are collected.

EARNINGS MAY AFFECT THE BENEFITS PAID

Social security benefits alone will probably not be enough to meet all living costs during retirement. A person may need to work to add to the income he receives. The amount that he earns has an effect on the amount of social security benefits he receives.

After an insured worker reaches 72, he is entitled to benefits regardless of the amount that he earns. But a person under 72 is not entitled to full benefits when his total earnings exceed $1,680 a year. Generally his benefits will be affected as follows: (1) $1 in benefits will be withheld for each $2 of earnings over $1,680 and up to $2,880, and (2) $1 in benefits will be withheld for each $1 of earnings over $2,880 until all benefits disappear.

There is one important exception to these restrictions. There will be no deduction from benefits for any month in which the insured person neither earns more than $140 working for someone else nor performs "substantial services" in a business of his own. There is no specific definition of "substantial services," but it generally means devoting more than 45 hours in self-employment during one month. This exception applies for any particular month, no matter how much the person earns in the rest of the year.

In figuring his earnings, the retired worker counts only such things as wages, salaries, commissions, tips, and what he nets from self-employment. The following kinds of income are not counted as earnings and thus do not affect one's benefits: pensions, endowments from insurance policies, dividends from stock, interest on savings, gifts or inheritances, and rentals from property one owns. A wife's earnings do not affect a retired worker's benefits. However, they can be counted against any social security benefits that she is drawing.

OBTAINING A SOCIAL SECURITY ACCOUNT NUMBER

If you work in a job covered by social security—and nine out of ten workers in this country do—you must have a *social security account number*. This number is used to identify your record of earnings. The social security benefits that you or your dependents may receive later will be determined by this record of earnings. The social security account number keeps your record of earnings from being confused with someone else's record.

A social security account number is also needed by persons filing federal income tax returns. The Internal Revenue Service uses this account number, which is issued to persons even though they are not covered by the social security program, as a taxpayer identification number for processing tax returns. Persons who are not working but who receive interest or dividends also need social security account numbers. Even a five-year-old child who has a savings account in his name and is receiving interest payments on it will be asked to give the bank a social security number.

To get a social security account number, it is first necessary to fill out an application form. This form may be obtained from one's employer, from the nearest social security office, or from a post office. The government then issues a *social security card* which bears the account number. A person should use the same account number during his entire life. If he loses the card, he may obtain a duplicate from a social security office. If a girl marries, a new card using her old social security number but giving her married name may be obtained.

Illus. 28-4. The upper half of the social security card may be carried by the employee so that he can show it to any employer; the lower half may be put away in a safe place.

Upper half

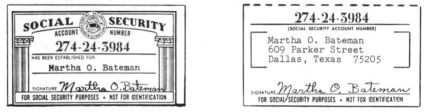

Lower half

If you want to know what your record of social security earnings is, you may request this information at any time by filling out a special card obtainable from your nearest social security office. You should check your account from time to time to make sure that your earnings have been correctly reported. If an error has been made, your nearest social security office will help to correct it. In general, no mistake that is much more than three years old will be corrected.

Developing Your Business Vocabulary

The following italicized terms should become part of your business vocabulary. For each numbered statement, find the italicized term that has the same meaning.

annuity
loss of income insurance, or
   disability income insurance
pensions

retirement, survivors, and
   disability insurance
social security account number
social security card
unemployment insurance

1. A private insurance plan designed to help replace income lost because of sickness or injury.
2. Insurance that provides cash payments for a limited time to people who are out of a job.
3. Payments made to retired workers under privately organized plans.
4. The amount of money that an insurance company will pay at definite intervals to a person who has previously deposited money with the company.
5. Government insurance that provides, among other things, for benefits to be paid to retired workers and their families.
6. The number used to identify one's record of earnings under social security laws.
7. The document bearing the social security account number.

Checking Your Understanding

1. Most disability income insurance policies do not provide for payments until after a specified waiting period. Is this a fair restriction? Explain.
2. What is the difference between unemployment insurance and workmen's compensation?
3. Who pays the tax to provide unemployment insurance?
4. How does a private pension plan differ from social security?
5. If a person buys an annuity contract, does he obtain the same kind of protection he would get from a life insurance policy?
6. Is the owner of a small retail store usually covered by retirement, survivors, disability, and health insurance?
7. How does the method of payment of social security taxes by an employee of a firm differ from the method of payment of such taxes by a self-employed person?
8. If a person retires at age 65, what should he do to receive his monthly social security benefits?
9. Nelson Schneider has been working in a job covered by social security. He decides to stop working at age 62. How much less will his retirement payments be if he starts drawing them at age 62 instead of age 65?
10. Will a 68-year-old worker who has qualified for social security benefits lose any part of his benefits if he earns: (a) $1,000 a year? (b) $1,500 a year? (c) $2,000 a year?
11. If a person loses his social security card, does he lose any benefits to which he may be entitled?
12. Suppose that you have been working for several years and want to know what your record of social security earnings is. How could you obtain this information?

Applying What You Have Learned

1. "Planning for our personal financial security in the future is more important to all of us today than it was for people a hundred years ago." Do you agree or disagree with this statement? Why?

2. Milton Kirsh has just been discharged from the military service, where he learned to be a radio technician. He is, however, having some difficulty finding a job in his home town. He has heard about workmen's compensation and unemployment insurance, but he does not know whether he would qualify for either. Which one should he investigate? Why?

3. Tom Hardy finds that if an annuity is to be received as long as either he or his wife lives, the annual annuity will be less than if it is to be received only during his life. How do you account for this difference?

4. Mike Rossi dies, leaving a widow 34 years old and two children, ages 12 and 6. He has been covered by retirement, survivors, and disability insurance; and benefits will be paid on the basis of average yearly wages of $6,600. According to the table on page 338, how much may his survivors receive each month:

   (a) In the fifth year after his death?
   (b) In the tenth year after his death?
   (c) In the twentieth year after his death?
   (d) In the thirtieth year after his death?

5. How much would Mr. Rossi's survivors have received each month during the year after his death if the following conditions had prevailed:

   (a) The older child was 18, married, and a full-time student?
   (b) The older child was 21, single, and a full-time student?
   (c) The younger child was 19, single, and enrolled in a special class one night a week?
   (d) The younger child was 28, unmarried, and seriously disabled as the result of being in an automobile accident when he was 17?

Solving Business Problems

1. Assume that the total tax rate for retirement, survivors, disability, and health insurance is 5.2% for an employer, 5.2% for an employee, and 7.5% for a self-employed person, and that this tax is levied on only the first $7,800 of a person's annual earnings. Now assume that a certain individual earns $7,000 a year.

   (a) What is the total annual tax on the employer and the employee if the person is employed?

(b) What is the total annual tax if the person is self-employed?

(c) Of these total tax amounts, how much is collected specifically for hospital insurance from both the employer and the employee?

(d) How much is collected specifically for hospital insurance from the self-employed person?

(Refer to the percentage breakdown in the appropriate lines of the schedules on page 336.)

2. Assume that all the figures given in the preceding problem are the same, except that the individual is earning $9,000 a year.

(a) What is the total annual tax on both employer and employee if the person is employed?

(b) What is the annual tax if the person is self-employed?

(c) Of these total tax amounts, how much is collected specifically for hospital insurance from both the employer and the employee?

(d) How much is collected specifically for hospital insurance from the self-employed person?

3. In 1970 Robbie Sherman, a self-employed singer, earned $8,200.

(a) What is the total cash amount that he should have paid in social security taxes when filing his income tax return? (See the schedule on page 336.)

(b) Assume that 5 years later, Robbie will be earning $1,000 a month as a self-employed singer. What will be his social security tax for that year?

4. Mr. Loman, a teacher at Anderson High School, plans to retire next summer when he is 62. He is trying to decide whether to start drawing social security benefits at age 62 or to wait until he is 65. At 62 his monthly retirement check would be $99.40. At 65 it would be $124.20. Assume that Mr. Loman lives to be 72.

(a) What is the total amount of social security benefits he will receive if he begins to draw retirement payments at age 62?

(b) If he retires at age 65, what will be his total benefits?

(c) How much more (or less) will he receive by starting to draw benefits at age 62?

5. Suppose that Mr. Loman lives to be 82.

(a) What is the total amount of social security benefits that he will receive if he begins to draw retirement payments at age 62?

(b) If he starts to draw such payments at age 65, what will be his total benefits?

(c) How much more (or less) will he receive by starting to draw benefits at age 62?

Enriching Your Business Understanding

1. Richard Wells, 65, has retired from a full-time job and is drawing social security benefits of $122 a month. After a year of not working, he decides to accept a job that requires about two-thirds of his time working as a salesman for a local real estate firm. How is his retirement pay affected:

   (a) If he works from January through December, earning $300 each month or a total of $3,600 for the year?

   (b) If he works 8 months at $400 a month and 4 months at $100 a month, for a yearly total of $3,600?

   (c) If when he is 73 years old he is earning $325 a month, or a yearly total of $3,900?

2. Assume that the employer's share of the social security tax is increased from the current rate to 7% or more. (a) Will the profits of a business be correspondingly decreased? (b) If any or all of this tax is passed on to someone else, to whom is it transferred and how is the transfer made?

3. Since most workers are protected by workmen's compensation, is not unemployment insurance for these same workers an unnecessary type of coverage? Explain your answer.

4. "Social security is nothing more than a form of charity." Do you agree with this statement? Present arguments for the stand you take on this statement.

5. You have learned that nine out of ten Americans work in jobs covered by social security. Find out from your nearest social security office who is not covered by social security in your city or county.

6. Savings, insurance, and investments in a home and other property contribute to economic security as well as to a higher standard of living. All of us can count on a happier and more successful life if we start planning now for our economic well-being. This might be called estate planning. How can one start his estate planning while he is still in high school? How can he continue this estate planning early in his working career?

Unit 7

Saving and Investing Money

PART 29
Making a Savings Plan

Those of us whose incomes are not large—and most of us are in this group—need to save carefully in order to be able to buy many of the things that we want. Now we may want to pay for a watch or a camping trip. Later we may want to pay college expenses, and still later we may want to pay for a home. If we are to be able to pay for these things, we must save regularly.

A person who has saved money can often take advantage of opportunities that otherwise would be lost. A watch that is just what you want may be offered at a special sale at a low price. If you have savings, you may be able to buy it. Or your parents may find that someone wants to sell a house quickly and is willing to sell cheaply. If they have savings, they may be able to buy it. Or a person may want to start a small business and work for himself instead of for someone else. If he has savings, he may be able to do this. In various ways, then, a person who saves part of his income is able to take advantage of buying opportunities.

Savings also offer protection against want in case of sickness, during old age, or in case of the death of a person who has dependents. In Part 28, you learned that the federal government and many businesses provide benefits for retired workers. Also, insurance makes it possible to decrease the risk of loss resulting from

TRY TO SAVE PART OF YOUR INCOME

a wage earner's sickness or death. But social security payments, pensions, and insurance often take care only of one's minimum needs. Savings provide the "extras."

SAVINGS INCREASE IN VALUE IF YOU INVEST THEM

Saving only a few dollars at a time may not seem to be very important, but even small savings can be put to work so that they earn an income. When savings are put to work to earn income, they become *investments*.

When savings are invested and the income earned from them is in turn invested, the increase over a number of years is larger than many people might think. Suppose that David Skinner, a mechanic, can save $50 a month. In a year, his savings will amount to $600; in 10 years, $6,000. He finds that he can deposit his money in a savings account and receive interest of 5%. If he does this, he will have at the end of 10 years, not $6,000, but about $7,775—$1,775 more than the amount deposited.

As an *investor,* David realizes the importance of this increase of $1,775. Thus, he does some more calculation to see how much the increase will be if he continues to save for a longer period. He finds that, at the rate of $50 a month, his savings and interest will amount to over $12,000 in 14 years. If this amount continues to earn interest at 5%, the interest received from it will amount to more than $50 a month. This means that if David saves $50 a month for 14 years and deposits it so that it will earn 5% interest, he can withdraw $50 a month after that time without decreasing the investment. Most young people do not think in terms of 14 years from now. But it does pay to think ahead. The increase in savings as a result of interest earned is shown in Illustration 29-1.

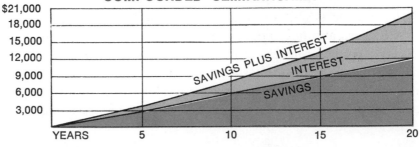

SAVINGS AND INTEREST FOR AN INVESTMENT OF $50 A MONTH FOR 20 YEARS AT 5% INTEREST COMPOUNDED SEMIANNUALLY

Illus. 29-1. Money kept in a mattress or in a sugar bowl is not an investment, but money deposited in a savings account is an investment.

Illustration 29-2 shows how rapidly monthly savings of different amounts increase when invested at 5%. The first column of the table shows the amount saved each month. The other columns show the total amount of the savings plus interest at the end of different periods. This table assumes that interest is calculated each 6 months (*semiannually*) and that the interest is added to the principal on which the income is calculated for the next 6 months. When interest is added to the principal on which future interest is calculated, we are said to have *compound interest*.

MONTHLY SAVINGS	END OF FIRST YEAR	END OF SECOND YEAR	END OF THIRD YEAR	END OF FOURTH YEAR	END OF FIFTH YEAR	END OF TENTH YEAR
$ 5.00	$ 61.64	$ 126.39	$ 194.43	$ 265.91	$ 341.00	$ 777.52
10.00	123.27	252.78	388.85	531.81	682.01	1,555.03
25.00	308.18	631.96	972.13	1,329.53	1,705.02	3,887.58
30.00	369.82	758.35	1,166.56	1,595.43	2,046.02	4,665.09
35.00	431.45	884.74	1,360.99	1,861.34	2,387.02	5,442.61
50.00	616.36	1,263.92	1,944.27	2,659.06	3,410.03	7,775.16

Illus. 29-2. This table shows the growth of monthly deposits with interest of 5% compounded semiannually for a selected number of years.

SAVINGS SHOULD BE INVESTED PROMPTLY

A person docs not usually receive at one time a large amount of money that he may invest. In fact, he may accumulate his savings a dollar or two at a time. He may wait until he has saved a considerable sum, perhaps $100, and then invest the whole amount at once. This plan is usually not desirable because the investor earns no interest while the sum is being accumulated.

A number of financial institutions allow a person to invest his money in small amounts as it is saved. They accept deposits as the depositor wants to make them, and they pay interest at regular periods. Examples of such institutions are banks, credit unions, and savings and loan associations.

SAVINGS SHOULD BE INVESTED CAREFULLY

Savings that are invested do increase in amount, but only if they are wisely invested. Suppose that you lend $40 to a friend with the understanding that he is to repay it with 6% interest at the end of a year. If payment is made, you will receive $42.40 at the end of the year. But if the borrower has no money at the end of the year, you may get nothing. You may lose both the $40 principal and the $2.40 interest. Investments are satisfactory only when the safety of both principal and interest is assured.

Not all investors need the same degree of safety. Suppose that a person has enough money to make 100 different investments. If he loses one of them, he still has the other 99, and his one loss may not be very important. On the other hand, suppose that a person has only a small amount of money and is able to make only one investment. If he loses this, the loss would be very serious to him. A person with limited funds should be very careful to make investments that will be as safe as possible.

SAVINGS SHOULD OFFER A GOOD RATE OF RETURN

A good investment should be safe, and it should also earn a reasonable income or offer a satisfactory rate of return. If a person receives 5% interest, for example, he is better off than if he receives only 3% or 4%. Illustration 29-3 shows the value of an original investment of $100 at the end of 20 years at the rates of 3%, 4%, 5%, and 6%. Note that at 3% the interest is only $81, but that at 6% it amounts to $226.

AMOUNT OF $100 INVESTED FOR 20 YEARS AT DIFFERENT RATES OF INTEREST

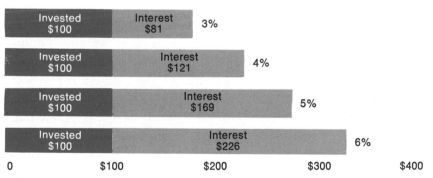

Illus. 29-3. An investment should offer a good rate of return. It should also be safe and should be reasonably liquid.

Usually, the higher the rate of interest offered by an investment, the greater the risk of loss. Loans to the federal government are safer than any others. If investors prefer to lend to individuals or to businesses, regardless of the danger of loss, they do so largely because they receive rates of interest higher than those paid by the government. For example, when the government is paying 5% interest, one business may be paying 6% and another business may be paying 8%.

The offer of a low rate of interest does not guarantee safety, because investors may be mistaken about the risk involved. Similarly, the offer of a high rate of interest does not mean that loss is bound to occur. The high rate does mean, though, that investors believe that the loan involves considerable risk. The borrower would not offer to pay a high rate of interest if his credit were good enough so that he could obtain a loan for less interest.

SOME SAVINGS SHOULD BE IN LIQUID FORM

When an investment can be turned into money quickly, it is said to be *liquid*. This feature of an investment is desirable, for one may need money quickly to take care of emergencies. Suppose, for example, that you have $1,000 on deposit in a bank. If you need money right away, you can withdraw it from the bank. On the other hand, suppose that you own a piece of land which you bought for $1,000. The land may be a safe investment and may eventually return a satisfactory income; but if you need money at once, you may not be able to get it. You may have trouble selling the land, or you may be able to get only part of the price you paid for it, perhaps $700. In this case, you will lose $300, not because the investment was unsafe but because it could not be quickly turned into money.

A person making a number of investments need not have all the investments in a liquid form. He will seldom need all his money at one time. However, he should have enough of his investments in a liquid form so that he can get money at once if he needs it.

A good investment, then, is one that is safe, earns a fair income, and is reasonably liquid.

Developing Your Business Vocabulary

The following italicized terms should become part of your business vocabulary. For each numbered statement, find the italicized term that has the same meaning.

compound interest	*liquid investment*
investment	*semiannual*
investor	

1. Savings put to work to earn income.
2. One who invests money for income or profit.
3. Twice a year.
4. Interest on both the principal and the interest previously earned.
5. An investment easily convertible into cash.

Checking Your Understanding

1. Name several reasons that these persons might have in mind in planning a savings program: (a) a high school boy or girl, and (b) the head of a family.
2. "Wally Kirkland has $1,000 that he wants to invest." What do you understand to be the meaning of this statement?
3. After having saved for several years, Gordon Woodruff accumulated $500. He lent this amount to a friend, who later was unable to pay any interest or to repay the loan. Was Mr. Woodruff as well off as if he had made no effort to save?
4. How does compound interest differ from ordinary interest?
5. Why are semiannual payments of interest better for the lender than annual payments?
6. Suppose that you want to invest $3 a week. Should you wait until the end of a year and invest $156 at that time, or should you invest $3 each week?
7. Is an investment that pays a high rate of interest better than an investment that pays a low rate of interest?
8. Bruce Nathans has $500 in a savings account and is receiving 5% interest on it. A friend, John Thurgood, asks to borrow the money and offers to pay 8% interest. What might be the advantages and disadvantages of making the loan to Mr. Thurgood?
9. Tell which of the following investments might be called liquid: (a) land, (b) a deposit in a bank, (c) a loan made to a friend in exchange for an oral promise to pay, and (d) a loan that is secured by a mortgage.
10. What will be the accumulated savings if $10 is deposited monthly at 5% interest compounded semiannually for a period of 10 years? (Use the table on page 351).

Applying What You Have Learned

1. Randall Fleming inherited $3,000 from an uncle and did not bother to invest this money. Assume that it could have been invested safely to earn 5% a year. How much did Randall lose each month by not investing his inheritance?
2. Frank Brokaw, a man of considerable wealth, invests $5,000 in a newly organized manufacturing company. Earl Chapman owns his home and also has $5,000 in a savings account. He knows of Mr. Brokaw's investment. Because Mr. Brokaw has a reputation for being a good businessman, Mr. Chapman decides to make a similar investment. Is the fact that the investment may be a good one for Mr. Brokaw sufficient indication that it may be a good one for Mr. Chapman?

3. Gerald Holt is more concerned with safety of investments than with the amount of interest earned. Therefore, he puts his money in investments where the income earned is 5% or less. He believes that in this way he will be sure to have investments in which there is no risk of loss. Do you believe that Mr. Holt can be sure he is investing his money safely?

4. Wayne Payton tells you that his father invested $1,000 forty years ago and since then has been paid $1,500 in interest. Was this a very good investment?

5. Jeanne Young, an art student, inherits $2,500 from her grandfather. This is the only money she has. She deposits $500 in a bank to use for her education. With the rest she buys some paintings that she believes will increase in value within the next few years. Under the circumstances, do you think her investment is a wise one?

6. Susan Gilligan has $1,500 that she plans to use while going to college, and she expects to enroll within two years. Do you recommend that she invest her money in real estate in the meantime?

7. Each of the following borrowed money at about the same time: the federal government; a small, newly organized company with limited earning power; and a company that had been operating for many years and that had made large profits each year. (a) Why should one of these three probably need to pay a higher rate of interest than either of the other two? (b) Which probably paid the lowest rate and which probably paid the highest rate?

8. Fred Reibling wanted to borrow $1,000 from Cliff Mathis. Mr. Reibling offered to pay 10% interest although the usual rate at that time was 5%. Suggest why the higher rate was offered.

Solving Business Problems

1. Ray Fess lends $500 to Bill Hedges, who is to pay interest of 7% a year in return for the use of the money.

    (a) How much interest does Mr. Hedges have to pay Mr. Fess each year?

    (b) If the interest is to be paid semiannually at the rate of 7% a year, how much would Mr. Hedges pay on each interest date?

    (c) How much less interest would Mr. Fess have received each year if he had deposited the $500 in a savings account paying 5% interest?

2. Brenda Nolan deposited in a bank $30 each month for 5 years.

    (a) What is the total amount of principal that she has invested?

    (b) How much do the deposits amount to if they earn 5% compounded semiannually? (See the table on page 351.)

    (c) What is the total amount of interest earned?

3. Brian Jordan deposited in a bank $5 a month for 10 years; Keith Griffin, $10 a month for 5 years; and Joe Walters, $35 a month for 1 year. According to the table on page 351:

(a) Which of these three people earned the most interest?

(b) How much more interest did he earn than was earned by each of the others?

4. Bob Maxwell finds that he can save $25 a month.

(a) If he receives no interest on his savings, how much will his savings amount to in 1 year? In 10 years?

(b) If he deposits his money monthly in a savings account and receives an income of 5% compounded semiannually (the rate used in the table on page 351), how much will he have at the end of 1 year? At the end of 10 years?

(c) At the end of 10 years, how much of the value of the savings as found in (b) will be made up of interest?

Enriching Your Business Understanding

1. If you deposit money in a savings bank, the bank will guard it for you and will return it to you when you ask for it. In the meantime, the bank will pay you interest on the amount deposited. (a) Is it fair for you to receive interest? (b) If so, what service are you rendering for which you should be paid?

2. Assume that a business borrows $100,000 and gives the lender a promissory note secured by a mortgage on its buildings. Assume also that in the next 20 years the business pays $120,000 in interest and still has to repay the debt of $100,000. The total amount paid the lender is thus $220,000 for a loan of $100,000. Why would a business be willing to pay the lender in principal and interest more than twice the amount that was borrowed?

3. Suppose that a person invests $1,000 at 5% and another $1,000 at 7%. He reinvests the interest on each investment at the same rate as the principal. Do you think that the difference between the amount of the two investments in 20 years is likely to be about $20, $200, $400, or $800? Explain.

4. Suppose that everyone saves his money and no one buys such things as cars, furniture, household equipment, and new houses. If no one is buying, merchants will not be making sales, factories will not need to produce goods, and many people will lose their jobs as a result. Under these circumstances, do you think that it is a good idea for a person to save part of what he earns, or would it be better if everyone spent all that he earns?

PART 30
Using Savings Accounts

We all approve of the idea of saving and investing our money to earn an income, but sometimes we have so little to save that it hardly seems worthwhile. Fortunately, even small amounts of money can be invested in the form of a savings account, and small amounts saved regularly do grow into important sums. Places where savings accounts can be maintained are to be found almost everywhere.

Almost all commercial banks maintain *savings departments*. A person can maintain an account in the commercial department which handles checking accounts, in the savings department, or both. As you learned in Part 13, a savings account differs from a checking account in two important ways: (1) checks may not be written on a savings account, and (2) a bank pays interest on the amounts deposited in a savings account.

REGULAR SAVINGS ACCOUNTS IN COMMERCIAL BANKS

The steps followed in opening a savings account in a bank are similar to those followed in opening a checking account. A person fills out a signature card, makes a deposit, and receives a savings passbook. The passbook shows the deposits and the withdrawals made by the depositor, the interest earned, and the balance of the account.

When the depositor makes a deposit, he fills out a deposit ticket much like that used in making a deposit in a checking account. He presents this ticket, the savings passbook, and the deposit to the bank clerk. The clerk then enters the deposit in the passbook. If the depositor forgets his passbook, the clerk accepts his deposit and gives him a receipt for it. The clerk enters the deposit when the passbook is presented at a later date.

A depositor cannot write checks to withdraw money from a savings account even though he may have both a savings account and a checking account in the same bank. If a depositor wants to withdraw money from a savings account, he fills out a withdrawal slip supplied by the bank. This slip, together with the savings passbook, is given to the bank clerk. Usually money cannot be withdrawn from a savings account unless the passbook is presented. If the book is lost, the bank will issue a duplicate. Before the duplicate is issued, however, the bank requires the depositor to sign certain forms for the protection of the bank.

SPECIAL SAVINGS ACCOUNTS IN COMMERCIAL BANKS

The savings departments of commercial banks commonly offer savings plans that are different from their regular savings accounts. These special savings accounts are given different names by different banks, but they all pay a higher rate of interest than do regular accounts. To earn this higher rate, the depositor must meet certain requirements. Two common requirements are:

1. An amount equal to or greater than a fixed minimum must be deposited. This amount may be $1,000 or more.
2. The depositor must agree to leave the money in the bank for at least a minimum period of time. This time is commonly three or six months.

The savings placed in these special accounts may be recorded on forms known as *certificates of deposit*. Or they may be recorded in special passbooks that are similar to the passbooks provided for regular accounts.

SAVING THROUGH MUTUAL SAVINGS BANKS

A *mutual savings bank* operates much like the savings department of a commercial bank in that it accepts for deposit the savings of individuals. Many mutual savings banks also perform other services, such as renting safe-deposit boxes, operating school savings programs, and selling savings-bank life insurance.

There are no stockholders in a mutual savings bank. Therefore, the earnings of such a bank are paid out only to the depositors. The amount paid to depositors is often less than the total earnings because the bank usually retains some of the earnings to provide for any losses that may occur in the future.

A depositor deals with a mutual savings bank in about the same way he would deal with a commercial bank. When a depositor opens an account, he fills out a form that is similar to the signature card of a commercial bank. Whenever he wishes, he brings additional money to the bank. Each amount is entered in his passbook. At regular times, usually every three or six months, the net earnings of the bank are distributed to depositors in the form of interest credited to their accounts.

SAVING THROUGH SAVINGS AND LOAN ASSOCIATIONS

Savings and loan associations operate for two main purposes. First, as you learned in Part 20, they lend money to individuals for use in building or buying homes. Second, they assist small investors by handling savings accounts in much the same way that banks handle savings accounts. Many savings and loan associations also offer check-cashing service, rent safe-deposit boxes, and sell travelers checks and U.S. savings bonds.

Most savings and loan associations are owned by those who hold accounts with them. The account holders are the co-owners, and they receive income in the form of dividends. This income is most commonly credited to their accounts. The rate of dividend paid by a savings and loan association depends on the earnings of the association. It is usually a good rate because savings and loan associations have low operating costs and are able to lend money to home buyers at favorable rates of interest.

SAVINGS CAN BE PLACED IN CREDIT UNIONS

Credit unions, as you learned in Part 20, are organized by a specific group to serve that group. Credit unions obtain their funds by selling ownership shares to their members. Those who direct the union's business affairs are elected by the members. Each member has one vote, whether he owns only one share or many shares. The funds collected through the sale of shares are usually loaned to members. Excess funds may be invested in loans to other credit unions, in government securities, or in savings and loan association shares.

Illus. 30-1. Persons can put their savings in regular savings accounts or special accounts in commercial banks, in mutual savings banks, in savings and loan associations, or in credit unions like this one.

The dividends paid by credit unions, like those of savings and loan associations, are commonly higher than the interest paid by savings banks. Dividends are not guaranteed and can be paid only if they are earned. The amount of a dividend thus depends to a considerable extent on the skill of those who manage the credit union.

ADVANTAGES OF INVESTING IN SAVINGS ACCOUNTS

Savings accounts are recommended for investors who want a high degree of safety, a reasonable rate of interest, and a convenient means of making deposits and withdrawals. They are very attractive for those who want to save for a definite time and for a definite purpose, such as a vacation or a Christmas fund. Some important advantages of savings accounts are:

(1) Deposits can be made conveniently. In almost every community a person has a choice of several places where savings accounts can be maintained. The term "deposits" as used in this discussion includes all amounts placed in mutual savings banks, savings and loan associations, and credit unions. In reality, these amounts are usually investments in the ownership of the business and are not actually deposits.

(2) Small deposits are accepted. An original deposit of at least $1 is usually required for a savings account. Other deposits of almost any amount can be made.

(3) A great degree of safety is assured. In almost all banks, each deposit of $20,000 or less is insured through the Federal Deposit Insurance Corporation. Similarly, each account in most

savings and loan associations is insured up to $20,000 by the *Federal Savings and Loan Insurance Corporation*.

(4) The interest and dividends paid are reasonable. Interest and dividends paid usually vary from 4% to 6%. This is a fair return on an investment with such a high degree of safety.

(5) The deposits can be withdrawn at any time they are needed. Some banks and savings and loan associations may require that a 30-day notice be given before withdrawals are made, but almost without exception they are able to give depositors money at any time that it is desired.

Persons who have larger sums of money to invest may want to place part of them in investments which offer higher rates of interest. Even these persons, though, may deposit part of their funds in savings accounts because of the availability and safety of such investments.

Developing Your Business Vocabulary

The following italicized terms should become part of your business vocabulary. For each numbered statement, find the italicized term that has the same meaning.

> *certificate of deposit*
> *Federal Savings and Loan*
>   *Insurance Corporation*
> *mutual savings bank*
> *savings department*

1. A division of a commercial bank that accepts deposits that draw interest.
2. A form used to record savings placed in special savings accounts.
3. A bank that has no stockholders and pays out earnings only to its depositors.
4. An organization that insures accounts up to $20,000 in a savings and loan association.

Checking Your Understanding

1. What steps are followed in opening a savings account in a commercial bank?
2. How does a depositor withdraw money from a savings account?
3. What are two common bank requirements for a special savings account?

4. Why is the interest paid to depositors of a mutual savings bank usually less than the bank's earnings?
5. What are the two chief purposes of savings and loan associations?
6. Why is the rate of dividend paid by savings and loan associations to their account holders usually a good rate?
7. Who elects the people who direct the business affairs of a credit union?
8. What determines the amount of dividends paid by a credit union?
9. What are five advantages of savings accounts?
10. Up to what amount are accounts in most banks and savings and loan associations insured through the Federal Deposit Insurance Corporation and the Federal Savings and Loan Insurance Corporation?

Applying What You Have Learned

1. Penny Thompson has a checking account and in one month drew only two checks against her account. She also has a savings account and during the same month made two withdrawals from this account. Even though there were two withdrawals from each account, the bank paid interest on the savings account but not on the checking account. Why does the bank pay interest on one account and not on the other?
2. What advantages of savings accounts make them especially desirable for high school students?
3. Commercial banks commonly pay a higher interest rate on some special savings accounts than they do on regular accounts. Give reasons why you think a bank can afford to pay a higher interest rate on special accounts.
4. Give the name of a commercial bank in your community that has a savings department. What rate of interest does it pay?
5. Give the name of a mutual savings bank or a savings and loan association in your community. What rate of interest has it paid recently?
6. List groups of people in your community who have organized or who might organize a credit union.
7. Find out whether banks in your community offer special Christmas club plans. If they do, answer the following questions.

(a) What arrangements are made for depositing money?
(b) What interest does the money in the fund draw?
(c) When is the Christmas fund available for use?

Solving Business Problems

1. The table below shows the amount of money in savings deposits in four different types of organizations for 1950 and 1970:

	Savings Deposits (in billions of dollars)	
	1950	1970
Commercial banks	$36.4	$208.7
Mutual savings banks	20.0	69.0
Savings and loan associations ...	14.0	146.7
Credit unions	0.8	15.5

(a) In which organization did savings deposits increase the most in dollars from 1950 to 1970? How much was this increase?

(b) In which organization did savings deposits increase the most in percent from 1950 to 1970? How much was this percent?

2. Mack Carlton receives a gift of $1,000 when he is 16 years old. Assume that he deposits this amount in a savings account and receives interest at the rate of 5% annually.

(a) If the interest received is not invested, how much will he receive each year?

(b) If the interest received is also invested each year at 5%, how much more will he receive the second year than he did the first?

(c) If the principal and the interest are always invested at 5% and if money at this rate doubles itself in 16 years, how much will the fund amount to when Mr. Carlton is 64 years old?

(d) What will be the income for a year when Mr. Carlton is 64 years old?

3. On December 31 Paul Gatto deposits $300 in each of two savings banks. On one deposit he receives interest at the rate of 5% annually. On the second he receives interest at the rate of 5%, payable quarterly. If in each case the interest is added to the principal, what will be the amount of each savings account at the end of a two-year period?

4. The savings departments of both the Northside Bank and the People's Bank pay interest at the rate of 5% a year. Both pay interest on the balance at the beginning of an interest period plus any deposits made during the first month of the period less any withdrawals. The Northside Bank pays 2.5% interest for each of two half years, January 1 to June 30 and July 1 to December 31. The People's Bank pays 1.25% interest for each of four quarters, January 1 to March 31, April 1 to June 30, July 1 to September 30, and October 1 to December 31.

Assume the following facts for a depositor during one year:

> January 1, balance in the account, $800
> January 10, deposited $200
> June 5, withdrew $300
> July 2, deposited $400
> October 1, deposited $500

(a) If interest is paid to the depositor as it is earned, how much interest would be paid on this account during the year by the Northside Bank? By the People's Bank?

(b) If interest is not paid to the depositor but is added to his account so that it will draw additional interest, what would be the balance of the account at the end of the year in the Northside Bank? In the People's Bank?

Enriching Your Business Understanding

1. Organizations that accept savings accounts do not all pay the same rates of interest. The difference between the lowest interest rate paid and the highest may be 1% or 1½% or even more. Why does not everyone in a community deposit his money where it will draw the highest rate of interest?

2. The Suburban Savings and Loan Association has the rule that it may require a depositor to give 30 days' notice of a withdrawal. The association has, however, always permitted depositors to withdraw amounts at any time without notice. Why does the association have such a rule if it never enforces it?

3. The government does not provide insurance that all investments will be successful. For example, it does not provide insurance for investments in land, stocks and bonds, or a small business. Since it does not provide insurance against loss in other investments, why should it set up the Federal Deposit Insurance Corporation and the Federal Savings and Loan Insurance Corporation to insure deposits in banks and in savings and loan associations?

PART 31
Investing In Bonds And Stocks

Businesses, government, and other organizations often need to raise money. When they borrow for a short period of time, such as two months or six months, they may borrow from a bank. But sometimes they may want to borrow for a longer period of time, perhaps 10 or 20 years. They may also want to borrow more than can be obtained from any one bank or other lending agency. How do they raise money in such cases? Two common ways are by selling bonds and by selling stocks. Many persons invest their savings in bonds and stocks issued by businesses, government, and other organizations.

The Marcroft Corporation has had satisfactory earnings for several years. The company's policy has been to use most of its earnings to develop new products and buy more equipment. This policy has enabled the company to increase its earnings from year to year and has also given it excellent prospects for the future. But spending so much to develop new products and buy equipment has kept the company from building up a very large cash balance.

The company needs a larger building and new equipment right away if it is to continue to grow as the management hopes it will. The company would therefore like to borrow $1,500,000 and repay the debt 15 years later. Its bank is not willing to make such a loan because commercial banks usually make loans only for

MANY BUSINESSES ISSUE BONDS

short terms, such as two months, six months, or perhaps even a year. An officer of the bank recommends that the company consider borrowing the needed money by selling bonds.

A *bond* is a printed promise to pay a definite amount of money, with interest, at a specified time. Bonds are thus similar to the promissory notes discussed in Part 20. Interest is usually paid twice a year. Each bond indicates the amount that it promises to pay. Often the amount of each bond is $1,000. If the Marcroft Corporation is to borrow $1,500,000 by issuing $1,000 bonds, it must issue 1,500 bonds.

A bond may be secured by a mortgage on the company's property. In that case, it is known as a *mortgage bond*. If a bond provides for no mortgage but is only a claim against the company's earnings, it is known as a *debenture bond*, or simply *debenture*. Usually debenture bonds are issued only by well-established businesses with good earnings records and good prospects for the future. To make their bonds attractive to investors, other companies must offer the additional security that a mortgage provides.

To issue its bonds, the Marcroft Corporation goes to an investment bank. An investment bank, as you learned in Part 12, specializes in providing long-term financing for corporations. The bank investigates Marcroft's past record and its prospects for the future. The bank is interested in the bonds only if everything indicates that the company will be able to pay both the interest and the principal when they are due. If the business' record and prospects are satisfactory, the investment bank—either by itself or with other dealers—will buy the bonds and sell them to investors.

THE FEDERAL GOVERNMENT ISSUES BONDS

The federal government sells several kinds of bonds, but Series E savings bonds are most popular with small investors. These bonds can be purchased in the denominations and at the prices shown in Illustration 31-1. After two months from the date of purchase, a savings bond can be cashed or redeemed at the cost price; after six months, it can be redeemed at a higher price. The cash value of a bond increases at the end of each six-month period until the date of maturity, which is currently five years, ten months after the date of purchase.

The difference between the purchase or issue price and the redemption value of a Series E bond is the interest that has been

United States Savings Bonds, Series E	Face Value	Cost or Issue Price
	$ 25	$ 18.75
	50	37.50
	75	56.25
	100	75.00
	200	150.00
	500	375.00
	1,000	750.00

Illus. 31-1. A United States Savings Bond, Series E. Face values and cost prices of the various bonds available are shown in the table.

earned on the investment. For example, a bond purchased for $56.25 and redeemed for $75 has earned $18.75 of interest. The face value of a bond plus a small bonus is paid when a bond is redeemed at maturity so that the average annual rate of interest is 5½%. If a bond is not kept until its date of maturity, the annual rate of interest is less. If the investor wants to do so, he may hold the bond after it matures; it will continue to earn interest at 5½%.

Investors can buy savings bonds from banks, some savings and loan associations, any Federal Reserve bank, or the Treasury Department in Washington, D.C. Bonds are usually redeemed at a bank, but they may be taken or sent for redemption to a Federal Reserve bank or to the Treasury Department. Since the smallest denomination of the Series E bonds costs $18.75, the bonds are not a convenient means of regularly investing a few dollars at a time. To offset this disadvantage, many businesses will—if the employee wishes—deduct a small amount from each paycheck and buy a bond for the employee when enough money has been accumulated.

BONDS MAY BE ISSUED BY LOCAL GOVERNMENTS

Your school district may find that because more students are enrolling each year, it must build a new high school. To pay for the building, extra taxes must be collected for a number of years and saved until enough money has been accumulated. This means, of course, that the school cannot be built for some time, and it may be needed right away. So it is likely that the district will obtain the necessary money by issuing bonds. It will then build the school and pay for it out of taxes over a period of years while the building is being used. If a city needs new streets, water mains, or sewers, it may also obtain the money for them by issuing bonds. All such bonds issued by a city are known as *municipal bonds*. Similar bonds are issued by counties, states, and school districts.

The interest paid by a city, county, state, or school district is not subject to the federal income tax. Their bonds are thus especially attractive to persons who have large incomes and pay high federal taxes. For this reason, these bonds often pay a rather low rate of interest, sometimes less than federal government bonds.

MANY INVESTORS PLACE THEIR MONEY IN STOCKS

In Part 5 you learned that the ownership of a corporation is divided into shares of stock, and a person who buys such shares is a part owner of the business. An investor may buy one or more shares, depending on the amount that he wants to invest in a single business. He thus becomes a stockholder, and his ownership in the business is shown by a printed form known as a *stock certificate*. If a business is profitable, part of the profits are paid to the stockholders in the form of dividends.

When stock is issued, each share may be given a face value, known as *par*. This may be any amount, such as $10, $25, or $100. If each share does not have a par value, it is known as *no-par stock*. The price at which stock can be bought or sold at any time is known as the *market value* or the *market price*. The market value depends largely on how much the business earns and what investors think it is likely to earn in the future. Market value changes frequently, often from day to day. The investor is chiefly concerned with the market value rather than the par value. The market value determines how much he will have to pay if he invests in a corporation's stock or how much he will receive if he sells stock that he owns.

The stock that a corporation issues may be divided into classes. *Preferred stock* has a preference in the payment of dividends and perhaps in the distribution of property if the business is closed. *Common stock* has no preference over other shares. If a corporation issues only one class of stock, as many do, it is all common stock.

If a person owns 6% preferred stock, he will be paid a dividend of 6% of the par before anything is paid to the common stockholders. Often, however, the income that a preferred stockholder receives is limited to a fixed rate, such as 6%. In this case, a very profitable business may pay a large dividend on common stock and pay only 6% on preferred stock. On the other hand, if the business has little profit, the preferred stockholders may receive 6% while the common stockholders receive nothing. If the business makes no profits, neither the preferred stockholders nor the common stockholders will receive any dividends.

Stocks are usually bought and sold through dealers known as *brokers*. A broker may buy stock from the one who owns it and then sell it to the new owner. Or he may arrange for the sale to be made directly by the seller to the buyer. Such sales are known as *over-the-counter sales*. The stocks of small and medium-sized corporations are usually sold over-the-counter by dealers in their communities.

The stocks of large corporations are bought and sold through central markets known as *exchanges*. When brokers place their customers' orders to buy and sell with the exchanges, they do not have the buyers and the sellers deal directly with each other. The prices at which stocks are bought and sold at different exchanges are quoted in daily newspapers.

The current dividend rate in dollars per year.

The hundreds of shares sold during the day.

The first price at which a sale was made.

The highest price at which a sale was made during the day.

The lowest price at which a sale was made during the day.

The last price at which a sale was made.

The net change between the closing price and the closing price of the preceding day.

Stocks	Div.	Sales in 100s	Open	High	Low	Close	Net Chg.
Abacus	.74t	4	12¼	12¼	12	12	. . .
AbbtLab	1.10	247	67½	67¾	67	67½	. . .
ACF Ind	2.40	27	42¾	44⅛	42¾	43½	+1
AcmeCleve	1	9	13⅞	14⅛	13¾	13¾	— ⅛
Acme Mkt	2b	5	41	41	40¾	40¾	— ½
AdmEx	1.24e	41	12¾	12¾	12½	12⅝	—1⅛
Ad Millis	.20	15	13¾	13¾	13¼	13½	— ¼
Address	1.40	94	27⅞	28	27½	28	+ ⅛
Admiral		19	8½	8½	8	8	— ⅜
AetnaLif	1.40	1007	40⅛	40¼	37⅛	37¼	—3
Aguirre Co		16	9¼	9½	9¼	9½	+ ⅛
Aileen Inc		22	32⅝	33	32⅝	33	+ ½
Air Prod	.20b	5	45⅝	45¾	45½	45¾	— ⅛
Air Pd	pf4.75	16	120	120	120	120	— ¾
Air Red	.60e	45	17½	17⅝	17⅜	17½	— ⅛
AJ Industries		62	4	4	3⅞	3⅞	. . .
Akzona	1a	76	29⅝	29⅝	29¼	29¼	— ½
Ala Gas	1.10	8	15	15⅛	14⅞	14⅞	— ⅛
Alaska Inters		121	23⅝	23¾	22½	22¾	— ⅜
AlbertoC	.28	x170	36½	36¾	36¼	36½	+ ⅜

Stocks	Div.	Sales in 100s	Open	High	Low	Close	Net Chg.
BunkR	pf1.50	5	29¾	29¾	29½	29½	— ⅛
Burl Ind	1.40	28	39⅞	40	39¼	39¼	— ⅝
BurlNor	1.77e	80	30	30¼	30	30	— ⅛
BurlNor	pf.55	6	6⅜	6½	6⅜	6⅜	
Burndy	.70	2	16½	16½	16¼	16¼	— ¼
Burrghs	.60	250	112	113⅜	111½	113	— ¼
Cabot Cp	.70	33	36⅝	36⅝	36	36	. . .
Cadence Ind		12	10⅝	10⅝	10⅜	10⅜	— ⅜
Cal Finanl		34	7⅝	7¾	7⅜	7¾	. . .
Callahn Mng		229	11¾	13½	11½	13⅛	+1⅜
CampRL	.45a	155	31½	34	31¼	33½	+2½
CampSp	1.10	53	29¼	29¼	28¾	28¾	— ½
Cdn Brew	.40	11	7¼	7¼	7⅛	7⅛	— ⅛
Cdn Pac	3.20	14	60⅝	61	60⅜	61	— ⅛
CanalRd	1.10	3	15	15	14¾	14¾	— ½
Cap C Bdcst		30	27½	28⅛	27½	28⅛	+ ⅜
Carbrun	1.50	6	46¾	46¾	46¾	46¾	— ¼
Carlisle	.60	9	13⅛	13⅜	13⅛	13¼	— ¼
Caro C&Oh	5	z100	58	58	58	58	+ ½
CaroPLt	1.46	37	22⅜	22¾	22¼	22½	. . .

Illus. 31-2. Quotations for a few of the stocks listed on the New York Stock Exchange.

WHY DO PEOPLE INVEST IN BONDS AND STOCKS?

A brief summary may help you to understand the differences between investing in bonds and investing in stocks:

1. When a person buys a bond, he is lending money.
2. When a person buys stock, he is buying a part interest in a business.
3. A bondholder is promised a fixed rate of interest.
4. A stockholder may, if the business is profitable, receive a part of the profits as dividends.

When an investor buys the bonds of a business, it is usually because they pay a higher rate of interest than he can obtain from other investments that he considers equally safe. Bonds of corporations, unlike the savings accounts discussed in Part 30, are not insured. Most businesses pay their bonds promptly when they are due, but sometimes one may not. Thus, bonds of a business are usually bought only by persons whose training or experience enables them to judge whether the bonds are reasonably safe.

Investments in government savings bonds are as safe as any investment can be. Because they are debts of the federal government, one can be sure that they will be paid on demand. There is no danger that the bonds will decrease in value because the redemption values are fixed. The bonds also earn a reasonable rate of return. The interest rate of 5½% for Series E bonds is usually considered acceptable for an investment with such a degree of safety.

Savings bonds are *registered,* that is, the name of the owner or owners is entered in the government's records. Since the ownership of each bond is registered, a bond can be replaced if it is lost, stolen, or destroyed. Series E bonds are issued only to individuals and not to businesses and other organizations.

As was mentioned earlier, municipal bonds are attractive to persons with large incomes because interest on these bonds is not subject to federal taxes. Municipal bonds also offer much of the safety of federal government savings bonds.

When a person buys stock in a corporation, he may receive as dividends part of the profits that are not needed to improve or expand the business. If the business does very well, the stockholder may receive large dividends which may be much more than the interest he would receive from a bond. Also, the stock's market value may increase. But if the business does not do well, the dividends may be quite small or there may be none at all. And the stockholder may not be able to sell his stock for as much as he paid for it. Care should thus be taken to invest in the stock of sound, profitable corporations.

Stocks and bonds and other written forms such as notes are sometimes grouped together and are called *securities*. This does not mean, however, that all investments in such forms are secure. Only if investments are well selected is a reasonable degree of safety or security provided.

Developing Your Business Vocabulary

The following italicized terms should become part of your business vocabulary. For each numbered statement, find the italicized term that has the same meaning.

bond
broker
common stock
debenture bond
exchange
market value or *market price*
mortgage bond
municipal bond

no-par stock
over-the-counter sales
par
preferred stock
registered bond
securities
stock certificate

1. A printed promise to pay a definite amount of money, with interest, at a specified time.
2. A bond that is secured by a mortgage on the issuing company's property.
3. A bond that is only a claim against the issuing company's earnings.
4. A bond issued by a city.
5. A printed form that shows ownership in a corporation.
6. The face value assigned to a share of stock.
7. Stock that has no stated face value.
8. The price at which a share of stock can be bought or sold.
9. Stock that has a preference in the payment of dividends.
10. Stock that has no preference over other shares.
11. A dealer in the stocks and bonds of a corporation.
12. Sales of stocks and bonds that are not made through an exchange.
13. A market where stocks and bonds are sold.
14. A bond that has the owner's name entered in the borrower's records.
15. A collective name for stocks, bonds, and other written forms such as notes.

Checking Your Understanding

1. Why are some companies able to sell 6% mortgage bonds when they cannot sell 6% debenture bonds?
2. What functions does an investment bank perform for a business that wants to issue bonds?
3. When is interest paid on U.S. savings bonds, Series E?
4. What are some advantages of buying Series E savings bonds?
5. For what purposes are cities and school districts likely to issue bonds?
6. Why are municipal bonds more attractive to people with large incomes than to people with small incomes?
7. Is the market value of a share of stock likely to be the same as the par?
8. Is preferred stock likely to be more valuable than the common stock of the same company?
9. Explain the difference between selling stock through an exchange and selling it over-the-counter.
10. What are some advantages and disadvantages of buying stock in a corporation?

Applying What You Have Learned

1. What are some of the differences between a bond and a promissory note similar to the one shown on page 241?
2. Company A wants to borrow $1,000. Company B wants to borrow $10,000. Company C wants to borrow $1,000,000. Which of these businesses is most likely to issue bonds? Why?
3. Assume that the Crawford Corporation issues both mortgage bonds and debentures and that the two have the same interest rates. Which would you prefer to own? Why?
4. Why did the Marcroft Corporation sell its bonds to an investment bank instead of to individuals who might want to buy the bonds as investments?
5. Why do bonds of a business usually pay a higher rate of interest than do government bonds?
6. Why does the government pay a higher rate of interest on Series E bonds held to maturity than on such bonds redeemed earlier?
7. Assume that you wanted to buy a Series E savings bond. Where in your community might you arrange to purchase the bond?
8. If you were going to buy a share of stock, would you prefer to buy a stock with no-par value or a stock with a par of $25, assuming that each could be bought for the same price, $38?
9. If an investor has a share of 5% preferred stock with a par of $5, how much can he hope to receive in dividends each year?

Solving Business Problems

1. Ronald Hizer decides to have his employer deduct $20 from his paycheck each month to buy savings bonds.

   (a) At the end of the year, how many Series E savings bonds, $100 face value, will Ronald have bought?
   (b) At the end of the year, how much will be available toward the purchase of another $100 bond?
   (c) At the end of 5 years, how many bonds with $100 face value will Ronald have purchased?

2. Verna Dickson owns 5 Morgan Enterprises bonds, each with a face value of $1,000. Morgan Enterprises pays 5% interest each year on the bonds it has issued. The interest payments are made semiannually to each bondholder.

   (a) How much interest does Verna receive every 6 months?
   (b) At the end of 20 years, how much interest will Verna have received?

3. The table below shows the market price and the annual dividend of 6 different stocks:

	Market Price	Annual Dividend
Consolidated Engineering	$48	$2.50
Electro-Jet Company	50	3.00
Federated Industries	30	1.60
Instrumentation, Inc.	30	1.30
Magus Corporation	38	1.90
Seaboard Steel	65	2.70

   What would be the rate of return on each of these stocks if it were bought at the price given in the table?

4. The Rand Company has issued 2,000 shares of 6% preferred stock with a par of $50 and 1,000 shares of no-par common stock. At the end of a year, $10,000 is to be paid as dividends.

   (a) What will be the dividend per share of preferred stock?
   (b) What will be the total dividend paid on preferred stock?
   (c) How much will be available for the dividend on common stock?
   (d) What will be the dividend per share on common stock?

   In another year, $15,000 is to be paid as dividends.

   (e) What will be the dividend per share of preferred stock?
   (f) What will be the total dividend paid on preferred stock?
   (g) How much will be available for the dividend on common stock?
   (h) What will be the dividend per share on common stock?

Enriching Your Business Understanding

1. Series E savings bonds at one time paid interest of less than 3% a year on bonds held to maturity. Later the rate was increased several times. Why do you think the interest rate was increased?
2. Check a book on law or finance to find: **(a)** the difference between a registered bond and a coupon bond, and **(b)** the advantages of each.
3. Within a few weeks the market price of a stock dropped from $110 to $85. Did this mean that the company is likely to fail or that its stock is not a good investment?
4. Suppose you want to invest in the stock of a company and you find that this company issues both common and preferred stock. Which kind of stock would you rather buy? Why?
5. The chart on the left below shows for a recent year the ages of people in this country who own shares of stock. The chart on the right shows the incomes of people who own stock. Study the charts, then answer the questions.

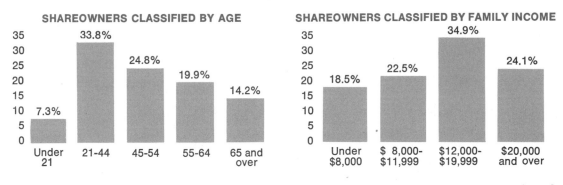

SHAREOWNERS CLASSIFIED BY AGE

Under 21: 7.3% 21-44: 33.8% 45-54: 24.8% 55-64: 19.9% 65 and over: 14.2%

SHAREOWNERS CLASSIFIED BY FAMILY INCOME

Under $8,000: 18.5% $8,000-$11,999: 22.5% $12,000-$19,999: 34.9% $20,000 and over: 24.1%

   (a) What percent of the stockholders were under 21 years of age? Under 45 years of age?
   (b) What percent of the stockholders had a family income of less than $8,000 a year? Less than $12,000 a year?

6. In the stock market quotations on page 369, small letters such as "t," "b," "e," and "a" are given after the dividend rate. In the newspaper in which these quotations were originally printed, the meanings of these letters were explained. Look at the stock market quotations in your daily newspaper for similar reference letters and find the meaning of each.
7. Consult a book on accounting or finance to find the meaning of the terms stock dividend and stock split-up. Assume that a corporation issues a 50% stock dividend. Do you believe that after the dividend is distributed, the market value of each share of the stock is likely to be **(a)** the same as, **(b)** more than, or **(c)** less than the market value of each share before the stock dividend? Explain.

PART 32

Investment Clubs and Mutual Funds

Dale Elliott had an investment problem—not because he had a lot of money to invest but because he had only a little. If he had had much money to invest, he might have subscribed to investment services and paid for investment advice. As it was, it seemed that he would have to depend largely on his own judgment.

Dale was 21 years old, a graduate of a technical school, and was employed as a draftsman. He had several savings bonds that he had bought through his company and a small savings account to take care of emergencies. He wanted to invest some of his future savings in common stocks because it seemed likely that they would pay him a better return in the long run than would other types of investments.

Dale expected to have about $20 a month to invest in common stocks. The fact that the amount was small did not in itself keep him from buying stocks. Members of the New York Stock Exchange have a plan for small investors known as the Monthly Investment Plan. Under this plan a person can invest as little as $40 in a three-month period. Although this plan made it possible for Dale to buy common stocks, he hesitated to do so. Which stock or stocks should he buy? With the small amount that he had to invest, he could buy stocks in only a few corporations, probably in only one or two. If he made a poor selection, he might suffer a serious loss. If the corporation did not make good earnings in the future, he might receive small dividends or none at all, and the stock might decrease in value.

FORMING AN INVESTMENT CLUB

During lunch hours and coffee breaks, Dale discussed investments with several of his friends. He found that they had problems much like his own. They all wanted to invest in common stocks, but each had so little to invest that buying common stocks did not seem to be practical.

A broker recommended to one of Dale's friends that they form an investment club and make their investments together. At his suggestion, they wrote to the National Association of Investment Clubs for information about how to organize and operate such a club. With the information they received, Dale and 14 of his friends met one evening and formed an *investment club*. They decided to call it the Security Investment Club. They all signed an agreement specifying, among other things, that:

1. The club was to be operated as a partnership.
2. Each partner was to contribute at least $20 a month to the club for investment.
3. All dividends received by the club were to be reinvested.
4. If it became advisable for a member to withdraw, he would after a month's notice be paid the value of his interest in the club at the time of his withdrawal.

OPERATING AN INVESTMENT CLUB

After the club was organized, the major problem was the selection of sound investments. Some of the stocks to be considered were suggested by the different members. Others were suggested by the broker whom they had selected to make their purchases and sales.

Each member was assigned one or more stocks for study. The club's broker referred them to several sources of information about stocks. The members were also aided in their studies by procedures and forms recommended by the National Association of Investment Clubs. After each member had completed the study of the stock or stocks assigned to him, he reported his findings to the club at one of its regular meetings. The stock or stocks to be purchased were selected by a vote of all members.

Dale and the other members of the Security Investment Club found that they received a number of benefits from the club. First, since each member agreed to invest $20 a month in the club, regular savings were encouraged. A member was permitted to skip a monthly investment if he needed to, and this was not unfair to the other members because the club's earnings were shared in proportion to the members' investments. Still, each member made a real effort to keep up his monthly investments and seldom failed to do so.

A second benefit was that each member was able to learn a good deal about how to judge a stock. Each member was usually assigned one stock at a time to study. He was helped in his study by suggestions and forms from the National Association, by the advice of his fellow club members, and by the club's broker.

A third benefit was that the club was able to buy stocks in a number of corporations. If one investment did not do very well, it might be offset by another investment that did extremely well. A single mistake was therefore not so serious as it would have been if it were the only investment of one person.

Dale stayed in the Security Investment Club for several years. During the club's first two years of operation, the profits were small. After that, however, the club did very well. Dale would have liked to continue as a member, but after six years his company transferred him to another city. He was no longer able to attend meetings of the club or take part in any of its activities. The club therefore permitted him to withdraw and paid him the value of his interest at the time that he withdrew.

Illus. 32-1. Investment clubs encourage regular saving by members, provide members with opportunities to learn about how to judge a stock, and make it possible to buy stocks in a number of corporations.

IBM

A MUTUAL FUND RESEMBLES AN INVESTMENT CLUB

After Dale was settled in his new job, he was again faced with the problem of what to do about investments. So far as he knew, there was no investment club that he might join, and he was not well enough acquainted in his new location to consider organizing a club. He thought about buying stocks himself, but at best he could buy only a few. A single mistake in selecting a stock might result in a larger loss than he could afford. He therefore decided to study the possibility of investing in the stock of a mutual fund.

A *mutual fund*, also known as an *investment company,* is a corporation that sells its own stock to the public and buys stocks, or stocks and bonds, of other corporations. It receives interest and dividends from its investments. From these amounts it first pays its operating expenses. The amount that is left is distributed as dividends to its stockholders.

A mutual fund is similar to an investment club in that it takes the money of a number of individuals and invests in the securities of many corporations. But a mutual fund is operated by highly skilled professionals who are paid for their services. An investment club is operated by amateurs who usually receive no pay for the work they do for the club. Also, a mutual fund is much larger than an investment club. One large mutual fund has more than 200,000 stockholders and more than $2 billion in investments.

MUTUAL FUNDS ARE OF SEVERAL TYPES

Mutual funds may be classified as open-end or closed-end. An *open-end fund* is one in which a person can invest at any time and can withdraw all or part of his investment at any time. In other words, the fund will sell its stock to investors whenever they wish to buy and will buy back the stock from investors whenever they wish to sell. A *closed-end fund,* on the other hand, has a fixed number of shares. These shares may be bought and sold on a stock exchange or over-the-counter like the stock of ordinary corporations. Most mutual funds are of the open-end type.

Mutual funds may also be classified according to the types of securities in which they invest. *Balanced funds* are those that invest in bonds, preferred stocks, and common stocks. They try to have their investments balanced so that they will earn a reasonable income regardless of changes in business conditions. *Common stock funds* buy common stocks only. And these common stock funds differ according to the types of stocks that they buy. Some look for "growth" stocks; that is, stocks that they believe will increase considerably in value in the future. Others tend to buy stocks that are paying good dividends or that are expected to pay such dividends in the near future. Still others invest in stocks in one industry, such as chemicals or public utilities.

A mutual fund is a large organization that has many expenses. It must pay commissions to those who sell its stock. It must pay the salaries of the skilled employees who select its investments. And it must pay the many other expenses of operating a business. All these expenses must be passed on to investors in the mutual fund. This is accomplished in two ways.

First, an open-end mutual fund will sell stock to investors and will buy stock back at any time. But the price at which it sells stock is usually about 8½% higher than the price at which it will buy stock. Illustration 32-2 shows the prices of a number of mutual funds on one day. For each fund, the "asked" price is the price at which the mutual fund will sell its stock; the "bid" price is the price at which the fund will buy its stock. Note that the difference between the two prices is commonly 8½% of the "asked" price. This difference is often as much as the stock will earn in about two years. For this reason, stock in a mutual fund is seldom bought as a short-term investment. It is usually bought only by those who wish to hold it for a number of years. Both the "bid" price and the "asked" price fluctuate as the prices of the fund's investments fluctuate, but the difference between the "bid" price and the "asked" price as a percentage remains about the same.

CHARGES FOR THE SERVICES OF MUTUAL FUNDS

	Bid	Asked		Bid	Asked		Bid	Asked		Bid	Asked
Aberdn	1.82	1.99	Col Grth	11.12	11.12	Fund Am	7.98	8.75	Luth Bro	10.86	11.87
Admiralty Funds:			ComS Bd	4.46	4.85	Gatewy	7.23	7.82	Manhtn	4.52	4.94
Grwth	5.78	6.33	Cwlth AB	1.20	1.30	Gen Sec	9.04	9.04	Mass Fd	10.27	11.25
Incom	3.62	3.97	Cwlth C	1.45	1.57	Gibraltr	6.34	6.40	Magna In	8.19	8.95
Insur	7.12	7.80	Comp As	8.54	9.36	Group Sec:			Mass Inc	14.29	15.62
Advisrs	4.83	5.28	Compet	6.08	6.66	Apex F	6.89	7.54	Mass Inv	10.52	11.50
Aetna Fd	8.62	9.42	Comp Bd	8.30	9.02	Bal Fd	8.16	8.92	Mass Tr	13.70	14.97
Affiliated	6.56	7.09	Comp Fd	8.66	9.41	Com St	11.77	12.87	Mates	3.48	3.48
Afutre	6.97	6.97	Comstk	3.87	4.23	GrthFd A	6.72	7.34	Mathers	11.29	11.29
All Am F	.58	.63	Concord	11.10	11.10	Grth Ind	17.45	17.45	Moody Cp	10.92	11.93
Allstate	9.73	10.46	Consol In	10.50	11.00	Guardn	22.40	22.40	Moody's	11.77	12.87
Alpha Fd	9.93	10.85	Contl MI	6.46	6.46	Hamilton:			MIF Fd	7.66	8.28
Amcap	5.32	5.81	Cont Gth	8.00	8.08	HFI	4.03	4.40	MIF Gth	4.58	4.95
Am Bus	3.06	3.31	Corp Ld	13.84	15.21	Gth	6.56	7.17	MuUS Gv	10.45	10.61
Am Dvln	9.67	10.57	Cnty Cap	11.19	12.09	Harbor	7.25	7.92	Mu OmG	4.85	5.27
Am Eqty	4.44	4.85	Crn WDiv	5.47	5.98	Hartwll	10.73	10.73	Mu Omin	9.64	10.48
Capit	7.27	7.95	Crn WDal	6.13	6.70	H&C Lev	8.60	8.60	Mut Shrs	13.53	13.53
Incme	8.46	9.25	deVgh M	60.27	60.27	Hedb Gor	6.79	6.79	Mut Trst	1.93	1.93

Illus. 32-2. Quotations of prices of mutual funds.

Second, a fund may use part of the dividends and interest it receives to pay its expenses. In this case, only the balance after all expenses are paid is distributed to stockholders as dividends. Some funds use only about 5% of their income from interest and dividends for their expenses, but other funds may require 10%, 15%, or even more.

A few mutual funds have the same "bid" and "asked" price. Such funds are called *no-load funds* because they do not add a commission or "load" to the sales price. But a no-load fund may use more of its income to pay operating expenses than does a "load" fund. The dividends that it pays to stockholders may therefore be smaller. In the long run an investor may find that he gains as much or even more by buying shares in a load fund than he would by buying shares in a no-load fund.

ADVANTAGES OF MUTUAL FUNDS

Mutual funds started about 40 years ago. Now they have more than 4 million stockholders and investments worth about $45 billion. The rapid growth in the number of stockholders and in the total investments has come about because investors have been impressed with three main advantages of mutual funds.

First, a mutual fund invests in the securities of many corporations—50, 100, or even more. As a result, there is no danger of serious loss if any one stock does not prove to be profitable.

Second, the investments of mutual funds are selected by highly skilled professional people. The earnings of a mutual fund may therefore be greater than the average earnings of all stocks.

Third, small amounts can be invested at one time, and earnings can be reinvested. It is therefore possible for an investor to accumulate a large amount even though he is not able to invest much at any one time.

Illus. 32-3. This chart shows the total amount accumulated by a $50-a-month investment in the stock of one mutual fund when all dividends are reinvested.

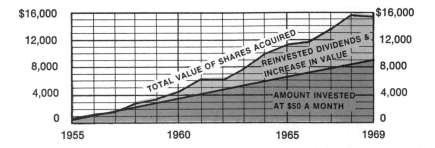

UNIT 7 / SAVING AND INVESTING MONEY

Developing Your Business Vocabulary

The following italicized terms should become part of your business vocabulary. For each numbered statement, find the italicized term that has the same meaning.

balanced fund	*mutual fund* or
closed-end fund	*investment company*
common-stock fund	*no-load fund*
investment club	*open-end fund*

1. A small group organized to invest money for its members.
2. A corporation that sells its own stock to the public and buys stocks, or stocks and bonds, of other corporations.
3. An investment company in which a person can invest at any time and from which he can withdraw all or part of his investment at any time.
4. An investment company with a fixed number of shares.
5. A mutual fund that invests in bonds, preferred stocks, and common stocks.
6. A mutual fund that invests in common stocks only.
7. A mutual fund that adds no sales commission to the sales price of its stock.

Checking Your Understanding

1. Why did Dale Elliott want to invest some of his money in common stocks instead of placing it all in savings accounts and savings bonds?
2. What risk would Dale take if he invested in common stocks?
3. What were four things specified in the agreement signed by members of the Security Investment Club?
4. Who decided which stocks should be bought by the Security Investment Club?
5. In what respects are investment clubs and mutual funds similar? In what respects are they different?
6. What is the difference between an open-end fund and a closed-end fund?
7. What is the "asked" price of a mutual fund? The "bid" price?
8. Why are the dividends that a mutual fund pays less than the interest and dividends it receives?
9. What are some advantages of investing in a mutual fund?

Applying What You Have Learned

1. Assume that a friend of yours has asked your advice about joining an investment club. What can you tell him about the advantages and the disadvantages of belonging to such a club?

2. Why might a broker be interested in helping a group of people form an investment club?

3. On January 1 the Quality Investment Club owned common stocks with a market value of $20,000. Dividends of $600 were reinvested in additional stocks during the year. The market value of the stocks at the end of the year (including the $600 reinvested) was $20,188. (a) What was the rate of return of the dividends based on the January 1 market value? (b) How do you account for a market value of only $20,188 at the end of the year when the $600 dividends had been reinvested in additional stocks?

4. One mutual fund is advertised as a "growth" fund. Another is advertised as an "income" fund. What would you expect to be the difference between the two funds?

5. What are some of the major expenses of a mutual fund?

6. Why is it reasonable for the "asked" price of a mutual fund to be higher than the "bid" price?

7. One mutual fund requires 5% of its income from interest and dividends to pay its operating expenses. Another requires 15%. Is the first necessarily a better investment than the second? Why?

8. Is the fact that the "bid" and "asked" prices in a no-load fund are the same, complete proof that a no-load fund is more desirable for the investor than other funds?

Solving Business Problems

1. On January 1 of a recent year, the Security Investment Club had common stocks with a market value of $36,000. During the year, dividends of $1,224 were received on these investments. On December 31 of the same year, these investments had a market value of $41,040.

   (a) What was the rate of return of the dividends on the market value on January 1?
   (b) How much did the stocks increase in value during the year?
   (c) What percent of the value on January 1 was the increase during the year?

2. Ray Clark invested $20 a month in an investment club. During the first year that he was a member of the club, the income was just equal to the expenses. At the end of the year, the value of the

club's investments was just equal to the cost. During each of the next two years, the dividends received by the club (after club expenses were subtracted) was 4% of the value of the investments at the beginning of the year. Dividends were reinvested. Starting with the second year, the market price of the investments increased 6% of the value at the beginning of the year.

(a) What was the value of Ray's investment in the club at the end of the first year?

(b) What was the value of his investment at the end of the second year?

(c) What was the value of his investment at the end of the third year?

3. Eva Kelly paid $1,854 for 100 shares of a mutual fund. At that time the "bid" price of the shares was $16.96 a share.

(a) How much more than the "bid" price did Eva pay?

(b) What percent was this difference of the cost of the 100 shares?

4. Assume that Peter Segoni, a young man only two years out of high school, is interested in putting some of his savings into stocks. After discussing with friends the stocks of some companies in which he is interested, he decides to buy the following:

10 shares of Wilcox Corporation at a market price of 17¼
15 shares of Zendix, Inc., at 9½
 6 shares of Type-Ray Terminal at 21⅞

(a) If Peter is successful in acquiring the stocks at the prices indicated and assuming a brokerage fee of $27, what is the total amount that he has to remit to the brokerage house?

(b) If a year later the market prices of the stocks were 26, 13¼, and 19 respectively, by what amount and percentage had his total investment increased (at least on paper)?

(c) Assume that the annual dividend on each share of stock was 60¢, 95¢, and $1.20 respectively. At the price at which Peter bought the stock, what was his rate of return on each stock?

Enriching Your Business Understanding

1. The National Association of Investment Clubs can be of great assistance to persons who want to form an investment club. Through research in your library or by writing to the NAIC, make a report on the specific aids it can give to persons interested in organizing an investment club.

2. Mutual funds report to their stockholders both income from investments and capital gains. What is the difference between regular

income and capital gains? (You may find the definition of capital gains in an unabridged dictionary to be helpful.)

3. The financial or business section of many daily newspapers includes a list of mutual funds and gives the "bid" and "asked" prices. Study such a list, then answer the following questions:

   (a) How many of the funds are no-load funds?
   (b) Which fund has the highest price per share? The lowest?
   (c) What does the price per share of the stock of a mutual fund indicate about its desirability as an investment?

4. As was mentioned earlier, members of the New York Stock Exchange have a method by which investors may buy stock with small but regular payments. This is known as the Monthly Investment Plan or the MIP. Under this plan, payments are usually made monthly, but they may be as small as $40 each three months. Assume that an investor is considering buying shares in one corporation under the MIP and buying shares in a mutual fund. What do you consider to be the advantages and disadvantages of each of these two methods of investing?

PART 33
Investing In a Home

In one way or another, we are all users, buyers, or sellers of real estate. *Real estate* is land and anything that is permanently attached to it. For most of us, this means a home. During your lifetime, you will spend from 15% to 20% of your income to rent or buy a home. Because this is a sizable investment, it is important for you to understand some of the problems involved in providing housing for yourself and your family.

About two-thirds of all families in this country are home-owners. Many buy homes because they find owning cheaper than renting. But most families have other reasons for buying a home. One of the most important reasons is pride of ownership—the satisfaction of owning something of value. Families who own property can change or improve it as they please. They can then be sure that they will receive the benefit when they paint or repair a house or plant trees or shrubs. And they can make these changes any time they want without having to consult a landlord. Also, owning a home provides many people with a sense of security. When a family owns its home, it knows that it can stay there without the probability of having to move.

ADVANTAGES OF OWNING A HOME

Illus. 33-1. Owning its own home gives a family a feeling of security and pride.

ADVANTAGES OF RENTING A HOME

Although more and more people are buying homes, renting does have some advantages. When a family rents, it is free to move at almost any time. By renting, a family is best able to take care of changes in family needs, such as changes in size. When a person rents, he is also freed of much of the upkeep of home ownership.

Renting also has the advantage of making it easier for a person to keep money available for immediate use. When a family invests all of its savings in a home, it may not have enough money to meet unexpected expenses or pay bills during a time when the family income is low. If a person buys a home, he should try to accumulate some savings in addition to the amount that he pays for the home. If he cannot do this, it will probably be better to continue renting for a time.

ESTIMATING THE COST OF OWNING A HOME

The actual cost of owning a home includes more than just the purchase price. It also includes taxes, insurance, upkeep, depreciation, interest that could be earned with another investment, and interest that must be paid on a home loan.

(1) Local property taxes are one of the certain costs of home ownership. They are not the same in all communities, and they may vary in one community from year to year. On the average, they are about 2% of the value of the property.

The tax rate is not based on the actual value of the property but rather on its *assessed value*. This is the amount at which, for taxation purposes, the property is listed on the books of the county or other government unit. This assessed value is usually quite a bit less than the actual market value of the property—in most cases, only one-half the actual value. For example, if a house can be sold for $20,000, its assessed value may be only $10,000.

The property tax rate may be stated as so many dollars per $1,000 of assessed value. If the tax rate is $40 per $1,000 of assessed value, the annual taxes on property assessed at $10,000 would be $400. This is 4% of the assessed value but only 2% of the $20,000 actual value of the property in our example.

Before a person buys a house, he should find out from his local town or county officials the assessed value of the property, the tax rate, and the taxes actually paid in previous years. Both the assessed value and the tax rate may change, but changes are usually relatively small. If a person is planning to build a new house, the value of the new property can be estimated for taxation purposes. If he is planning to buy a house that is new and not yet assessed for taxes, the assessed value of similar houses in the neighborhood can be learned.

(2) The cost of insurance is considerably less than the cost of taxes, but it is still an important expense of home ownership. The cost of insurance is affected by the value of the house, the material from which it is made, the location in relation to other buildings, and the availability of the local fire protection. An insurance agent can give the rate on a particular house that a person is thinking of buying. The annual cost is usually not more than ½ of 1% of the value of the house, or $5 for each $1,000 of property value.

(3) Homeowners find that keeping their property in good condition results in frequent expenses. Total annual *upkeep* costs probably average about 2% of the value of the house. These costs do not necessarily occur every year. Many repairs and replacements can be put off so that for a year or two it seems that the costs of upkeep are small. But if repairs are delayed too long, the house falls into poor condition and the cost of bringing it into good repair increases.

(4) Depreciation, as you learned in Part 25, is the decrease in the value of property caused by use and time. If a house is kept in good condition, depreciation may amount to very little. In fact, a house in a neighborhood that is favorably located and in which the property is well kept up may actually increase in value over

Illus. 33-2. Many persons find that buying mobile homes is a practical way to achieve home ownership. Attractive mobile home parks like this one have grown up across the country.

Lear Siegler, Inc.

the years. Since depreciation may or may not be an important cost, we shall not include it in our estimates. It should be remembered, however, that depreciation is certain to be a cost if a generous amount is not spent for upkeep from year to year.

(5) The interest on the money invested is an important cost of owning a home. If the owner must borrow to pay for his home, he can easily learn the amount of interest that he will have to pay. He will also have some of his own money invested in the property. If this were invested elsewhere, it could be earning interest. The amount that the owner could receive by investing his money somewhere else is therefore one of the costs of owning the property. This amount is only an estimate. But by inquiring about the amount of interest paid by savings banks and savings and loan associations, the owner can learn how much interest his money could be earning. He can therefore make his estimate of cost rather accurately.

(6) When a family buys a home, it usually borrows part of the money from a savings and loan association, a bank, or some similar source. Usually it agrees to pay the lender about ¾ of 1% of the amount of the loan each month. For example, if the amount borrowed is $15,000, each monthly payment may be $112.50, or a total of $1,350 for the year. Not all of this $112.50 a month is an expense. Part of it is a saving. For example, if the interest rate is 7%, the interest during the first month is $87.50 ($15,000 × .07 × 1/12 = $87.50) and the payment on the loan is $25 ($112.50 payment — $87.50 interest).

As the debt decreases, the amount required for interest decreases and the amount applied to the loan increases. If the interest is figured on the new balance at the beginning of each month, the home should be completely paid for in 259 months, or about 21½ years. The amount of the monthly payment will vary according to how quickly the loan is to be repaid. If it is to be repaid completely in 15 years, the monthly payment will be much larger than if it is to be repaid in 25 years.

SCHEDULE OF
DIRECT LOAN REDUCTION
Amount of Loan $15,000 — Interest Rate 7%
Monthly Payment $112.50

PAYMENT NUMBER	PAYMENT ON INTEREST	PRINCIPAL	BALANCE OF LOAN
1	$87.50	$25.00	$14,975.00
2	87.35	25.15	14,949.85
3	87.21	25.29	14,924.56
4	87.06	25.44	14,899.12
5	86.91	25.59	14,873.53
6	86.76	25.74	14,847.79
7	86.61	25.89	14,821.90
8	86.46	26.04	14,795.86
9	86.31	26.19	14,769.67
10	86.16	26.34	14,743.33
11	86.00	26.50	14,716.83
12	85.85	26.65	14,690.18
247	$7.95	$104.55	$1,257.54
248	7.34	105.16	1,152.38
249	6.72	105.78	1,046.60
250	6.11	106.39	940.21
251	5.48	107.02	833.19
252	4.86	107.64	725.55
253	4.23	108.27	617.28
254	3.60	108.90	508.38
255	2.97	109.53	398.85
256	2.33	110.17	288.68
257	1.68	110.82	177.86
258	1.04	111.46	66.40
259	.39	66.40	—0—

Illus. 33-3. Schedule showing how a loan may be paid in equal monthly payments, with the interest calculated on the balance owed after each payment. The principal decreases only about $310 ($15,000−$14,690.18) during the first year, but it decreases more than 3½ times as much during the last year.

AN EXAMPLE OF THE COST OF OWNING A HOME

Raymond Monteleone is considering buying a home for $22,000. Of this amount, he estimates that $4,500 is the value of the lot and $17,500 is the value of the house. He has $5,500 that he can invest, and he can borrow $16,500 at the rate of 7%. He estimates that each year he will have to pay out:

Taxes (2% of the cost of the house and lot) ..	$ 440
Insurance (½% of the cost of the house)	87.50
Upkeep (2% of the cost of the house)	350
Payment on loan and interest (¾% of the loan each month)	1,485
	$2,362.50

If Mr. Monteleone buys this property, he should be prepared to make payments of $2,362.50 a year, or about $197 a month. Of course, not all of this is an expense. In about 21 years the home will be paid for. After that time the amount spent each year should be only $877.50, or about $73 a month.

As mentioned earlier, the amounts actually spent each year do not represent the true cost of owning a home. After the loan is repaid, Mr. Monteleone will have invested $22,000. If this money had been invested in some other way so that it would earn 5%, he would have had an income of $1,100 a year. The actual cost of owning the home might be considered to be the sum of this amount and the annual payments for taxes, insurance, and upkeep —a total of $1,977.50 a year, or about $165 a month.

LOOK CAREFULLY AT THE VALUE OF PROPERTY

Because of the difference in individual preferences, a house may not be worth exactly the same to several families. However, the value of one house can be determined rather closely by comparing it with the values of others. After a person has examined the size, location, and surroundings of a number of houses, he can usually form a rather accurate opinion of the relative value of each. Then he can determine about what he is willing to pay for one that he is interested in buying.

A person can also get some information about a property's value by finding out how much he can borrow on it. Before a lending agency will lend money on property, it has the property *appraised*. This means that it has the property examined by professional *appraisers* who estimate its value. If a lending agency is usually willing to make a loan equal to three-fourths of a property's value, it probably will lend as much as $12,000 on property worth $16,000. If it is willing to lend only $10,500 on a particular property, it probably considers the value of that property to be about $14,000.

INVESTIGATE THE OWNERSHIP OF PROPERTY

When a person is buying real estate, he should be as certain as possible that he is obtaining a good title to it. In other words, he should be sure that he is obtaining complete and clear ownership of the property. As a general rule, the buyer can receive no better title than the seller has to give. Even though the seller does own the property, there may be claims against it for which the new owner will be responsible. For example, if there are unpaid taxes on the property, these taxes are a claim against the property itself. If they are not paid, the property may be taken and sold so that the government may collect the taxes. Also, the former owner may have borrowed money and given a mortgage on the property as security for the loan. Until this loan is paid, the buyer of the property may be held responsible for payment.

These examples illustrate the need for a person to be sure that he is actually receiving a good title to real estate. Most persons are not trained to examine legal records, so a lawyer may be employed to make a title search. Certain companies known as *title insurance companies* operate to guarantee that titles are good. If the title that is guaranteed by such a company does not prove to be a good one, the insurance company will pay the amount of the loss to the buyer of the property.

There is some risk of loss when investing in a home. The buyer may have considered the property to be worth more than its actual value. Property values in general may decrease. Sometimes the town or the city grows in such a way that property in a certain area becomes less valuable. These dangers cannot be avoided entirely, but they can be decreased by carefully examining the property and comparing that property with others.

When a person buys a home, there is often a danger that he will buy a more expensive one than he can afford. As a result, his income may not be large enough to pay all necessary expenses. Buying a home is generally a good investment, but it is not a good one if it involves an expense greater than the family can afford.

BUYING A HOME INVOLVES RISKS

Developing Your Business Vocabulary

The following italicized terms should become part of your business vocabulary. For each numbered statement, find the italicized term that has the same meaning.

appraise	*assessed value*	*title insurance company*
appraiser	*real estate*	*upkeep*

1. Land and anything permanently attached to it.
2. The value placed upon property as a basis for taxation.
3. Keeping property in good repair.
4. To estimate the value of property.
5. One who is expert in estimating the value of property.
6. A company whose business is guaranteeing that titles to real property are good.

Checking Your Understanding

1. What are some advantages of owning a home and some advantages of renting a home?
2. What items, in addition to the original investment, are included in the cost of owning a home?
3. On the average, the annual cost of taxes is about what percent of the value of the property?
4. Where can a person find out his local tax rate?
5. What influences the amount charged for insurance on a house?
6. What percent of the value of the house do the annual costs of upkeep generally average?
7. If a house is kept in good condition, will the depreciation usually be large?
8. Why should interest be considered as an expense of owning a home?
9. Explain how the total cost of owning a home is estimated.
10. Give examples of claims that may be held against real estate which a prospective buyer should know about.
11. How can a buyer be sure that he will receive a good title to property?

Applying What You Have Learned

1. A tax rate is often quoted in mills, or tenths of a cent. The rate in a certain town is 40 mills on a dollar. What are the annual taxes on a house that is assessed at $8,000?
2. Charles Morehead is planning to buy a house and lot. How can he estimate the amount of taxes that he will have to pay if he makes this purchase?
3. Harley Leatham is paying $125 a month as rent on his home. He could buy a house by making a payment of $6,000 in cash and by giving a mortgage for $18,000 at 7%. The interest on the mortgage would be less than the rent that he is now paying. Do you believe that Mr. Leatham could reduce his expenses by purchasing the house?
4. Jerome Slattery owns a house that cost $12,000. For the past 3 years the upkeep has averaged less than $50 a year. May Mr. Slattery assume that $50 is a fair estimate of the annual expenses of maintenance?
5. Neil Bellow buys a house and lot for $17,000. He pays $8,000 in cash and gives a mortgage for $9,000 at 7%. He states that his interest cost will be $52.50 a month. Is he correct?
6. John Chepko is considering buying a house for $18,000. Suggest ways of estimating whether this is a fair asking price.

7. If a person borrows money to buy a home and makes monthly payments of $120 on the loan, is all of this amount an expense? Explain.

Solving Business Problems

1. Michael Chesson is considering buying a house and lot for $24,000. Of this amount, the house is worth $20,000 and the lot is worth $4,000. Mr. Chesson has $6,000 for a down payment, and the balance of the purchase price would have to be borrowed at the rate of 7%. He estimates that the annual cost of owning the property would be:

Taxes, 2% of the cost of the property
Insurance, .4% of the cost of the house
Upkeep, 1.5% of the cost of the house
Interest on the loan, 7%
Interest on the investment, 5% of the down payment

  (a) What is the total estimated annual cost of owning the property?
  (b) At the present time Mr. Chesson is paying rent of $150 a month. If he buys the house, will his expenses for housing be increased or decreased? By what amount?
  (c) Assume that Mr. Chesson buys the property and must pay $135 a month to apply on the principal and the interest on the mortgage. How much should he provide in his monthly budget to take care of all the amounts that he must pay in cash?

2. William Haub is considering buying a house and lot for $17,000. Of this amount, the house is worth $15,000 and the lot is worth $2,000. Mr. Haub has $4,000 for a down payment, and the balance of the purchase price would have to be borrowed at 7%. He estimates that the annual cost of owning the property would be:

Taxes, 2% of the cost of the property
Insurance, .5% of the cost of the house
Upkeep, 2% of the cost of the house
Interest on the loan, 7%
Interest on the investment, 5% of the down payment

  (a) What is the total estimated annual cost of owning the property?
  (b) Mr. Haub is now paying rent of $160 a month. If he buys the property, will his expenses for housing be increased or decreased? By what amount?
  (c) Assume that Mr. Haub buys this property and must pay $97.50 a month to apply on the principal and the interest on the mortgage. How much should he provide in his monthly budget to take care of all the amounts that he must pay in cash?

3. Hugh Maguire buys a house and lot for $20,000, making a down payment of $5,000 and giving a mortgage for the rest at 7%.

   (a) If the loan is to be repaid at the rate of ¾ of 1% a month, what is the amount of each monthly payment?
   (b) How much of the first monthly payment is interest and how much is payment on the loan?
   (c) How much of the second monthly payment is interest and how much is payment on the loan?

Enriching Your Business Understanding

1. The tax rate in many cities tends to increase each year. Why?
2. The Perez family is renting an apartment for $130 a month. Mr. Perez reads in the newspaper that the tax rate on real estate for the coming year will be increased by 40¢ per $100. Since Mr. Perez is a renter and pays no real estate taxes, will this increase in the tax rate make any difference to him?
3. In the problems in which the cost of owning a home was found, income taxes were not considered. The amount of these taxes is influenced by a number of things, such as the amount of income, the number of persons in the family, and the deductions allowed for various purposes. But income taxes often do have a bearing on the difference between the cost of owning property and renting. Rework (a) and (b) of Problem 1 on page 393 with the following assumptions:

   Mr. Chesson's income tax rate is 25% of his taxable income.
   Property taxes and interest paid are expenses that are deductible before the income tax is determined.
   Interest received is taxable.

4. Assume that William Haub pays income taxes at the rate of 20% of his taxable income. Rework (a) and (b) of Problem 2 on page 393, assuming that taxes and interest paid are deductible from taxable income and that interest received is taxable.
5. Cooperatives and condominiums are becoming more and more popular as a means of home ownership. Through research in your library, find out what cooperatives and condominiums are and make a report on the advantages and disadvantages of ownership for either a cooperative or a condominium.
6. Make an estimate of the annual cost of owning a home in your community. Assume that the house is worth $17,500 and the lot is worth $2,500. Use your local tax and insurance rates, but use the estimate for upkeep given in this part.

Unit 8

Practical Money Management

PART 34
Planning The Use Of Income

Have you ever stopped to think how much money you will earn during your lifetime? Suppose that you start working part-time at 16, graduate from high school at 18, accept a full-time job, marry at 22, and work until 65. During that time, you might expect to earn $350,000 to $500,000 or even more.

This is a great deal of money, but there are many demands on it. Food, shelter, clothing, medical care, education, insurance, transportation, and other expenses must be paid. Some people do not know how to deal wisely with such demands. Recently two articles dealing with family incomes and spending habits appeared in a leading magazine. In one article, a family was described as "earning $12,000 a year and going broke." In the other article, a family was "living and saving money on $9,000 a year." What accounts for this situation? It can be accounted for largely in terms of *money management*. The first family was very possibly not as good at money management as the second family.

Good money management does not mean doing without, but rather getting the most for your income. It does not mean being a miser, but rather spending for the things that you really want and can afford to buy. Money management does not mean having less fun, but rather gaining the most satisfaction from careful planning and spending.

WISE MONEY MANAGEMENT IS A SKILL TO BE LEARNED

Skill in money management is like any other skill: it has to be learned. No one sits down at a typewriter for the first time and types at 60 words a minute. And even the most skilled typist sometimes makes errors. It takes time and effort to learn the skill of money management, and even the most skilled money manager can make mistakes. But good money management will help you get the things you really want and need before careless spending eats away your income.

What is involved in good money management? It includes setting goals for yourself, learning to live within your income, buying wisely, using properly those things you buy, planning contributions, and saving. These factors will be discussed in the paragraphs that follow.

GOALS ARE ESSENTIAL IN MANAGING MONEY

If a family is to obtain the goods and services it wants most, *goals* must be set. A family's short-term goal, for example, might be paying off all its debts or having some remodeling done on its house. A longer-range goal might be a new house, a vacation trip, or a college education for one of the children.

Goals are very personal. They are not the same for all persons, or even for all persons within a given age group. Your goals will be affected by such factors as your age, where you live, and your interests and values. A family's goals will be affected by similar factors, plus its size.

Goals also change from time to time. A family's goals will change as its physical needs change. For example, an apartment or a small house might best suit the needs of a newly married couple. A young, growing family might set the goal of buying a larger house to meet its needs. Stop and think about how your goals may have changed in the last few years and what your goals may be at age 21 or 31.

No matter how much goals change, they are important to good money management. Working to achieve a certain goal probably gives an individual or a family the best reason for practicing good money management.

The goals you set must be realistic in terms of the resources available to you. *Monetary income* is a main resource that enables you to achieve the goals you have set, but there are others as well.

Time is a resource. Every person has the same amount of time, but the wise person plans the use of his time. He decides how much of his time should be spent studying, how much working, and how much playing. Your health and energy are important resources. So are the knowledge and skill you possess and the equipment and facilities that you and your family own. Also, resources made available by the community and government—public parks, swimming pools, libraries, and so on—help people meet goals they have set for themselves.

Do you have trouble living within your income? Most people do. Did you ever think that doubling your allowance and other income would solve your money problems? Doubling your income would certainly make it possible for you to buy more things, but the income would still have to be managed wisely if you were to buy the right things. Living within your income is a problem that you and your family will always have. Merely increasing income does not solve the problem of using it properly.

The amount of income that a person or a family has depends upon a number of factors. The occupation one enters determines income to a great extent, because some types of work pay more than others do. Some jobs require more education and skill or are more demanding of time and energy than other jobs that pay less. Location also affects income. Workers in large cities generally

"The electric bill is over the budget again, so for 30 days
the TV goes off at 9 and everybody brushes teeth manually."

Copyright 1970 by the Kiplinger Washington Editors, Inc.

*Illus. 34-1. Part of good
money management is
learning to live within
one's income.*

earn more than do workers in rural areas or small towns. Of course, the cost of living is generally higher in large cities than it is in rural areas or small towns. The number of family members who are working also obviously affects the total family income. Many women now hold full-time or part-time jobs. A wife may work during the first few years of marriage, quit to raise a family, then go back to work after the children are older.

A high school student can usually find opportunities to earn some income on a part-time basis. Baby-sitting, mowing lawns, delivering newspapers, and stocking shelves in grocery stores are some of them. Working part-time brings you in contact with adults who hold full-time jobs. These contacts will help you learn more about these jobs and about the wages paid for different kinds of work.

WE MUST PLAN FOR WISE BUYING

Few of us are ever able to have all the things we would like to have. But by planning carefully and by practicing *thrift,* we can have now or in the future many of the things we really want. You have already learned that too much impulse buying may mean that you will not have enough money left to buy the goods and services to satisfy your basic needs and meet the goals you have set. Part of planning your purchases is deciding whether you need one item more than another. The following paragraphs give three rules to help you make this decision.

Is the article you are thinking of buying really more desirable than something else? Sometimes we buy an item simply because other people are buying similar items, and we give little thought to whether the item is actually needed. When a person's income is limited—and most of our incomes are limited—buying one thing may make it impossible to buy something else. Each purchase should be judged according to whether it will give more satisfaction than something else.

Will a purchase result in more expense in the future? Many families decide that they can afford to make the down payment on a new house and to make future payments as they come due, without considering such expenses as property taxes and upkeep of the house. If a purchase will result in larger expenses in the future, these future expenses should be planned for—perhaps even more carefully than the first cost.

Illus. 34-2. A part-time job, such as that of a clerk-typist, may provide a student with both income and work experience.

Otis Elevator

Do you need the article right now, or will you need it in the near future? Sometimes you can save money by buying goods at special sales before the goods are actually needed. You should be careful, though, not to provide for your needs too far in advance. Conditions may change so that something you want very much now may not be wanted at all later. Also, using your money to buy things you do not need right away may mean that you cannot buy other things you really need.

POSSESSIONS SHOULD BE USED CAREFULLY

The person who plans his purchases carefully and then uses them carelessly is not a good money manager. Use your possessions carelessly, and you can lose money. A radio left in an unlocked desk can be stolen. A lawn mower left out in the rain will rust. Failing to keep a car properly lubricated can shorten its life. Small tears and neglected stains in clothing will soon make it unwearable. These are just a few examples of how the careless use of possessions can add to the cost of living.

CONTRIBUTIONS MUST BE PLANNED

In money management, a person should decide how much responsibility he has to worthy charities and to other groups that are supported by public contributions. Among such groups are churches, the American Red Cross, the Salvation Army, the Heart Fund, the American Cancer Society, and the United Appeal. In making *contributions,* the good money manager should be sure that the cause is a worthy one. He should also be sure that the person to whom he gives his contribution has the right to collect it. Whether to give and how much to give are questions that each person must answer for himself.

WE MUST PLAN OUR SAVINGS

Did you ever hear someone say, "On the first of the year I'm going to start saving money," or "As soon as I earn $250 a month, I'll start saving." You may have made such statements yourself. Sometimes these plans are successful, but usually they aren't. The way to save is to begin saving now and to develop the habit of saving regularly, no matter how small each amount may be.

Some people develop the saving habit by having a goal for saving, such as buying a typewriter or a watch. Some save by deciding not to spend a certain amount—such as 10 cents—out of every dollar they earn. Do this regularly, and the amount saved can grow to a sizable sum in a rather short time.

As you learned in Unit 4, the money that you save should be put to work for you—in savings accounts, in government bonds, or in some other form of investment. Savings left idle around the house earn nothing for you. And there is always the chance that the money will be lost or stolen or that you will be tempted to spend it.

Developing Your Business Vocabulary

The following italicized terms should become part of your business vocabulary. For each numbered statement, find the italicized term that has the same meaning.

contribution	*money management*
goal	*thrift*
monetary income	

1. Planned control of financial income and expenditures.
2. Something that an individual or family seeks to achieve.
3. Salary, wages, commissions, or other financial rewards.
4. The careful use of one's time and money.
5. An amount given to charity or other public service agency.

Checking Your Understanding

1. Why do some people who have a good income still seem unable to make ends meet?
2. What are six important aspects of good money management?
3. Why are goals essential to good money management? Why do goals change?
4. Name several factors which determine the amount of income of an individual or a family.
5. What are some common part-time jobs open to high school students? Can you name some not mentioned in the text?
6. No one can have everything he would like to have. Mention three important rules that will help you decide which of several purchases you may want to make.
7. Being able to make a down payment on a car or some other item does not necessarily mean that the person can afford to buy it. Explain.
8. Show, by giving examples, how a careful buyer but a thoughtless user of what he buys may be a poor money manager.
9. Name at least six public welfare agencies that are supported by our contributions.
10. "How much is saved is not so important as developing the habit of saving regularly." Explain this statement.

Applying What You Have Learned

1. The income of the Kozman family is well above the national average. Therefore, they do not feel that it is necessary to plan the use of their income. They find, though, that they are having difficulty making ends meet. Suggest some specific reasons why the Kozman family is having financial difficulty.
2. What is the difference between short-term and long-term goals of an individual or a family? Give several examples of each of these two types of goals.
3. Explain how the use of resources—other than financial resources—can have the effect of adding to family income.
4. The first cost of an item may be only a part of the total cost. For each of the items listed below, name some common expenses incurred in using the item:

   (a) dog   (c) television set
   (b) minibike   (d) camera

5. Describe what special care is needed in order to get the most use out of each of the items listed on page 406:

(a) paint brushes (d) shoes
(b) power lawn mower (e) typewriter
(c) woolen sweater (f) rug

6. The Kroner family sets aside $1 out of every $20 earned for contributions to charity. The Harmeyer family contributes 6 cents out of every dollar earned. (a) Which family contributes more? (b) What are some reasons why some persons contribute a larger part of their income to charity than others do?

7. On a sheet of paper draw two columns and write the headings "Part-Time Job" on the left and "Career Possibilities" on the right. In the left column list four part-time jobs that could lead to full-time careers. Directly opposite in the right column, write the career or careers into which each part-time job could develop.

Solving Business Problems

1. The Malora family has some lawn furniture that is falling apart. Rebuilding and painting the old furniture would take about 10 hours of work; lumber and nails would cost about $12; and the paint and brush would cost about $7.50. If Mr. Malora rebuilds the furniture, he estimates that it will last another 3 years. He is undecided whether to rebuild the old furniture or to buy new furniture for $97.50.

   (a) If the new furniture will last for about 10 years, what is the yearly cost of wear and tear?
   (b) What will be the yearly cost of the rebuilt furniture (not including a charge for labor)?
   (c) Should Mr. Malora consider his time as a part of the cost of rebuilding the old furniture?
   (d) If Mr. Malora decides to buy the new furniture, what are some things, other than cost, that he might consider?

2. Five students with different earnings and allowances have different saving plans. These amounts and saving plans are:

Student	Weekly Earnings and Allowances	Amount or Percent Saved Each Week
Ellen Lovens	$ 6.00	60¢
Gene Ramsey	10.00	7%
Dick Ackeman	12.50	4%
Marie Caruso	6.50	30¢
Jan Tobin	8.75	20¢

   (a) For each student, calculate his savings for one week.
   (b) For each student, calculate his savings for an entire year.

3. Tim Boerger is a camera fan. He takes one roll of twelve pictures about every two weeks. About a year ago he decided that the cost of the film, developing, and printing was using up too much of his allowance. Thinking that he could save money by developing and printing his own pictures, he bought a developing and printing outfit including the following items:

> 3 developing trays @ 49¢ each
> 1 darkroom light @ $1.19
> 1 printer @ $11.96
> Supply of developer and fixer, $3.85
> Supply of printing paper, $6.25
> 3 ferrotype plates @ $1.12 each

At the end of the year he had used up all of his supplies; but his trays, light, printer, and ferrotype plates were in excellent condition and worth about $13.

(a) What was the total cost of all items purchased?
(b) How much would the developing and printing have cost him in a year if he had had the work done by a processor at a cost of 64¢ per roll of film?
(c) How much did his supplies and equipment decrease in value during the year?
(d) Did he save or lose money by developing and printing his own pictures? How much?
(e) How much per roll of film did the developing and printing cost him when he did his own processing?

4. Employees of the Greensburg Manufacturing Company contributed a total of $8,240 to the United Appeal. They decided by majority vote to request that each local organization receive percentages of this amount as follows:

Organization	Percent
Red Cross	18%
Salvation Army	15%
Boy Scouts	5%
Girl Scouts	4%
Mental Health Association	12%
Children's Home	15%
YMCA	5%
Community Center	13%
Girls' Town	6%
Legal Aid Society	7%

What amount was each local group to receive?

Enriching Your Business Understanding

1. Listed below are some unusual buying opportunities. Which of these might result in a wise purchase and which in a careless purchase? Tell why in each case.

   (a) Buy an "as is" power lawn mower at the end of the season for $35.
   (b) Pick up all the fallen apples you want at 50¢ a bushel.
   (c) Your pick of any five used automobile tires at $5 each.
   (d) Ladies' dresses, stained by smoke from a fire, at $2 each. Examination not permitted. No returns allowed. No more than six to a customer.
   (e) A person unknown to you stops you on the street and explains that he is from out of town, has lost his wallet, and needs cash quickly. He offers to sell you a beautiful ring for $15 and shows you his driver's license to prove his identity.

2. It has been said that almost anyone could be wealthy if he started saving and investing one-third of his income from the time that he was twelve years old. How do you feel about this? Is it a practical idea? If so, why don't more people follow this practice?

3. Dave Glickman graduated from high school two years ago. Since then he has held at least six different jobs, none of which paid him a satisfactory income. He now complains that he never gets any breaks, that no good opportunities come his way. (a) Can you suggest some possible reasons for his bad breaks? (b) Is it possible for a person to improve his opportunities? How?

4. Some people seem to be born money managers. They are able to earn and save money, and they always seem to have needed spending money. Some resolve that they will start being better money managers "tomorrow" or "next year." Others keep hoping for the "Midas touch." (a) What is the "Midas touch"? (b) Outline the qualities of a good money manager.

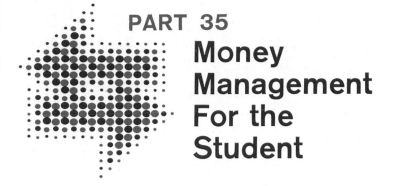

PART 35

Money Management For the Student

Steve Barstock is a high school student. He receives an allowance of $3 a week from his parents, and he earns about $7 a week cleaning up at a nearby gas station. Steve didn't think he was a careless spender, and he tried to save some money. But by the end of a week he never seemed to have money left over for savings. In fact, many times his money was gone before the end of the week so that he couldn't buy even things he needed.

Steve brought up his money problems to his parents, hoping that they would increase his allowance. Instead they suggested that he try to manage his money more wisely. So Steve decided to set up a saving and spending plan that he could follow. Such a plan is called a *budget*.

Since Steve knew what his average weekly income was, his main job was to plan his *expenditures* so that he would get the most from this income. He decided first on the amount he wanted to save. He did this because he knew from past experience that if he decided first on how to spend the money, he would probably have nothing left to save. Steve felt that he should be able to save $2 a week. He then estimated his weekly expenses based on his past experiences and his future needs. The budget he prepared is shown in Illustration 35-1.

BUDGETS DIRECT HOW MONEY SHOULD BE SPENT

Steve Barstock
Weekly Budget
February 1, 19--

Estimated Income		Estimated Expenditures	
Allowance	3 00	Savings	2 00
Part-time work	7 00	Lunches	3 00
		School Supplies	90
		Personal Expenses	1 50
		Recreation	2 00
		Gifts & Contributions	60
Total	10 00	Total	10 00

Illus. 35-1. A budget of income and expenditures for a week.

After Steve had prepared his budget, he tried to follow it, but he kept no records to show how he was actually spending his money. At the end of a few weeks he found that he hadn't saved anything, but he couldn't remember where his money had gone. So Steve concluded that he needed not only a budget but also records to show exactly how his money was being spent.

RECORDS SHOW HOW MONEY WAS ACTUALLY SPENT

A budget directs how money should be spent; records show how money has actually been spent. Both are necessary, but records can become burdensome if they are too detailed. They should be kept as simple as possible and yet provide the information that is needed. Steve decided to keep his record of income and expenses in the form shown in Illustration 35-2. Study this illustration carefully, and follow along with the steps Steve went through in filling out this record.

(1) Steve first wrote down the total amount budgeted and the amount budgeted for each item. These amounts were to remind him at all times of how much he was allowing for each item. He then ruled a line across the whole page so that he would not confuse his budget amounts with the amounts he received and spent.

(2) On April 4, the day he started the record, Steve had $8.50 in cash. To distinguish between this beginning balance and the amounts to be received during the week, he wrote the word "Balance" in the Explanation column. Note how the year, month, and day were entered in the date column.

(3) Also on April 4, Steve received his allowance of $3 and spent 60 cents for lunch at school. Note how these two entries were made.

	Date	Explanation	Totals — Receipts	Totals — Payments	Savings	Lunches	School Supplies	Personal Expenses	Recreation	Gifts and Distribution
				Steve Bardock — Income and Expense Record						
(1)		Budget $10.00	—	—	2 00	3 00	90	1 50	2 00	60
(2)	April 4	Balance	8 50							
	4		3 00	60		60				
(3)	5			1 50		55	60		35	
(4)	6			1 00		65		35		
(5)	7			1 70		50	20		1 00	
	8			1 70		60		1 10		
(6)	9		7 00	3 10	2 00				1 10	
	10			40						40
(7)	10	Totals	18 50	10 00	2 00	2 90	80	1 45	3 45	40
(8)	10	Balance		8 50						
			18 50	18 50						
(9)	April 11	Balance	8 50							
(10)	11		3 00	60		60				
	12			50		50				
	13			1 10		65	45			
	14			1 75		55	10		1 10	
	15			2 50		50		2 00		
	16		7 00	2 00	2 00					
	17			50						50
	17	Cash Short		70				70		
	17	Totals	18 50	9 65	2 00	2 80	55	2 70	1 10	50
	17	Balance		8 85						
			18 50	18 50						
	April 18	Balance	8 85							

Illus. 35-2. A personal income and expense record.

(4) A similar entry was made for each day of the week. When amounts were spent for two or more purposes, the total was entered in the Payments column and the individual amounts were entered in the Distribution columns. Note the entries for April 5.

(5) Steve proved his record at the end of each week to be sure that he was keeping it accurately. After his last entry for the first week, he found the totals of the Receipts and Payments columns. He wrote these totals in small pencil figures directly under the last line on which he had recorded an entry. At any time, the difference between the total of the Receipts column and the total of the Payments column should be the same as the cash on hand. The difference between Total Receipts and Total Payments was $8.50, which Steve wrote in small pencil figures in the Explanation column. Steve counted his pocket money and found that he had exactly $8.50. So he assumed that his record was correct.

(6) Steve found the totals of each Distribution column and wrote these totals in small pencil figures. He then added these

totals and compared the sum with the total of the Payments column. The two amounts were the same.

(7) Satisfied that his records were correct, Steve ruled a single line across all money columns to indicate addition and then entered the totals of all columns in ink.

(8) He added the cash balance ($8.50) to the total of the payments and then brought down to the next line the totals of the Receipts and Payments columns. This showed that the Receipts equaled the sum of the Payments and the Balance.

(9) Steve then ruled a double line across the Date column and all the money columns to show that his record book had been balanced. To show the amount of money on hand at the beginning of the second week, he brought down the balance of $8.50 in the Receipts column. If the page had been about full, Steve would have carried the balance to the top of the next page.

(10) Receipts and payments were recorded during the second week as they were during the first. When the Receipts and Payments columns were totaled at the end of the second week, the cash balance was found to be $9.55. But when Steve counted his pocket money, he found he had only $8.85. He probably had lost 70 cents or had forgotten to record a payment. So he entered 70 cents in his record as a personal expense. He usually did not write an explanation of an entry, but in this case he did write "Cash Short" in the Explanation column. He thought that he might be interested in noting how much his cash was short from week to week. After making the entry for cash short, Steve ruled and balanced his record as he had done at the end of the first week.

SAVINGS AND EXPENSES ARE COMPARED WITH THE BUDGET

Steve had written his budget *allowances* in his record form as a reminder of how much to save and spend. But at the end of each week he wanted to know exactly how his savings and expenses compared with his budget allowances. To obtain this information, he used a form like that shown in Illustration 35-3. Study it to see how Steve prepared this record.

(1) Steve entered his budget allowances for the week of April 4 to 10.

(2) He entered the amounts that he had actually saved and spent during the first week, obtaining this information from the income and expense record.

Steve Barstock Comparison of Savings and Expenses with Budget Allowances								
Date 19--	Explanation	Savings	Lunches	School Supplies	Personal Expenses	Recreation	Gifts and Contributions	Totals
April 4-10	Budget	2 00	3 00	90	1 50	2 00	60	10 00
	Saved and Spent	2 00	2 90	80	1 45	2 45	40	10 00
	Carried Forward	—	10	10	05	(45)	20	—
	Budget	2 00	3 00	90	1 50	2 00	60	10 00
April 11-17	Available	2 00	3 10	1 00	1 55	1 55	80	10 00
	Saved and Spent	2 00	2 80	55	2 70	1 10	50	9 65
	Carried Forward	—	30	45	(1 15)	45	30	35
April 18-24	Budget	2 00	3 00	90	1 50	2 00	60	10 00
	Available	2 00	3 30	1 35	36	2 45	90	10 35
	Saved and Spent	2 00	3 00	80	65	2 95	70	10 10
	Carried Forward	—	30	55	(30)	(50)	20	25
April 25- May 1	Budget	3 75	3 00	90	2 00	3 25	1 10	14 00
	Available	3 75	3 30	1 45	1 70	2 75	1 30	14 25

Illus. 35-3. Comparison of savings and expenses with budget allowances over a three-week period.

(3) The differences between his budget allowances and the amounts he actually saved and spent told him how well he had kept within his budget. For example, he saved exactly $2 as he had planned. He had allowed 90 cents for school supplies but spent only 80 cents, thus having 10 cents to carry over to the next week. He spent 45 cents more for recreation than he had planned. To show that he exceeded his budget allowance for this item, he encircled the 45 cents.

(4) Steve again entered the amounts that he had budgeted for the week.

(5) He added the amounts carried forward and the budget allowances to find the amounts available for the second week. For example, the amount available for school supplies was found to be $1.00; but the amount available for recreation was only $1.55 since during the first week he had exceeded his budget on this item by 45 cents.

Budget allowances are estimates, and sometimes they have to be revised. Maybe the first estimate was not very accurate. Then too, every person's requirements change from time to time. At the end of the third week, Steve decided that he should make some changes in his budget allowances. For one thing, his employer

BUDGETS MAY HAVE TO BE CHANGED

wanted him to work a few extra hours a week, so this meant that he could earn an extra $4 a week. Also, Steve knew that several school parties were coming up and that he would probably be spending more for recreation and personal expenses. There would also be gifts to buy for his mother's and sister's birthdays. And he wanted to put aside another $1.75 a week in savings.

After considering each of these factors, Steve revised his budget estimates as follows:

Savings	$ 3.75
Lunches	3.00
School supplies	.90
Personal expenses	2.00
Recreation	3.25
Gifts and contributions	1.10
Total estimated savings and expenses	$14.00

These new budget allowances were recorded in the comparison form (Illustration 35-3) and were added to the amounts carried forward to show the budget amounts available for the fourth week.

If a budget is carefully planned, estimates will not need to be changed very often. If the amount allowed for a particular item is too small, it may be due to one of several reasons: (1) an unusual expense may have occurred; (2) the cost of the item may have increased; or (3) the person may have been careless in his spending. It should be remembered that increasing an allowance for one item requires a decrease in the allowance for one or several other items.

Developing Your Business Vocabulary

The following italicized terms should become part of your business vocabulary. For each numbered statement, find the italicized term that has the same meaning.

allowance   *budget*   *expenditure*

1. A definite plan for saving and spending income.
2. An amount actually spent for food, clothing, or other items.
3. A limitation or an amount granted for a special purpose.

Checking Your Understanding

1. When a budget is being prepared, why should the income be estimated before payments are planned?
2. In planning his budget, why did Steve decide to list first the amount of money he wanted to save?
3. How can past expenditures assist in planning a budget?
4. A budget is of little value without records. Explain the difference between a budget and a record.
5. Why did Steve write his budget estimates in his income and expense record before he entered any of his transactions?
6. Steve totaled all columns in his income and expense record at the end of the week. (a) Why did he find these totals? (b) How would this help to prove the accuracy of his record?
7. What entry did Steve make when he found that his cash on hand was less than the balance shown by the record?
8. When Steve spent more for an item than he had allowed in his budget, how did he show this fact on his comparison form? Why?
9. Under what conditions might it be necessary to revise budget estimates?

Applying What You Have Learned

1. In this part you learned that a good budget and recordkeeping system should be simple. If a more detailed system would provide a person with much more helpful information, why should he not be encouraged to maintain such a system?
2. Peggy Monroe says that she can't possibly keep a budget because she never knows exactly how much her income will be or how much money she will spend. (a) Explain how she might make an estimate of her income and expenses. (b) Is Peggy likely to save much money?
3. By examining the completed income and expense record on page 411, you will note that only the amount of savings was exactly equal to the budget. What, then, was the value of having the budget and keeping records?
4. Rather than recording daily expenditures in a form similar to that in Illustration 35-2, how else might a student keep an accurate tally of what he actually spent during a day or a week? What advantage or disadvantage would this method have over the one Steve Barstock used?
5. Suppose that Steve Barstock had found the 70 cents unaccounted for at the end of the second week in his income and expense record. How should this amount be recorded when it is located?

6. At the end of each week shown on the comparison record on page 413: **(a)** Which expenditures were exactly the same as the budget allowances? **(b)** Which were less? **(c)** Which were more?

7. Kathy Brendamour made every effort to prepare an exact budget. Each week she transferred to savings any amount that was not spent. If she needed to spend more for an item than she had budgeted, she withdrew this amount from her savings. Is Kathy following a good money management plan? Explain.

Solving Business Problems

1. The personal income and expense record on page 411 shows how Steve Barstock kept a record of his income, savings, and expenses for a period of two weeks from April 4 to April 17. In this problem you will keep Steve's record for the next week, from April 18 to April 24. Draw up a form similar to that used in Illustration 35-2, or use the form included in your *Activities and Projects*.

(a) Write on the first line of the record Steve's budget allowances as shown in Illustration 35-2 and rule a line across the entire page.

(b) Write on the second line the balance of cash on hand as of April 18, obtaining this information from Illustration 35-2.

(c) Enter in the record form the following transactions that Steve completed during the week of April 18 to 24:

April 18   Received allowance, $3; lunch, 55¢; paid for developing a roll of film, 65¢ (charge to personal expense).

        19   Lunch, 70¢; coke and hamburger, 45¢ (charge to recreation).

        20   Lunch, 60¢; contribution for gift for classmate, 30¢.

        21   Bought paper for school use, 40¢; lunch, 50¢; received week's salary, $7.

        22   Bought magazine for English class, 40¢; lunch, 65¢; made deposit in savings account, $2.

        23   Ticket for basketball game, $2; refreshments at game, 50¢.

        24   Church offering, 40¢.

(d) Rule and balance the record in the same manner that Steve used at the end of the first and second weeks. Refer to Illustration 35-2. Steve's cash on hand at the end of the third week is $8.75.

(e) Now prepare a comparison form similar to that on page 413. Draw a form similar to this one or use the form given in your *Activities and Projects*.

(f) On the first line of the comparison form, record the amounts available for the week of April 18 to 24, obtaining this information from Illustration 35-3.

(g) On the second line of the form, enter the amounts saved and spent. Then determine the amounts carried forward and enter them on the third line.

2. As was explained on pages 413-414, Steve's budget allowances were changed at the end of the third week. The revised budget allowances should now be used in Steve's records.

(a) On the next available line of the comparison form, enter the new budget allowances as given on page 414. Calculate the amounts available for the week of April 25 to May 1 and record them on the following line.

(b) Prepare a second page for the income and expense record or use the form given in your *Activities and Projects*. On the first line, write Steve's revised budget allowances and rule a line across the entire form. On the second line, write the balance of the cash on hand, $8.75.

(c) Record the following transactions that Steve completed during the week of April 25 to May 1:

April 25 Received allowance, $3; lunch, 50¢; birthday gift for sister, $1.50.
26 Ballpoint pen for school use, 25¢; lunch, 55¢.
27 Lunch, 50¢; haircut, $2.
28 Lunch, 50¢; paperback book for school use, 60¢.
29 Received week's salary, $11; deposited $3.75 in savings account; lunch, 65¢.
30 Movie and refreshments, $3.00.
May 1 Church offering, 40¢.

(d) Rule and balance the record. Steve's cash on hand is $8.55.

(e) Complete the comparison form for the week.

Enriching Your Business Understanding

1. Frequently the statement is made that "a budget must be balanced." Explain the meaning of this statement as it applies: (a) to an individual; (b) to a family; (c) to a town or city government; and (d) to the federal government.

2. Listed below are a number of points of view which have been expressed about following personal budgets. Examine each of these statements and express your opinion about them. Be prepared to defend your point of view.

   (a) "I know how much I earn, how much I want to save, and how much I can spend. Why keep a record?"
   (b) "I pay all my bills by check. My checkbook is my record."
   (c) "I keep a record only of major expenses—there is no point in bothering with penny and nickel items."
   (d) "I have a complete record of every cent I have received and spent since I was 12 years old."

3. Suppose that you are chairman of the arrangements committee of the Business Club in your school. Your club, composed of 25 members, is planning a two-day trip to a nearby city.

   (a) Develop a budget for the trip, including four meals, overnight room accommodations, transportation, and $18 for incidentals.
   (b) Assume that you have half of the necessary amount in your club treasury. Suggest a plan by which your club could earn the balance.

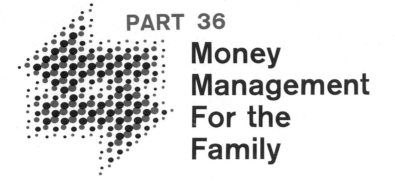

PART 36

Money Management For the Family

It is even more important for the Barstock family to manage its income wisely than it is for Steve to manage his income wisely. This is true because several persons are spending the family income and because more than one person may be contributing to the family income. The family that has a good money management plan can enjoy a higher style of living than it would have without the plan. Following a budget does not necessarily mean scrimping and doing without. But it does require the regular setting aside of definite amounts to go toward buying what the family wants.

FIRST STEPS IN PREPARING A FAMILY BUDGET

When a family budget is being prepared—just as when an individual budget is being prepared—the amount to be saved should be decided upon first. If this amount is not considered first, the allowances for expenses may take up all the income and leave nothing for savings. It is fairly easy to fix allowances for *regular expenses*, such as rent and food. *Irregular expenses* are much more difficult to estimate. For example, medical and dental expenses may not occur very often, but they may be large when they do occur. Such expenses should be provided for somewhere in the budget. If allowances are not made for them, irregular expenses may use up a large part of savings.

A budget must be tailor-made to fit the family; no standard budget can be made to fit all families. However, printed budgets and the experiences of others are useful when a family does not have complete records of past expenditures on which to base its budget estimates. Standard budgets are also useful in checking actual expenditures at the end of a year to see if any of them seem too large. If a family makes most of its payments by check, the checkbook record is also very helpful in planning a budget.

THE BARSTOCKS MAKE A BUDGET

Steve Barstock's father, Ted Barstock, has a *net income* of $7,400 a year, or $620 a month. This is the amount Mr. Barstock receives after taxes and other deductions have been withheld from his earnings. Mrs. Barstock has a part-time secretarial job which gives her a net income of $1,200 a year, or $100 a month.

To obtain information on which to base their budget, the Barstocks read several booklets on family income planning. They learned that family savings and expense items are often classified under eight main divisions:

1. *Savings* (including savings accounts in banks and other similar institutions, government bonds, life insurance premiums, and principal payments on mortgage on home).
2. *Food* (including food eaten at home, meals eaten away from home, milk and dairy products, beverages, candy, and bakery goods).
3. *Clothing* (including clothing for all the family, dry cleaning, sewing appliances, and shoe repairs).
4. *Household* (including rent, interest on mortgage, taxes, fire insurance, gas and electricity, coal or fuel oil, telephone, water, household furnishings, household supplies, and painting and repairs).
5. *Transportation* (including payments on automobile, automobile upkeep and operation, fares for public transportation, and auto and drivers' licenses).
6. *Health and personal care* (including medical and dental expenses, drugs, eyeglasses, hospital and nursing expenses, accident and health insurance, barber and beauty shop, toilet articles, and children's allowances).
7. *Recreation and education* (including books, magazines, newspapers, theaters, movies, concerts, vacations, school expenses, hobbies, radio and TV, musical instruments, and club dues).
8. *Gifts and contributions* (including church, Community Chest or United Appeal, charitable organizations, and personal gifts).

The Barstocks believed that they could save $100 a month. This included the payment on their home mortgage, less interest, and the sum they planned to deposit each month in a savings account. The Barstocks first made an estimate of their past expenditures based mainly on their checkbook record. Then they prepared the budget shown in Illustration 36-1.

The Barstock Family Monthly Budget January, 19--			
Estimated Income		Estimated Expenditures	
Husband's Income	620 00	Savings	100 00
Wife's Income	100 00	Food	160 00
(after tax deductions)		Clothing	75 00
		Household	120 00
		Transportation	80 00
		Health & Personal Care	55 00
		Recreation & Education	60 00
		Gifts & Contributions	70 00
	720 00		720 00

The Barstocks' budget was a plan. They had to know whether they were following the plan, so they needed a record of actual income and actual expenditures. They wanted a record system that was easy to maintain and yet was complete enough to provide the information they needed. The income and expense record adopted, shown in Illustration 36-2, was similar to Steve's income and expense record shown on page 411. However, there is a difference in the number of columns and in the column headings.

Entries for savings were made whenever money was transferred to some form of savings. On January 10 a payment of $95 was made on the Barstocks' home mortgage. Their passbook from the savings and loan association which granted the loan showed how much of each payment was interest and how much was applied to the principal of the loan. For this payment, $37 was applied to the loan and was recorded in the Savings column. The interest expense of $58 was recorded in the Household column. As the interest is calculated on the balance of the loan, it will gradually decrease from month to month. The amount saved—that is, the amount applied to the loan—will increase correspondingly each month.

Entries for expenses were recorded each Saturday and at the end of the month. These entries were made much as Steve made

THE BARSTOCKS SET UP THEIR INCOME AND EXPENSE RECORD

The Barstock Family
Income and Expense Record

Date	Explanation	Totals		Distribution of Savings and Expenses							
		Receipts	Payments	Savings	Food	Clothing	House-hold	Trans-portation	Health & Personal Care	Recreation & Education	Gifts & Contri-butions
	Budget, $720	—	—	100 00	160 00	75 00	120 00	80 00	55 00	60 00	70 00
Jan. 1	Balance	300 00									
7			80 25		33 10	9 80		16 40	8 40	6 55	6 00
10	Payment on Mortgage		95 00	37 00			58 00				
13		310 00									
14			110 20		36 45	15 90	7 60	8 65	19 25	15 10	7 25
21			116 75		35 20		12 40	38 20	7 15	8 20	15 60
28			81 56		29 13	13 65	9 43	10 10		9 25	10 00
31		410 00	159 85	50 00	23 76	17 14	19 95	3 20	12 65	12 15	21 00
31	Totals	1,020 00	643 61	87 00	157 64	56 49	107 38	76 55	47 45	51 25	59 85
31	Balance		376 39								
		1,020 00	1,020 00								
Feb. 1	Balance	376 39									

Illus. 36-2. Income and expense record.

similar entries in his income and expense record. Incomes were entered on the days they were received. The Barstocks ruled and closed their record as Steve did, except that their record was ruled and closed at the end of the month.

THE BARSTOCKS COMPARE THEIR RECORD WITH THEIR BUDGET

At the end of each month, totals of the columns in the income and expense record were entered on the comparison form shown in Illustration 36-3. Note that Mr. Barstock circled those amounts that represented expenditures greater than the budget allowed.

When the Barstocks set up their budget, they had $300 in cash on hand and in their checking account. They decided to keep about this amount in reserve to meet any unusual expenses. So this amount was not budgeted for current expenses. That is why the $300 is shown in the income and expense record but not in the comparison form.

As far as the Barstocks could tell from their records, they were following the budget satisfactorily. At the end of January, the clothing category had a fairly large balance. However, Mr.

The Barstock Family
Comparison of Savings and Expenses with Budget Allowances

Month 19--	Explanation	Savings	Food	Clothing	House-hold	Trans-portation	Health & Personal Care	Recreation & Education	Gifts & Contribution	Totals
January	Budget	100 00	160 00	75 00	120 00	80 00	55 00	60 00	70 00	720 00
	Saved and Spent	87 00	157 64	56 49	107 38	76 55	47 45	51 25	59 85	643 61
	Carried Forward	13 00	2 36	18 51	12 62	3 45	7 55	8 75	10 15	76 39
February	Budget	100 00	160 00	75 00	120 00	80 00	55 00	60 00	70 00	720 00
	Available	113 00	162 36	93 51	132 62	83 45	62 55	68 75	80 15	796 39
	Saved and Spent	97 90	148 27	87 87	143 03	94 95	50 75	39 95	61 25	723 97
	Carried Forward	15 10	14 09	5 64	(10 41)	(11 50)	11 80	28 80	18 90	72 42
March	Budget	100 00	160 00	75 00	120 00	80 00	55 00	60 00	70 00	720 00
	Available	115 10	174 09	80 64	109 59	68 50	66 80	88 80	88 90	792 42

Illus. 36-3. Comparison of savings and expenses with budget allowances over two-month period.

Barstock remembered that the family had planned to take advantage of end-of-winter sales to buy some clothing for the children, so this would reduce the clothing balance considerably by the end of March. In other categories, the balances were fairly close to the budget allowances.

THE BARSTOCKS KEEP A RECORD OF UNPAID BILLS

The Barstocks receive monthly bills for such expenses as utilities and also make a monthly payment on their house. Since these payments are made regularly each month, there is little chance that the Barstocks will forget about them. But other bills need to be paid at less regular intervals. For example, life insurance premiums are due twice a year, in March and September. Property taxes must be paid in June and December. If there is no record to remind the Barstocks when such bills will be due, they may fail to budget for them.

The Barstocks bought a file box similar to the one shown in Illustration 36-4. The box contains a folder for each month of the year. As bills are received, they are placed in the folder for the month in which they are to be paid. There is also an extra folder marked "Next Year" in which the Barstocks keep all bills and papers, plus reminders about such things as property taxes and insurance premiums, to be taken care of in the following year.

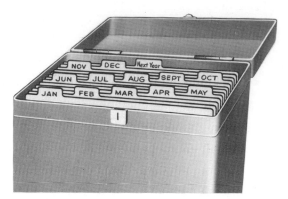

Illus. 36-4. A file for memorandums and unpaid bills. Bills that have been paid are removed from the box and filed in another container.

BUSINESS PAPERS MUST BE FILED

Current bills, receipts, canceled checks, income and property tax records, wills, securities, insurance policies, deeds to property—all are important in a family's business affairs. Records such as these must be kept in an orderly manner so that the information they contain can be located easily when it is needed. Certain papers, such as wills, securities, and insurance policies, should be kept in a safe-deposit box. Other records, such as canceled checks and receipts for paid bills, should be stored in home files. Stationery and office supply stores sell a wide variety of filing equipment for home use. A family should select the type of equipment which is best suited to its needs.

Some business and personal papers should be filed for long periods of time. An insurance policy, for example, should be kept until the contract has been fulfilled or canceled. Records involving the transfer of property should be held for as long as the property is owned. Copies of tax returns must be retained for at least three years from the deadline date for filing the returns.

Receipts for payment of bills, especially those involving large sums of money, should be kept until there is no possibility that payment will be demanded a second time. Other important papers should be kept as long as necessary to establish the legal rights of the individual.

THE BARSTOCKS DETERMINE THEIR FINANCIAL WORTH

It is sometimes desirable for a family to determine what it is worth financially. This can be done by listing everything the family owns (its *assets*) and what it owes (its *liabilities*). The value of some assets is determined by estimating their present resale value. The value of life insurance policies can be determined from the cash value tables in the policies themselves. Information helpful in preparing a statement of family worth is available from the expenditure records of previous years.

The Barstocks' statement of *net worth* is shown in Illustration 36-5. As you can see, the family's net worth is determined by subtracting the family's liabilities from its assets. If a family prepares such a statement every two or three years, it can obtain a fairly good idea of how well it is doing with its money management. A net worth that increases from year to year usually indicates that the family is making financial progress and is practicing good money management.

The Barstock Family
Statement of Net Worth
December 31, 19--

Assets		Liabilities and Net Worth	
Cash (Checking Account)	$ 312.50	Baker National Bank	$ 150.00
Cash (Savings Account)	965.15	G. Wilcox & Co.	175.00
U. S. Savings Bonds	210.75	Uptown Savings & Loan	12,000.00
Life Insurance	1,126.00	Capitol Finance Co.	800.00
Clothing	680.00	Family Net Worth	20,259.40
House and Lot	22,950.00		
Household Furnishings	5,040.00	Total Liabilities	
Automobile	2,100.00	and Net Worth	
Total Assets	$33,384.40		$33,384.40

Illus. 36-5. A family's statement of net worth.

Developing Your Business Vocabulary

The following italicized terms should become part of your business vocabulary. For each numbered statement, find the italicized term that has the same meaning.

assets	*net income*
irregular expenses	*net worth*
liabilities	*regular expenses*

1. Expenses, such as rent and food, that are paid at regular intervals.
2. Expenses that are paid at infrequent times, such as once in three years or at unforeseen times.
3. The amount a person receives after social security, income tax, and other similar items have been subtracted from his earnings.
4. Everything of value that a family owns.
5. Debts that a family owes.
6. The difference between a family's assets and its liabilities.

Checking Your Understanding

1. Why is it even more important for a family to plan the use of its income than it is for an individual to plan the use of his income?
2. Mention several kinds of family expenses for which the amount spent each month is about the same. List several kinds of expenses that are not the same each month and are thus more difficult to estimate.
3. Family savings and expenses are commonly classified in eight main divisions. (a) What are these divisions? (b) What items are commonly included in each of these divisions?
4. Why is part of the mortgage payment of $95 recorded in the Barstocks' income and expense record as savings and part as household expense?
5. At the end of January, the Barstocks had spent $18.51 less than they had allowed for clothing. Does this mean that they overestimated their budgeted clothing needs? Explain.
6. Explain the plan Mr. Barstock used to keep a record of unpaid bills.
7. Why is it important to file family business papers and personal records so that they can be located easily?
8. How does a statement of net worth indicate whether a family is making financial progress?
9. What are some of the ways in which a family can determine the value of its assets? Its liabilities?

Applying What You Have Learned

1. Consider a family of five people: the father, working as a salesman for a local furniture store; the mother, a housewife; and three children, 14, 9, and 2 years old. (a) What are some typical regular expenses that this family might be required to meet weekly or monthly? (b) What are some irregular expenses that the family might be required to meet?
2. Since their daughter Marilyn is in college, Mr. and Mrs. Torreano find it necessary to plan their expenditures carefully. They bought a book on budgeting and recordkeeping and tried to follow a budget based on an average family's expenditures. After trying for several months to follow the budget, they found that their expenditures could not be made to agree with the budget they had adopted. (a) Explain why they might have had difficulties with their budgeting efforts. (b) What do you recommend that the Torreano family do?

3. Edward Foreman estimates that the expenses for medical and dental services for his family will average about $200 a year. In the first year after he began to keep records, these expenses amounted to $85. In the second year they amounted to $79. Should Mr. Foreman change his budget allowance for this item in the third year? Why?

4. Refer to the Barstock family's comparison record on page 423 and answer the following questions:

    (a) At the end of January, for which items had they spent more money than the budget allowed?

    (b) At the end of February, for which items had they spent less money than the budget allowed?

    (c) At the beginning of March, for which item did they have the largest surplus over the regular budget allowance? How could this have happened?

5. Mrs. DuBois keeps all her personal and business papers in a shoe box. She places them in the box in the order in which they are received. Would you say that Mrs. DuBois is using an effective filing system for her records? Explain.

6. Tell whether you agree or disagree with each of the following statements, and be prepared to justify your viewpoint.

    (a) "A large income is necessary to security and happiness."
    (b) "Budgets take the fun out of spending."
    (c) "Members of the family should decide together how income should be used."

Solving Business Problems

1. In this problem you will continue the Barstock family's record of income and expenses for the next month, February. Draw up a form similar to that in Illustration 36-2, or use the form included in your *Activities and Projects*.

    (a) Write on the first line of the record the Barstocks' budget allowances for February, obtaining this information from Illustration 36-1. Rule a line across the entire form.

    (b) Write on the second line the balance of cash on hand as of February 1, $376.39.

    (c) Enter in the record form the following transactions that the Barstocks completed during February. Use Illustration 36-2 on page 422 as a guide.

    Feb. 4 Payments: food, $32.40; household, $6.75; toothpaste, cosmetics, etc., $14.25; church, $8.

10   Made monthly payment on mortgage, $95: payment on principal, $37.90; payment of interest, $57.10.

11   Payments: food, $31.45; clothing, $17.90; household, $3.98; gasoline and oil, $4.95; magazines, newspapers, and theater tickets, $7.75; church, $7.

15   Income, $310.

18   Payments: food, $36.42; clothing, $19.20; household, $10.80; gasoline, $4.65; children's allowances, $6; cosmetics, $3.50; car repairs, $16.75; dental bill, $15; magazines and film, $8.25; church, $10.

25   Payments: food, $24.40; clothing, $24.65; household, $12.60; payment on car, $36; furniture, $15.75; gasoline, $5.45; theater tickets, $15; church, $8.

28   Income, $410.

28   Payments: food, $23.60; clothing, $26.12; household, $36.05; gasoline and car repairs, $27.15; prescription drugs, $6; children's allowances, $6; school supplies, $8.95; deposited $60 in savings account; United Appeal, $28.25.

(d) Rule and balance the Barstock family's record for February. Cash on hand was $372.42.

(e) Now prepare a comparison form similar to that on page 423. Draw a form similar to this one or use the form given in your *Activities and Projects*.

(f) On the first line of the comparison form, record the amounts available for February, obtaining this information from Illustration 36-2.

(g) On the second line enter the amounts saved and spent as shown in the income and expense record.

(h) Calculate and record the amounts carried forward at the end of the month.

2. In this problem you will continue the Barstock family's record of income and expenses for the next month, March.

(a) On the comparison form, enter the budget allowances for March.

(b) Calculate and record the amounts available for March.

(c) Enter on the income and expense record the following transactions that the Barstocks completed during March.

March   4   Payments: food, $16.10; dinner at restaurant, $12.50; towels and linens, $15.65; gasoline, $6.85; phonograph records, $7.95; church, $12.

8   Paid premium on life insurance, $62.16.

10   Made monthly payment on mortgage, $95: payment on principal, $38.60; payment of interest, $56.40.

11   Payments: food, $38.10; children's shoes, $14.90; refrigerator repairs, $28.50; gasoline, $6.10; subscription to magazine, $6; wedding present, $10; church, $10.

15   Income, $310.

18   Payments: food, $38.40; automobile and driver's licenses, $22.50; prescription drugs, $8.20; children's allowances, $6; newspapers and magazines, $3.60; church, $12.

25   Payments: food, $34.93; suit, $65; household, $17.93; payment on car, $36; gasoline and oil, $7.20; tickets to high school play, $5; school expenses, $12; contribution for flowers for fellow worker who is ill, $2; birthday present, $10; church, $12.

31   Income, $410.

31   Payments: food, $19.65; gasoline, $4.90; doctor's bill, $12; medicine, $8.50; dental bill, $13; children's allowances, $6; club dues, $5; phonograph records, $8; contribution to orphanage, $10; deposited $60 in savings account.

(d) Rule and balance the Barstock family's record for March. Cash on hand was $310.80.

(e) On the next available line of the comparison form, enter the amounts saved and spent.

(f) Calculate and record the amounts carried forward at the end of the month.

(g) Enter the budget allowances for April.

(h) Calculate and record the amounts available for April.

Enriching Your Business Understanding

1. Talk with your parents about the extent to which they maintain financial records of their income and expenditures. On the basis of your discussions with them and on the basis of what you have learned in this part, outline an income and expense record that you feel would meet the needs of your family.

2. Explain how each of the following might require a change in the family budget. Be as specific as possible.

   (a) A daughter enters college.
   (b) The family income increases by one-fourth.
   (c) The family moves to the suburbs.
   (d) The family buys a second car.
   (e) An aged parent moves in with the family.
   (f) Two teenagers start driving the family car.
   (g) A family which had been renting buys a home.

3. From newspapers and other sources, try to find out how much money was budgeted for the following items by your town, county, or district.

   (a) School needs.
   (b) Streets or highways.
   (c) Police department.
   (d) Fire department.
   (e) Public welfare.
   (f) Mayor's office.
   (g) Public library.
   (h) Parks.

4. Every family has the problem of arranging certain materials in an orderly way. Suggest a plan for filing and organizing each of the following materials so that a particular item can be located quickly when it is needed.

   (a) Canceled checks.
   (b) Children's health records.
   (c) Christmas card list.
   (d) Recipes.
   (e) Family birth certificates.
   (f) Manufacturers' instructions for care and use of appliances.
   (g) Manufacturers' instructions for care of wearing apparel.
   (h) Newspaper clippings.
   (i) Photographs.
   (j) Telephone numbers.

PART 37

The Rising And Falling Values of Money

One of the most important uses of money is as a standard or measure of value. We may say that a trumpet is worth $100, a TV set, $200; and a car, $3,000. This means much more to us than to say that a car is worth 15 TV sets or 30 trumpets. Money is used to measure values just as the mile is used to measure distances and the quart is used to measure liquids.

Some standards of measurement are always the same. A mile is always a mile and a quart is always a quart. A dollar is something different as a measuring device. The fact that a book can now be bought for $4 does not mean that the same book would have cost $4 ten years ago or will cost $4 ten years from now.

Suppose that a school lunch cost 40 cents a few years ago and that a similar lunch now costs 50 cents. Obviously, the price of lunches has increased one-fourth, or 25%. A 25% change in the price of one item may not seem to mean much. But if the average price of all goods and services has gone up 25%, a person needs $1.25 to buy the same thing he used to be able to buy for $1.

It is not easy for a person to judge for himself how much prices are changing. Even when prices are generally rising, the

BUYING POWER OF MONEY IS NOT ALWAYS THE SAME

Illus. 37-1. One thing that good money managers consider is that the buying power of money is not always the same.

Ewing Galloway

prices for some things may not change, and the prices for others may even decrease. Even the items that do increase in price may not all increase at the same rate.

To make information about price changes available to everyone, the federal government publishes price indexes, one of which is the Consumer Price Index. A *price index* is a series of numbers showing how much prices have changed over a number of years. The *Consumer Price Index* shows the changes in the average prices of goods and services bought by consumers.

Illustration 37-2 gives the Consumer Price Index for 1940 to 1970. In compiling the chart, the average prices for some 300 goods and services in 1957-59 were taken to represent 100%. The figure given for each year is a percent of this average. For example, the amount 49 for the year 1940 means that the average price consumers paid for all items in 1940 was about one-half of the average price for similar items in 1957-59. In 1970 the average price of all items was 134, or about one-third above the 1957-59 average.

The line for the Consumer Price Index on the chart does not seem to go up very rapidly, so that changes in prices may not seem important. But over a number of years the changes may be very important. You cannot determine from the chart exactly how much prices changed each year. But it can be determined mathematically that prices increased, on the average, a little over 3% a year, compounded annually. A 3% increase in prices does

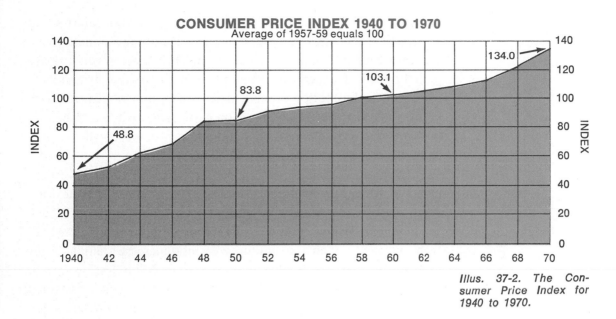

CONSUMER PRICE INDEX 1940 TO 1970
Average of 1957-59 equals 100

Illus. 37-2. The Consumer Price Index for 1940 to 1970.

not seem to be too burdensome for anyone, but note the total increase over the 30-year period.

The Consumer Price Index was about 49 in 1940; in 1970 it was 134. The prices of goods and services increased 173% in the 30 years (134 − 49 = 85 increase; 85 ÷ 49 = 1.73, or 173% increase). A person with take-home pay of $400 a month in 1940 would have needed, in 1970, take-home pay of about $1,100 a month to be equally well off.

An increase in the general price level is called *inflation*. With inflation there is a decrease in the purchasing power of a dollar. A decrease in the general price level is called *deflation*. With deflation there is an increase in the purchasing power of a dollar.

Inflation occurs whenever the demand for goods and services tends to be greater than the supply. In a period of prosperity when almost everyone has a job, many people become too optimistic. They spend their earnings freely and greatly increase their credit purchases, especially those made on the installment plan. As a result, the demand for goods of all kinds tends to increase rapidly. What happens? Prices rise.

As prices rise, wages and salaries also tend to rise. If increases in wages and salaries are offset by increased production, there is

WITH INFLATION, MONEY HAS LESS BUYING POWER

no effect on prices. But if increases in wages and salaries are greater than increases in production, there are more dollars to be spent for a limited amount of goods, and prices are given another push upward. To meet the demand or the expected demand for more goods, businesses expand. They build new stores and factories and spend large amounts for equipment. All this spending in turn increases demand and tends to add to the upward movement of prices.

Local and federal governments may also contribute much to inflation. Governments spend enormous amounts of money for defense, public buildings, roads, and many other kinds of goods and services. If governments raise enough in taxes to match all their payments, their expenditures do not increase demand. For each dollar they spend, the public has one dollar less to spend. But if governments borrow large amounts from banks and then spend those amounts, they increase demand. Governments spend their borrowed funds, but the amount that the public has to spend is not decreased.

WITH DEFLATION, MONEY HAS MORE BUYING POWER

Deflation tends to occur when the supply of goods and services exceeds the demand. When prices become high because of inflation, consumers may decrease their purchases. This may happen either because they think that prices are too high or because they have already bought to the limit of their money and credit.

Because of the decreased buying by consumers, businesses have less demand for their products. They may decrease the number of their employees or have employees work shorter hours. Then the employees have less money to spend, and they decrease their buying. The decreased buying by employees still further decreases demand and makes deflation even more serious. As business becomes less active, stores and factories may delay expansion. This again decreases demand and helps to push prices down.

Deflation is also encouraged when government increases taxes more than it increases spending. When it does this, it takes money away from consumers that they might otherwise spend, and does not make an offsetting increase in its spending. This decreases the total demand for goods and services and tends to cause prices to decrease.

As individuals, we cannot do very much to affect either inflation or deflation. When prices seem to be too high, we may postpone making some purchases. If many consumers do this, the demand for goods may fall off, and prices may decrease as a result. But most of us are not able to postpone many of our purchases. We must spend regularly for food, clothing, and shelter. And if we need or want something like a new car or a refrigerator, we probably want it now and not three or four years from now when prices may be lower. Also, we have no assurance that prices will be lower in the future; they are more likely to be higher.

Government, acting for all of us, can do much to combat inflation. Among other things, it can:

1. Increase taxes. An increase in taxes takes money away from consumers and thus reduces their purchases of goods and services.
2. Reduce government spending. A reduction in spending, especially when accompanied by higher taxes, decreases demand and thus decreases prices.
3. Increase interest rates. Through the Federal Reserve System, higher interest rates can be encouraged. Higher interest rates make it cost more to borrow the money that a person needs to buy such things as a car or a house. Higher interest rates also increase what a business must pay if it wants to borrow to expand its facilities. Some buying may therefore be postponed or avoided entirely. Decreases in purchases may result in a decrease in the demand for goods that may help bring about a decrease in prices.

WHAT CAN BE DONE TO COMBAT INFLATION?

WHAT CAN BE DONE TO COMBAT DEFLATION?

To combat deflation, government can follow policies just the opposite of those used to combat inflation. Among other things, it can:

1. Decrease taxes. A decrease in taxes leaves more money in the hands of consumers and thus makes possible an increase in the purchase of goods and services. An increase in spending by the general public will help to increase prices.
2. Increase government spending. An increase in spending that is not offset by an increase in taxes increases demand and, thus, prices.
3. Lower interest rates. Through the Federal Reserve System, lower interest rates can be encouraged. Lower interest rates tend to encourage individuals and businesses to borrow in order to buy. With increased borrowing, consumers have more money to spend. This helps to increase the demand for goods and eventually will provide a support for prices.

WHY MORE IS DONE ABOUT DEFLATION THAN INFLATION

When deflation threatens, prompt action is usually taken. Everyone notices the slowing down of business and the loss of jobs that deflation brings. Public officials are encouraged to do whatever they can to avoid the hardships that deflation causes. Furthermore, the actions taken to combat deflation are usually well received. Almost everyone likes to have his taxes reduced. Few object to increased spending for public works or services that benefit them. Also, few object to lower interest rates, especially if they want to borrow to buy a home or for any other purpose.

But when inflation threatens, such prompt action is not likely to be taken. The strong demand for goods and services that usually occurs at the beginning of a period of inflation makes businesses prosperous and jobs plentiful. Wages and salaries are increasing. Prices may be increasing even more rapidly; but increases in prices, occurring a little here and a little there, are not so noticeable at first. So before inflation becomes really serious, most people do not want anything done that will disturb the seemingly prosperous conditions. Often nothing is done to control inflation until it has gone so far that it cannot be completely avoided but can only be slowed down or kept from increasing.

Usually the means of combating inflation are unpopular to us as individuals. Few people like to pay higher taxes or higher interest rates. Reduced government spending is approved in principle by many people, but few favor reductions in the public works or services that affect them and their jobs.

Some people contend that a little inflation each year is desirable, but there is general agreement that the price level should be reasonably stable. In the past, the price level has moved up in some years and down in others. Over a long period of time, however, there has been a tendency for prices to increase. This tendency is likely to continue, especially since the means of combating inflation are not popular with many people. Individually, we can do very little to prevent either inflation or deflation. However, we can support those government officials who advocate policies that will help to avoid extremes of either inflation or deflation. And, as you will see in the following part, we can also plan our own financial affairs so that we will be harmed as little as possible by inflation or deflation.

INFLATION AND DEFLATION IN THE FUTURE

Developing Your Business Vocabulary

The following italicized terms should become part of your business vocabulary. For each numbered statement, find the italicized term that has the same meaning.

Consumer Price Index *inflation*
deflation *price index*

1. Any series of numbers showing how prices have changed over a period of years.
2. A price index that shows the changes in the average prices of goods and services bought by consumers.
3. An increase in the general price level.
4. A decrease in the general price level.

Checking Your Understanding

1. Is money a good measure of the value of different things at one time? Explain.
2. If the price level rises, does the buying power of money rise?

3. Who prepares the Consumer Price Index? Is this index based on the retail prices of goods only?

4. How much did the Consumer Price Index increase from 1940 to 1970? (See Illustration 37-2 on page 433.)

5. Would a person with take-home pay of $700 in 1970 be as well off as a person with take-home pay of $500 in 1945? Why or why not?

6. Are we likely to have inflation when the supply of goods is greater than the demand?

7. What can each of us as individuals do to combat inflation?

8. What can the government do to combat inflation? Explain how each of these actions by the government affects inflation.

9. What can each of us as individuals do to combat deflation?

10. What can the government do to combat deflation? Explain how each of these actions by the government affects deflation.

11. Why is the government more likely to take prompt action to combat deflation than it is to combat inflation?

Applying What You Have Learned

1. If Mr. Beckemeyer puts $1,000 in a safe-deposit box in a bank, how much will it be worth in five years? Can he expect that at the end of the five years the money in the safe-deposit box will buy more than, the same as, or less than it would have when it was put in the box? Explain.

2. Suppose that sugar sold for 5¢ a pound in 1940 and 12¢ a pound in 1970. Did the price of sugar increase more or less rapidly than the Consumer Price Index?

3. The average price of electricity sold for residential use was 3.8¢ per kilowatt hour in 1940 and about 2¢ in 1970. (a) Compare the change in the cost of electricity per kilowatt hour with the change in the Consumer Price Index from 1940 to 1970. (b) Suggest reasons for the difference.

4. Will a large increase in installment sales tend to cause inflation or deflation? Why?

5. Will an increase in the average production of all workers that is greater than the average increase in wages and salaries tend to cause inflation or deflation? Why?

6. Which is more likely to increase inflation: (a) an increase in government spending with no increase in taxes? (b) an increase in government spending with an equal increase in taxes? (c) a decrease in government spending with an increase in taxes?

7. Does a large decrease in buying by consumers tend to cause inflation or deflation? Why?

Solving Business Problems

1. Refer to the Consumer Price Index on page 433.

   (a) In which 10-year period, beginning with 1940, was there the greatest increase in the index? How much was this increase?
   (b) In which 10-year period was there the least increase in the index? How much was this increase?

2. Assume that the price of shoes changes at exactly the same rate as the Consumer Price Index. If a pair of shoes sold for $4.88 in 1940, how much did the same grade of shoes sell for:

       (a) In 1950?   (b) In 1960?   (c) In 1970?

3. Assume that the price of bread increases at exactly the same rate as the Consumer Price Index. If a loaf cost 10¢ in 1940, how much would it cost:

       (a) In 1950?   (b) In 1960?   (c) In 1970?

4. If Jim Berryman had weekly take-home pay of $100 a week in 1960, how much would he need in 1970 to be equally well off? Assume that Jim's expenses increase at the same rate as the Consumer Price Index.

Enriching Your Business Understanding

1. The Consumer Price Index below gives a breakdown of price increases of services, food, nondurables with the exception of food, and durables. Study the chart carefully, than answer the questions on page 440.

COMMODITIES AND SERVICES. CONSUMER PRICE INDEX

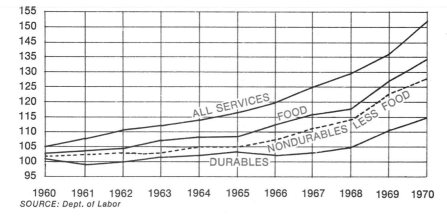

SOURCE: Dept. of Labor

(a) Which one of the items charted increased the most during the ten-year period? What might account for this large increase?

(b) What might account for the fact that there was less of an increase in the price of durables than in the prices of other items?

2. The Consumer Price Index and the Wholesale Commodity Price Index for 1950, 1960, and 1970 are given below. Study the table, then answer the questions.

Year	Consumer Price Index	Wholesale Commodity Price Index
1950	83.8	86.8
1960	103.1	100.7
1970	134.0 (est.)	117.0 (est.)

(a) Explain the difference between what is measured by the two indexes. (Dictionary definitions of "wholesale" and "commodity" may help you understand the second index.)

(b) Which index showed the greater increase in the 20-year period?

(c) Suggest reasons why one index should rise more rapidly than the other.

3. Possible trends toward inflation and deflation in our economy are of interest to many people. Look through newspapers for the last several days. Clip news stories that deal with economic events and problems. Be prepared to read and explain to the class two or three of the most interesting items from your collection of clippings. Indicate why you consider these items to be of economic importance, and try to relate them to topics you have studied so far in this class.

PART 38
Money Management And the Price Level

In 1945 the Donald Kneiberts were pleased with their financial worth. Their home was more than half paid for, and they had some other savings. As an electrician, Mr. Kneibert earned enough so that he and his family could live very comfortably. He also had enough life insurance to assure his family a reasonable income if he should die. Their financial needs for the immediate future seemed to be well taken care of. But they were concerned about what their income would be after Mr. Kneibert retired.

Mr. Kneibert expected to retire in 1970. After that, he would have social security benefits, a pension from his company, and some income from a savings account. His total income would be enough so that he and his wife could live fairly well if they watched their pennies. But if they were to maintain their present style of living, they felt that they would need some other income. So to supplement their income, Mr. Kneibert bought an annuity policy from an insurance company. The terms of the policy provided that he pay premiums annually through 1969. Starting in 1970, the insurance company would pay a fixed amount each month to him or to his wife as long as either lived.

THE KNEIBERTS MAKE THEIR RETIREMENT PLANS

After Mr. Kneibert retired in 1970, he and his wife were somewhat discouraged because their income did not seem to provide for them as well as they had hoped. The amount was actually a little larger than they had expected when they first made their retirement plans in 1945. But it did not seem to provide the style of living they wanted.

The main reason for this situation was that in 1970 almost everything cost much more than it had when their retirement plans were made in 1945. This increase in prices disturbed the Kneiberts, especially since they had no way of knowing what increases there might be in the future. Their income was fixed and could not be expected to increase. Further increases in prices would mean that they could buy just that much less.

In making their financial plans, the Kneiberts had not considered possible changes in the price level. And as you learned in Part 37, the price level does change. In the rest of this part, we shall discuss inflation and deflation as they relate to using credit, buying insurance, and making investments.

RELATION OF THE PRICE LEVEL TO CREDIT

Credit may be used for a few days or a few weeks in ordinary charge accounts. Or it may be used for several months or even years in installment plans. Such credit transactions are not directly affected by the price level. In a period of inflation, workers are likely to be earning good salaries and to be able to pay their accounts promptly. In a period of deflation, workers may have less income because of lower wages or shorter working hours and may be less able to pay their accounts promptly. But these differences are not a direct result of changes in the price level.

Now consider another type of credit transaction: obtaining a loan for a long period of time, such as a 20-year loan for the purchase of a house. Suppose that the price level rises an average of 3½ % a year during the 20-year period. If the value of the house increases as rapidly as the price level, it may be worth about twice its original cost at the end of the 20 years. Also, wages and salaries will probably increase as the price level increases. It will thus take a constantly decreasing share of the buyer's income to make regular payments on the house.

Illus. 38-1. Persons on fixed incomes, such as retired persons, are hurt most by a period of rising prices.

The situation is just the opposite in a period of falling prices. The value of a house will tend to decrease from year to year. Also, if wages and salaries are decreasing, the payments on the house will take a constantly increasing share of the borrower's income.

Obviously, rising prices are likely to benefit persons who have long-term debts. As a result, these persons often favor some inflation. Lenders who are receiving a fixed interest income will be more interested in maintaining a stable price level.

RELATION OF THE PRICE LEVEL TO INSURANCE

Changes in the price level do not have any bearing on the purchase of short term insurance, such as insurance on cars and other property. It is true that insurance costs rise as prices rise, but such insurance is bought for the present. A person should buy what he needs now regardless of what prices may be in the future.

Life insurance is quite different. Benefits from a life insurance policy may be received many years after the policy was taken out. If the price level has risen during that time, the amount received for the policy may buy much less than was expected when payments on the policy were first started. This does not mean that life insurance should not be bought. It only means that a person should not make the accumulation of life insurance too great a part of his savings program.

RELATION OF THE PRICE LEVEL TO INVESTMENTS

As you learned in Part 29, a good investment is one that is safe and that earns a fair income. But an investor is interested in more than the amount of money he will receive from his investments; he is also interested in what that money will buy. He is thus concerned with how the buying power of his invested money will be affected by rising or falling prices. As far as inflation and deflation are concerned, investments may be divided into two classes: short-term and long-term.

Short-term investments are those made for a few months or a few years at the most. For example, you may save throughout the school year for a trip to a summer camp. Or you may save for several years to build a fund for college expenses. In such cases, it is not likely that either inflation or deflation will make much difference. Prices may change, but the price level probably will not change enough within a few months or even a few years to noticeably affect the amount that your dollars will buy.

Long-term investments are those that extend over a period of years—10 years, 15 years, or even more. For example, a family may save for several years to accumulate enough money for a down payment on a house. When they finally do buy the house, they may expect to keep it for a long time. Or a man may invest money in order to provide income after he retires. In such cases, the possibility of inflation or deflation is important. Either may affect the value of the investment in terms of what it will buy in the future.

INVESTMENTS IN A PERIOD OF DEFLATION

Investments that pay a fixed amount in dollars are most desirable in a time of falling prices. For example, assume that a person has invested $1,000 in a 6% bond due in 10 years. Each year he receives $60 interest. If prices fall during the 10-year period, the buying power of each $60 increases. Also, the $1,000 that he receives when the bond is paid will buy more than it would have when the bond was purchased.

Similarly, depositors in savings banks and in savings and loan associations benefit somewhat from falling prices. It is true that in a period of falling prices the demand for loans may decrease because fewer people may be buying homes. As a result, the earnings of savings banks and of savings and loan associations may decrease. They may therefore decrease their interest or dividend rates. But the amount on deposit will not be changed by a change in the price level. If the price level is lower when the deposit is withdrawn than it was when the deposit was made, the investor gains that much in purchasing power.

Investments that tend to increase in value as the price level rises are most desirable in a time of inflation. For example, assume that a family buys a home and keeps it for 10 years. If the price level increases 15% in that time, the prices of houses will probably also increase. This does not mean that every house will increase equally in value. Some may not increase at all, and some may actually decrease. But well-maintained houses will tend to increase in value as prices rise.

Common stocks are a popular investment when prices are rising. Rising prices help businesses make satisfactory profits and thus make it easier for them to pay attractive dividends. As the prospect for future increases in dividends seems to be good, the prices of the stocks will tend to increase. Not all common stocks will increase equally in price. In fact, if a business is not well managed, the price of its stock may actually fall during a period of rising prices. But a general increase in the price level is likely to be accompanied by an increase in the price of common stocks.

Study Illustration 38-2. In this chart, common stock prices and consumer prices are assumed to be 100% in 1945. The common stock line extending generally upward shows the yearly change in common stock prices determined as a percent of the 1945 prices. Similarly, the consumer price line indicates the changes in consumer prices as a percent of the 1945 average price.

The increase in the average price of common stocks was about four times greater than the average increase in consumer prices. Several factors were responsible for this large increase. The prices of many stocks rose because managers and employees were efficient in operating the businesses. The stocks of most corporations also became more valuable from year to year because the corporations retained part of their earnings to expand and thus to increase earnings in future years. But some of the increase probably resulted from the change in the price level, which tended

INVESTMENTS IN A PERIOD OF INFLATION

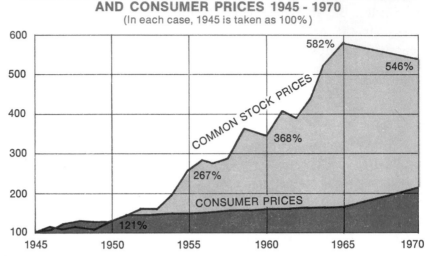

COMPARISON OF INCREASES IN COMMON STOCK PRICES AND CONSUMER PRICES 1945 - 1970
(In each case, 1945 is taken as 100%)

COMMON STOCK PRICES

582%

546%

368%

267%

CONSUMER PRICES

121%

600

500

400

300

200

100

1945   1950   1955   1960   1965   1970

Illus. 38-2. Comparison of increases in common stock prices and consumer prices from 1945 to 1970.

to make everything that the corporations owned more valuable. As prices increased, it was also easier for businesses to sell their goods at favorable prices and thus earn satisfactory profits.

PERSONS SHOULD BALANCE THEIR INVESTMENTS

It is hard for the average investor to be certain whether the price level will rise or fall in the future and how rapidly it may move in either direction. It is therefore desirable for a person to try to balance or distribute his investments. In doing this, he will have some that will benefit from falling prices and some that will benefit from rising prices.

The Donald Kneiberts did not balance their investments. They assumed a stable price level, and their retirement income was a fixed amount at a time when the price level was rising. The annuity that Mr. Kneibert bought in 1945 paid a definite amount each month. That was the only kind of annuity that insurance companies offered at that time. Now some insurance companies offer *variable annuities*. With the funds received from buyers of variable annuities, insurance companies invest in securities, such as common stocks, that tend to increase their yield as the price level increases. This enables the insurance companies to increase the payments on the annuities. The increases in the payments may not be as large or occur as rapidly as the increases in the price level, but they should offset those increases to a great extent.

Illus. 38-3. Everyone should try to balance his investments so that he is hurt as little as possible by a rise or a fall in the price level.

Mr. Kneibert's pension was also a fixed amount. With increases in prices, there were some increases in the interest paid on his savings accounts. Also, the benefits received from social security were increased. But these increases were not equal to the increases in the general price level. The Kneiberts would have been better off if they had placed part of their savings in mutual funds or in good common stocks.

Developing Your Business Vocabulary

The following italicized terms should become part of your business vocabulary. For each numbered statement, find the italicized term that has the same meaning.

long-term investment
short-term investment
variable annuity

1. An investment made for a few months or, at most, a few years.
2. An investment made for a number of years.
3. An annuity that tends to fluctuate with the price level.

Checking Your Understanding

1. What sources of income did the Kneiberts expect to have after Mr. Kneibert retired?
2. Why did the Kneiberts' retirement income fail to provide for them as satisfactorily as they had hoped it would?

3. Is the use of a charge account made undesirable by a possible change in the price level?

4. Tom DeJockemo, a high school student, works after school and on Saturdays and hopes to save money to pay for college expenses later on. Should Tom consider possible changes in the price level when he is investing his savings?

5. Mr. Johannsen is considering buying a new home. To do so, he will have to obtain a loan that will be paid off over a 20-year period. Does it make any difference to Mr. Johannsen whether the price level is rising or falling during that time? Explain.

6. Is the buying power of the amount received from an insurance policy increased or decreased by inflation? By deflation?

7. If you thought it likely that the price level would increase 3% a year, what would you do:

   (a) About the purchase of automobile insurance?
   (b) About the purchase of homeowners insurance?
   (c) About the purchase of life insurance?

8. Tell which of the following will be made a more attractive source of income by the possibility of deflation:

   (a) an annuity
   (b) bonds of a corporation
   (c) one's own business
   (d) municipal bonds
   (e) pensions
   (f) real estate
   (g) a savings account
   (h) social security benefits
   (i) stocks of corporations
   (j) U.S. savings bonds

9. Tell which of the items listed in Question 8 will be made a more attractive source of income by the possibility of inflation.

10. Henry Knowles bought stock in ten different corporations. In this way he hoped to avoid the risk of having too much money in one investment. Is this what is known as "balancing investments"?

Applying What You Have Learned

1. Mr. Deaton plans to retire in about 10 years. After he retires, he and his wife should receive about $250 a month in social security benefits. He should also receive $250 a month from a pension and $40 a month from interest on a savings account. If Mr. Deaton has additional savings to invest, what kinds of investments would you recommend that he consider?

2. Mr. Katz also plans to retire in about 10 years. He owns his home. He receives about $250 a month as dividends on common stocks that he owns. He also expects to receive social security benefits of about $230 a month. If Mr. Katz has additional savings to invest, what kinds of investments would you recommend that he consider?

3. In 1950 Mr. Boyers bought a common stock for $12 a share. From the chart on page 446, can you estimate how much the stock was worth in 1970?

4. Miss Pollitt is considering buying an annuity to provide additional retirement income. Under what circumstances do you recommend that she buy (a) an annuity that pays a fixed amount each month, or (b) a variable annuity?

Solving Business Problems

1. In 1950 Floyd Polinsky paid $1,000 for common stock. In 1970 the market price for this stock was four times the original cost.

   (a) What was the market price of the stock in 1970?
   (b) If the dividends paid in 1950 were 3% of the cost price, what was the amount of the dividends in dollars?
   (c) If the dividends increased so that in 1970 they were 3% of the market price, what was the amount of the 1970 dividends in dollars?
   (d) What percent of the original cost price was the amount of the dividends found in (c)?

2. Les Altergate bought $1,000 of common stocks in each of the years 1945, 1950, 1960, and 1970. Assume that these stocks increased in price at the same rate as the index of common stock prices given on page 446.

   (a) In 1970, what was the current price of the stock purchased in 1945?
   (b) In 1970, what was the total market price of the stocks purchased in all four years?

3. Dillon Routt is considering making one of two investments: a bond costing $1,000 that pays $60 a year interest, or 25 shares of stock at $40 a share. The stock pays an annual dividend of 60¢ a share. Dillon decides to buy the stock because he believes that it will increase in value. How much per share should the stock increase in value each year to make up the difference between the dividend and the interest that might have been earned on the bond? (Any possible effect of income taxes may be ignored.)

Enriching Your Business Understanding

1. In 1950 Todd Ruben bought two 4% bonds of a corporation. Would you expect the price of these bonds to increase from 1950 to 1970 the same as the price index for common stocks? Give reasons for your answer.

2. Which of the following has risen (or fallen) the most in price between 1965 and the latest date for which you can find information: (a) common stock prices? (b) Consumer Price Index? (c) Wholesale Price Index? Calculate the change as a percentage. (Data may be found in the *Statistical Abstract of the United States,* but more current data can be obtained from the *Federal Reserve Bulletin* or from other financial publications.)

3. For several years after 1965 there was a gradual decrease in the value of long-term government bonds issued before 1965. Did this indicate any doubt on the part of investors that the government would pay the interest or the principal of the bonds?

4. Some mutual funds invest only in common stocks; others invest only in bonds; and some invest in both stocks and bonds. Describe a situation in which you would recommend that a person buy the stock of a mutual fund that:

   (a) Invests only in common stocks.
   (b) Invests one-third of its funds in bonds and two-thirds in common stocks.
   (c) Invests only in bonds.

Unit 9

Communication and Transportation

PART 39
Communication And Transportation In Our Economy

We are a nation of more than 200 million people, scattered over more than 4 million square miles. In land area, our country is the fourth largest in the world. Yet within this vast area, we live together as a unified nation rather than as isolated states or communities.

Much of the unity we have as a nation is based on good communication and good transportation. Thanks to communication, persons from Juneau, Alaska, to Trenton, New Jersey, can learn of a President's election at the same time. Or a father in Bangor, Maine, can talk to his son in Honolulu. Thanks to transportation, persons in Kansas can eat fresh oranges, and persons in Florida can have wheat to make bread. And thanks also to transportation and travel, we can visit other parts of the country so that the Rockies, the Grand Canyon, or the Black Hills become more than just pictures in a geography book.

Communication is the sharing of information. There are many different ways of sharing information with someone else. When we think of communication, we usually think of spoken or written messages, but people can communicate through any one of the five senses. Even objects—a traffic light, for instance—can communicate. A green light gives you the information that you can go ahead.

THE ROLE OF COMMUNICATION IN OUR ECONOMY

Today we can communicate quickly with other persons in almost any part of the world. Planes carry mail between cities or across the country in a matter of hours instead of the weeks or months that used to be required. Telegraph messages may be sent and delivered almost instantly over distances of thousands of miles. We can talk by telephone to people across the nation and even across the ocean. While he is in his car, a driver may talk with another person miles away. A pilot may talk with someone on the ground thousands of feet below him. A passenger on a steamship may carry on a conversation with someone on shore.

Television allows us to watch history being made, such as man's first step on the moon. We can be part of the audience when the President addresses Congress, when two pro football teams meet in a playoff game, or when a Shakespearian play is being performed. Radio, too, brings us entertainment and news from all over the world.

Thanks also to man-made satellites, great distances no longer separate people who want to communicate with each other. Early Bird, the world's first commercial communications satellite, was launched in 1965. It aids in transmitting radio, telephone, and television signals to all parts of the world. It was the first of a series of satellites that will eventually form a global communications network.

Illus. 39-1. A television broadcast being produced in a studio. Television is an important means of communication between people in our country and in other countries.

Panasonic

A modern economic system like ours depends upon rapid, efficient transportation of people, raw materials, and merchandise. Travel and transportation are sometimes considered to be the same thing. In our discussion, however, we shall consider *transportation* as the physical movement of goods from one place to another. *Travel*, which will be discussed in the next section, will be thought of mainly as the movement of people.

Without our transportation system, farms could not market their fruits, grains, and livestock. Stores would close because they could not obtain merchandise to sell. Factories would close for lack of materials. Even if some factories did not immediately run out of materials, they would be unable to ship their products to buyers. Without the services of railroads, trucks, ships, planes, and cars, many cities and towns would perish.

Mass production could not exist without a good transportation system. In making the thousands of parts that go into a single car, for example, 53 different types of material—from aluminum to zinc—are used. Without transportation to bring these materials together, there could be no car. Because of our transportation network, various regions of our country can specialize in producing certain products. Lumber can be produced in the Northwest and sold in the East. Natural gas from the Southwest can be piped to consumers in Illinois. Citrus fruits can be grown in Florida and California and shipped to New England.

Another economic value of transportation is its ability to extend a firm's market area. For example, a bakery in one city can provide daily service to smaller cities within a 50-mile radius. A department store located downtown or in a major shopping center can draw trade from a 100-mile radius. A fertilizer manufacturer can sell and deliver his products in nearby states. A shoe manufacturer can locate near the source of labor or raw materials and can market shoes all over the country.

Transportation allows all of us to enjoy a higher style of living. It enables us to use and enjoy products grown or made elsewhere in this country or in other countries. Transportation can result in lower prices for the goods we buy. This is because all regions of the world can specialize in producing goods that their resources enable them to produce most efficiently.

Mobil Oil Corp.

Illus. 39-2. Our economy has a well-developed system for the transportation of goods. This giant ocean-going supertanker is used to transport huge quantities of petroleum.

WHY TRAVEL SERVICES ARE IMPORTANT TO US

For many of us, travel is necessary to earn a living. Every day millions of workers commute by bus, train, or car from their homes to the places where they work. Many salesmen for business firms travel almost all the time calling on customers in distant cities. Businessmen may travel throughout the country to carry on the business affairs of their firms.

People also travel for pleasure. In about half our states, vacation travel is one of the three most important sources of income. A few states claim that it is their most important industry. Personal and family incomes are increasing. Gradually we are getting longer vacations and more leisure time. Transportation companies carry on appealing advertising campaigns urging us to travel. Many companies offer special low-cost package trips and liberal credit arrangements. Because of these and other factors, *tourism* is becoming an increasingly important industry.

Our needs and wants for travel services are creating some serious problems. It is predicted that by 1975 there will be more than 110 million cars on our nation's highways. Highways are already overcrowded, and more and better ones need to be built. The smog that shrouds many of our cities is blamed at least in part on exhaust fumes from vehicles. Thus, federal regulations now require that all new vehicles sold in the United States be equipped with air pollution controls.

Some metropolitan areas are building or planning *mass transit facilities*. They are working to develop faster, more efficient commuter train service and better bus service. The objective of such

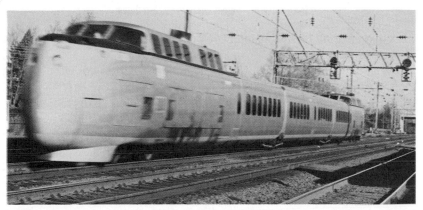

Sikorsky Aircraft

Illus. 39-3. High-speed trains like this one may be part of the mass transit facilities of the future. This Turbo-Train, on a test run, reached a speed of nearly 171 miles per hour.

services is partly to encourage people to leave their cars at home during working hours and thus reduce traffic congestion.

Air travel is becoming more and more popular both for business and pleasure. The jumbo jet, developed to carry greater loads of passengers and freight, is currently in operation on continental and intercontinental flights. Airliners with loads of more than a thousand passengers each are possible within the next 20 years. Many airports are already unable to keep up with the volume of air traffic. New airports are being built to handle more safely and efficiently the current and future volume of air traffic.

Developing Your Business Vocabulary

The following italicized terms should become part of your business vocabulary. For each numbered statement, find the italicized term that has the same meaning.

communication   *transportation*
mass transit facilities   *travel*
tourism

1. The sharing of information with others.
2. The physical movement of goods from one place to another.
3. The movement of people from one place to another for business or pleasure.
4. The traveling of people from one place to another for pleasure.
5. A system of modern transportation to meet the needs of commuters in urban areas.

Checking Your Understanding

1. Give examples of what might happen if suddenly we were without means of communication and transportation.
2. What are some of the methods of communication commonly used today?
3. How does communication assist business in carrying on its activities?
4. How does transportation contribute to our economy?
5. Why would mass production be impossible without a good transportation system?
6. How do transportation facilities enable businesses and regions to specialize in production of goods?
7. Why is it said that transportation enables us to enjoy a higher style of living?
8. What changes would you have to make in your present way of living if travel services as we have them today did not exist? Explain by giving four or more examples.
9. State three or four reasons for the growth of the travel industry in recent years.
10. Name several problems that our nation faces as a result of the growing demand for travel services.

Applying What You Have Learned

1. Why do we have more than one form of communication?
2. Messages are frequently communicated by telephone, telegraph, television, and radio. Suggest a situation in which each of these methods might be used by: (a) a retail merchant, (b) a police station, (c) a newspaper.
3. Prepare a list of five different business firms in your city or in a city near you which provide communication services and five which provide transportation services. Name the specific type of service provided by each.
4. What types of communication activities might be typical of: (a) an insurance company, (b) a passenger airline, (c) a wholesale produce firm.
5. Transportation and travel assist us in many ways in our daily lives. List the ways in which various forms of transportation are used: (a) by individuals, (b) by business firms, (c) by government agencies.
6. In many ways, our style of living depends upon transportation to bring us products and services we use in our everyday lives. Make a list (three or four items) for each of the following questions:

(a) Which products do you and your family use that are not produced in the United States?

(b) Which products do you and your family use that are made in this country but that are shipped in from another state?

After reviewing your lists and those of others in your class, to what degree would you say that we are dependent upon transportation?

7. Tell how traveling is of benefit (a) to the traveler and (b) to the state or country in which he is traveling.

Solving Business Problems

1. The table below shows the number of employees for three groups of the communications industry in 1960 and 1969.

	1960	1969
Telephone communication	706,000	883,000
Telegraph communication	38,000	32,000
Radio and television broadcasting	92,000	131,000

(a) What was the total number of communications employees in 1960? In 1969?

(b) By what percent did the total number of communications employees increase from 1960 to 1969?

(c) From 1960 to 1969, which group of communications employees had the largest increase in number of employees?

(d) From 1960 to 1969, which group of communications employees had the largest percentage increase in employees?

(e) Which group had a reduction in the number of employees? By what percent?

2. The table below shows the growth in telephone service and population of the U.S. from 1960 to 1969.

	1960	1969
Total telephones in service:	74 million	115 million
Business	21 million	32 million
Residential	53 million	83 million
Average daily conversations	285 million	462 million
Total population	180 million	203 million

(a) What was the number of telephones per 1,000 population in 1960? In 1969?

(b) Did business service or residential service account for the largest percentage increase in telephone service from 1960 to 1969?

(c) What was the average number of daily conversations per telephone in 1960? In 1969?

(d) What was the average number of daily conversations per person (based on total population) in 1960? In 1969?

3. In a recent 12-year period, the revenues of domestic air carriers increased as follows:

Passenger revenue: from $1,065,000,000 to $4,260,000,000
Mail revenue: from $61,000,000 to $170,000,000
Express & freight
revenue: from $62,000,000 to $287,000,000

(a) What was the total increase in revenue from these three sources during the 12-year period?

(b) Rank the revenue sources according to the largest dollar increase.

(c) Rank the revenue sources according to the largest percentage increase.

Enriching Your Business Understanding

1. The Federal Communications Commission and the Interstate Commerce Commission are two government agencies that have important responsibilities relating to communication and transportation. Find out from resources in your library what the major responsibilities of these two agencies are.

2. Write a brief paper describing the needs for transportation and communication that an industrialized country has that a primitive country might not have.

3. There are many fine career opportunities for young people in fields related to tourism. Prepare a report describing the various kinds of jobs that are available in the travel industry. In your report, explain also why opportunities for employment in these kinds of jobs will increase in the future.

4. The communication, transportation, and travel industries are customers as well as producers of services. You can probably imagine what would happen if the services of these three industries were suddenly unavailable to their customers. Now consider the other side of the coin. What would be the effect on those who supply goods and services to these industries? Be specific in your answer.

PART 40
Communication By Telephone And Telegraph

Millions of miles of telephone and telegraph wires link cities and communities in our country. We have so many telephones that there is, on the average, one phone for every two persons. More than 450 million phone conversations are held every day. For about 30 years before 1877, all rapid long-distance communication depended upon the telegraph. Today the telephone has taken over many of the jobs that the telegraph used to perform. However, the telegraph is still an important means of communication, mainly for businesses.

Telephone subscribers have a choice of line service. If a telephone line is used by one subscriber only, it is a private line. If it is used by two or more subscribers, it is a party line. Although only one of the subscribers can use the line at one time, a party line may be satisfactory if a subscriber does not make calls too often. Private lines are more expensive than party lines.

YOU MAY USE DIFFERENT KINDS OF TELEPHONE SERVICE

Telephone calls may be either local or long distance. Long distance calls are those made outside the area served by the subscriber's telephone exchange. About 95 out of every 100 calls made are local calls. Most subscribers pay a fixed monthly rate for their telephone service and can make as many local calls as they want. In many cities, though, a subscriber may pay a lower monthly rate and then pay an additional amount for each local call over a certain number. In either case, a separate charge is made for each long distance call.

There are two kinds of long distance service. When you call *person-to-person*, the one you call must speak to you in order to complete the call. Charges begin when you start talking with that person. If that person cannot be located, there is no charge for the call. When you call *station-to-station*, the connection is made with a certain telephone, and it is assumed that you are willing to talk to anyone at that telephone. Charges start from the moment the connection is made. Station-to-station calls are more easily and quickly completed than are person-to-person calls. For this reason, station-to-station calls are less expensive.

All person-to-person calls must be placed by an operator. Most station-to-station calls can be dialed directly by the caller rather than being placed by the operator. This is referred to as *direct distance dialing*. The charges for long distance calls differ according to whether the call is made person-to-person or station-to-station, the distance of the call, the time when the call is made, and how long the call lasts. The minimum charge is for a definite period of time, usually three minutes. An overtime charge is made for each extra minute used. Charges for long distance calls are usually less in the evening or on weekends or holidays.

Both person-to-person and station-to-station calls may be made as *collect calls*. This means that charges are billed to the telephone being called rather than to the person who is calling. If you want to call your parents long distance from a friend's house, you can tell the operator to reverse the charges and place them on your parents' telephone bill. A person who is called collect is asked by the long distance operator whether he will accept the charges.

Long distance calls may also be charged on a credit card that the telephone company issues to the subscriber. Businessmen who travel a great deal and make many long distance calls find this service convenient. The businessman or his company is billed once a month for all calls made and charged during the month.

PACIFIC TIME
SUBTRACT 3 HOURS

MOUNTAIN TIME
SUBTRACT 2 HOURS

CENTRAL TIME
SUBTRACT 1 HOUR

EASTERN TIME

British Columbia 604
Alberta 403
Saskatchewan 306
Manitoba 204
807
Ontario
705
Quebec 819
418
Newfoundland 709
New Brunswick 506

Alaska 907
Washington 206 / 509
Montana 406
North Dakota 701
Minnesota 218
906
Montreal 514
Maine 207
N H
Nova Scotia 902

Oregon 503
Idaho 208
Wyoming 307
South Dakota 605
612
715
Wisconsin 507
608
Michigan 416
Toronto 613
New York
Vt
Mass
Rhode Island 401
Conn

916
Nevada 702
Utah 801
Colorado 303
Nebraska 308 / 402
Iowa 319 815
Illinois
219
Ohio
814
Penna 717
New Jersey

California 408
805
714
Arizona 602
New Mexico 505
806
Kansas 316
Missouri 816
217
Indiana
618
Kentucky
West Va 304
703 Virginia
North Carolina
Delaware 302
Maryland 301
District of Columbia 202

913
417
314
502
615
704 919

Oklahoma 405
918
Arkansas 901
Tennessee
South Carolina 803

Hawaii 808
915
817 214
Texas
Mississippi 601
Louisiana 318
Alabama 205
Georgia 404
912

Mexico 903
512
713
504
904
Florida 813
305

Bermuda and the Caribbean Islands 809

Illus. 40-1. Knowing the time and code of the area into which you are calling can help you complete the call more quickly.

Telephone companies offer special kinds of telephone equipment and services to customers, particularly businesses. Some telephones are equipped for automatic dialing. When a Card Dialer is used, the names and numbers of persons and firms frequently called are listed on special cards. When one of these numbers is to be called, the appropriate card is inserted in the proper position, and the number is automatically dialed.

There are now telephones capable of feeding data into a computer using regular telephone lines. A *Data-Phone* enables computers to exchange information by "talking" to each other. Machine language is changed to electrical tones that are sent over telephone wires, then changed again into machine language at the receiving end. The Touch-Tone telephone, which replaces the conventional rotary dial with push buttons, can also be used to feed data to a computer. Many businesses use Touch-Tone telephones to "consult" a computer about orders, billings, bank balances, and credit authorizations.

BUSINESSES USE SPECIAL KINDS OF TELEPHONE SERVICE

Businesses which make many long distance calls to many different places may use WATS (Wide Area Telephone Service). Instead of paying for each separate call it makes, the business is billed under WATS at either a full-time subscription rate or at a measured subscription rate. With a full-time subscription rate, the business can make as many long distance calls as it wants over one line for a flat charge. With a measured subscription rate, the business is billed at a fixed price for the first 10 hours of long distance calls and is billed at a reduced overtime rate for extra hours of usage on one line.

Another special service which telephone companies can provide is the *conference call*. This enables three or more persons anywhere in the world to talk together at the same time over the regular telephone network. These calls must be placed through an operator. Up to ten phones in different places may be connected at one time.

Mobile telephone service allows telephones to be placed in moving vehicles. This service has enabled police, fire, and forestry conservation departments to protect life and property more effectively. Some calls to mobile telephones may be dialed direct. Others must go through a long distance or mobile service operator.

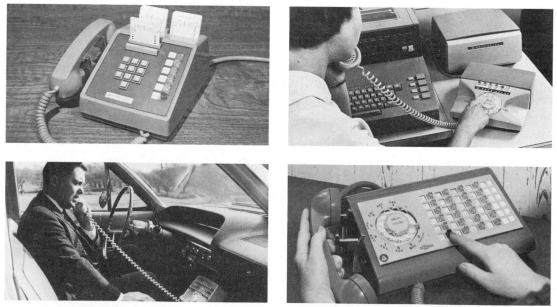

Illus. 40-2. Special kinds of telephone equipment.

Telegraph wires extend both over land and under the ocean. Telegraph messages sent over land wires are called *telegrams*. Telegraph messages sent from one continent to another by wires laid on the bottom of the ocean are known as *cablegrams*. Those sent by radiotelegraph between stations not connected by wires are known as *radiograms*.

When we think of telegraph communication, we usually think of written messages or telegraphic money orders. But today nearly any type of information can be transmitted by telegraph. Weather maps, blueprints, sketches, statistics, graphs, and many other types of data can be sent great distances in a matter of minutes. At a special rate, your opinion on a political issue can be telegraphed to any elected official. You can telegraph greetings on special occasions such as birthdays and holidays. Through many telegraph offices you can even send a message that will be delivered in song. And through telegraph service you can arrange to have candy or flowers delivered in other parts of the country.

You can send a telegraph message in one of two ways. You can go to a telegraph office and write out the message on a special form the office provides, or you can telephone the message to the telegraph office. The telegraph office then sends the message by wire to the destination city. In the destination city, the telegraph company delivers the message by telephone or by messenger. If the message is telephoned, a copy will be mailed upon request. If the message is addressed to a business office, the telegraph company may deliver it to the office over a special wire.

If you were to send a telegraph message, you could choose to send it as a full-rate or fast telegram or as a night letter. The *full-rate* or *fast telegram* is sent promptly after it is received at the telegraph office. The charge depends on the distance the telegram is being sent and on the length of the message. No charge is made for the signature. The minimum charge is the charge for a 15-word message. If the message is longer, there is a charge for each additional word. If a person does not specify the kind of message he wants to send, it will be sent as a full-rate telegram.

During the night the telegraph company has less demand for its services than it has during the day. It therefore offers a reduced

MANY KINDS OF DATA ARE SENT BY TELEGRAPH

CHARGES FOR TELEGRAMS VARY

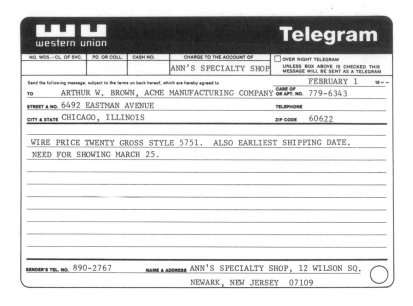

western union   **Telegram**

NO. WDS.–CL. OF SVC.	PD. OR COLL.	CASH NO.	CHARGE TO THE ACCOUNT OF	☐ OVER NIGHT TELEGRAM
			ANN'S SPECIALTY SHOP	UNLESS BOX ABOVE IS CHECKED THIS MESSAGE WILL BE SENT AS A TELEGRAM

Send the following message, subject to the terms on back hereof, which are hereby agreed to   FEBRUARY 1   19– –

TO   ARTHUR W. BROWN, ACME MANUFACTURING COMPANY   CARE OF OR APT. NO.   779-6343

STREET & NO. 6492 EASTMAN AVENUE   TELEPHONE

CITY & STATE CHICAGO, ILLINOIS   ZIP CODE   60622

WIRE PRICE TWENTY GROSS STYLE 5751. ALSO EARLIEST SHIPPING DATE.
NEED FOR SHOWING MARCH 25.

SENDER'S TEL. NO. 890-2767   NAME & ADDRESS ANN'S SPECIALTY SHOP, 12 WILSON SQ.
NEWARK, NEW JERSEY 07109

Illus. 40-3. A full-rate telegram.

rate for relatively long overnight messages. Messages sent during the night at the low night rate are known as *night letters.* Night letters are accepted up to 12 midnight for delivery the next morning. In almost all instances, the minimum charge is the charge for a 100-word message. For a longer message, there is a charge for each additional word. The charge for a 100-word night letter is about two-thirds of the cost of a 15-word fast telegram.

The cost of a telegraph message is usually paid by the person sending it. If the message is telephoned to the telegraph office, the cost of the message can be added to the sender's telephone bill. If the message is sent from a pay telephone, it may be paid for with coins like a long distance call. The telegraph company will then collect from the telephone company. When a telegram is sent collect, the amount charged is paid by the person or firm accepting the message. A telegram is often sent collect when it is sent upon the request of or as a favor to the one receiving the message.

TELEGRAPH SERVICES FOR BUSINESSES

Most telegrams today come from businesses and go to other businesses. Businesses that send a large volume of telegrams may use telegraph tie lines. These are direct wires between the business and the local telegraph office. Four other types of telegraph service that are important to businesses are facsimile service, teleprinter service, Telex, and private wire systems.

Facsimile telegraph is the sending of exact copies of messages, drawings, or pictures. With one type of facsimile machine, the *Desk-Fax,* the message is first placed on the cylinder of the machine. A tiny electric eye scans the material to be transmitted and flashes an exact copy of it to the nearest high-speed telegraph center. The center then flashes the copy on to its destination city. Telegrams are received in the same manner.

Illus. 40-4. A telegram is often delivered by the telegraph company to a business office by means of a Desk-Fax. This machine automatically reproduces the entire telegram. It may also be used by a business to send a message.

Western Union Telegraph Co.

A teleprinter is a special machine with a keyboard resembling a typewriter. With a teleprinter, the message is typed in the business' office and is recorded immediately on a tape or message form in the telegraph office. The telegraph office then transmits the message on to its destination.

Telex is a direct-dial two-way teleprinter service that links major cities in the United States and many countries in other parts of the world. It allows one business to get in touch with another business instantly if that business has a teleprinter.

A private wire system is really a private telegraph system for a single business that sends many telegrams to its branch offices and plants. Such a system is designed and maintained by the telegraph company on a lease basis.

The telegraph company offers some other special services to businesses. Delivery of parcels, shopping service, providing commercial news service and advertising aids, sending a single telegram to a number of people at the same time, and keeping a company's clocks on time—these are among the many services the telegraph company makes available to businesses.

Developing Your Business Vocabulary

The following italicized terms should become part of your business vocabulary. For each numbered statement, find the italicized term that has the same meaning.

cablegram	*full-rate* or *fast telegram*
collect call	*night letter*
conference call	*person-to-person call*
Data-Phone	*radiogram*
Desk-Fax	*station-to-station call*
direct distance dialing	*telegram*

1. A long distance call in which the caller asks the operator to connect him with a particular person.
2. A long distance call in which the caller will speak to anyone answering the telephone at the number called.
3. A method of making a long distance station-to-station call by dialing the area code and the telephone number.
4. A telephone call, the charge for which is paid by the person called.
5. A telephone that enables machines to transmit information back and forth over regular telephone wires.
6. A telephone call in which several persons located in different places talk together at the same time.
7. A telegraph message sent over land wires.
8. A telegraph message sent by wires laid on the bottom of the ocean.
9. A telegraph message sent between stations not connected by wires.
10. The fastest type of telegraph service.
11. A telegraph message accepted up to 12 midnight for delivery the next day.
12. Telegraph equipment which sends exact copies of messages, drawings, or pictures.

Checking Your Understanding

1. Why is a station-to-station call less expensive than a person-to-person call?
2. Under what conditions might a telephone credit card be convenient for an individual?
3. What is a Card Dialer?
4. Explain how Touch-Tone telephones may be used in businesses.
5. What is WATS? How may businesses be billed for telephone service under this system?

6. How may an individual send a telegraph message?
7. Why are night letters less expensive than full-rate or fast telegrams?
8. In what ways may the cost of a telegraph message be paid?
9. Explain how facsimile service, teleprinter service, Telex, and private wire systems are used by businesses.
10. In addition to transmitting messages, what other services does the telegraph company offer to businesses?

Applying What You Have Learned

1. During one week Tad Hirotaka, a traveling salesman, made the five long distance phone calls described below. What type of service should he have asked for in each case?

   (a) On Monday Mr. Hirotaka received an order from a customer who asked him to telephone the order to the company at once.
   (b) On Tuesday Mr. Hirotaka wanted to call his home.
   (c) On Wednesday a customer asked for quotations on some special material. It was necessary for Mr. Hirotaka to talk with the sales manager to get this information.
   (d) On Thursday Mr. Hirotaka wanted to call a real estate salesman about the purchase of a house. The salesman had told Mr. Hirotaka that he would be home between 5 and 8 p.m.
   (e) Mr. Hirotaka was informed by letter that prices on some new items would be available on Friday and that he should call his office then.

2. The Watsonian Hotel wants to hire a girl to run its telephone switchboard. What qualities do you think are desirable in a person holding such a position? Explain why you consider each one to be desirable.

3. Assume that it takes an average of ten minutes to complete a long distance call. Using the time-zone map on page 465, indicate the latest time on a given day when a businessman in the Central time zone can make the following calls:

   (a) To talk with a bank in San Francisco which closes at 3 p.m.
   (b) To place an order with a supplier in Philadelphia who closes telephone orders at noon for the next day's shipment.
   (c) To contact a company salesman in Denver before he leaves a client's office at 5 p.m.

4. Don Simpson's parents are expecting him to arrive on the 4:17 p.m. plane, Flight 397, from Pittsburgh on Tuesday. Local weather conditions forced cancellation of the flight, and Don will not arrive home until 10 p.m. on that day. Would you advise Don to telephone or to telegraph his parents about his change in plans?

5. Harry Watterson has ordered some merchandise by letter. He expects shipment to be made on Wednesday. On Wednesday morning he decides that the order needs to be doubled. What telegraph service might enable him to reach the merchant before the original order is sent?

6. Assume that it takes 5 minutes to send a telegram between New York and Chicago, 5 minutes between New York and St. Louis, 10 minutes between New York and Denver, and 15 minutes between New York and Los Angeles. From the time-zone map on page 465, find at what time telegrams sent at 4 p.m. from New York will be received in each of the other four cities.

Solving Business Problems

1. In one community, the monthly cost of a private telephone line is $6.50. The monthly cost of a two-party line is $4.90.

   (a) How much more is the monthly cost of private line service than two-party line service? What percent is this figure of the cost of two-party service?

   In another community, the cost of a private line is $5.05. The cost of a two-party line is $3.60. Four-party line service is also available for $2.90 a month.

   (b) How much more is the monthly cost of private line service in the first community than in the second community? What percent is this figure of the cost of service in the second community?

   (c) Expressed as a percent, how much more expensive is private line service in the second community than four-party service in that community?

2. The long distance rates from Cincinnati, Ohio, to selected points are given in the table on page 473. David Heron completed the following calls during one month. None exceeded three minutes.

   (a) To L.B. Barnhart in Chicago, day rate.
   (b) To the residence of Joseph Steiner in Miami, evening rate.
   (c) To the residence of Charles MacKenzie in Seattle, night rate.
   (d) To Charles MacKenzie in Seattle, day rate.
   (e) To a business firm in Baltimore, day rate.
   (f) To Nelson Abrams in Detroit, day rate.
   (g) To the residence of Fred Zorski in Baltimore, late night rate.
   (h) To Edward Pruitt in Mobile, night rate.
   (i) To the residence of Michael Detzel, Chicago, weekend rate.
   (j) To a business firm in Washington, D.C., day rate.

Find the cost of each call and the total cost of the long distance calls placed by Mr. Heron.

From Cincinnati to	Station-to-Station				Person-to-Person	
	Day	Evening	Night & Weekend	Late Night	Day	Night & Weekend
Alabama, Mobile	1.40	1.00	.75	.65	2.40	2.05
D. C., Washington	1.05	.80	.60	.60	1.55	1.30
Florida, Miami	1.40	1.00	.75	.65	2.40	2.05
Illinois, Chicago	1.30	.90	.70	.60	2.20	1.90
Maryland, Baltimore	.90	.70	.60	.60	1.45	1.20
Michigan, Detroit	1.30	.85	.65	.60	1.80	1.50
Washington, Seattle	1.70	1.25	1.00	.75	3.30	2.85

3. The telegraph rates for Cleveland, Ohio, are given in the table below. During November, Fuller & Anderson Building Supplies sent the following messages:

(a) A 15-word telegram to Springfield, Ohio.
(b) A 65-word night letter to San Francisco, California.
(c) A 107-word night letter to New York City.
(d) A 32-word telegram to St. Louis, Missouri.
(e) A 140-word night letter to Akron, Ohio.
(f) A 12-word telegram to Knoxville, Tennessee.

Find the cost of each message and the total cost of the messages sent during the month.

From Cleveland to	Full-Rate Telegram		Night Letter	
	15 Words or less	Each Additional Word	100 Words or less	Each Additional Word
Destination inside State of Ohio	$2.35	8¢	$1.40	1¢
Destination outside State of Ohio	$2.85	9¢	$1.80	1.5¢

4. The senior class of the high school at Brentwood, in your state, has rented costumes for a play from the Elizabethan Costume Company of Dillonvale, in your state. The play is to be given on Friday night. On Thursday morning the costumes have not yet been received. As the secretary of the class, wire the Elizabethan Costume Company that if the costumes are not delivered by Friday morning, they cannot be accepted.

Enriching Your Business Understanding

1. In this part you learned about some special kinds of telephone equipment. Several other kinds of telephone equipment are listed below. Explain what each kind of equipment is. (The telephone company should be able to provide you with printed information describing the equipment.)

   (a) Speakerphone.
   (b) Call Director.
   (c) Volume control handset.

2. The rates charged by telephone companies are carefully regulated by the government. Why should the government be concerned with regulating the charges for telephone services when it does not regulate the prices of such things as food and clothing, which make up a much larger part of the average family's budget?

3. From your telephone directory or local telephone office, find out what the universal information code is and how it is used.

4. Listed below are several special services of Western Union. Prepare a report describing one or more of them. (Special printed leaflets available at your local telegraph office will provide you with the basic information you need.)

   (a) Candy-Grams.
   (b) One-To-Many Message Service.
   (c) Operator 25 Service.
   (d) Purchase-Pack-Ship Service.

5. Western Union features a public opinion message telegraphic service. Describe this service and indicate how it differs from standard holiday and greeting messages that Western Union also makes available.

6. The microwave radio beam system is one of the newest developments in telegraph communication. Using leaflet material available at your telegraph office, describe this system. Be sure to include in your report how messages are transmitted and the advantages of this system over the telegraph key and the teletypewriter.

PART 41
Communication By Letter

How do you communicate in these situations? You're working on a school project dealing with how businesses hire employees, and you want to gather information from a business firm located in a distant state. Or you've seen a new record album advertised in a magazine, and you want to order the album. Or you've read a newspaper ad for a summer job, and you want to apply for it. Probably the most efficient way for you to communicate in these situations is by letter.

Much of the world's business is carried on through letters. Every day millions of letters—80 billion a year—flow through the business and government offices of our country. A business may write letters to its customers, to its suppliers, to service businesses, or to persons within its organization. Communicating by letter is not as fast as communicating by telephone or telegraph. However, letters often can give more information and are usually less expensive—especially for long messages—than are the telephone and telegraph. Also, the letter provides a written record of the message.

Many of the business letters written are *sales letters*. They are written to introduce a person to a product and, hopefully, to persuade him to buy. You may have received sales letters offering

BUSINESSES WRITE MANY KINDS OF LETTERS

for sale such merchandise as records, cosmetics, or transistor radios. Some businesses do all their selling by mail. Besides sales letters, a business may write letters in response to customers' inquiries, to acknowledge the receipt of an order, to answer a customer's complaint or make an adjustment, and to request information from a supplier.

Good letter communication is basic to the operation of almost any type of business. In fact, a letter may even spell the difference between success or failure in some business dealings. A well-written letter responding to a customer's complaint, for example, can keep the customer's goodwill. A poorly written letter can mean that the customer will never come back to that business again.

WHAT MAKES UP A GOOD LETTER?

Writing a good letter takes skill, just as writing a good short story or a novel takes skill. What characterizes a good letter? A good letter is (1) carefully planned; (2) brief and to the point; (3) accurate; (4) complete; (5) courteous in statement and tone; and (6) attractive in appearance and in proper form.

(1) One of the reasons why many persons do not write good business letters is that they give little time to planning just what they want to say. Time and attention should be given to the points that the writer wants to make. For certain types of letters, such as one written to order merchandise, it is helpful to jot down the points the letter will make. If the writer starts writing before he has in mind what he wants to say, the letter may not be clear and some important facts may be left out.

(2) Business letters tend to be more formal than personal letters, yet business letters should say in simple and easily understood language what they have to say and then close. The finest writers are noted for the simplicity of their writing. In a letter, a person should write much as he talks. He should be careful to use complete, well-constructed sentences and to avoid slang. But he should try to visualize the person to whom he is writing and should write as if he were talking to that person.

(3) In a business letter, accuracy of information—facts, figures, directions, observations—is important. A misstatement creates more work and more correspondence to clear up a matter that a single letter could have resolved. After a letter has been

written, the writer should read it over carefully to be sure that it makes sense.

(4) A letter may be accurate in terms of what is included and still leave out some important information. Suppose that a girl writes a letter ordering a blouse and forgets to state the size. The blouse will be delayed in getting to her, and more correspondence will be needed to see that the order is filled properly.

(5) A letter is an individual's personal representative. It reflects his personality. Courtesy and tact in a letter show the writer's consideration for the person to whom he is writing. That individual cannot see him personally, so how the writer says what he has to say is often as important as what he says. Just as a voice on the telephone can make or lose friends by its tone, so can the tone of the letter one writes.

(6) When you meet a person for the first time, you are impressed by the way he speaks and looks. A business letter, too, creates a first impression. If the letter is attractive, the first impression is good. If the letter is unattractive, the first impression is bad. An attractive appearance, then, makes it easier for a letter to accomplish its purpose.

Many styles of business letters are acceptable, but most firms choose one style and follow it. Two satisfactory styles—one for penwritten letters and one for typewritten letters—are shown on pages 478 and 479. Study each of these illustrations carefully.

LETTERS SHOULD BE ATTRACTIVE IN APPEARANCE

A carbon copy of each business letter should be made and filed. It serves as a record of what has been said and done. Making a carbon copy is quite important for letters involving times and dates for appointments, accompanying the payment of bills, requesting reservations, ordering products and services, and applying for a job. Making a carbon copy takes very little extra effort; it often saves much time, expense, and further correspondence.

The form of the address on an envelope is similar to the address used in the letter. Even though the letter is to be delivered in the same city in which it is mailed, the name of the city should be given in the address. An envelope that is simply addressed "City" may be delayed or lost. It is also important to be sure that the writer's return address appears on the envelope.

875 Westlawn Road
Denver, Colorado 80205
January 29, 19--

Western Electronics, Inc.
221 Sands Boulevard
Las Vegas, Nevada 89109

Gentlemen

A friend whom I visited recently told me that he bought his multi-band portable radio from your firm. I was impressed with the quality of the radio's sound. I do not remember the name of the radio or all its features. My friend bought it from you last year and paid about $50 for it. I think it was a five-band radio.

Could you please tell me whether you still carry this radio, what its present cost is, and how I might obtain one? Thank you for any assistance you can give me.

Sincerely yours
Dylan Jones

The *heading* contains the writer's address and the date. The ZIP Code is placed after the name of the state. Note the punctuation used. No punctuation is required at the end of each line unless the line ends with an abbreviation.

The *address* to which the letter is being sent is placed a little below the heading at the left side of the page. In penwritten letters, both the heading and the address may be indented. No punctuation is required at the end of each line unless the line ends with an abbreviation.

The *salutation* begins at the left margin. No mark of punctuation is required after the salutation, but a colon is often used. When a letter is addressed to an individual, the salutation usually includes "Dear" and the name of the person addressed. The word "Gentlemen" is ordinarily used as the salutation when the letter is addressed to a business.

The first line of each paragraph in the *body* of the letter is indented about one-half inch. Ordinary rules of good English writing are followed in paragraphing and punctuating the body of the letter.

The *complimentary close* begins at about the middle of the line of writing. It need not be followed by a mark of punctuation; but if a colon is used after the salutation, a comma is used after the complimentary close.

The *signature* is the penwritten name of the writer.

Illus. 41-1. An acceptable form for a handwritten business letter.

221 SANDS BOULEVARD
LAS VEGAS, NEVADA 89109
Telephone 521-1000

February 11, 19--

Mr. Dylan Jones
875 Westlawn Road
Denver, CO 80205

Dear Mr. Jones

Thank you for your letter of January 29 concerning
the availability of a portable radio similar to
your friend's.

From the brief description you gave in your letter,
I assume that you are referring to our Wonderworld
Globemaster 5-band portable radio. This radio has
12 transistors, full-range tone control, and a
telescopic antenna. Its price is $48.95. This does
not include shipping charges.

I am sending you, under separate cover, a catalog
describing our radios and other products. The radio
you inquired about is described on page 9. Please
let us know if we can be of further help to you.

Very truly yours

J. C. Penwick

J. C. Penwick, Manager
Mail Order Department

sb

The name and address of the business are printed on a *letterhead*; thus, the typed heading includes the date only. Note the placement of the date in relation to the letterhead, right margin, and address.

The address is typed four spaces below the date line. Each line of the address begins at the left margin. The two-letter state abbreviation is especially designed for use with an Optical Character Reader, a new device that helps post offices to speed up the handling of mail. No mark of punctuation is required at the end of each line unless the line ends with an abbreviation. No period follows the two-letter state abbreviation.

The salutation begins at the left margin and is separated by a blank line from the address and the body of the letter. It may be followed by a colon, although no mark of punctuation is required.

When the body of the letter is typed with single spacing, a space is left between paragraphs. The first line of each paragraph may start at the left margin or may be indented.

The complimentary close is started at the center of the page, one double space below the last line of the body. If a colon is used after the salutation, the complimentary close should be followed by a comma.

The name and title of the writer are usually typed below the penwritten signature.

When a letter is typed by someone other than the dictator, the typist's initials are placed in the letter's lower left corner. These initials are called *reference initials*

Illus. 41-2. An acceptable form for a typewritten business letter.

Postcards are often used for business communication when the message to be sent is brief. The arrangement of the copy on the card is similar to the form of a business letter. Often, though, the address of the person being written is omitted to save space, and no space is used between paragraphs. Stamped government postal cards may be purchased from post offices for less than the postage cost of a letter. They may be mailed without additional postage.

```
                                        3710 North Street
                                        Tampa, FL  33620
                                        April 13, 19--

Dear Harvey

     There will be a meeting of the Seminole Youth
Club next Thursday, April 19, at the Park Street
School.  The time of the meeting is 7:30 p.m.
     This is our second meeting this month, and we
hope to finalize plans for the fund-raising drive
for our new clubhouse.  A local civic group has
offered to match every dollar we raise for this
purpose.  Do come and help us with the planning.

                                   Susan Wilson
                                   Secretary
                                   Seminole Youth Club
```

SPEEDING UP THE FLOW OF BUSINESS CORRESPONDENCE

Because businesses handle so much correspondence, many of them have adopted time-saving ways of taking care of their letter writing. To save time, many businessmen dictate either into a dictating machine or to a stenographer who takes the letter in shorthand. The letter is then transcribed by the stenographer. Some large firms have centralized dictation systems. A businessman can pick up the telephone, dial a certain number, and dictate the letter. When he calls, a dictating machine is automatically turned on to record his letter. The belt or disc on which it is recorded is then given to a stenographer, who transcribes the letter. It is given to the dictator when it is finished.

Businessmen who write many routine letters, such as those acknowledging the receipts of orders, often use guide forms. This means that the bulk of the message is standardized and does not have to be composed each time a letter must be written. A stenographer is told to use Form Paragraphs #1, #2, and so on. She fills in the appropriate date, name, address, and figures for the person who is to receive the letter.

If a business wants to send exactly the same letter to many different people, the letter may be printed. In this case, the salutation may be an impersonal "Dear Friend" or "Dear Reader." Sales letters are often prepared in this way. However, if the business wants to give a more personal tone to the letter, it may use an *automatic typewriter*. With such a machine, the body of the letter is typed only once; a perforated or magnetic tape is prepared as the typing is done. When letters are to be prepared, the tape is placed in the machine and the machine automatically types the letter. It will stop at predetermined points to allow the operator to type in the date, name, and address for each person on the mailing list.

Many businesses also use special mail processing equipment. Some machines will open letters automatically. Others can fold letters and other materials and insert them in envelopes. Other machines address envelopes automatically. *Postage meters* seal the envelope, imprint the postage on it, and stack the envelopes in one operation. Postage for the meter is obtained by taking the meter to the post office. The meter is set for the exact amount of postage the business pays for. When it has printed the amount it was set for, it locks.

Illus. 41-4. A postage meter is one of the machines that businesses use to speed the flow of correspondence.

Pitney-Bowes, Inc.

Developing Your Business Vocabulary

The following italicized terms should become part of your business vocabulary. For each numbered statement, find the italicized term that has the same meaning.

automatic typewriter *postage meter* *sales letter*
letterhead *reference initials* *salutation*

1. A letter whose primary purpose is to persuade a person to buy a certain product or service.
2. A sheet printed with the name and address of an organization.
3. A greeting to the person who is to receive a letter.
4. The initials of the typist of a letter, often placed in the letter's lower left corner.
5. A machine which types letters automatically but stops to allow the operator to type in certain information.
6. A machine which automatically seals, stamps, and stacks mail.

Checking Your Understanding

1. What are some types of letters that businessmen frequently write?
2. List and explain briefly six characteristics of a good letter.
3. What are the six major parts of a business letter?
4. What information is ordinarily given in the heading of a letter when a letterhead is used? When a letterhead is not used?
5. What information is commonly printed on a letterhead?
6. What salutation may be used if you write a letter to the Prescott Furniture Company? To Mr. Charles Prescott?
7. Why should a carbon copy of each business letter be kept?
8. Even though a letter is to be delivered in the same city in which it is mailed, the name of the city should be included in the address on the envelope. Why?
9. In what ways may the form of a message written on a card differ from that of a message written on business stationery?
10. Describe several types of equipment that businesses use to speed up the letter communication process.

Applying What You Have Learned

1. Bring to class two letters that you or your parents have received recently from business firms. Analyze them, using as a basis the six characteristics of a good letter presented in this part. How would you classify these letters according to the purpose of each letter?

2. The advertisement below appeared in the "Help Wanted" section of a newspaper. What details would a person interested in this job want to include in the application letter he would write?

ORDER CLERK—INSIDE SALESMAN
Must have sound administrative and clerical abilities with pleasant telephone personality. Experience preferred in building material industry. Knowledge of doors and windows very helpful. Responsibilities will include taking orders, customer relations and pricing. Growth opportunity. If interested please write letter or resume describing qualifications to Box J595, Enquirer. Include salary history please.

3. Judy Cameron is preparing to write a letter requesting a reservation at Boothbay Lodge for a weekend holiday. What facts should Judy include in her letter?

4. Bring to class letterheads used by local business firms. Select two of them and point out the information the letterheads contain, the size and style of type used, and the arrangement of the materials on the sheet.

5. What advantages and disadvantages do cards have for communicating business messages?

Solving Business Problems

1. Arrange the following letter properly on a sheet of paper measuring 8½ by 11 inches. Use today's date and your school address. Sign your own name.

Mr. Clarence F. Haeckel, 3709 Blue Rock Road, Cheyenne, Wyoming 82001. Dear Mr. Haeckel: Thank you for sending me a copy of "The Air Around Us." Before I read this pamphlet, I had never fully realized the great need for us to solve the problems of air and water pollution in our country today. (New paragraph) This pamphlet will help me to prepare my term paper on "Conserving Our Natural Resources." I appreciate your sending the pamphlet to me so promptly. Sincerely yours.

2. Assume that you are secretary of your high school business club. The club has decided to ask Dr. Howard Kaufmann, a professor of marketing at a university in a nearby city, to give a short talk at the regular monthly meeting of the club. The meeting is to be held on Wednesday afternoon of next week. Dr. Kaufmann is to be in your city that day to address a meeting of the American Marketing Association.

As secretary of your club, write a letter to Dr. Kaufmann asking him to speak to your club. Use paper measuring 8½ by 11 inches. Use your school address and sign your name. For Dr. Kaufmann's address, use a real or imaginary name of some university and the name of some nearby city. Mention in your letter to Dr. Kaufmann that the meeting is to be held in the school auditorium at 3 p.m. and that there will be at least 100 persons in attendance.

3. Suppose that you want to order the following items from A.J. Morganthal and Company, a mail-order house:

A turtleneck sweater, #7G6715F, size 34, $6.97, black and grey. Two-way stretch pants, one pair, red, nylon knit, $9.95, #6G9317F. #6G8463, figure skates, size 6½, $13.49, white. $5.44, black pouch handbag, #8G109E.

The company's address is 6956 Ironstone Road, Memphis, Tennessee 38108. Use your own return address. There is no tax on the items ordered, but parcel post charges that must be paid by the buyer amount to $1.87. Write a letter ordering the merchandise and assume that you enclose a check in payment of the goods and postage. Rearrange and include all necessary information in a manner so that your order can be read easily and filled quickly.

Enriching Your Business Understanding

1. The ZIP Code system divides the country into mail delivery units of five-digit numbers. Report on the meaning of each of the digits.
2. A new device called OCR (Optical Character Reader) works with ZIP Code to speed the handling of mail by the post office. Find out and report on how OCR operates. Also obtain from your local post office the abbreviations for the 50 states as used with ZIP Code and OCR.
3. Talk with two businessmen who dictate their letters to a stenographer and two who dictate their letters to a dictating machine. Report on why the businessmen prefer one method over the other.
4. By visiting an office using mail handling equipment or by obtaining advertising literature on the equipment, prepare a brief report on one or both of the following topics:

   (a) How a folding machine operates.
   (b) Sealing and stamping envelopes by machine.

5. Interoffice correspondence is an important aspect of written communication in businesses. Obtain from two or three businesses in your area and from two or three government offices samples of their interoffice communication forms. Report on the similarities and differences of the forms.

PART 42
Communication Through Advertising

Every day you are informed, warned, appealed to, entertained, and persuaded by mass communication. What is mass communication? A television or a radio program is mass communication. So is a billboard, a poster in a subway station, or a sign painted on the outside of a city bus. Your daily newspaper is a kind of mass communication. So are magazines and movies. *Mass communication* is the conveying of a message to a large number of people at the same time.

The means of communication that you have learned about so far in this unit are person-to-person means of communication. Mass communication is different, and it has its good points and its bad points. When many people are addressed at the same time, there is little chance for personal contact and appeal. But it would be much too expensive—in both money and time—to communicate with a great many people on a person-to-person basis. Through mass communication, a message can be conveyed to many people at a very small cost per person.

Many different groups use mass communication. Businesses, government, educational institutions, charitable organizations, and others convey messages through mass media. But the greatest use of mass communication is to advertise goods and services that

ADVERTISING IS A FORM OF MASS COMMUNICATION

businesses offer for sale. *Advertising* is any nonpersonal, persuasive communication about ideas, goods, or services.

Most advertising seeks to bring about action from those who receive the message. The desired action is usually for the prospect to buy what the advertiser is selling. The advertiser may ask his audience to buy a certain make of car, to switch to his brand of toothpaste or soap, or to have their dry cleaning done at his plant. This kind of advertising, which is designed to get people to buy a specific product or service, is called *promotional advertising*.

Another type of advertising is used by businesses to create goodwill for their company rather than to promote the sales of a specific product or service. For example, advertising of a large drugstore chain might stress the years of testing it conducts before offering its products to the public. A bank might advertise how it supports community activities such as the Boy Scouts. Such advertising is called *institutional advertising*.

You have probably also seen ads trying to persuade people to take a certain stand on proposed legislation or to apply for a job with a certain company. You may also have seen *public service advertising* encouraging the public to "Drive Carefully," "Help Fight Cancer," or "Buy a Savings Bond Today." And most of us have probably used advertising for personal reasons. As publicity director of your school drama club, for example, you might advertise an upcoming play in the newspaper.

ADVERTISING IS PLACED IN VARIOUS MEDIA

The advertising business, like all other businesses operating on a national scale, has grown over the years. In 1970, more than $20 billion was spent on local and national advertising—more than $95 for every person in the United States. About $12 billion of this amount was spent for national advertising; the rest went for local advertising. This huge amount of money was spent in six major media: (1) newspapers, (2) broadcast media, (3) direct mail, (4) magazines, (5) outdoor advertising, and (6) transportation advertising.

(1) Many businesses, especially small ones with a local market, use newspapers to carry most of their advertising messages. More money is spent on newspaper advertising than is spent in any other medium. Newspapers bring the advertiser's message right to

Illus. 42-1. A public service advertisement that appeared in various media.

the customer's doorstep. Nearly all communities in the United States have a newspaper published either locally or in a nearby city; few homes are without a daily newspaper. Newspaper advertising is a fairly inexpensive way of reaching prospects in a local area.

(2) The medium of television has become second only to newspapers in the amount of advertising it carries. Television combines the impact of seeing a product advertised with the impact of hearing about it. And since more than 94% of the homes in this country have one or more television sets, an advertiser can take his messages into almost every home.

The biggest drawback of television advertising is its expense. A 60-second commercial on a national network may cost as much as $55,000. Small advertisers thus turn their attention mainly to radio if they want to use a broadcast medium. Radio also reaches

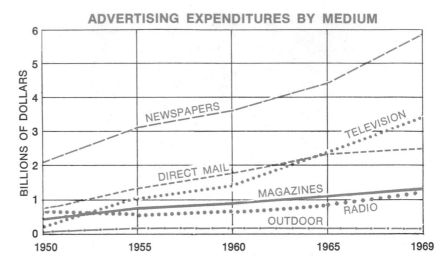

ADVERTISING EXPENDITURES BY MEDIUM

Illus. 42-2. Expenditures in selected advertising media from 1950 to 1969.

many people—Americans own nearly 200 million radios—and costs less than television advertising. Also, radio can reach people when they are driving a car, doing housework, lying on the beach, or performing almost any other activity.

(3) When businesses want to give their messages a more personal appeal, they may use *direct mail advertising*. For example, a business might put its advertising message in the form of a letter and send it only to persons on rural mail routes in a certain area. Or it might put its message in the form of a catalog or brochure and send it to all retailers in a given state or to all physicians in New England. With television, radio, or newspaper advertising, a message goes to anyone who happens to be watching or reading. Direct mail allows a business to be more selective in communicating an advertising message.

(4) There are several different types of magazines. *Consumer magazines* are those of general interest to most ultimate consumers. *Trade, technical,* or *professional magazines* are those which appeal to certain business and professional groups. There are magazines directed to engineers, teachers, hardware merchants, and many other special groups. A business can choose the type of magazine best suited to advertising its product. The manufacturer of an electric toothbrush would most likely advertise in a popular consumer magazine. The manufacturer of a new woodworking tool might well advertise in a builder's trade magazine.

Magazine advertising can be quite expensive. A full-page ad run in only one issue of a popular consumer magazine, for example, may cost more than $80,000. However, magazines offer a longer life for ads than do other media. A magazine may be kept for several weeks or months and passed on to different people. A newspaper, for example, may be read quickly and thrown away.

THE TOP 15 CONSUMER MAGAZINES: THE WINNERS AND LOSERS

RANKING	ADVERTISING REVENUES		ADVERTISING PAGES	
	1969	% CHANGE FROM 1968	1969	% CHANGE FROM 1968
1. Life	$153,272,371	0	2,392.31	−13
2. Time	95,328,209	+ 6	2,928.74	+ 1
3. Look	77,366,363	0	1,358.18	− 2
4. TV Guide	67,575,226	+18	2,046.25	+ 9
5. Newsweek	63,742,045	+21	3,317.29	+10
6. Reader's Digest	57,219,244	0	1,111.49	− 4
7. McCall's	41,625,338	+ 2	936.26	− 2
8. Ladies' Home Journal	39,267,851	+14	1,127.73	+16
9. Better Homes & Gardens	38,929,292	+ 6	987.14	+ 3
10. Sports Illustrated	35,269,142	+17	2,168.51	+ 4
11. Good Housekeeping	35,119,881	+ 1	1,288.63	− 1
12. Playboy	32,219,026	+27	912.43	+14
13. U.S. News & World Report	27,474,255	+10	1,898.96	− 4
14. The New Yorker	25,778,513	− 6	4,710.72	−10
15. Redbook	23,132,692	+27	1,107.22	+22

Publishers Information Bureau, Inc.

Illus. 42-3. The top 15 consumer magazines.

(5) Some businesses, particularly retailers, do a good deal of outdoor advertising. There are several kinds of outdoor advertising. One kind is the sign painted or pasted directly onto a building. Another kind is the electric spectacular frequently found in the downtown areas of cities. A third kind is the billboard which you often see along streets and highways. Many people have complained that the billboards along highways are a blight on the landscape. Some states have even passed laws to control the use of such advertising.

(6) One form of transportation advertising is the *car card*. This is an advertisement placed inside a public transit vehicle such as a bus. Another form of transportation advertising is the *station poster* placed inside railroad stations, bus depots, and airline terminals.

Illus. 42-4. Outdoor advertising includes both billboards and electric signs.

ADVANTAGES WE DERIVE FROM ADVERTISING

You have seen that businesses spend a great deal of money to advertise their goods and services. Is advertising worth it? Does it really benefit the producer or the consumer or society?

One of the benefits of advertising is that it is informative. It enables the consumer to learn about new products on the market and about improvements in existing products. Advertising can give the buyer information that he can use to judge product quality. Advertising does not relieve a person of the responsibility for being a careful buyer. But it can give him information he needs to use his buying power skillfully. Many people have come to rely on the information ads provide when they plan their buying.

A second advantage of advertising is that it helps make mass production possible because it creates demand for goods. As you have learned, it is usually less expensive to produce goods in large quantities than it is to produce goods in small quantities. It is not necessarily ten times more expensive to make 100,000 units of a given product than it is to make 10,000 units. This is because savings are realized through the use of highly specialized labor and automated equipment. The savings may result in increased profits to the producer, lower prices to the consumer, or both.

A third advantage of advertising is that by increasing the demand for goods and services, it helps to create more jobs. The demand for goods causes retailers to place more orders with wholesalers. Wholesalers in turn order more goods from the factories. To fill these orders, the factories hire more workers and buy greater quantities of raw materials, equipment, and supplies. Providing more jobs benefits not only those who are hired but society as a whole.

A fourth advantage of advertising is that it can help change our style of living. Each year billions of dollars are spent on developing products to make our lives more enjoyable. When a new product is introduced, though, few people will buy it immediately. People have to be told about it. Advertising introduces the public to new or better goods and services: new or better types of insurance, health-saving medicines, and labor-saving devices, for example.

Some indication of advertising's effect on our economy was revealed when New York City newspapers were shut down by a strike. The impact of the strike was dramatic. Department store sales fell off nearly 25%. Job applications decreased sharply. Theaters were almost empty. After the strike was settled, a survey was taken. People were asked, "What did you miss most in not having your newspaper?" Nearly half of the persons responding to the question replied, "The ads."

You have just read about some of the benefits claimed for advertising. However, some people today question whether advertising really benefits us. Critics point to the often exaggerated claims made for some products. They question whether making people style conscious or fashion conscious actually does improve our style of living. Is the purchase of a highly advertised mouthwash so necessary for success in making friends? Critics of advertising also feel that producing the many different models of a single product—the demand for which was created by advertising—may increase rather than decrease the price consumers pay. In addition, they feel that advertising can create a demand for products which may be harmful to our health, such as cigarettes.

Because of the great size of the advertising business and because of its influence on all of us, there has been much pressure for more control over it. It is true that some advertisements have

CONTROLS HAVE BEEN PLACED ON ADVERTISING

been misleading or in poor taste; such ads bring discredit upon all reputable advertisers. The advertising industry thus tries to police itself by living up to a code. An example of one such code is the code adopted by the American Association of Advertising Agencies. Individual advertisers, broadcasters, trade associations, and others also try to regulate their own advertising activities.

Federal legislation, such as the Wheeler-Lea Act, has been passed to correct some of the more flagrant misuses of advertising. This law, sometimes called the Truth in Advertising Act, makes misleading and false advertising a federal offense. It imposes penalties on those who violate the act. A number of other acts require that products be labeled fully and accurately to reveal their content.

In recent years, two federal agencies in particular have stepped up their programs to eliminate advertising that is false, misleading, or in poor taste. These two agencies are the Federal Trade Commission and the Federal Communications Commission. Some states have laws and agencies that serve a similar purpose and that are designed to protect the consumer's interest.

Today's shopper is deluged by competing, often conflicting, claims about the virtues of various products. Despite the controls placed on it, not all advertising is truthful. We on the receiving end of advertising need to keep ourselves informed about all goods and services that meet our needs and wants. We should read advertisements intelligently and make wise use of them. But we should not be oversold by them.

Developing Your Business Vocabulary

The following italicized terms should become part of your business vocabulary. For each numbered statement, find the italicized term that has the same meaning.

advertising
car card
consumer magazine
direct mail advertising
institutional advertising
mass communication

promotional advertising
public service advertising
station poster
trade, technical, or
  professional magazine

1. The conveying of a message to a large number of people at the same time.

2. Any nonpersonal, persuasive communication about ideas, goods, or services.

3. Advertising that seeks to increase the sales of a particular product or service.

4. Advertising that seeks to build goodwill for the firm doing the advertising.

5. Advertising that tries to get the public to act in socially desirable ways.

6. Letters and other mailable advertising materials sent directly to customers.

7. A magazine containing articles of interest to the general public.

8. A magazine containing articles of interest to a special group.

9. An advertisement placed in or on moving vehicles.

10. An advertisement placed inside transportation terminals.

Checking Your Understanding

1. What is the difference between mass communication and person-to-person communication?

2. What is the principal advantage of using mass communication? What is the principal disadvantage?

3. What is the greatest single use of mass communication?

4. What are the six major advertising media?

5. Why are television and radio so extensively used by advertisers?

6. Give several examples of direct mail advertising.

7. Why do some advertisers use popular consumer magazines while other advertisers use magazines that are read by persons engaged in a single occupation?

8. Name four ways in which advertising benefits us as consumers and society as a whole.

9. How does advertising help to provide more jobs and more income?

10. Why do some people today question whether advertising really benefits us?

11. What are some controls exercised over advertising today?

Applying What You Have Learned

1. Some media are better suited to the advertising of certain products than they are to others. Name an advertising medium that you feel would best promote the sale of each of the products listed on page 494. Give reasons for your selections.

(a) Gasoline (f) Motor scooters
(b) Television repair services (g) New homes
(c) Teenage girls' dresses (h) Used cars
(d) Men's work shoes (i) Cake mixes
(e) Ski equipment (j) Office furniture

2. Select a type of article usually available for purchase, such as breakfast cereal. Make a list of all the different media in which you find this type of article advertised. Identify specific ads that have appeared in these media.

3. Why is a direct mail campaign considered a form of mass communication whereas letter correspondence is considered as person-to-person communication?

4. Suppose that you are involved in a debate on the merits of various advertising media. You are asked to tell what advantages television advertising has over other forms of advertising. What would your response be?

5. Many persons are fearful of the influence of advertising upon individual consumers and upon society as a whole. Do you believe this concern is justified? If so, why?

6. It has been said that few, if any, businesses can survive unless they attract repeat sales. What effect does this have on truth in advertising?

7. Select five advertisements from current magazines. Try to choose ads that differ from each other as much as possible. Prepare an analysis of each ad, reporting on the following points:

   (a) What specific information does the advertisement contain about the contents of the item?
   (b) What appeals are used?
   (c) What "puffs" or meaningless statements are included?

Solving Business Problems

1. As the advertising manager for your school yearbook, you want to try to sell enough advertisements to cover the cost of printing 400 yearbooks at $3 each. You believe that you can charge the following prices for space in the yearbook: full page, $30; half page, $20; quarter page, $10; 2-inch ads (two to a quarter page), $6.

   (a) How much money will you have to raise to cover the cost of the yearbook?
   (b) If you have six class members do all the selling of advertisements and you want to assign them equal quotas, what will be the quota assigned to each?

Suppose that your salesmen turn in money for the following advertisements:

Salesman	Full Page	Half Page	Quarter Page	Two-Inch
Bacovin	2	5	4	7
Hummel	1	4	6	3
Wittenberg	6	0	2	5
McClure	5	4	5	5
Fioresi	4	7	4	7
Podesta	2	1	10	3

(c) How much in ads was sold by each of the six salesmen?
(d) What percent of his quota did each salesman sell?
(e) What percent of the total advertising quota was sold?

2. The American Foods Corporation introduced a new breakfast cereal. In one year it sold 31 million packages of this cereal. Its local and national advertising costs for this cereal were $1,116,000. If this cereal sold for 45¢ a package:

(a) What was the total revenue from the sale of the cereal?
(b) What was the advertising cost per package?
(c) What percent of total revenue was spent for advertising?

3. The Exline Company's figures for advertising expenses, total expenses, and sales volume for two different years are given below.

	First Year	Second Year
Advertising expenses	$ 78,750	$ 97,020
Total expenses	525,000	882,000
Sales volume	656,250	1,078,000

For each of the two years, find:

(a) The percent of total expenses represented by advertising expenses.
(b) The percent of total sales spent for advertising.

On the basis of your figures, would you conclude that the company's advertising program appears to be successful? Why?

4. A company wants to introduce a new product to as many people as possible within a certain region and at the lowest cost. The management believes that by advertising in various media it can achieve the following results:

Medium A can reach 60% of the population at a cost of $750
Medium B can reach 80% of the population at a cost of $850
Medium C can reach 40% of the population at a cost of $440

Medium D can reach 90% of the population at a cost of $500
Medium E can reach 40% of the population at a cost of $500

Compute the cost-per-person-reached for each advertising medium. Assume that there are 50,000 people in the geographical region the company is interested in.

Enriching Your Business Understanding

1. A classmate claims that there is no difference between advertising and publicity. What do you think? Explain your answer with examples.
2. By calling your local newspaper, determine and compare the cost of advertising a used motorcycle in the classified section with the cost of a one-inch display advertisement. What are the advantages of one type of advertisement over the other? Also, find out what the various groupings are in the classified section.
3. In direct mail advertising, one of the most important things is to obtain or prepare a list of good prospects. For each of the products or services listed below, give one or two sources from which prospect lists might be developed.

   (a) Portable typewriters.
   (b) Home furniture.
   (c) Travel tours.

4. Learn what you can about "bait" advertising. What is its purpose?
5. An advertising agency is a business that assists other businesses in all phases of their advertising. Contact an agency in your city or community and make a report on the types of services the agency performs.
6. Suppose that your class in school is going to present a play to raise money for class activities. The name of the play is "It's Never Too Early," a comedy. Giving your imagination free rein as to the plot of the play, write an advertisement which you could insert in the school newspaper as a full-page ad. Use 8½- by 11-inch paper, and illustrate the ad with sketches if you would like.
7. Advertising is a fast-growing business in which there are many job opportunities. By consulting books and career pamphlets on advertising, prepare a list of ten or fifteen jobs in this field.

PART 43
Transportation Of Goods

You have probably had to stop many times at railroad crossings and wait until a long freight train passed by. It may have carried automobiles from Michigan, farm machinery from Illinois, or dried fruit from California. There may have been tons of meat and fresh fruits in the refrigerator cars. There may have been tank cars filled with gasoline or chemicals, open cars loaded with coal and scrap iron, and flatcars loaded with machinery or pipes. These goods and many others that the train may have carried are essential to us as consumers and to our economy. Think what would happen in your community if all means of transportation came to a complete stop.

An individual or a company that is engaged in transporting goods or people is called a *carrier*. Goods that are transported are called *consignments*. They may also be referred to as shipments or freight. The person or company making the shipment is known as the *consignor* or *shipper*. The person or company receiving the consignment is known as the *consignee*.

There are two main types of carriers: private and public. *Private carriers* are used by their owner to move his own products or employees. The truck that a farmer uses to haul his supplies or produce is a private carrier. So is the truck that a retailer uses

MAJOR MEANS OF TRANSPORTATION

to deliver customers' orders. *Public carriers* are used by their owners to move goods or people for others. There are two types of public carriers. A *common carrier* holds itself open to the general public. A *contract carrier* sells its services to one or more individuals or businesses under contract and is not available to others.

Our principal means of transporting goods in this country are railroads, trucks, inland waterways, pipelines, and airplanes. Every shipper must decide which of these means will best serve his needs. This decision may depend upon such factors as the kind of goods to be shipped, the time required for delivery, the cost of shipping, and the destination of the goods.

Illus. 43-1. This chart shows how much cargo is moved by various types of intercity carriers. A ton-mile represents one ton of freight carried one mile.

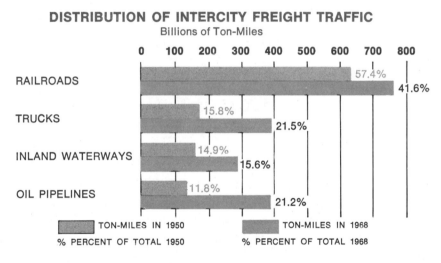

DISTRIBUTION OF INTERCITY FREIGHT TRAFFIC
Billions of Ton-Miles

RAILROADS CARRY THE MOST FREIGHT

A vast network of railroad lines extends throughout our country. We have nearly a quarter of a million miles of rail, almost one-third of the world's total. Rail transportation is best suited to handling bulky, heavy commodities in large quantities and at a reasonable speed. It often has cost advantages for such items, especially over long-distance routes.

Railroads also offer the shipper many special facilities. For example, a railroad can build a spur or sidetrack to a new factory or can put a freight car on a siding for several days, thus giving the consignee a warehouse on wheels from which he can sell or make deliveries. To compete with trucklines, railroads offer door-to-door pickup and delivery service to shippers. They also build special cars to handle the business of a shipper with unique requirements. Examples are tank cars to handle chemicals, rack cars for new automobiles, and refrigerator cars for perishable foods. Railroads also offer transfer privileges. They will switch a car from one railroad company to another as it goes toward its destination. This is why you may see cars from different railroads on a single freight train. This method reduces costs to the shipper, since goods do not have to be loaded and unloaded several times.

Most railroads have adopted a policy of not accepting shipments of less than a full carload. Shippers sending smaller items may turn them over to firms known as *freight forwarders*. These firms consolidate many small shipments into a full carload.

Railroads have many advantages, but other means of shipping goods are competing vigorously. This competition has meant lower costs and better service for shippers. Even with strong competition, however, railroads still haul nearly as much as all other public carriers put together. And they will probably continue to carry a large share of bulky, heavy shipments.

There are about 15 million trucks on our streets and highways. You probably see many trucks every day, and those that you see really represent three different kinds. One kind consists of all the trucks that businesses own and use to serve their customers. These are private carriers. Examples are the delivery trucks of dry cleaners, laundries, retail stores, and milk route men. The second kind consists of trucks owned and operated by individuals or businesses for their own use. These are also private carriers. They include trucks that farmers use to haul supplies and produce, and trucks that factories use to haul raw materials and supplies. The third kind consists of trucks owned by individuals and by motor freight companies that sell their trucking services. These may be common or contract carriers. Some motor freight lines own thousands of vehicles and operate many terminals.

Trucks are the railroads' biggest competitor for the shipper's business. Trucks have increased their share of cargo hauling in recent years because of a number of advantages. First, they can go almost anywhere to almost any town, right to the doors of the shipper and the consignee. Second, their time schedules are very

TRUCKS TAKE FREIGHT ALMOST EVERYWHERE

flexible. A truck can begin its run as soon as a load is picked up; a railroad or an airline operates on a fixed schedule. Trucks also accept small shipments and consolidate a number of them to make a truckload. For fragile cargo, trucks offer the advantage of less handling of the shipment and thus lessen the chance of breakage. Special equipment enables trucks to carry almost any kind of cargo. There are dump and construction trucks, refrigerator trucks, parcel delivery vans, household moving vans, cattle trucks, auto and boat haulers, and tankers for all kinds of liquids.

Trucks are likely to increase their share of freight transportation as our country becomes even more urbanized. There will be greater need for trucks to handle short hauls within cities and suburban areas and between towns that are close together. Our modern expressways speed up traffic flow and cut driving time for trucks. This reduces the cost of truck operation, even when trucking companies pay truck-rate tolls and fees for the privilege of using such roads.

PIGGYBACK COMBINES TRUCK AND RAIL SERVICE

A service offered by trucks and railroads together is called *piggyback* service. With this service, goods are loaded into a trailer at the factory or some other point. The trailer is hauled by truck to a railroad siding and is lifted onto a flatcar. When the shipment reaches its destination, the trailer is lifted off the flatcar and moved by truck to the consignee. The handling of goods from factory to consignee is kept to a minimum. A similar service, called *fishyback*, is available for water shipments. An adaptation of piggyback and fishyback is called *containerization*. With this service, goods are packed by the shipper in large containers which can be carried on railroad cars, trucks, or ships. These containers are not as heavy and bulky as the trailers used with piggyback and fishyback.

WATERWAYS OFFER LOW-COST TRANSPORTATION

Cargo being shipped by water often goes by barge or small ships on inland waterways and by larger ships in ocean trade. *Inland waterways* are lakes, rivers, and channels within the United States. An important inland waterway leading to the Atlantic Ocean is formed by the Great Lakes and the St. Lawrence Seaway. The Seaway, opened in 1959 by our country and Canada, brings

Southern Pacific Railroad

Illus. 43-2. Piggyback is a combination truck-rail freight service. Here a crane is unloading a piggyback trailer from a railroad car. Later the trailer will be loaded onto a truck and moved to its destination.

ocean-going vessels to such cities in the nation's heart as Chicago, Cleveland, Detroit, and Duluth. Other important inland waterways are our rivers, especially the Mississippi, the Ohio, and the Delaware.

Ships that carry cargo between cities along one coast—from Boston to Baltimore, for example, or from Seattle to Los Angeles—are engaged in *coastal trade*. Ships carrying goods from the Atlantic ports to the Pacific ports are engaged in *intercoastal trade*. Our country's great volume of trade with other countries is carried on mainly by ships.

The greatest advantage of shipping by water is that its cost is relatively low. Water is ideal for shipping heavy, bulky cargo to cities that can be reached by water. Coal, iron ore, lumber, grains, gravel, cement, chemicals, and petroleum products are often shipped by water. They make up about 90% of the freight carried on the Great Lakes and our rivers and canals.

There are several disadvantages of shipping by water. First, water traffic is slow. Second, the routes are inflexible because waterways do not go everywhere. But for heavy, bulky products when slow delivery is permissible, waterways will continue to be widely used.

PIPELINES CAN MOVE CERTAIN COMMODITIES

There are about 450,000 miles of pipeline across our nation, and pipelines are an important means of transportation for certain commodities. Pipelines are widely used to transport crude oil, gasoline, and industrial gas. Even powdered coal, cement, and wood pulp are being transported by pipelines. In addition, there are almost three-quarters of a million miles of pipeline transporting natural gas to home and industrial customers.

Pipelines are built both underground and on the surface. Pumping stations along the lines keep the liquids or gases moving under pressure. An advantage of a pipeline is that once it is built, operating costs are low. For example, the cost of moving petroleum products by pipeline is about half that of moving them by rail.

AIR FREIGHT IS BECOMING MORE IMPORTANT

Even though air freight accounts for less than 1% of the nation's freight, the cargo is often valuable and vitally needed. We used to think of air shipments as being limited to small packages, but this is no longer true. Large all-cargo aircraft can carry shipments of up to 45 tons. Smaller shipments often go aboard passenger aircraft. A shipment by air freight between any two cities in the continental United States usually takes no more than two days.

Air freight is more expensive than surface transportation, but things other than rates alone need to be considered. Air freight may actually be less expensive than other forms of transportation when the time factor is important. For example, it may be the best method of shipping clothing that is subject to seasonal use or quick changes in style. Foods and other perishable merchandise may best

Illus. 43-3. Air freight may actually be less expensive than other forms of transportation when the time factor is important.

United Air Lines

UNIT 9 / COMMUNICATION AND TRANSPORTATION

be shipped great distances by air freight. Also, the fast shipment of machine parts may far offset higher transportation rates if a factory's operation depends on those parts. For example, parts for an oil drilling rig can be flown into an otherwise inaccessible region.

Developing Your Business Vocabulary

The following italicized terms should become part of your business vocabulary. For each numbered statement, find the italicized term that has the same meaning.

carrier	*consignor* or *shipper*	*inland waterways*
coastal trade	*containerization*	*intercoastal trade*
common carrier	*contract carrier*	*piggyback*
consignee	*fishyback*	*private carrier*
consignment	*freight forwarder*	*public carrier*

1. An individual or company that is engaged in transporting goods or people.
2. A shipment of goods.
3. The person or firm who ships something.
4. The person or firm to whom something is shipped.
5. A transportation unit used by its owner to move his products or employees.
6. A transportation firm that is engaged in transporting passengers and goods for hire.
7. A public carrier that offers its services to the general public.
8. A public carrier whose services are available to persons or businesses under contract.
9. A firm which consolidates small shipments to make a full railroad carload.
10. A shipping service in which loaded trailer trucks are carried on railroad flatcars.
11. A shipping service in which loaded trailer trucks are carried on ships.
12. A shipping service in which specially designed containers can be carried on railroad flatcars, trucks, or ships.
13. Lakes, rivers, and channels within the United States.
14. Trade engaged in by ships carrying goods between ports on one coast.
15. Trade engaged in by ships carrying goods from Atlantic ports to Pacific ports.

Checking Your Understanding

1. Which means of transportation carries the greatest volume of intercity shipments within the borders of our country?
2. Which means of transportation has shown the greatest increase in amount carried since 1950?
3. What factors does a shipper consider in choosing a method of shipping goods?
4. Name several advantages that railroad shipping offers.
5. Give examples of the three different kinds of trucks found on our nation's streets and highways.
6. What advantages of motor freight transportation will likely cause trucks to haul an increasingly large proportion of all freight shipments?
7. What are the advantages and disadvantages of shipping by water?
8. What type of cargo makes up most of the shipments that go by inland waterways?
9. Give examples of products that are commonly transported by pipeline.
10. Give examples of goods that might best be moved by air freight.

Applying What You Have Learned

1. Can you distinguish between types of carriers? Give reasons for your answer in each of the following cases.

   (a) Frank Moretti runs a small farm and has a cattle truck that he sometimes uses to haul livestock and supplies. He also advertises that he will haul livestock to market for other people. Is he a public carrier or a private carrier?
   (b) Bruce Gill owns a fleet of 10 dump trucks that he leases to 2 large construction companies. Is he a public carrier or a private carrier?
   (c) The Gidding-Hayes Corporation has a fleet of 60 vehicles and 2 aircraft that it uses to transport parts, supplies, and employees. Is this fleet in the public carrier classification?
   (d) Charles Haverkos owns a semitrailer van and moves household goods for families. Is he a contract carrier?

2. Prepare a list of 10 different companies that carry shipments from your city to other cities. Include in the list as many different kinds of companies as possible. If you live in a community which has fewer than 10 transportation companies, list all that are available.
3. Generally, no one method of transportation can make a complete delivery. Do you agree with this statement? Explain your answer.

4. A manufacturer wants to ship a refrigerator weighing about 200 pounds to a retail appliance store in a small town about 100 miles away. **(a)** How should the manufacturer determine which transportation company offers the kind of service needed for this shipment? **(b)** What kind of shipping service do you think the manufacturer should use?
5. Select for consideration one of the following items owned by most families: automobile, electric stove, or sofa.

    (a) What raw materials were used in making the item you selected?
    (b) Where were these raw materials most likely obtained?
    (c) How were they probably transported to the point where the final product was made?

Solving Business Problems

1. The approximate rates for shipping 30,000 pounds of textbooks 800 miles by three different carriers are:

Truck	$2.45 cwt.
Rail	2.30 cwt.
Piggyback	1.15 cwt.

    (a) For each carrier compute the total textbook freight charge.
    (b) For each carrier determine the cost per mile of moving one ton of textbook freight.

2. The table below gives the percentages of workers employed in the different types of transportation businesses in a recent year:

Type of Business	% of Workers
Railroad	26.1
Local and interurban passenger	10.3
Trucking	38.8
Air	11.0
Pipeline	.7
Other	13.2

    (a) Assuming that the total number of transportation workers was 2,657,000, what was the number of workers employed in each type of transportation business?
    (b) If the hourly wage averaged $3.50 per worker, how much did each type of transportation business contribute to the economy during the year (40-hour week) in terms of salaries and wages paid?

3. The table on page 506 gives the amount of freight carried on this country's inland waterways during a recent year:

System	Billions of Ton-Miles
Atlantic coast rivers	27
Gulf coast rivers	28
Pacific coast rivers	8
Mississippi River system	125
Great Lakes system	115

(a) What was the total amount of freight carried on inland waterways?

(b) What percentage of the total did each system account for?

(c) Prepare a pie chart showing the share of total freight carried by each system.

Enriching Your Business Understanding

1. The importance of transportation has been recognized by the federal government to the extent that a Department of Transportation was recently established. What are the responsibilities of this department?

2. Make a map of your state showing the major railroad lines, airline routes, and waterways. On the map mark the location of major cities. Be prepared to give a short oral report on what parts of your state have to rely mainly on truck transportation.

3. When goods are shipped by freight, several different forms must pass between the consignor and the consignee. Find out what the following forms are and be prepared to describe them to the class: (a) bill of lading, (b) freight bill, (c) waybill, and (d) notice of arrival.

4. Individually or as part of a committee assigned by your teacher, visit the shipping department of a factory, store, or other firm that prepares packages for shipment. Observe how these packages are wrapped and shipped.

5. Prepare a brief written report on an occupation in the transportation industry. This occupation may be that of a truck driver, bus driver, dispatcher, traffic manager, or any other occupation that you want to learn about.

PART 44
Postal And Other Shipping Services

Our economy depends on the shipment of vast quantities of goods from one part of the country to another. Our large factories depend on our transportation system to bring them raw materials of all kinds and to distribute their products to consumers. Our farms and ranches of hundreds and even thousands of acres would not be profitable without a complete transportation system. Gasoline for our automobiles and often natural gas to heat our homes are available because of thousands of miles of pipeline.

These examples illustrate the need for our major means of transportation which were discussed in the preceding part. They are railroads, trucks, barges and ships on our waterways, and pipelines. But an individual who has a small package to ship is not primarily concerned with the advantages and disadvantages of the major means of transportation. Rather, he is concerned with the various services available to him. Also, many businesses have the problem of sending small packages to their customers. For such shipments, the United States mail and several types of express services are commonly used.

Mail that goes to points within the United States and its possessions is called domestic mail. Mail that goes to other countries is called international mail. Domestic mail is classified as first class, second class, third class, and fourth class or parcel post.

THERE ARE FOUR CLASSES OF DOMESTIC MAIL

Illus. 44-1. In the United States we send and receive about 80 billion pieces of mail each year —about two-thirds of all the mail in the world. Our Post Office Department operates nearly 35,000 post offices and employs over a half million men and women to handle this volume of mail for us.

Post Office Annex, Cincinnati, Ohio

The types of mail handled, the service the mail receives, and the postage charged differ in each class.

First-class mail is commonly thought of as consisting of handwritten and typewritten matter such as personal letters, business letters, and postcards. And these are important types of first-class mail. But any package that is sealed against inspection by postal authorities must be sent first class. Sealed first-class mail may not be opened by anyone in the postal service unless the mail cannot be returned to the sender. In that case, sealed first-class mail may be opened by people employed for that purpose in offices known as dead-letter offices. First-class mail is therefore desirable not only for personal and business letters but also for various other personal items. For example, you would use first-class mail to send a savings passbook to a bank, football or theater tickets to a friend, or a check to a firm to which you owe money.

First-class matter may be sent anywhere in the United States and its possessions for a small charge for each ounce or fraction of an ounce. The rate for first-class mail sent to Canada and Mexico is the same as that for similar mail sent within the United States. Letters to all other countries require a higher amount of postage. Unless you are certain about rates, weights, and other regulations for foreign mail, you should check at the post office for correct information.

Second-class matter consists of newspapers, magazines, and other publications that are issued at least four times a year to a list of subscribers or members. Publishers of these periodicals are given special mailing rates in order to make news and information available to the public at a low cost. Rates for second-class mail will vary according to the weight and type of publication and the mailing distance. Publishers must file an application for a permit with the post office and pay a fee for the privilege of mailing their publications at the second-class rate.

Individuals may remail printed matter, for which publishers have already obtained second-class privileges, at a rate that is a little higher than that given to publishers. If a package of newspapers or magazines is heavy enough so that the fourth-class rate is lower, it may be sent at the fourth-class rate.

Third-class mail includes almost everything not in first class or second class and weighing less than 16 ounces. Third-class mail is less expensive than first-class mail. Third class is therefore often used by individuals to mail small packages weighing less than 16 ounces. Businesses frequently use third-class mail for large mailings of advertising materials, including brochures and light-weight catalogs.

Fourth-class mail is also called *parcel post*. This class includes all packages that weigh one pound or more and that may be opened for postal inspection. Parcel-post rates change according to the distance the package is to be sent, as well as according to the weight. In calculating the amount of postage to be charged, the pound is the smallest unit to be considered. The same charge is made for a fraction of a pound as is made for a full pound.

For parcel-post mailing purposes, our country is divided into postal zones as shown in the table on page 510. The postage required is the same for a given weight for all points in one zone. The postal zones are measured from the place of mailing. The table shows the distance that is included in each zone. A local zone includes any point within the delivery limits of the post office from which the package is mailed.

There are limits on the size and weight of packages that can be sent by parcel post. Ask your post office if you are in doubt about whether a package will be accepted. You may seal a parcel-post package if you give the postal authorities permission to open

ZONES	DISTANCE
Local	Local Post Office
1 & 2	Up to 150 miles
3	150 to 300 miles
4	300 to 600 miles
5	600 to 1,000 miles
6	1,000 to 1,400 miles
7	1,400 to 1,800 miles
8	Over 1,800 miles

it. This may be given as part of a printed label or by writing "May be opened for postal inspection" on the package.

Educational materials may be shipped, regardless of distance, at a lower rate if they carry the notice "Special Fourth-Class Rate" and give the nature of the package contents. Such educational materials include books, 16-millimeter films, printed music, records, and manuscripts.

SENDING MAIL TO OTHER PARTS OF THE WORLD

Packages may be sent by surface mail or airmail to foreign countries. A *customs declaration*, furnished by the post office, must be attached to each such package. The customs declaration must give a complete, accurate description of the package's contents. Rates, weight limitations, and other regulations are not the same for all countries. You should ask your local post office about requirements applying to your shipment.

There are special postal services for sending packages to American servicemen overseas. For packages marked PAL (Partial Airlift), the sender pays the regular parcel post rate to the U.S. port plus a small charge for air service. For packages up to five pounds marked SAM (Space Available Mail), only parcel post rates to the U.S. port are paid. The packages are carried by rail or truck to the port city, then airlifted overseas as air space becomes available.

SOME SPECIAL SERVICES OF THE POST OFFICE

Our post offices have a number of special services. These services include (1) airmail, (2) registered mail, (3) special handling, (4) special delivery, (5) certified mail, (6) insurance, and (7) COD service. Some of these services are available for all classes of mail; some apply only to certain classes.

(1) Sending mail by air greatly speeds delivery, especially over long distances. Mail carried by train from San Francisco to New York, for example, usually takes about three days just for the trip. The same trip is less than five hours by jet. Today much ordinary mail is sent by air. However, one must pay higher postage to assure airmail service. Special envelopes and stamps may be used for airmail materials, but their use is not required. The word "Airmail" should be stamped or written on the address side of flat mail and on the top, bottom, and sides of packages.

(Reprinted by permission from *Sales Management, The Marketing Magazine* © Sales Management, Inc., 1969)

Illus. 44-3. Airmail provides more rapid service than that of surface mail.

(2) At its low rates, parcel post usually is delivered to the destination post office more slowly than is first-class mail. If a person wants a package sent as quickly as first-class mail, he can send it marked *special handling*. For this service, a fee is charged in addition to regular postage.

(3) A letter or package sent *special delivery* is delivered promptly after being received at the destination post office. This service is quite useful on weekends, nights, and holidays when no regular delivery service is scheduled. Special delivery service is open to all classes of mail at an extra charge. For packages, special delivery also includes special handling; that is, delivery to the destination post office as quickly as first-class mail.

(4) You may obtain added protection for first-class mail by having it *registered*. In accepting registered mail, the post office assures you that every possible care will be taken to deliver it. If the mail is lost, the post office is responsible for its value or the

amount for which it is registered, whichever is lower. When you send registered mail, you are given a receipt. This should be kept in case a claim must be made because your mail was lost. For a small extra fee, you can get a return receipt signed by the person to whom your mail was addressed. This receipt is valuable if you want to know whether your registered mail was delivered.

(5) *Certified mail* is like registered mail in that it provides proof that first-class mail was actually delivered. But certified mail does not provide payment if the mail is lost or damaged. For this reason, fees for certified mail are less than for registered mail. Return receipts can be requested for a small extra fee.

(6) Both third- and fourth-class mail may be insured. A small charge, in addition to regular postage, is made for this service. Postal insurance is limited to $200, so very valuable merchandise is usually not sent by parcel post. It may, however, be sent first-class and registered at a higher value.

(7) When a package is sent *COD (collect on delivery),* the post office collects the value of the package from the addressee before giving the package to him. If the sender wishes, he may also have the post office collect the postage and the charge for the COD service.

PACKAGES ARE SHIPPED BY PRIVATE FIRMS

If for some reason you do not want to send a package by mail, you can send it by a private transportation firm. You can choose from among the following shipping services: (1) REA Express, (2) air freight, (3) parcel delivery service, (4) bus service, and (5) motortruck express.

(1) REA Express is a shipping service widely used by both businesses and individuals. Its services are available in many communities throughout the United States. Unlike parcel post, it accepts packages of any size. In addition, REA Express provides pickup and delivery service in some areas. The REA Express Company uses railroads, trucks, and ships for its regular service. It also offers air express service that ships packages via airline companies.

(2) Air freight is similar to REA air express except that it is a service offered to shippers by an airline company itself. Because air freight gives rapid service, it is usually classified as a form of express shipping. Airlines offering air freight service ship

cargo not only on passenger aircraft but also on regularly scheduled all-cargo flights. Air express and air freight take about the same amount of time in the air. Air express includes pickup and delivery as part of the cost of sending the shipment; air freight does not. However, the airlines will arrange for pickup and delivery services for an extra charge.

(3) Parcel delivery firms operate largely within cities and suburban areas, but some such firms also operate between cities. They are used chiefly by retail and wholesale businesses in shipping small packages to customers, but they also provide special package messenger service for individuals.

United Parcel Service

Illus. 44-4. One well-known parcel delivery firm is United Parcel Service, which has branches in many cities throughout the country.

(4) Many bus lines will carry shipments on their regular passenger schedules. This assures rapid delivery if the destination city is on the bus' direct route. Packages must be taken to and picked up from the bus station.

(5) Some motor freight companies offer special express service between major cities, often overnight. These trucks operate on a faster-than-normal schedule. Cargo does not have to be changed from one truck to another but goes direct to its destination. Motor freight is very useful to business firms in shipping such things as merchandise and manufactured parts. Individuals use it mainly for shipping household goods; other shipping services are more convenient for small items.

Developing Your Business Vocabulary

The following italicized terms should become part of your business vocabulary. For each numbered statement, find the italicized term that has the same meaning.

certified mail
COD (collect on delivery)
customs declaration
first-class mail
fourth-class mail or *parcel post*

registered mail
second-class mail
special delivery
special handling
third-class mail

1. Mail that includes handwritten and typewritten matter and all mailable matter sealed against postal inspection.
2. Mail consisting mainly of newspapers, magazines, and other such periodicals.
3. Mail consisting of such materials as small packages weighing less than a pound.
4. Mail that includes all packages weighing one pound or more that may be opened for postal inspection.
5. A form which must be attached to parcel-post packages sent to any foreign country and which indicates the nature of a package's contents.
6. Postal service that enables a parcel-post package to be sent to the destination post office as quickly as first-class mail and then to be delivered by regular carrier.
7. Postal service in which mail is delivered by a postal messenger ahead of the regular mail delivery.
8. First-class mail on which the post office has a liability to the sender if it fails to make delivery.
9. Mail which provides a means of proof that first-class mail has been delivered, but does not cover payment of possible losses.
10. A service that provides for the collecting of money at the time of the delivery of merchandise.

Checking Your Understanding

1. Describe the kinds of materials commonly sent in each of the four domestic mail classifications.
2. Under what conditions may a sealed letter be opened by postal authorities?
3. What determines the charges for mailing a parcel-post package?

4. What types of materials may be sent at the special fourth-class rate?

5. Explain the meaning of PAL and SAM as they apply to sending packages to American servicemen overseas.

6. What is the difference between special delivery and special handling for parcel post?

7. What is the advantage of paying an additional fee for a return receipt on registered or certified mail?

8. What is REA Express?

9. Since we have the use of both airmail and air express services, of what benefit is air freight to us?

10. Why do we as individuals seldom ship packages by rail or motor freight?

Applying What You Have Learned

1. What type of postal service should be used to mail each of the items below?

   (a) A magazine containing an article you want a friend to see.
   (b) A rare family photograph weighing four ounces.
   (c) A package of seeds weighing three ounces.

2. Tell under what circumstances you would prefer to send a package:

   (a) By regular parcel post.
   (b) By parcel post, special handling.
   (c) By parcel post, special delivery.
   (d) By airmail.

3. Evelyn Dattilo wants to send a letter with an enclosure valued at $60. Her friend Susanne tells her that the safest way to send the letter is by special delivery. Do you agree with Susanne? If not, what method would you recommend?

4. Alan Silberg sent a small birthday gift by registered mail to his aunt. He discovered later that she never received the gift. What should Alan do to locate the package or to obtain payment for its loss?

5. The Wilmark Jewelry Company wants to mail a small package worth $1,000 to a customer in another state. Should the company insure or register the package? Why?

6. The Scandia Publishing Company receives a $67 order from a new customer, a bookstore in another city. How may it ship the order so that it will be sure to receive payment for the books?

7. George Kahle has a package weighing 92 pounds that he wants to ship by parcel post or express. Which method would you recommend that he use?

Solving Business Problems

1. Assume that the rates for parcel post are those shown in the following table:

Weight, 1 pound and not exceeding—	Local	1 and 2 Up to 150 miles	3 150 to 300 miles	4 300 to 600 miles	5 600 to 1,000 miles	6 1,000 to 1,400 miles	7 1,400 to 1,800 miles	8 Over 1,800 miles
Partial Table of Fourth-Class (Parcel-Post) Zone Rates				*Zones*				
2 pounds .	$0.50	$0.60	$0.60	$0.65	$0.70	$0.80	$0.85	$0.90
3 pounds .	.50	.65	.70	.75	.85	.95	1.05	1.15
4 pounds .	.55	.70	.75	.85	.95	1.10	1.20	1.35
5 pounds .	.55	.75	.80	.90	1.05	1.25	1.40	1.60
12 pounds .	.70	1.15	1.25	1.50	1.85	2.15	2.55	2.90
13 pounds .	.70	1.20	1.35	1.55	1.95	2.25	2.70	3.10
14 pounds .	.75	1.25	1.40	1.65	2.05	2.40	2.85	3.25
15 pounds .	.75	1.30	1.45	1.75	2.15	2.50	3.00	3.45
22 pounds .	.90	1.65	1.90	2.25	2.80	3.30	4.05	4.70
23 pounds .	.90	1.70	1.95	2.30	2.90	3.40	4.20	4.85
24 pounds .	.95	1.75	2.00	2.35	3.00	3.55	4.35	5.00
25 pounds .	.95	1.75	2.05	2.45	3.05	3.65	4.50	5.20

Calculate how much the Stonemill Gift Mart pays for postage in one day if it sends out the following items:

(a) 1 3-pound parcel sent to Zone 4.
(b) 2 22-pound parcels sent to Zone 2.
(c) 1 15-pound parcel sent to Zone 8.
(d) 3 4-pound parcels sent to a local address.
(e) 1 12-pound parcel sent to Zone 6.
(f) 1 25-pound parcel sent to Zone 7.
(g) 2 13-pound parcels sent to Zone 3.
(h) 1 5-pound parcel sent to Zone 5.

2. Assume that special delivery and special handling rates for parcel post are as follows:

Special delivery:
    Not more than 2 pounds, 65¢
    More than 2 pounds but not more than 10 pounds, 75¢
    More than 10 pounds, 90¢

Special handling:
    Not more than 2 pounds, 25¢
    More than 2 pounds but not more than 10 pounds, 35¢
    More than 10 pounds, 50¢

Using these figures and the parcel-post rate table in Problem 1, calculate the postage required to send each of the items below.

(a) 1 13-pound parcel sent special delivery to Zone 4.
(b) 1 4-pound parcel sent special handling to Zone 7.
(c) 2 24-pound parcels sent special delivery to a local address.
(d) 1 14-pound parcel sent special handling to Zone 2.
(e) 3 2-pound parcels sent special delivery to Zone 5.

3. Airmail postage charges for four different parcels are as follows:

(a) A 5-pound parcel sent to Zone 3, $2.60.
(b) A 15-pound parcel sent to Zone 8, $12.08.
(c) A 3-pound parcel sent to Zone 6, $2.11.
(d) A 23-pound parcel sent to Zone 7, $16.67.

In each case, how much more does it cost to send the parcel by airmail than by regular parcel post?

4. The table below gives some comparative costs of express, parcel post, and motor freight. Examine the appropriate columns which present the needed information, then answer the questions.

| Item to Be Shipped | Shipment From Cincinnati, Ohio to: | | | |
	Detroit	New York City	Miami	Los Angeles
1. A teacher ships 50 lbs. of books:				
REA Express (pickup and delivery).	$ 6.84	$ 8.42	$ 6.28	$ 8.98
Parcel Post (special fourth-class rate)	3.06	3.06	3.06	3.06
Air Freight (no pickup or delivery).	10.00	10.00	10.00	15.50
Air Express (pickup and delivery).	8.00	11.65	16.30	25.95
2. A couple sends a 15-lb. box of Christmas gifts:				
REA Express	8.05	9.55	10.90	14.15
Parcel Post	1.45	1.75	2.15	3.45
Air Freight	10.00	10.00	10.00	15.50
Air Express	8.00	8.00	8.00	11.00
Air Parcel Post	7.40	7.73	9.79	12.08

(a) What percent would the teacher save by sending the books to New York by the least expensive method as compared with the most expensive method?
(b) Notice that it would cost the couple more to send a 15-pound box of gifts to Los Angeles by air freight than by any other method. How much more is this cost, in terms of a percent, than if they were to send the box by air express?

Enriching Your Business Understanding

1. From your local post office, find out the cost of mailing a 7-pound package to an address in the sixth zone by each of the following methods:

    (a) Regular parcel post.
    (b) Regular parcel post, insured for $200.
    (c) Parcel post, special handling.
    (d) Parcel post, special delivery.
    (e) Airmail.
    (f) First class.
    (g) First class, registered for $500.

2. What does the term "franked mail" mean? Who uses it and why are they given this privilege?

3. Assume that you are sending three packages to the same destination, a place of your choice within 400 miles of your home. Compare the charges of three or four transportation services available in your vicinity for the shipment of these packages:

    (a) A two-pound box of candy.
    (b) Books weighing 8½ pounds.
    (c) A box containing clothing and other personal items and weighing 18 pounds.

4. Make a study of employment opportunities in the postal services. Consider such things as the types of work available, training requirements, and opportunities for advancement.

5. If REA Express is available in your community, find out the following information about it:

    (a) Does it pick up and deliver shipments?
    (b) When delivery service is offered, what are the limitations on distance?
    (c) For what amount does REA Express insure shipments without making an extra charge?
    (d) What limitations are placed on the amount for which an REA Express shipment can be insured?

PART 45
How Americans Travel

We Americans like to be on the move. Visit a large airport, a railroad station, or a bus terminal and you'll see many people on their way from one place to someplace else. Many businessmen travel as part of carrying on their business activities. Other people, vacationers, travel just for the fun of it. We are intrigued by the thought of distant cities, of foreign countries, of faraway places that are new or different from what we have at home. For any one of several reasons, we all travel or expect to travel.

People used to do most of their traveling on foot, horseback, stagecoaches, or by sailing ships. None of these means offered much comfort or speed, but travelers had little choice if they needed to get from one place to another. Now we can choose to travel by the means of transportation that suits us best: automobiles, planes, buses, trains, or ships.

OUR MAIN MEANS OF TRAVELING

(1) We rely more on the automobile for our travel than on any other means of transportation. More than 90% of all vacation trips, for example, are made by car. Many families prefer to drive their cars on vacations because cars are convenient, private, and generally less expensive than other means of transportation. Businessmen may prefer to use cars because this frees them from having to depend on plane, train, and bus schedules.

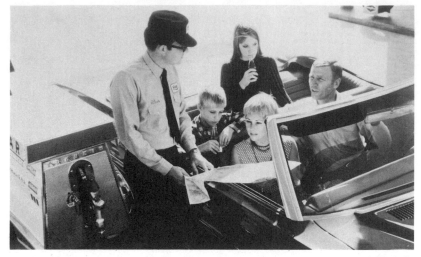

Swift & Co.

Americans own more than half of all the automobiles in the world. With this many automobiles, good highways are essential. About 43,000 miles of highway will eventually be part of the Interstate Highway System. When this system is completed, it will link almost all communities of 50,000 or more people.

Persons traveling on business often fly into a city and then rent a car to use while they are there. Vacationers may also rent cars, perhaps for as long as several weeks. Rental costs are based on the length of time a car is kept and usually on the number of miles driven. Rates vary according to the kind of car desired and the length of time it is used.

(2) Airplanes are the second most popular means of travel, especially for businessmen. The main advantage of air travel is its speed. For the vacationer, air travel can give an extra day or two at his destination. For the businessman, air travel can mean that he does not have to spend as much time away from his firm.

On most airlines there are two main classes of service, first class and coach. First class is more expensive, but seating and other accommodations are more comfortable. On some airlines and for some flights, other classes of service are available. These may be given such names as economy fare, night coach, and commuter class. Airlines also offer special discount rates for children under 12, for students, for families traveling together, and for military personnel. Excursion fares are also less expensive, but one usually must stay at least a week before returning.

(3) Buses are most popular as a means of traveling to smaller towns and cities. Bus transportation is usually less costly than even the lowest fares for train or air travel. Bus lines usually do not provide meals, but lunches and snacks may be furnished on a few luxury buses.

The Greyhound Corporation

Illus. 45-2. Buses are a popular form of public transportation, particularly as a means of traveling to smaller towns and cities.

(4) Passenger trains now account for less than 2% of all intercity travel. In the last two decades, railroads have cut out more than two-thirds of their passenger trains. In 1959 there were nearly 1,200 passenger trains operating; today there are only about 450. Most of the passenger trains still in operation are commuter trains used on short runs. The government is studying the problem of declining railroad passenger service. One suggested solution is the establishment of an independent firm which would handle only passenger train service. This firm would work with the railroads but would leave the railroads free to haul the more profitable loads of freight.

(5) Rapid air travel and the jumbo jet have almost eliminated the steamship as a means of traveling between continents. Today most steamships are used for pleasure cruises; they are

Pan American Airways

Illus. 45-3. Inside and outside the Jumbo Jet— a great innovation in modern travel.

really like floating resort hotels. Modern cruise ships are air-conditioned, have rooms with private baths, and offer such special services as beauty salons, outdoor cafes, gift shops, and planned social activities. A traveler can select a cruise that may range from a few days among the Caribbean islands to a few months around the world. Depending on his pocketbook, he can pay from $100 to $3,500 or more for a cruise.

SELECTING THE BEST TRAVEL ACCOMMODATIONS

No one means of travel is best at all times for all people. What one traveler wants may not be suitable for someone else. One vacationer may want to travel leisurely but luxuriously. Another, knowing that his time and budget are limited, may want to get where he is going as quickly and cheaply as possible. A government official on an important assignment may want to get to his destination as fast as possible, whatever the cost. One businessman may feel that he can take more time traveling and can work enroute on writing a report. Another businessman might want to combine business and pleasure by taking his family along. Different people traveling for different reasons have different travel needs.

To choose a means of travel wisely, a person must have the facts about the various services that are available. One way to get information on schedules and prices is to ask passenger sales agents at airline terminals, bus and train depots, and ticket offices of transportation companies. The traveler should compare rates that have been quoted to him, however, because rates may vary. Air fares, for example, may vary considerably even between the same two points. This may be due to such factors as time of the flight and class of service.

It may be easier to compare the services of one company with those of another if travel information is in printed form. Thus, *timetables* are issued free by all the major transportation companies. The timetables of many different companies are combined in official guides. Three that are widely used are the *Official Guide of the Railways, Official Airline Guide,* and the *Official National Motor Coach Guide*. These guides are available in ticket offices, at hotels, and in many businesses.

Directories of information about motels, hotels, trailer courts, and campsites are also available. Some directories have complete information about the accommodations provided and the prices charged. These directories may be obtained from several different sources: city chambers of commerce, automobile clubs, travelers' information booths, and service stations, among others. The traveler should usually make reservations to assure that a hotel or motel room will be ready when he arrives. In many resort or vacation areas, rates for lodging vary according to the season of the year. Thus, highest rates may be in effect in Florida during the winter. In Maine, rates may be highest in the summer. It is wise to take this into account when planning trips to areas such as these.

American Hotel and Motel Assn.

Illus. 45-4. Motels, like this one, are likely to be in suburban areas and near airports, though some may be downtown in the city. Hotels are more likely to be in the business districts of cities and towns. One staying at a motel can usually keep his car close to his room and take baggage from it as needed. Also, the car is available for short trips. Hotels, however, are more likely to be close to shops, theaters, and restaurants.

Illus. 45-5. For vacation travel, many families camp out. Campsites are available in state and national parks and other public areas and at private campgrounds. Information on location, cost, and reservations for public and private campgrounds may be obtained from Highway Department maps, vacation guide literature from a state's Development Commission, and camping associations such as the North American Family Campers Association.

PERSONS USE SERVICES OF TRAVEL BUREAUS

If a person needs help in planning a trip, he can contact a travel bureau. Such a business offers vacation ideas, trip suggestions, and information on costs of transportation and lodging. Travel bureaus will also make reservations, obtain tickets, and provide other services for the traveler. Some vacationers like group tours where a guide takes care of tickets, baggage, hotel accommodations, and many other matters. Of course, many people prefer to travel independently. Travel bureaus will make full or partial trip arrangements to suit a person's special needs. The services of a travel bureau can help make a trip more enjoyable and perhaps less expensive than if one were to work out all the details himself.

Travel bureaus receive their incomes mainly from airlines, steamship companies, hotels, and other such organizations. This income comes in the form of commissions on the tickets and services sold. Travel bureaus generally do not receive a commission from railroads. Because they receive their incomes from other sources, travel bureaus usually do not charge travelers for their services. However, services such as special prearranged tours almost always require a charge.

MANY AMERICANS TRAVEL TO OTHER COUNTRIES

More than three million Americans travel abroad every year. To travel in many countries, a person needs a *passport*. This is a form, issued by the country of which he is a citizen, giving the reason for his traveling in other countries. Passports are good for five years. Applications for passports may be obtained from the federal building in most major cities or from a travel bureau. A *visa* is permission granted by a government to enter a country and is required by most foreign nations. This is usually stamped on the passport by a consular representative of the country to be visited. When he applies for his passport, the traveler can find out about the inoculations he may need before traveling in certain foreign countries.

A person planning a trip to a foreign country can obtain information from transportation companies, travel bureaus, and often from banks and other financial institutions. These firms are glad to help travelers since they may sell tickets, travelers checks, and other services as a result. Large cities may also have offices of consular officials and other foreign government representatives who can give information about travel in their countries.

When traveling in a foreign country, a person must have his American money changed into the currency of that country. He can make the exchange at banks, American Express offices, and many hotels and business firms.

Although they may already be covered by life and health insurance, some persons want additional or special protection while traveling. Such protection is available through *travel policies*. They are designed mainly to pay benefits for death, loss of limb

TRAVELERS MAY BUY SPECIAL INSURANCE

Gamble-Skogmo

Illus. 45-6. For the person interested in a group tour—a "package" trip with all details handled by a guide or director who travels with the group—travel bureaus can be helpful in presenting a variety of choices. At least for their first trip abroad, some people prefer to go on a group tour where the guide takes care of many of the travel details.

or sight, and medical and hospital costs resulting from an accident. Whether or not one should buy travel insurance depends in part on what other regular insurance he carries. Existing policies may provide enough protection.

One type of travel policy covers a person for a specific trip on a certain type of public carrier, such as a plane, train, or bus. Another type of policy covers the insured while traveling on almost any type of conveyance. There is also insurance to cover travelers for almost any kind of accident, whether in a vehicle or not, for a stated period of time. This period is typically from one week to not more than six months. This kind of insurance is often called a vacation policy. Special policies are also sold to cover loss of or damage to baggage and personal belongings while one is traveling.

If a person is planning a long trip by car, he should check in advance with his insurance agent. Most automobile insurance policies cover a person as a driver in our 50 states and Canada, but not in other countries. The agent can also give him instructions on what to do in case of accident and injury while he is away from home.

PERSONS MAY ASK TRAVELERS AID FOR HELP

What does a person do if he needs help while he is traveling and perhaps is alone in a strange city? What should he do, for example, if he has lost his wallet or his tickets? Such persons can turn to *Travelers Aid*. This organization is the nation's only social service agency devoted solely to meeting the needs of traveling people in trouble. Besides the typical traveler, it may help migrant workers, military personnel, the physically handicapped, elderly persons, and refugees.

Most Travelers Aid offices are located in transportation terminals. There are Travelers Aid offices in more than 80 major cities throughout the United States, Canada, and Puerto Rico. There is no charge for the services of Travelers Aid. The organization is supported mainly by contributions through such agencies as the Community Chest. However, it also receives some of its support from transportation companies.

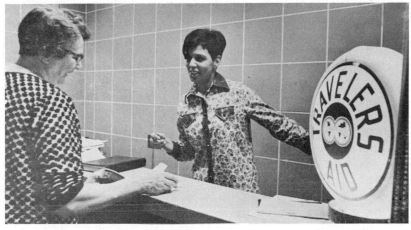

Michigan Bell Telephone Company

Illus. 45-7. Offices of Travelers Aid are maintained in many railroad, bus, and air terminals. But the services of Travelers Aid are for all travelers, including those who travel by automobile. The address of the nearest Travelers Aid agency can be found in the telephone directory.

Developing Your Business Vocabulary

The following italicized terms should become part of your business vocabulary. For each numbered statement, find the italicized term that has the same meaning.

passport   *travel policies*
timetable   *visa*
Travelers Aid

1. A printed form giving schedules and services of a transportation company.
2. A form showing the country of which a traveler is a citizen and giving the reason for his traveling in other countries.
3. Permission granted by a government to enter its country.
4. Insurance covering certain kinds of losses resulting from accidents while on a trip or vacation.
5. An organization that maintains offices to give information and help to travelers.

Checking Your Understanding

1. Why do many individuals and families prefer travel by car to using public transportation?
2. How does air coach class differ from first class?

3. For what special groups do airlines give discount rates? Why do you think they do this?
4. For what types of travel are buses most popular?
5. What is one proposed solution to the problem of declining railroad passenger service?
6. Why have steamships become less important as a means of traveling between continents?
7. Where may a traveler obtain information about means of transportation and about travel services?
8. Describe some of the services of a travel bureau.
9. What sources of information are available to a person planning a trip to a foreign country?
10. What are some of the limitations of a travel insurance policy?
11. Why should a person check with his insurance agent before he plans on driving in a foreign country?
12. Describe the services rendered by Travelers Aid.

Applying What You Have Learned

1. Mr. and Mrs. Abner Schumaker are planning to take a 2,000-mile vacation trip by car. Make a list of the expenses they should consider in preparing their vacation budget.
2. A family of four is planning its vacation. Father and son propose that they rent a house trailer to provide the needed lodging and kitchen facilities. Mother and daughter would prefer staying in motels. They suggest that the family plan to eat one meal a day in a restaurant and make the other two light meals that can be prepared in roadside parks. Discuss the advantages and disadvantages of the two plans.
3. Meals or snacks are commonly served without charge on airplanes. Why do you think this service is not customary on trains and buses?
4. Tim Kolper, a sportswriter, rents a car in Chicago and at the end of three weeks turns the car in at St. Louis. It would have been less expensive for Tim to fly to St. Louis instead of driving. What reasons might Tim have for driving a rental car this distance and this length of time?
5. Kim Barnett is planning to go to a summer resort in Maine for her vacation. She would like to know what services are offered by the different hotels at this resort before making a definite choice. From what sources can Miss Barnett obtain this information?
6. Suppose that you want to take a trip and are uncertain whether you should go by plane, train, or bus. Prepare a list of the information you ought to obtain about each method of transportation before you make a decision.

Solving Business Problems

1. Ed Gallenstein and two of his college friends decided to rent a car while vacationing at Blue Sea Beach. They rented the car for all day Saturday, Sunday, and Monday and for three hours on Tuesday. The rates charged were: weekends (Saturday and Sunday only), $6 a day plus 11¢ per mile; weekdays (Monday through Friday), $10 a day plus 11¢ per mile; hourly rates, $1.75 plus 11¢ per mile. When the boys turned in their rented car, the mileage indicator showed that they had driven 187 miles.

    (a) What was the amount charged for the time the car was used?
    (b) What was the amount charged for mileage?
    (c) What was the total cost of the rental service?
    (d) The boys divided the expenses equally. What did each pay?

2. Mr. and Mrs. Nelson Barber and their two sons plan to take a 10-day trip by car. They estimate that they will travel about 1,450 miles. Mr. Barber finds from his past records that his car averages 14½ miles to a gallon of gasoline and that the average cost of gasoline is 37¢ a gallon. He also estimates that miscellaneous automobile expenses will amount to $20.

The Barbers estimate that they will spend an average of $5.50 a day for each person for meals for 10 days and $20 a night for motels for the family for 9 nights. They also estimate that entertainment expense will amount to $10 a day for 10 days. An allowance of $40 is made for miscellaneous expenses.

Prepare a budget showing the amount estimated for each type of expenditure.

3. In a recent year Americans traveled abroad for a variety of reasons, as indicated below:

Personal reasons	36.6%
Pleasure	41.4
Business	8.1
Government business	9.2
Other	4.7

Prepare a pie chart from these figures and choose an appropriate heading for it.

Enriching Your Business Understanding

1. Many American families, in order to travel at an economical cost, are camping and preparing their own meals on vacation. Make a list of resources available to the camper that would provide information on public and private campsites, facilities that are available, and costs.

2. More students are traveling today than ever before. Find out from transportation companies and from such sources as the National Student Travel Association what special rates and services are available to this group of the traveling public.

3. Select a place in a nearby state that you would like to visit for one week. Report to the class on the following:

   (a) What types of suitable transportation to this place are available?
   (b) What are the comparisons in cost and travel time among the available methods of transportation?
   (c) What method of transportation would you choose? Why?
   (d) Make a rough estimate of what a one-week trip would cost you. Include your transportation costs and then estimate your other expenses under such headings as food, lodging, entertainment, sports, or miscellaneous.

4. Plan a trip to any city that is at least 300 miles away. Determine the various methods of travel that you might use, the time required for each, and the cost of each. For the method that you prefer, find the time that you will leave your home city and the time that you will arrive at the destination city. Also, find the time of departure and arrival for the return trip.

5. Most of our hotels are operated on the European plan. Hotels in resort areas, however, are often operated on the American plan. Find out what is meant by the American and European plans. Also, why do you think the American plan is especially suitable for hotels in resort areas?

6. Select one of the following questions and be prepared to give an oral report on your findings to the class:

   (a) What services do modern hotels and motels offer their guests in addition to room and restaurant facilities?
   (b) What are the advantages and disadvantages of going on a group tour?
   (c) How much baggage can you carry without charge on a plane? A bus? A train? A ship?

Unit 10

Government, Business and Labor

PART 46
Government's Role in Our Economy

It would be difficult to play football without having rules and a referee. Rules are not intended to interfere with the freedom of any one player but rather to make sure that all players are treated fairly. Business activities, like a football game, must be conducted according to rules of fair play.

We are involved in business as consumers, employees, employers, investors, and owners. Since everyone is affected by business operations in some way, the conduct of business concerns us all. No one group or individual should be allowed to have an unfair advantage over another. Our government serves as a kind of referee for business.

Suppose that Peter Martino decides to start a small restaurant in a new shopping center. He is free to start a business of his own, but government requires that he follow certain rules and regulations so that the welfare of others will not be harmed. For example, Mr. Martino must meet standards set up by the local department of health. His building must have the approval of the local fire department. His working conditions and wages must comply with state labor laws. Regulations for operating a restaurant also benefit Mr. Martino as a businessman. Because of regulations, other restaurants will have to compete fairly and honestly with him.

WAYS IN WHICH OUR GOVERNMENT SERVES US

"We, the people of the United States"—the first words of the Preamble to the Constitution. And we, the people, make up our country's government. Locally we elect mayors, sheriffs, councilmen, school board members, and other officials to represent us. On the state level we elect governors, legislators, and other leaders. At the national level we elect a president, vice president, representatives, and senators.

Government officials serve us; we do not serve them. They are responsible to us for passing and enforcing laws needed for the welfare of all. What are some of the services they provide us? They operate public schools, hospitals, and libraries. They build and maintain streets, highways, and water supply systems. They provide parks and other facilities for recreation. They maintain police and fire departments and our armed forces. They collect and deliver mail. They print and coin money. They develop programs to conserve natural resources.

Such services are necessary for our welfare, and government can perform them better than we can as individuals. Our government assumes many other responsibilities for us. In this part, however, we shall limit our examples to some of the important relationships of government and business.

Illus. 46-1. One important government service—and one which we often take for granted—is the operation of schools so that everyone may receive an education.

Chemical Bank

Most businessmen operate fairly and honestly, but a few may try to take unfair advantage of their customers or competitors. Government seeks to prevent this. For example, many businesses have to ship goods by railroad. If a railroad gives one shipper a lower rate, that shipper has an unfair advantage over other shippers. Government regulations prevent this inequality. They require that a railroad charge everyone the same rate for the same kind of shipment over the same route.

Many laws have been passed to prevent unfair business practices. Some cities and states regulate the purity and quality of certain food products, such as milk and meat, that are sold by local businesses. Federal law prohibits the adulteration or misbranding of any food, drug, device, or cosmetic sold in *interstate commerce*. A product is *adulterated* if it fails to meet minimum standards of purity and quality. *Misbranding* is the failure to state correctly certain required facts on a product's label. Most local and state governments also provide for regular inspection of food products and of scales and measures used in selling goods.

A *public utility* regularly supplies a service or a commodity that is vital to the public welfare. Examples are telephone companies, railroads, and companies that provide gas, water, and electricity. Government limits competition among public utilities. This is done so that the citizens may be better served. One public utility such as a telephone company can give a city better service than could several companies. If your city had six different telephone companies instead of one, each with its own telephone lines and expensive equipment, the service you would get would probably be more expensive and less efficient.

Governments give special privileges to public utilities. For example, cities give permission for their streets to be used by electric, telephone, and telegraph companies for their wires; by gas and water companies for their mains; and by bus companies for their buses. The right of privately owned public utilities to use the streets is usually limited so that no more than one company of each kind will serve a certain city. The city gives the utility the right to supply certain services and keeps out all competing companies.

OUR GOVERNMENT PREVENTS UNFAIR COMPETITION

COMPETITION IS LIMITED AMONG PUBLIC UTILITIES

MONOPOLIES IN BUSINESS ARE LIMITED

When a business has control of a commodity or a service, a *monopoly* exists. Some monopolies are desirable; others are not. Although one telephone company can give citizens better service than six could, the same is not true for most other businesses. For example, it is not good for a single firm to be the sole seller of groceries in a city. That firm might have stores in all parts of the city so that each family would be fairly near a store. But because of lack of competition, customers might receive poor quality merchandise, prices might be too high, and service might be inefficient.

When there are many similar businesses competing for the customer's dollars, each business will do all it can to attract customers and give them quality merchandise and good service. For this reason, government forbids monopolies in most lines of business. When government does permit a business, such as a telephone company, to operate as a monopoly, it reserves the right to regulate the business and its prices so that public interests are served.

ENFORCEMENT OF CONTRACTS IS A FUNCTION OF GOVERNMENT

The enforcement of contracts is a vital function of government. If Mr. Carew promises to pay the Hillwin Plumbing Company $150 for a water heater, he knows that he must pay. Similarly, the Hillwin Company must do what it promised to do for a payment of $150. Mr. Carew knows that if he does not pay, he can be taken to court and forced to pay. The provisions of legal contracts can be enforced in our courts. Businesses could not operate successfully if government did not use its authority to enforce contracts through the courts.

PROPERTY RIGHTS ARE PROTECTED BY GOVERNMENT

As you learned in Part 1, anything that we lawfully acquire and that we may freely use or sell is known as private property. *Public property* is made up of those things owned in common by the people of a city, state, or nation. Post offices, public schools, public playgrounds and parks, and streets are some examples of public property.

Government protects our right to private property. The city, state, or nation can take private property for use only when it is necessary to do so for the public good. The owner is paid a fair price for the property taken. The power to purchase, at a fair price, private property for necessary public use is known as the right of *eminent domain*.

Patent and copyright laws were passed to encourage and reward people who create useful things. A *patent* gives an inventor the exclusive right to make, use, or sell his invention for a period of 17 years. A *copyright* gives an author, composer, or artist the exclusive right to use what he has produced. This right exists for 28 years and may be extended for another 28 years. Inspect the front pages of your textbooks, and you will see examples of statements of copyrights.

Businesses may also be granted the sole use of *trademarks* in marketing their products. Trademarks that have been registered for protection by the government include such familiar ones as those shown in Illustration 46-2.

GOVERNMENT GIVES SPECIAL PROPERTY RIGHTS

Illus. 46-2. How many of these trademarks can you identify?

Government is concerned not only with the protection of property rights; it is also much concerned with the protection of human rights. For example, government does not permit businesses to employ persons and pay them a wage that is far too low to meet their basic needs. Laws have been passed to assure that each employee receives at least a reasonable basic wage. These laws are called minimum wage laws. They state that no person may be employed in a business covered by minimum wage laws and be paid less than a specified rate per hour.

You have also learned that government, through unemployment compensation laws, provides an unemployed person with

HUMAN RIGHTS ARE PROTECTED BY GOVERNMENT

funds that assist him in supporting himself and his family until he can find a job. In some cases government will provide him with the training or retraining needed to get a new job. Also, it will help him locate a job.

Businesses cannot engage in certain other practices that may harm human rights. The federal government, states, and cities have passed laws forbidding discrimination against persons because of their race, religion, sex, or other factors. Also, more attention has recently been directed toward enforcing open housing. This means that lodging offered for rent or sale is available to all citizens who want it and can afford it.

GOVERNMENT GIVES HELP TO PRIVATE BUSINESS

Our local, state, and national governments aid private business in many ways. One important service is the collection and reporting of information that businessmen can use in planning for the future. The Bureau of Labor Statistics, the Small Business Administration, the Department of Agriculture, and many other federal agencies collect information on a nationwide scale. They make available information on how people earn, save, and spend their incomes; on employment and unemployment; on business failures; on the cost of living; and on many other phases of economic life.

Direct aid is also given to business. Through agencies of the federal government, loans may be granted to small business firms and to farmers. Homebuilders, veterans, and others may also borrow needed funds from federal agencies and some state government agencies.

The federal government also provides aid in the form of subsidies and tariffs. A *subsidy* is aid given in the form of a direct payment. For example, subsidies may be given to farmers who are unable to produce crops or raise livestock at a profit. A *tariff* or *customs duty* is a tax on goods imported into our country. When a tariff is levied on imported goods, the selling price is increased to cover both the cost of the goods and the tax. This makes it possible for businesses in this country to compete favorably with imports that might otherwise be sold at lower prices. Our government also aids and protects American business interests abroad.

SOME SERVICES YOUR TAX DOLLAR PAYS FOR

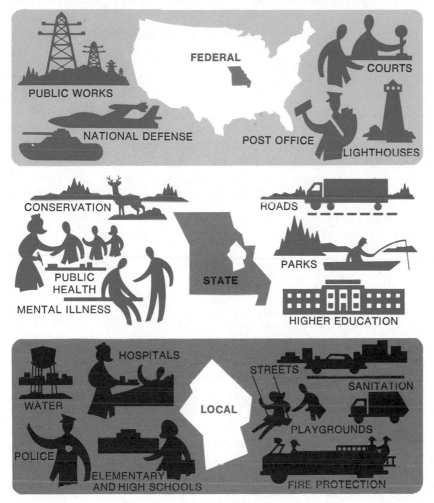

Illus. 46-3. These are only some of the services that our tax dollars pay for.

Businesses could not thrive if there were no public roads to transport goods and people. Businesses could not survive long if government did not use its authority to enforce contracts. They could not operate freely if government did not keep public order so that life and property are protected.

All of us agree that government has certain responsibilities for the general welfare. But to what extent should government aid and regulate? The final answer rests with the citizens. By using their voting rights, they must decide on the responsibilities government is to assume.

HOW MUCH GOVERNMENT PARTICIPATION?

Developing Your Business Vocabulary

The following italicized terms should become part of your business vocabulary. For each numbered statement, find the italicized term that has the same meaning.

adulterated

copyright

eminent domain

interstate commerce

misbranding

monopoly

patent

public property

public utility

subsidy

tariff or *customs duty*

trademark

1. Trade among states.
2. The failure of a product to meet minimum standards of purity and quality.
3. The failure to state correctly certain required facts on a product's label.
4. A business that provides essential services or products for the public at prices usually determined by government regulations rather than by competition.
5. Exclusive control of a commodity or service.
6. Things owned by a city, state, or nation.
7. The right of government to purchase, at a fair price, privately owned property for necessary public use.
8. The exclusive right given an inventor to make, use, or sell his invention for a period of 17 years.
9. The exclusive right of an author, composer, or artist to use or sell what he has produced for a period of 28 years.
10. A word, letter, or device indicating the origin and ownership of the article to which it is applied.
11. Money granted by the government to assist in the establishment or support of an enterprise considered to be of benefit to the public.
12. A tax on imported goods.

Checking Your Understanding

1. In what ways does government serve or assist a small businessman like Peter Martino?
2. List six major responsibilities that we entrust to our government for operation and control.
3. Do you think that each of the responsibilities listed for the preceding question can be better assumed by government than by private business? Give reasons for your answer.

4. Give some examples of government regulations that have been established to prevent unfair competition in business.

5. Why is free competition not permitted in public utilities? Name several public utilities in which no competition is allowed.

6. Under what circumstances is a monopoly desirable?

7. What is the difference between private and public property? Give some examples of each.

8. Explain why special property rights in the form of patents and copyrights are issued.

9. Give examples of how government protects human rights in the business world.

10. What are some specific aids that government gives to private business?

11. Who decides the extent to which government should regulate business?

Applying What You Have Learned

1. One law requires that promises made under certain conditions must be fulfilled. Another requires that advertising must be truthful. A third requires that food offered for sale must be wholesome. How does each of these laws aid business?

2. Make a list of the public utilities in the community in which you live. (a) What services do they render? (b) Do you believe it would be better to have any of these services offered by several business enterprises under free competition?

3. Why are railroad companies, bus companies, and airlines required to have the fares that they charge approved by the government?

4. Assume that five additional acres of land are needed to enlarge your high school. How could your school district acquire this property?

5. Give at least one good reason for each of the following:

   (a) Government regulates railroad rates but not the price of bread.
   (b) Government inspects meat and meat products but not automobile tires.
   (c) Government inspects scales but not automobile speedometers.

6. Max Grote claims that government regulation of business activities seriously limits the freedom of a businessman in the conduct of his business. He feels that we would be more prosperous if we had no government regulation of business. Do you agree?

7. Paul and Mary Jo are discussing the fact that "government is our biggest business." Paul feels that some government activities are in direct competition with private business and that this is unfair. He feels that government should limit its activities only to those that private business cannot or will not undertake. Mary Jo feels

that government should undertake any business activities that it can perform better or less expensively than private business. What do you think? Give examples of types of business activities undertaken both by private business and by government.

Solving Business Problems

1. Below are the cash receipts and disbursements for a one-year period for a town's public library association:

Receipts:

Cash on hand, beginning of year	$ 850
Town and state appropriations ...	18,000
Income from investments	1,495
Membership dues and gifts	1,643
Fines from overdue books	549
Miscellaneous income	176

Disbursements:

Salaries and related costs	$ 9,455
Books and periodicals	6,687
Utilities (heat, light, telephone) ..	721
Insurance	343
Equipment and supplies	1,068
Cleaning and repairs	295
Summer and in-service programs .	1,215
Library binding	679
General administrative expenses ..	481

(a) What was the total amount of cash on hand and received during the year?

(b) How much was paid out during the year?

(c) What percent of the total cash received was accounted for by town and state appropriations?

(d) What percent of total disbursements was accounted for by salaries?

(e) What was the cash balance of the library association at the end of the year?

2. In a city in which there are 90,000 employed workers, 18,000 are public employees. Of this number, 6,000 are employed by the federal government, 8,000 by the state government, and 4,000 by the city.

(a) What percent of all workers are public employees?

(b) What percent of the public employees are employed by the federal government?

(c) What percent of the public employees are employed by the state government?

(d) What percent of the public employees are employed by the city?

3. The voters of Millvale are asked to approve a bond issue to buy property and develop a park for the community. City officials state that the cost over a 20-year period will amount to an extra 20 cents per hundred dollars in yearly taxes on the assessed value of property. They further state that the increase in taxes for the average homeowner will be only $10 a year.

(a) What will be the yearly increase in property taxes for Mr. Floyd Alcorn, a Millvale resident who owns a home valued at $22,000 but assessed at 30% of its value?

(b) What is the average assessed value of the homes in Millvale?

4. The proposed budget for a town as presented to the town meeting for approval was as follows:

General government	$ 94,850
Public safety	66,433
Highways	135,000
Sanitation and waste removal ...	9,875
Health and welfare	28,320
Interest and redemption of debt	180,500
Education	985,000
Capital expenditures (equipment and land purchase)	92,650
Miscellaneous unlisted	7,072

(a) What was the total of estimated expenditures for the town for the year?

(b) What percent of the total budget was to be accounted for by highway expenditures and interest and redemption of debt?

Enriching Your Business Understanding

1. Sometimes, because of rapid changes in technology, some workers lose their jobs. Private business and government work together to provide the retraining necessary to prepare such workers for new jobs. By contacting your local state employment service or by interviewing an employment officer in a local business firm, find out what you can about such programs that may be available in your community.

2. Explain the difference between interstate commerce and intrastate commerce. Why does the federal government regulate one and not the other?

3. Select one of the laws listed below and write a brief report on the major provisions of that law:

   (a) Sherman Antitrust Act.
   (b) Robinson-Patman Act.
   (c) Food, Drug, and Cosmetic Act.
   (d) Equal Pay Act.

4. By referring to the *Statistical Abstract* or some other current source, determine how many patents were applied for in a recent year and how many were issued. Can you give some reasons why many more patents were issued to corporations than to individuals?

5. If you write a popular song, you can obtain a copyright on the work for 28 years. No other person has the right to reproduce it without obtaining your permission. Is it fair for the government to give you this protection and deny many other people the opportunity to use the song in any way they wish?

6. What is the purpose of each of the following government-sponsored or government-initiated programs?

   (a) Community Action Program.
   (b) Vista.
   (c) Job Corps.
   (d) Neighborhood Youth Corps.

7. Mr. and Mrs. Hullsman, who are in their 50's, own valuable business and residential property in Millvale. They do not have children living with them now and they personally do not have the time or the desire to use the park that is proposed in Problem 3 on page 545. The Hullsmans are very much opposed to the park project, which would cause a substantial increase in their taxes.

   (a) Do you feel that the Hullsmans are acting as good citizens in opposing the bond issue?
   (b) Can you offer some arguments showing that the passage of the bond issue might be of benefit to the Hullsmans?

PART 47
Meeting the Cost of Government

If we want telephone service, electricity in our homes, or milk delivered to our door, we each pay the bills. But suppose we want to protect our homes against fire? Should we each buy our own fire-fighting gear? Should everyone in a certain neighborhood join together and buy a fire engine? Or should everyone in the community buy protection by helping to pay for a well-equipped, well-staffed fire department?

The most practical way to get fire protection is for everyone in a community to share the cost of maintaining a fire department. The same applies to sharing the cost of protection provided by police and our armed forces. These services, along with those you learned about in Part 46, can be better provided by government than by us as individuals.

Like private business, government produces certain goods and services for the public. And these goods and services, shared by everyone, cost money. State and local governments build and run schools. City and county governments build and maintain roads. Government owns land, buildings, forests, and mines. It provides businesses and individuals with electric power. It builds ships in government-owned shipyards. It provides medical care. It lends money to businesses and farmers through its credit programs or

GOVERNMENT IS A PRODUCER AND A CONSUMER

insures money that is lent by private firms. It is a landlord in that it builds and rents lodging. Some local government units own and operate hospitals and municipal water and transit systems. And to provide manpower for these and other activities, government employs one out of every eight persons in the American labor force.

Government is also a large customer of thousands of privately owned business firms. These firms supply the goods and services government needs to provide for the public welfare. Businessmen must be paid for paper, office machines, trucks, clothing, food, and thousands of other items that they sell to the government. Federal, state, and local governments spend more than $300 billion each year for the goods and services they buy to carry out their responsibilities. This figure represents about one-third of the total national expenditure for goods and services.

As citizens and consumers in a representative form of government, we help to control the services that government provides. The more services we demand, the higher the cost of running the government. Most of the money needed to run our government comes from taxes. Taxes are the payments that individuals and business firms make to cover the costs of government services. The power to impose taxes is basic to the power to govern.

Illus. 47-1. The more government services we demand—from building expressways to maintaining national parks—the higher the cost of running the government. Individuals and businesses pay taxes to cover the cost of government services.

Ewing Galloway

The amount of money government collected in taxes in a recent year represented about $1,500 for every person in the United States. This sum was made up of: (1) taxes on property; (2) taxes on goods and services; (3) taxes on imports; (4) taxes on income; (5) taxes on estates, inheritances, and gifts; and (6) social security taxes.

(1) There are two types of property taxes. One type is taxes on real estate, including land and such permanent attached improvements as houses, factories, and stores. The other type is taxes on personal property such as farm machinery, cars, furniture, merchandise, livestock, and stocks and bonds. Property taxes are collected by many different types of taxing units: state, town, county, and city governments; school districts; townships; sewer districts; and so on. Most property taxes are collected and used by local governments. The federal government and state governments obtain most of their revenue from other sources.

(2) Nearly every day we pay taxes on many of the things we buy. In most states and in some cities the consumer pays a *sales tax*. This may be from 2% to 5% of the amount of each purchase. Another type of tax that the consumer pays on the purchase of certain goods and services is an *excise tax*. This tax is imposed only on certain goods and services such as gasoline, cigarettes, and air travel. Excise taxes are generally included in the price of the good or service being purchased. The sales tax is added to the cost of the purchase. Excise taxes are essentially federal taxes; sales taxes are state and city taxes. In some cases consumers pay both an excise tax and a sales tax on things they buy.

(3) Only the federal government can collect taxes on imports. States cannot impose taxes on goods that are imported from foreign countries or shipped in from other states. About a hundred years ago, tariffs provided more than 90% of the federal government's total income. Today the amount collected from tariffs is less than 1% of the federal government's total income.

(4) *Income taxes* on individuals and corporations produce about two-thirds of the federal government's total income. More than half the states also impose income taxes. In addition, some cities levy taxes on the earnings of locally employed workers.

THE FEDERAL GOVERNMENT DOLLAR BUDGET FOR 1971

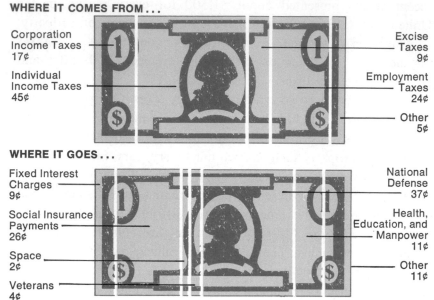

WHERE IT COMES FROM...

Corporation Income Taxes 17¢

Individual Income Taxes 45¢

Excise Taxes 9¢

Employment Taxes 24¢

Other 5¢

WHERE IT GOES...

Fixed Interest Charges 9¢

Social Insurance Payments 26¢

Space 2¢

Veterans 4¢

National Defense 37¢

Health, Education, and Manpower 11¢

Other 11¢

Illus. 47-2. Where the federal government gets its money, and how that money is spent.

The corporation income tax is levied on the corporation's yearly profits and is paid directly to the federal government. This results in a kind of double taxation. The corporation must pay taxes on its profits, and the stockholders must pay taxes on their share of the profits received as dividends. Partnerships and sole proprietorships do not pay a federal income tax in the same manner. Instead, each partner and each proprietor pays an individual income tax only upon his share of profits from the business.

Under the present tax law, employed persons pay all or a large part of their federal income tax during the year in which they receive their income. Employers are required by law to withhold the tax from employees' earnings and forward the tax to the government. Persons who receive much income from sources other than wages and salaries estimate the amount of their income for the year. They pay the tax on it directly to the government, either in one amount or in quarterly installments. Each taxpayer must file an income tax return each year. At that time an adjustment is made for any overpayment or underpayment of the total tax due.

The federal income tax is levied against taxable income. Taxable income is determined by subtracting certain deductions and

THE STATE AND LOCAL GOVERNMENT DOLLAR
REVENUE & EXPENDITURES FOR 1968

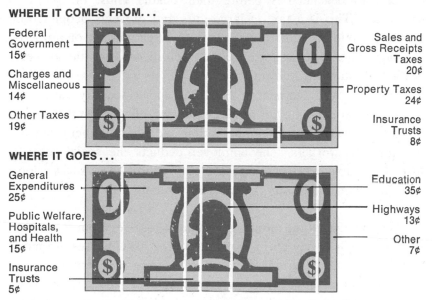

WHERE IT COMES FROM...

Federal Government 15¢

Charges and Miscellaneous 14¢

Other Taxes 19¢

Sales and Gross Receipts Taxes 20¢

Property Taxes 24¢

Insurance Trusts 8¢

WHERE IT GOES...

General Expenditures 25¢

Public Welfare, Hospitals, and Health 15¢

Insurance Trusts 5¢

Education 35¢

Highways 13¢

Other 7¢

Illus. 47-3. Where state and local governments get their money, and how that money is spent.

exemptions from total income. Allowable deductions might include contributions to religious or charitable organizations, business losses, interest charges paid, losses from theft and accidents, and certain taxes and other business expenses. Exemptions usually refer to allowances for dependents. These are members of the family that the taxpayer is supporting, including the taxpayer himself. For example, if a taxpayer is the head of a family consisting of himself, his wife, and three children, he may claim a total of five exemptions. For 1970, $625 of gross income is exempted from tax for each dependent. This amount is to be increased in several steps until it is $750 in 1973 and later.

In times of special financial need, the federal government may add a *surtax*. This amount is a certain percent of the regular income tax. It must be paid, in addition to the regular tax, by all taxpayers.

(5) Taxes on estates and inheritances are levied by both the federal government and state governments. They are imposed at the time of a property holder's death. The *estate tax* is based on the total amount of the estate left by the owner. The *inheritance tax* is based on the amount inherited by an individual.

To avoid these taxes, many persons used to transfer their property to beneficiaries before their death. Thus, the *gift tax* was levied. This is a tax on large gifts and prevents people from avoiding estate and inheritance taxes. A large amount of property can no longer be transferred either before or after the owner's death without being subject to a tax.

(6) As you learned in Part 28, social security taxes are levied on both employers and employees. These taxes provide funds for unemployment compensation and for retirement benefits for qualified workers. The employer deducts the social security taxes from employees' wages. He then forwards these taxes, along with his share of the tax, to the government.

INCOME FROM TAXES MAY NOT EQUAL EXPENSES

In some years the money government receives from taxes may not be enough to pay all its expenses. When its expenses are more than its income, government may borrow from individuals, banks, insurance companies, and other organizations. It borrows by issuing short-term notes or long-term bonds. When government borrows money on such notes or bonds, it is not receiving income. The money it receives is strictly a loan. The money must be paid back to the investors with interest. The interest on our national debt—on all notes and bonds that the federal government has issued—is over $13 billion a year. Part of our tax money must be used to pay this interest. Tax money must also be used to pay off the government's debts.

Government income depends to a considerable extent on business conditions. When there are thousands of prosperous businesses employing millions of workers, government collects great sums in taxes. For example, when large amounts of goods are made and sold, government income from sales taxes increases. When business is good and corporation profits and personal incomes are large, the receipts from income taxes are large. But if many businesses fail and many workers lose their jobs, the amount of taxes that can be collected decreases.

THE BUSINESS OF GOVERNMENT IS OUR BUSINESS

As taxpayers, we should insist that good business management be followed in the conduct of government. Those we entrust to run our government should:

1. Decide the purposes for which government money is to be used.
2. Decide how much money will be needed to fulfill these purposes.
3. Decide how to raise the money needed.
4. Make sure that money set aside for a particular purpose is used for that purpose and no other.
5. Prepare careful budgets and operate within those budgets.

We can help see that these things are done by:

1. Being interested in government affairs.
2. Electing capable, honest people to government positions.
3. Studying and then voting intelligently on the issues presented to us.
4. Conveying our views to our elected and appointed officials.

Our government officials must find ways to obtain the money to pay for the services that we want. But we must remember that if we expect more in government services, we must be willing to pay for these services through higher taxes.

Developing Your Business Vocabulary

The following italicized terms should become part of your business vocabulary. For each numbered statement, find the italicized term that has the same meaning.

estate tax	*inheritance tax*
excise tax	*sales tax*
gift tax	*surtax*
income tax	

1. A tax on consumer goods in general, added separately to the purchase price.
2. A tax on specific commodities that is generally included in the prices quoted to the purchaser.
3. A tax on the earnings of individuals and corporations.
4. An extra tax that is a certain percent of the regular income tax.
5. A tax based on the total amount of property left by a deceased person.
6. A tax on the amount inherited by an individual, imposed at the time of the death of a property holder.
7. A tax imposed on large amounts of property given away.

Checking Your Understanding

1. What are some government services which must be paid for mainly through taxes?
2. List six kinds of taxes levied and collected by government.
3. In addition to federal and state governments, what other types of taxing units are there?
4. Give an example of a real estate tax and an example of a personal property tax.
5. How does a sales tax differ from an excise tax?
6. Explain how a corporation income tax is a form of double taxation.
7. How does an individual determine the amount of his taxable income against which the federal income tax is applied?
8. Why does government levy gift taxes?
9. Why does government borrow money? How is this usually done?
10. In what ways does government income depend on business conditions?
11. State five principles of good business management that can be used in the conduct of government.
12. What control do we, the governed, have over the operation and cost of government programs and services?

Applying What You Have Learned

1. Below is a list of some of the public services undertaken by government. For each service, indicate whether federal, state, or local government would most likely have the major responsibility for financing the service:

   (a) Fire protection
   (b) Education
   (c) Parks and recreation
   (d) Water distribution
   (e) Intercity highways
   (f) Airports
   (g) Aid to low income groups
   (h) Sewage and refuse disposal
   (i) Mass transit
   (j) Police protection
   (k) Public libraries
   (l) Urban planning and renewal
   (m) City streets
   (n) Communicable disease control

2. The Blainesville Volunteer Fire Department feels that it could give better service to the community if it were better equipped and had more money with which to operate. The Department is studying the following possibilities for raising more money:

   (a) Hold a series of barbecues and sell tickets to them.
   (b) Seek an appropriation through the budget of the town government.

(c) Request that the Department be included in the Community Chest fund-raising drive.

(d) Conduct its own fund-raising drive.

What do you see as advantages and disadvantages of each of these plans?

3. Tom Feddersen is a stockholder of the Middle States Construction Company. Mr. Feddersen states that as an owner of this company, he is being taxed twice. First, the profits of the corporation are taxed. Second, when he receives his share of the earnings in the form of dividends, he must pay a personal income tax on these profits. Is Mr. Feddersen correct in his reasoning that he is subject to double taxation?

4. Elaine Coffaro is an employee of the Hilltop Dairy Company, which is owned and operated by Al Osborne. What kinds of federal taxes may Mr. Osborne have to deduct from Miss Coffaro's wages?

5. For each of the following kinds of taxes, indicate those paid directly to the government by taxpayers and those collected for the government by business.

(a) Individual income taxes   (e) Inheritance taxes
(b) Payroll taxes   (f) Excise taxes
(c) Sales taxes   (g) Corporation income taxes
(d) Property taxes   (h) Tariffs

6. How is money received by the government through the sale of bonds different from money received through taxes?

Solving Business Problems

1. The Elmwood School District is located in a city of 20,000 people. The student enrollment is 4,000. The current property tax rate for the city is $34.20 per $1,000 of assessed valuation. Of this tax rate, $17.10 per $1,000 is budgeted for educational needs. The assessed valuation of all city property is $126 million.

(a) How much revenue should the city receive this year from the property tax?

(b) What percent of the property tax is budgeted for educational needs?

(c) How much of the total annual revenue is budgeted for educational needs?

(d) What is the average amount of revenue received by the school district per student enrolled?

2. The Village Record and Radio Shop is a small business in a city of about 30,000 people. Its sales for the year amounted to $42,760, and its assessed valuation for property tax purposes is $39,500. The city's tax rate is 39 mills. The state has a sales tax of 4½%.

   (a) What must the owner of the shop pay in property taxes for the year?
   (b) What must he remit in sales taxes to the state?

3. The chart below gives the annual property tax levy in a community over a 5-year period:

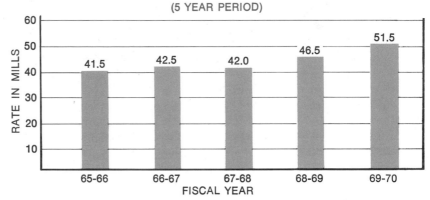

ANNUAL PROPERTY TAX LEVY
(5 YEAR PERIOD)

The tax rate is the same for real and personal property. Assume that your family lives in this community and presently owns the following taxable property:

Property	Assessed Value
Family residence	$13,800
Two cars	$900 and $700
Household furniture	$ 1,500
Two-family house (rented) .	$14,600

   (a) What is the total assessed value of the family's taxable property?
   (b) How much did the family have to pay in taxes in the latest year?
   (c) If the family had owned the same amount of taxable property in 1965-66, what would have been the amount of tax it would have had to pay?
   (d) By what percent has the mill rate increased over the five-year period?

4. The table on page 557 gives examples of what a family of four would have had to pay in taxes in a recent year:

THREE EXAMPLES OF TODAY'S TAX BITES

FOR A FAMILY OF FOUR —	$10,000 ANNUAL INCOME	$20,000 ANNUAL INCOME	$30,000 ANNUAL INCOME
Federal income tax	$1,120	$3,200	$5,910
Social security tax	$ 374	$ 374	$ 374
State income tax	$ 170	$ 550	$1,100
Property tax	$ 200	$ 400	$ 600
Sales and excise taxes	$ 740	$1,160	$1,370
TOTAL TAXES PER FAMILY	$2,604	$5,684	$9,354
TAXES AS PERCENTAGE OF ANNUAL INCOME	26%	28.4%	31.2%

NOTE: Figures assume family owns a home and itemizes deductions, on federal income tax return, equal to 15 percent of income.
SOURCE: Estimates by U.S. News and World Report

(a) What percent of the total annual income would a family have paid if it was in the $10,000 bracket? In the $20,000 bracket? In the $30,000 bracket?

(b) A family in the $30,000 bracket earned three times or 300% of the amount earned by a family in the $10,000 bracket. But the amount of income taxes paid by a family earning $30,000 was what percentage of the amount paid by a family earning $10,000?

(c) What percent of annual income was paid to the federal government as income tax by the family in the $10,000 bracket? In the $20,000 bracket? In the $30,000 bracket?

5. Spending by federal, state, and local governments keeps rising. This happens because our population keeps growing; we keep demanding more and more services; and the prices that government must pay for the goods and services it needs keep increasing. The table below shows the increase in government spending over the last 30 years:

CALENDAR YEARS	SPENDING BY GOVERNMENTS (BILLIONS) FEDERAL	STATE AND LOCAL*	TOTAL
1939	$ 8.9	$ 8.6	$ 17.5
1945	$ 84.6	$ 8.1	$ 92.7
1950	$ 40.8	$ 20.0	$ 60.8
1955	$ 68.1	$ 29.5	$ 97.6
1960	$ 93.0	$ 43.1	$136.1
1965	$123.5	$ 63.4	$186.9
1969	$195.0	$100.0	$295.0

*Excluding federal aid.
SOURCE: 1939-65, U.S. Dept. of Commerce; 1969, estimate by U.S. News and World Report

(a) How much has federal spending increased over the 30-year period?

(b) What percentage increase is this?

(c) How much has spending by state and local governments increased over the same period?

(d) What percentage increase is this?

(e) During this 30 years, which type of government spending has shown the greatest increase?

Enriching Your Business Understanding

1. Government usually borrows on notes or bonds, but there are other business papers given by the government as evidence of debt. Look in the financial pages of a daily newspaper and see if you can find out what these other business papers are.

2. Today federal income taxes are withheld from each paycheck. In earlier years this was not done; the taxpayer received his full income and then paid his tax directly once a year. Why was the change made?

3. In some occupations, a person's earnings may fluctuate during a year. Thus, it is not always possible for an individual or his employer to determine the full amount from which "pay as you go" income tax deductions should be made. The federal government therefore asks each such person to file and, if need be, pay on an estimated tax return. From a federal tax guide or from the local office of the Internal Revenue Service, find out what you can about the estimated tax. Look particularly for how the estimated tax is determined, who must file that type of return, and when estimated taxes must be paid.

4. A hundred years ago, about 90% of the federal government income was received from taxes on imported goods. Today the income from tariffs is less than 1% of the total federal income. What are some factors that might be responsible for this great change?

5. The sources of money for the public school systems of the nation as a whole are: local government, 56%; state government, 40%; and federal government, 4%. Most of the funds received by schools are used to meet current operating expenses. For your school system, find out the amount budgeted for each of the current operating expenses, such as administrative salaries, teachers' salaries, textbooks, attendance and health services, and maintenance of plant. Calculate the total operating expenditures for the year and determine the cost per student enrolled.

PART 48
The American Tax System

When a homeowner receives his property tax statement, he knows the exact amount of his property tax and the basis upon which it is figured. But when a consumer looks at the price tag on a television set, he does not know the amount of the taxes contained within the selling price. The price includes a part of the taxes of the manufacturer who made the television set. It includes part of the taxes of the trucking firm that delivered the set to the store. And it includes part of the taxes of the store that sold the set to the consumer.

We thus pay taxes both directly and indirectly. This is one characteristic of our tax system. Two terms that describe this characteristic are impact and incidence. The *impact* of a tax indicates who pays the tax to the government. For example, when a homeowner pays the tax on the house he lives in, the impact of the tax is on him. The *incidence* of a tax indicates who really bears the burden of the tax. In the case of the homeowner, the incidence of the tax is also on him.

The impact and incidence of a tax are not always on the same person. The person who pays the tax may often be able to shift the tax to someone else. And he probably will shift the tax if he can. In the case of the television set, for example, several persons shifted the tax on to someone else.

In the following paragraphs, you will learn that the incidence of a tax is likely to fall on the one who consumes the goods or services affected by the tax. Most taxes, then, are finally paid by consumers. Also, the tax falls on each consumer about in proportion to what he spends for goods and services.

IMPACT AND INCIDENCE OF PROPERTY TAXES

A homeowner receives the benefits from the use of his home. A real estate tax on that home is thus a tax on consumers. A real estate tax on rental property is also a tax on consumers, but this may not be as obvious.

The tax on rental property is usually paid by the owner or landlord. The landlord considers this tax to be one of the costs of maintaining the rental property. In this respect, the tax is like such costs as painting and repairs. The landlord must try to take in enough in rent to pay all the costs of maintaining the property and to earn a profit. If he cannot do this, it would be better for him to invest his money somewhere else.

If property taxes are raised, a landlord may not raise rents right away. And if taxes are lowered, a landlord may not lower rents right away. But in the long run, higher property taxes will mean higher rents, and lower property taxes will mean lower rents. When taxes go up, the landlord will need more income to pay his costs. His competitors will have the same increase and will scarcely be able to offer lower rents than he does. Thus, he can make the increases he considers necessary. But when real estate taxes are lowered, more investors will be interested in providing rental property. The increase in the supply of rental property will result in more competition among landlords. This in turn will encourage the offering of lower rentals.

Whoever occupies a home actually bears the burden of the tax on that home. This is true whether the occupant is the owner who pays the tax to the government or a renter who makes payments to a landlord. In both cases, the tax is on the consumer.

Taxes on business property are also passed on to consumers. For example, a store owner pays taxes on his real estate, merchandise, and equipment. These taxes are a part of his operating expenses and make up part of the price of the merchandise he sells. Each time a consumer buys something, he is actually paying part

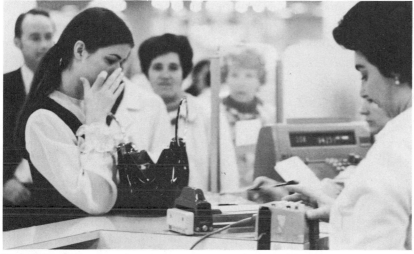

Transamerica Corp.

Illus. 48-1. The incidence of a tax is likely to fall on the one who consumes the goods or services affected by the tax. Thus, consumers finally pay most taxes.

of the store's property taxes. His share in these taxes is in proportion to the amount he buys.

Most property taxes are passed on to consumers, but a few are not. Take the case of a wheat farmer in the Midwest. The price of his product is fixed in national and world markets. It is not affected by expenses in one small area. So if the farmer's county or school district increases its tax rate, both the impact and the incidence of the tax fall on the farmer. He must pay the tax, and he has no chance to pass it on by increasing his prices. Similarly, when a tax is levied on a business that is competing with other businesses not subject to the tax, the business may not be able to pass the tax on to consumers.

A sales tax is obviously a direct expense of the consumer. If an item sells for $1 and the state sales tax is 4%, the merchant collects $1.04 from his customer. The merchant then pays 4 cents to the state, but the consumer is the one who provides the money for the tax.

An excise tax is also paid by the consumer, but it may not be quite as obvious that this is so. The federal government, for example, levies an excise tax of 4 cents a gallon on gasoline. When a customer buys gasoline, the price quoted includes this excise tax. The customer pays the excise tax just as surely as he pays a sales tax, even though the excise tax is not quoted separately.

IMPACT AND INCIDENCE OF SALES AND EXCISE TAXES

IMPACT AND INCIDENCE OF CORPORATION INCOME TAXES

When the federal government needs more money, higher taxes on corporation incomes are often favored. Many people believe that corporations are large and wealthy and well able to share their profits with the government. They also believe that such taxes come from the corporations' profits and have no effect on individuals.

Sometimes it may be true that none of a corporation's income tax is passed on to consumers. If a corporation is producing goods for export, it probably is competing with foreign producers. Thus, it may not be able to increase its prices to balance an increase in its income tax. Similarly, a corporation may be competing with foreign companies that import to this country. In such a case, no price increases may be possible to offset an increase in the income tax.

Many corporations, however, do not compete with foreign businesses. They compete with other corporations that also operate only in this country. All are subject to the same income taxes. They tend to regard an increase in income taxes just as they would an increase in any other expense. Prices are gradually increased to offset the added tax. Suppose that a corporation has been making a profit of 3% of its sales. It probably will be able to adjust its prices so that it can keep on making a profit of 3% of sales even after an increase in the tax rate. In such a case, the added income tax is not really a burden to the corporation. Instead it is passed on to the consumers who buy its goods and services. The impact of the tax is on the corporation, but the incidence is on the consumer.

IMPACT AND INCIDENCE OF PERSONAL INCOME TAXES

As you learned in Part 47, the largest single source of income for the federal government is the income tax on individuals. Those who pay this tax are also consumers, so the tax may be said to be a tax on consumers. But the tax is levied on what is earned, not what is spent. The tax may thus be looked on as a tax on earners, not consumers, even though the two groups are largely the same.

Although personal income taxes are chiefly the expense of those who pay them, even some of these taxes are passed on to consumers. Everyone is concerned with his take-home pay—his pay after all deductions have been made. If an increase in the income tax rate requires the employer to deduct more from wages and salaries, take-home pay is reduced. Employees may then seek increases in wages and salaries to offset the increases in deductions. These increases in wages and salaries become part of each business' expenses. They are passed on to consumers in higher prices. To the extent that this is done, even personal income taxes are passed on to consumers.

All of us want the services our government provides, and the tendency is to want more and better services all the time. But few of us like to pay the taxes that make these services possible. We are not inclined to be happy about any tax, and we are seldom pleased when taxes are raised. Still, we do agree that some taxes are necessary. We also are likely to agree that a good tax system should, among other things, have the following characteristics: (1) it should provide stable income for the government; (2) it should be easy to collect; and (3) it should be fair to all taxpayers.

QUALITIES OF A GOOD TAX SYSTEM

(1) The job of running government is easier if officials know how much money they will receive during a year. A school system, for example, needs to know how much tax income it can count on. Then it can balance this income against the planned expenses for salaries, maintenance of buildings, books and supplies, and so on. This is one of the reasons why a tax on real estate is so widely used. A tax of, say, $40 per thousand on real estate assessed at $20,000 will bring a tax revenue of $800. This amount is fixed and will not be affected by business conditions. The school district can count on receiving its share of this amount and can set up its budget accordingly.

(2) A satisfactory tax is one that can readily be collected from everyone who is subject to it. This is another reason why a tax on real estate is so widely used. Real estate cannot be hidden. If the tax is not paid, the taxing authority may seize the property and sell it so that the taxes may be collected. On the other hand, personal property such as stocks, bonds, jewelry, and money can be hidden from the taxing authority. Some persons may try to evade paying taxes on this kind of property. Thus, in many areas personal property is not taxed at all or is taxed at a very low rate.

A sales tax is another tax that is easy to collect. The consumer pays it each time he buys something. Since the tax is paid as purchases are made, there is little chance that it will be evaded.

(3) It is hard to determine what is each person's fair share of a tax. It is even harder to develop a law that distributes a tax with complete justice.

Some have suggested that a person or family should pay taxes in proportion to the benefits it receives. This seems reasonable as a theory. However, it is impossible to measure the value of the many benefits that we all receive from government. Also, many persons who receive extensive benefits have little with which to pay taxes. For these reasons, taxes are not levied according to benefits received. They are levied on property owned, on amounts spent, and on income.

A *proportional tax* is one with a uniform rate regardless of the amount involved. The tax on real estate is largely a proportional tax. Some states give minor exemptions to homeowners who live in their own homes. But with these exceptions the tax on real estate is in direct proportion to its assessed value. This may not be completely fair. A person living in a $30,000 home is not necessarily twice as able to pay taxes as a person living in a $15,000 home. He may be more able; he may be less able. Still, those owning real estate are on the average probably able to pay taxes in proportion to the value of their property.

Illus. 48-2. Taxes that are levied should provide a stable income for the government, should be easy to collect, and should be fair to taxpayers. A tax on real estate meets these criteria.

H. Armstrong Roberts

A sales tax is also a proportional tax. It is levied on sales at a fixed rate, such as 3% or 4%. In many states the tax does not apply to some items. Common exemptions are food and drugs. With these exceptions, the tax is proportional. The tax on a $10 sale, for example, is exactly ten times the tax on a $1 sale. A sales tax is often thought to be unfair because everyone is taxed at the same rate regardless of his ability to pay the tax. But because sales taxes provide large and dependable revenues and can easily be collected, they are used by all states and some cities.

Safeway, Inc.

Illus. 48-3. Items that are commonly exempted from sales taxes are food and drugs.

A *progressive tax* is one that increases the rate as the amount taxed increases. Our federal income tax is mainly a progressive tax. As taxable income increases, the rate also increases. For example, the tax on a taxable income of $20,000 may be almost three times the tax on a similar income of $10,000. The progressive feature of the federal income tax is generally accepted. It is generally believed that those with large incomes should pay a larger share of their incomes as tax than should those with small incomes.

Because most taxes are passed on to consumers, almost any reasonable tax proves to be fair to everyone in the long run. But large changes in tax rates may cause temporary unfairness. For example, a large increase in the real estate tax rate may be costly to a business because the business may not be able to raise its prices at once. A large decrease in the tax rate may provide a windfall for a business because prices may not decrease quickly. The fairness of a tax, then, depends not only on the nature of the tax. It also depends on whether the tax is stable and is one that everyone can adjust to.

Developing Your Business Vocabulary

The following italicized terms should become part of your business vocabulary. For each numbered statement, find the italicized term that has the same meaning.

impact (of a tax)   *progressive tax*
incidence (of a tax)   *proportional tax*

1. That which indicates who pays the tax to the government.
2. That which indicates on whom the burden of the tax finally falls.
3. A tax with a uniform rate regardless of the amount involved.
4. A tax that increases the rate as the amount taxed increases.

Checking Your Understanding

1. Give an example of a tax on property that is a direct tax on a consumer.
2. Give an example of a tax on property that is paid to the government by a business but that is passed on to consumers.
3. Are all business taxes passed on to consumers? Explain.
4. Are the impact and the incidence of a sales tax on the same person? Explain.
5. Do consumers avoid taxation by having taxes levied on corporations?
6. Is a personal income tax ever passed on to consumers other than those who actually pay the tax? Explain.
7. Do all of us pay a share of almost every tax?
8. What is meant by "stable income" for a government?
9. Why should a tax be easy to collect?
10. Give examples of taxes that are (a) easy to collect and (b) difficult or expensive to collect.
11. Should taxes be levied according to the benefits received by each taxpayer?
12. Give an example of a proportional tax and an example of a progressive tax.

Applying What You Have Learned

1. When a new tax or an increase in taxes is proposed, are you more interested in the impact or the incidence of the tax? Explain.
2. Ray Coombs believed that the real estate tax was too high. Partly to avoid this tax, he sold his house and rented an apartment. Did he actually succeed in avoiding the tax?
3. Give an example of a situation in which a corporation may be able to pass its income tax on to consumers. Give an example of a situation in which a corporation may not be able to pass its income tax on to consumers.
4. Which tax would you consider to be more stable: a tax on real estate or a tax on amusements? Explain.
5. People with expensive jewelry are usually well able to pay taxes. If, therefore, the government needs additional money, would you recommend a large tax on jewelry?
6. Why is it important that tax rates should not be changed greatly from year to year?

Solving Business Problems

1. Glen Fretcher owns a home that he offers for rent. During a period of years the assessed value has been increased from $9,600 to $10,500 and the tax rate has been increased from $26.00 a thousand to $37.60 a thousand.

   If the increases in taxes are not to decrease Mr. Fretcher's rental income, how much will he have to increase the rent per month?

2. The Corbin family has a total income of $9,000 a year. Of this amount, $3,600 is spent for items subject to sales tax. The Landon family has total income of $14,600 a year. Of this amount, $4,425 is spent for items subject to sales tax. In each case the sales tax is 4%.

   (a) Which family uses the greater percentage of its income for sales taxes?
   (b) How much is the difference between the percentages required for sales taxes?

3. Don Lieber earns $160 a week. From this salary the following deductions are made:

Pension	2½%
Social security	5.2%
Insurance	$ 2.00
Income tax	$23.10

   How much is Don's weekly take-home pay?

4. John Planter owns two pieces of real estate, valued at $12,600 and $18,900 respectively. They are assessed at two-thirds of their value. The tax rate is $43.20 per $1,000 of assessed valuation.

   How much is Mr. Planter's annual real estate tax?

5. Stan Rudolf has $5,000 to invest. He is considering investing in 5½% municipal bonds or in 8% corporation bonds. The income from the municipal bonds is not subject to income tax.

   (a) Which will bring him the greater return after deducting income taxes if Mr. Rudolf's tax rate is 20%? 25%? 30%?
   (b) How much is the difference in each case?

Enriching Your Business Understanding

1. From a dictionary or a textbook on economics, find the meaning of the term "regressive tax." Why is a sales tax sometimes said to be regressive?
2. Assume that the federal government places a tax on imports of certain goods.

   (a) On whom is the impact of the tax?
   (b) Give an example of a situation in which the incidence of the tax might be on the consumer.
   (c) Give an example of a situation in which the incidence of the tax might be on the producer.

3. Most states and some cities have sales taxes. Others do not. Present arguments for and against sales taxes.
4. In Part 47 you learned about the different kinds of taxes levied by government. Suppose that Jeff Torres earns a salary of $9,200 a year and rents his home. (a) Which of the kinds of taxes discussed in Part 47 does he probably pay? (b) Which of these kinds of taxes are paid by others but are passed on to him as part of the cost of the goods he buys?

PART 49
Labor's Role In Our Economy

On your way to school this morning, you probably saw many people working at their jobs or traveling to them. You may have seen a lineman climbing a telephone pole, a farmer plowing a field, or a work crew repairing a street. You may have seen an owner unlocking the door of his store, or a route man delivering milk.

These people and many others produce goods and services for us. If you think about it, you will get some idea of how many workers are needed to supply you with the goods and services you use. Each one of these jobs is important.

In Part 1 you learned that three kinds of economic resources are needed to produce the things we need and want. These are natural resources, capital resources, and human resources or labor. Natural and capital resources would be of little value without labor to make use of them. Without labor our tools, machinery, and buildings would not be built. And without labor this equipment could not be put to good use in producing goods and services.

The term *labor* includes all human effort, both mental and physical, exerted to produce goods and services. It includes all men and women who grow or take products from nature, convert raw materials into useful products, and who market these products.

LABOR IS ONE OF OUR ECONOMIC RESOURCES

It includes people who render services to others—services ranging from baby-sitting to brain surgery. Labor also includes those who supervise others and who manage business operations. Some economists consider management as a separate factor of production. For our purposes, though, it is logical to include this group as a necessary part of labor.

THE SEGMENTS OF OUR LABOR FORCE

Most of us will spend many years as part of a vast army of American workers. Our *labor force* is comprised of all persons 16 years old or older who are working or looking for work. There are about 85 million people in this group. Most workers are employed either part-time or full-time in business, industry, or government. But the labor force also includes professional people, such as doctors and lawyers, and other self-employed people, such as farmers.

In the ranks of our labor force are machinists, coal miners, janitors, garment workers, teachers, salesmen, accountants, company executives, government officials, military men, artists, and clergymen. In fact, it is sometimes easier to describe the labor force by stating who is not included in it. Persons not considered part of the labor force are mainly students, housewives, retired persons, those under 16, and those unable or unwilling to work. Students are included in the labor force if they are over 16 and if they work part-time while in school.

NOT IN LABOR FORCE: IN LABOR FORCE:

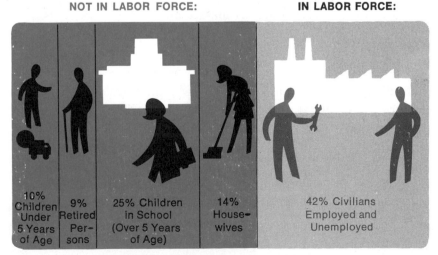

| 10% Children Under 5 Years of Age | 9% Retired Persons | 25% Children in School (Over 5 Years of Age) | 14% House-wives | 42% Civilians Employed and Unemployed |

Illus. 49-1. This chart shows who is included in our labor force and who is not.

You have probably heard the motto, "United we stand, divided we fall." As workers, many of us unite for causes we consider important. Almost every worker belongs to some special organization that is concerned with the welfare of its members. Physicians belong to the American Medical Association. Lawyers join the American Bar Association. Millions of farmers are members of the American Farm Bureau or the Grange. Employers are active in local employers' councils and merchants' associations. Many businessmen belong to the Chamber of Commerce and the National Association of Manufacturers. There are special societies for sales managers, actors, farmers, and countless other groups.

Having a strong group speak for its members is a common means of expression in a democracy. Many persons in our labor force—about 19 million of them—obtain such expression through labor unions. Nearly 16 million of these workers belong to unions that are affiliated with one very large labor organization. This is the American Federation of Labor-Congress of Industrial Organizations, or the AFL-CIO. There are also powerful independent unions. The International Brotherhood of Teamsters, the United Mine Workers, the Brotherhood of Locomotive Engineers, and the United Auto Workers are some of them.

Before the 1800's, we were largely an agricultural economy. Most businesses were small. The owner of a business hired only a few workers, and he knew them personally. In the 1800's, the widespread use of machinery and mass production enabled businesses to grow larger and larger. Small shops mushroomed into large factories. When hundreds or perhaps thousands of workers were on the payroll, it was impossible for owners and managers to know each one personally.

In those times, many factory workers labored under conditions that we would consider unbearable. Work days of 12 or 14 hours were not unusual. Working conditions were very often unsanitary and sometimes unsafe. Women and children were often hired to do heavy, tiring work. Pay was frequently so low that workers could buy only the bare necessities. A worker who complained about such conditions was often fired. He was also usually blacklisted; that is, his name was circulated among other businesses

WORKERS UNITE TO ADVANCE THEIR INTERESTS

THE START AND GROWTH OF LABOR UNIONS

as being a troublemaker. If employees banded together to express their discontent, they were at times prosecuted in the courts. Some of the early conflicts between employers and employees were violent.

Despite opposition, groups of employees kept trying to improve their working conditions. They gained strength and wider coverage when the AFL was established in 1886. In 1935 a group broke away from the AFL and formed the CIO, but the two were reunited in 1955.

In 1935 the legal status of unions in the United States was firmly established. That year saw the passage of the National Labor Relations Act, sometimes called the Wagner Act. It affirms the right of employees to join unions. It provides that employees have the right to hold fair elections to determine which union they want. It also states that employees have the right to select representatives from their unions to make agreements with employers about working conditions.

TODAY'S LABOR UNIONS HAVE GREAT INFLUENCE

Employees were not always right in their earlier conflicts with employers. But there is justice in the idea that labor unions were needed to resolve differences with employers. Now most people support the basic purposes and activities of unions. Owners and managers of large businesses cannot know each employee personally. The union serves as a means of communication between employees and management.

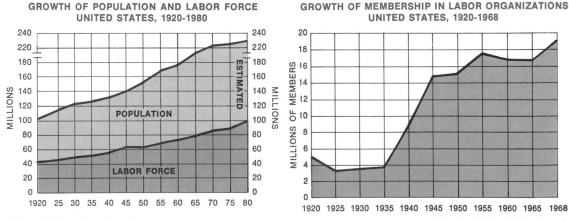

GROWTH OF POPULATION AND LABOR FORCE
UNITED STATES, 1920-1980

Illus. 49-2. Growth of population and labor force in the U.S.

GROWTH OF MEMBERSHIP IN LABOR ORGANIZATIONS
UNITED STATES, 1920-1968

Illus. 49-3. Growth of membership in labor unions in the U.S.

UNIT 10 / GOVERNMENT, BUSINESS, AND LABOR

In recent years unions have succeeded in attracting to membership groups of workers who used to show little interest in unions. For example, it is estimated that more than two million government employees now belong to unions. Ten years ago, only about one million were union members. Workers holding white-collar jobs are joining unions in greater numbers. Also, the number of women belonging to unions continues to increase.

Labor unions have become so powerful that laws have been passed to regulate their power. For example, one provision of the Taft-Hartley Act of 1947 forbids a *closed shop* agreement. This means that it forbids a shop in which only members of a union may be hired by the employer. The law does permit a *union shop* agreement. This means that an employer may hire employees who are not union members but that they must join the union within a specified time. In 1959 another law was passed to regulate the administration of unions. The object of legislation passed in recent years is to protect workers' rights while preventing unfair practices on the part of unions.

WAYS IN WHICH UNIONS HELP THEIR MEMBERS

The main objectives of labor unions have been to get for their members higher wages, fewer hours in the standard work week, and safer and more pleasant working conditions. To assure that workers have continued economic well-being, unions often insist that an *escalator clause* be included in long-term agreements with employers. This clause, sometimes called a cost-of-living clause, specifies that a wage adjustment will be made as the cost of living rises during the contract period. This helps protect the worker against inflation.

Providing job security for members is another major concern of unions. Much unemployment is due to changes in business conditions. When business is good, many persons are employed to produce the goods and services the public demands. But when business is poor, there is less need for so many workers, and some are laid off. Also, some employment is seasonal. In some fields, there is more demand for workers during one time of year than another. For example, more salespeople are needed during the Christmas season than at any other time. Some unemployment is caused by changes in technology. For example, a new machine may be invented which will do the work of several employees.

Unions try to get job security for their members in several ways. They try to persuade employers not to discharge suddenly large numbers of employees. Unions may try to get employers to agree to retrain workers and place them in other jobs. Unions may urge employers to guarantee their workers enough employment to earn a minimum annual income. Unions also strive for employers to recognize seniority rights, to consider the length of time a worker has been with the company.

In recent years, unions have given more attention to gaining for their members compensation other than salary or wages. The *fringe benefits* they bargain for include sick leave with pay, paid vacations, life and health insurance, pensions, profit-sharing plans in which the employees share in the company's earnings, paid holidays, and free health services on the job. Unions have also worked for the passage of legislation which provides other benefits for workers. By lobbying and by supporting candidates for political office, unions have prompted the passage of laws providing for workmen's compensation, social security, and unemployment insurance.

HOW UNIONS GET RESULTS

Suppose that an employee in a large company is not satisfied with his wages or working conditions. If he presents his complaints in person to the employer, he may not get much consideration. If he says he will quit, the employer may not be concerned. He can usually hire someone who will be satisfied with the present arrangements. A worker usually cannot get very far with individual bargaining.

On the other hand, if many workers present a united front, employers will generally hear their complaints. Negotiations between an organized body of workers and an employer, dealing with wages and working conditions, is called *collective bargaining*. If differences cannot be resolved through collective bargaining, the employees may threaten to *strike* and refuse to return to work until their demands are met. The strike is a powerful weapon of organized labor because it brings production to a halt. In many industries, most or all of the factory employees are members of unions. Work stoppage by a strike seriously affects both the business and the employee.

Illus. 49-4. Collective bargaining is an important tool of labor unions.

During a strike, employees may apply pressure through *picketing.* Union members carry signs telling the public that the company is "unfair to labor." Many union members and others who sympathize with the union will refuse to deal with the business that is being picketed. Sometimes union members will refuse to transport and handle or buy the products of a business involved in a labor dispute with another union. This action is a *boycott.*

Because strikes are so costly to both workers and employers, both groups prefer to settle their differences through compromise. They often have long periods of bargaining in an attempt to establish a union contract between the two groups. If the representatives of the employees and the employer cannot reach an agreement, they may ask an outsider to act as an umpire or *arbitrator.* They agree to abide by his decision.

Day-to-day complaints are usually settled through grievance procedures that have been agreed upon and included in the union contract. A union member's grievance is presented to his supervisor by the union representative, or *steward.* If the grievance cannot be settled, it is taken to a higher management level. If it still cannot be settled, most union contracts call for an arbitrator to decide the case.

WORKERS AND BUSINESS FIRMS ARE PARTNERS IN PRODUCTION

When representatives of labor unions and of business firms sit around a conference table to bargain, they usually realize that they must agree on certain basic points. Both sides want the firm to be successful. If it is not, it will not be able to pay dividends to owners, pay adequate wages to employees, or expand and create new jobs. With few exceptions, both sides want to safeguard the freedoms that characterize our economic system.

Intelligent employers and employees realize that they are in active partnership. One cannot survive without the other. If we are to continue to be a strong nation, conflicts between employers and employees must be kept to a minimum. Management and employees often have differences, but fortunately they strive to resolve their differences peacefully around the bargaining table.

Developing Your Business Vocabulary

The following italicized terms should become part of your business vocabulary. For each numbered statement, find the italicized term that has the same meaning.

arbitrator *labor*
boycott *labor force*
closed shop *picketing*
collective bargaining *steward*
escalator clause *strike*
fringe benefits *union shop*

1. All mental and physical effort directed toward the production of goods and services.
2. All persons 16 or older who are working or looking for work.
3. An agreement to employ only persons who are already members of a union.
4. An agreement requiring workers to join a union within a specified time after employment.
5. A provision in a union contract calling for wage increases as the cost of living rises.
6. Things such as pensions, vacations, and insurance that are granted to employees in addition to wages.
7. The method by which representatives of employers and employees reach decisions about wages and working conditions.

8. A work stoppage by employees in order to compel an employer to yield to workers' demands.
9. The placement of union members before a place of business to urge workers and the public not to deal with the business.
10. Combining in refusing to have dealings with a person or business.
11. A person chosen to settle a dispute between employer and employees.
12. A union representative in the shop.

Checking Your Understanding

1. Why is labor so important a factor in the productive process of a nation?
2. Who is included in the U.S. labor force? Who is not?
3. Name five or more groups, other than workers in labor unions, that have formed associations. Which of these organizations are likely to have members in your community?
4. What conditions in the past have contributed to the rise and growth of unions?
5. What is the AFL-CIO?
6. What is another name for the Wagner Act? Why is this act of special importance to workers?
7. The Taft-Hartley Act forbids a closed shop agreement but permits a union shop agreement. What is the main difference between these agreements?
8. Why do unions give so much attention to job security for their members? How do they try to obtain job security for their members?
9. Prepare a list of benefits that unions have helped obtain for workers. Have workers who are not members of organized unions shared in these benefits? Explain.
10. Why is collective bargaining more effective than individual bargaining?
11. Why do both workers and employers generally prefer to settle disputes by collective bargaining rather than by strikes or other tactics?

Applying What You Have Learned

1. Some people are considered part of our total labor force; some are not. Tell whether each individual described on page 578 is or is not considered part of the labor force.

(a) A college student not engaged in outside work.
(b) A nightclub singer.
(c) The French Ambassador stationed in Washington.
(d) An airline stewardess.
(e) A bank president.
(f) A machinist out of work because of a union strike.
(g) A U.S. soldier stationed in Europe.
(h) A housewife.
(i) The President of the United States.
(j) A writer of mystery stories.
(k) An 18-year-old high school graduate interviewing for a job.
(l) A retired businessman.
(m) A dentist.
(n) Your teacher.
(o) A disc jockey.
(p) A farmer.

2. The workers at the Green Mountain Manufacturing Company are on strike. What groups, other than the workers and the owners of this company, are affected by the strike? In what ways?

3. Some persons claim that government workers, since they are public servants and may hold jobs upon which public safety depends, should not have the right to strike. What do you think?

4. The drivers for a large trucking firm are engaged in a dispute with the management of the firm. They threaten to strike unless their demands are met. Management officials, like the truck drivers, are employees and are part of the labor force of this firm. Would it not be reasonable and fair, therefore, for management to support the drivers, even to the point of joining them in a strike, rather than to oppose them? Explain.

5. "Workers and employers should solve their own problems without any interference from government." Do you agree with this statement? Explain.

Solving Business Problems

1. Assume that in the community in which you live and work, there are 22,500 persons, of whom 13,700 are members of the labor force. Of those in the labor force, 3,690 are members of a labor union. Membership is distributed as shown in the table on page 579. The table also shows the percent of change in membership over last year. Study the table, then answer the questions on page 579.

Employees	Present Membership	% Change Over Last Year
Automobile workers	700	+4.2%
Retail clerks	820	+6.9
State, county, and municipal employees	490	−0.4
Federal government employees	275	+3.8
Teachers	348	+2.1
Laborers	1,057	+5.9

(a) What percent of the persons in the community are members of the labor force?

(b) What percent of the persons in the labor force are members of labor unions?

(c) If the present membership figures include the increase in membership over a year ago, what was the membership in the three largest unions at that time?

2. Listed below are the hourly wages for building trade journeymen in eight cities as of 1969. These are the average union wage rates agreed upon through collective bargaining.

Atlanta, Georgia	$5.39
Chicago, Illinois	6.19
Cleveland, Ohio	7.15
Dallas, Texas	5.32
Jacksonville, Florida	4.78
Milwaukee, Wisconsin	5.86
San Francisco, California	6.50
Newark, New Jersey	6.51

(a) What is the average hourly wage rate for building trade journeymen in these eight cities?

(b) In terms of percent, how much greater is the highest wage than the lowest wage?

(c) Assume that a worker in each of these cities works an average of 40 hours a week for a full year at the pay rates given above. Each receives 2 weeks vacation with pay. What were the yearly earnings of the one receiving the highest pay? The lowest pay? What was the difference between the two?

3. The U.S. Department of Labor reports that in a recent month there were 85,000,000 persons in the labor force. Of this number, 3,000,000 were unemployed. Strikes accounted for 132,000 of those unemployed.

(a) What percent of the labor force was out of work?

(b) What percent of the labor force was unemployed because of strikes?

(c) What percent of the unemployed was out of work because of strikes?

Enriching Your Business Understanding

1. American unions are organized basically as craft (or trade) unions or as industrial unions. Check with your school or public librarian for references describing these two kinds of unions. Explain the differences between each and give examples of each type of union.

2. Discuss the questions below with acquaintances who are members of labor unions. Summarize in writing the information you receive from your discussions and be prepared to give an oral report to the class.

   (a) What social and welfare advantages does the union provide for its members?

   (b) What does it cost to maintain membership in the union?

   (c) What voice does the membership have in the operation of the local union? In the national union?

3. Listed below are a number of terms that are frequently used in conversations and news stories about the activities of American workers. Some of these terms have very interesting origins. Find out what you can about these terms and be prepared to explain their usage to the class.

   (a) featherbedding
   (b) layoff
   (c) lobbying
   (d) mediation
   (e) right-to-work law

   (f) secondary boycott
   (g) seniority
   (h) scab
   (i) strikebreaker
   (j) wildcat strike

4. Make an appointment to talk with a union representative about that union's contract with a particular employer. Find out: (a) the length of time the contract is to run; (b) whether grievance procedure is set forth; (c) whether the contract includes an escalator clause; and (d) what new provisions appear in the contract that were not included in the last one the union had with the company.

PART 50
World Trade And Our Economy

Every day people buy hundreds of things—food, clothing, cars, magazines, insurance, tickets to football games, TV sets, and many other items. Other people sell these goods and services. This buying and selling is called *trade*. If you want to trade, you must find someone who has what you want. You must also have what he wants. And the two of you must agree on values.

The buying and selling of goods and services goes on continuously throughout the world. But all of the goods sold in a particular community may not be produced in that community. In fact, a community probably provides very few items for itself. Like individuals, communities are interdependent.

Suppose a person in Lincoln, Nebraska, buys a car from his local dealer. The car was probably manufactured in Detroit. But the heater, battery, tires, and others parts may have been produced in communities in other states. And many of the materials used to make these parts may have come from other nations. For example, all the natural rubber used in making the tires may have come from Malaysia.

You can see that the customer in Lincoln, Nebraska, would not have had his car if it were not for trade among communities in the United States and trade between the United States and other countries. Trade among people and businesses in the same country is called *domestic trade*. Trade among different countries is called *world trade* or *international trade*.

TAKING ADVANTAGE OF ADVANTAGES

What did some members of your family have for breakfast this morning? Coffee, cereal, and sliced bananas, perhaps? But they might have had only cereal if it were not for our trading with Brazil for the coffee and with Honduras for the bananas. The sugar on your table may have come from the Philippines. Even the paper your morning newspaper was printed on may have come from Canada.

Our country has many natural resources, a skilled labor force, and modern machines and methods of production. Yet we are not self-sufficient. We go beyond our borders to get many things we need and want. We have carried on trade with as many as 150 foreign countries in one year. Why do we trade with other countries? To answer this question, let's first look at why there is trade among different sections of our own country.

The various sections of our country have certain unique assets. These assets may be such things as climate, deposits of natural resources, rich soil, or a favorable location. These unique assets enable a state or a region to produce a certain good or service of higher quality or at a lower cost than another state or region. A state or region which can produce a product more efficiently than another state or region can is said to have a *comparative advantage*. Florida has a comparative advantage over Wisconsin for growing oranges. Hawaii has a comparative advantage over Ohio for growing pineapples. Washington has a comparative advantage over Wyoming for catching and canning fish.

Trade allows each state or region to specialize—to devote most of its resources to producing the kind of goods it produces best. Florida grows the oranges and leaves the cheese-making to Wisconsin. Hawaii grows pineapples and leaves the tire-making to Ohio. Washington catches and cans the fish and leaves the sheep-raising to Wyoming. And each state exchanges its special products for the special products of other states. What is the result for us as consumers? We benefit by having many different kinds of products that are generally better in quality and lower in price than if each state or region tried to supply most of the things its people need.

These trade advantages hold true also for the nations of the world. Many nations have unique assets that give them comparative advantages for certain products. Brazil has a comparative advantage over the United States in the production of coffee; Honduras, a comparative advantage in growing bananas. And, compared with these and many other countries, we have a comparative advantage in the production of cars. Because of trade, nations can specialize in the kind of production they do best. And consumers everywhere benefit.

THE IMPORTANCE OF OUR IMPORTS

As consumers, we want many goods that we do not produce in our country. Many products in our country are not produced in sufficient quantity to satisfy our needs and wants. But, thanks to world trade, we can have these products.

Those things we buy from other countries are called *imports.* Imports account for our total supply of bananas, coffee, cocoa, spices, tea, silk, and crude rubber. About half the fish we buy comes from other countries. Imports also account for 20 to 50% of our supplies of carpets and rugs, sugar, leather gloves, dishes, and sewing machines. To keep making industrial and consumer goods, we depend on importing tin, chrome, manganese, nickel, copper, zinc, and several other metals.

Prudential-Grace Lines

Illus. 50-1. Many products move in world trade by means of oceangoing freighters such as this.

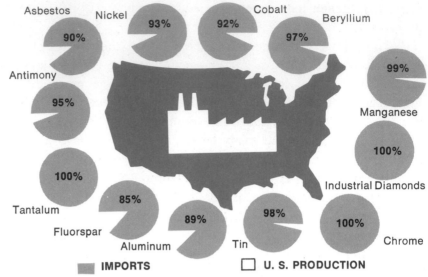

Illus. 50-2. The United States produces only small amounts of many minerals and metals that are needed in our industries. This illustration shows how essential strategic imports are.

Asbestos 90%
Nickel 93%
Cobalt 92%
Beryllium 97%
Manganese 99%
Antimony 95%
Tantalum 100%
Fluorspar 85%
Aluminum 89%
Tin 98%
Industrial Diamonds 100%
Chrome

■ **IMPORTS**   □ **U. S. PRODUCTION**

If we could not import certain raw materials, we would have to do without many of the products we use today. Without world trade, many of the things we want and need would cost more than they do now. Because of the principle of comparative advantage, we can buy goods from other nations at prices lower than we would have to charge if we produced the same goods.

Many of us prefer to buy certain imported goods—even at higher prices—because of their uniqueness or quality. For example, you may like the taste of imported Dutch chocolates better than the American brands. So you may buy from the Dutch producers even though their costs are higher. Or perhaps you are willing to pay more for a German-made microscope or a Swiss-made watch because you have confidence in the quality and workmanship of these products.

THE IMPORTANCE OF OUR EXPORTS

The goods and services we sell to other countries are called *exports*. Just as imports benefit us, exports benefit the peoples of other countries. People in nations throughout the world run their factories with machinery made in the United States. They till their land and harvest their crops with American-made implements. They eat food made from many of our agricultural products. They use our chemicals, commercial fertilizers, medicines, and plastics. They see our movies and read a good deal of our printed matter.

Two segments of our economy—machinery and agriculture—are especially dependent on selling in foreign markets. Our exports in the machinery and transport equipment field include diesel engines, buses, tractors, oil-drilling rigs, earth-moving equipment, jet planes, computers, and air conditioning and refrigeration equipment. Large amounts of farm products are also sold abroad each year. Farmers who grow such crops as tobacco, cotton, wheat, and rice depend on selling in foreign markets.

The jobs and incomes of millions of American workers depend directly on our success in exporting. And the profits of many businesses depend in part on the demands of other countries for our products.

Suppose that each of our 50 states had a different kind of money, each with a different value. Imagine the trouble you would have in traveling through New England if you had to change your "Massachusetts Money" into "Rhode Island Money" and then into "Connecticut Money." Or if you lived in Chicago and were ordering products from Oregon, you would need to convert your "Illinois Money" into "Oregon Money" to make payment. This is what we must do when we travel in or trade with other countries. It is one reason why world trade is so much more complicated than domestic trade.

HOW WE PAY FOR FOREIGN TRADE

Each nation has its own type of money and its own banking system. In the United States, we use dollars; Mexico uses pesos; France, francs; India, rupees; and so on. When American businessmen buy olive oil from Italy, for example, arrangements are made to change American dollars into liras, the Italian money. If you were to visit Spain, you would need to obtain pesetas to pay for meals and other expenses. When Spanish people come to this country, they need to change their pesetas into dollars.

Because of the differences in value of the monies of the world, rates of exchange are established among countries. The *rate of exchange* is the value of the money of one country expressed in terms of the money of another country. If the Mexican peso is listed as .08, this means that the peso is worth 8¢ in our money and that an American dollar could be changed into 12½ pesos. The approximate values of the currencies of several foreign countries on a recent date are given on page 586.

Country	Money Unit	Value in U. S. Money
Canada	Dollar	98¢
England	Pound	$2.40
India	Rupee	13¢
Japan	Yen	28/100 of a cent
Portugal	Escudo	3.5¢
Venezuela	Bolivar	23¢
West Germany	Deutsche mark	27.5¢

The problem of foreign exchange is solved by the foreign exchange market, which is comprised mainly of banks from around the world. The banks are willing to buy and sell the currencies of the various countries. They provide the needed—and often very complex—services which allow traders to make and receive payments.

OUR BALANCE OF TRADE AND BALANCE OF PAYMENTS

An expression often used in world trade is *balance of trade.* This simply means the difference between the amount of a country's merchandise exports and the amount of its merchandise imports. If a country sells more to other countries than it buys from them, it is said to have a favorable balance of trade. If it buys more than it sells, it is said to have an unfavorable balance of trade.

For a number of years, the United States has had a favorable balance of trade. In a recent year, for example, our merchandise exports totaled over $36 billion and our merchandise imports totaled over $35 billion. This gave us a favorable balance of trade of about $1 billion. However, we should not assume that we have a financial advantage over other countries because of our favorable balance of trade. Instead, to get a better picture of our financial condition in world trade, we need to consider all transactions with other countries.

If we know the dollar value of all our economic transactions with foreign countries, we can find our *balance of payments.* **This** is the difference between our total payments to other countries and our total receipts from other countries. Included in our payments and receipts are all purchases of imports, all sales of exports, money spent and earned on travel, military expenditures overseas, loans to and money borrowed from foreigners, and other such transactions.

If, after adding up all these transactions, we find that we are spending more in other countries than we are receiving, we say that we have a deficit in our balance of payments. If we were receiving more than we were spending, we would have a surplus in our balance of payments. Just as you try to balance your spending with your earnings, so do countries try to balance their spending with earnings.

BALANCE OF PAYMENTS OF THE UNITED STATES, 1969
(IN BILLIONS OF DOLLARS)

PAYMENTS		EXPLANATION OR EXAMPLE
Imports of merchandise	$35.8	Our purchases of bananas, tin, cars, etc., from foreign countries.
Travel	3.4	American tourists spending money abroad.
Purchase of services	11.1	American using foreign airlines and ships, etc.
Payment for foreign investment	4.5	Profits, interest, dividends earned on foreign investments in the United States and returned abroad.
Foreign aid	3.8	United States economic aid to other countries.
Private investment	5.4	United States businesses building factories overseas; United States citizens buying foreign stocks and bonds and putting their money in foreign bank accounts.
Transactions unaccounted for	2.9	Errors and omissions in collecting the statistics.
TOTAL PAYMENTS	$66.9	
RECEIPTS		**EXPLANATION OR EXAMPLE**
Export of merchandise	$36.5	Sale of machinery, computers, wheat, etc., to countries.
Travel	2.1	Foreigners spending money in the United States as tourists.
Export of services	9.1	Foreigners using our ships, airlines, etc.
Income from foreign investment	7.9	Profits, interest, dividends earned on United States investments abroad and returned to the United States.
Foreign investment in the United States	4.1	Foreign businesses and individuals investing money in the United States.
TOTAL RECEIPTS	$59.7	
EXCESS OF PAYMENTS OVER RECEIPTS	$ 7.2	The deficit in our balance of payments.

Illus. 50-3. The balance of payments of the United States.

THERE ARE BARRIERS IN WORLD TRADE

In the United States, people are free to trade in any of the 50 states. Almost no barriers are placed in the way of trade from one state to another. The most important restriction on trade among nations is the tariff. As you learned in Part 47, this is a tax which a government places on imported products. Suppose you wanted to buy a bicycle made in England. The English bike producer sets a price of $60. Our government places a 20% tariff

($12) on the bike when it is imported. If the shipping charges are $10, you must pay $82 for a bike which would cost only $60 in England.

The $12 tariff which you would pay on the bike would go to our government. Some governments use the tariff as a means of raising revenue. But in most industrialized countries, tariffs bring in only a very small part of total government revenue. Tariffs are generally used as a means of protection. Tariffs are included in the price consumers pay for imported goods. This can mean that the price of the imported goods will be higher than the price of goods of domestic producers. Imposing tariffs can thus reduce the amount of imported goods that consumers will buy. In our bicycle example, if a bike of comparable quality is made and sold in this country for $75, you will probably buy it rather than the $82 English bike. But what if there were no $12 tariff on the English bike? You might well prefer to buy it at the $70 price.

There are several reasons why protection from imports is desired. A government may want to protect those industries which produce goods necessary for national defense. If a country depends entirely on imports for its supply of certain products, such as steel, that supply might be cut off in wartime. Therefore, the government may wish to protect with tariffs an industry which is important to national defense, even though the industry may not produce as cheaply as the same industry in other countries.

Another reason for imposing tariffs is to protect new industries. When new industries get started, they usually cannot produce as efficiently as established ones. So they may have trouble competing against more efficient producers in other countries. Nations often set up tariff barriers to give "infant industries" the protection they need to get started.

Still another reason for our tariffs is that they protect American workers. Some people argue that without tariffs on imports from countries where labor costs are low, our producers might have to reduce wages in order to compete in price. Thus, it is said, our workers would either get lower incomes or perhaps lose their jobs. On the other hand, it is argued that the important point is not how high the hourly or daily wages are but how productive the worker is.

TRADING PARTNERS OF THE UNITED STATES

1969 EXPORTS TO (MILLIONS)	COUNTRY	1969 IMPORTS FROM (MILLIONS)
$9,138	Canada	$10,390
3,490	Japan	4,888
2,335	United Kingdom	2,121
2,118	West Germany	2,603
1,450	Mexico	1,029
1,262	Italy	1,204
1,195	France	843
708	Venezuela	940
672	Brazil	616
605	Switzerland	452
517	India	344
477	Sweden	355
374	Philippines	423
303	Colombia	240
205	Denmark	250
118	Ireland	123
106	Soviet Union	52

Illus. 50-4. Some of the trading partners of the United States.

There are other barriers to foreign trade which are not classed as tariffs. One example is the *import quota*. This is a limit on the amount of a given commodity that may be imported within a given period of time. Our government has placed quotas on such goods as sugar, cattle, petroleum products, and dairy products. Some countries also have buying regulations, licensing requirements, and laws to control their imports.

WORLD TRADE IS TWO-WAY STREET

We need many kinds of products from other countries, and they in turn need products from us. But we cannot for long sell our goods to other nations unless we are also willing to buy their goods. Since other countries need dollars to pay for our goods, and the principal means of obtaining dollars is by selling their products to us, trade must be a two-way street.

As we develop good trading relationships with other countries, we also have the opportunity to strengthen our friendship with those countries. By exchanging films, dramatic and musical productions, books, magazines, and other goods and services, nations can learn more about each other. By exporting machinery and modern equipment, we can help other countries raise their styles of living. In its broadest sense, international trade can help to develop better understanding and greater respect among peoples of the world.

Developing Your Business Vocabulary

The following italicized terms should become part of your business vocabulary. For each numbered statement, find the italicized term that has the same meaning.

balance of payments   import quota
balance of trade   imports
comparative advantage   rate of exchange
domestic trade   trade
exports   world trade or international trade

1. The buying and selling of goods and services.
2. The buying and selling of goods and services among people and businesses within the same country.
3. Trade that is carried on among different countries.
4. The ability or capacity of a state or country to produce certain things more efficiently or suitably than can be done in another state or country.
5. Goods and services we buy from other countries.
6. Goods and services we sell to other countries.
7. The price paid in the currency of one country for a unit of the currency of another country.
8. The difference in value between the merchandise exports and the merchandise imports of a country.
9. The relationship between our total payments to other countries and our total receipts from other countries.
10. A limit on the amount of a particular commodity that may be imported into a country during a specified period of time.

Checking Your Understanding

1. "Like individuals, communities are interdependent." Do you agree with this statement? What does it mean to you?
2. Explain how both domestic and international trade are involved in the production and sale of an automobile, or some other commodity of your choice.
3. What examples can you offer to show that there is regional specialization of production in the United States? In the world?

4. How do the questions in the preceding exercise relate or apply to the concept of comparative advantage?
5. We buy products from foreign countries for basically the same reasons foreign countries buy from us. Can you give three good reasons to explain why people of one country buy goods from other countries?
6. What two segments of our economy are particularly dependent on international trade?
7. Under what conditions may a country be said to have a favorable balance of trade?
8. In international business, is a nation's balance of trade the same as its balance of payments? Explain.
9. Various barriers have been set up which tend to limit international trade. Mention two such barriers and explain how each works.
10. State four reasons that are given by some countries for imposing tariffs on imports.
11. In order to thrive, why does world trade need to be a "two-way street"?

Applying What You Have Learned

1. Explain how world trade contributes to a higher level of living for many people in various countries.
2. Suppose the United States was completely self-sufficient. Would it make good sense for us as a highly productive nation to follow a policy of exporting our goods and not importing anything?
3. An American manufacturer of electric toasters wishes to sell his product to the people of Turkey. Can you think of some of the difficulties that this businessman might have in entering the Turkish market?
4. What are "infant industries"? Give a few examples of such industries. Should an infant industry be protected by a high tariff? If so, for how long?
5. Robert Webber maintains that we should impose high tariffs on compact cars that are imported from other countries. Give arguments in support of Mr. Webber's position. Can you also offer a few arguments against such tariffs?
6. In each of several recent years, the United States has had a favorable balance of trade but at the same time an unfavorable (or deficit in) balance of payments. What are some possible causes for these plus and minus differences? (A study of Illustration 50-3 on page 587 will help you answer this question.)

Solving Business Problems

1. Assume that a tourist pays the amounts stated below for certain goods and services in selected countries. For each expenditure, give the equivalent cost in U.S. money. Indicate also whether you feel that the value received is high, about the same, or low when compared with similar purchases in your community. (Refer to the table on rates of exchange on page 586.)

   (a) In Portugal, 40 escudos for a full-course dinner.
   (b) In India, 3 rupees for an American (imported) bar of soap.
   (c) In Japan, 1,650 yen for one ticket to a movie theater.
   (d) In Venezuela, 3 bolivars for dry cleaning of a suit.
   (e) In West Germany, 10 deutsche marks for a man's haircut.
   (f) In England, 18 pounds for a hotel room for three days.

2. In a recent year, U.S. merchandise exports amounted to $30,470,000,000; and its imports, $26,990,000,000. During this same year, total receipts from all transactions (including the exports) amounted to $50,830,000,000. Total U.S. payments for all transactions (including the imports) amounted to $53,870,000,000. From these world trade figures, determine the following:

   (a) Did the U.S. have a favorable or unfavorable balance of trade? In what amount?
   (b) Was there a deficit or a surplus in our balance of payments? In what amount?

3. Refer again to Problem #2. During the year in question, Americans traveling in other countries spent $3,200,000,000. If for some reason none of us would have been permitted to travel outside the U.S. during that year, how would our balance of payments have been affected? What would have been the revised amount?

4. Copy the table on page 593 on a separate sheet or refer to the same table in your *Activities and Projects*. Complete the table by (a) adding a line at the bottom for Totals and (b) adding a column at the right of the table with the heading "U.S. Balance."

   Analyze and interpret the data in the completed table by responding to the following questions:

   (a) What is the total of all imports? Of all exports?
   (b) What is the balance of trade for each merchandise group? In the added columns, place a (—) before each figure that shows an unfavorable balance; place a (+) before each figure that shows a favorable balance.
   (c) For total merchandise imports and exports, did we have a favorable or an unfavorable balance of trade? What was the amount?

UNIT 10 / GOVERNMENT, BUSINESS, AND LABOR

(d) What group of merchandise made up the largest amount of our exports? How much was this?

(e) What single merchandise group accounted for the largest unfavorable balance of trade? What was the amount of the unfavorable balance?

(f) What single merchandise group accounted for the largest favorable balance of trade? What was the amount?

U.S. Imports and Exports by Merchandise Groups for a Recent Year (000,000's omitted)		
Merchandise	Imports	Exports
Food and live animals, including animal and vegetable oils and fats	$ 4,740	$ 4,160
Beverages and tobacco	790	700
Crude materials, inedible, except fuels ..	3,350	3,540
Minerals, fuels, and related materials ...	2,530	1,060
Chemicals	1,140	3,290
Machinery and transport equipment	7,990	14,460
Other manufactured goods	11,500	6,090
Other transactions, including estimates for low-value shipments	1,220	930

Source: *Statistical Abstract of the United States.*

Enriching Your Business Understanding

1. Review your family's food purchases over the past few weeks and look through the stock of food supplies that may presently be on hand. Make a list of the ingredients that you believe were probably imported. Indicate, too, where some of these items might have come from. How seriously would your meals be affected if imports of these items were suddenly completely stopped?

2. On page 584 is a chart showing how dependent the United States is on other countries for certain important minerals and metals. Work with your teacher in selecting some or all of the materials listed. Describe briefly—in nontechnical terms—what the product is and give examples of its use in our economy. Also try to find out from what countries we obtain each of these materials.

3. Divide into small committees of three or four students. Arrange to talk with local business people who have knowledge of the kinds of goods imported for sale in your community. These business

people may be owners of small stores or department managers or buyers in large firms. Make a list of up to 20 commodities that are imported by a business such as the following: drugstore, gift shop, music store, delicatessen, sporting goods store, women's apparel department, or grocery store.

Whenever possible, indicate the country from which each item was imported. Also try to find out the amount of tariff that may have been levied. (Work closely with your teacher in planning these committee projects. He may approve of other types of businesses to survey and advise you on how to obtain and organize your information.)

4. What are reciprocal trade agreements? Do you feel it is in the interest of international goodwill for countries to enter into such agreements? Why?

5. What is the European Economic Community (EEC), which is better known as the Common Market? What are the member countries? What is the purpose of the Common Market? (Work with your teacher in preparing either a written report or an outline for an oral report.)

6. Reproduced below is a Foreign Exchange listing for September 9, 1970, given in U.S. dollars and decimals of a dollar:

Argentina, peso ...	$ .2520	Israel, pound	.2875
Australia, dollar ...	1.1155	Italy, lira	.0016
Brazil, cruzeiro ...	.2170	Japan, yen	.0028
Canada, dollar	.9841	Mexico, peso	.0801
France, franc	.1813	Norway, krone	.1400
Great Britain, pound	2.3890	Philippines, peso ...	.1600
Holland, guilder ...	.2780	South Africa, rand .	1.3915
Hong Kong, dollar .	.1650	Spain, peseta	.0144
Iraq, dinar	2.8300	Switzerland, franc ..	.2325

Examine the financial page of the current edition of a large city newspaper (or *The Wall Street Journal*) and locate the Foreign Exchange section. From the information in the above listing and from your current paper, prepare a five-column chart showing for each country the information indicated by the headings below:

FOREIGN EXCHANGE				
Country	*Monetary Unit*	*Exchange Rate Sept. 9, 1970*	*Exchange Rate (latest date)*	*Difference in rates (+ or —)*

Unit 11

Living and Working in Our Economy

PART 51
Looking At Your Work Motives

Why do we work? One answer to this question is simple. We work to earn a living, to supply ourselves with the essentials of life: food, clothing, and housing. If nature had supplied primitive man with pleasant weather all year round or with warm, comfortable caves, he would not have had to build shelters for himself and his family. If there had been plenty of food and water outside each cave entrance, man would not have had to work for his food by hunting, fishing, or planting crops. If he had not been threatened by wild animals, he would not have had to work to make weapons to protect himself. But man was forced to work to survive. As he worked to protect himself and to supply his wants, he moved out of his primitive state.

Survival is still the main reason why people work. But in a modern, industrialized country like ours, there are other reasons why people work. There is more to working than just making money.

Most people today look for work which gives them more than just enough money to live on. All of us want to be comfortable and to enjoy some luxuries. We are not satisfied to live as our grandparents lived. We all want cars, TV sets, freezers, air conditioners, and many other things to add to our comfort. We

SOME REASONS WHY WE WORK

want to travel and to have good entertainment. Most of us work to attain a better style of living.

But most of us want other things, not measured in dollars and cents, from our work. People work to provide a living for themselves and their families, but they also work: (1) for personal satisfaction, (2) for recognition, (3) to be of service to others, and (4) for security. These rewards are often called *psychic income*.

(1) The person who enjoys his work is fortunate. He probably has the energy and the initiative to do his job well. He likes to go to work and is not bored by it. His efforts give him personal satisfaction. For example, the secretary takes pride in knowing that her thoughtfulness in scheduling appointments helped her boss through a busy day. The good salesman takes pride in knowing that he helped his customer buy exactly what was needed at the right price. The bookkeeper gets satisfaction in knowing that his financial statements are accurate. The craftsman is proud of the product he has made or the repair he has done. Most of us, then, work partly for personal satisfaction.

(2) Many people work for the recognition that may come to them. Recognition on the job may be in the form of praise from supervisors, promotions, salary raises, or certificates of merit. Some people like to work in occupations where they receive recognition from others—in medicine, law, or teaching, for example. For others, the self-recognition of knowing they have done a job well is enough.

(3) Many people work because they want to be of service to others. In this group are nurses, teachers, social workers, and clergymen. People in other types of jobs also can feel that they are of service to others. Salesmen, office receptionists, repairmen, contractors, and many other workers can take pride in helping others.

(4) People also work for security, to earn enough income so that they can be self-supporting throughout life. People now are living much longer than they used to; the period of retirement is longer. Elderly people, like all others, prefer to be independent—to go where they please and to do as they please. While they are young, persons should make some plans to provide for independent old age.

Some people think that having many material goods is all there is to working and living. But real success is measured in more than just a good income to buy the things you want. Success in living and working involves accepting four basic responsibilities for: (1) development of self, (2) participation in *civic* affairs, (3) improvement of human relationships, and (4) economic awareness.

(1) A person owes it to himself and others to develop his abilities through education and training. This involves deciding upon a career, planning his education, getting the job he wants, and working hard at it. But self-improvement means more than this. It means developing hobbies, being aware of current events, and learning to appreciate fine art, music, and literature. It also means recognizing that all activities operate on the highest level when governed by what is basically right and wrong.

(2) You are familiar with the statement "government of the people, by the people, for the people." This is exactly what democracy means. But democracy can work only as citizens take part in government. They can do this by discussing political issues, by joining in local civic programs, and above all by expressing themselves at the ballot box. The person who fails to do these things has little right to complain about civic conditions that do not suit him.

(3) It is very difficult—perhaps impossible—to live an isolated life. The world's population is increasing rapidly. In the past few years, you may have seen a number of new housing developments spring up in your community. The school population continues to grow. Within minutes, rapid means of communication bring to us events that are happening halfway around the globe. And within a few hours, jet planes can whisk us thousands of miles away to other places.

Our world is constantly growing smaller. If we are to live together in this shrinking world, we must work toward improving our relationships with all other people we contact. We must work especially on improving relationships with the people we contact most often outside of our family and friends: fellow citizens in our community, our employers, and our fellow workers.

In every community there is a lot of work to be done. A community may have problems relating to schools, equal housing for all, fair taxation, health conditions, rapid transportation facilities, parks and recreation facilities, and others. Such problems are solved only as citizens work together, learn to respect each other's points of view, and learn to live in harmony.

Persons should also strive to build good relationships with their employers. The success of any organization that employs people depends greatly upon their efficiency, cooperation, and loyalty. Both the employer and the employee depend on each other to perform business tasks. The employer wants to hire workers who fit into his organization and who earn their pay. The employee wants a job that will pay him a satisfactory income and will fulfill his other work needs.

In almost all jobs, we must work with other people. Offices, stores, factories—all have workers with different educational, religious, racial, and economic backgrounds. We must learn to work together. When we do our share and perhaps a little more, fellow workers tend to do the same.

Cheerfulness, a cooperative attitude, and a regard for others are qualities that help build good *human relations*. These qualities are especially important on certain occasions. For example, you may be asked to work overtime to finish an important job. You may have to do some extra work because another worker is sick. You may disagree with someone on such minor matters as room temperature, arrangement of equipment, and staggering of lunch hours and coffee breaks. Calmly discussing problems with fellow workers and supervisors will usually solve them.

For his own peace of mind, every employee should be interested in the work he is doing. If he is unhappy with his job, he should discuss his grievance with his supervisor. Perhaps he is in the wrong kind of work. This may mean that he should seek a transfer to another department or perhaps look for another type of job.

(4) No person, regardless of his occupation, can escape his economic responsibilities. Successful personal and family economics depends on earning a living. But you have already learned that just earning a living is not enough. The job one holds should give him other rewards.

The person with economic awareness understands many of the businessman's problems. The businessman must make decisions

Illus. 51-1. All workers in a business are members of a team. It is as a team that they are best able to produce the goods and services consumers want. Every worker should try to make his job pleasant and profitable for himself and his fellow workers.

Zenith Radio Corporation

about what and how much to produce and about where and how to sell his product. He is constantly faced with the problem of hiring good workers and of keeping them happy. He must find ways of raising money to start a business and to keep it operating. He must determine what prices to charge for products so that he can pay fair wages and make a reasonable profit.

To a great extent, our economic welfare depends on jobs being available to all qualified workers. Otherwise, persons will not be able to buy the goods and services they want. The aware citizen is concerned about matters that affect working opportunities and conditions. For example, if a strike occurs, employees may be out of work for some time. Businesses may be forced to shut down or to cut back production. The resulting shortages of goods can mean that consumers will have to do without some goods or pay higher prices for scarce items. Employees, employers, investors, and consumers all suffer from such a situation.

The aware citizen also understands that government provides services the public demands and that these services are paid for out of tax money. He understands that as the cost of services increase, taxes must increase—that we may have almost any government service we want but that we must pay for it. The aware citizen votes intelligently for laws that have merit and for public officials who seem honest and dependable.

OPPORTUNITIES EXIST IN MANY FIELDS OF WORK

A young man entering college was asked by his counselor what he wanted to study. The young man replied, "The field that has the most opportunities." What was wrong with his point of view?

The truth is that there are many opportunities in any field of work. They are there for those who are willing to prepare themselves and who are willing to work. For example, many people can play a guitar or a piano a little bit. But how many are willing to spend the time practicing every day to become really skillful? Many people can type fairly well. But how many are willing to spend the time and energy to become expert? The same is true of any other area of study, from mathematics to foreign languages to business administration. Of course, some persons can do some things better than others, but this is no excuse for accomplishing nothing. Every kind of job that produces useful goods and services is important. And in every job there are chances to do good work.

While it is true that there are opportunities in any field of work, you do need to use some care in choosing what you are going to do. There are certain areas of work that will probably always be with us: law, teaching, ministry, medicine, dentistry, and so on. But there are many other fields of work that are constantly developing. Hundreds of jobs that people work at today did not exist a quarter of a century ago. There are opportunities everywhere for young people. In the rest of this unit, you will learn about some of them.

Developing Your Business Vocabulary

The following italicized terms should become part of your business vocabulary. For each numbered statement, find the italicized term that has the same meaning.

    civic   *human relations*   *psychic income*

1. Nonmonetary satisfactions or rewards.
2. Pertaining to governmental or citizenship activities.
3. Working with others in a cooperative manner.

Checking Your Understanding

1. What are some of the reasons, in addition to the need to earn a living, why people work?
2. Mention four basic responsibilities for success in living and working.
3. "Self-development means more than preparing for an occupation and obtaining a job." Explain.
4. Give some examples of civic duties in which each citizen ought to participate.
5. Name three groups of persons with whom one should try to develop good human relations.
6. What are some problems that are likely to arise between an employee and his fellow workers? Can you suggest how these problems might be resolved?
7. Name three things that characterize the person who has economic awareness.
8. "As citizens we may have whatever government services we wish, but we must pay for them." Explain.
9. Why is it said that there are opportunities in all fields of work?

Applying What You Have Learned

1. Make a list of four jobs: one in an office, one in a retail store, one in a factory or on a farm, and one in a profession such as law, medicine, or teaching. (a) For each job, describe the ways in which a person might gain satisfaction from that job. (b) List the dissatisfactions that might arise from each job.
2. Today a large number of married women work outside the home. Many such women really do not need the income they earn. If this is so, why do you think they work? What satisfactions do they receive from working?
3. Choose two occupations in which you are interested. For each, make a list of ways in which you might gain recognition on that job. In what ways are the two lists different? In what ways are they the same?
4. The word "success" means different things to different people. Prepare a statement of what success means to you.
5. Almost every group of persons has economic problems of some kind. Mention three economic problems of your class in school or of a club to which you belong. Suggest steps that might be taken to solve each of these problems.
6. A good education is becoming more and more important to successful living. Still, some people with a good education fail, and a few people with little formal education are highly successful. Suggest reasons why this is true.

7. Study the bar chart below. In which occupational groups are women in the majority and in which are they in the minority? How do you account for these facts?

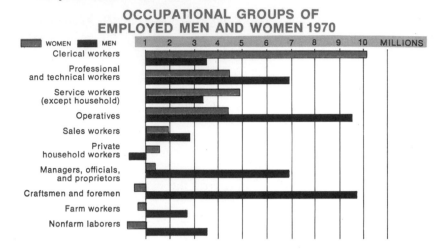

OCCUPATIONAL GROUPS OF EMPLOYED MEN AND WOMEN 1970

Solving Business Problems

1. In a recent survey, teenagers were asked what factors they considered important for happiness in their future careers. In all, 860 teenagers were contacted. Of this number, 490 responded. The table below gives the facts about their responses.

Work Factor	Number Mentioning This Factor
Future salary	302
Good fellow workers	250
Good fringe benefits	191
Good supervisors	238
Good working conditions .	297
Importance of the job	200
Job security	315
Personal interest in work..	396
Opportunity for promotion	297
Serving others	300
Starting salary	199

(a) What percentage of the teenagers contacted responded to the survey?

(b) For each work factor, indicate the percentage of respondents citing that factor.

(c) What three work factors appear to be most important to the teenagers surveyed?

(d) Which factors were cited as important by more than 50% of the teenagers?

2. In a recent year and for the nation at large, the percentages of Americans who had achieved their highest levels of education were:

Years of Schooling	Percentage
Less than 5 years	5.4
5-7 years	9.3
8 years	13.3
1-3 years of high school ..	18.2
4 years of high school ...	33.6
1-3 years of college	9.6
4 years of college or more	10.6

Assuming that you live in a community of 42,000 people and that this community is typical of the nation at large, how many persons would fall into each educational grouping given above?

3. National income figures (in billions of dollars) of different industries in the United States for three separate years are shown below.

	1960	1965	1969
Agriculture, forestry, and fisheries ...	$ 16.9	$ 21.0	$ 23.8
Mining and construction	26.5	35.2	48.1
Manufacturing	125.8	172.6	229.1
Transportation	18.2	23.2	29.0
Communications and public utilities .	17.1	22.6	30.2
Wholesale and retail trade	64.4	84.3	112.6
Finance, insurance, and real estate ..	45.8	61.9	85.2
Services	44.5	64.1	94.4
Government and government enterprises	52.9	75.2	114.8

(a) Did the income for each industry show an increase for the nine-year period?
(b) What was the total national income for each of the three years?
(c) For 1969, what percent of the total income was government income?
(d) Of all the figures given, which showed the greatest dollar increase between 1960 and 1969? What was the percent of increase?

4. It is estimated that over the next eight-year period, the percentage of people changing jobs in selected occupational groups will be:

Professional and technical	29.7%
Service workers	27.3%
Skilled blue collar	16.4%
Semiskilled blue collar	6.8%

Assuming that in a given community the number of workers in each of these four groups is 876, 1,493, 1,219, and 954 respectively, determine how many persons in each of these groups are likely to change jobs.

Enriching Your Business Understanding

1. Think of the types of volunteer activities in which people in your community are engaged. These would include a volunteer fire department, helping to raise funds for public health nursing, and so on. List the activities and tell briefly how they contribute to the betterment of the community. If people were not willing to give their time, effort, or money, what would be the effect upon the community?

2. In our country, eight million men and women 18 years of age and over can read or write no better than the average 10-year-old fifth grader. Many of these recognize their need for getting more education to pursue a hobby, improve job skills, or aid in self-development. Adult basic education programs are designed to meet the needs of these people. Find out what you can about any adult basic education programs in your community.

3. In a recent year, the following percentages of our work force obtained their incomes in the following ways:

Private wages and salary	73%
Government employment	13%
Self-employed	12%
Family workers	2%

Prepare a bar chart to show this information.

4. "Business is a cooperative endeavor, and all who contribute to the production of goods and services are entitled to a share in the returns of production."

    (a) Do you agree with this statement? Why?
    (b) What is the name of the share received by each of the following: investor, property owner, manager, employee? How is the amount that each receives determined?
    (c) Does government share in the returns of production? How? Why? How is the amount that government receives determined?

PART 52

The Changing Job World

Our country is made up of thousands of communities, from small towns and farming communities to large cities. Every day a vast army of civilian workers—about 80 million men and women—leave their homes to go to work. In addition, several million men and women are serving in our armed forces. Some of the civilian workers are self-employed, but the vast majority are employed by someone else. They help a businessman or a government agency produce goods or services that increase our country's wealth.

A LOOK AT THE JOB WORLD OF TODAY

You can gain a better understanding of our army of workers by studying Illustration 52-1. In this chart, the workers are divided into nine large groups. Notice that the largest groups are the operatives and the clerical workers. The smallest groups are the agricultural workers and the laborers.

Some of these workers, supervisors, and managers are *salaried*. This means that they earn a given amount of money for each week, month, or year they work. Some are *hourly workers*—they earn so much for each hour that they work. Still others are *piece-rate workers*. They are paid a given amount for each item they produce or for each service they render. Other workers in the sales field may be paid a *commission*. This means that they are paid a percentage of each sale they make.

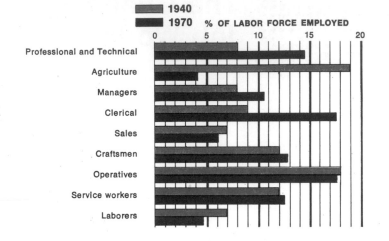

MAJOR OCCUPATIONAL GROUPS IN THE UNITED STATES
Employed Persons, Men and Women

■ 1940
■ 1970   % OF LABOR FORCE EMPLOYED

| | 0 | 5 | 10 | 15 | 20 |

Professional and Technical
Agriculture
Managers
Clerical
Sales
Craftsmen
Operatives
Service workers
Laborers

Illus. 52-1. As the chart shows, there has been a change in job opportunities over the years. More people are employed in professional and technically skilled jobs, in managerial positions, and in office and service occupations. This means that employment is growing fastest in occupations requiring at least a high school education and that many jobs require education beyond high school.

The chart gives only an overall picture of the kinds of work that are being done in this country. Actually, there are many different kinds of jobs in each occupational group. For example, included in the "Operatives" group are filling station attendants, apprentice plumbers, and miners, among others. Other groups, likewise, include many different kinds of jobs.

TRENDS IN THE JOB WORLD

A famous writer recently said that this is the first time in history that parents are not living in a world like the one their children will live in. This statement suggests how fast the whole world is changing. The job world is changing just as rapidly. A few occupations are performed about as they were in your grandfather's day. But most have changed and will keep on changing as new methods and new machines are introduced. The many changes taking place in the labor market mean new and different job opportunities for you. The following trends are among the important ones that affect the amount of skill and education you will need.

(1) More highly skilled workers are needed. There is less demand for unskilled or semiskilled workers. Industry needs *technicians,* skilled workers who also know the principles of mathematics and science which apply to a field, such as electronics. In offices and stores, too, workers with more skills are needed.

The unskilled person finds himself today unemployed or in danger of unemployment.

(2) More supervisory and managerial people are needed. As offices, stores, factories, and other firms become larger, there is more need for supervisory personnel. For the person skilled at scheduling work, supervising others, and making decisions, there is great opportunity for advancement.

(3) More jobs are open to women. Many women are filling positions in fields formerly open only to men. Increasingly, women are handling managerial positions in offices and retail stores. They also can find job openings in such high-income fields as real estate and insurance and in professions such as law, medicine, social work, and teaching.

(4) More workers must be mobile. They are discovering that to obtain the kind of employment they want, they must be able and willing to move from one community to another. This *mobility* is especially important if an employer is one who advances employees from one job to another in different plants or units of the firm. For example, future supervisors and managers of retail chain stores are given chances to learn by being moved from one store to another. Not everyone wants to move away from parents and friends, but some occupations demand this mobility.

You can help yourself be mobile by getting the right kind of education. Develop the basic skills of reading, speaking, writing, and mathematics. Improve your ability to work with others. Train for jobs that are in demand even though opportunities may not be available locally.

(5) Fewer jobs are bound by discrimination. Employers are now opening up jobs to any applicant regardless of race or creed. There is probably still some racial and religious discrimination in jobs, but times are changing. The young person now can depend on his own education and training to get him the first job. Then he must prove that he can perform well if he is to advance. Also opening up are ownership opportunities for those from minority groups who have the capital and the management know-how.

(6) More people are holding more than one job. According to a recent survey, nearly 5% of all employed persons hold two or more jobs. They do this to earn extra money or to try

another line of work. Such persons are called *moonlighters*. Most of the people working at two jobs are married men.

Changes in occupations today and those predicted for the future mean two things for you. First, there will be much opportunity for a satisfying career in a variety of occupations. Second, the chance of being successful in this career depends on your getting all the education and training you can and on continuing your improvement while you are working.

A LOOK AT THE JOB WORLD AS YOU MAY KNOW IT

As a young person, it is natural for you to think of jobs as they exist now. But full-time employment is still a few years away for you. You should look at the world of work as it will probably be in the next decade or so and be prepared for change. A good way to do this is to look at the estimates made of what will happen to various occupations.

Study Illustration 52-2 for a moment. The chart shows that there will be increases in most types of jobs between 1970 and 1980 and that the demand for employees will continue to increase. Note these highlights:

1. Almost all groups of occupations will increase except those of farmers, farm laborers, and unskilled workers. Only two out of twenty-five workers will be in these occupations.
2. Occupations increasing most rapidly are those requiring some education and training beyond high school.
3. One out of five workers will be in a professional or technical occupation.
4. At least one out of four workers will be in an office or sales occupation.
5. Skilled craftsmen are and will continue to be in great demand.
6. Opportunities are increasing rapidly in service occupations such as teaching, nursing and medical technology, food and lodging occupations, and social work.

THIS IS THE TIME TO GATHER JOB INFORMATION

It is possible that you will work in some occupation 40 years or more. This is a long time, and you can afford to spend some time now gathering information about different occupations. You may change your mind several times before you decide definitely on your occupation. But it is good to develop the habit of learning about occupations that interest you. Successful persons select their occupations; those who have no plan just drift from job to job.

HOW EMPLOYMENT OPPORTUNITIES WILL LOOK BY 1980

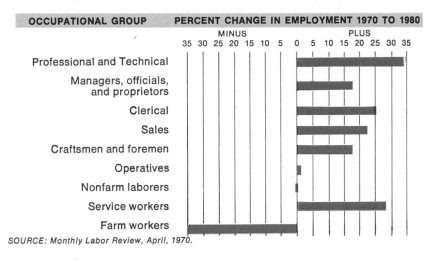

OCCUPATIONAL GROUP	PERCENT CHANGE IN EMPLOYMENT 1970 TO 1980

SOURCE: Monthly Labor Review, April, 1970.

Illus. 52-2. From this chart, you can see that the biggest increases in employment are taking place in the occupations that require the most education and training.

The U.S. Department of Labor publishes the *Dictionary of Occupational Titles,* which describes all the occupations in this country. In it are listed more than 26,000 occupations known to exist in this nation. Each listing describes a single job title, such as file clerk. Many jobs, though, are actually part of a *cluster of jobs*; that is, a number of jobs with something in common so that skill in one job can be used in another. For example, the job of clerk-typist is part of the office occupations family, and a typist should be able to do the work of a file clerk. The *Dictionary* can help you see what each job requires in terms of duties to be performed and education and training required. The *Dictionary* also points out that if you are trained for a cluster of related jobs, your skills are more salable in the labor market. The same government agency also publishes the *Occupational Outlook Handbook,* which describes fields of work in the future.

There are a number of other sources of information about jobs and job requirements:

1. Consult your teachers and counselors.
2. Watch for announcements about jobs in newspapers and magazines.
3. Note job announcements released by employment agencies, the Civil Service Commission, and local firms.
4. Visit factories, stores, offices, or other places of business to observe people at work.

5. Interview a person who is doing the kind of work you are interested in.
6. Note job information that you may get from radio and television programs.
7. Ask your school and public librarians for help in locating books and pamphlets on job opportunities and requirements.

Make use of as many sources as you can. You should look for these kinds of job information: a description of the job, the duties performed, paths of advancement to higher-level jobs, personal qualities required, education and training needed, and incomes earned by typical workers in this occupation.

GUIDELINES THAT HELP IN MAKING A CAREER CHOICE

Choosing your career is one of the most important decisions you will ever make. The world of work provides many opportunities for you if you take time to learn about the market and train yourself to acquire the necessary skills. Remember, your first choice may not be your last, but it is important to get started by choosing a field of interest. The following guideposts may help you do this.

(1) Am I enthusiastic about this occupation? Is this what I really want to do? Will I enjoy doing this kind of work more than any other that I know about? Am I willing to learn as much as I can about this occupation?

(2) What are the requirements of this occupation? What skills or other abilities are needed? How much education and training are necessary?

(3) Am I suited for this occupation? Do I have the physical, mental, social, and emotional qualities necessary for success in this occupation? If I do not have them, am I willing to develop them? Am I willing to spend the time, energy, and money needed to prepare myself for this occupation?

(4) Will I be able to advance myself in this occupation? Does it lead to higher-level jobs with greater responsibility and higher pay?

(5) What benefits are there in this occupation? Is it one that provides training even though the beginning salary is relatively low, or is it one with a high beginning wage but a dead-end job future? Are the skills of this occupation useful in others in case I want to change, or is the job one in which I will have to stay even though I want a change?

Developing Your Business Vocabulary

The following italicized terms should become part of your business vocabulary. For each numbered statement, find the italicized term that has the same meaning.

commission
hourly worker
job cluster
mobility

moonlighter
piece-rate worker
salaried worker
technician

1. An employee who is paid a stated amount for a given period of time regardless of the number of hours worked.
2. An employee who is paid a given amount for each hour worked.
3. An employee who is paid according to the amount of work he produces.
4. A percentage of each sale made or service rendered, paid to an employee as salary.
5. A skilled worker who also knows the principles of mathematics and science of a field.
6. The ability of a person to move from one community to another to find employment or to obtain a job promotion.
7. A worker who holds two or more jobs.
8. A number of jobs with something in common so that skill in one job can be used in another.

Checking Your Understanding

1. Explain how salaried, hourly, and piece-rate workers are paid.
2. Describe at least four job trends that will affect the type of employment you may obtain.
3. How does education help a worker be mobile so that he can obtain a job?
4. What are two things that occupational changes mean to you?
5. According to the text, which occupational groups are growing most rapidly? Least rapidly?
6. Explain the difference between "selecting" an occupation and "drifting" into an occupation. Which is more likely to lead to success? Why?
7. What information is contained in the *Dictionary of Occupational Titles*?
8. How does a worker benefit from being trained for a cluster of jobs?

9. Describe at least four ways you can obtain information about job opportunities and job requirements.
10. Most workers are interested in advancing themselves in their fields of work. Explain why this is true.
11. Mention five guideposts that will be of help to you in choosing an occupation.

Applying What You Have Learned

1. If you were to examine a chart of major occupational groups in the United States in the year 1900, how would it differ from the chart in Illustration 52-1?
2. Some kinds of occupations require mostly physical effort; others require mental effort; still others require both physical and mental effort. List as many occupations as you can think of in each of these three groups.
3. Discuss with your friends reasons why different people choose different occupations. Write down these reasons and present your report in class.
4. Refer to the chart on page 613 and answer the following questions:

    (a) What reasons can you give for the expected large increases in the highly skilled occupations?
    (b) Which of the growing job areas require a college education?
    (c) If you had to start in an unskilled job, how could you get into a better occupation?

5. Find out from your relatives, friends, or neighbors whether they think job opportunities have changed in the last few years in your community. Summarize your findings in a brief list.
6. Today more and more women are entering occupations formerly open only to men. But in many lines of work, women are in reality prevented from entering or prevented from moving into top levels. A few become engineers, doctors, or draftsmen, for example, but most do not. (a) Is there an economic loss if skilled, educated women are not allowed to work at jobs for which they are trained? (b) What factors do you think cause women to be denied entry or advancement in certain occupations?
7. Select an occupation in which you are interested.

    (a) Describe the duties of a worker in this occupation.
    (b) What special personal qualities must a person have or be willing to develop?
    (c) What training or education is needed by a worker in this occupation?
    (d) Where may such training or education be obtained?

Solving Business Problems

1. Examine the pie charts below, then answer the questions.

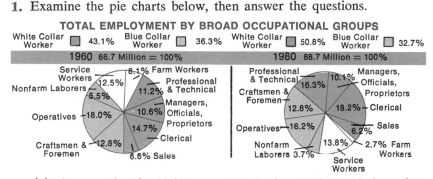

TOTAL EMPLOYMENT BY BROAD OCCUPATIONAL GROUPS

(a) Assume that in 1960 your state had a total population of 2 million workers and that the percentage in each occupational group was the same as that for the nation as a whole. How many workers were there in each of the nine categories given?

(b) For the nation as a whole, which occupational groups are expected to increase their percentage of workers? Which ones will decrease by 1980?

(c) As compared with the percentage of the total work force in blue collar jobs in 1960, will this group increase or decrease by 1980?

2. Assume that you have been offered a job as a salesman, with a choice of three different kinds of pay for your work:

Plan A: A straight salary of $560 a month.
Plan B: A commission of 8% on sales. (You believe that your sales will amount to about $7,500 a month.)
Plan C: A guaranteed salary of $350 a month plus a commission of 4% on estimated sales of $7,500.

(a) Calculate your earnings for one month under each plan.
(b) Calculate your earnings for one year under each plan.
(c) How much greater is the largest yearly amount than the smallest?

3. Factory workers in the Neptune Novelty Company are paid 37¢ each for items completed. If they complete more than 50 items a day, they are paid an additional amount according to the following schedule: 51 to 60 items completed, 3¢ each; 61 to 70 completed, 5¢ each; more than 70 completed, 7¢ each. The workers listed below completed in one day the following number of items:

Worker A, 52 items   Worker D, 74 items
Worker B, 58 items   Worker E, 70 items
Worker C, 64 items   Worker F, 50 items

How much did each worker earn that day?

Enriching Your Business Understanding

1. The term "full employment" is used to describe a situation when most people are working, even though several million people may actually be unemployed.

   (a) Do you suppose it will ever be possible to have 100% employment? Explain.
   (b) What are some conditions that seem to keep some of our workers unemployed? Explain which of these conditions you think might be improved or even removed. Why?

2. The statement is sometimes heard that "anyone who really wants to work can find employment." Do you agree or disagree with this statement?

3. Our society is now making conscious efforts to open up job opportunities to many who previously were denied such opportunities. By searching news magazines and other current periodicals and newspapers, try to discover and report to the class on what attempts are being made to provide employment opportunities to the following: (a) the undereducated, (b) those with jail sentence records, (c) those with physical handicaps, and (d) those with mental handicaps.

4. As directed by your teacher, find out from the local office of your state employment service what the job opportunities are in your community, your county, or your state. If your teacher wants you to do so, individually or as part of a committee, make up some tables or charts showing employment in various occupations.

5. Select some occupation in which you are interested. As directed by your teacher, write a letter to a personnel manager or a person in this occupation. Ask him what the job opportunities are, what the requirements for employment are, and how to prepare for that occupation.

PART 53
Planning Your Career

Most people do not stay in the same occupation throughout their working lifetime. But each person has to make a start in some occupation. It is wise to make a tentative choice of an occupational family while still in school. By doing this, a person can lay a foundation of study for the work he is to do.

Maybe you have already decided that you want to be a salesman, a store manager, a secretary, a nurse, a teacher, a mechanic, or an engineer. Maybe you have two or three different occupations in mind. In any case, you should make some plans now about the kind of work you want to do. In your plans, you will want to study your own abilities, interests, and personality. You will want to learn as much as possible about the job or jobs in which you are interested. Also, you should compare your talents with the job requirements. And you should consider the kind of education you will need.

Your work will make up a large part of your lifetime from about age 20 or so to about 65. Your enjoyment of life will depend in part on how successful you are in your work. People generally do best those things that they enjoy doing and for which they have the proper talent and training. To find the job that is best for you, you must understand yourself.

KNOW YOURSELF BEFORE YOU CHOOSE A CAREER

(1) Consider your likes and dislikes. Ask yourself questions such as these. Do I enjoy the challenge of leading others? Which do I like better—working alone or as part of a team? Does working with my hands satisfy my desire to create? Am I willing to move away from my home and family? Am I willing to gamble by taking a job now for the good it may do me in getting a better one later? Does work requiring attention to detail and accuracy appeal to me? Is it important to me to work outdoors? Do I prefer working with ideas rather than tools and machinery?

(2) Consider your abilities and special talents. Ask yourself questions such as these. Can I sing or play a musical instrument? Do I speak with ease before groups? Do I draw or sketch well? Do I like mathematics? Am I a good writer? Am I good at persuading people? Am I a fast reader who knows what he has read? Do I have a good memory? Do I have special physical strength so that I can work long hours and still have energy?

(3) Consider your school record. Do you do equally well in all subjects? What are your most difficult subjects? What are your easiest subjects? What subjects do you want to continue studying? Where do you want to continue your education after high school?

Special tests can sometimes reveal special interests and abilities. Among such tests are general ability tests, reading ability tests, interest inventories, and various kinds of *aptitude tests*. These tests can give you a further indication of your interests and abilities. But do not expect tests alone to tell you what you should or should not do. Ask your teachers and counselors about tests you can take and about how to interpret the test results. Also, you might take the tests offered by your state employment service when you are eligible.

(4) Consider your hobbies. Hobbies can reveal special interests and abilities. Many hobbies have vocational values and can lead to careers later. Among such hobbies are music, writing, art, and working with tools.

(5) Consider your physical qualities. Some jobs require more physical energy than others. For example, construction workers, mechanics, and factory workers often must have more than average physical strength. Other jobs require mental concentration for long periods of time or the physical stamina to travel and meet new people all the time.

What do you mean when you say, "She has a pleasing personality"? *Personality* is not easy to define. In a practical sense, personality consists of those qualities that make an impression upon others. And this impression is based largely on three qualities: appearance, voice, and behavior.

(1) Impressions are influenced by your appearance. Your appearance is determined by such things as your posture, dress, and grooming. Think about how you stand and walk. Are your clothes appropriate for the occasion? How about personal cleanliness?

(2) Impressions are influenced by your speech. In most occupations today, the ability to communicate is a key requirement. A good voice can be cultivated, but it is of little value if you use language carelessly. To other people, carelessness in pronouncing words and errors in grammar often indicate carelessness in other things.

(3) Impressions are influenced by your behavior. Here are six things to remember if you want your behavior to make a favorable impression:

1. Be honest. No one can be considered completely honest if he is honest in most things but is dishonest in little things that he thinks may not harm anyone.

Pitney-Bowes, Inc.

Illus. 53-1. Your personality is your complete self—your physical being, grooming, clothing, cleanliness, speech, and behavior. You are in command of most of these factors. Only you can decide to become the kind of personality you want to be.

2. Be cooperative. A football team would get nowhere without the cooperation of each player. There are few jobs where one can do everything by himself. Teamwork is the key to success in the office, store, or factory.

3. Be dependable. Do you keep your promises? Do you report to class on time? If you serve on a committee, do you finish a job you agreed to do? If you are unable to keep an appointment with someone, do you notify him?

4. Be thoughtful and considerate of others' feelings. Show an interest in the activities of others. Congratulate people on their achievements, and be a good loser. Don't pry into others' personal affairs.

5. Develop good work habits. Plan the use of your time. Organize your class assignments. Hand work in on time, and make it neat and accurate.

6. Use good manners. Good manners can help your business success and social popularity. Knowing how to do the right things makes you feel at ease.

EDUCATION IS AN INVESTMENT IN YOURSELF

In modern industry it often takes an investment of $25,000 or more in tools, equipment, and buildings to provide a job for one employee. Employers are willing to invest such a large amount in order to make a profit. Are you willing to invest in yourself by getting an education that will profit you?

If you dropped out of school today, what kind of job could you get? How much money could you earn? Some young dropouts call themselves pushouts. They feel that the school did not serve them and that they were really "pushed out." Maybe they did not take advantage of what the school offered in vocational education or work experience programs. Still, the dropout or pushout—whatever the reason—will have trouble in the labor market. He is the last to be hired and the first to be laid off. The rate of unemployment among dropouts is three times higher than among high school graduates. In many parts of the country, few dropouts can get a job at a wage that is above the poverty level for a family.

The dropout or pushout must face facts in today's labor market. To get a decent job, he needs some training through manpower retraining centers, job corps programs, private schools, or vocational schools. When he faces facts, he knows also that he should complete his high school education, even if at night, in a completion center or through the military service educational programs.

Finishing high school and continuing your education in some way after high school does not guarantee that you will be financially successful. But it does help your chances. Note in Illustration 53-2 the relationship between education of the head of the family and the family income.

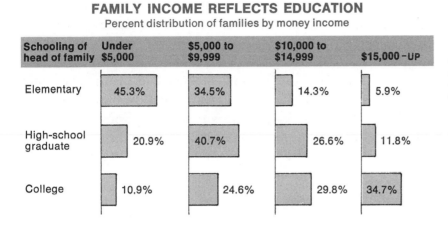

FAMILY INCOME REFLECTS EDUCATION
Percent distribution of families by money income

Schooling of head of family	Under $5,000	$5,000 to $9,999	$10,000 to $14,999	$15,000–UP
Elementary	45.3%	34.5%	14.3%	5.9%
High-school graduate	20.9%	40.7%	26.6%	11.8%
College	10.9%	24.6%	29.8%	34.7%

Illus. 53-2. No one should work for money alone, but education will pay off in other ways. One important way in which it benefits you is in helping you find a career that is personally satisfying to you.

CAN EVERYONE OBTAIN AN EDUCATION?

How can you obtain more education after you leave high school? You may believe that you and your family are not rich enough to give you a good education. But many opportunities are open to you. In fact, visitors from foreign countries are often amazed at the kinds of public education our citizens support.

Some students can live at home while attending a two-year or four-year college, a community college, a technical institute, or a private business school. Some can work part time or during the summer to earn some of their fees and expenses.

On the other hand, perhaps you should work for one or two years after high school. With a sound savings plan, you should be able to put aside enough for at least a couple of years of schooling. Also, the extra maturity and work experience may help you to be a better student.

There are other ways to finance education beyond high school. You might attend a junior college, a community college, a technical institute, or a private business school part time. You might work in the daytime and take courses offered at night. A wide range of evening school courses is offered at low cost by adult education centers and vocational-technical schools. In addition, many scholarships are being offered by colleges, government, private foundations, and business firms.

The federal government and some state governments are now offering loans to young people who want to continue their education. Many of these loans are offered without an interest charge or at a very low rate of interest. Some government loans have *forgiveness clauses*. This means that part of the loan need not be paid back if the student teaches for one or more years after graduation.

THE CHOICE OF A CAREER IS UP TO YOU

When you have studied your abilities and personal qualities and the requirements of occupations in which you are interested, you have taken two important steps in planning your future. You are then ready for the next step. This is the matching of your abilities and qualities with the job requirements. No person is a born salesman, a born teacher, or a born anything else. But almost everyone has certain qualities that match certain job requirements better than others.

WHERE YOU CAN CONTINUE YOUR EDUCATION FOR EMPLOYMENT AFTER HIGH SCHOOL

TYPE OF SCHOOL	LENGTH OF COURSES OF STUDY	OCCUPATIONAL STUDY AREAS USUALLY OFFERED
1. 4-Year College or University	4 years; some have 2-year curricula, also evening school	Professional curricula such as business administration, engineering, nursing, and agriculture
2. Junior or Community College (Public or Private)	1-year and 2-year curricula (full time)	Engineering, health occupations, secretarial administration, marketing, accounting, data processing, agricultural technician
3. Private Business or Trade School	Few months to 2 years (full time or part time)	Secretarial-clerical, accounting, sales, skilled industrial trades or technician training
4. Vocational/Technical Institute	Few months to 2 years (full time)	Secretarial/clerical, bookkeeping, industrial trades, commercial art, distributive education
5. Adult Study Center	Individual courses each semester, often 1 or 2 evenings a week	Apprenticeship, business, industrial, supervisory and management training, small business operation, home economics, health occupations
6. Employer or Union School	Short duration such as few weeks	Specialized job training for job skills and supervisory abilities
7. Correspondence Study Schools	Each course varies according to student's study habits	Specialized courses in various vocational areas

Illus. 53-3. This table shows the kinds of educational institutions that may exist near your home.

No one can tell you exactly what occupation to follow. You may not be ready now to select the specific job you want to do, but you can begin studying the field you are interested in. As you gather more information and gain more experience, you will be able to narrow down your job choices.

Developing Your Business Vocabulary

The following italicized terms should become part of your business vocabulary. For each numbered statement, find the italicized term that has the same meaning.

aptitude tests
forgiveness clause
personality

1. A means of determining special abilities that a person may have.
2. The qualities of a person that make an impression upon other people.
3. A provision in a government loan which states that part of the loan need not be repaid if the person receiving it teaches for a prescribed period of time after graduation.

Checking Your Understanding

1. In planning for a career, what are four things you will want to do?
2. How may your likes and dislikes help you in choosing an occupation?
3. How can your school record help in deciding what you would like to do?
4. What are some different kinds of information about yourself that tests can give you?
5. What are some qualities by which one may judge the personality of another?
6. How can one improve his appearance?
7. What might errors in grammar and carelessness in pronunciation reveal about a person?
8. What are five things to remember if you want your behavior to make a favorable impression?
9. Why is it said that education is a way of investing in yourself?
10. In what ways could you possibly finance your education after high school graduation?

Applying What You Have Learned

1. Two statements which have often been made are: "A man's life is his work" and "A person is known by his occupation."

    (a) What is meant when we say that a man is known by his occupation?

    (b) How does a person's occupation affect, if at all, his home life, his church and community life, his health, and his recreation and hobbies?

    (c) Should a person, in considering his life's occupation or a change in jobs, consider the effects on his home, health, and social life?

2. Phil Renneberg is a freshman at McMillan High School. Phil says that he doesn't want to be concerned about his career until after he graduates from high school. He feels that then he will have a better idea of what he wants to do. Do you agree or disagree with Phil? Why?

3. Give as many reasons as you can that you think cause high school students to drop out of school or think of themselves as being pushed out before graduation. What could be done in your area to reduce the number of dropouts?

4. Studies made of the reasons why people fail on a job show that many employees do not succeed because they lack certain desirable personal traits. Some of the most important traits required for successful employment are described below and on page 627. Make an analysis of your own employment traits by rating yourself on each one. Write the letters *a, b, c, d, e, f, g,* and *h* in a column. Then after each letter write the word *Excellent, Good, Fair,* or *Poor* to indicate your rating.

    (a) *Attitude.* You make an effort to work as well as you can; you do not try to avoid work; you seldom complain about having to work.

    (b) *Thoroughness.* You finish what you start out to do; you make an effort to be completely accurate; no one has to remind you that your work is incomplete.

    (c) *Mental alertness.* It is easy for you to learn new things; instructions for work do not have to be repeated frequently; it is easy for you to understand something that has been thoroughly explained.

    (d) *Cooperation.* You work well with other people; you enjoy working with others on a group project; you do not criticize how other people do their work.

    (e) *Promptness.* Work assignments are completed on schedule; you seldom ask for more time to complete your assignments; you never fail to meet commitments on time.

(f) *Initiative.* You can make independent decisions about what to do; you seldom have to be shown what to do; you do not wait to do something that needs to be done until someone tells you to do it.

(g) *Health.* You are not absent from school frequently because of minor illnesses; you are careful to maintain good health habits so that illness does not interfere with your activities; you seldom suffer from long periods of illness.

(h) *Personal appearance.* You never wear messy clothing to school; you constantly make an effort to keep yourself and your clothes neat and clean.

Solving Business Problems

1. Howie Crockett learned that last year the cost of providing an education at his high school averaged $648 per student.

   (a) If the cost remains the same, what will be the cost for one student for the four years that he remains in high school?

   (b) What was the total cost of maintaining the high school for the year if there were 792 students enrolled?

2. The number of students enrolled in public elementary and secondary schools and the number of teachers within the public schools for certain years are shown below.

Year	Students (in thousands)	Teachers (in thousands)
1920	21,578	657
1940	25,434	875
1960	36,087	1,381
1969	45,619	2,014

   (a) For each of the years shown, calculate the average number of students for each teacher.

   (b) What was the amount of increase in the number of students enrolled during the 49-year period?

   (c) By what percent did the number of students increase?

   (d) What was the amount of increase in the number of teachers during the 49-year period?

   (e) By what percent did the number of teachers increase?

3. Assume the median annual income of elementary school graduates, high school graduates, and college graduates to be:

   Elementary school, $4,778
   High school, $7,244
   College, $10,090

(a) In a period of 40 years, how much more does a high school graduate earn than does an elementary school graduate?

(b) In the same period, how much more does a college graduate earn than a high school graduate? Than an elementary school graduate?

Enriching Your Business Understanding

1. Choose one of the following fields of business work: bookkeeping and accounting, stenographic and secretarial, merchandising and selling, and general clerical. List all the specific jobs that you can name that relate to the field you select. Place an asterisk (*) in front of each job that you consider as a possible beginning job— a job that a responsible high school graduate could hold.

2. Select one of the specific jobs listed in the preceding question and prepare a job description of it. You may want to prepare a chart or table describing this job under such headings as:

Summary of duties (work performed)
Qualifications for the job (education, special training, special abilities)
Working conditions (hours, surroundings, vacations, etc.)
Opportunities for advancement (promotion policies, future growth)
Special requirements (tools, uniforms, workers' organizations, etc.)
Advantages and disadvantages of the job.

3. The federal government in recent years has passed legislation to help overcome the problem of the hard-core unemployed by providing them with job training. One of these programs is administered through the Office of Economic Opportunity (OEO). Find out all you can about the OEO programs in your area. Consult the OEO coordinator in your city or the director of vocational education in your school. Find out who is eligible for training, how much allowance a person gets while in training, what types of jobs he may be trained for, and what he does after training.

4. To find out more about educational opportunities available to you, make a list of the types of educational institutions in your town or city or within easy driving distance. For each type of educational institution, state briefly the courses of study offered and tell whether part-time students are accepted.

5. Using information available from your teacher or school guidance department, find out how much it would cost to attend a two-year or four-year college you might want to attend. Suggest some ways in which you might finance your education.

PART 54
Getting
That
Job

It is easy for us to overlook the importance of what we are doing now. But from day to day you are writing a personal record that is important in preparing for a career. The courses you take in school are part of your record. They give you the abilities and knowledge you need on the job. They enable you to gain insights into possible careers and also indicate your areas of interest. The grades you earn are also part of your school record. So are the rating sheets about you and your work that your teachers and counselors may fill out. So is the work experience you get.

Future employers are likely to examine your school record carefully. It will also be examined by officials of other schools or colleges you may want to enter. Your school record is a permanent one; it is important to establish the best record you can.

In most areas the job market is very competitive. And in later years competition will probably be even stiffer than it is now. Larger numbers of young people are graduating from high school, and many are getting some form of post-secondary career training. They add more well-educated, well-trained applicants to the labor market. Competition for low-skill jobs is increasing because there are fewer such jobs available.

Despite the competition, there is a career available for you. But it is up to you to get ready and be prepared to compete.

TRY TO GET WORK EXPERIENCE

While you are in school, part-time and vacation jobs can mean valuable experience as well as money. Try for a job that is related to the work you may want to do in the future. For example, if you want to be an engineer or a skilled mechanic, look for part-time or summer work in construction or in repair shops such as garages. If you want to be a secretary, a part-time job as a clerical worker will help you get experience. Being a volunteer clerk-typist for a charitable organization such as your church or the Red Cross can also give valuable experience. If you want a career in advertising, sales, or marketing and merchandising, you might look for a job as a stockboy, checker-cashier, or salesperson. You might also work in a restaurant or drive-in to learn more about dealing with people.

In many places you can get valuable work experience through your school. Your school may have a placement service, a work experience program, or a cooperative occupational training program. If it does, it can help you find a job that meets your interests and your career goals. There may also be work opportunities, either for pay or credit, within the school in the cafeteria, the school office, the school store, or maintenance or audiovisual departments.

Sometimes it will not be possible to get a part-time job directly in the field you have chosen for a career. All employment can give you valuable experiences. In any job, you can form good work habits. And in any job you can develop poise in meeting people and facing new situations. You can also learn more about our economic system and how others earn a living.

HOW TO LOOK FOR A JOB

When you are ready to look for a job—whether full time or part time—don't be satisfied with taking the first one that comes along. Try to locate the best available job by using the sources of help listed below and on page 631.

1. Select a number of places in which you would like to work and then apply in person. Employers are impressed by the initiative of a young person who effectively presents his qualifications.
2. Tell friends about your desire for work. They may know of job openings where they work or somewhere else.
3. Let your counselors and teachers know of your job needs.
4. Register with public and private employment service offices.

Illus. 54-1. A girl who wants to be a secretary might seek a part-time job as a clerical worker or as a receptionist in an office.

5. Study the "help wanted" columns in your local papers and follow up quickly on those openings that interest you. You may also want to run a "job wanted" advertisement yourself.
6. Interview business agents or other officials of local unions. Ask them for information about apprenticeships, job placement services, union membership requirements, and the current job market.
7. Inquire at your city hall, county seat, or post office about job vacancies, qualifications, and examinations that may be given for government work.

Many employers now use *employment agencies* to find workers. These agencies are either publicly or privately owned. For example, state governments operate employment services in cooperation with the federal government. Offices are usually found in larger towns and cities. These offices test job-seekers' abilities and aptitudes. They counsel job seekers and try to match each person with the requirements of the job opening. Because the state employment service is operated with tax money, no fees are charged either to job seekers or employers. Other public, non-profit employment agencies that charge either no fees or very small ones are operated by schools, unions, and organizations such as the YMCA, YWCA, B'nai B'rith, and the Urban League.

Private employment agencies are in business to make a profit, and they charge a fee for their services. For some jobs, the employer will pay the fee if the job seeker is hired. For other jobs, the job seeker must pay it. The fee is usually a percentage of the salary earned for the first month or several months. Most private employment agencies are trustworthy and may be very helpful. However, the job seeker should investigate an agency before using its services.

EMPLOYERS HAVE DIFFERENT HIRING PROCEDURES

Different employers have different hiring procedures. In small firms, the hiring is usually done informally on the basis of a personal interview with the owner or manager. Most large firms have a *personnel department*. This department begins looking for new employees by using some form of *job specification*. This describes the duties of a job and specifies what skills, knowledge, training, and experience the qualified worker must have. The personnel director and his staff recruit employees through advertisements, visits to schools and colleges, and requests to public and private employment agencies. The staff interviews applicants, may give tests, and may refer the applicant to a department head or supervisor for interviews. Finally, they make a job offer to those they feel are qualified. After the employee is hired, the personnel department is usually responsible for his training. It is also responsible for his job ratings and decisions about his promotions.

PREPARING YOUR DATA SHEET

Some large firms require that job seekers write letters of application. This is a way of screening out those who seem best qualified. These persons are then invited for a personal interview. Other firms may invite job seekers to apply in person for a job, with no letter of application required. In either case, a *personal data sheet* should be prepared. It summarizes important information about the applicant. Well-prepared, it can make an excellent impression on prospective employers.

A copy of a personal data sheet may be enclosed with a letter of application. This makes it possible to write a short, to-the-point letter. Data sheets may also be given to employment agencies or used during an interview. Data sheets should be short and should outline the data in brief, readable form. Elizabeth Wilcox's personal data sheet on page 633 shows the kinds of information that such a sheet may contain and the form in which it may be prepared.

```
                          Personal Data Sheet of
                              Elizabeth Wilcox
                              1690 Woodlawn Court
     249-3845 (after 5 p.m.)  Hartford, CT  06101      May 1, 1971


     EDUCATION

         1967 - Present   Wilson High School.  Am presently a senior and will
                          be graduated in June, 1971.  Am combining college
                          preparatory subjects with business electives.

                          Business Subjects Studied
                              General Business
                              Bookkeeping
                              Typewriting
                              Office Machines
                              Business Law

                          Activities
                              General Business Club - 1 year
                              Secretary of Boosters Club - 1 year
                              Treasurer of Future Business Leaders Club - 1 year
                              Yearbook Business Manager - 1 year

                          Scholastic Record
                              Grade average is in upper one-third of class

     EXPERIENCE

         1969 - Present   Brand Company, Hartford.  General office work consist-
         (Part-time and   ing of typewriting, filing, data processing, record-
         summers)         keeping, and duplicating duties.

     PERSONAL

         Age, 18; height, 5'4"; weight, 115 pounds; health, excellent; hobbies,
         reading, sewing, swimming.

     REFERENCES

         Mr. Ford Sebring, Personnel Director
         Brand Company
         678 Sigmund Street
         Hartford, CT  06103

         Mrs. Rose Wilding, Guidance Counselor
         Wilson High School
         Elm and Ninth Streets
         Hartford, CT  06102

         Mr. William Sullivan
         Head, Business Department
         Wilson High School
         Elm and Ninth Streets
         Hartford, CT  06102
```

If you are answering a job advertisement or are following up a friend's lead, writing a *letter of application* may be the first step. Its purpose is to get you a personal interview. The letter of application should be written so that it makes the employer interested in seeing you. It should be a simple, frank, yet courteous sales letter.

Like any good sales letter, your letter of application should gain the employer's attention and interest. It should create in him a desire to see you. And it should stimulate him to take the

WRITING YOUR LETTER OF APPLICATION

desired action—inviting you to come for an interview. Examine the letter in Illustration 54-3 to see how the writer followed the basics of preparing a good letter of application. The letter is carefully and neatly prepared, courteous, and brief and to the point. A carelessly written letter may cause the employer to judge you as a careless worker. Remember, too, that your letter must compete favorably for attention with other letters.

Illus. 54-3. A letter of application may be prepared in a form similar to this.

```
                                         1690 Woodlawn Court
                                         Hartford, CT  06101
                                         May 1, 1971


        Mr. C. P. Martin
        Personnel Manager
        The Ag-Rex Company
        Vinton and Highland Streets
        Hartford, CT  06105

        Dear Mr. Martin

        In Sunday's Hartford Courant I read your advertisement for a
        general office clerk.  I wish to apply for that position.

        This June I shall be graduated from Wilson High School.  I
        have taken such general education courses as English, history,
        and mathematics, and have also studied a number of business
        subjects.  I can operate most of the common office machines,
        including basic data processing equipment, and can type letters
        and straight copy material accurately at an average rate of 60
        words a minute.

        For the past two years I have worked part-time and during sum-
        mers in the office of the Brand Company here in Hartford.  This
        work has enabled me to obtain general office experience and has
        also increased my interest in office work.  I would someday like
        to advance to the position of office manager with a business
        firm.

        Enclosed is a personal data sheet giving my qualifications in
        more detail.  May I have an interview with you at your conve-
        nience?  I may be reached at 249-3845 after 5 p.m. on any week
        day.  Thank you for your consideration.

                                         Sincerely yours

                                         Elizabeth Wilcox

                                         Elizabeth Wilcox


        Enclosure
```

Most companies ask the job seeker to fill out a printed application form. This is especially true if he has not previously applied for the job in writing. The purpose of the application form is to secure information about a job applicant. Most application forms ask the applicant to give his name, age, address, list of references, and information about education, previous employment, or other qualifications. The employer uses this information to decide whether an applicant is worthy of further consideration.

Illus. 54-4. A job applicant should fill out the application form neatly, accurately, and honestly.

APPLICATION FOR EMPLOYMENT

The Ag-Rex Company

Name _Elizabeth Ann Wilcox_   Date _May 12, 1971_

Address _1690 Woodlawn Court_   Phone No. _249-3845_

City _Hartford_ State _Connecticut_ ZIP Code _06101_   Soc. Sec. No. _771-210-652_

Date of Birth _3/22/53_ Place of Birth (City & State) _Albany, New York_

Do you live with parents? _Yes_ Board? _____ Rent? _____

High School attended _Wilson High School_

City & State _Hartford, Connecticut_ Year Graduated _____

Business subjects studied _General Business, Bookkeeping, Typewriting, Office Machines, Business Law_

Are you in school now? _Yes Will be graduated in_ If yes, where? _Wilson High School_
June, 1971

What grade do you most often receive? _Grade average in upper one-third of class_

In what activities have you participated? _General Business Club, Boosters Club (Secretary), Future Business Leaders Club (Treasurer), Yearbook Staff (Business Manager)_

What hobbies or sports do you enjoy? _Reading, sewing, swimming_

In the space to the right indicate your present speed in shorthand and typing, if you have these skills. Place an (X) after the office machines you can operate.	Shorthand		Typing	60	Dictaphone	X
	Billing Machine		Bookkeeping Machine		Mimeograph	X
	Addressograph	X	Calculator	X	PBX Board	
	Comptometer		Key Punch	X	Adding Machine	X
	Verifier	X	IBM Tabulator	X	Other	

Indicate the two most recent positions held. (Most recent first.)

NAME OF COMPANY	POSITION HELD	DATE YOU BEGAN
Brand Company, Hartford	Office Clerk	June, 1969

References:

NAME	ADDRESS	OCCUPATION
Mr. Ford Sebring	678 Sigmund St., Hartford, Conn.	Personnel Director, Brand Company
Mrs. Rose Wilding	Elm & Ninth Sts., Hartford, Conn.	Guidance Counselor, Wilson High School
Mr. William Sullivan	Elm & Ninth Sts., Hartford, Conn.	Head, Business Dept Wilson High School

By signing this application I affirm that all statements made herein are true to the best of my knowledge.

Elizabeth Wilcox
Signature of Applicant

SOME COMPANIES GIVE TESTS

After the application has been made but before your interview, you may be asked to take certain tests. Tests are given for several reasons. The employer may want to see you demonstrate your skills, such as typing. He may also want to determine your special aptitudes. Or he may use tests to find out more about your personality. You should try to do as well as you can on these tests. However, the staff of the personnel department knows that you feel under pressure, and it takes that into account when grading your tests.

PREPARING FOR THE INTERVIEW

If the company is satisfied with your application and the test results, you may be asked to come for a personal interview. This gives a company interviewer the chance to make judgments about your dress, manners, use of English, voice, and other personal characteristics. Plan your interview as carefully as you would plan a personal data sheet or letter of application. Keep the following points in mind:

1. Be on time for the appointment.
2. Go alone to the interviewer's office. Do not ask friends or relatives to go with you.
3. Be careful of your conduct while waiting to see the employer. Receptionists and others in the office may also be forming opinions about you, based on your appearance and behavior.

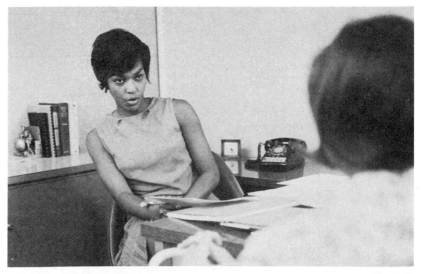

Illus. 54-5. A personal interview gives the employer an opportunity to judge the job applicant's personal characteristics.

Monsanto

UNIT 11 / LIVING AND WORKING IN OUR ECONOMY

4. Try to be calm during the interview. Do not talk too much. Answer and ask questions intelligently. Let the interviewer guide the discussion.

5. Plan to leave when the interviewer indicates that he wants to close the interview. Do not prolong the discussion. Thank him for the chance to present your qualifications.

6. After the interview, send a note to the person who interviewed you, thanking him for his time and consideration.

WORK TO BUILD A GOOD REPUTATION

After accepting a job, you should immediately notify other employers who may still be considering you. Also let the school placement office or employment agencies with whom you have registered know that you have been placed.

Not all efforts to obtain jobs are successful. You may have applied for a job for which you were not fully qualified. You may have made an unfavorable impression. There may not have been any vacancies at the time. Business conditions may have been poor. You may have applied for a high-level job for which you did not have the proper experience. Try to analyze as objectively as possible why you failed to get the job. Be honest with yourself. If you made mistakes, plan to correct them.

In your school work, in your social activities, in applying for jobs, and while working on the job, you will want to build a favorable reputation. A favorable reputation will reward you both in your personal life and in your career.

Bethlehem Steel Corp.

Illus. 54-6. Building a good reputation with your employer, co-workers, and friends will help make both your career and your personal life more satisfying.

Developing Your Business Vocabulary

The following italicized terms should become part of your business vocabulary. For each numbered statement, find the italicized term that has the same meaning.

employment agency　　　*personal data sheet*
job specification　　　　*personnel department*
letter of application

1. An organization that attempts to place qualified workers in satisfactory jobs.
2. The part of a business whose main responsibility is that of hiring employees and working with them in various ways.
3. A description of what the duties of a job are and the qualifications demanded of the worker.
4. A brief description of an individual's education, experience, and other information used in seeking employment.
5. Actually, a sales letter selling a prospective employer on the qualifications of a job applicant.

Checking Your Understanding

1. Of what does your personal record consist? Why is building a good personal record important?
2. What is the meaning of the statement, "Prepare for increased job competition"?
3. What can you learn from work experience that might help you be successful in your career after graduation?
4. Give seven suggestions on how to go about looking for a job.
5. What services do employment agencies provide? In what ways are public and private agencies usually different?
6. Explain how the procedures for hiring workers may differ in a small business and in a large business.
7. Explain how a personal data sheet is different from an application blank.
8. Why is a letter of application often considered as a kind of sales letter?
9. Why should the applicant for a job be especially careful in filling out application blanks?
10. What types of information may an employer get about an applicant during the interview that he could not get from a letter of application?

11. Mention at least five important points to keep in mind when being interviewed for a job.
12. What does a worker who was not hired gain by sending a thank-you note to the interviewer?

Applying What You Have Learned

1. Study the chart given below. What do the facts presented in this chart indicate? Is there any relation between the data shown here and the statement, "Prepare for increased job competition"? Explain. (Note: Prior to 1959 no classification was available for the 18-21 age group.)

RISING LEVEL OF EDUCATION

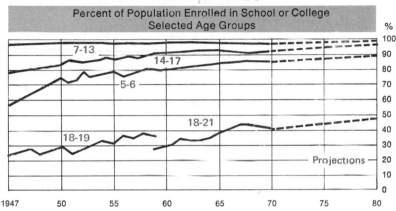

2. Select an occupation in which you would be interested as a career. List as many part-time or summer jobs as you can think of that would give you skills and experience that would be helpful in this career.
3. Charles and Susan were discussing their high school plans of study. Charles said that he planned to take only regular academic courses, get a broad education, and later acquire any special skills needed after he got his job. Susan planned to take a number of academic courses also, but she intended to take some business courses. She said that a business firm has a right to expect an applicant for a business job to possess some business understandings and skills. With whom do you agree and why?
4. The personnel manager for the Reliable Insurance Company requires each applicant for a stenographic position to fill out an application blank, interview the supervisor of the stenographic department, and take a shorthand and typewriting test. If these steps are completed satisfactorily, the applicant is then notified to

return for a final interview with the personnel manager. Explain why the company requires an applicant to complete each of these steps.

5. If you were the personnel manager of a company and were charged with hiring a receptionist-stenographer for your firm, what qualities would you look for in applicants for the job? How would you expect to obtain information about these qualities from each applicant?

6. The ad below appeared in the "Help Wanted" section of a recent newspaper:

> **BOOKKEEPER**
>
> Experienced, responsible person. Knowledge of complete payroll, including payroll taxes. Accounts receivable and payable and post to the ledger to the trial balance. 8 a.m. to 5 p.m. Downtown location. $135 per week. Reply with handwritten letter only. Box W571, Evening News.

(a) Why might the employer want applicants for this job to write a handwritten letter of application? (b) Why might the employer have the letter addressed to the newspaper box number rather than identifying itself and having letters go directly to its personnel department?

7. Mike Harris was graduated from high school where he had taken business courses, including bookkeeping. After looking unsuccessfully for a job for two weeks, he registered with a private employment agency. Through the agency, he secured a job as an account clerk at a beginning salary of $85 a week. He agreed to pay the agency a registration fee of $25 and a placement fee of 20% of his first 12 weeks' salary. (a) Was Mike wise to use the services of a private employment agency after two weeks of job-hunting? (b) How much did Mike have to pay the agency for finding a job for him? Do you believe this fee was justified? Why or why not?

Solving Business Problems

1. The average earnings and work hours of production workers in manufacturing in the United States for two recent years were:

	1965	1969
Average weekly earnings per worker	$108.77	$129.50
Average number of weekly working hours	41.2	40.7

(a) What were the average hourly earnings per worker for each of the years?

    (b) By what percent did the average weekly earnings increase from 1965 to 1969?

    (c) By what percent did the average hourly earnings increase from 1965 to 1969?

    (d) If the Consumer Price Index increased from 109.9 in 1965 to 127.7 in 1969, was the worker better or worse off in 1969 than in 1965?

2. You have received information about three different jobs:

    (a) An office job, assembling and stapling papers, folding leaflets, and sealing and stamping envelopes.

    (b) A job in a refreshment stand in a park during the summer.

    (c) A part-time job in a gift shop, stocking shelves, checking shipments, and preparing packages for mailing.

Write a letter applying for one of these jobs. Supply the name and address of the employer. Refer to the illustration in this part as a guide for necessary information to include in your letter.

3. Draw up an application form similar to the one on page 635 (or use the form in your *Activities and Projects*) and supply whatever information you think necessary to apply for one of the jobs mentioned in Problem 2.

4. Prepare your own personal data sheet that you might use to accompany a letter of application for a job. Use the personal data sheet on page 633 as a guide.

Enriching Your Business Understanding

1. The chart below indicates the type of work in which young people from 14 to 17 are engaged on a full- or part-time basis:

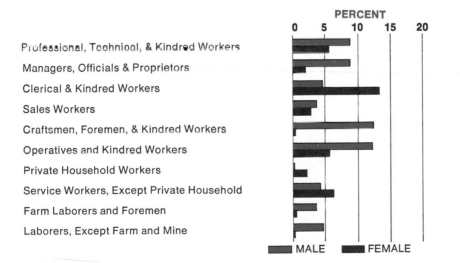

(a) What type of work attracts mostly boys? Mostly girls?

(b) What type of work attracts both boys and girls in about equal percentages? Why might this be so?

(c) What specific jobs would be representative of each of the major types of work shown on the chart?

2. Secure a copy of the classified advertising section of a Sunday newspaper published in a medium- to large-size city. Examine the "help wanted" columns, particularly the advertisements of private employment agencies.

(a) In the listing of the private agencies, what do the terms, "no fee" and "fee paid" mean?

(b) Salaries for some jobs are listed as "open," "to $600," or "$350+." What do these terms mean?

(c) Compare the regular "help wanted" columns with the advertisements of employment agencies. What differences do you find in the types of jobs advertised?

3. Write a letter addressed to your teacher, principal, or former employer requesting permission to use his name as a reference when you apply for a job.

APPENDIX A
Finding Useful Information

Success in school, in personal life, and at work often depends on how well a person can locate and use information. It has been said, for example, that a good lawyer is not one who knows facts, but one who knows where to *find* the facts. You, too, will often need to locate certain information for school reports or projects. You may want to obtain information to prove a point with friends. Many times you will want information just to satisfy your own curiosity.

In this appendix a number of important sources of information are described. By knowing what type of information is available in each source, you will be able to locate facts and figures quickly when they are needed.

PUBLIC AND SCHOOL LIBRARIES

The services of public and school libraries are available to you. You are free to visit public libraries to read newspapers and magazines. Some libraries keep files of clippings on important topics. In some of the larger libraries, recordings of fine music and pictures can be borrowed. Public, high school, and college libraries contain those reference books most likely to be used by students and others who need to find specific information on almost any subject. Trained librarians will assist you in finding desired information.

In some parts of the country, traveling libraries—called *bookmobiles*—circulate throughout rural and suburban areas. Special libraries are maintained by many of the larger business firms, trade associations, and clubs. Microfilms of rare documents or technical and scientific reports may sometimes be obtained from government and university libraries.

GENERAL REFERENCE SOURCES

Many books are designed purposely as sources of information. When you want information of any kind, consider first the possibility of finding it in a general reference book. If one of the popular reference sources does not contain the information needed, consult a librarian or the card index in the library.

Dictionaries. The dictionary is probably our most useful reference book. Its chief purpose is to give the spelling, pronunciation, and meaning of words; but most dictionaries provide other useful information. Some of the more commonly used types of dictionaries are listed on page 644.

1. *Unabridged dictionary.* This is a complete dictionary giving more information about words and their meanings than smaller editions do. Unabridged dictionaries, often containing more than 2,500 pages, provide us with additional information such as the following:

Guide to pronunciation.
Abbreviations.
Punctuation and grammar.
Rules for spelling, forming plurals, and capitalizing.

Forms of address.
Drawings and illustrations.
Tables of measures and weights, kinds of money used throughout the world, and common foreign language phrases.

2. *Abridged dictionary.* This is a condensed or shorter version of a larger dictionary. It is usually the size of an average book and is handy for quick reference on the spellings and the meanings of words.
3. *Thesaurus.* This is a book of synonyms (words similar in meaning) and antonyms (words opposite in meaning).
4. *Special-field dictionaries.* Special kinds of dictionaries are published for use in such fields as medicine, law, and business. There is even a dictionary showing correct shorthand forms. Dictionaries in French, Spanish, Italian, and other languages are also available.

Encyclopedias. The most complete single source of general information is the encyclopedia, which contains information taken from all fields of knowledge. It is usually published in several volumes because it gives information on so many different subjects.

Encyclopedias, like dictionaries, are published in brief as well as in comprehensive editions. Both one-volume editions and complete sets are available. There are also junior editions published for the use of school-age children.

Encyclopedias are also published for special fields of interest, such as business, education, engineering, sports, religion, and ethnology (the study of various races of people). The *Reference Encyclopedia of the American Indian,* for example, presents much information on the characteristics and culture of the American Indian, including brief biographies of leaders among this group of people.

Almanacs. An almanac is a publication filled with facts and figures about government, population, industries, religions, museums, education, cost of living, national defense, trade, transportation, and many other subjects. The *World Almanac* and the *Information Please Almanac* are two books of facts that are published annually. They are among our most popular up-to-date references. Paperbound editions of these almanacs can be purchased at many newsstands.

Atlases. An atlas is a book containing various kinds of maps of regions and countries of the world. It includes information on population, products, climate, history, and commerce. An atlas is very helpful in learning the location or the size of a city or a country, the pronunciation of a geographical name, or the agricultural and commercial products of an area.

Directories. A directory is a book listing names of people living in a certain place or engaged in a particular business, trade, or profession.

1. *Telephone.* The telephone directory gives the names, addresses, and telephone numbers of subscribers. Some telephone directories contain a civic section that provides a highway map of the city, information about the industry and

commerce of the city, a list of parks and playgrounds, and a summary of traffic rules. Many telephone directories have a classified section—the yellow pages. This is a listing of the names, addresses, and telephone numbers of suppliers of goods and services. The names are arranged in alphabetical order under headings that describe the types of businesses and services.

2. *City*. A city directory lists the names, occupations, and addresses of persons 18 years old or older who reside in the city for which the directory is compiled. Other information usually given includes the names of business firms, streets, clubs, churches, museums, and other institutions in the city.

3. *Government*. The *United States Official Congressional Directory* contains information about the various departments, bureaus, and boards of the federal government, and gives the names of government officials and members of Congress. The *Book of the States* and the *Municipal Yearbook* provide similar information about state and local governments. Another important source, published annually by the federal government, is the *United States Government Organization Manual*. This is a valuable reference book for students, teachers, businessmen, lawyers, and others who need information about the functions, publications, and services of U.S. government agencies.

4. *Special types*. Special types of directories include those of national businesses, public school teachers and administrators, clubs, associations, and newspapers and periodicals.

Books of Statistical Information. Statistics are facts that can be stated in the form of numbers. There are several excellent sources of statistical information. In addition to the almanacs referred to on page 644, there are the *Statistical Abstract of the United States,* the *Statesman's Yearbook,* the *Census Reports,* and many others too numerous to include here.

Readers' Guide. Magazines or periodicals contain many articles on various subjects not to be found in books. Because there are so many magazines, it is impossible for anyone to find all the desired information without some aid. This aid is supplied by the *Readers' Guide to Periodical Literature.* The *Readers' Guide* provides an index to articles appearing in more than 100 current magazines. It is published twice a month, except for one issue in July and one in August. Once a year, one large volume is published that combines all the articles listed in the indexes issued during the preceding 12-month period.

Newspapers. Almost all of us refer to daily newspapers for information on radio and television programs and for announcements of movies showing at the theaters. If we are planning a trip, we may check on weather forecasts and road condition reports. Newspapers also inform us of scheduled lectures, exhibits, concerts, school affairs, sports events, and other activities. Major newspapers print information about economic conditions, prices of commodities, cost of living, prices of stocks and bonds, and other information of interest to businessmen and consumers.

SPECIALIZED REFERENCE SOURCES

There is a wealth of information in almost any special field. You may be familiar with such special references as *Scott's Standard Postage Stamp Catalog* for stamp collectors, the *Official Baseball Guide* for sports fans, and the *Radio Amateur's Handbook* for "ham" radio operators. For speakers and writers, there are reference books on quotations, jokes, and anecdotes. Directories, yearbooks, handbooks, and other references are available to hobbyists, artists, musicians, entertainers, workers in technical trades and professions, ethnic groups, and many others. A few of the more widely used special reference sources are described in the paragraphs that follow.

Information for Travelers. Two commonly used sources of information for travelers are:

1. *Road maps.* In addition to highway routes, many road maps show places of interest, camping sites, parks, lakes, street layouts of larger cities, and other details.

2. *Guides and directories.* The *Official Guide of the Railways* contains timetables of all U.S. railroads and many airlines and steamship lines. Also included are timetables for railways and steamships in Canada and Central American countries.

   The *Hotel & Motel Red Book* gives information about the location and size of hotels and motels, room rates, and hotel services for more than 6,000 hotels, motels, inns, and resorts in the U.S. and in many foreign countries.

   The *Official Airline Guide* contains airline schedules, fares, and information such as airmail rates, car rental services, and conversion of dollars to foreign currencies.

   The *Travel Trailer Guide,* revised annually, contains a listing of over 15,000 travel trailer parks in the United States and Canada.

Information for Consumers. Two popular monthly magazines, *Consumer Bulletin* and *Consumer Reports,* contain advice and facts about products and services used by most consumers. The American Council on Consumer Interests (Stanley Hall, University of Missouri, Columbia, MO 65201) provides specific and helpful information through its *Newsletter* and *Journal of Consumer Affairs.*

Many useful government bulletins, most of which cost very little, can be ordered from the Superintendent of Documents, U.S. Government Printing Office, Washington, DC 20402. Many libraries have *The Monthly Catalog of United States Government Publications,* which lists by subject all federal government publications issued during the preceding month. Bulletins of value to consumers are often available from Better Business Bureaus, unions, colleges, government agencies, and other public and private organizations.

Information for Businessmen. The U.S. Department of Commerce releases many reports and studies of value to large and small business firms. It publishes *Survey of Current Business,* a monthly periodical with articles and statistics on business activity and economic conditions. The Department of Labor issues the *Monthly Labor Review,* which gives information on prices, wages, and employment. National, state, and local chambers of commerce also provide many kinds of useful reports.

The *Economic Almanac* is prepared by the National Industrial Conference Board. It is a standard source of facts on current business and economic developments.

The *Business Periodicals Index,* which lists articles from more than 170 business publications, is a very helpful source of information on current trends and thought in business, economics, and industry.

Much information about business affairs can be found in the financial pages of daily newspapers. Other publications such as *The Wall Street Journal, Fortune,* and *Business Week* are devoted primarily to business and its problems. A business can subscribe to special newsletter services, such as *The Kiplinger Washington Letter,* for information not usually published in newspapers and magazines.

Many handbooks describing principles, practices, and methods for certain specialized fields of business are available. Among the handbooks of special interest to businessmen are:

1. *Accountants' Handbook*—a general reference book in accounting, containing answers to accounting problems and presenting the principles of accounting.
2. *Financial Handbook*—a guide to solving financial problems such as financing the growth and operation of the business and raising new capital for expansion.
3. *Foreign Commerce Handbook*—a guide that deals with exporting and importing operations.
4. *Office Administration Handbook*—a comprehensive volume focusing attention on the human relationships involved in the management of offices. It includes chapters on testing, hiring, supervising, training, and promoting office workers; and on office systems, policies, work procedures, correspondence, layouts, equipment, and data processing developments.
5. *Marketing Handbook*—a reference book that discusses all phases of the marketing process such as advertising, sales promotion, and research.

Almost every field of business has its special trade directory. For example, special directories are published for persons in such businesses as advertising, retailing, insurance, real estate, banking, plastics manufacturing, air transportation, and frozen food processing.

Information about People. Encyclopedias tell about great men and women of history. Other reference books give information about men and women now living. The best-known books of this type are *Who's Who* and *Who's Who in America. Who's Who* gives a summary of the lives and the achievements of outstanding people living throughout the world. *Who's Who in America* lists mainly those leaders living in the United States. Books similar to these are also published for special groups, such as *Who's Who in Commerce and Industry, Who's Who in American Education, Who's Who of American Education, Who's Who of American Women,* and *American Men of Science.* Another popular reference about people is *Current Biography,* which includes sketches about individuals, many of various nationalities, who have become prominent because of their recent accomplishments.

Information about Occupations. Two important publications giving information on occupations are the *Dictionary of Occupational Titles* and the *Occupational Outlook Handbook* (see page 613). Another very worthwhile reference for junior and senior high school students is *The Encyclopedia of Careers and Vocational Guidance.* This extensive compilation is published in two volumes. Volume I contains practical vocational guidance material and broad articles on opportunities in some 70 major industries or areas of work. Advertising, air transportation, data processing, insurance, law, retailing, teaching, and foreign trade are some of the areas covered. Volume II contains more than 200 articles on specific occupations, such as bank teller, stenographer, travel agent, hotel manager, buyer, economist, accountant, stewardess, automobile mechanic, glazier, and watch repairman. These articles give detailed information about the nature of the work, requirements, methods of entry, earnings, and sources of additional information.

APPENDIX B
Arithmetic Review

This arithmetic review will be especially helpful to you in solving many of the end-of-chapter problems in this textbook and the common arithmetic problems you will encounter in your personal business transactions. These suggestions deal with a few of the most bothersome kinds of arithmetic calculations you will need to make. Different people have difficulties with different kinds of problems. Use the inside covers of your workbooks to write down ideas for making other calculations that will be especially helpful to you.

MULTIPLYING NUMBERS ENDING WITH ONE OR MORE ZEROS

In multiplying two numbers, if one or both of the numbers have zeros at the extreme right, place the zeros to the right of an imaginary line, multiply the numbers to the left of the line, and bring down the total number of zeros to the right of the line.

For example:

$$
\begin{array}{r}
4\,7\,| \\
\times\ 2\,3\,|0\,0 \\
\hline
1\,4\,1\,| \\
9\,4\,| \\
\hline
1\,0\,8,\!1\,|0\,0
\end{array}
\qquad
\begin{array}{r}
4\,7\,|0\,0 \\
\times\ 2\,3\,| \\
\hline
1\,4\,1\,| \\
9\,4\,| \\
\hline
1\,0\,8,\!1\,|0\,0
\end{array}
\qquad
\begin{array}{r}
4\,7\,|0 \\
\times\ 2\,3\,|0\,0 \\
\hline
1\,4\,1\,| \\
9\,4\,| \\
\hline
1,\!0\,8\,1,\!|0\,0\,0
\end{array}
$$

DIVIDING BY NUMBERS ENDING WITH ONE OR MORE ZEROS

When the divisor is 10, 100, 1,000, etc., move the decimal point in the dividend one place to the left for each zero. Moving the decimal point one place to the left divides a number by 10; two places to the left, by 100; three places to the left, by 1,000; etc.

For example:

$$14.2 \div 10 = 1.42 \qquad 4685 \div 1000 = 4.685$$
$$231.7 \div 100 = 2.317$$

$$168.2 \div 20 =$$
$$2\ )\ \underline{16.82}$$
$$8.41$$

When the divisor is 20, 400, 3,000, etc., drop the zeros in the divisor, move the decimal point in the dividend one place to the left for each zero, and divide by the remaining number 2, 4, 3, etc.

Other examples:

$$72.8 \div 400 = \qquad 6729 \div 3000 =$$
$$4\ )\ \underline{.728} \qquad\qquad 3\ )\ \underline{6.729}$$
$$.182 \qquad\qquad\qquad 2.243$$

USING DECIMALS

Some students find the use of decimals a bit bothersome. Knowing and following a few simple rules will help improve your calculations involving decimals.

1. Adding numbers with decimals—keep all decimal points in line.

For example:

Add:	84.25	34.7
	1.89	1.98
	625.00	362.
	16.93	.459
	———	16.16
	728.07	8.73
		———
		424.029

2. Subtracting numbers with decimals—keep decimal points in line.

For example:

392.6 ◄—fill out spaces to the right with "0's"—► 392.600
—8.794   —8.794
                                                    ———
                                                    383.806

Subtract 9.876 from 74   74.000
                         —9.876
                         ———
                         64.124

3. Multiplying numbers with decimals.

For example: Multiply 6.34 by 6.3

6.3 4   a. Keep right margin even
  6.3
——————   b. Keep figures in line
1 9 0 2
3 8 0 4   c. To locate decimal point, count all digits to the right
——————   of the decimal point in the two original figures—in
3 9.9 4 2   this case *three*—count off that number of places
                from the right in the product, and set the point.

4. Always multiply by the simpler number.

For example: Multiply 2.4 × 375.1. This is the same as multiplying 375.1 by 2.4, which is simpler.

Other examples:

3 7 5.1	× $	6 8|	× $	1 7 2|
2.4		3.5|0		6.5|0
1 5 0 0 4		3 4 0|		8 6 0|
7 5 0 2		2 0 4|		1 0 3 2|
9 0 0.2 4		$ 2 3 8.0|0		$ 1,1 1 8.0|0

5. Dividing numbers with decimals.

First example: (Dividend) 129.54 ÷ .34 (Divisor) =

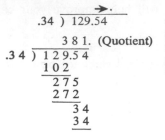

```
         ➔.
.34 ) 129.54
```

```
        3 8 1. (Quotient)
.3 4 ) 1 2 9.5 4
        1 0 2
          2 7 5
          2 7 2
            3 4
            3 4
```

To the right of the decimal point in the dividend count as many places as are to the right of the decimal point in the divisor. Set the decimal point in the quotient at this point. Keep figures in line.

Second example: 420 ÷ 75 =

```
          5.6
7 5 ) 4 2 0.0
        3 7 5
          4 5 0
          4 5 0
```

Decimal point is always at extreme right of whole number, although not shown. In dividing, a decimal point may be placed at the right of the dividend and 0's added as needed.

MULTIPLYING BY PRICE FIGURES SUCH AS $2.98, $13.99, ETC.

Dealers frequently price items for sale at such figures as 99 cents, $4.98, $99.98, etc. This is done because a price of $99.98, for example, seems less to the prospective buyer than an even $100.

Let us assume that 27 items are purchased at $19.99 each.

The usual method of multiplication:

```
$  1 9.9 9
×      2 7
   1 3 9 9 3
   3 9 9 8
$ 5 3 9.7 3
```

A simpler method:

```
        27
×  $ 20.00
     540.00
 −      .27
   $539.73
```

(1) Multiply by the next higher number containing zeros—in this case $20.00.
(2) If the price figure ends in 99¢, subtract 1¢ for each item purchased—in this case 27¢.

Other examples:

If the price figure ends in 98¢, subtract 2¢ for each item purchased—in this case 64¢.
($.02 × 32 = $.64).

32 items at $4.98

```
        32
×  $   5.00
   $160.00
 −      .64
   $159.36
```

If the price figure ends in 97¢, subtract 3¢ for each item purchased—in this case $2.13.
($.03 × 71 = $2.13).

71 items at $9.97

```
        71
×  $  10.00
   $710.00
 −     2.13
   $707.87
```

USING CERTAIN FRACTIONAL PARTS OF $1.00 IN MULTIPLYING

While merchandise may be priced at any figure, prices are frequently expressed in fractional parts of $1.00, $10.00, $100.00, etc., that can be calculated easily and quickly. For example, 50 cents is ½ of $1.00; 25 cents is ¼ of $1.00; 33⅓ cents is ⅓ of $1.00. Thus:

24 items selling for $1.00 each would cost	$24.00
24 items at 50 cents each would cost ½ of $24 or	$12.00
24 items at 25 cents each would cost ¼ of $24 or	$ 6.00
24 items at 33⅓ cents each would cost ⅓ of $24 or	$ 8.00

With a little practice, many similar calculations can be made mentally. While there are many fractional parts of $1.00, the ones shown below will be very helpful to you from time to time in making your arithmetic calculations.

Table 1

Fractional Part of $1.00	Halves	Thirds	Fourths	Sixths	Eighths
⅛					$.12½
⅙				$.16⅔	
¼			$.25		
⅓		$.33⅓			
⅜					$.37½
½	$.50				
⅝					$.62½
⅔		$.66⅔			
¾			$.75		
⅚				$.83⅓	
⅞					$.87½

You already know several of the above fractional parts of $1.00, and with practice you will be able to use those and others quickly and accurately. Four different types of calculations are involved. Perhaps you will not be able to master all of them, but certainly you can master some of them.

First type:

1. Numerator of fractional part is "1," that is, ⅛, ⅙, ¼, etc.
2. There *is no remainder*; that is, the calculations come out to even dollars.

For example:

24 × $.25 = $6.00

How to calculate:

24 items at $1.00 each would cost	$24.00
25¢ is ¼ of $1.00, hence at 25¢ 24 items will cost ¼ of $24 or	$ 6.00

Other examples:

$32 \times \$.12\frac{1}{2}$ $(32 \times \frac{1}{8}) = \$\ 4.00$
$36 \times \$.16\frac{2}{3}$ $(36 \times \frac{1}{6}) = \$\ 6.00$
$48 \times \$.25$ $\quad(48 \times \frac{1}{4}) = \$12.00$
$39 \times \$.33\frac{1}{3}$ $(39 \times \frac{1}{3}) = \$13.00$
$48 \times \$.50$ $\quad(48 \times \frac{1}{2}) = \$24.00$

Second type:

1. Numerator of fractional part is "1."
2. There *is a remainder*; that is, the calculations will result in dollars and cents.

For example:

$33 \times \$.25 = \$8.25$

How to calculate:
33 items at $1.00 each would cost $33.00
25¢ is ¼ of $1.00, hence at 25¢ 33 items will cost ¼
   of $33 or $8¼; ¼ of $1.00 is 25¢, thus ...... $ 8.25
(*Note:* The fraction of a dollar obtained will always be one of the fractions illustrated in Table I, so that once these fractional parts are mastered there is nothing new to be learned.)

Other examples:

$41 \times \$.12\frac{1}{2} = \$\ 5\frac{1}{8} = \$\ 5.13$ $(\frac{1}{8} = .12\frac{1}{2}$ changed to .13)*
$39 \times \$.16\frac{2}{3} = \$\ 6\frac{3}{6} = \$\ 6.50$ $(\frac{3}{6} = \frac{1}{2} = .50)$
$37 \times \$.25 \quad = \$\ 9\frac{1}{4} = \$\ 9.25$
$28 \times \$.33\frac{1}{3} = \$\ 9\frac{1}{3} = \$\ 9.33*$
$25 \times \$.50 \quad = \$12\frac{1}{2} = \$12.50$

(*Since 1¢ is our smallest coin, if the final fraction is ½ or **more**, the last figure is raised 1 penny; if less than ½, the fraction is dropped. *Note:* Some retailers convert every fraction to 1¢, even if the fraction is less than ½.)

Third type:

1. Numerator is other than "1."
2. There *is no remainder*.

For example:

$48 \times \$.75 = \$36.00$

How to calculate:
Think of $.75 as ¾ of $1.00 and solve by cancellation

$$48 \times \$.75 \ (\overset{12}{\cancel{48}} \times \frac{3}{\cancel{4}}) = \$36.00$$

Other examples:

$$24 \times \$.37\frac{1}{2} \ (\overset{3}{\cancel{24}} \times \frac{3}{\cancel{8}}) = \$\ 9.00$$

$$32 \times \$.62\frac{1}{2} \ (\overset{4}{\cancel{32}} \times \frac{5}{\cancel{8}}) = \$20.00$$

$$36 \times \$.66\frac{2}{3} \ (\overset{12}{\cancel{36}} \times \frac{2}{\cancel{3}}) = \$24.00$$

$$16 \times \$.75 \quad (\overset{4}{\cancel{16}} \times \frac{3}{\cancel{4}}) = \$12.00$$

$$18 \times \$.83\frac{1}{3} \quad (\overset{3}{\cancel{18}} \times \frac{5}{\cancel{6}}) = \$15.00$$

$$72 \times \$.87\frac{1}{2} \quad (\overset{9}{\cancel{72}} \times \frac{7}{\cancel{8}}) = \$63.00$$

Fourth type:

1. Numerator is other than "1."
2. There *is a remainder*.

For example:

$$34 \times \$.62\frac{1}{2} = \$21.25$$

> *How to calculate:*
> Think of $\$.62\frac{1}{2}$ as $\frac{5}{8}$ of $\$1.00$; but since 8 does not **divide** evenly into 34, first multiply by 5 and then divide by 8.
>
> $$\$\ 34 \times 5 = \$170$$
> $$\$170 \div 8 = \$\ 21\frac{2}{8}$$
> $$\$\ 21\frac{2}{8} \qquad = \$\ 21.25$$

$$34 \times \$.62\frac{1}{2} \quad (34 \times \frac{5}{8} = \frac{170}{8}) = \$21.25$$

Other examples:

$$61 \times \$.37\frac{1}{2} \quad (61 \times \frac{3}{8} = \frac{183}{8}) = \$22.88$$

$$43 \times \$.66\frac{2}{3} \quad (43 \times \frac{2}{3} = \frac{86}{3}) = \$28.67$$

$$21 \times \$.75 \quad (21 \times \frac{3}{4} = \frac{63}{4}) = \$15.75$$

$$51 \times \$.83\frac{1}{3} \quad (51 \times \frac{5}{6} = \frac{255}{6}) = \$42.50$$

$$23 \times \$.87\frac{1}{2} \quad (23 \times \frac{7}{8} = \frac{161}{8}) = \$20.13$$

Note: You will observe that after the number is multiplied by the numerator, the remaining calculation is exactly like that in the *second type* above.

Fractional parts of other amounts. To the student who is interested in developing further his skill in calculating fractional parts of other amounts, a few additional examples will demonstrate the larger number of applications possible.

First example:

.05 is ½ of	.10	
.50 is ½ of	1.00	
5.00 is ½ of	10.00	Thus:
50.00 is ½ of	100.00	
500.00 is ½ of	1,000.00	

$$24 \times \ \ \ \ .05 = \ \ \ \ \ \ 1.20$$
$$24 \times \ \ \ \ .50 = \ \ \ \ \ 12.00$$
$$24 \times \ \ \ 5.00 = \ \ \ \ 120.00$$
$$24 \times \ \ 50.00 = \ \ 1,200.00$$
$$24 \times 500.00 = 12,000.00$$

Second example:

.02½ is ¼ of	.10	
.25 is ¼ of	1.00	
2.50 is ¼ of	10.00	Thus:
25.00 is ¼ of	100.00	
250.00 is ¼ of	1,000.00	

$$430 \times \ \ \ \ .02\frac{1}{2} = \ \ \ \ \ \ 10.75$$
$$430 \times \ \ \ \ .25 \ \ = \ \ \ \ \ 107.50$$
$$430 \times \ \ \ 2.50 \ \ = \ \ \ 1,075.00$$
$$430 \times \ \ 25.00 \ \ = \ \ 10,750.00$$
$$430 \times 250.00 \ \ = 107,500.00$$

APPENDIX C
Percentage and Interest

USING PERCENTAGES

What does *percent* mean?

Some students get confused when the term "percent" is mentioned. Actually the "percent" concept is very simple. Percent is derived from two Latin words, "per centum," meaning "by the hundred." This is why percent is easy—you are using a fraction whose denominator is always 100. The percent sign is %. Every percent figure can then be expressed as either a common fraction or as a decimal fraction.

For example:

Percent		Common Fraction		Decimal Fraction
3%	=	$\frac{3}{100}$	=	.03
5%	=	$\frac{5}{100}$	=	.05
7%	=	$\frac{7}{100}$	=	.07

In fact, you never use the percent figure in calculating percent. You always change the percent figure to either a common fraction or a decimal fraction. To illustrate:

To find:

4% of $300: multiply $300 $\times \frac{4}{100} =$ $12.00; or $300 $\times$ .04 = $12.00

6% of $250: multiply $250 $\times \frac{6}{100} =$ $15.00; or $250 $\times$ .06 = $15.00

CALCULATING INTEREST

Interest is expressed as a percent; but in calculating interest, both the percent and the length of time are considered.

For example:

8% interest on $400 for 1 year $= $400 $\times$ .08 $\times$ 1 = $32.00

5% interest on $550 for 3 years $= $550 $\times$ .05 $\times$ 3 = $82.50

One method of calculating interest for less than one year is explained in Part 20 of this textbook; another method of calculating interest for less than a year is explained below.

THE 60-DAY, 6% METHOD OF FINDING INTEREST

Both bankers and businessmen often use a simple method of finding interest, known as the 60-day, 6% method. As this name indicates, the method is based on a period of time of 60 days and a rate of 6%. This method of finding interest will be explained through the use of several problems.

Problem 1. Find the interest on $100 for 60 days at 6%.

　　Step 1: Find the interest for one year.
　　　　　　$100 × .06 = $6

　　Step 2: Find the interest for 60 days.
　　　　　　In interest problems a year is considered to be 360 days.

　　　　　　Therefore $\frac{60 \text{ days}}{360 \text{ days}}$ = ⅙ of a year

　　　　　　$6 × ⅙ = $1, the interest on $100 for 60 days at 6%

Since the interest on $100 for 60 days at 6% is $1, it will be observed that the interest on any amount for 60 days at 6% can be found simply by *moving the decimal point two places to the left.*

Examples: Interest on $100.00 for 60 days at 6% = $1.00
　　　　　　Interest on $550.00 for 60 days at 6% = $5.50
　　　　　　Interest on $275.50 for 60 days at 6% ▬ $2.755, or $2.76

The 60-day, 6% method may be used when the time is not 60 days.

Problem 2. Find the interest on $1,000 for 30 days at 6%.
　　Solve for 60 days:
　　　　The interest on $1,000 for 60 days at 6% = $10
　　30 days is ½ of 60 days; therefore:
　　　　$10 × ½ = $5, the interest on $1,000 for 30 days at 6%

Problem 3. Find the interest on $500 for 90 days at 6%.
　　Break down the 90 days into 60 days and 30 days, as follows:
　　　　The interest on $500 at 6% for 60 days = $5.00
　　　　The interest on $500 at 6% for 30 days = 2.50
　　　　The interest on $500 at 6% for 90 days = $7.50

To find the interest for any number of days, break down the 60 days into periods of time that are simple fractions of 60 days.

Examples: 30 days = ½ of 60 days
　　　　　　20 days ─ ⅓ of 60 days
　　　　　　15 days = ¼ of 60 days
　　　　　　10 days = ⅙ of 60 days

Problem 4. Find the interest on $420 for 105 days at 6%.
　　　　The interest on $420 at 6% for 60 days = $4.20
　　　　The interest on $420 at 6% for 30 days = 2.10
　　　　The interest on $420 at 6% for 15 days = 1.05
　　　　The interest on $420 at 6% for 105 days = $7.35

To find the interest for 1 day or for a few days, first find the interest for 6 days. 6 days are ¹⁄₁₀ of 60 days.

Examples: The interest on $720 for 60 days at 6% = $7.20
　　　　　　The interest on $720 for 6 days at 6% = $ .72 (¹⁄₁₀ of $7.20)

It will be observed that the interest on any amount for 6 days at 6% can be found by *moving the decimal point three places to the left*.

Examples: The interest on $720 for 6 days at 6% = $.72
The interest on $720 for 1 day at 6% = $.12 (⅙ of .72)
The interest on $480 for 6 days at 6% = $.48
The interest on $480 for 1 day at 6% = $.08
The interest on $42 for 6 days at 6% = $.042
The interest on $42 for 1 day at 6% = $.007 = $.01

Problem 5. Find the interest on $412.50 for 97 days at 6%.

The interest on $412.50 at 6% for 60 days = $4.125
The interest on $412.50 at 6% for 30 days = 2.0625
(carry to 4 decimal places)
The interest on $412.50 at 6% for 6 days = .4125
The interest on $412.50 at 6% for 1 day = .0688
(⅙ of $.4125)
The interest on $412.50 at 6% for 97 days = $6.6688 = $6.67

The 60-day, 6% method may be used when the rate is other than 6%.

In order to find the interest on any amount at any rate of interest, first solve for 6%; divide by 6 to obtain the interest at 1%; then multiply by the desired rate.

Problem 6. Find the interest on $360 for 75 days at 5%.

First, solve for 6%:
The interest on $360 at 6% for 60 days = $3.60
The interest on $360 at 6% for 15 days = .90
The interest on $360 at 6% for 75 days = $4.50

Next, find the interest at 1%:
$4.50 ÷ 6 = $.75, the interest at 1%
Then, multiply by the desired rate of interest:
$.75 × 5 = $3.75, the interest on $360 for 75 days at 5%

Problem 7. Find the interest on $580 for 127 days at 7%.

The interest on $580 at 6% for 60 days = $ 5.80
The interest on $580 at 6% for 60 days = 5.80
The interest on $580 at 6% for 6 days = .580
The interest on $580 at 6% for 1 day = .0967
The interest on $580 at 6% for 127 days = $12.2767
$12.2767 ÷ 6 = $2.0461, the interest at 1%
$2.0461 × 7 = $14.3227, or $14.32, the interest
on $580 for 127 days at 7%

CALCULATION OF INTEREST ON INSTALLMENT LOANS

The method of calculating the rate of interest on installment loans presented in Part 20 is sufficiently accurate for most purposes. For a more exact calculation of interest, the following method is presented.
Problem. Martin B. Allen borrowed $120 from the small loan department of his bank and signed a note for $126. He agreed to pay back the balance in 8 equal monthly installments of $15.75. What annual rate of interest did he pay for the use of the $120 that he actually received?

Solution. The cost of the loan was $126 - $120 = $6. Assume that an interest rate of 12% a year, or 1% a month, was charged for the loan. On this basis the interest would have been:

$120.00 borrowed for 1 month @ 1% would cost . . . $1.20
—15.75 1st payment

104.25 borrowed for 1 month @ 1% would cost . . . 1.04
—15.75 2nd payment

88.50 borrowed for 1 month @ 1% would cost 89
—15.75 3rd payment

72.75 borrowed for 1 month @ 1% would cost 73
—15.75 4th payment

57.00 borrowed for 1 month @ 1% would cost 57
—15.75 5th payment

41.25 borrowed for 1 month @ 1% would cost 41
—15.75 6th payment

25.50 borrowed for 1 month @ 1% would cost 26
—15.75 7th payment

9.75 borrowed for 1 month @ 1% would cost 10
—15.75 8th payment

Interest cost if the money had been borrowed at 1% a month, or 12% a year . . . $5.20

It will be observed that the interest was figured on the total $120 for the first month only, because the borrower had the use of the entire amount only during that month. During the second month the interest was figured on $104.25, as $15.75 was repaid at the end of the first month. The amount on which the interest was figured was decreased in a like manner for each month during the time of the loan.

At 1% a month, or 12% a year, the interest would have been $5.20. The actual cost of the loan was $6. How many times greater was this actual cost than $5.20? This may be found by dividing $6 by $5.20:

$$\$6 \div \$5.20 = 1.1538$$

The amount actually paid was, then, 1.1538 times greater than the amount would be if the rate had been 1% a month, or 12% a year. Since interest rates are given on a yearly basis, the actual rate was:

$$12\% \times 1.1538 = 13.85\%$$

CALCULATION OF INTEREST ON INSTALLMENT PURCHASES

The method of calculating the rate of interest on installment purchases presented in Part 21 is sufficiently accurate for most purposes, but the following method is more exact.

Problem. Larry Simms bought a radio on the installment plan from the Ace Radio Shop for $102. A down payment of $12 was made at the time of the purchase, and $9 was paid at the end of each of the following 10 months. The radio could have been purchased for $92 in cash. What rate of interest was paid for the privilege of buying on installments?

Solution. The amount that Larry paid for the privilege of buying on installments is found by subtracting the cash price of the radio from the installment price of the radio.

$102 the installment price of the radio
—92 the cash price of the radio
$ 10 the amount paid for the privilege of buying on installments

The radio could have been purchased for $92 in cash. A down payment of $12 was made. The cash price was therefore $80 more than the down payment. Larry could have bought the radio for cash if he had borrowed $80 from some other source. He was, then, in reality borrowing $80 from the Ace Radio Shop. This may be shown as:

$ 92 the price that would have been paid if the purchase had been for cash
—12 the down payment at the time of the purchase
$ 80 the amount borrowed from the dealer

If Larry had borrowed $80 from some other source at a rate of 1% a month, or 12% a year, the interest would have been found as follows:

$80 borrowed for 1 month @ 1% would cost . . . $ .80
—9 1st payment
71 borrowed for 1 month @ 1% would cost 71
—9 2nd payment
62 borrowed for 1 month @ 1% would cost 62
—9 3rd payment
53 borrowed for 1 month @ 1% would cost 53
—9 4th payment
44 borrowed for 1 month @ 1% would cost 44
—9 5th payment
35 borrowed for 1 month @ 1% would cost 35
—9 6th payment
26 borrowed for 1 month @ 1% would cost 26
—9 7th payment
17 borrowed for 1 month @ 1% would cost 17
—9 8th payment
8 borrowed for 1 month @ 1% would cost 08
—9 9th payment
Interest cost if the money had been borrowed at 1% a month, or 12% a year . . . $3.96

You will observe that the interest was figured on $80 for the first month only, since Larry had the use of this amount during that month only. During the second month the interest was figured on $71 because $9 was repaid at the end of the first month. The amount on which the interest was figured was decreased in a like manner for each installment paid.

At 1% a month, or 12% a year, the interest was $3.96. The actual cost for the loan was $10 ($102 — $92 = $10). How many times greater was this actual cost than $3.96? This may be found by dividing $10 by $3.96:

$$\$10 \div \$3.96 = 2.5252$$

The amount actually paid, then, was 2.5252 times greater than the amount would have been if the rate had been 1% a month, or 12% a year. The actual rate, then, was:

$$12\% \times 2.5252 = 30.30\%$$

GLOSSARY

A

ABA number: the number assigned to a bank by the American Bankers Association.

account: the record that a bank keeps of a customer's deposits.

adulterated: the failure of a product to meet minimum standards of purity and quality.

advertising: any nonpersonal, persuasive communication about ideas, goods, or services.

allowance: a limitation or an amount granted for a special purpose.

annuity: the amount of money that an insurance company will pay at definite intervals to a person who has previously deposited money with the company.

appraise: to estimate the value of property.

appraiser: one who is expert in estimating the value of property.

aptitude tests: a means of determining special interests and abilities that a person may have.

arbitrator: a person chosen to settle a dispute between employer and employees.

articles of partnership: a written agreement made by partners in forming their business.

assessed value: the value placed upon property as a basis for taxation.

assets: everything of value that a person, family, or business owns.

automated data processing: processing data by using automatic machines that require little human attention.

automatic typewriter: a machine which types letters automatically but stops to allow the operator to type in certain information.

automation: the process of using electronic and mechanical equipment to perform a series of operations with a minimum of human effort.

B

balanced fund: a mutual fund that invests in bonds, preferred stocks, and common stocks.

balance of payments: the relationship between our total payments to other countries and our total receipts from other countries.

balance of trade: the difference in value between the merchandise exports and the merchandise imports of a country.

bankbook: a depositor's book in which a bank enters his deposits.

bank draft: a check that a bank draws on its own deposits in another bank.

bank money order: a form often purchased from banks for use in making small payments.

bank reconciliation: a statement showing how the checkbook balance and the bank statement balance were brought into agreement.

bank statement: a report given by a bank to a depositor showing the condition of his account.

basic health coverage: a combination of hospital, surgical, and regular medical expense insurance.

bearer: the one who holds a check or other negotiable instrument.

beneficiary: the person named in an insurance policy to receive the insurance benefits.

bill: a form generally used to show charges for services.

blank endorsement: an endorsement consisting of a name only.

board of directors: a group of people elected by stockholders to manage a corporation.

bodily injury liability insurance: insurance protecting the insured person against claims resulting from accidental injuries or deaths he is responsible for.

body (of a letter): the main part of the letter.

bond: a printed promise to pay a definite amount of money, with interest, at a specified time.

boycott: combining in refusing to have dealings with a person or business.

brand name: a trade name placed on merchandise by manufacturers or middlemen.

broker: a dealer in the stocks and bonds of a corporation.

budget: a definite plan for saving and spending income.

budget plan: a credit plan which is similar to an open charge account but spreads payment over a few months.

business: any organization that supplies persons with the goods or services they want.

C

cablegram: a telegraph message sent by wires laid on the bottom of the ocean.

canceled check: a check that has been paid by a bank.

capacity: the factor in credit that has to do with a customer's ability to earn.

capital: the factor in credit that has to do with the property a customer owns.

capitalism: an economic system in which individuals own most of the capital resources and carry on business activities with a minimum of government control.

capital resources: tools, machinery, and other equipment used to convert natural resources into goods and services.

car card: an advertisement placed in or on moving vehicles.

carrier: an individual or company that is engaged in transporting goods or services.

cashier's check: a check that a bank official draws on funds in his own bank.

cash value: the amount that an insurance company will pay to the insured if a policy is given up.

certificate of deposit: a form used to record savings placed in special savings accounts.

certified check: a personal check that is guaranteed by a bank.

certified mail: mail which provides a means of proof that first-class mail has been delivered, but does not cover payment of possible losses.

channel of distribution: the path that a product takes on its way from the producer to the consumer.

character: the factor in credit that has to do with a customer's honesty and probable willingness to pay.

charge account: a credit plan under which the total amount due is ordinarily paid within a month.

charter: a document, generally issued by a state government, granting permission to start a corporation.

check: an order written by a depositor directing a bank to pay out money for him.

checkbook: a bound book containing blank checks and check stubs or a check register.

checking account: a bank account against which a depositor may write checks.

check protector: a machine that imprints the amount of the check on the check form.

check register: a form used instead of check stubs for a record of checks written.

check stubs: forms in a checkbook on which a depositor keeps a record of his deposits and checks.

civic: pertaining to governmental or citizenship activities.

clearance sale: using a price reduction to sell items that a merchant no longer wishes to carry in stock.

clearinghouse: a place where banks exchange checks drawn on each other.

closed-end fund: an investment company with a fixed number of shares.

closed shop: an agreement to employ only persons who are already members of a union.

coastal trade: trade engaged in by ships carrying goods between ports on one coast.

coinsurance clause: a provision in which a person agrees with his insurance company to pay a percentage of his medical expenses.

collect call: a telephone call, the charge for which is paid by the person called.

collective bargaining: the method by which representatives of employers and employees reach decisions about wages and working conditions.

Collect on Delivery (COD): a service that provides for the collecting of money at the time of the delivery of merchandise.

collision insurance: insurance covering damage to one's car caused by collision or by turning over.

commercial bank: a bank that handles checking accounts, makes loans to individuals, and provides other banking services.

commission: a percentage of each sale made or service rendered, paid to an employee as salary.

common carrier: a public carrier that offers its services to the general public.

common stock: stock that has no preference over other shares.

common-stock fund: a mutual fund that invests in common stocks only.

communication: sharing information with others.

communism: an economic system in which government owns most of the property and has tight control over the production and distribution of goods and services.

comparative advantage: the ability or capacity of a state or country to produce certain things more efficiently or suitably than can be done in another state or country.

competition: the rivalry among businesses to sell their goods and services to buyers.

complimentary close (of a letter): the words used immediately before the signature to conclude a letter.

compound interest: interest on both the principal and the interest previously earned.

comprehensive major medical insurance: a combination insurance policy that includes basic health coverage and major medical protection.

comprehensive physical damage insurance: insurance covering losses of or damages to the insured automobile, except those caused by collision or by turning over.

conditional sales contract: a contract under which ownership of the goods remains with the seller until the buyer completes all payments.

conference call: a telephone call in which several persons located in different places talk together at the same time.

consignee: the person or firm to whom something is shipped.

consignment: a shipment of goods.

consignor: the person or firm who ships something.

conspicuous consumption: the practice of buying goods and services to impress others.

consumer: one who uses goods and services.

consumer finance company: a company which specializes in making small loans without requiring the borrower to put up security.

consumer magazine: a magazine containing articles of interest to the general public.

Consumer Price Index: a price index that shows the changes in the average prices of goods and services bought by consumers.

containerization: a shipping service in which specially designed containers can be carried on railroad flatcars, trucks, or ships.

contract: an agreement to exchange goods or services for something of value.

contract carrier: a public carrier whose services are available to persons or businesses under contract.

contribution: an amount given to charity or other public service agency.

convertible policy: a term life insurance policy that may be changed into another type of insurance.

cooperative: a business owned by the members it serves and managed in their interest.

copyright: the exclusive right of an author, composer, or artist to use and sell what he has produced for a period of 28 years.

corporation: a business made up of a number of owners but authorized by law to act as a single person.

credit: promising to pay at a future time for something of value received now.

credit card: a card which identifies a person and gives him the privilege of obtaining goods and services on credit.

credit memorandum: a form used to show the value of merchandise returned or an allowance for unsatisfactory merchandise.

creditor: one who sells or lends on another's promise to pay in the future.

credit rating: an individual's reputation for paying his debts on time.

credit union: a cooperative association which accepts deposits and makes small loans to its members.

customs declaration: a form which must be attached to parcel-post packages sent to any foreign country and which indicates the nature of a package's contents.

customs duty: a tax on imported goods.

D

Data-Phone: a telephone that enables machines to transmit information back and forth over regular telephone wires.

date of maturity: the date on which a note comes due and must be paid.

debenture bond: a bond that is only a claim against the issuing company's earnings.

debtor: one who buys or borrows and promises to pay later.

decreasing term insurance: term life insurance on which the premiums remain the same during the term but the amount of protection gradually decreases.

deductible clause: a part of an insurance policy which states that the policy pays only a certain percent of any loss or that the policy does not cover losses below a certain amount.

deductions (payroll): amounts subtracted from total income for social security taxes, income taxes, and other items.

deed: a written form showing the right of ownership to real estate.

deflation: a decrease in the general price level.

department store: a large retail store that is organized into departments and that sells many different kinds of merchandise.

deposit: money that is placed in a bank account by a customer.

depositor: one who places money in a bank account.

deposit ticket (deposit slip): a form that accompanies a deposit and shows the items deposited.

depreciation: the decrease in the value of property caused by time and use.

Desk-Fax: telegraph equipment which sends exact copies of messages, drawings, or pictures.

direct distance dialing: a method of making a long distance station-to-station phone call by dialing the area code and the phone number.

direct mail advertising: letters and other mailable advertising materials sent directly to customers.

disability income insurance: *see* loss of income insurance.

discount: interest deducted in advance from the total amount borrowed.

discount store: a self-service retail store that sells general merchandise at lower prices than those of other stores selling the same merchandise.

distribution: *see* marketing.

distributor: *see* middleman.

dividend (insurance): part of the unused premium returned to the holder of a participating insurance policy.

dividend (stock): profits of a corporation paid to stockholders.

division of labor: specialization by workers in performing certain portions of a total job.

domestic trade: the buying and selling of goods and services among people and businesses within the same country.

down payment: part of the purchase price of an item, paid at the time of buying.

drawer (of a check): the person who signs a check.

E

economic resources: all the means with which we produce the things we need and want.

economic risks: the chance of losing the financial value of something.

economics: the study of how people decide what, how, and for whom goods and services should be produced.

economic system (economy): the plan that a nation develops for making decisions on how best to use its economic resources.

electronic data processing (EDP): the use of computers to process data and produce reports or solve problems based on that data.

eminent domain: the right of government to purchase, at a fair price, privately owned property for necessary public use.

employment agency: an organization that attempts to place qualified workers in satisfactory jobs.

endorsement: writing on the back of a check that transfers ownership of the check.

endorsement in full: an endorsement including the name of the person to whom the check is transferred.

endorser: the person who endorses a note and is responsible for payment if the original borrower does not pay.

endowment life insurance: a life insurance policy payable to the beneficiary if the insured should die or payable to the insured himself if he lives beyond the number of years in which premiums are paid.

escalator clause: a provision in a union contract calling for wage increases as the cost of living rises.

estate tax: a tax based on the total amount of property left by a deceased person.

exchange: a market where stocks and bonds are sold.

excise tax: a tax on specific commodities that is generally included in the prices quoted to the purchaser.

expenditure: an amount actually spent for food, clothing, or other items.

exports: goods and services we sell to other countries.

express money order: a form purchased from an express company for use in making payments.

extended coverage: additional protection of property against losses from such causes as windstorms, explosions, riots, and vehicles.

extractors: businesses that grow products or take raw materials from nature.

F

face of a note: the amount shown on a note as the amount borrowed.

family income policy: a policy that combines a standard whole life insurance policy with a decreasing term rider.

fast telegram: *see* full-rate telegram.

Federal Deposit Insurance Corporation: an organization that guarantees bank deposits up to $20,000 for each account.

Federal Reserve System: a nationwide banking plan set up by our federal government to assist banks in serving the public more efficiently.

Federal Savings and Loan Insurance Corporation: an organization that insures accounts up to $20,000 in a savings and loan association.

finance charge: the charge that covers a merchant's cost of handling a particular credit account.

financial responsibility laws: laws providing that if a driver causes an accident and cannot pay for damages either through insurance or through his own savings or property, his driver's license will be suspended or revoked.

first-class mail: mail that includes handwritten and typewritten matter and all mailable matter sealed against postal inspection.

fishyback: a shipping service in which loaded trailer trucks are carried on ships.

forged check: a check signed by someone without the authority to do so.

forgiveness clause: a provision in a government loan which states that part of the loan need not be repaid if the person receiving it teaches for a prescribed period of time after graduation from college.

form utility: usefulness that is added to materials by changing their shape or structure.

fourth-class mail: mail that includes all packages weighing one pound or more that may be opened for postal inspection.

fraud: the act of deceiving or misrepresenting.

freight forwarder: a firm which consolidates small shipments to make a full railroad carload.

fringe benefits: things such as pensions, vacations, and insurance that are granted to employees in addition to wages.

full-rate telegram: the fastest type of telegraph service.

G

gift tax: a tax imposed on large amounts of property given away.

goal: something that an individual or family seeks to achieve.

goods: the tangible things we use in our everyday lives.

Gross National Product: the total value of all goods and services produced in a country during a year.

gross profit: the difference between the selling price and the cost price of an article.

group health insurance: health insurance available to members of a group as a unit.

group life insurance: life insurance issued to members of a group as a unit.

guarantee: a promise that a product is of a certain quality or that defective parts will be replaced.

guaranteed insurability option: a provision that enables the holder of a straight life or endowment policy to buy additional insurance even though he has become uninsurable.

H

heading (of a letter): the complete address of the writer and the date.

health insurance: insurance which protects against unexpected medical expenses.

homeowners policy: a package policy covering a wide range of risks for the owners of homes.

hospital expense insurance: insurance that pays part or all of the charges for room, board, and other hospital expenses that the insured person incurs.

hourly worker: an employee who is paid a given amount for each hour worked.

human relations: working with others in a cooperative manner.

human resources: the people who work to produce goods and services.

I

impact (of a tax): that which indicates who pays the tax to the government.

import quota: a limit on the amount of a particular commodity that may be imported into a country during a specified period of time.

imports: goods and services we buy from other countries.

impulse buying: the purchase of goods that a consumer had not planned to buy but was prompted to buy because he saw the goods attractively displayed.

incidence (of a tax): that which indicates on whom the burden of the tax finally falls.

income: money earned by labor, business, or government.

income tax: a tax on the earnings of individuals and corporations.

industrial insurance: insurance sold in small amounts and for which premiums are often collected weekly or monthly.

inflation: an increase in the general price level.

inheritance tax: a tax on the amount inherited by an individual, imposed at the time of the death of a property holder.

inland waterways: lakes, rivers, and channels within the United States.

installment buying: buying merchandise and promising to make weekly or monthly payments on it.

installment contract: the written agreement signed by a customer buying on the installment plan.

installment credit: a type of credit in which a debt is repaid in a series of payments.

installment loan: a loan repaid with interest in a series of payments.

institutional advertising: advertising that seeks to build goodwill for the firm doing the advertising.

insurable interest: a financial interest in insured property; also, a financial interest or other benefit derived from the continued life of a person.

insurance: the protection provided by the sharing of economic risks.

insurance agent: a person who sells insurance.

insurance company: a firm that makes insurance available to others.

insured: one who carries insurance.

interchangeable parts: parts that are made precisely the same so that they can be used to replace similar parts that are worn or broken.

intercoastal trade: trade engaged in by ships carrying goods from Atlantic ports to Pacific ports.

interest: an amount paid for the use of money.

international trade: trade that is carried on among different countries.

interstate commerce: trade among states.

inventory: a list of goods showing the cost of each item and the time it was bought.

investment: savings put to work to earn income.

investment bank: a bank that handles the transactions of businesses that need to obtain large amounts of money.

investment club: a small group organized to invest money for its members.

investment company: *see* mutual fund.

investor: one who invests money for income or profit.

invoice: a form used by wholesalers and manufacturers for listing items sold to retailers.

irregular expenses: expenses that are paid at infrequent times, such as once in three years or at unforeseen times.

J

job cluster: a number of jobs with something in common so that skills in one job can be used in another.

job specification: a description of what the duties of a job are and the qualifications demanded of the worker.

joint account: a bank account that is used by two persons.

L

label: a statement attached to merchandise describing its nature or contents.

labor: all mental and physical effort directed toward the production of goods and services.

labor force: all persons 16 or older who are working or looking for work.

letterhead: a sheet printed with the name and address of an organization.

letter of application: actually, a sales letter selling a prospective employer on the qualifications of a job applicant.

level term insurance: term life insurance on which the amount of protection remains the same during the term.

liabilities: debts that an individual, family, or business owes.

liability insurance: insurance against loss because of responsibility for injuries to other people or for damage to their property.

license: a document giving permission to carry on a certain kind of activity.

limited-payment policy: permanent life insurance on which premiums are paid only for a stated number of years.

liquid investment: an investment easily convertible into cash.

loan credit: credit that is used to borrow money.

long-term investment: an investment made for a number of years.

loss of income insurance: a private insurance plan designed to help replace income lost because of sickness or injury.

M

mail-order house: a retail firm that sells merchandise through catalogs and ships goods directly to customers.

maintenance charge: a fixed monthly charge made by a bank for maintaining a checking account.

major medical expense insurance: insurance designed to help offset very heavy medical expenses resulting from serious or long ailments.

maker: the person who signs a note and promises to make payment.

margin: *see* gross profit.

marketing: the various activities that are involved in moving goods from producers to consumers.

market value (market price): the price at which a share of stock can be bought or sold.

mass communication: the conveying of a message to a large number of people at the same time.

mass production: the use of machines to produce goods in large quantities.

mass transit facilities: a system of modern transportation to meet the needs of commuters in urban areas.

maturity value: the value payable at the maturity of a bond or note.

Medicaid: medical expense assistance provided by state governments.

medical payments insurance: insurance providing medical expense protection for those persons injured while in the insured person's car.

Medicare: health insurance provided under social security laws.

merchantable goods: goods that are fit to be used by the buyer.

middlemen: persons or businesses which supply the various services in moving goods from producers to consumers.

misbranding: the failure to state correctly certain required facts on a product's label.

mobility: the ability of a person to move from one community to another to find employment or to obtain a job promotion.

money income: the amount of money that a family or an individual earns during a certain period of time.

money management: planned control of financial income and expenditures.

monopoly: exclusive control of a commodity or service.

moonlighter: a worker who holds more than one job.

mortgage: a legal paper giving a lender a claim against a borrower's property in case the borrower does not repay a loan.

mortgage bond: a bond that is secured by a mortgage on the issuing company's property.

mortgage insurance: a life insurance policy that assures the payment of debts on real property if the insured dies.

mortgage loan: a loan for which property is pledged as security.

municipal bond: a bond issued by a city.

municipal corporation: an incorporated town or city.

mutual fund: a corporation that sells its own stock to the public and buys stocks or stocks and bonds of other corporations.

mutual savings bank: a savings bank that has no stockholders and pays out earnings only to its depositors.

N

national bank: a bank that operates under banking laws of the federal government.

natural resources: materials supplied directly by nature and that may be used in producing goods and services.

needs: things that humans must have to survive.

net income: the amount that a person receives after social security, income tax, and other similar items have been subtracted from his earnings.

net profit: the amount left over after the cost price and all expenses are deducted from the selling price of an article.

net worth: the difference between the assets and the liabilities of an individual, a family, or a business.

night letter: a telegraph message accepted up to 12 midnight for delivery the next day.

ninety-day plan (three-pay plan): a type of budget plan in which a customer makes a purchase and pays for it in equal payments over a period of three months.

no-load fund: a mutual fund that adds no sales commission to the sales price of its stock.

noninstallment credit: a type of credit in which a debt is repaid in one payment.

no-par stock: stock in a corporation that has no stated face value.

nonparticipating policy: an insurance policy that does not pay dividends to the policyholder.

note: *see* promissory note.

O

on trial (on approval): a sale in which goods do not become the buyer's property until he has given his approval of them.

open charge account: a credit plan in which a customer may charge a purchase at any time but must pay the amount owed in full at the end of a specified period.

open-end fund: an investment company in which a person can invest at any time and from which he can withdraw all or part of his investment at any time.

ordinary life insurance: *see* straight life insurance.

output per man-hour: the amount of goods that one worker, on the average, can produce in one hour.

outstanding check: a check given to the payee but not yet returned to the bank for payment.

over-the-counter sales: sales of stocks and bonds that are not made through an exchange.

P

par: the face value assigned to a share of stock.

parcel post: fourth-class mail.

participating policy: an insurance policy that entitles the policyholder to a refund of part of the premium at the end of the policy year.

partnership: an association of two or more persons operating a business as co-owners and sharing profits or losses.

passbook: *see* bankbook.

passport: a form showing the country of which a traveler is a citizen and giving the reason for his traveling in other countries.

patent: the exclusive right given an inventor to make, use, or sell his invention for a period of 17 years.

patronage refund: earnings that are returned to a member of a cooperative in proportion to the amount of his purchases.

payee: the person to whom a check or note is made payable.

pensions: payments made to retired workers under privately organized plans.

per capita output: the figure that results from dividing the GNP of a country by the population of that country.

personal data sheet: a brief description of an individual's education, experience, and other information used in seeking employment.

personality: the qualities of a person that make an impression upon other people.

personal liability insurance: insurance against loss because of one's responsibility for injury to other persons or for damage to property.

personal property: property not attached to the land.

personnel department: the part of a business whose main responsibility is that of hiring employees and working with them in various ways.

person-to-person call: a long-distance call in which the caller asks the operator to connect him with a particular person.

picketing: the placement of union members before a place of business to urge workers and the public not to deal with the business.

piece-rate worker: an employee who is paid according to the amount of work he produces.

piggyback: a shipping service in which loaded trailer trucks are carried on railroad flatcars.

place utility: usefulness added when goods and services are available where they are wanted.

policy: a contract between one who buys insurance and one who makes it available.

policyholder: one who carries insurance.

possession utility: usefulness that comes from owning or having the right to use a particular good or service.

postage meter: a machine which automatically seals, stamps, and stacks mail.

postal money order: a form issued by a post office for use in making payments.

post-dated check: a check dated later than the date of issue.

preferred stock: stock that has a preference in the payment of dividends.

premium: the amount paid for insurance.

price: the amount that a consumer must pay to obtain a good or service.

price index: a series of numbers showing how prices have changed over a period of years.

principal: the amount of money borrowed.

private carrier: a transportation unit used by its owner to move his products or employees.

private enterprise: the right of individuals to start or invest in any legal business with the hope of earning fair profits.

private property: the right to own, use, or sell things of value.

proceeds: the net amount of money a borrower receives after the discount is subtracted from the principal.

productivity: *see* output per man-hour.

products: the tangible things we use in our everyday lives.

profit: the amount left over from sales after the costs of running a business have been paid.

profit motive: the desire to benefit financially from investing time and money in a business, realizing that there is risk of loss.

program: a set of detailed instructions that direct the operation of a computer.

progressive tax: a tax that increases the rate as the amount taxed increases.

promissory note: a written promise to repay borrowed money at a definite time.

promotional advertising: advertising that seeks to increase the sales of regular merchandise or to draw trade.

promotional sale: selling items below regular cost to increase the sales of regular merchandise or to draw trade.

proof of loss: the evidence which the insurer requires of the insured in order to establish the loss and determine the extent of liability.

property damage liability insurance: insurance providing protection against claims of damage to other people's possessions.

proportional tax: a tax with a uniform rate regardless of the amount involved.

psychic income: nonmonetary satisfactions or rewards.

public carrier: a transportation firm that is engaged in transporting passengers and goods for hire.

public property: things owned by a city, state, or nation.

public service advertising: advertising that tries to get the public to act in socially desirable ways.

public utility: a business that provides essential services or products for the public at prices usually determined by government regulations rather than by competition.

R

radiogram: a telegraph message sent between stations not connected by wire.

raised check: a check whose amount was increased by a dishonest person.

rate of exchange: the price paid in the currency of one country for a unit of the currency of another country.

real estate: land and anything permanently attached to it.

real income: the amount of goods and services that a family or an individual can buy with the amount of money earned during a certain period of time.

real property: land and anything permanently attached to it.

receipt: a written acknowledgment that money has been received.

reference initials: the initials of the typist of a letter, often placed in the letter's lower left corner.

registered bond: a bond that has the owner's name entered in the borrower's records.

registered mail: first-class mail on which the post office has a liability to the sender if it fails to make delivery.

regular expenses: expenses, such as rent and food, that are paid at regular intervals.

regular medical expense insurance: insurance that provides for payment of a physician's ordinary bills.

renewable term policy: a term life insurance policy that the policyholder can continue for one or more terms without taking a physical examination.

repossess: to take back what was sold on the installment plan if payments are not made as agreed.

restrictive endorsement: an endorsement that limits the use of a check to a specific purpose.

retail credit bureau: an organization which keeps records on persons in a community who have done business on credit with local firms.

retailer: a middleman who sells directly to ultimate consumers.

retirement, survivors, and disability insurance: government insurance that provides, among other things, for benefits to be paid to retired workers and their families.

revolving charge account: a credit plan in which purchases can be charged at any time and at least part of the debt must be paid each month.

rider: a special provision attached to a standard insurance policy.

S

safe-deposit box: a compartment in a bank vault for the storing of valuables.

salaried worker: an employee who earns a stated amount for a given period of time regardless of the number of hours worked.

sales credit: credit that is used to acquire goods and services and pay for them at a later time.

sales letter: a letter whose primary purpose is to persuade a person to buy a certain product or service.

sales tax: a tax on consumer goods in general, added separately to the purchase price.

salutation: a greeting to the person who is to receive a letter.

savings account: a bank account on which interest is paid.

savings and loan association: an organization that provides savings account services for its depositors and makes loans to individuals for use in buying homes.

savings bank: a bank that accepts only savings deposits.

savings department: a division of a commercial bank that accepts deposits that draw interest.

second-class mail: mail consisting mainly of newspapers, magazines, and other such periodicals.

securities: a collective name for stocks, bonds, and other written forms such as notes.

security: something of value pledged to insure payment of a loan.

semiannual: twice a year.

service charge: a charge made by a bank for checking account services.

service credit (in banking): a decrease in the service charge allowed for a bank account with a large balance.

service credit (in buying): sales credit that is used to acquire services.

services: those things that other people do for us.

shareholder: *see* stockholder.

short-term investment: an investment made for a few months or, at most, a few years.

signature card: a card, kept by a bank, that shows the signatures of persons authorized to draw checks against the account.

signature loan: a small loan obtained for a short time by signing a note.

single-line store: a retail store that carries only one kind of merchandise or a few related kinds.

single-payment loan: a loan repaid with interest at the end of a definite time.

socialism: an economic system in which the government owns and operates a number of basic industries and provides for some degree of private property and private enterprise.

social security account number: the number used to identify one's record of earnings under social security laws.

social security card: the document bearing the social security account number.

sole proprietorship: a business owned by one person.

special delivery: postal service in which mail is delivered by a postal messenger ahead of the regular mail delivery.

special handling: postal service that enables a parcel-post package to be sent to the destination post office as quickly as first-class mail and then to be delivered by regular carrier.

standard fire policy: a basic type of property insurance that protects against loss resulting from fire and lightning damage to a home.

state bank: a bank that operates under the banking laws of the state in which it is located.

statement of account: a form sent to customers showing a complete record of business transactions for a period, such as a month.

station poster: an advertisement placed inside transportation terminals.

station-to-station call: a long-distance call in which the caller will speak to anyone answering the telephone at the number called.

steward: a union representative in the shop.

stock: a share of ownership in a corporation.

stock certificate: a printed form that shows ownership in a corporation.

stockholder: a person who owns stock in a corporation.

stop-payment order: a written order instructing a bank not to make payment on a certain check.

straight life insurance: permanent life insurance on which the insured pays unchanged premiums throughout his life.

strike: a work stoppage by employees in order to compel an employer to yield to workers' demands.

style of living: the quality and quantity of goods or services, plus economic or social advantages, that are available to individuals, families, and nations.

subsidy: money granted by the government to assist in the establishment or support of an enterprise considered to be of benefit to the public.

supermarket: a retail store that sells mainly food items and is characterized by self-service.

surgical expense insurance: insurance that provides benefits to cover the cost of operations.

surtax: an extra tax that is a certain percent of the regular income tax.

T

take-home pay: the net amount of money that an employee receives after all deductions are made.

tariff: a tax on imported goods.

technician: a skilled worker who also knows the principles of mathematics and science of a field.

technology: the application of scientific and technical knowledge and methods to the production of goods and services.

telegram: a telegraph message sent over land wires.

telegraphic money order: a message directing a certain telegraph office to pay a specific amount of money to a particular person.

term insurance: a life insurance policy that protects against risk only for a specified period of time.

third-class mail: mail consisting of such materials as small packages weighing less than a pound.

thrift: the careful use of one's time and money.

timetable: a printed form giving schedules and services of a transportation company.

time utility: usefulness added to goods and services by being available when they are wanted.

title: ownership of goods or services, or the form that is evidence of ownership.

title insurance company: a company whose business is guaranteeing that titles to real property are good.

Touch-Tone telephone: a telephone which replaces the conventional rotary dial with push buttons.

tourism: the traveling of people from one place to another for pleasure.

trade: the buying and selling of goods and services.

trade association: an organization of firms engaged in one line of business.

trademark: a word, letter, or device indicating the origin and ownership of the article to which it is applied.

trade, technical, or professional magazine: a magazine containing articles of interest to a special group.

transportation: the physical movement of goods from one place to another.

travel: the movement of people from one place to another for business or pleasure.

Travelers Aid: an organization that maintains offices to give information and help to travelers.

travelers checks: forms sold by banks, express companies, and various other establishments to take care of the financial needs of travelers.

travel policies: insurance covering certain kinds of losses resulting from accidents while on a trip or vacation.

trust company: a bank that manages the money and property of others.

U

uncollectible accounts: amounts owed by credit customers who do not pay their bills.

unemployment insurance: insurance that provides cash payments for a limited time to people who are out of a job.

uninsured motorists protection: insurance protecting the policyholder against losses if he is injured by a hit-and-run driver or by a driver who carries no insurance.

union shop: an agreement requiring workers to join a union within a specified time after employment.

upkeep: keeping property in good repair.

V

value: the worth of a good or service to a consumer, measured in terms of how much he is willing to pay for it.

variable annuity: an annuity that tends to fluctuate with the price level.

variety store: a retail store that is similar to a department store but that sells lower-priced goods and fewer bulky items.

visa: permission granted by a government to enter its country.

W

wants: those things that are not necessary to survival but that make life much more enjoyable.

warranty: *see* guarantee.

whole life insurance: permanent life insurance that includes premium payments either for a lifetime or for a limited number of years.

wholesaler: a middleman who buys goods in large quantities from producers and sells them in smaller quantities to retailers.

workmen's compensation: payments made to employees for injury and loss of income caused by accidents on the job.

world trade: trade that is carried on among different countries.

INDEX

A

ABA number, 159
Ability tests, 620
Address in a business letter, 478, 479
Adulterated, 537
Advertising, 485; advantages of, 490; controls on, 491; direct mail, 488; expenditures by medium, 488; institutional, 486; media, 486; as part of mass communication, 485; promotional, 486; public service, 486; as source of product information, 112; Truth-in-Advertising Act, 492; Wheeler-Lea Act, 492
AFL-CIO, 571
Air express, 512
Air freight, 502
Airmail, 511
Air travel, 459, 520
American Bankers Association (ABA) number, 159
American Express, money order, 195; travelers checks, 197
Annuity, 335, 446
Application blank, for a charge account, 264; for a job, 635
Applying for a job, 632
Appraisal of property, 390
Aptitude tests, 620
Arbitrator, 575
Area codes for direct distance dialing, 465
Articles of partnership, 58
Assessed value of property, 386
Assets, 424
Automated data processing, 72; invention of, 72; punched card in, 73; summary of procedures in processing data by, 73
Automatic typewriter, 481
Automatic vending, 90
Automation, 72; applications of computers, 75; automated data processing, 72; components of computer, 75; electronic data processing, 75; how machines affect jobs and workers, 76; invention of automated data processing machines, 72; processing machines, 72; processing

data by computer, 74; program, 74; summary of procedures involved in processing data by automatic machines, 73
Automobile insurance, 287; bodily injury liability, 288; collision, 290; comprehensive physical damage, 290; cost of, 291; deductible clause, 290; discounts on premiums, 293; financial responsibility laws, 287; medical payments, 288; property damage liability, 290; protection provided by, 287; rates in five cities, 292; summary chart of basic coverages, 291; uninsured motorists protection, 289
Automobile travel, 519

B

Balanced mutual funds, 378
Balance of payments, 586
Balance of trade, 586
Balancing investments, 446
Bankbook, 160
Bank credit card plans, 232
Bank draft, 192
Bank money order, 193
Bank number, 159
Bank reconciliation, 181
Banks, ABA numbers of, 159; bank drafts, 192; cashier's checks, 192; central credit plans, 232; checking account services of, 146, 157, 179; clearing checks between banks, 206; commercial, 149; deposits accepted by, 145; deposits insured by Federal Deposit Insurance Corporation, 158; Federal Reserve System, 150, 158; government regulation of, 150; interest paid by, on savings accounts, 147; investment banks, 149; investment services of, 148; loans made to customers, 148, 240; money order, 193; mutual savings, 358; national, 150; profits earned by, 150; safe-deposit boxes in, 147; savings, 149; sav-

ings account services of, 147, 357; savings departments of commercial, 357; state banks, 150; trust companies, 148; trust services of, 148
Bank statements, information contained on, 181; reconciling, 183
Basic health coverage, 332
Beneficiary of life insurance, 309
Better Business Bureau, 135
Bill, 266; receipted, 269; record of unpaid, 423
Blank endorsement, 204
Blue Cross and Blue Shield, 324
Board of directors, of cooperative, 63; of corporation, 62
Bodily injury liability insurance, 288
Body of a letter, 478, 479
Bonds, 365; of businesses, 365; debenture, 366; differences between, and stocks, 370; of federal government, 366; of local governments, 367; mortgage, 366; municipal, 368; registered, 370; savings, 366; why people invest in, 370
Borrowing, from banks, 148; calculating interest on installment loans, 245; calculating interest on single-payment loans, 242; discounted note, 243; interest must be paid for money borrowed, 242; loan credit, 229; promissory note must usually be given, 241; security may have to be offered, 241; where loans may be obtained, 240; why people borrow, 239
Boycott, 575
Brand names, 123
Broadcast advertising, 487
Brokers, 369
Budget, classifications for a family, 420; compared with family's income and expense record, 423; compared with student's income and expense record, 412; may have to be changed, 413; preparing, for a family, 419; preparing, for a student, 409
Budget charge account, 231

planning savings, 404; planning for wise buying, 402; possessions should be used carefully, 403; and the price level, 441; records for a family, 421; records for a student, 410, 412; skill to be learned, 399; for a student, 409

Money order, bank, 193; express, 195; postal, 194; telegraphic, 196

Monopoly, 538

Monthly Investment Plan of New York Stock Exchange, 375

Moonlighters, 612

Mortgage, 241

Mortgage bond, 366

Mortgage insurance, 311

Motels, 523

Motivation for work, 599

Motorcycle insurance, 293

Multiplier effect of a business, 48

Municipal bonds, 368

Municipal corporation, 62

Mutual fund, 378; advantages of, 380; amount accumulated by monthly investment in, 380; balanced fund, 378; charges for services of, 379; closed end, 378; common stock fund, 378; load fund, 380; no-load fund, 380; open-end fund, 378; quotations of, 379; similarity of, to investment club, 378

Mutual savings bank, 358

N

National Association of Investment Clubs, 376

National banks, 150

National Bureau of Standards, 136

National Labor Relations Act, 572

Natural resources, 5

Needs, 3; spending for, 98

Net income, 420

Net profit, 48

Net worth of a family, 425

Newspaper advertising, 486

New York Stock Exchange, 369, 375

Night letters, 468

Ninety-day charge plan, 231

No-load mutual funds, 380

Noninstallment credit, 230

Nonparticipating insurance policies, 315

Nonprofit corporation, 62

No-par stock, 368

Note, discounted, 244; parts of, 241; proceeds of, 243; as security for loan, 241

O

Occupation, *see* Job

Occupational Outlook Handbook, 613

Official Airline Guide, 523

Official Guide of the Railways, 523

Official National Motor Coach Guide, 523

On approval, 132

On trial, 132

Open charge account, 230

Open-end mutual fund, 378

Ordinary life insurance, 311

Outdoor advertising, 489

Output per man-hour, 27

Outstanding checks, 182

Over-the-counter sales of stock, 369

P

PAL (Partial Airlift), 510

Parcel delivery service, 513

Parcel post, 509

Par stock, 368

Participating insurance policies, 314

Partnership, 56; articles of, 58; example of starting a, 58; number of, in this country, 56

Party telephone lines, 463

Passbook, 160

Passport, 524

Patent, 539

Patronage refund, 64

Payee, of a check, 169; of a note, 241

Pensions, 335

Per capita output, 26

Personal data sheet, 632

Personality, 621

Personal liability insurance, 303

Personal property, 299

Personnel department, 632

Person-to-person calls, 464

Physical damage insurance, 290

Picketing, 575

Piece-rate workers, 609

Piggyback, 500

Pipeline transportation, 502

Place utility, 42

Policy, insurance, 280

Policyholder, 280

Population, growth of, and labor force, 572; trends, 29

Possession utility, 42

Postage meter, 481

Postal money order, 194

Postal services, *see* Mail

Postcard, 480

Post-dated check, 172

Preferred stock, 368

Premium, insurance, 280; on automobile insurance, 291; comparison of cash value with, 315; for different types of life insurance policies, 314; for Medicare, 327

Price, 109

Price index, 432

Price level, 441; relation of, to credit, 442; relation of, to insurance, 443; relation of, to investments, 444

Principal of a note, 241

Private carriers, 497

Private enterprise, 16

Private enterprise system, 16

Private property, 16

Private telephone lines, 463

Private wire telegraph system, 469

Proceeds of a note, 243

Producers, 43; buying goods directly from, 87

Producers' cooperative, 63

Production, *see also* Automation; adding utility to goods and services, 43; depends on transportation, 457; division of labor, 71; factors of, 5; how machines affect jobs and workers, 76; increases in, 28, 70; Industrial Revolution, 69; interchangeable parts, 72; mass, 70; output per man-hour, 27; specialization of, 71; technology, 70; workers and business are partners in, 576

Productivity, 27; increases in, 28

Products, *see* Goods

Profit, 16; after taxes, of large corporations, 48; gross, 47; net, 48; reward for business risks, 47

Profit motive, 16

Program for computer, 74

Progressive tax, 565

Promissory note, 241

Promotional advertising, 486

Promotional sales, 120

Proof of loss, 303

Property, assessed value of, 387; determining value of, 390; investigating ownership of, 390; personal, 299; private, 16; public, 538; real, 299; rights protected by government, 538

Property damage liability insurance, 290

Property insurance, 299; cost of, 302; coverage should be based on property's current value, 302; as expense of home ownership,

387; fire and extended coverage, 301; homeowners policy, 299; insurable interest in property, 301; inventory of household goods, 303; kinds of property, 299; payment for losses, 303; personal liability, 303; proof of loss, 303; standard fire policy, 301

Property tax, as expense of home ownership, 386; impact and incidence of, 560; kinds of, 549

Proportional tax, 564

Protection against uninsured motorists, 289

Psychic income, 600

Public carriers, 498

Public property, 538

Public service advertising, 486

Public utility, 537

Punched card, 73

Purchasing, *see* Buying

Q

Quota, import, 598

Quotations, mutual fund, 379; stock market, 369

R

Radio advertising, 487

Radiograms, 467

Railroad transportation, 498

Rail travel, 521

Raising a check, 169

Rate of exchange, 585

REA Express, 512

Real estate, 385

Real income, 101

Real property, 299

Receipt, 268; for bank deposit, 160; canceled check as, 268; how long to keep a, 269; for money withdrawn from savings account, 358; and stub, 269

Reconciliation, bank, 181

Records, businesses keep, 45; filing, 424; personal, 410, 421, 424

Reference initials, 479

Registered bond, 370

Registered mail, 511

Regular checking account, 180

Regular expenses, 419

Regular express, 419

Regular medical expense insurance, 322

Regular savings account, 358

Renewable term insurance, 311

Renting a home, 386

Repossession, 255

Resources, *see* Economic resources

Restrictive endorsement, 204

Retail credit bureau, 265

Retailer, 88; clearance sales of, 120; promotional sales of, 120; as source of product information, 113; types of, 88

Retirement, survivors, and disability insurance, 336

Revolving charge account, 232

Rider, 312

Risks, *see* Economic risks

S

Safe-deposit boxes, 147

Salaried workers, 609

Sales, in retail stores, 120

Sales credit, 230

Sales letters, 475

Sales tax, 549; impact and incidence of, 561

Sales ticket, 265

Salutation in a letter, 478, 479

SAM (Space Available Mail), 510

Savings, importance of, 349; income from invested, 350; liquidity of, 353; planning, 404; rate of return on, 352; safety of, 351; should be invested carefully, 351; should be invested promptly, 351; table of, 351

Savings account, 147; advantages of, 360; in banks, 147; certificates of deposit, 358; in credit unions, 359; deposits in, 147, 358; how to open a, 357; interest on, 147, 350; in mutual savings bank, 358; passbook, 357; regular, in commercial banks, 357; in savings and loan association, 359; special, in commercial banks, 358; withdrawals, 358

Savings banks, 149

Savings bonds, 366

Savings department of commercial bank, 357

Savings and loan association, 240, 359

Second-class mail, 509

Securities, 371

Security for a loan, 241

Series E savings bonds, 366

Service charge, for checking account, 179; for stopping payment of a check, 173

Service credit, in buying goods, 230; for checking account, 180

Services, 3; growth of service businesses, 44

Shareholders, 56

Ship, travel by, 521

Shipping goods, *see* Transportation

Shop, closed, 573; union, 573

Shopping, *see* Buying

Short-term investments, 444

Signature, for a business, 171; on a check, 170; on a letter, 478, 479; for a school organization, 171

Signature card, 158; for an individual account, 159; for a joint account, 159

Signature loans, 241

Single-line store, 89

Single-payment loan, 242

Small Business Administration, 540

Socialism, 18

Social security, 336; account number, 339; benefits under, 337; card, 340; earnings may affect benefits paid, 338; examples of monthly benefits, 338; Medicare, 327, 336; rates, 336; record of earnings under, 340; retirement, survivors, and disability insurance, 336; taxes, 336, 552; types of payments, 337; who is covered by, 336; who pays for, 336

Sole proprietorship, 56, 157

Special checking account, 180

Special delivery, 511

Special handling, 511

Special savings account, 358

Specialty shop, 89

Standard fire policy, 301

State banks, 150

Statement, bank, 181; of credit account, 233, 267; of net worth, 425

Station poster, 489

Station-to-station calls, 464

Steward, 575

Stock certificate, 60, 368

Stock exchanges, 369

Stockholders, 56

Stock quotations, 369

Stocks, 56; broker, 369; certificate, 60, 368; common, 368; comparison of increases in common stock prices and consumer prices, 446; difference between bonds and, 370; dividends on, 62, 368; exchanges, 369; investing in, 368; market value of, 368; in a mutual fund, 378; no-par, 368; over-the-counter sales, 369; par, 368; preferred, 368; quotations of, 369; why people buy, 370

Stop-payment order, 173

Stores, kind of retail, 89

Straight life insurance, 311
Strike, 574
Stub, *see* Check stub
Style of living, 28
Subsidy, 540
Supermarket, 89
Surgical expense insurance, 322
Surtax, 551

T

Taft-Hartley Act, 573
Take-home pay, 98
Tariff, 540, 549, 587
Taxes, characteristics of good tax system, 563; estate, 551; gift, 552; impact and incidence of, 560; income, 549; inheritance, 551; progressive, 565; property, 386, 549; proportional, 564; sales, 549; social security, 336, 552; surtax, 551
Technicians, 610
Technology, 70; *see also* Automation, Production
Teenage charge accounts, 234
Teenage spending patterns, 110
Telegraph, 467; cablegrams, 467; charges for telegram, 467; data sent by, 467; Desk-Fax, 469; facsimile, 469; full-rate telegram, 467; how to send a telegram, 467; money order, 196; night letter, 468; private wire system, 469; radiograms, 467; special services for businesses, 468; telegrams, 467; teleprinter, 469; Telex, 469; tie lines, 468
Telegraphic money order, 196
Telephone, 463; area codes and time zones, 465; Card Dialer, 465; collect calls, 464; conference call, 466; credit cards, 464; Data-Phone, 465; direct distance dialing, 464; local calls, 463; long-distance calls, 463; mobile service, 466; party lines, 463; person-to-person call, 464; private lines, 463; station-to-station call, 464; Touch-Tone, 465; WATS, 466
Teleprinter, 469
Television advertising, 487
Telex, 469
Term insurance, 310; accumulates no cash value, 316; convertible policy, 311; decreasing term, 311; level term, 311; premiums of, 314; renewable policy, 311
Tests for job applicants, 636

Third-class mail, 509
Three C's of credit, 264
Three-pay budget plan, 231
Thrift, 402
Time of a note, 241
Timetable, 523
Time utility, 42
Time zones, 465
Title, to goods, 132; to a home, 390
Title insurance companies, 391
Touch-Tone telephone, 465
Tourism, 458
Trade, *see* World trade
Trade associations, 134
Trademarks, 539
Trade, technical, or professional magazine, 488
Train, travel by, 521
Transit facilities, mass, 458
Transportation, 457, 497; by air, 502; cargo moved by various intercity carriers, 498; common carriers, 498; consignee, 497; consignments, 497; consignor, 497; containerization, 500; contract carriers, 498; fishyback, 500; freight forwarders, 499; piggyback, 500; by pipeline, 502; private carriers, 497; public carriers, 498; by rail, 498; role of, in our economy, 457; by truck, 499; by water, 500
Transportation advertising, 489
Travel, 457, 519; by airplane, 520; by automobile, 519; by bus, 521; to foreign countries, 524; group tours, 525; importance of, in our economy, 458; insurance, 525; selecting travel accommodations, 522; by ship, 521; sources of information about accommodations, 523; by train, 521; Travelers Aid, 526; travelers checks, 197; using services of travel bureau, 524
Travelers Aid, 526
Travelers checks, 197
Travel and entertainment credit cards, 233
Travel policies, 525
Trucking, express, 513; freight, 499
Trust companies, 148
Truth-in-Advertising Act, 492
Truth-in-Lending Act, 256

U

Uncollectible accounts, 222
Unemployment insurance, 334

Uniform Consumer Credit Code, 257
Uninsured motorists protection, 289
Unions, *see* Labor unions
Union shop, 573
United Parcel Service, 513
United States savings bonds, 366
Unordered merchandise, 134
Upkeep of home, 387
Utilities, public, 537
Utility, 41

V

Value, 109
Variable annuities, 446
Variety store, 89
Vending machines, 90
Visa, 525
Vocation, *see* Job

W

Wagner Act, 572
Wants, 3; are unlimited, 6; spending for, 98
Warranty, 133
Waterways, transportation by, 500
WATS (Wide Area Telephone Service), 466
Wheeler-Lea Act, 492
Whole life insurance, 311; cash value of, 315; combining policies to meet special needs, 312; endowment, 312; guaranteed insurability option, 312; limited-payment policies, 311; premiums for, 314; straight life, 311
Wholesaler, 90
Workers, *see also* Labor, Labor unions; and business are partners, 576; commission, 609; hourly, 609; major occupational groups, 610; mobility of, 611; moonlighting, 611; motives for working, 599; opportunities for, 604, 612; piece-rate, 609; salaried, 609; trends affecting, 610
Workmen's compensation, 325
World trade, 582; balance of payments, 586; balance of trade, 586; barriers in, 587; comparative advantage, 582; customs duty, 540; how we pay for, 585; import quota, 598; is two-way street, 589; tariff, 540, 549, 587; trading partners of U.S., 589; U.S. exports, 584; U.S. imports, 583